The Foster Parenting Toolbox

The Foster Parenting Toolbox

A practical, hands-on approach to parenting children in Foster Care

Edited by Kim Phagan-Hansel

EMK Press • Warren, New Jersey

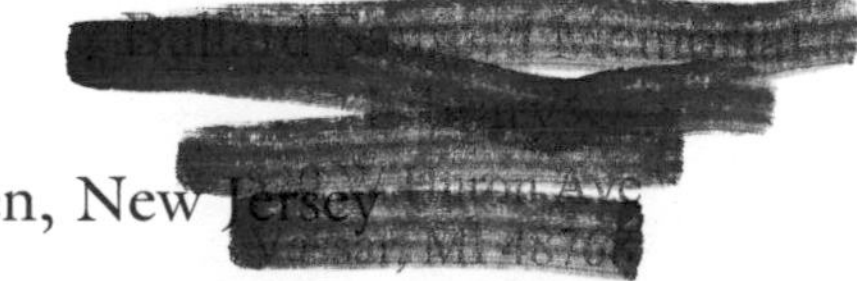

EMK Press, a subsidiary of EMK Group, LLC
16 Mt. Bethel Road, #219
Warren, NJ 07059
www.emkpress.com

This book is based on information from sources believed to be reliable, and also includes the subjective opinions of the authors of each of the articles. We have made every effort to ensure accuracy and completeness based on the information available at the date when each article was written. However, completeness and accuracy cannot be guaranteed. This book may contain mistakes and some information presented as fact may instead be an author's judgement and/or opinion. Readers should use this book as a general guide and not as the ultimate source of information about any topic discussed herein. This book does not replace consultations with licensed doctors, therapists, agency caseworkers or social workers. This book is sold without warranties of any kind, express or implied, and the publisher, editor, authors, and all individuals associated with the publication of this book expressly disclaim responsibility for any liability, loss, or damage resulting from the contents of this book.

Publisher's Cataloging-in-Publication Data

Phagan-Hansel, Kim.
The foster parenting toolbox : a practical, hands-on approach to parenting children in foster care / edited by Kim Phagan-Hansel.
p. cm.
Includes bibliographical references and index.
ISBN 9780972624466

1. Foster parents. 2. Foster home care. 3. Foster children. 4. Adoption. I. Title.

HQ759.7 .F643 2012
362.73/3 --dc22 2011943714

Manufactured in the United States of America

I want to thank my parents and extended family for
providing me with a loving, nurturing childhood,
so I could understand the importance of a family
and that every child deserves one.

I want to thank my husband and children
for sacrificing their time with me and
understanding my desire to improve
the lives of children in foster care.

And finally, I want to thank those
who step up to the plate every day
to make a difference in the life of a child...
your work is invaluable.

Kim Phagan-Hansel

Throughout the book you will find a series of postcards that have been created as a national community art project by those who have experienced foster care first hand...from being in the system. This project is intended to build the alumni community at the same time they educate foster care professionals and providers, and the general public about the culture of foster care. Learn more about this project and also how to create your own postcards from the Foster Care Alumni Association of America's website: www.fostercare-alumni.org/postcard_project.htm

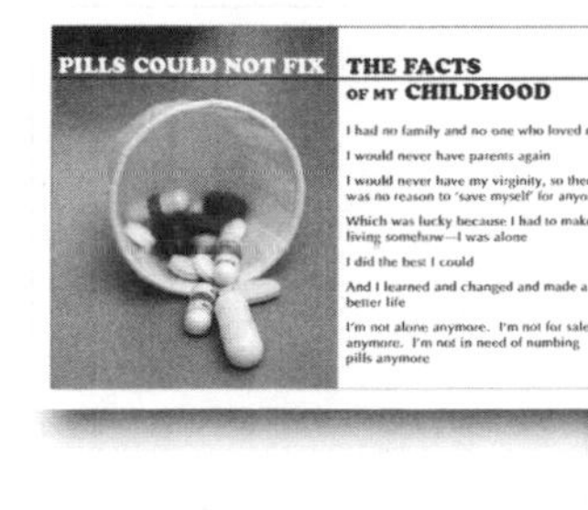

Why Foster 1-22

Perspectives 23-46

Transitions 47-76

Teamwork 77-92

Birth Family Connections 93-112

Loss, Grief & Anger 117-148

Attachment & Trust 149-174

Trauma & Abuse 175-196

Family Impact 197-220

Discipline 221-246

School Tools 247-276

Parenting Teens 277-298

Nurturing Identity 299-316

Allegations 317-334

Respite & Support 335-354

Reunification, Adoption & Beyond 335-384

For additional resources, visit www.emkpress.com.

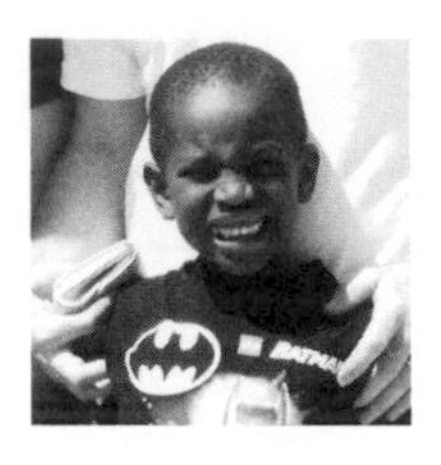

Your Personal Toolbox

Creating Connections with Fostering
By Kim Phagan Hansel

Today more than 420,000 children live in out-of-home placements, or foster care, and of those more than 114,000 are waiting to be adopted (Adoption and Foster Care Analysis and Reporting System FY 2009). Some of those children live with relative guardians and others live with licensed resource parents, more commonly known as foster parents.

In the last few years, more and more attention has been drawn to the children waiting in the foster care system – waiting to return to biological parents, waiting to be adopted, waiting to age out of "the system." From increased legislation to assist children as they age out of foster care to national campaigns to raise awareness about children who need to be adopted, more information is available about foster children and their specific challenges than ever before. However, as the awareness has gradually risen about children living in foster care, the myths about foster care in general and the people who "raise" these children continue to linger. Called to help, thousands of foster parents across the country care for children who live in their care for a day, a week, a year or longer.

Foster parents face unique parenting challenges. Most of the children they care for have suffered abuse and neglect in some form that required their placement into foster care. The trauma these children experience in unsafe environments can create a myriad of challenges for the children. In addition, the children also suffer trauma from being physically removed from everything they know and placed into a new home with new people and new rules. Overnight, their lives are turned upside down. For children, this creates an incredible impact on their lives, causing them to struggle with behavioral issues, fall behind in school, suffer from post-traumatic stress disorder and so many other issues.

Foster parents are trained and licensed to be the calm in the storm for these children, to mend them and restore them for however long they are in their care. To do this, foster parents are required to maintain their license, transport children to and from appointments with caseworkers, birth parents, siblings, doctors and therapists on a regular basis – and they're also expected to at the very least show them love. Foster par-

ents are professional parents entrusted with the lives of children who have been abused, battered, neglected and forever affected by their experiences. Because of the nature of foster care, foster parents must keep the children's information confidential, thus creating little opportunity to bring attention to themselves or the children in their care. This circle of confidentiality prevents society from understanding the depths of the challenging work foster parents undertake. This unfortunately, leaves foster parents often feeling alone, misunderstood and with little support as they tackle raising some of the nation's most challenging children.

So for two reasons, the Foster Parenting Toolbox has been created. First, similar to the magazine, Fostering Families Today, for which I have been editor for the past 10 years, this book will serve as a resource and training tool for foster parents. It's a book that foster parents can flip through to find ways to handle difficult behaviors such as lying or stealing. Second, the Foster Parenting Toolbox, should be considered a safe place for foster parents to turn to, or becoming like a best friend who understands because the stories shared in this book are stories from other foster parents walking a similar path.

Whether it is midnight and foster parents are in crisis with their newest foster child or if it's the need to learn more about foster parenting before jumping in, this book will hopefully provide some answers. The Foster Parenting Toolbox has been created in an easy-to-read format with quick bites of information that foster parents can read while stirring dinner or snuggled in a chair after the kids are off to bed. For whatever your need, during whatever down time you have, this book should serve as a guide and a stepping stone on your foster parenting journey. Good luck!

Kim Phagan-Hansel, editor Fostering Families Today

Strengths Based Language

By Donna D. Petras, PhD, MSW, and Eileen Mayers Pasztor, DSW

Language is what connects a culture. So the words we use, in whatever language, can be affirming or they can sound harsh. Some of the language used in the child welfare field over the decades and even centuries has tended to be negative and even evoke painful feelings in the children or families to whom the words refer. For example, the expression, "up for adoption," comes from the "Orphan Train" era in the late 1800s and early 1900s in which hundreds of thousands of orphaned, destitute and street children from New York City were sent on trains to families in Midwest communities as child labor. It was the beginning of the formal foster care system as we know it today. But when the trains arrived at their destinations, the children were arranged on the train station platforms, or paraded to church halls, or theater stages to be viewed and selected by the families waiting there to pick out their child. These children were literally "up" for adoption. That expressed has remained to this day. Or what about the terminology "home study" that foster care and adoption agencies use to "screen" prospective foster and adoptive parents? That really began as a "house study," when well-water and floor space were considered critical issue for the "orphan train" children, and "home study" is still used these many decades later.

And while some words have stuck with the child welfare system, others have been slowly been eliminated to improve the way children and families in the child welfare system are explained. One expression that was dropped in the 1980s was "natural parent" or "real parent" to differentiate between birth and foster or adoptive parents. Other expressions that stigmatize and even blame children and that are not strengths-based include "hard to place" child, or "aging out." Children who are abused and neglected will of course act out their hurt and pain. Those behaviors then cause the adults, who caused the trauma, to label the children "hard to place," and ostensibly given us a "pass" on having to find safe, nurturing families to raise them. And, if we grew up with our parents, or have adult children, the idea of becoming 18 years of age and having contact severed would never occur to us. Yet young people in foster care will use the expression "aging out" on a regular basis.

It is essential that all of us involved in child welfare – whether the children in our care or in our caseloads – continue to improve language so many of the stigmas and negative language can be eliminated and children and families can be viewed in a more positive light. Referring to children as "cases" or "placements" also could be reframed. Asking "how many placements will that home take?" should be restated as "How many children can that grandparent care for, or could that foster or resource parent work with?

Definitely consider the word "home." Let's consider "home" as a four letter, negative word as it relates to child welfare. A home does not heal or hurt children, but the people living there do. Homes don't have feelings, families have feelings. So when caseworkers state that they are going to visit a home, they are really going to talk with a family. There are implications and outcomes for that "visit." Even that word should be re-considered. Are we really going to "visit" a family, as it isn't a social call? Aren't we going to meet with or consult with the parents to discuss the safety, well-being, and permanency issues for the children living there? By substituting the word "family" for "home" we focus on the people, their interactions and feelings rather than the structure in which they live. However, the concept of "home" can evoke positive feelings – and the strong connection we often feel with the place called home, such as the phrase "home for the holidays." The point is to focus on the people, not the place.

Here's a chart that considers some of the more historical deficit language and the more positive, strengths-based reframing language that conveys the intent of the communication

Historical, "Deficit" Language	Strengths-Based Language
Hard to place child	Families who can protect and nurture children are hard to find
Natural/real parent	Birth parent
Pulled/removed from home	Separated from their families
Foster homes	Resource families
Slots/homes/beds	Families available to care for a child
Weeding out/screening out	Selecting in
Damaged child	Child with special needs
Home study	Mutual family assessment
Referring to children and families as "cases"	Children and Families
Caretaker	Caregiver
Substitute care	Family Foster Care, Residential Care, Group Care, Kinship Care (there is no substitute for the birth parent)

It is challenging to change words and phrases that have been in our child welfare culture for so long, but with some effort those changes can be made to benefit families and children. If each one of us commits to use more positive, strengths-based language, perhaps others will start using it as well, in essence, changing ideas and actions to be far more child and family-friendly.

The idea of moving from deficit to strengths-based language was originally developed by Dr. Pasztor for the curriculum, *Adoption Clinical Training (ACT)* offered by the California-based Kinship Center.

This perspective is also explained in the following publication: Pasztor, E.M., Petras, D., & Rainey, C. (2011). *Collaborating with Kinship Caregivers: A Research to Practice Competency-based Training Program for Child Welfare Workers and Their Supervisors.* Washington, DC: CWLA.

With Thanks

A book of this sort doesn't just happen.

The Foster Parenting Toolbox has been a year-long endeavor to bring to foster parents throughout the country an easy-to-read, meant for them resource that can help guide their foster parenting journey. The idea for the book was created by two women – Carrie Kitze of EMK Press and Kim Phagan-Hansel of ***Fostering Families Today*** – who saw a need for more resources for foster parents who have an incredibly profound impact on this nation's most vulnerable population – kids in foster care. This book is a compilation of many voices and experiences from a variety of people involved in the child welfare system in different ways.

Special thanks to all the foster parents represented in this book including Denise Kendrick, Veronica Brown, and Cheryl Peterson who have woven incredible tales of their foster parenting journey and triumphs and tribulations along the way.

Professionals like Eileen Mayers Pasztor, Donna D. Petras, and James Kenny, have provided valuable insight into the world of foster care after many, many years of being entrenched in the battle to improve the lives of kids in care as well as many others.

The foster care alumni who created perspectives that were essential: Noelle Hause, Misty Stensile, Adam Robe, and all the voices of alumni who are scattered through this book, either through their words or postcards. We hope that by sharing their wisdom and realities that things will change for the better for the youth in foster care.

These and all of the wonderful writers in this book have openly shared their knowledge, stories of joys and pains, and a little piece of their lives to help others. This book never would have been created without any of them. The people who have stepped forward to share their stories are the real heroes – the ones walking the journey everyday with a child's hand in theirs. These are the people who make a difference and we thank them.

To those who read this book in it's various incarnations; your comments and insights have helped to shape this book, and we thank you.

And to Chi-Ying Jan who tirelessly tracked permissions, read for common sense and understanding, and came away changed with a new understanding and perspective and Cindy McCabe, Quark guru and the consistency police, we appreciate your efforts on behalf of this book.

And to each of you who continued to ask "When will this book be done?" as we struggled with the sheer complexity of it and the enormity of task. We hope it was worth the wait.

Kim Phagan-Hansel, Editor
Carrie Kitze, Publisher

Why Foster?

The Starfish Story
By Loren Eiseley

Once upon a time, there was a wise man who used to go to the ocean to do his writing. He had a habit of walking on the beach before he began his work.

One day, as he was walking along the shore, he looked down the beach and saw a human figure moving like a dancer. He smiled to himself at the thought of someone who would dance to the day, and so, he walked faster to catch up.

As he got closer, he noticed that the figure was that of a young man, and that what he was doing was not dancing at all. The young man was reaching down to the shore, picking up small objects, and throwing them into the ocean.

He came closer still and called out "Good morning! May I ask what it is that you are doing?"

The young man looked up, and replied "Throwing starfish into the ocean."

"I must ask, then, why are you throwing starfish into the ocean?" asked the somewhat startled wise man.

To this, the young man replied, "The sun is up and the tide is going out. If I don't throw them in, they'll die."

Upon hearing this, the wise man commented, "But, young man, do you not realize that there are miles and miles of beach and there are starfish all along every mile? You can't possibly make a difference!"

The young man bent down, picked up another starfish, and threw it into the ocean. As it met the water, he said, "It made a difference for that one."

Loren Eiseley was an anthropologist who wrote extensively. He was the 'wise man' in the story who was walking along a beach after a storm and encountered the fellow throwing the starfish back.

The Day That Changed My Life

By Michele Burnette

Don't touch me! You're not my mommy! I want my mommy!

February 3, 1997 was a day that forever changed my life. That was the day my family opened our home and hearts to foster care. It was a colder than average Friday afternoon when I got the call. Two brothers, age 3 and 18 months, were coming "into care." Would we be able to take them? Without hesitation I said, "YES."

With nervous anticipation I opened the door that afternoon to two sets of coal black, blood shot eyes looking up at me with pure fear and confusion. I quickly tried to usher them into my "gingerbread" home, filled with toys and the scent of fresh baked cookies wafting in the air. But instead I was met with screams of "Don't touch me! You're not my mommy! Don't touch me!" I began to get flustered. The weeks of resource parent training and books that I had read about foster care never prepared me for this reaction! The worker rattled on about court, antibiotics, phone numbers, blah, blah, while echoes of "Don't touch me, you're not my mommy. I want my mommy," rang through my head. Then suddenly she was gone. My own children were intertwined in my legs chanting "why they crying? We got toys? Are they our new brothers?"

When the sudden realization of what was happening settled upon me, I began to cry. As a tear ran down my cheek, I thought to myself, "I want my mommy." At that moment something occurred to me, I wasn't the only one feeling overwhelmed and scared right then. I quickly put aside my fears and moved on to the task at hand.

I popped in a video for my children, which to my surprise, charmed the 18-month-old. He went over to the TV and stood mesmerized by the big purple dinosaur singing and dancing in front of him. Winning over the 3-year-old proved more challenging.

Cautiously, I approached and asked if he wanted to watch TV. He screamed, "NO." I asked if he wanted something to eat. Again there were screams of "no." I asked if I could sit by him. His silence was the closest thing to acceptance I had so I seized the opportunity. I slid down next to him on the top stair and just sat. After what seemed like ages, I felt him lean against me. I put my arm around him and began to stroke his head. Within minutes he was asleep.

The next few weeks proved to be as challenging as the first few days. From rigging our seven passenger van to accommodate five car seats and working around food differences to navigating phone calls that sent the 3-year-old into a maddening rage – it was tough! But we were surviving. The children were thriving and a fragile trust was being formed. We had those boys four weeks before they were sent back to their parents. They had come to us sick, dirty and broken. They returned clean, healthy and on the way to being mended and I was mad – no, I was furious. I had gone into foster care with the intention of saving a child. How could I do that when I was only perpetuating the situation? I was giving them false hope. How could they trust me? Wouldn't they think that I was just sending them back to the deplorable situation they came from?

After much discussion with my husband, we decided to keep our home open and try again. Within days we got the next call. This time a newborn needed care for a week while his mom was incarcerated. That child was followed by a 10-month-old who stayed two months, who was followed by another 10-month-old who stayed three weeks. Each child came into our home with his or her own set of baggage and stayed for varying amounts of time.

It was about six months after our first boys left our home that I received a call from my licensing worker. She told me that the boys had come back into care and the oldest had asked to come back to our home. I was crushed. We had just taken two other children so our home was full. I wouldn't be able to help them. The worker told me that she wasn't calling to ask us to take the boys. She was calling us to tell us that the boys had remembered us. She said, "One day you will understand why I called you."

That night as my mind kept drifting off to her words I had my epiphany. I got into foster care to "save a child." But what I had done was so much more than that – I had given a child the opportunity to be a child – even if it was only for four weeks. During that short time he was with us he could play, grow, thrive and not have to worry about when he was going to eat again or where he was going to sleep that night or if his mom would come back to get him. That had made enough of an impression on him that he remembered.

Today our home is still a foster home. We have fostered for more than 13 years, taking in more than forty children in that time. Our family has grown from three to seven children. Two weeks ago I received an important phone call. A young man who we had fostered five years ago for a period of two years found my number and called me. We chatted for about 30 minutes. As I was thanking him for calling, I mentioned that he was always welcome in our home and he should come by to visit some time. He quickly replied, "How about tomorrow?" He spent the whole next day with us playing, laughing and reminiscing. As I dropped him off that night at his home, I realized that this is what foster care was really about. Foster care is about making a connection – a connection intended to last a lifetime.

Michele Burnette has been a foster parent since 1997, fostering more than 40 children. She is a mom to seven and became a foster parent after seeing drug addicted babies left in the hospital where she worked as a nurse. She is married and currently serves as the president of the Maryland Foster Parent Association – Region 3, vice president for the National Foster Parent Association and the newly elected president of the Resource Parent PTSA, Parent, Teacher, Student Association.

Selecting Foster Parents: What To Expect and Ask

By Eileen Mayers Pasztor, DSW, and Donna D. Petras, PhD

> *Veronica is 10 years old, with a 5-year-old sister and 3-year-old brother. Veronica was caught shoplifting at a convenience store. She took crackers, soda, milk, and candy. She told the police that her mother has been gone for several days, probably looking for drugs or in jail because of drugs. Veronica has not been going to school in order to watch over her siblings. There are no grandparents or aunts and uncles that Veronica knows of. Veronica and her siblings need a foster family for an indefinite period of time.*
>
> *Denetria is 30 years old; with four children younger than age of twelve. She was laid off from her job because of budget cuts, and the whereabouts of the two fathers of her children are unknown. She and her children were living in her car near a park when discovered by the park police. The police took the children into protective custody and referred Denetria to a women's shelter. Denetria said to the police, "Please take away my problems, not my children."*
>
> *What if a child in your family (your birth child, a niece or nephew, a grandchild, or perhaps the child of a close family friend) had to be separated from every relative he or she knows and go immediately to live with a family totally unknown to that child or to you? What if you were the child welfare caseworker, supervisor, or administrator charged with the responsibility of ensuring that those "strangers" could provide a safe, nurturing family for a few days, months, or even years until this child could return to you?*

Foster Parents Have an Essential Role

On a daily basis, in these circumstances and countless others, child welfare agencies will turn to foster parents to take care of infants, children, and teens when it has been established that relatives or other extended family members aren't able or willing to do that. Foster parents are the foundation of every foster care program.

In 1991, the NCFFC – a joint effort by the Child Welfare League of America (CWLA) and the National Foster Parent Association (NFPA) – changed the long-established language of foster family care to family foster care. This was to emphasize that fostering takes place in a family setting. More recently, there has also been an emphasis on using the words foster family, instead of foster home. This is because when children have been hurt from abuse or neglect, it will not be their foster homes that heal their hurts but, instead, it will be the members of their foster families who will make the positive difference in their lives. Make a commitment right now: every time you hear someone say "foster home" change it to "foster family." Remember, homes don't have feelings, families have feelings!

What is a foster parent?

Foster parents are *licensed*, *certified*, or *approved* depending upon their respective jurisdic-

Definitions:

Child protection agencies, whether public or private, have the legal mandate to provide family foster care services. By law or policy, they have the right to choose the foster families with whom they wish to work. Individuals and couples who wish to be licensed, certified, or approved have the right to accept or decline the invitation to become a member of that agency's foster care team. The following definitions may be helpful in understanding some of the pieces.

• ***Family foster care:*** A mandated child welfare service for children and parents who must live apart while maintaining legal and, almost always, affectional ties. When children and parents must be separated because of the tragedy of neglect, physical or sexual abuse, or other special circumstances, family foster care provides a planned, goal-directed service in which the care of children takes place in an agency-licensed, certified, or approved family. The value of family foster care is that it responds to the unique individual needs of children and their birth parents through the strength of family living with community supports. The goal of family foster care is to provide opportunities for healing, growth and development leading to healthier children and families, with safe, nurturing relationships intended to last a lifetime. (National Commission on Family Foster Care. 1991. *A Blueprint for Fostering Infants, Children, and Youths in the 1990s.* Washington, DC: CWLA, p. 121).

• ***Foster parents/foster family:*** An individual or couple who is licensed, certified, or approved to provide round-the-clock protecting and nurturing for children in the custody of a public or private child welfare agency, lasting for a few days, weeks, months, or years.

• ***License, certification, or approval:*** An array of expressions used by different jurisdictions to indicate that an individual or family have met their standards for foster parenting, and are qualified to foster. This is usually for a specified period of time, requiring a new license, recertification, or re-approval after one or perhaps two years.

• ***Child welfare agency:*** A governmental department with a legal mandate to provide child protection services; or a private, not-for-profit agency that has a contract with the public agency to provide child welfare services. For-profit agencies are not common; some states do not allow foster care to be provided by for-profit agencies.

• ***Out-of-home care:*** The overall term for child welfare services that are provided for children and parents who are not living together, including family foster care, emergency shelter care, kinship care (relatives taking care of younger family members), group homes, or residential treatment facilities.

tions and whether the program is run by public/government or private/non-profit agencies. Each foster parent/family that a child protection agency selects to license, certify, or approve must have the ability, willingness, and resources to be partners in helping the agencies with which they are affiliated to achieve federally required goals of child safety, child well-being, and permanency. Each agency and each foster parent must mutually determine if the foster parent can fulfill this commitment. The process by which this happens historically has been known as a "homestudy." That term dates back to the 19th century "Orphan Trains," when orphaned and destitute European immigrant children roaming the streets of New York were sent on trains to live with families in the growing West. The "study" was not much more than the local town leaders nodding their assent if the family had enough well water and floor space, i.e. a house or homestudy.

If you are Veronica on your way to live with a foster family, what are you feeling? What behaviors will reflect those feelings? What do you want your new foster parents to be like? How do you want them to help you? What do you want to know about them? How do you know that the child welfare caseworker driving you to your new "family" – someone you may have never met before – will find the right foster parents for you? Oh, you are expecting that you and your little brother and sister are going together, aren't you? Or did the caseworker tell you there were no foster parents who could take you together, so the three of you are being separated? Now how do you feel about the caseworker and the people you are going to live with?

If you are Denetria, how do you feel about your children being taken away to live with foster parents? What do you want to know about these people? Are you afraid they will judge you? What do you want them to do for your children? Do you want them to help you see your children and get them back? Like Veronica, you are expecting that all of your children will stay together, aren't you? What happens to your ability to see your children if they are divided among four different foster families who may live in four different parts of your city?

What if someone in your family needed foster care? What do you want to know about the foster parents being selected? How will you know they are qualified? How do you know the child welfare staff is qualified to make those decisions?

Finding the right parent for the child

Today's children needing family foster care have experienced physical abuse and neglect, sexual abuse, and the chaos that comes from living with drug-involved families. They express their life experiences in their behaviors. In the 1970s, the child welfare field coined the expression "hard to place" child to excuse itself from having to find the right match for children. That is no longer acceptable. Children can't be labeled as "hard to place" because of the trauma that adults inflicted upon them. We can only say that skilled foster families are hard to find, as are the child welfare workers who collaborate with and support them. The process of determining ability, willingness, and resources to foster has been reframed from "homestudy" to "culturally competent strengths/needs family assessment," although "homestudy" is still common.

Responsibility to the children
Child protection agencies, whether public or private, have the legal mandate to provide family foster care services. By law or policy, they have the responsibility and the right to choose the foster parents with whom they wish to work. Individuals and couples who wish to be licensed, certified, or approved have the right to accept or decline the invitation to become a member of that agency's foster care team.

What to Expect

Government and private agencies charged with the responsibility to provide foster care have the legal and ethical obligation to ensure, to the best of their ability, that children are placed with foster parents/families with the willingness, ability, and resources to fulfill that role. There are standards or criteria for foster parents/families to meet. There must be an assessment and selection process to determine whether those standards are met. In turn, individuals and families must determine if they wish to work with that agency. This process often includes a series of personal interviews, group preparation sessions for potential foster parents, review of certain records, reference checks, and completion of required paperwork.

Although specific requirements in foster parent standards vary, most states have standards that address the following issues and engage in similar efforts to assess the standards. The major areas addressed in foster parent standards correspond to the following categories of foster parent competencies that were initially established by the NCFCC in 1991 and later adopted by the PRIDE Model of Practice (Parent Resource for Information, Development, and Education), published by CWLA:

Can you provide a safe and nurturing environment for children, including:

a. Do you have integrity, and no adult in your family has been convicted of a crime that may indicate a potential risk to children?
b. Are the living quarters of your house adequate to accommodate additional children, and free of foreseeable hazards and risks to children?
c. Is your family currently experiencing a critical period of change or stress that may diminish your capacity to respond to the needs of children entering your family?

Can you meet children's developmental needs and address any developmental delays, including:

a. Can you provide positive, age-appropriate structure and discipline in accordance with standards that prohibit corporal punishment, withholding of food, and other harsh punishments?
b. Can you provide the basic needs of children in the areas of nutrition, physical care, health care, emotional support, education, recreation and other developmental needs?

Can you support children's relationships with birth parents and other relatives and work to achieve continuity in the children's history and to support the children's cultural identity including:

a. Can you support the children's visits and other contacts with their birth families?
b. Can you avoid derogatory comments and other negative communications about the children's families?
c. Can you provide information to the children's birth families about the children's development and progress and engage the birth parents in activities with the children as provided for in the children's service plans?
d. Can you support the children's cultural heritage and provide religious and/or spiritual training consistent with any that the children's birth families have or request?

Can you help connect children to safe and nurturing relationships intended to last a lifetime:

a. Can you work with the agency to achieve the permanency plans for the children, typically to reunite the children with the birth parents or relatives?
b. Can you work toward adoption for children when reuniting them with birth parents is not possible? In many instances foster parents are asked to engage in "concurrent planning," or working toward reuniting the children with their birth families and beginning planning for adoption in case the birth parents are unable to change sufficiently to create a safe and nurturing environment for the children.
c. Can you help insure that youths who reach the age of 18 and for whom neither reunification with birth parents nor adoption is possible will stay connected to your family due to the safe and nurturing relationships you have established?

Can you participate as members of a professional team:

a. Can you keep confidential all personal information about the children's families and circumstances that led to the placement and ongoing services of the children?
b. Can you welcome agency representatives into your house, including caseworkers, licensing workers, and others involved with the children's care?
c. Can you participate in meetings and other activities required by the service plans, such as taking children to therapy?
d. Can you participate in ongoing training and professional development?

Therefore, you can expect that assessment of these standards includes:

- Individual discussions with an agency representative.
- Group meetings and training to discuss your willingness, ability, and resources to address these challenges, and to learn new skills.
- Individual interviews with the members of your family and any other adults living there.
- Personal references and criminal background checks (applicants and all adult members of their households must be fingerprinted in order for the criminal background check to be completed)
- Measuring home floor space to confirm that space requirements are met, observing living space to confirm that adequate furnishings to accommodate the children such as beds and drawer and closet space are present and that provisions to protect against fire, poisoning, and other potential risks identified in the state's standards are observed.

While this may seem intrusive, consider the following scenario: What would you want to know about a family that would step in to take care of someone you love? How long would it take you to make this assessment? How would you know you made the right assessment?

Preservice training helps you make an informed decision.
Many agencies use what is called "preservice training" or "group preparation/selection" as an important part of the selection or assessment process. Working in a group with other prospective foster parents provides the opportunity to become more aware of fostering issues, to know and understand more about the program and, most important, to apply what is learned to your own individual and family situation. This will help you and the agency make an informed decision if foster parenting is right for you and your family. If it is not, you don't want to find out after a child has been placed with you. This becomes another rejection for that child, and a sad experience for you and your family. Make every effort to work with an agency that provides preservice training as a way to complete your assessment. Any agency that would invest many hours in preparing you – before you even decide to take one of their children – has got to be an agency that cares about people. Make sure that training is co-led by an experienced foster parent, too!

Typically Asked Questions

Here are two categories of questions that should be raised during the foster parent selection process. The first category are questions that typically are asked by prospective foster parents. These are followed by issues that prospective foster parents should raise, but may not because perhaps they are not aware of their significance. Because agencies have mandates by federal, state, or county laws, every agency may have its own set of criteria and ways of answering the questions. The depth of the answers may also vary among staff, depending upon the quality and quantity of training and supervision they receive, and how frequently agency policy manuals are updated.

- Ask if your agency has a brochure or a manual for prospective foster parents.
- Seek out foster parents in your community (perhaps through a place where you worship or where children go to school).
- Learn if your city, county, or state has a foster parent association that you can connect with. Go online to the National Foster Parent Association at www.nfpainc.org for valuable information and support. For example, the NFPA website will link you to many excellent resources, such as each state's requirements for training; it will also give you general answers to some typically asked questions about foster parenting.

What is the application process?
What are all the steps involved in becoming a foster parent? How do I get an application form? Is there a checklist of my responsibilities? Is there one specific person I should connect with?

What training or preparation will I receive?
What is the process to participate in the training? Is it in a group or online?

How much does it cost to be a foster parent?
Will I have to pay to get a license or certification or approval? When I participate in training, what expenses are involved in that such as mileage and babysitting?

What is the monthly reimbursement rate for foster parenting?
Isn't foster parenting typically a voluntary experience with no salary provided? Doesn't the child placing agency that has custody of the child provide for the costs of caring for that child, such as room and board, medical care, and clothing? How is the reimbursement related to the age of the child? Are there guidelines as to how these funds can be used?

Can I choose the children I want?
What are the ages of the children needing foster care? What is the greatest need? Could I be an effective foster parent for siblings, or children with special medical needs? How do you match the needs of children with the strengths of prospective foster parents?

I have biological children – what do I tell them about fostering?
What kind of training and support or guidelines will you provide to help me talk with my children about being a foster family? How will your assessment and licensing or certification process address this? What about preparing other family members or friends for our fostering experience?

In what ways is fostering similar to and different from parenting birth children?
Am I expected to adopt the child or children placed with me? What does "concurrent planning" mean? What kind of support will I (and my family) get to help us let go of a child to whom we have become attached or, conversely, to prepare to adopt a child we had planned to return to birth family?

In what ways is fostering similar to and different from adoption?
Am I expected to adopt the child or children placed with me? What does "concurrent planning" mean? What kind of support will I (and my family) get to help us let go of a child to whom we have become attached or, conversely, to prepare to adopt a child we had planned to return to birth family?

What about the ethnicity and culture of children I may be asked to foster?
Would I be asked to foster a child who may be of a different ethnicity, culture, or religion than that of me or my family? If so, what kind of training and support would I/we get to help this child get adjusted? What kind of support or preparation might the child get to be placed with a family who will be "different?" What about the impact on the birth parents?

What kinds of references are needed?
Do you want to talk with members of my family, friends, people at my place of worship, or colleagues from work? Will you talk with my children's school teachers?

Why is fingerprinting required?
Would a past criminal conviction automatically prevent me (or a member of my family)

from becoming a foster parent? What if I had a record as a teenager?

Essential Issues to Discuss

What is the role of foster parents at your agency?
Are they considered clients (someone needing help with a problem), or team members, or even team leaders? In many jurisdictions, the term "resource families" is used to refer to foster and adoptive parents as essential members of the child protection team. While foster parenting is not a specific job with a salary, is there a kind of "job description" or something that lists the roles and responsibilities of foster parents in the agency? Does the agency use the National Foster Parent Association Code of Ethics for foster parents, or is there an adaption at your agency? Does my state or county have a foster parent bill of rights law? If not, does the agency have a list of foster parent rights that it uses? The NFPA has posted its Code of Ethics for Foster Parents as well as foster parent bill of rights laws from several states on their website at www.nfpainc.org.

What about being accused of abuse?
(See pgs 317-334 for more information)
What happens if I or someone in my family is accused of abusing a child placed with us? What will happen? What supports and resources would be available? What could be the impact on the individual members of my family: the children and adults?

Valuable Information and Support

Visit the National Foster Parent Association at www.nfpainc.org for valuable information and support. For example, the NFPA website will link you to many excellent resources, such as each state's requirements for training; it will also give you general answers to some typically asked questions about foster parenting.

Do I need any special insurance to be a foster parent? Is insurance provided by the agency, or do I get or need my own?

Might I be asked to foster a young person whose sexual orientation is different from that of members of my family or me? If so, what kind of training and support would I/we get to help this young person get adjusted? What kind of support or preparation might the child get to be placed with a family who will be "different?" What about the impact on the birth parents?

Summary

When children cannot safely remain with their birth families, then our communities turn to foster parents to step in and help ensure that these children experience all the benefits of family life. Before you decide that foster parenting is for you, talk over the following issues with everyone close to you, and with your child welfare agency representative:

Becoming a foster family is a life-changing event for everyone involved. What changes are you expecting?

Being a foster parent is not a lifetime commitment to a child. It is a commitment to be meaningful to a child's lifetime. Children who come to live with us may stay for a few weeks or for years. They may not appreciate our contribution to their lives until they are much older. One of the most compelling aspects of being foster parents is that almost all children who come to live with us will have been abused or neglected before we meet. This requires considerable sensitivity.

Becoming a foster parent is a privilege, it is not a right. But for a child to be free from abuse and neglect, that's a right, not a privilege. Ensuring this right for children is an extraordinary contribution not only to those children, but to their parents, kin, and our communities. Thank you.

Eileen Mayers Pasztor, DSW, is experienced as a public agency caseworker and supervisor; as a curriculum developer and trainer; and as a foster and adoptive parent for children with special needs who, now as adults, continue to require her support. She teaches child welfare and social policy advocacy courses at the School of Social Work at California State University, Long Beach (CSULB), and edits the journal ***Reflections – Narratives of Professional Helping****. She was the national program director for family foster care, kinship care, and adoption at Child Welfare League of America (CWLA). She is recognized internationally for her leadership to create programs to develop, train, select, and support foster and adoptive parents (Nova, MAPP, PRIDE), and she continues to consult and train nationally.*

Donna D. Petras, MSW, PhD, has many years of experience in the field of child welfare as a caseworker, supervisor, trainer, administrator, professor, consultant in program development, and author. She is the former Director of Foster Care for the Illinois Department of Children and Family Services and Past-President of the U.S. National Association of State Foster Care Managers. Donna has conducted research and published in the areas of child neglect, kinship care, and parenting. Since 2004, Donna has worked in Ethiopia and Tanzania to create social services for orphaned and vulnerable children and their families. Donna is Director of Models of Practice and Training Development at CWLA.

Foster Parent Stipends: Are They Doing it for the Money?

By Sarah Gerstenzang, MSW

Having been a foster parent I can say that the people that do it are not in it for the money. We were given ten dollars a day ($300/month) to feed, cloth, house, drive, and take care of a ninth grader. (1996 standards) You cannot take care of a teenage child for only ten dollars a day. Yes they also gave as a very small clothing allotment, but that was not near what it takes to clothe a teenage girl. Wife and [I] will never do it again. Way too much hassle with all levels of the establishment. (Comment from "pharmacist" in response to an article about cutting stipends in Utah as a budget saving measure.)

Despite the fact that every prospective foster parent is screened and licensed to ensure that they are stable and capable, one of the most often repeated phrases with regard to foster parenting is that they "do it for the money." My husband and I were often asked about this as foster parents – no one implied that we were actually profiting from providing care and all expenses for the little girl in our home in exchange for about $500 a month but that others did this. In fact, the money we received obviously did not cover the expenses of caring for a baby in New York City; I spent $10 an hour on 10 hours a week of babysitting so that I had $100 left each month for everything else! Like all other foster parents we met, we paid for all other expenses out of our pocket. And like the majority of other foster parents we knew, this was ok because we were foster parenting because we loved parenting and wanted to help children. Unfortunately, this reality limits the families that can be recruited to those that have money to spare or to those that live below the poverty line so that the reimbursement is in keeping with their spending on their own family.

There is much confusion, on the part of both foster parents and caseworkers, about stipends and whether they are a payment to foster parents. I recently had a woman and her husband who had cared for teenage boys for a decade tell me that the children had gotten more difficult and yet they hadn't received a "raise" in all that time. Although they were licensed foster parents, no one had explained to them that the money was in no way a salary.

The federal government requires states that accept federal funds to pay for foster care to reimburse parents for the "cost of (and the cost of providing) food, clothing, shelter, daily supervision, school supplies, a child's personal incidentals, liability insurance with respect to a child, reasonable travel to the child's home for visitation, and reasonable travel for the child to remain in the school in which the child is enrolled at the time of placement." 42 U.S.C. 675 (4) (A). As noted in our personal experience above, most states are in violation of this policy and do not actually reimburse foster parents for actual costs as required by law. Foster parents are challenging this violation of federal law in court in California and New York.

Reimbursement to foster parents for expenses are referred to as stipends, subsidies or board rates. Overtime, states have enhanced the payment system in an effort to attract enough foster parents to care for especially challenging children because if there are not enough available families, children are placed in institutions. While each state develops its own child welfare law and policy under the federal umbrella, it is common that states have three levels of care – basic, special, and exceptional. The level of care is determined by the child's needs. For example, a child who receives the highest rate would have exceptional medical or emotional challenges.

Americans have developed law and policy to keep children living with families because living in an institution is not only terrible for children's development and long-term outcomes, it is also far more expensive. In New York State, for example, it costs about $29,000 for a child to live with a foster family and $123,000 to live in a residential treatment center and $205,000 in an institution for hard-to-place youth. (New York State Office of Children and Family Services budget estimates 2010). The majority of the cost of keeping a child in foster care goes to administrative expenses with roughly a fifth of the money being spent to reimburse the foster parents for expenses.

Foster parents in the United States have been reimbursed for some of the expenses of the children in their care for more than 100 years. This practice started to discourage foster parents from putting children to work to earn their keep. Foster parents have always been volunteers – unlike all others in the system such as social workers, lawyers, judges, etc. – and therefore do not earn salaries, benefits such as vacation days, health insurance or social security entitlements. They also have no rights that employees have, such as the right to organize by forming a union.

So why the "doing it for the money" stereotype? Partly the media is to blame for focusing on negative stories where foster parents abuse or neglect children in their care – a very, very tiny percentage of the total hundreds of thousands of families who provide loving care. Otherwise, negative perceptions are drawn because many of the Americans who step forward as foster parents are poor. The overrepresentation is due to numerous factors: the vast majority of children who come into foster care are poor and friends and relatives are often recruited to care for them. Foster parenting is very demanding, requiring many trips to appointments and visits with birth family, and working families can't always accommodate their schedules or they have other options to bring children into their home such as international adoption. Middle and upper class Americans who have little interaction with the child welfare system make assumptions about the people who do step forward – maybe in an effort to distance themselves or provide an excuse as to why they are not doing it themselves. And sometimes it seems that caseworkers have a hard time empathizing with the stresses that come with foster parenting – perhaps thinking that foster parents are paid – or even worse taking advantage of neglected children to line their pockets, helps caseworkers justify their feelings.

Reimbursing foster parents for the full cost of the caring for children in foster care in accordance with the law would go a long way to recruiting a larger pool of families. And educating everyone on the intent and purpose of stipends would make it much easier to retain families. A recent ad in my local paper noted that foster parents would receive "tax free earnings" – this type of misinformation sets up a negative relationship between the foster parents and the caseworkers, in a job that already comes with many challenges!

Sarah Gerstenzang, MSW, is the executive director of the New York State Citizens' Coalition for Children. Her child welfare policy and practice experience includes research and publication on a range of foster care and adoption issues as well as presentations at national and international conferences. Her most recent book is ***Another Mother: Co-parenting with the Foster Care System****. She has been a foster, kinship, adoptive parent, and support to siblings from foster care.*

Tough and Rewarding...

Being a foster parent is the toughest job there is, but at times it is also the most rewarding. I have been doing foster care for almost four years now, and have had many children come through my home. All of the children come with their own stories, habits and baggage. Many of the kids have never done the things that we, as a family, take for granted. Watching movies at the theater, visiting a park, going camping or even eating at a restaurant that doesn't have a drive-thru have all been firsts for the kids in our care. We take these children into our home and into our lives, giving them all of the things that we give to our own children. Sometimes the little things that we take for granted make these foster kids light up like a kid on Christmas. Actually seeing the looks on their faces as they share Christmas traditions with us and learn new ones from us is even more amazing.

When we have done our part and the time comes for them to return home to their parents, it is bitter sweet. You know that you have made a difference in their lives, but not nearly as much as they have made a difference in yours. Then when the time comes and you see them out and about, you always wonder if you should speak to them and if you do, will they remember you? How will they respond? Most often they will come up to us, give us hugs like there's no tomorrow and share something they remember about us. Sometimes they have a whole list of things.

– David Gibbons, foster care alumnus and foster parent

Foster parents can best help the children they care for by truly showing an interest in the kids, as if they were their own. Foster parents should put themselves in the children's shoes and think of how they would feel if their parents were to abandon them.

– Tiffany Diaz, former foster youth

The most challenging thing about being in foster care I'd say is moving constantly. It's challenging because it's one home to another and there's no stability in that. You meet new people, make new friends and then next thing you know, you're moving again just when you got settled down. Sometimes you don't get the chance to tell anyone...it just happens and you're gone.

– Crystal Frazier, foster youth

Navigating the System

By Emily Parks, LMSW

The excitement of foster parenting is often challenging with the overwhelming abundance of rules, regulations, deadlines, and feelings of being completely lost. I am a social worker, former foster parent, and adoptive parent of my son. I have felt all of those feelings. Ironically enough, I felt this even being familiar with the foster/adoption system so the reality is that foster parenting can be completely overwhelming!

There are a few things I always recommend to new foster parents trying to understand how fostering works.

1. Understand you always have the right to ask and if you don't understand or agree with the answer, ask someone else. It's important to understand that in many foster/adoption agencies, funding for staff salaries is limited and many caseworkers are new and may also be learning how the system works. So ask questions and don't be afraid to ask a supervisor for clarification.

2. Get involved in a community support group or online group. This is a great way to find out what other foster parents are doing, where they are finding resources, and what's available in your community. Be open to trying new approaches and finding creative ways to handle situations. There has always been someone with a similar situation who can offer some great advice.

3. Build relationships with professionals such as caseworkers, therapists, speech therapists, the child's doctor, school teachers, school counselors, ECI workers, special needs workers, and others. Keep in mind that these professionals are often trying to keep up with changing rules and regulations when it comes to foster/adoption services. Understand that we are all in this together and sometimes a positive approach is more helpful than a negative one.

Emily Parks, LMSW, has more than 15 years experience working with children in the foster care system, juvenile justice, and residential treatment. She advocates not only for the children and youth of Texas, but also for her son who was adopted out of the foster care system.

Foster Parent Links

For Links to Foster Parent Associations in your city or state, visit these websites for the most up-to-date listing:

www.nfpainc.org/reploc/
www.fosterparents.com/states3

Why I Stay

By Amy Bates

I often wish I could go back to a time where I believed that all children in our city were being raised by attentive, good parents. Before I became a foster parent I deluded myself into thinking that all children had clean clothes, nutritious meals, and loving parents who read books to them. It would never enter my mind that a 2-year-old would scrounge for food to feed a 1-year-old sibling. I would never think that children could be so frightened by their own parent's angry outbursts that they had to hide under their bed, shaking in terror. I would not know about the 12-year-old who was brutally raped because she was at a party where she should not have been with no parent waiting up, expecting her to come home. Going back to a time before I was a foster parent would mean my biggest concern in life would be what to make for dinner, not worrying about who does not have dinner.

However, I cannot go back to that time of blissful ignorance and as tough as it is sometimes, I would not want to go back. Being a foster parent has meant having my heart broken many times. As I have heard the stories about the little ones who come into my home, I have wept for the lives that they have lived so far. "Life is not fair" has new meaning for me as I look at my own children and their friends. They have no idea how blessed they are to live the life they do. As I say goodbye to yet another child I have loved so dearly, I wonder why I choose to stay a foster parent.

It certainly is not the money. As hard as it may be to believe, animal kennels get paid more to care for a dog per month than foster parents receive to care for a child. Come to think about it, the hours are not that great, either. I remember once getting up every two hours to feed a premature baby who had been born addicted to meth. It is not the respect I get from people. Most think I have lost my mind and wonder aloud if I am endangering my own children. So why do I continue?

A close friend of mine, who also works in child welfare, has a personal motto, which I love, "Making the world good enough for our children." She once expressed to me that she stays in this field not only to help the families she works with, but to help her children as well. For every child she touches with kindness, she hopes he or she will some day grow into a responsible, healthy adult who will positively affect the world.

Along with that, I would add that it is my fervent hope that something I do or say will stick. That the children will remember that once someone cradled them close and whispered, "I love you." I pray that in times of darkness and fear, those children will hum our favorite bedtime song and know they are special and worth loving. That, as they grow into adults, those children will recall that there is an alternative lifestyle, and chooses better for themselves. I am often told that I can't save them all and that is true. I don't want to save them all, just the ones who pass through our home on their personal journey through life. I stay a foster parent because I have to believe what I do makes a difference in a child's life, and some day down the road, that will matter.

Amy Bates is mom to 10 kids who miraculously came to her through adoption, birth, and foster care. She and her husband have been foster parents for 11 years and she works for a non-profit agency that emphasizes family preservation and child safety.

My Decision to be a Foster Parent

By Judy Bledsoe

When I turned the big age of "50," I wondered, "what in this life have I always wanted to do, but never done?" The answer was exploring what it meant to be a foster parent. Though I had a respect for the word "foster" parent, I truly did not know what all was involved. My oldest daughter, at that time 33 years old, knew foster parenting always intrigued me so she encouraged me to inquire more about it. I called the local Department of Social Services to find out if someone could answer my questions.

Through that phone call, my husband and I were invited to attend some workshops on foster parenting to help us understand the role foster parents play and get answers to my questions. The classes were interesting and informative on what was actually happening to children throughout the country, but especially right in my own community. Once we saw the **great need** to **love** these children, we decided on foster/adoption.

I interviewed several foster/adoptive parents who shared foster parenting stories and I was told that fostering brings with it a "roller coaster" of emotions! I mentioned to my husband that if we had fostered children in our home for several years, and the chance to adopt came up, I wanted to because I simply could not easily give up the children I had nurtured for so long.

After several months of "screening," background checks, retrieving records, and attending workshops on being foster/adoptive parents, we received a call that there were four children who needed a family. My husband was motioning a big "NO" wave with his hands because we never expected such a large bunch. That week our son had also been in a car accident and he was going to need some therapy and assistance, so we decided against the placement. My heartstrings tugged over the fact that four little children needed a family and we were not able to provide it for them.

Less than four weeks later, we received yet another call from the agency that four more children from a different family needed a family. Their ages were younger than the first group of siblings – 11-month-old Mary, 2-year-old Selena, 3-year-old Jada and a 4-year-old. We were surprised about their young ages because the agency had told us during our training that most foster children are older. I chuckled to my husband that the Lord was simply "preparing" us to get ready for four children because **He** wanted them with us.

To make a long story short, those children changed our lives for the better and forever. After three years of fostering them, we adopted all of them except Jada. Jada has a different daddy than her siblings and her paternal grandmother is now raising her. But we still see her and she remains in contact with her siblings.

Our children love their home with us and they love attending their church as well. They are active in their children's club at church. My husband and I are truly blessed to have these children to love and share our lives with. My challenge to anyone who has a special love for special children, please get involved and open your home and heart, because these children need you so desperately.

Judy Bledsoe is a foster mom who has always had a love for children and her family. Her faith in the Lord is her strength!

Best Laid Plans...

By Kate Thompson

In a rare quiet moment the other day I reminisced about the strange looks I would get in the supermarket with four children at my side some 20 years ago. That was around the time that 2.2 children per family became popular and somewhat the "norm." I guess my explanation is I have never fit the "norm" and even more so now. My trips to the supermarket these days are either late at night by myself or with at least five or six of my current brood. You see, our foster parenting journey began after our four children grew up, and we now have a new family of eight children younger than eight for a grand total of twelve! We didn't have empty nest syndrome as many people think. God just opened our eyes and hearts one day and we saw abused and neglected children sitting almost next door with a desperate need for Christian parenting, so we became foster parents.

The first phone call came on a Friday afternoon. There were 20-month-old twin boys who had just come into foster care. The caseworker asked if we would take them and the answer "yes" was out of my mouth before I even had time to think. Suddenly I realized that we were not yet approved, but the caseworker said since we had completed all of our training we could be approved quickly because of the urgent need to place these children. In no time I was on my way to pick them up. There were all sorts of things running through my mind, the first being that my husband Roger was on a flight home from a business meeting and had no idea we had just gained two more children, or infants, I should say. I needed clothes, strollers, and car seats.

Our plan had not included infants; we were thinking older children, at least older than three. I had done my diaper duty and was not planning on going back.

Our plan had not included infants; we were thinking older children, at least older than three. I had done my diaper duty and was not planning on going back. With my 83-year-old mother-in-law in tow, I walked into the agency and my heart melted as I saw two identical little boys sitting on two different caseworkers' laps. Their faces were blank, devoid of expression as they gazed at me when I knelt down in front of them. One had a large bruise that streaked across his left cheek, and as I looked further they both had on clothes that were too small and uncomfortable. Their hair was blonde but unkempt and hung to their shoulders with their bangs just about covering their big blue eyes. Those eyes were so vacant. They clutched two dirty looking bottles in their hands as if they were the only possession they knew or recognized.

I fell in love straight away. I knew I shouldn't, but the mother instinct to protect them from all their hurts rose up in my heart so fiercely that it surprised me. I had heard all the stories and even had seen the pictures, but these were real live little boys, hurting from neglect and abuse. They were sitting in front of me and the emotions they evoked came from deep within. In that instant I knew that I would fight for these kids above and beyond the call of duty.

We borrowed two infant car seats from my caseworker and settled them in the car. They began screaming and obviously did not like being restrained. I would later find out that they had often been locked in their car seats for hours, hence the intense dislike of being held in place. I called home to have my older children prepare something for them to eat. Remembering that children shouldn't be given anything too unfamiliar in those first couple of days, I requested mashed potatoes and hot dogs. My daughter Louise reminded me that she had a game that night and then my son Ben reminded me that I was his transportation out that night. I suddenly also remembered my poor husband. He was due in at the airport at 9:30 pm Well, we were in for some fun!

The first shock came when I realized that the boys had obviously never eaten mashed potatoes. Didn't every kid eat that? I guess not ones who came from their circumstances. They just didn't know what to do with the food. They rolled it around in their mouths becoming familiar with the feel, and luckily for me, and my busy night, they decided they liked it. With dinner over, it was transportation time. I loaded in mum-in-law, the twins and Ben and off we went. First drop off was Ben and then to the K-Mart in hopes of finding a stroller, as the boys were unsteady on their feet, and some clothes in the right size. Of course each time I loaded and unloaded the car the boys screamed and protested. I would become used to people looking and wondering what the commotion was about.

Somehow, Nana and I survived K-Mart and emerged with at least three changes of clothes, two umbrella strollers, some new bottles and a couple of toys that the boys could amuse themselves with. Next stop was the airport. The boys finally went to sleep on the way and we pulled them gently from the car into their new strollers to meet their new 'Daddy.' Nana had gotten new life from this whole adventure and was gamely keeping up with me as we wheeled the boys into the baggage area to pick up Roger.

I was first around the corner and he spotted me straight away. "Who is this? One of Louise's babysitting jobs?" he asked. But before I could answer Nana appeared with an identical replica of the mine. "Oh," he sighed softly as his eyes welled up. "I think I know where these two come from." He bent down and in his wonderful gentle manner said a soft "Hi" to the boys. Of course they just stared back blankly. No smiles, no tears, no frowns, just nothing.

Luckily we had a room set up, not with cribs but with two beds and cuddle toys waiting for the two children we were hoping to adopt. The boys slept so long that at 11 a.m. the next morning we woke them up. They had big bags and dark shadows under their eyes and still no expression whatsoever. Word had gotten around my neighborhood and my neighbors brought everything from toys, clothes, shoes, car seats, and much more. It took a week for them to wake up. I honestly believe they were drugged from second hand smoke or so sleep deprived that they just didn't move off the couch. But finally they woke up and then the fun really began.

We called them "chipmunk cheeks." They would eat so much food that they stored it in their cheeks like chipmunks. It was like they weren't sure there was going to be another meal so they were going to eat as much as they could. I have so many wonderful memories and pictures of their first foods from ice cream cones to broccoli. They soon learned to love food and were willing to try anything.

Even though from the moment they arrived it was like they were part of us and belonged to us. But it is not always like that. Our little boys were meant to be in our family and my heart knew that instantly when I saw them for the first time. Today, Dustin and Devin have been in our home for more than thirteen years. In March 1999, we officially made them ours when we adopted them.

Kate Thompson became a foster parent in 1997 and fostered more than 60 children. She has had experience with many disorders such as ADHD, OCD, Bi-Polar, physical disabilities such as Cerebral Palsy and deafness. She has cared for Downs Syndrome and brain damaged children, as well as those that were neglected and delayed. She has adopted eight children from the Department of Children's Services, including three sets of twins. She currently has custody of a Liberian child who is the product of a broken adoption. She lives on a small hobby farm with her husband, nine children aged 8 to 15, nine chickens, seven goats with four new "kids," and two mini horses that were rescued due to the economy. She is also a singer songwriter, an actress, director, and author of ***Is Eight Enough – God Knows and He Ain't Telling****.*

Is It Worth It?

By Amy Bates

"Is it worth it?" she asks.

Sleepless nights, endless to-do lists, judgment from people who have no right, Loss of time with friends, husband, children…self. Lack of money as you add another to the table and in line at the amusement park.

"Tell me please, I have only just begun. Is it worth all this? Do you help anyone?"

The question weighs on me. "Sure it is," is what I want to quickly reply. You are helping a lost soul, a child who has no one. The need for parents like you is immense. The answer stills on my tongue as I pause to respond.

Looking back over the years I had to consider, is it really worth it? Interacting with parents who rarely appreciate your commitment to their child. The idea that somehow drugs, violence, and neglect are not to blame for you stealing their children. Demands insisted upon seem silly when compared to reasons the children were removed. You become the enemy, an easy target for resentment and hate.

The "system" can also be difficult to work with at times. Caseworkers who can't be bothered to return calls to you, a simple babysitter. Judges who make decisions endangering the children you love. Always living in a glass house, where every mistake is discussed around a table as a "team." Being told help, but don't interfere.

Love, but not too much…

Then I think of the children, all of the little ones who could finally stop being mom to their younger siblings and just be a kid. The sweet angels continually crying as they go through withdrawals. Each of them who marveled at the amount of food in the cupboards. The meaning of full, taking a long time to understand.

Christmas gifts that get to stay,
Spilling milk, waiting for the blow that never comes,
New clothes, a bed of their own, and a room to keep it all in.
Birthday cakes, full belly, homework, parks, rules, bedtime stories, traditions.
Regardless of age, these are some things first experienced in my home.

My mind then wanders to earlier in the day when one of "my" kids burst through the door. "Coming to play," he says and I know this is true. The reasons however, go deeper than that. Opening our door again because he is hungry, tired of the fighting, needs a getaway. **He comes because he knows…here is calm, peace, love.**

Our family gives him the ability to visualize a different future for himself. Knowing he has us in his corner, cheering him on, hoping, praying for his success. Time spent with our family gave him something valuable, which can never be taken away. The difference in his life and others who have passed through our house is real. Making all other sacrifices seems insignificant, small, worthless.

"Yes" I reply. "It is worth it."

Amy Bates is mom to 10 kids who miraculously came to her through adoption, birth, and foster care. She and her husband have been foster parents for 11 years. She is continually amazed at the strength of the children who pass through her doors and is honored to get to know each and every one of them.

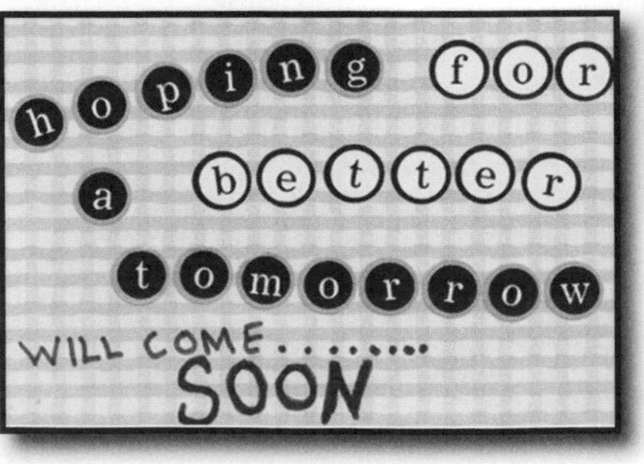

Perspectives

"You never truly know someone until you've walked a mile in his shoes."

We Need More Than the Obvious

By Tamarra Lestage

We are coming from the worst and it is disappointing when your last bit of faith and hope is crushed by someone who gets paid to do the exact opposite.

"It takes a village to raise a child." How many of you heard that saying before? I've heard it so many times, yes 21-year-old me heard this saying many, many times. People still say those things, and everyone knows exactly what it means. Whatever happen to the significance of it?

As I speak to some elders in my community, you know the type, the ones who start every last one of their speeches with "back in my days" as if they don't want to claim today being theirs too (even if they are alive and kicking). Who could blame them? I wouldn't either, because their yesterday isn't like today.

They painted a picture in my head where no kid went without food, clothes, or an education. Sounds like heaven doesn't it? Yeah, they were also generous when it came to reprimanding a child. Boy were they generous. Imagine a whole town chasing you with their hands held high to give you the spanking of your life when you misbehave. Does it still sound like heaven? No? Okay, I may have gone overboard with my imagination but I got the significance of it from just listening to those stories.

So when you sign up to be a foster parent you've enlisted yourself to be part of that village. I hope you are well aware that in a foster youth's mind your title isn't so popular. There is a reason why I said your title instead of saying foster parents. In my book, a couple of bad cops doesn't determine the faith of the rest of the cops. And it isn't any ones fault (not even the system for wanting quantity instead of quality), but the bad cops who come with alternative motives.

That is coming from someone who had a horrible experience with a foster parent. She gave me sheets that looked like the rags on a homeless person. I remember waiting outside in the cold, rain, and heat for them to come home after a long day of school and work. However, she didn't have a lock on the fridge which was one of the main reasons I said yes when my caseworker asked me if I wanted to live with her. Later on, I found out the reason she didn't lock it was because she didn't have food stored in it.

I Put on a
FAKE SMILE
So people don't
Know I'm Hurting!

So imagine me being allergic to eggs, peanuts, and milk and chlorine. I also had indoor and outdoor allergies. I had to take pills, eye drops, and nasal spray. Guess who fed me in order for me take my medicine? My boyfriend, with his teenage part time job salary. That wasn't his responsibility. But as I said before, one bad cop doesn't determine the faith of the rest. We are coming from the worst and it is disappointing when your last bit of faith and hope is crushed by someone who gets paid to do the exact opposite.

As a teenager, I wanted that parental love and support. I wanted a couple of awkward talks of the bird and the bees. I wanted a father greeting my date at the front door with a shot gun so he would know that his life could end because he simply brought me home three seconds past my curfew. I wanted a mother to teach me her favorite recipes. I am not asking anybody to shoot anyone on my account, just treat us like your child and stop branding us to society every time you introduce us to your friends. Every time you introduce us as your foster child it puts us in an awkward position. We might as well say "hey look at me, poor old me! My parents didn't want me so this wonderful family took me in and sometimes they just like to parade me around and remind me of my fortunes. However, I am very grateful so let's throw a parade and shout all hail to this family."

That would be so wrong, but you know what? It is deserved because now the kids at school pick on me for being a foster child and your kids look down on me and you're just filling the case book because it is required of you. What about protection? What about giving me a little bliss from the simplest things I never received? Yes those things are required of you by being a foster parent. What else does a foster child need? Think of them as your child then you will know.

Tamarra Lestage is a former foster child who loves to write and share her perspectives. She is a member of Florida Youth SHINE.

I think the best way foster parents can help the kids they care for is to stay open minded, patient, don't take much personally. Be prepared for a little (or a lot) of chaos. I know I've bitterly pushed away my foster parents when I really just wanted to be closer to them. It's taken me a while to come around and realize everything they do for me and show gratitude. And even years after placement old issues still come up, so be open minded to whatever is going on and be patient with us. We just want to know that you're not going to leave us too.

– current foster youth

Tough Starts Matter

By Adoption Learning Partners Staff

When Mike and Megan brought their son Peter home, they were prepared for sleepless nights; they knew there would be an adjustment period. But they were not ready for what lay ahead: learning issues at school, monumental melt downs over the slightest thing, lashing out. All of it, unexplained – even Peter couldn't tell them why. When their counselor told them Peter's behavior was a result of his infant care, it made no sense to Mike and Megan. How could what he can't remember continue to affect him? What should they do to help him? And how are they going to keep the rest of their lives together while they figure it all out?

Peter's story is not unique. Children living in or adopted from foster care, children adopted internationally, and children adopted domestically as infants may have all experienced, in different ways, a tough start in life. Your job, as parents, is to help these children get what they missed before they came into your home and to help them develop the skills to work around the challenges life has handed them. But that isn't always so easy to figure out.

Children who come from foster care often get a ***Tough Start*** in life. They may have suffered prenatal substance exposure or malnutrition; their early care may have been substandard with multiple care givers unable to truly meet their needs. They may have experienced neglectful, chaotic, or abusive environments. Regardless of the reason, this type of trauma impacts our children's brains. Understanding that a child's behavior may not be completely willful, but rather the product of a Tough Start is the first step. It may be "can't" vs. "won't."

Understanding the impact

"I don't know what happened to me before I was adopted, but I still have nightmares about it." – adult adoptee

Before children develop recall and are able to communicate their feelings and fears, they have what is called state memory. For some children the trauma happened before they were even born. For others the impact occurs early on. In the first years of life, a child's experiences are stored in state memory. Typically, they cannot recall the traumatic events, the difficulties of their beginnings, or explain their feelings. However, they have the fear of being hungry or harmed, they have the sense of being rejected, and they have an awareness of feeling unwanted or unloved. These feelings often manifest themselves in behaviors that even the most experienced parent may find hard to understand and manage.

Recognizing the importance of early diagnosis

"We hoped it was something John would outgrow. Everyone else said he would. So we waited. We didn't get help until he had been with us for three years." – adoptive parents

Parents often hesitate to get a diagnosis fearing that their child will forever be labeled as having a problem. But a diagnosis defines treatment. And since the brain is more flexible the younger the child is, the earlier treatment begins, the greater the recovery potential. There are many pieces of assessment that fit together to form a diagnosis. A comprehensive assessment gathers information about your child through observation, interviews and testing. Receiving an accurate diagnosis helps to prioritize possible treatments as well as to secure appropriate services from a school or insurance provider. It also arms you as parents with the tools you need to better help your child.

Adjusting your parenting style to suit your child's needs

"Once we began to understand the "whys" of his behavior, we could begin to figure out the "hows" of helping him change it." – foster and adoptive parents

The goal of "therapeutic parenting" is to help your child develop the coping skills he or she needs to better function in life, now and in the future. You are providing the loving nurture that your child should have had from the beginning of life. This may require you to learn some new parenting tactics. You can't fall back on the "that's how I was raised and I turned out okay" mentality. You can't parent on autopilot – you have to be in the cockpit with your eye on the controls at all times. Why? Because your child is more vulnerable. Therapeutic parenting maximizes your strengths and your child's strengths. It can help you to offset and work around triggers and vulnerabilities. This allows you to respond more insightfully to your child. It gives you the ability to appropriately redirect your child's negative behavior and to encourage healing and the development of new coping skills.

Taking care of yourself, and the rest of your family

"This is not about how much you can take before you break; it's about taking a break before you do." – adoption professional

Now you have learned about possible causes for your child's behavior, how to get the appropriate resources, how to teach coping skills and manage triggers at home…what about you? What about your other children? Many parents feel guilty taking time for themselves; your tough start child requires so much time and energy, your other children need whatevers left. However, it is important to recognize the toll that raising a tough start child can take on you, your relationships and your other children, and to marshal your resources of time and energy to best effect. There are simple, small and practical steps and exercises to build your strength, help your relationships and open communication with your other children. Having a child in your life is a blessing. But having a child with a tough start also presents challenges, to everyone involved.

Samantha, Mike and Megan's therapist, worked with them as a family and each of them individually. She helped them understand the fear that drove Peter's behavior. She taught them that he didn't remember why, and couldn't tell them he was afraid, but the fear existed. Once Mike and Megan understood how trauma affected Peter's brain, they could begin helping him manage his behavior and felt a little less overwhelmed.

Finding resources that help families understand and address all of these areas is challenging. That's why Adoption Learning Partners has a series of online courses one entitled, ***Tough Starts Matter****. The* ***Tough Starts Matter*** *courses include modules on brain development, treatment options, parenting strategies, and family resources. Find this course (and others) at www.adoptionlearningpartners.org.*

A Foster Child's Perspective

By John Morgan

As foster children we go through rough times. We are dealing with things that no human being on this planet should ever experience, including rejection, abandonment, neglect, and abuse from the ones we trusted and loved so dearly.

We are confused and hurt. Our actions and behaviors that we display are not acceptable by society. It's the only way we can figure out to get that pain out into the open. It is our cry for help so to speak. Through this, foster parents, teachers, caseworkers, and so on truly need to understand that we are still kids and we need direction, structure, TLC, a shoulder to cry on, and most importantly, open ears.

I was lucky enough for my first (and longest placement) to have all of these things and more. I will never forget my time in that family. My first day, I was defensive and unsure of my future. I wouldn't even sit down for the first couple of days in that place because of my confusion, pain, and paranoia. I stayed quiet and very shy, with little interaction with the family.

But remember this, be patient and understanding. The child will open up his or her shell rather quickly if you show that you are there to assist during his or her time of need.

This family did this by acting more like a friend and providing a support system. They didn't push or attempt to invade my life. From that time I began to trust them. I slowly began to open up, and with it came more trust. Within a few months, I accepted them as family. Which they also did with me. But don't get discouraged if this process doesn't happen overnight, as it never will.

Be prepared for troubled times and when they happen, remember the times that the youth has shared appreciation, and shown that they have given you what trust they can muster up. Hopefully, within time, they will accept you as their family just as what you are trying to do for them. That should be the ultimate (if not the only) reward you should look forward to for being a foster parent to those children unfortunate to have to go through such an ordeal.

On behalf of foster children throughout this beloved country, let me say thank you for showing and proving that you care when so few seem to show lack of concern for our leaders of tomorrow!

John Morgan is a former foster youth and an advocate for foster youth throughout Florida.

"The Jigsaw Puzzle Child"

By Eileen Mayers Pasztor, DSW

Every adult who interacts with children in foster care must understand average, expectable, or "normal" child development principles, and the often devastating impact of neglect and physical and sexual abuse on child well-being. As a foster care caseworker who grew up to become a foster and adoptive parent, here are two stories about child development that demonstrate what happens when caseworkers don't have grounding in child development, and offers a tool that helps look at child development from a more realistic perspective.

My decision to be a child welfare worker was not a career calling. I sought any job where a college diploma was required, and the county welfare department (as social services was called a long time ago) was seeking college graduates. With the qualifications of only a bachelor's degree in history and a driver's license, I was hired as a foster care caseworker. I didn't even know what foster care was because I was fortunate to grow up in a family with nurturing parents.

On my second day at work, I was sent to see a foster mother who had been fostering for more years than I was old. We had a disagreement about the age of a child in her care. According to the case record, the child was about one year of age. The foster mother said the child was three years old. I did see the child, but I didn't stay long. When I returned to the agency, I told my supervisor, who recently earned a masters in social work, about what happened. My supervisor asked me what the child was doing, as a way to determine who was correct: the case record or the foster mother. I told my supervisor that the child was riding her tricycle most of the time. Everyone but myself was astonished that I didn't know a one-year-old couldn't ride a tricycle... I didn't learn that as a history major. Years later, after I gained some experience in child development and of course much more, I returned to the agency and ran into that foster mother. She told me that I was the dumbest case worker she had ever met. Think of the mistakes that are made when basic information such as child development is not known.

Many years later, after having the privilege of working with literally thousands of wonderful foster parents and child welfare professionals around the country, and becoming a foster parent, my husband and I decided to add to our family by adopting a child with special needs. He was chronologically ten years old, and had been in two residential facilities since the age of six. My parents were thrilled at the addition of who would be their only grandson. But it didn't take long for them to be frustrated with his behaviors, least of which was his "excess energy" and inability to focus on any activity for more than a few minutes. Try as I might to prepare them that he was going to be "different" from other ten year olds, we were all struggling. So I invented the "jigsaw puzzle" activity to show them how he wasn't really ten years old.

The Jigsaw Puzzle Tool

Children have eight parts to their development: their age in years; appearance age; IQ age; academic age (grade in school); emotional age; social age; whether they are an ethnic match with the family they are living with, and how many years of customs, values, and traditions they share; and their life experience age. Most people – like my parents – were expecting that a ten-year-old would look between 9 and 11 years of age, would be in the fifth grade, would be of average or above intelligence; would be white like us, and would share our family values and traditions.

Children who have experienced the tragedy of abuse and neglect and sexual abuse have fragmented pieces. See the puzzle below – that's the puzzle for a child born with the blessings of good genes and good environment. The puzzle on the right – that's my son. He was 10 years old in years, but he looked eight (small for his age). He processed information like an eight-year-old according to his IQ test and, academically, he didn't read or write when he came to us: not one word. So he was academically preschool age.

Regarding trust, why should any child who has been abused or neglected by adults

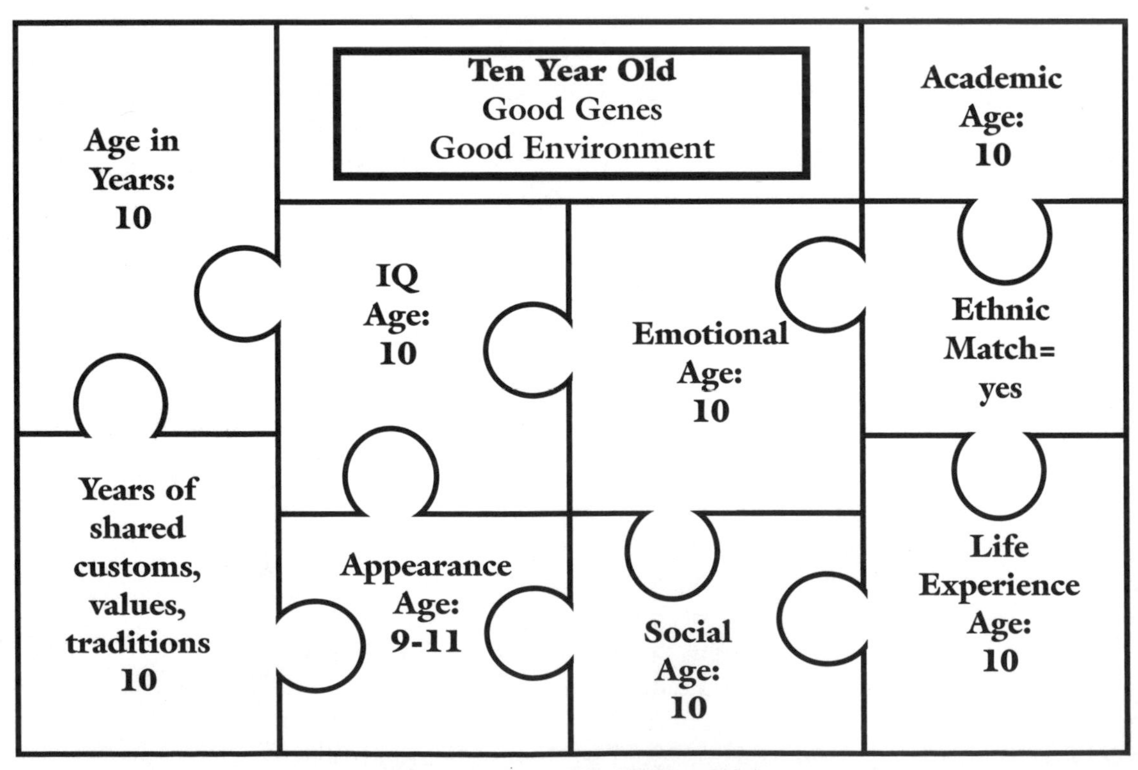

The Typical Ten Year Old

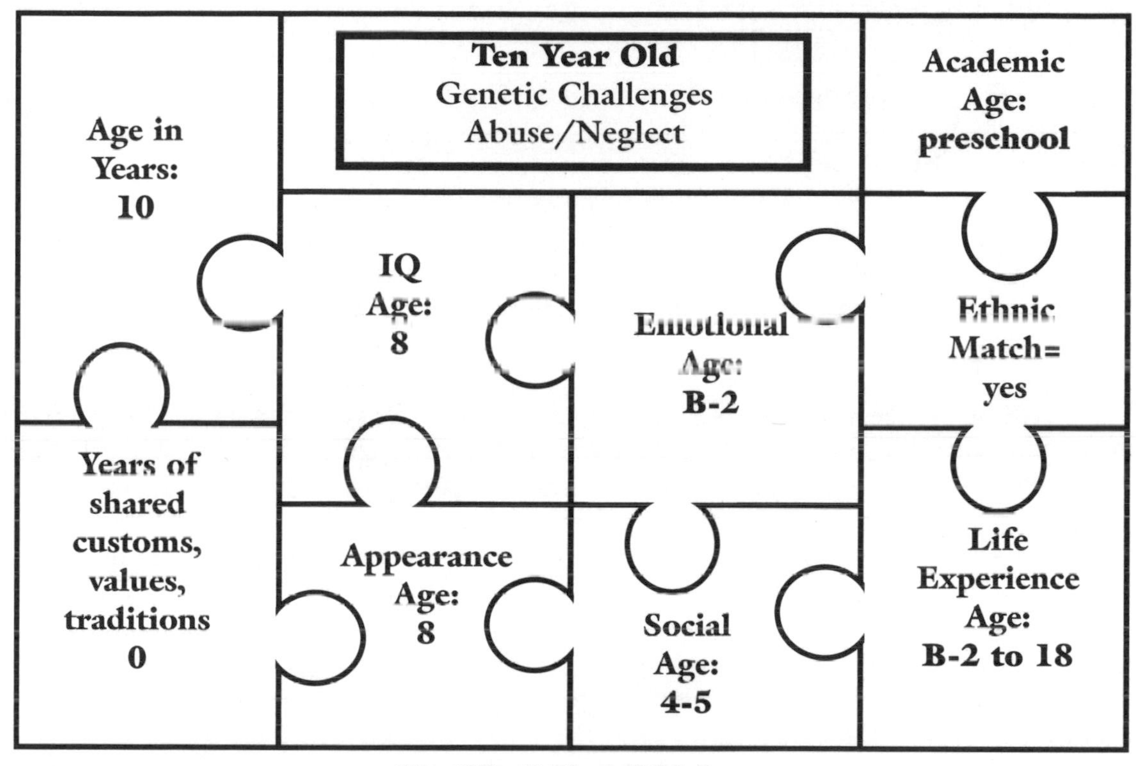

My "Ten" Year Old Son

trust any of us? We think of families as safe havens. Children coming into the foster care system typically see families as places where children get hurt. Mom neglects you when she is high; her boyfriend abuses you because you're just a reminder that she had sex with someone else. Families can be scary places. This can be especially true if you've lived with many previous foster or even adoptive parents who started off by saying, "I love you," and then called for your "removal" (like you were garbage or snow) when your behaviors acted out your normal feelings of fear and anger.

Socially, after living in a residential setting with other challenged children, our son could do parallel play but not interactive play, which made him socially at the preschool age. We were an ethnic match, but we had zero years of shared customs, values, and traditions. He wanted to sleep with us because that was what he had been taught before he was sent away to residential; and he wanted to be sure we wouldn't abandon him in the middle of the night. As another example, when our foster daughter came to live with us, she had the custom of sleeping with her shoes on her pillow. That's because, where she used to live, she never knew who would try to molest her in the middle of the night; she used her shoes as a weapon or to run.

To assess the "life experience" age, you look at the range from the youngest age to the oldest age of functioning. In my son's situation, this would place his youngest age of functioning at his emotional age, which was "birth through two" – when basic trust is established. For most children who have been abused or neglected, typical attachments and trusting relationship are suspect. His oldest age of functioning I list as 18 plus years of age. This is because children who have been sexually abused have experienced activities that many people don't know about until they at least go to R-rated movies or have had some of their own more "grown up" or intimate relationships.

How Does This Work?

In every child welfare class I teach, in every workshop I do, in every keynote I give, I demonstrate the "jigsaw puzzle child" activity. I usually do it with two pieces of flip chart paper. First I diagram the "typical" ten-year old. Then I diagram my son. And then I rip the pieces apart and throw them on the floor. This is because the child welfare and other "systems" don't typically deal with children in foster care from a developmental perspective and in a unified way. The case record documents the date of birth or chronological age. Anyone who meets the child sees the appearance age. Schools interact with a different piece of the child, and so on. And if a foster parent has three children in their care, that's actually 24 different ages and stages to protect and nurture.

Consider the risk factors for children whose pieces of their jigsaw puzzle do not fit together. What are the risks for a girl who is emotionally, socially, and cognitively 12 but looks like she's 16? What are the risks for boys who look older than their abilities? And for young people of color, the risks are greater. Latino and African American males tend to get referred to juvenile corrections while Anglos are more likely to go to mental health facilities.

What happens when these "jigsaw puzzle children" turn 18 years of age and the alarm on their independent living clock rings? Now, at the chronological age of 18 years, they are supposed to be "emancipated." They "age out." Listen to how awful those words sound, how unnatural they are. What do they sound like to a child? How can we expect safe and responsible behavior from someone who is 18 in years only, but socially, emotionally, academically, and cognitively much younger? And here's another critical question:

Who is responsible for putting all the "pieces" back together again?

From now on, every time you think about a child in your care, your caseload, your classroom or even the courtroom, think of all the pieces of the puzzle. Put a jigsaw puzzle diagram in their records. Discuss the "jigsaw puzzle" pieces when getting ready to place children. It may be that the placing caseworker does not know what all the pieces are. It may be that some children have to live with foster parents for a while before their foster parents can determine what the "ages" are. Tell the judge. Remember, when you are considering sending children back to their parents, the parents have jigsaw puzzles pieces, too. It's just their chronological ages are higher. Otherwise, their pieces look a lot like those of their children. How do we ensure child safety, well-being, and permanency when we send "jigsaw puzzle" children to live with "jigsaw puzzle" parents?

Fast forward the clock: Our son is now in his thirties. He is a client of county mental health services. He cannot work; my husband and I help him with most of his tasks of daily living. He has a wonderful relationship with my 90-year-old parents, who accepted him many years ago, once they put the pieces of the puzzle together. I didn't expect to be a mom to someone who is thirty-something in years, but emotionally and socially much more like a 14-year-old. However, I am humbled that, through his challenges, and those of my foster daughter, I was taught the lessons that enabled me to create and share these activities. I would have preferred, of course, that they had not had the experiences. But our adult "children" are safe, and we're still a family. I hope this "jigsaw puzzle" tool will help facilitate safety, well-being, and permanency for the children in your care and in your caseloads, too.

Adapted from:
Child Welfare League of America. (2009). Foster PRIDE/Adopt Pride – Preservice Training for Foster and Adoptive Parents, Trainer's Guide. Washington, DC: Child Welfare League of America, p. 243.

Pasztor, E.M. & McCurdy, M. (2009). *When work comes home and home goes to work – child welfare social workers as foster and adoptive parents.* In E. Grise-Owens & K. Lay, (eds.), *Reflections – narratives of professional helping.* Special Issue: *Inside Out – Reflections on Personal and Professional Intersections*, Spring, Volume 15, #2, 95-105, p. 95; and p. 98.

Pasztor, E.M., Polowy, M., Leighton, M., & Conte, R. (1991). *The ultimate challenge: Foster parenting in the 1990s.* Washington, DC: Child Welfare League of America.

Eileen Mayers Pasztor, DSW, is experienced as a public agency caseworker and supervisor; as a curriculum developer and trainer; and as a foster and adoptive parent for children with special needs who, now as adults, continue to require her support. She teaches child welfare and social policy advocacy courses at the School of Social Work at California State University, Long Beach (CSULB), and edits the journal Reflections – Narratives of Professional Helping, and she continues to consult and train nationally.

Taking off the Mask

By Anne Birdsong Giberson

The other night I felt miserably sorry for myself. I had gotten some negative feedback about my kids and that's a sensitive spot for me. Whenever I hear disparaging remarks about my life's work I make a supreme effort to square my shoulders, raise my chin a notch and open my ears to listen without being defensive. I listen in order to take in what they have to say, weigh it for merit, and implement any action that might be needed.

What Other See

I know that my children are not perfect and they are a continual work in progress. Shaping and molding is hard work. I am forever turning over in my mind how I can tweak the system in order to get the best "output." Output in this case being strong, healthy, straight-A students who help little old ladies cross the street as soon as they finish all of their household chores with a smile on their shiny faces.

Overall, I feel pretty proud of my crew, though they are by no means a "finished product" and there is much work to be done to nip certain problems in the bud. But on most days I feel good about myself and my kids. Last night was different. Coming from two places (both near and dear), I felt shadow was being noticed instead of light. And even more in question than my children's character was my way of doing things. Everything about how these kids are raised is my domain: what they eat, how much time they spend in front of screens, how white their teeth are, how many responsibilities they have and how well they do them, how short their toenails are and the list goes on. If they're falling short, that means I am falling short because their life training is my job.

Staying Neutral

So yeah, I try to remain neutral so I can take in feedback and make it work for me, but I'm not always so good at the neutral thing. I get emotional where my kids and my sense of self-esteem are concerned. What I have to keep foremost in my mind is, how do I feel I'm doing? How do I feel about how my kids are turning out? If I know I'm doing a good job (I do), then I have to continue to take in the feedback and use it for what it's worth, but not let other people's opinions overshadow my own.

This is difficult territory for any mom, but even more so for those of us raising children not born of our loins. For some reason, that immediately turns the spotlight onto everything we do. Every action or inaction is dissected and analyzed. Need a reason for children misbehaving? Look no further than the fact that they were born to another mother. Third party child-rearing seems to become the scapegoat for every misdeed or hair out of place. Have you ever noticed that if there's a news item of some atrocity that was committed by a person who was once adopted or a foster child, that is generally the first thing mentioned after the crime itself? It's supposed to be an "aha" moment for the audience, so we can make sense out of the tragedy. Why do I never hear my favorite newscaster say,"... he is responsible for the senseless deaths of countless puppies and kittens. You know, he was raised by his biological family..."

What's worse is that we let this phenomenon bury us ever deeper into the mire of make-believe. We get so tired of people looking for the bad in our kids and then making that connection to foster/adopted kids that we tend to gloss things over. We put our spin on the account in order for others not to have their self-righteous "I told you so" moments. The danger in this, though, is that we set ourselves up for isolation. Support systems are vital not only for our kids, but for our own mental and emotional well-being. If we have no one with whom to share Johnny's missteps because we can't take our happy face mask off, how will we cope? How long can it last?

The Illusion of Perfection

We all savor the image in our minds of the perfect family beside the picket fence. The smiling, stress-free mom who has taken these kids in to give them a better life. The fanciful notion that if you provide a kid with a loving home, a pretty room, nice clothes, and a trip to Disney, the troubled youngster will magically morph into a warm, carefree, and loving child who does no wrong and has reconciled all past troubles and traumas. It's a fine image, but it truly does belong only in the daydream recesses of our minds. If we try to portray that to the world at large, we are doing ourselves, our kids, and the foster/adoption community a disservice.

But I know I am indeed guilty of that. Because I believe so strongly in fostering and adopting, I want the rest of the world to jump on board. In order for people to want to parent these children themselves, they need to see positive images of families who are making it work. So I generally go into my auto-pilot walking advertisement mode whenever I walk out of my home. I ensure everyone looks well-groomed and appropriately dressed. I give the manners and rules lectures before we step through the doors of any establishment. If any of my kids begin to act up, I endeavor to keep my mask in place and not let any of my frustrations shine through. I try to ensure people see just "regular kid" issues as opposed to "adoption/foster" issues.

Again, there is a danger in that. Soon enough, that mask goes on. It goes on not just when you walk out of your house, but when you have close friends over, or when you talk on the phone with a trusted family member. When we become disconnected, not just with random strangers, but with those closest to us, and finally, even with ourselves, we get to the point where we feel like we're emotionally hyperventilating.

Being Honest With Yourself

It is vital that we identify the people in our lives that we can be ourselves around when we're in the thick of our child-rearing stress. As parents, we are the front line of helping these children resolve their past traumas and losses. Make no mistake, being in that position can take its toll. We need to ensure that we have ears to bend and shoulders to cry on when we need them. To that end, I would encourage every foster/adoptive parent to make a list of those they can be honest with in regards to their parenting struggles. Mentally flip through the Rolodex and ask yourself who you can turn to and expose your shortcomings and frustrations as a parent. A few to consider would be (in no particular order): Spouse, Listserv of foster/adoptive parents, Partner, Parents, Sibling, Pastor, Friend, Therapist.

Of course, the first person on that list should be yourself. If you can't be honest with yourself about your frustrations, you don't have much hope in opening up to anyone else.

So at the end of the day, sit quietly and review all that you did as a parent that you were pleased with. But then be sure to examine the things you did or said that left you feeling less than proud. And tell yourself that it's okay that you fell short of your mark. To hit a couple of clichés at once, being aware is "half the battle" and "tomorrow is a new day."

When you feel comfortable being honest with yourself, try it out on the person at the top of your trust list and see how that goes. The goal here is to wear that mask of perfection less and less, around fewer and fewer people. If you can manage that, it won't seem such a crisis when one of your darlings acts up, and you won't feel the neurotic impulse to brush everything under the welcome mat the minute behavior goes awry. You want to become confident enough to say that your child is making bad choices, showing poor impulse control or acting like a flippin' lunatic. No one is going to fault you for that. Those around you will realize that even though your kids are no Stepford Children, they are real kids with real issues and you are still alive and well. They'll realize that, yes, kids from "the system" may have issues, but it doesn't mean they cannot be a part of a family that cares about them. It doesn't mean they cannot learn good behavior. And it certainly doesn't mean they are not capable of love.

So take off the mask. Wearing it fools no one.

Anne Birdsong Giberson is the mother of six children. Three of her kids joined her family by birth, and three were born to other mothers and joined the family later in life, at the ages of 5, 10, and 13. Anne lives on a small hobby farm in rural Pennsylvania with her husband of 20 plus years where she and the kids watch over their horses, goats, dogs, and other assorted critters. Between mucking out the barn and resolving disputes between children, she occasionally updates her blog at www.bringingboryahome.blogspot.com.

To the Honorable Judge Michael Usan

I am writing to you in regards to Alexander Mcleod who is currently incarcerated for violation of community control and is set to appear in front of you on 10-7-2010.

My name is Mackenzie Ramsay and I met Alex Mcleod in the foster care system at the Impact Group Home in Fort Lauderdale, Florida in 2003; we were both 17 years of age.

First I want to present a brief literature review:

I feel it is safe to state children are one of society's most vulnerable populations. So one can imagine youth in foster care are especially vulnerable. I view them as innocent victims of both parents who created an environment of maltreatment and innocent victims of the foster care system. Using the system's theory perspective, the manifest and latent functions stemming from childhood trauma of being removed from your home and placed in the foster care system can and will have detrimental effects on the overall quality of life. According to Krinsky (2010), 25,000 youth transition out of the foster care system every year and without the anchor of a family. Former foster youth disproportionately join the ranks of homeless, incarcerated and unemployed. The average age of financial independence in America is 26 years of age; however, we presume that foster youth can somehow attain financial and emotional independence by age 18. Instead, these adolescents are woefully unprepared for independent adult life, and when they stumble, too many times no one is there to provide any type of support. I feel a result of this is clearly illustrated by these facts: former foster youth are 10 times more likely to be arrested than youth of the same age, race, and sex and one in four youth who age out of foster care will end up in jail within the first two years after leaving care (Krinsky, 2010). Other studies have confirmed this and also found high rates of homelessness, incarcerations, poor physical and mental health, limited educational attainment, high unemployment, high rates of pregnancy, and high rates of substance abuse (Collins, 2001; Courtney & Dworsky, 2005; Reilly, 2003).

Throughout my teenage years and early adulthood I became another statistic and fell victim to the self-fulfilling prophecy. I have made many legal and personal mistakes which I am not proud of. I sat in front of Judge Susan Lebow and plead openly under the youthful offender motion. I scored out to prison time, however, I was placed on three years of probation after finishing a year-long term of house arrest. I was fortunate and blessed to receive more than a second chance, but more like a fifth chance. I was able to turn my life around and I earned a bachelors of social work degree from Florida Gulf Coast University graduating Summa Cum Laude. I will graduate in May with a masters of social work. Afterward I will seek a masters in criminal justice, and finally a juris doctor degree in family law. I am currently working for The Department of Children and Families in Ft. Myers and I will become a Child Protective Investigator this May. You may ask yourself "how does one foster youth succeed and one does not?" The answer is social support and resilience.

Social support is a crucial ingredient in the recipe of success. Without adequate social support, one's health and well-being could be in jeopardy. Often foster care youth have no social support, let alone a positive mentor or role model. According to Daining &

DePanfilis (2007) mentoring has been identified as a potential way to meet youths' critical needs for continuous supportive connections and more recent studies revealed that youth who have a positive and significant relationship with at least one adult tend to fare better in the challenging transition into adulthood (Ahrens, DuBois, Richardson, Fan, & Lozano, 2008; Munson & McMillen, 2009). Ahrens et al. (2008) found mentored youth, who reported having a mentor before 18 years of age and for at least two years, fared better on self-reports of overall health, educational attainment, physical aggression, suicide risk, and risk of sexually transmitted infection than did non-mentored foster care youth. According to Munson & McMillen (2009) older foster care youth who had engaged in a natural mentoring relationship for more than one year reported lower levels of stress and were less likely to have been arrested by the age of 19 than were non-mentored youth.

I could go on and on with scholarly literature backing my viewpoint on foster youths' struggles to transform into a productive member of society; however, I know your time is valuable. In my case, Kristen Guerrise, executive director of the FLITE Center in Ft. Lauderdale, served as my mentor who entered my life when I was 18. I have also been blessed with the ability to be resilient throughout my life. Alexander Mcleod also demonstrates resiliency and as of the past several months Guerrise, who worked wonders in my life, is mentoring Mcleod. Throughout my years of knowing Mcleod I realized he was a follower, socializing with the wrong crowd. I personally have been acting as a positive role model in Mcleod's life as well. There are several foster youth whom I know, currently incarcerated, and I would

Be There

By Veronica Brown

As a teenager, I worked at a summer day camp. Attending the program was a boy with Downs Syndrome. At different times, he would take off from the group and hide in a quiet spot within the community center. It was my job to find him and get him back on track. When I located him, I would join him on the floor. We'd talk and I would try to figure out what was wrong. After ten minutes or so of talking, I'd convince him to rejoin the group. I was pretty pleased with myself. I thought of myself as a master problem solver or at the least, a great persuader. I was confident in my ability to connect with this disabled child.

Then one day that summer, this same boy ran away again. I remember being annoyed at the time. Whether it was because he'd done it so often or I was just particularly busy that day, I was losing my patience. I found him in his usual spot and just sat with him quietly, not talking at all. About ten minutes later, I looked at him and asked, "Are you ready to go back?" He nodded and back we went.

Many times since, when dealing with different foster kids, I am reminded of that summer and the lesson I learned. I don't always have to be the one talking, fixing, or motivating. Sometimes, it's enough just to be there. Be there to give time. Be there to provide space. Be there to show support. Be there to demonstrate my confidence in their ability. Just be there.

Veronica Brown has been a foster parent in Canada since 1995.

never advocate on their behalf. Mcleod is different: he is a bright, likable, and a kind young man who never had the luxury of having a positive role model in his life. He now has two!

I know Mcleod is a grown man and must be held accountable for his actions and he is aware of this as well. I am not asking for a slap on the wrist with Mcleod, as he should be disciplined and there will be consequences for his actions. I am asking to look at the literature that is available on foster youth, look at my situation, reflect back on your life to see how important family, friends, and your social support was in your success, and to reinstate Mcleod on community control (perhaps with a suspended sentence) to allow Guerrise and myself to continue working with him.

Sincerely,

Mackenzie Ramsay, BSW

Mr. Ramsay, BSW, was removed from his biological mother due to neglect and substance abuse at 3 months of age. He stayed in eight different foster homes and was removed from three of those eight foster homes due to abuse. He was adopted by age 3 and was removed from that home when he was 14, was returned to the foster care system and aged out at 18. He faced many hardships and struggled in many areas of his life but he has turned things around. His passion is child welfare and he has decided to make working with children and foster youth his main career choice.

References

Ahrens, K. R., DuBois, D. L., Richardson, L. P., Fan, M. Y., Sc Lozano, P. (2008). *Youth in foster care with adult mentors during adolescence have improved adult outcomes.* Pediatrics, 121(2), e246- e252.

Collins, M. E. (2001). *Transition to adulthood for vulnerable youth: A review of research and implications for policy.* Social Service Review, 75(2), 271– 291.

Courtney, M. E., & Dworsky, A. (2005). *Early outcomes for young adults transitioning from out-of-home care in the USA.* Child and Family Social Work, 11, 209– 219.

Daining, C, Sc DePanfilis, D. (2007). *Resilience of youth in transition from out-of-home care to adulthood.* Children and Youth Services Review, 29, 1158-1178.

Munson, M. R., 8c McMillen, J. C. (2009). *Natural mentoring and psychosocial outcomes among older youth transitioning from foster care.* Children and Youth Services Review, 31, 104-111.

Reilly, T. (2003). *Transition from care: Status and outcomes of youth who age out of foster care.* Child Welfare, 82(6), 727– 746.

A Loving Perspective on Foster(ing) Care

By Wilma Ice

From the uncommon vantage point of being the daughter of a former foster child, a former foster child, a former foster parent, and an adoptive parent of former foster children, I feel I can offer some valuable perceptions on several generations of foster care. Life for the participants in foster care is changing, but these changes are not broad or deep enough, to connect us to ourselves or to one another.

As a young person, I learned to view foster care as a kind of imaginary parent and I grew up feeling a certain loyalty. Although somewhat embarrassed about my status as a foster child, I felt protective of the people I associated with foster care. Perhaps, this was because the protection foster care gave to me, as a child, appeared greater than what I had been separated from.

But, I now know that along with any benefits it brings, foster care inflicts the added wounds of separation, even isolation, for children and their parents. The severity of what I am going to call "separation wounds" were hardly recognized, and barely understood until the most recent years of my life. I did not understand that neither foster care nor society copes well with the wounds that are so deep they literally tear us apart, separating us from what is within, and also from each other.

The birth parents of my children have taught me about the experiences of separation they had while passing through the programs, services, and legal proceedings designed to connect with them and improve the lives of their children. They speak as if the help that was offered was really not much help at all. I am left questioning why and wondering who will be responsible for changing this?

Foster care services do not extend broadly or deeply enough to connect the hearts of birth parents and foster parents, social workers and trouble-making adolescents, community members and lawmakers. Recognizing and honoring "oneness of heart" is the only real basis for healing our experiences of separation.

The birth parents of my children tell me that their separation has felt like isolation, rejection, even hatred. I understand their message and its impact. When I was a child and in foster care, I felt as shamed and blamed as my children's birth parents without knowing why. My own birth mother, a child of foster care, later felt alienated from the professionals she hoped would teach her to raise her children. Foster care is not the direct cause of these alienating experiences, and in some cases it successfully connects families to

I did not understand that neither foster care nor society copes well with the wounds that are so deep they literally tear us apart, separating us from what is within, and also from each other.

resources that help them heal. Yet, the foster care system relies on cautiously similar and familiar options generation after generation.

It does sometimes happen that laws, professionals and participants in foster care come together to create healing resources that work. When this happens successfully, it is done not state-by-state, nor agency-by-agency, but rather individual-by-individual. It is done compassionately and fearlessly, without loyalty to history. If we all had the willingness to go where we have not gone before, and to take chances on what we may not totally understand, it could be the beginning of a final era for foster care, as it now exists. We must forget about calling things wrong or right, and instead look for what works, restores and connects us.

Relationships are frequently not at the top of our list of priorities – not for foster care workplaces, communities, or even families. Other things become more important. It seems to me that in foster care, in particular, more energy is spent deciding "What is the most responsible thing to do? Or, the most highly regarded thing to do? Or, the safest (least risky) thing to do?" In order for the wounded hearts and spirits of foster children and their families to be healed, the real question is, "What is the most loving thing to do?"

My life has been more than ordinarily challenging at times. My early hardships were similar to what many children in foster care have experienced, and included poverty, domestic violence, physical abuse, emotional abuse, neglect, parental mental health and substance abuse issues, frequent moves, and so much more. Once I finished high school, these hardships were no longer present in my life, and after many years of emotional work I felt that I had healed all that I could, and focused my energies on functioning as well as possible.

I was professionally successful, active in my community, and others frequently assured me that I was a woman with a generous spirit, open mind, and gift of compassion. It seemed that I had risen above any personal and generational hardships, ending a cycle of pain. But had I?

My understanding and misunderstanding of myself was hidden behind socially acceptable walls of high education, social practice, and psychological sophistication. I did not know who I was, and for most of my life I did not know that I did not know. My life experiences had divided me, and separated me from my goodness. This, too, was the experience of my children, who all entered foster care early, and each of whom had multiple placements prior to adoption.

Loyalty, effort, action, and support from a small group of long-time friends, a bit of special concern from a couple of current foster care workers, and the dedication and guidance of one courageous, love-centered man helped me reclaim what I had lost…a belief in my own goodness. Having people in my life who were willing to be loved in the grimmest of times, changed how I see the world and how I see myself.

Some of the biggest challenges to living lives of loving action come from desires to be financially prosperous, well-educated, and to protect a professional image or personal understanding that we identify with. Although these desires can be positive, life has taught me that anything we decide we can't bear to lose is potentially the greatest hindrance to our progress. To create a more loving world, including the world of foster care, we must be willing to change our beliefs about ourselves and about life.

Establishing loving relationships as a priority is a change that I don't believe most people yet understand or invite with open arms. Some ask, "Isn't this what we are already doing?" Others say, "What you speak of is too idealistic and won't happen. I believe that love based relationships are within our reach, but we have yet to individually choose this path.

Loving relationships pass on healthy tools to foster children, and they are also essential for the adults who choose what opportunities will exist for families and children. Foster care currently reflects the scarcity of healing relationships that are present in society.

We can heal and prevent trauma only if we create a culture where loving relationships are second to nothing. The golden rule is a spiritual law taught in some form throughout all of history, without regard to religious creed or practice. Teaching our children that we do not stand alone, and that God is not outside of us but within, is a radical application of the golden rule. "Treat others as you wish to be treated" – or to state it differently – "What I give to you I also give to myself" is a recognition that we are spiritually only one, and that choices which increase the experience of separation promote conflict.

Transformation of core beliefs and the changing of lifelong understanding are associated with spiritual awakening, not science. It takes a lot of love to transform the beliefs of kids and adults in foster care, but when we meet up with love in a measure equal to the trauma we have known, healing happens.

We do not yet have the research tools to communicate love-based spiritual successes in measurable scientific ways, and society generally still values the experimental design of Newtonian physics more than it appreciates the potential of theoretical or quantum physics. Therefore, the tools and laws of spirituality are not easily adopted by medical, business or social science communities.

For any organization whose work is human healing, foster care for instance, we must learn to measure degrees of consciousness, sensitivity, awareness, and oneness of heart and spirit. How do we measure wisdom? Can we design tools to study the ability to discern what risks must be taken to know love, embrace truth, and more deeply feel joy?

All of us who are members of the foster care network have the responsibility to practice love. A model of love will be based on spiritual laws, not religious creeds or evidence based science. A model of love is based on sensitivity, awareness, wisdom, heartedness – (or what some call mindfulness).

If foster care is about fostering care, then we are on the wrong track. We must use the laws and principles of "oneness" spirituality, teaching our children that what I give to you, I also give to myself. Then, consciously practice as we teach!

Wilma (Willie) Ice is a single mom to three children adopted from foster care. Courtney is 15, Rose and Charlie are 8. Wilma is a registered nurse with the Commonwealth of Virginia, Department for the Blind and Vision Impaired. She is a former foster child and daughter of a former foster child.

I just want to fit in
Just want to be like a normal family
I wish I could pick out my own clothes
I want to invite friends over and go to friends' houses
I would like to attend after school activities
I want to feel love when I walk in the door
I need someone to take on the adult responsibilities
I just want to be like a normal kid
I hope to be a good parent some day
I never want to leave my kids
Will someone listen to me?
Let me decide
I want some closure
I'm tired of taking care of my siblings
Who will come to my band concert?
THIS IS JUST BETWEEN US
I can't remember what my dad looks like
why didn*t my parents come to see me?
Is my dad still in jail?
Can I see my brother?
IS MY MOM STILL TAKING DRUGS?
When will we go to court?
What did the judge say?
Where will I live?
What if I don't like it there?
Can my sisters come?
Do they really want me?
Will they send me back?
Don't tell anyone about this.
Why did my parents leave me?
ARE THEY COMING BACK?
Will I ever see them again?
Did I do something wrong?

The author is an advocate for abused and neglected children in the foster care system. Her submission represents the voices of children experiencing the pain of being separated from their families.

Foster Care Reflections

By Tina Severance-Fonte

We became foster parents more than five years ago. When we first received our license, it seemed like only two hours later we were being called for our first placement! Since graduating from the MAPP classes, I only possessed the book knowledge of being a foster parent. Now it was time for the rubber to meet the road.

Sketchy details were quickly explained to me: there was a teen mom who was removed with her 16-month-old baby, and they were asking if we could take them both. Since this would be among our first placements, I really panicked at the thought of a teenager. I was only in the market for the little ones. What if this young teen was disrespectful? What if she was dishonest? How would I deal with youth issues? Was I equipped? Was she a bad mother?

We made the decision to only take the baby. I agonized over our choice. They told me that the biological mother would go to a group home since she was aging out of the system soon. I second-guessed myself... was I a bad person for only taking one child? Our little "Frances," arrived, but would not speak. For six weeks, this child would not utter a single word. When she was thirsty or hungry, she would simply point at the refrigerator. We developed our own system of sign language and symbols. Speech therapy began, and continued several times a week.

One sunny, summer day while on my father's boat, Frances began to make sounds. We started to hear "ba, ba, ba, ba," and "da, da, da, da" – syllables of the beginnings of wondrous language! It was a true victory! As time went on, our former mute would not stop talking. She really came into her own. She loved school, church, and soccer. She even ended up in time-out frequently in preschool for speaking too much! Frances became a part of our family in every way.

Meanwhile, the goal in her case changed many times. Four times it shifted back and forth from termination to reunification. One caseworker passed away, one took a promotion, one was let go – so many players for one little girl. One child advocate approached us with the idea of doing Sunday evening phone conferences with her mother. While we were reluctant at first, we agreed. We felt that if this idea went haywire, we could always change our contact number. The phone conferences carried on for more than two years. The result was a positive partnership and unofficial mentoring opportunity. We never expected to actually become friends, especially when the relationship between foster parents and biological parents can be so adversary.

After more than four long years, a judge formally ordered a reunification on June 28, 2010. We had 24 hours to act upon this decree. Our 16-month-old baby was now a big girl, ready to start Kindergarten in the fall. Most foster parents would be beside themselves. Although a part of us was saddened, we knew that we had a direct connection to the biological mother and that this would not be a situation of a final division. In fact, we now continue to call and visit on a regular basis. Because we have an open relationship, we did not suffer psychological and emotional pain as we did with so many other placements when reunification took place.

I truly believe that "it takes a village," and we are so happy to stand by our Frances, but now in a different way. Regardless, we NEVER have to wonder what ever happened to this child. We are there to guide and support this young mother. It has been a pleasure to assist and coach in this unique situation. She, in fact, was not a bad mother, just a young person in great need of guidance and support. Not only is Frances' family, but her mom is too.

I went on to become the president of the Broward Foster and Adoptive Parent Association. We meet each month for training, support, legislative, and advocacy issues. It is my wish to change the current model of separation. So many negative effects can result from the way that reunification takes place now. It was a pleasure to be a temporary home for Frances, but now I can look out of the picture window and see a new family that I am pleased to have helped put back together.

We have not yet taken a new placement. I just want to make it to the six-month mark until the case is formally closed. If something should go wrong, we are willing to do this all over again.

Tina Severance-Fonte is a foster parent and president of the Broward Foster and Adoptive Parent Association www.brfapa.org.

How can foster parents best help the children they care for?

By Mariah Berry

- By being honest with them.
- By teaching manners and social responsibility.
- By teaching them how to keep their bodies clean and safety habits.
- By not feeling sorry for the kids and letting them get away with stuff.
- By keeping in touch after they leave.
- By preparing them for a realistic view of adoption
- By taking care of the tiny memory items that a child has.
- By not letting the children feel like they are just a job.
- By actually taking them to dental and doctors appointments like a real parent.
- By giving them clothes that help them fit in.

– Mariah Berry, 17, was in and out of foster care since age 3. She was finally adopted at age 14. She was in more than 30 foster homes in Florida, is hearing impaired and has overcome much.

Don't blame yourself nor give up. It may seem hard to cope with at times but take advantage of this opportunity. Some might say this isn't an opportunity but if you look at it in a different perspective, it is. Being in foster care can help you learn new skills you may not have known before and it can help you pay your way through college. So don't frown upon it even if at times it doesn't seem like anything is going your way.

– Corsica Parker, foster care youth

Numbers

By Veronica Brown

People always ask
For a number
Ask a lot really
Foster kids . . .
How many have you had?

I don't know
Haven't counted
Haven't wanted to count
I could, but why?
How do you count? Who do you count?
How do you count one weekend?
Two months? Eleven years?

Sam reminds me of one, "Do you count him?"
Oh . . . him. If I did, I'd count him twice

I remember names, not numbers

What does a number really tell you?
What answer do they want?
A bunch? Too many? Not enough?
Do I get a prize?

The kids count
How many homes
One, two, three . . .

Shawn was my first
I was his sixth
He was nine
He stopped remembering names
So he just called them by a number

Transitions

"When we are no longer able to change a situation, we are challenged to change ourselves." – Victor Frankl

Life Links: Transitioning Children in Foster Care with Less Trauma

By Jennifer Winkelman, MA, LPC, NCC

The synonym for the word "transitions" give a better glimpse of what our children face when they move: ***change, conversion, flux, shift, switch, turn, upheaval.***

With sweaty palms and a dry mouth, I sat knowing a headache would come with hurricane force once the session was over. Mom and Dad sat next to each other on their living room couch, and Reagan took the ottoman in front of the easy chair. Their room was decorated to feel cozy, but the news we were about to break would be far from it.

Their stomachs in knots, lumps in their throats, tears stinging their eyes, Mom and Dad dropped the bomb: "Reagan, we can't live together anymore." It didn't take long for Reagan to understand that Mom and Dad would remain together, she would be the one moving on, and the adoption wasn't going to happen.

We spent the next couple of hours talking as gently as we could about what happens next. The county caseworker would come in the morning. Mom and Dad still wanted to be a part of Reagan's life, so there'd be visits and phone calls from time to time, as long as it appeared healthy for Reagan. She would live with a previous foster family. But she wouldn't have to go back to her former school.

Reagan had never been told by anyone except a caseworker that another move was imminent. There were never adults who wanted to maintain contact, even though they couldn't parent long-term. She had never had a therapist involved for emotional support at this stage of a transition. Her behavior had always been blamed as the reason for the disruption. But this time was different, because even in the midst of tragedy, Reagan's caregivers were committed to **Life Links**.

One of the most significant facets of my job is supporting families as they transition children from one home to another. It is a necessary component of foster care, and at the same time, each time it happens, I grieve again for what the children must endure.

According to Miriam Webster's online dictionary, a "transition" is "passage from one state, stage, subject or place to another." Not so bad, right? But "transition's" synonyms give a better glimpse of what our children face when they move: change, conversion, flux, shift, switch, turn, upheaval.

During a move from one home to another, children's lives are turned upside down – even if positive feelings are associated with the change. Transitions, even in the best of circumstances for our children, are also traumas. They are usually sudden or unexpected and confusing. The meaning our children assign to their moves often contributes to a negative sense of self and poor self-esteem. And none of this weighs the impact of the losses children face when they move – caregivers, pets, foster siblings, teachers, playmates, the familiarity of their school/daycare, the blanket that smelled "just so," the "right kind" of milk, the rhyme and rhythm of that family. Each time they move, there is an infinite list of losses along with a shuffle into an inconsistent and unpredictable world.

From my experience in child welfare during the last 14 years, here are some all too common circumstances when children are moved through the foster care system:

- Emergency moves, where the child has little notice, sometimes in the middle of the night or while the child is sleeping.
- Being moved by a person who is a stranger to the child.
- Being moved with no explanation.
- Belongings transported in trash bags and items are sometimes lost in transit.
- Arrival at the new home with clothes that are too small, dirty, or in poor condition.
- Arrival at the new home in desperate need of a bath or with untreated illness.

Unfortunately, these things happen even when children are moving from one state licensed foster home to another. And they happen on the watch of well-meaning adults who lead the charge, but have lost sight of the highest priority: the souls of the children in care. We must take greater care with the part we play, in the midst of these traumas called "transitions."

It is easy to assign the burden to caseworkers, who are sometimes tragically the most consistent adult in a child's life. There is convenience in relying on the child's therapist to provide guidance and call the shots. Or maybe the families on either side of the transition should be responsible for dictating the process of moving a child. The tension is this: No one party should bear full responsibility for something so significant in a child's life. And at the same time, each party should feel the full weight of advocating for the child's best interest. But what do we advocate for? There is no single recipe or prescription to fit the unique needs of each child when it comes time to move. While we can't tackle transitions with a cookie-cutter approach, there are some principles that apply across foster care. No matter what your role, you can champion efforts to help kids transition with less trauma.

Be familiar. Just before, during, and after transition is the worst time for the players to change. Every time a child meets a new worker, this too, is another transition. So, the person who directly facilitates the transition should be someone with whom the child is familiar – someone in whom the child finds comfort, who is available on both ends, and all the way through. Contrary to popular practice, this person could even be the current foster parent. Familiarity and felt safety for the child during this process is essential. On a case-by-case basis, consider:

- When we have the luxury of scheduling visits between families as part of a child's transition, who facilitates? And how is the visit facilitated?
- Are there promises made to the child, aloud or implied, being broken with this transi-

tion? And what are the promise-breakers doing to help the child integrate this information, protecting the child's self-image?

- What is his or her perception of time? How fast or slow should the transition for this child go?

Prepare the next home and family for the child(ren). Share what you know! One family received a letter from a previous caregiver about their son. The previous foster mom wrote with detail about how she helped this little guy calm down by massaging his arms and back with lavender lotion while she sang "You Are My Sunshine." The new family mimicked her intervention, which yielded great results for his stress management. What a gift all these foster parents gave to this boy by communicating and utilizing what helped him in times of stress. These are the details that make a significant difference in minimizing trauma during moves.

Answer Questions, Tell the Story. When it comes time for children to move, we may wrestle with how to present it. While it is important to be mindful about how children will internalize what is shared with them, it is equally important to tell the truth – gently. Often, the reasons children move from one home to another is connected with their behavior. To transition children with less trauma, we must understand behavior is only one "language" through which children give voice to the things they've learned and how they feel about their life experiences. So instead, we must take responsibility for how we have been unable to adapt parenting strategies to better meet their needs. It's truthful and gentle. Work with a therapist during this phase if you have questions. There are many gifted clinicians who can offer support or consultation.

Before, after, and during the transition, it is important to answer children's questions, even if they aren't asked aloud. As you tell the story, help children to understand what has happened and what will happen next, weaving in answers to: "Why can't you keep me?" "What does this mean about who will be in my life from now on?" Because children in the system are often acclimating to a new environment, they hardly ever have the time to grieve where they were before. When you tell the story, you provide a forum for the grief process. It gives the children an opportunity to create meaning and make sense, with your healthy and grounded influence, of the changes they are experiencing. In the hustle and bustle of all of it, we must connect with the children's experiences, giving the implicit message that what is happening to them matters. Telling their story communicates, "Kiddo, you matter!"

Provide consistent sensory input. I get a much better night's sleep in a hotel room if I bring a pillow from home. There's a reason for that – I'm bathing my system in sensory input consistent with my home environment, and it regulates my system. The same is true for our kids. It may sound silly, but exploit the senses to minimize trauma; the sense of smell is especially linked to memory storage and emotional state, so maintain sensory input, in whatever ways you can. If you are the receiving family, find out what detergent the previous family used, the brand of toothpaste used and favorite foods. Purchase the CD the foster father used as part of the bedtime routine. I know one ambassador for consistent sensory input who is an adoptive mother. She wore the previous caregiver perfume for weeks, even though she was allergic to it! She wanted to provide a consistent smell for her youngster as a means of minimizing changes. Brilliant!

Exercise Awareness x 2. I will never forget a late night drive across town to move two little boys from their foster home. I felt sick, fretting about what elements of our night-time emergency would be triggers for them as they got older. Would they always have a fear of women with brown curly hair? Would the sight of a white Honda always bring them waves of anxiety? I knew what I had to do because of the unavoidable circumstances, but with everything in me, I didn't want to do it this way. During the drive, I talked with a co-worker, who reminded me how terrified the children would be about what was happening. The high levels of adult stress I was experiencing due to our "emergency" would have meant a lack of attunement to the boys' experiences with the move, making me emotionally unavailable to them. She coached me to "feel" as calm and safe as possible, for their sake. She nudged me to take care of my own business. We must assess where we are and tell the truth to a co-worker, teammate, supervisor, or even yourself about our own levels of stress. If we can't dial into ourselves, it will be impossible for us to tune into the children and authentically meet their needs. And we have to make sure we do some processing about the experience with someone else within 24 hours of helping children move. We want kids to be able to discuss their challenges, and this is one way for us to "walk the talk." Plus, it's a way to keep ourselves healthy, and the healthier we are, the healthier transitions we'll facilitate.

Give Roots. For kids who get shuffled around, often many details of their lives are lost along the way. When you have children in your care, consider yourself a biographer and historian. Make the most of lifebooks and photos. Write letters to children as an adult about what is happening in their lives. Keep a journal as a record you will send on with the child. These efforts bear witness to children's lives today, and give a springboard for tomorrow, when children will work to integrate all the pieces of their puzzle – making sense of where they lived, with whom, why and for how long.

The most challenging part about being in foster care was trying to find out who I really was in a world that was always changing. I had moved so many times in my stay in foster care, that I found myself trying to "fit in" everywhere I went. There were so many ethnic backgrounds and beliefs thrown at me, I stayed confused. It wasn't until I found myself at a group home in Gardendale, Alabama that I really found who I was, and found the peace with God that helped me. It helped that I had the best friends, and house parents a child could have asked for.

– Jessika Walker is a former foster child. She came into the system at 9 and ended up aging out at 18. She is now an Army wife, full time college student, and a mother of two daughters.

Give Dignity. This is "Transitions 101," so it should go without saying that kids deserve to be moved with their dignity in tact. Their belongings should not be packed in trash bags. Consider, for a moment, the message we send our youngsters when their possessions are transported by the same vessels we use for what we send to the city dump. If you are involved with the foster care system and may be responsible for helping children pack their things, you should invest in some duffle bags, suitcases or backpacks. It is a small price to pay for dignity.

As you turn the page into the next chapter, when you think about transitions, commit to one thing that you will change or be aware of the next time you participate in a child's move. Ask yourself, "If it were me having to move today, how would I want it to go?" Remember, moves go best when we are flexible, creative, adaptable, collaborative, and mindful of a child's individual needs. It's in the details, and a minute action on your part may make all the difference in trauma reduction for children.

Jennifer Winkelmann, MA, LPC, NCC, is the founder and clinical director of Inward Bound, LLC. As a psychotherapist for individuals, couples, and families, Jennifer's primary clinical focus is adoption and foster care issues, including the impact of early trauma and the spectrum of relationship difficulties that result from disrupted attachments. Learn more by visiting www.InwardBoundCo.com.

The most difficult thing about foster care was adjusting to each placement I went to. Every house had different rules and different ways of doing things. It was also hard to get a sense of "belonging" since I bounced around so much.

– Amanda Spight, former foster youth

The most challenging thing about being in foster care is that no one cares about the things that are special to you: That some foster parents and DCF people don't care about your things and special things like photos and memories get lost or destroyed.

– Mariah Berry, former foster youth, entered care at age 3, was adopted at 14 after being in more than 30 foster homes.

My First Night

By Adam Robe, MSW

My first night in foster care was difficult for me. Although I was with my sister, I still had no idea what was happening to me. My foster parents tried to help me feel more comfortable, but I was in a state of shock. As the days went by and I knew my mother wasn't coming back for me, I felt pure dread. I didn't know it at the time, but I was becoming depressed and withdrawn. Because I didn't have the words for what was happening to me, it wouldn't be until much later in my life that I would fully understand that I was going through the stages of grief and loss. Within 24 hours, I had lost my mother and brother, friends, neighborhood, and way of life. I felt powerless and afraid. I hid my fear and pain by putting an invisible barrier around me.

I found that people treated me differently when I was in foster care. My peers at my school were leery of me and it was difficult for me to make friends. I saw kids come and go in my foster home, and I knew that I needed to behave a certain way or I would be moved too. I pushed my own "self" away and became someone else in order to protect myself. Relationships became superficial and short-lived. I walked around not having a clear understanding of who I was and what life held in store for me.

After I was adopted, I kept myself protected from my adoptive parents and extended family. And even now, after all my years of social work training, and self-reflecting, I am still opening doors in myself that were closed long ago. In fact, several months ago, I finally grieved for the small Adam that I left behind years ago.

By sharing my journey with you, I can only hope that it will help you understand what a child in foster care may go through. There are so many factors that contribute to the long-term success of a child who has experienced foster care, but I hope that you keep a few things in mind:

- When children come into foster care, they have experienced a traumatic event.
- Children will go through the stages of grief and loss, although these stages may not be identified as such. A therapist may treat the symptoms a child displays without recognizing the issue for what it really is. Medication may dull a child's senses and make him or her feel better, but the underlying issues will not be dealt with.
- Children in this situation feel powerless and will find ways to find control, whether they demonstrate this by misbehaving, shutting down or through some other behavior. Food is often a huge control issue.
- A child's self-esteem and identity are affected.
- Adoption doesn't make all of the above go away.

It's important for me to point out that I'm not drawing the above conclusions simply as a result of my own experiences. Instead, these are conclusions that I've reached after working, as a trained professional, with children in the system for more than a dozen years.

Adam Robe, MSW, is a foster alumni and a trained social worker working with the foster care community. He is also the author of several books that can be found on his website at www.robbietherabbit.com.

This story tells about Robbie Rabbit's journey into foster care. Robbie is removed from his birth mother's home and placed with foster parents. He meets his new foster family, learns what a foster kid is and experiences some commonplace behaviors as he adjusts to his new life. The ending is intentionally vague: Children don't know whether Robbie will end up with his mother or whether he'll ultimately be placed for adoption.

Robbie Rabbit learns he must move to a new placement after his foster mom is no longer able to care for him. We learn how Robbie feels about moving and see how the child welfare professional lays the groundwork to help him improve communication.

Robbie Rabbit meets his court-appointed special advocate (CASA) for the first time. Kelly, his CASA, explains (in kid-friendly terms) what a CASA is, what CASAs do, and how the work of a CASA differs from the work of other child welfare professionals. Included in the back of the book is a game designed to promote communication between the child and the important people in his life.

The author of these books, Adam Robe, was abandoned at age five and adopted at age nine. Adam is now in his forties and has helped hundreds of foster children and their families adjust to tough life changes. His experiences range from working as a family-centered service worker in the Children's Division, supervising CASAs, directing foster care programs, serving as a regional director of an adoption and child welfare agency, teaching human services courses at the college level and delivering trainings and keynote speeches. His academic credentials include both an undergraduate and a master's degree in social work.

Adam's personal experiences with foster care and adoption, combined with his experiences as a child welfare professional, contribute to his unique insight into children's behaviors and interactions.

Easing the Pain of Separation

By Noelle Hause, EdD, LPC

Separating from loved ones can be painful and confusing. Children entering foster care often receive minimal warning as they are delivered to strange homes and expected to stay with strange people. Because young children make sense of the world through magical and egocentric thinking, they may believe they are responsible for certain events because of an action they took, or something they said or thought. For example, a child may believe the reason he has been moved to foster care is because he did not pick up his toys or because he was mad at his mother and wished for a nicer one. He is simply unable to take the perspective of another or to think logically and believes all events revolve around him.

Barton was a 4-year-old boy who spent many days and nights alone with his 8-year-old sister. His mother often went out on the weekends with friends leaving his sister in charge. Before leaving, his mother would often tell them to "...stay busy and clean your rooms. They are a mess!" One night, a neighbor woman made a call to the police when she suspected that the children were home alone. A welfare check by a police officer and human services worker ultimately resulted in a foster care placement. During the first week in placement, the foster mother was talking to Barton about visiting his mother when he suddenly blurted out, "My mom can't live with me because my room is messy."

Furthermore, with the inability to engage in abstract thinking, young children may be preoccupied with concrete problems such as, "Will I still sleep in my own bed? How will I get food?" As a result, children may experience feelings such as confusion, guilt, anxiety, grief, depression, panic, anger, and even rage and behaviors such as change in eating or sleeping habits, regression such as baby talk or bed wetting, acting out, and denial.

What can you do to help your young foster child adjust to this new situation?

- Make sure the child knows the placement in foster care is not a result of him or her being "bad." He or she is never responsible.
- Tell the truth appropriate to the child's age. Saying "Mommy is okay" when she is crying sends the child mixed messages and results in confusion. Talk about your feelings.
- Don't criticize or talk negatively of biological parents. Children are an extension of their parents and can feel defensive, responsible and in general feel like they are "bad" if they hear negative information about their parents.
- Furthermore, give your foster child permission to love his or her parents regardless of the reasons he or she is placed in your home. Children should not have to choose sides. Remember, each child is an extension of his or her primary caregiver.
- Try to answer questions as simply as possible.
- Give plenty of advanced warning before children visit their parents. This can be a challenge. Sometimes visits change at the last minute. Do the best you can to set up a regular schedule.
- Listen to concerns and questions posed by your child.

- Let your child express emotions and recognize them.
- Be concrete. Explain what life may be like in the near future.
- Each child should have his or her own bed and space to keep belongings without fearing that he or she must protect these items from other children.
- Nurture your foster children. Communicate that you are there to help and protect him or her.
- While physical touch and hugs are a way to express affection and nurturing, go slow. Remember, your newly placed foster child does not know you and may have had experiences with unpleasant touch prior to placement.
- Maintain a predictable daily schedule.
- Allow the child to be a child.
- Don't promise things you can't commit to or offer false hopes.
- Visitation schedules should be designed to be regular and dependable. Consideration should be given to the child younger than 2. In this case a child may feel more secure with day visits only.
- Be an advocate for developmentally appropriate skills, expectations and practices for the young child in your care.
- To make the transition for visits easier, your child could benefit from having photographs of parents or important personal belongings such as a blanket, stuffed animal, doll, or pet.

If you have concerns about your child's adjustment, ask yourself: Am I giving my child enough time to adjust? Are my child's behaviors or reactions interfering with his or her ability to function over time? If you do not feel like your child is making a timely adjustment professional help may be necessary.

Noelle Hause EdD, LPC, is an early mental health specialist for North Range Behavioral Health, Director of Community Health Resources for the North Colorado Medical Center Foundation, and adjunct faculty at the University of Northern Colorado. This article originally appeared in ***Fostering Families Today****.*

Feeling Fostered

By Missy Kenny-Corron, MSW

> *"You have no parents, your Mom doesn't want you."*

There were weeks and weeks of newspapers piled everywhere with attendant chaos and mess. The refrigerator was completely empty and cobwebs were in every corner of the apartment. The Christmas tree was still up though it was probably 80 degrees outside and there were a few scattered unwrapped gifts under it. I remember that specifically because my marshmallow maker was under there, and I wanted desperately to open it up and start making marshmallows but, somehow, between Christmas in December and that day in June, it was never the "right" time according to my parents. We had no phone, so I guess she must have left us alone in the house to go to the corner to call – or maybe she went to a neighbor, I honestly can't recall. Years after I heard her version of the day's events so many times I almost felt as if I had been there listening. "I called the police and told them that I would jump off the pier and take all three kids with me if someone didn't come right now and take them." "Them" of course was me and my younger brother and sister. I was six and the caller was my 26-year-old mother.

At some point that day some grown-ups (social workers) came and in quiet voices they herded me and my two siblings out of the apartment and away from my hysterical mother. My mom always tended toward the dramatic, but she wasn't exaggerating. Things were about as bad as could be. My alcoholic father had disappeared weeks ago and without his meager earnings we were starving. I don't think anything else could have persuaded her that this was necessary but she also was too depressed to care whether we ate or not and that I think was the deciding factor.

After spending most of the day in a big office, we were summarily dropped on the doorstep of a house with nothing more than the dirty clothes on our backs. If anyone thinks that a six-year-old cannot feel humiliated or shamed by circumstances beyond her control – well, you would be wrong. I felt it alright – had been feeling it since the moment those grownups walked into our filthy apartment and took us. We were introduced to some more people – and more than a few kids. Ranging in age from 18 months to 17 years the family had five children of their own and then we showed up. The family seemed nice and after the other grown-ups (actually more social workers) left, they put us in the back seat of a huge car and drove us to a toy store. We were given permission to pick one toy that we could have forever and that would be ours alone.

My brother, two years younger than I, had dragged his only possession with him, an old smelly brown teddy-bear; my sister who was barely 18 months and I had nothing. We walked up and down the aisles and to be honest, I don't remember what I chose – probably some ridiculous pink plastic thing. It really doesn't matter – what matters is that three dirty, scared, and friendless children were being given the chance to have one single thing that belonged to them alone. It was exactly what we needed at that moment. I don't know whether I loved my foster parents from that moment or one of the myriad that

Neither one could have been responsible for me alone – that is my Mother started me – but my Foster Mother is the one that taught me to strive for excellence and achievement.

followed – but I know it was love.

Aunt Mary and Uncle Larry (as we called them) freed up one bedroom and stuck the three of us in there together again – exactly the right thing to do. Years later I would find out that we were only supposed to be there for 24 hours because after 20 years of fostering they had decided to stop accepting long-term placements and stick to emergency care. Apparently there was no one family willing to take all three of us, so, they found three different families willing to take each of us individually. I think Aunt Mary must have known that would have been a disaster for us – she decided to keep us and keep us together.

We endured a lot those four years. Taunts of our peers – "You have no parents, your mom doesn't want you." At one point my little sister became distraught, the result of neighborhood kids' relentless teasing that she had no father, and so the social workers tracked ours down and forced him to make the one and only visit we got from him during the whole four years. We never saw him again after that day – and he subsequently died a few years after. Besides our mother, we had no contact with any relative at all during the time we spent in care. I know that at school I felt that the adults were all part of some great conspiracy – pitying us and offering cold charity when we needed it. Somehow, in spite of that we managed to do well.

One weekend four summers later we were planning to spend the weekend with our mother – who by then had been working and had a nice apartment. Lately, the overnight visits had increased so we didn't think anything amiss when she picked us up and took us to her apartment with small bags. Once we arrived she said, "Surprise! This is it! You are home! You are not going back to Aunt Mary and Uncle Larry's house!! We are back together as a family." I am sure a part of me was thrilled – but I also know that I was so darn mad! Furious even! I demanded she take us back right away since our stuff was still there, but it wasn't, all of it was in my mother's apartment. I don't suppose it was a coincidence but our foster family was planning a move to Florida and by the time we unpacked our little bags – our foster family was on its way to somewhere in Florida and we were never to see them again.

I cried for weeks at night – I couldn't cry during the day, I was aware of how that would make my mother feel – so I kept my feelings to myself crying only after I went to bed or during the rare moments I was alone. I felt betrayed and abandoned yet again. I wanted to go back to my foster mom's house – very clearly. We were happy there and with Mom visiting, it was the perfect arrangement according to my 10-year-old rationale. Why would we want to live in the chaos that my mom represented when we could live in a nice house with a mother AND a father who was not drinking and hitting people; it was clean, had plenty of food, had other kids to play with and some semblance of normalcy. I have only happy memories of the time spent in foster care. Other than the embarrassment of being IN foster care – which other kids and sometimes grown-ups would inflict – it was still so much nicer. I adored my foster siblings. Most importantly, we were loved by the entire family AND our mom.

I am grateful in large measure because of the rocky road I have traveled.

Over the years we came to accept the decision made by people we never really knew in offices far away. Our mom was great in a lot of ways – but stability and security were never quite achievable and much of our life with her was one of scrimping by. I never for one second forgot my foster mom. I would send her a silent thank you when someone praised me for an accomplishment – and while verbally thanking my mother I would harbor a secret that really I was the product of two mothers. Neither one could have been responsible for me alone – that is my mother started me – but my foster mother is the one who taught me to strive for excellence and achievement. I don't think I recognized that as being all that weird or unusual but I accepted it on some level because I rarely, if ever, spoke about it to my mother and certainly never mentioned that I had secretly wished we had been adopted by our foster parents.

What took longer was the resolution of the shame I carried as a former foster child. I took some pains for a long time to ensure that the conversation never took a turn in that direction. Like so many other previously neglected children I had a litany of things I felt shame over – alcoholic father, foster care, welfare, poverty, homelessness, a single mother and most of all the shame of disloyalty to my mom in feeling that my foster mother would have done a better job of raising us. Shame is toxic – in covering up my life I was living a lie in a sense – it wasn't until I was confronted with the choice to live that way forever or make a new decision that I finally came to terms with the fact that I was carrying around baggage that did not rightly belong to me. I had not made those choices – they had been made for me since I was the child. When, at last, I mentioned my four-year stint in foster care, I was surprised by the level of understanding and acceptance that others had. I mean, clearly people could distinguish between my own decisions and the decisions of those responsible for me. Today, it is a matter-of-fact item from my past, something that makes me who I am – but not the thing that defines me in anything other than the compassion I feel for the kids who are now struggling in some sort of care.

Eventually I looked up my foster family's name to see if I could get a phone number. I located a half a dozen names and numbers and thought, "Great! I will start dialing and maybe one of these will turn out to be right!" But when I reached for the phone I was hesitant and nervous. I was concerned that they might have passed on or that they wouldn't remember me. I held on to the numbers for a few years and in passing mentioned it to my sister. She immediately picked up the phone and dialed and we hit it on the first try. Sadly our foster dad had passed on the year before – but all the kids and our foster mom were fine! They had NOT forgotten us and were thrilled we finally tracked them down and reached out.

We talked to our mom about it and she was happy for us and sent along some messages of her own. Mom was also able to express her gratitude for the loving care we received while she was unable to manage it herself. I was finally able to say thank you to Aunt Mary and get some of the missing information about how we had ended up with her family. I re-established contact with the foster sister I had missed most and with my foster mom.

Though life was often no fiesta with my mother – she did her best and there was never a moment that I didn't understand how much she loved me or my siblings. I suppose that is the reason it got complicated. I understood how much she loved us but I also knew that her love came with a price that was paid by her children. It was so much more uncomplicated with my foster mom. Though I know there were times I wished it had been easier – that there were no divided loyalties to sift through, I also know that I lived with these two women as my mothers all my life. I accepted that who I am in every sense of the word is a combination of both.

I suppose that I could have turned out to be an angry person, full of resentments, regrets, and endless "why me" questions. I am nothing like that! I am grateful in large measure because of the rocky road I have traveled and where I am is no place I could have dreamed of as a child. I also know that plenty of people discounted me and my aspirations on account of where I started – as if my ability to achieve was solely directed by the road I was traveling rather than the traveler I am. They were wrong to do that – it is not that important in the end how many mothers I had or fathers I did not have – rather it is important that I had people who cared at all.

I am now a mother to three internationally adopted children. My parenting approach is like my general approach to life – akin to filling a plate from a buffet table. A little from here and a little from there – all piled on one plate next to each other changing the taste and texture of whatever each individual item is – and creating something new and whole.

Missy Kenny-Corron was placed into foster care at the age of 5 with her two younger siblings for four years. Eventually they were returned to their mom. After 25 years Kenny-Corron was able to locate and thank her foster mom in person. She writes about her kindergarten photo, above, "looking at myself as a 5-year-old helped me to understand that NO 5-year-old can be responsible for the choices that the adults in her life make. Recognizing that the 5-year-old in that picture – my 5-year-old self – was not bad or impossible to love... was healing on so many levels." Kenny-Corron and her husband live in New York with their three children who were adopted from China. Kenny-Corron is an assistant dean at Stony Brook University – the same university where she earned a bachelors in English Education and a masters degree in Social Work. She is also a licensed foster parent. This article originally appeared in ***Pieces of Me: Who Do I Want to Be?*** *published by EMK Press.*

To Be Concerned? Or Not To Be Concerned? That is the Question!

By Noelle Hause, EdD, LPC

> *I remember when my husband and I moved to a new home 12 years ago. Our 11-month-old son was on the verge of walking and talking prior to our move. However, due to the delay in the construction of our new home and the prompt sale of our old home, a two-week hotel stay was required while all of our personal belongings went into storage. My son's development appeared to well ... just "stop" – no words, no walking for the next three months. It was at that point that I realized how difficult it is for young children to adjust to change in their routines, caregivers, homes, families, and support systems.*

Such disruptions can result in development delays and negative behaviors as the child attempts to adapt to these changes. This does not mean that the child will be delayed or display challenging behaviors forever. With the right supports, understanding, and relationships, young children can make those developmental adjustments. It is important to sort out typical development and responses to change from more serious mental health or social-emotional and behavioral issues.

If you have concerns related to your child's behaviors, start by asking yourself the following questions:

- Has there been a change in my child's routine?
- Has there been a change in relationships such as a caregiver or child care provider?
- Has my child been ill?
- Is my child's behavior developmentally appropriate?
- Have I been emotionally available to my child?
- Does my child have delays in any area of development, such as speech-language, motor or cognitive development?
- Does my child lack the appropriate skills to be successful?
- Has my child's behavior been reinforced by someone or something in the environment?
- Does this behavior happen across all settings or just in certain settings such as school or home?

If you answered "yes" to any of these questions, were unable to answer any of these questions or are just interested in learning more about your child's behavior, try the following:

1. ***Keep a regular schedule and routine.***

2. ***Keep a log or journal of concerns related to development and behavior.***

3. ***Don't assume that your child knows how to behave.***
   It takes years to teach young children basic social skills.

4. ***Expect a change in behavior or delay in development when major life changes occur.***

5. ***Visit with your child care provider and observe your child in other settings.***

6. Ask yourself: Who does this behavior bother? Me? My child? The teacher? Other children?

Know your developmental stages: (Figure in a three- to four-month plus or minus factor because some children will master them early, some later).

1. Typically developing babies are eager to relate and explore the world around them – including other people.

2. When you think of a 2-year-old, does the word "NO" come to mind? Prior to this stage, infants have limited knowledge of themselves being separate from their caregivers. They are simply part of the adult who cares for them. As they are increasingly able to physically move to and from their caregiver, toddlers begin to realize their separateness. This recognition of being separate leads to "individuation" or the development of the infant's ego and sense of identity. So what should the social-emotional development of a toddler look like?

3. Toddlers approaching 36 months are trying to figure out where and how they fit into the world around them. While a toddler's use of "NO" is annoying and inconvenient, it is an important developmental stage. If a child has been recently separated from a primary caregiver, distress may result and separation anxiety may be heightened. A child may even show signs of bereavement if the separation is an extended one

4. "That's not fair." "Why don't I get to go?" "Did I do it better?" "Let's pretend that..." "Can I play with my friend?" "I want the same shoes as her." "I will help you if you give me some candy." Sound familiar? Fairness, belongingness, competition, pretend play, friendships, likenesses and differences, awareness of gender, and negotiation all characterize the fourth and fifth year of social-emotional development in young children.

Be reasonable with your expectations of developmental milestones. A child with cerebral palsy may have a more difficult time calming than a child without cerebral palsy. Contact your local child find organization, pediatrician, or mental health center for access to a full developmental screening or evaluation with an emphasis on social-emotional development.

Young children who are competent in social-emotional development have the ability to tolerate frustration better, persist in tasks, follow directions, problem solve and manage conflict with peers, develop good relationships overall, identify, understand, and communicate their own feelings, regulate their emotions and behaviors, and develop empathy. In addition, they are physically healthier, less impulsive, more focused, have greater academic achievement, and experience a sense of confidence and competence. In short, children who are competent in social-emotional development have increased school readiness and the ability to maintain long lasting relationships. Healthy, normal social/emotional development is an essential foundation for all other learning.

Noelle Hause, EdD, LPC, is an early mental health specialist for North Range Behavioral Health, director of Community Health Resources for the North Colorado Medical Center Foundation, adjunct faculty at the University of Northern Colorado and author of ***The Early Years*** *column for* ***Fostering Families Today*** *magazine.*

Developmental Stages

End of 3 months

- Develops social smile.
- Benefits from short, frequent interactions when alert.
- Appears to recognize and is comforted by primary caregivers.
- Is interested in and enjoys playing with others.
- Responds positively to touch.
- Communicates more with face and body.
- Imitates some movements and facial expressions.
- Becomes aware of body parts and realizes they are attached; such as observing their hand.
- Can latch on to bottle or breast.

End of 6 months

- Enjoys and imitates social play, such as beginning to play peek-a-boo.
- Interested in mirror images, responds to others' expressions.
- Shy or anxious with strangers.
- Body typically relaxed.
- Can calm within a half hour by sucking on a hand or pacifier, or responding to a blanket.
- Likes to be picked up or held and enjoys mealtimes.
- Communicates hunger and illness through different cries.
- Can eat within 30 minutes without gagging or vomiting.
- Stays awake for an hour or longer and falls asleep easily.
- Normal bowel movements.

End of 12 months

- Prefers familiar people.
- Expresses several emotions such as joy, pleasure, distress, interest, disgust, displeasure and discomfort.
- Communicates hunger, pain or tiredness.
- Responds actively to language.
- Shows displeasure when a toy is taken away/dropped.
- Shows anxiety when separated from caregiver.
- Feeds self using fingers, holds cup and drinks with help.
- Babbles sounds; blows "raspberries."
- Will assist caregiver in getting dressed by holding out arms and legs.
- Laughs.

End of 24 months

Social

- Imitates behavior of others.
- Shows concern by looking when another child cries.

- More aware of him or herself as separate from others.
- More excited about company of other children.
- Can be helpful by putting a toy on a shelf.
- Shows intense feelings for parents and others.
- Likes praise.
- May be aggressive if unable to communicate needs (biting).

Emotional

- Increasing independence.
- Self-conscious emotions emerge: shame, guilt, pride and embarrassment.
- Shows defiance; uses the word "no."
- Begins to use basic emotion words: "happy" and "sad."
- Recognizes and smiles at self.
- Initiate and play by themselves.
- Self-regulation involving ability to inhibit behavior.
- Curious about body and toileting behaviors.
- Trust in caregiver increases.
- Separation anxiety may result in nightmares.

End of 36 months

Social

- Imitates others.
- Will spontaneously show affection for familiar people.
- Can take turns with another.
- Understands concept of "mine" and "his or hers."
- Eager to please and look for approval from others.
- Wants to feel needed and included.
- Notices how he or she impacts others, as well as how others affect him or her.

Emotional

- Expresses a wide range of emotions.
- Identifies mad, scared, happy and sad in self.
- Uses emotion language in pretend play.
- Talks about causes and consequences of some emotions.
- Talks about emotions in the:

    Past: "He lost his dog, he was sad."
    Present: "I am happy. This is my birthday party."
    Future: "I am going to grandma's house, that makes me happy."
- Separates easily from parents.
- Objects to major changes in routine.

End of 48 months

Social
- Interested in new experiences.
- Cooperates with peers.
- Plays "Mom" or "Dad."
- Develops friendships.
- Creativity in fantasy play.
- Dresses and undresses self.
- Negotiates solutions to conflicts.
- More independent.
- Shows interest in gender differences.

Emotional
- Unfamiliar images may be "monsters."
- Views self as a whole person involving body, mind and feelings.
- Often cannot distinguish between fantasy and reality.

End of 60 months

Social
- Wants to please and be like her friends.
- Likes to sing, dance and act.
- More independence.
- Some understanding of moral reasoning (fairness and good/bad).
- Compares self to others.
- Tries to assimilate others rules into what has already been learned.
- More likely to agree to rules and is interested in fairness but may not be fair.

Emotional
- Aware of gender and gender differences.
- Able to distinguish fantasy from reality.
- Sometimes demanding or eagerly cooperative.
- Realizes that the same event can cause different emotions in different people – one person can win a game and another person can lose.
- Understands that one's feelings can persist after the event that caused them.

Saying Goodbye, Saying Hello!

By Hollee McGinnis, MSW

Please don't go,
Please don't go,
Oh, no! Please don't go!

I would much rather say, "Hello!"
It makes me feel very sad,
When you have to go.

It makes me wonder if you're mad.
It makes me wonder if I've been bad.
It makes me feel kind of lonely.

I feel worried when you have to go!
Are we no longer friends?
Will I ever see you again?

Please don't go,
Please don't go,
Oh, no! Please don't go!

I wonder what you will do,
When you are away from me.
If you go, will you remember me?

I want you to stay.
I rather like it when we play.
I don't like it when you have to go!

Why do we have to say goodbye?
Why can't you stay forever by my side?
I will miss you so much and cry!

Please don't go,
Please don't go.
Oh, no! Please don't go!

People come and people go,
But how much more I like "Hello!"
Even though when saying hello,
Makes me sometimes nervous, you know?

So what is the good in saying "bye?"

Well, if we never said goodbye,
How could birds learn how to fly?
How could we learn how to grow?
If we were always with the same things, you know?
Every night we say goodbye,
To that shiny sun outside.
But every morning we say hello!
Because the sun always comes back we know.
Sometimes for something new to begin,
Something else must come to an end.
And some goodbyes are good too,
When something hasn't been fun to do!

So why is it so hard to say "goodbye?"

Why? It's because of all those feelings inside:
And sometimes no matter how we try,
It's just hard to say goodbye.
Especially when we know it's the end,
And we may not see each other again.

So, it's okay to want to cry,
When you have to say goodbye.
It's hard to feel there's anything good.
When you feel all gloomy inside.

You might feel more like we should say:
"Sad-bye!"
"Bad-bye!"
"Mad-bye!"
Poo! Of all those choices,
"Goodbye" is better,
Don't you think that's true?

"Goodbye" means:
We are wishing each other well,
On a journey where we can't tell –
Where we might go, and who we might see,
And what kind of adventures there might be!

Even though we say goodbye,
Doesn't stop us from being friends inside.
We carry each other deep in our heart,
And nothing could ever take away that part!

There are things we can do, so we won't forget
All of the time that we spent:
We can make a card, or give a gift,
We can write a book, and draw pictures in it.

Just as a book has a beginning and an end,
That doesn't mean we can't read it again!
So, too, even when we say goodbye,
We can always revisit our memories inside.

Saying "Goodbye" is hard to do,
But over time it can be easier, too.
When you believe down deep in your heart,
That every good-bye can be a new start.

Hollee McGinnis, MSW, was inspired to write this poem by a 6-year-old boy in foster care who had gone through 12 placements in his short life. Her work with him was to create a good-bye that was different from all the others. It is dedicated to everyone who has found it hard to say goodbye.

First Night Strategies

By Foster Parents in the Trenches

Allow the children to remain in the clothes/pyjamas from their last placement so that they smell familiar!

Take them immediately to a store and let them buy one or two things that will be theirs forever. Many foster kids leave behind or lose precious objects and belongings. Having one thing to call one's own... is important.

Explain to them what they can/can't do if they wake up in the night and when they wake up in the morning. There's nothing worse than not knowing what you're expected to do. Also explain the next day a little before bed.

If you can prepare a meal with food that is familiar to the children – ask what they would like to eat... but don't be surprised by either poor or large appetites. Show the children where food/drink is and offer them the opportunity to have some snacks at will... food is often an issue and kids will relax a bit if they know they will eat regularly and have access to some snacks. Let kids know what the rules are, for example eating only in the kitchen or no snacking after bedtime, etc. Let them know when meals will be with a schedule or some other timetable they can understand. Keep fruit out or handy so they can help themselves.

Don't "smother" or overwhelm the child with chatter or affection. No one likes this from someone they barely know!

Try to find out the bedtime routine that they are used to and stick to it as much as possible for the first few nights.

If there was chaos and no bedtime ritual... ASK what they would have liked... have new toothbrush and toothpaste (some kids will not have had regular access to these) brush your teeth with them so they know how to do it without it being obvious. Teach them a "normal" routine.

Meet children on their level. Kneel down to look at them at their height when you first greet them.

My friend immediately bathed the toddler who was placed in her home. To this day, (four years later) he is terrified of baths. That taught me to not do anything too dramatic their first night. I don't put any huge demands on them, and love them as they are.

We have developed a strange tradition (simply because we were getting in the car to go when the call came for our first few placements) of going to Costco after a quick tour of the house. We have dinner at the food court there and the child can pick out foods (and if needed clothes) that are comforting. It's an easy way to get to know the child and it seems less stressful for them because they aren't the total focus.

Preparing for Adoption

By Claudia Fletcher

Life as a foster parent is living a life of paradox. While we are commissioned to help facilitate reunification with birth parents, are also aware that this may not take place and the children may become legally available for adoption. We also know that in the cases where children become legally free, we may be given the option of adopting them.

In many states, "concurrent planning" and foster-adopt programs make this dichotomy a bit easier to navigate. Families who are interested in adopting have children placed with them who are legally free and have an adoption plan or are likely to go down that road. In this situation, foster parents have a clear role and begin the process of claiming the children early in the relationship.

The waters muddy for foster parents who have children placed with them who they do not plan to adopt. Foster parents do not plan to adopt the children in their care for many reasons – they could be "too old" in their own minds, they could see their interests as being a temporary one wanting to help many different children, or they may have dreams of retiring from parenting at some point, (which foster parents can do, whereas other parents never really retire from parenting, no matter the age of their children).

What happens when a foster family finds themselves having to say goodbye to a child they have grown to love as he or she moves on to an adoptive home? What can foster parents do to make the transition easier and to help adoptive parents bond with the children? These and other questions surface when social workers begin to talk about recruiting an adoptive family for a foster child living in their home.

Even foster parents who have decided they do not want to adopt may suddenly have second thoughts when the idea of the child leaving their home becomes more of a reality. As parents' rights are terminated and the conversations at the monthly visit start to lean toward recruitment, many foster parents are surprised by their strong feelings. They are asked by the workers, and sometimes even pressured, to reconsider their decision to not adopt.

The first step in helping prepare children for adoption is making a final decision quickly. The entire process is often on hold for months while foster parents waver and social workers can see that the best scenario for the child would be to remain in the foster home. However, time for the child continues to be lost, which may damage the child if the final conclusion remains that the foster parents will not adopt. Once the decision not to adopt has been made, the foster parents assume the primary role of preparing the child for adoption. From the time children are legally free until an adoptive family has been identified, the foster parents must:

Process the concept of adoption with the children at an age appropriate level on a daily basis. Many children have no concept of the difference between a "birth family," a "foster family" and an "adoptive family." Help them to understand the legal and emotional differences and talk about adoption as a positive experience that offers the permanence foster care does not.

Re-affirm your love for the children and explain that it is okay to love many different people. Often children think they must stop loving their birth parents or their foster parents in order to start loving their adoptive parents. Let them know that they need not choose to love one or the other, but can love all of these people congruently.

Keep hope alive. Children are often discouraged when the process takes a long time and wonder if they will ever find an adoptive family. If foster parents and social workers do not believe the children will be adopted, that attitude will transfer, subtly or not, to the children. Those working on behalf of children need to believe that a home will be found. They need to talk to the children and the social workers about adoption as a future reality. Occasionally, social workers will need to be reminded that there is a family for every child: and that family simply needs to be found.

Work on a timeline or a lifebook with the children. Many foster parents do not feel that this is their responsibility. However, many caseworkers do not have time to do this, and if foster parents don't take it on, it will not happen. Childhoods are passing by as these children live with you, and every child deserves to have some kind of history (events such as when they lost their first tooth or rode a bike for the first time). One of the greatest gifts you can give to an adoptive family and to the children is a history of these events. When our foster son, who lived with us from 9 months to right before his third birthday, moved in with his biological grandmother, he took a scrapbook with him documenting every month of his life with us. He eventually returned to our home, and we were given permanent guardianship. He still has that book. Had he not returned, he would have had memories of our time together. Social workers can help provide details and allowing children to help piece together their years can be a healing time as well.

Keep expectations real regarding the type of family you feel the children should be matched with. Many foster parents do not understand the guidelines in place and how families are recruited by social workers. For example, the Multi-Ethnic Placement Act is specific regarding how much race may be an issue in selecting a family. In addition, the number of families willing to adopt older children is quite small in comparison to the number of children available. It would be ideal if a two-parent family who shares your faith, lives in the same kind of neighborhood, is the same race as the children, and does not already have "too many kids," would be selected, but it is more likely the social worker will be unable to find the ideal family despite their efforts. If you keep your expectations real, it will be easier for you to help the children.

Help the children to keep their expectations real. Talking about what a child might prefer in an adoptive home may provide quality insight for social workers who are recruiting. However, it is important to help children remain open-minded. Help them to understand that money, possessions and material things are not the most important things a family can offer. Let them talk and dream, but help them to be realistic. Once an adoptive family has been identified and revealed to the children, the foster parents' most important work begins.

Foster parents can be the key to an excellent transition. Here are some suggestions:

Talk frequently with the adoptive parents. It's a fine line between wanting to be supportive and helpful and appearing to be needy and controlling. Relax and help the adoptive parents relax. Give them a balanced perspective of the children and their strengths and needs. Paint a picture that is accurate but not negative.

Allow the children to talk about the future and encourage them to discuss their feelings. Let them talk about their fears and what they are excited about. Ask them questions to help them understand their emotions. Spend time talking about adoption and what it means.

When the social worker has given you the green light, facilitate conversations between the adoptive parents and the child. Phone, e-mail, video chats, letters and other forms of communication can make the time go by quickly and help the parents begin bonding. Make this your responsibility.

Organize paperwork for the family at placement. Find out from the social worker what things you have that the family will need. Be thorough, but don't over-do it (Four of Maggie's drawings from kindergarten would be wonderful to have, but 40 might be over-doing it.) Provide the family with things that will help the children to remember and connect the dots of their lives.

Decide what to send and what not to send with the children. A family I worked with received boxes of stuff that purportedly belonged to their new daughter. However, it included a lot of knick-knacks that were marked with garage sale tags. Packing a foster child to move into an adoptive home does not mean cleaning house and dumping it on the new family. Make sure that the clothing you send fits the children and belongs to them. Make sure toys work before packing. Make realistic decisions about things like bicycles – would it be cheaper to buy a new bike than to ship an old bike? Try to think about what you would want coming into your house. (Note: This is NOT the time to get rid of the favorite stuffed animal, even if it is ripped, ugly, smelly and irreparable).

Provide a list of things that comfort the children – smells, foods, textures, toys – for the new parents. List what laundry detergent you use and if you use fabric softener. What were their favorite activities or games they liked to play. Make a list of their favorite foods – you could even send recipes.

Develop a plan for continued contact between the foster parents and the children that is comfortable for the adoptive parents. This can be done in a relaxed way and will facilitate a great further relationship.

Finally, it is time to say goodbye. During this time, be authentic and open. It's a good thing that foster parents cry when a child leaves. Would YOU want someone to be happy if you were moving away? Remember to be real, grieve, and give the children freedom to move on.

The above lists are not all-encompassing. They are a beginning. Foster parents are central to a smooth transition and the focus must be on the children during this time. If you can facilitate an emotionally honest and thoughtful move from your home to the adoptive home for children, the adoptive parents and the children will experience great benefits not just in the immediate transition, but for years to come.

Claudia Fletcher and her husband Bart are parents of 12 children, born between 1986 and 1998, 10 adopted domestically from the child welfare system and two adopted internationally from Guatemala. A former college administrator, Claudia is an adoption worker for Permanent Family Resource Center and an Adoption Specialist for the Adopt America Network. Bart and Claudia published their first book in 2009: ***Out of Many, One Family: How Two Adults Claimed Twelve Children through Adoption****. (www.outofmanyonefamily.com).*

To Grandmother's House We Go: At the Intersection of Kinship Care and Foster Care

By Ron Huxley, LMFT, and Catie Hargrove, MS

For some children, a trip to grandmother's house is more than a casual one. It can be a safe haven from a living situation that is chaotic, unsafe, or confusing, and may be a more long-term living arrangement for the child. This placement arrangement, children living with relatives or near-kin, is known as "kinship care" and has similarities and differences to the more formal institution of foster care.

Historical Basis for Kinship Care

Although it was not until the 1990s that the term kinship care became mainstream, there is overwhelming evidence that kin and near-kin caregivers are not a new phenomenon in child welfare. In many cultures, relatives are the parents of choice in various circumstances, and are most always the alternative in situations where one or both parents are unavailable. Kinship arrangements may occur when birth parents are deceased, unable to parent, or to afford opportunities for education or to learn a trade. No matter how kinship arrangements evolve, family members stepping up to care for their own is as old as time and a natural part of our history across cultures.

Kinship Care vs. Foster Care

Although a kin caregiver can also be a foster parent, this latter designation is usually understood to be a more formal, court-mandated living arrangement for children. Children who have been removed from their homes due to abuse or neglect live with guardians who have been approved and licensed by social service agencies. Along with this formal arrangement comes extra support. Foster parents are guaranteed a monthly stipend to help defray the costs of care and to cover any medical care or treatments for the child. While in foster care, the legal responsibility for the child resides with the court and/or public agency responsible for oversight of the child's well-being. Therefore, foster parents are required to obtain permission from the agency or the court to do things with and for the child (for example, taking the child on vacation, administering medication as prescribed by a physician, or even getting a haircut). The physical care of the child is the responsibility of the foster parent, and they must abide by all rules, guidelines and stipulations set forth from the agency that has the legal responsibility and places the child in their care.

Kinship care is often similar to foster care, although there can be some significant differences depending on the type of legal arrangement that exists. Children can reside with relatives under any of the following arrangements:

1. Informal Kinship Arrangement – occurs when the parent or parents of the child arrange for the child to be cared for by a kin or near-kin, without the involvement of the legal system. This is the most common form of kinship care.

2. Kinship Caregiver – occurs when a child has been removed by authorities from the care of parents and is placed with a family member or near-kin caregiver. The caregiver has physical, but not legal custody of the child. The caregiver may access

some services directed toward kinship caregivers, although most of them are designed to assist low-income caregivers. Not all caregivers will be eligible to access these services, depending on specific eligibility criteria.

3. Kin Guardianship – a similar arrangement to the kinship caregiver, although the caregiver has physical and legal guardianship of the child, giving them the right to make decisions on behalf of the child. In some states additional services are available to Kin Guardians, including financial assistance and Medicaid coverage for the child.

4. Kinship Foster Care – occurs when the kinship caregiver is also a licensed foster parent. This typically allows the kinship caregiver to access more services and programs. Legal responsibility remains with the agency that placed the child in foster care, and kinship foster parents must meet and abide by all agency and court policies, procedures, and guidelines.

Benefits and Concerns of Kinship Care Homes

A recent study (Sakai, et al 2011) detailed the benefits of kinship care. It found that children placed with a relative had fewer behavioral and social skill problems than children in foster care but they had a higher risk of substance abuse and pregnancy as teenagers. This study also brought to light the reality that kinship care providers are more likely to be older, unemployed, single' and poorer than foster parents. Consequently, the researchers advocated for more support services to kinship caregivers to improve children's outcomes.

Because kinship care is often done outside the child welfare system, it often does not include the financial or legal support inherent in the foster care system. Additionally, there are unanticipated emotional challenges that raising a kin member can also bring. Some of these challenges include:

- Dual roles/relationships – for example, a grandparent is both parent of their own child and "parent" of their grandchild.
- Confusion about who has final say on the welfare of the child.
- Feeling forced into a role of secrecy to avoid legal conflict and having children placed in the "system."
- Conflicted loyalty over making the child's placement permanent versus being able to prevent further harm to the child.
- Dealing with personal guilt over choices their child has made and how this has affected their grandchild.
- Holding on to child rearing practices that may conflict with current social standards and from the child welfare system.

Who Belongs To The Child?

Historically, placement of a child has been in the service of adults. Children were seen as property and expected to be appreciative of anyone who would take them in. Decisions about permanency depended on who has the "rights" to a child. This line of reasoning makes sense from a legal perspective but what happens when we see the situation through the eyes of the child? Instead of asking the question "Who does the child belong to?" What different decisions would be made by asking "Who belongs to the child?" Who is important to the child and where would the child feel safest? The answers that come from this new perspective will dramatically alter social work practice and placement decisions. History and research suggest that the fewer disruptions for a child, the better the outcome. This makes kinship care a natural solution for child placements decisions when and where possible.

When a child's preferences and needs cannot be met by a kin placement, then foster placement with a non-relative is a viable next choice. Even in this scenario, openness of relationship with kin is vital to the well-being of the child and will lead to better permanency outcomes. This open attitude, with visitation and honoring of relationships with the family of origin will prevent detrimental placement disruptions.

Relatives, especially grandparents, who become caregivers for their kin should be applauded for their dedication to keeping their family together. Alternatively, those who cannot become caregivers, but who are persistent in maintaining relationships with their kin, contribute to the health and welfare of their family's children by being supportive to the foster parents who partner with them to provide safety and well-being for children.

Ron Huxley is a licensed child and family therapist and the director of Kinship Center services in San Luis Obispo, Calif. He is the author of the book ***Love and Limits: Achieving a Balance in Parenting*** *and founder of the ParentingToolbox.com blog.*

Catie Hargrove is director of Kinship Center's Education Institute in Salinas, Calif. She produces educational videos and develops curriculum for foster and adoptive parents, kinship caregivers and the professionals who support them.

References:

Berrick, J. D. (1998). *When children cannot remain home: foster family care and kinship care.* The Future of Children, 8(1), 72-87.

Hegan, R. L., Scannapieco, M. (1999). *Kinship Foster Care: Policy, Practice and Research.* New York: Oxford University Press.

Sakai, C., Lin, H., Flores, G. (2011). *Health outcomes and family services in kinship care: analysis of a national sample of children in the child welfare system.* Archives of Pediatrics and Adolescent Medicine, 165 (2): 159.

Happy To Meet You

By Veronica Brown

Why would you believe me when I said
"happy to meet you?"
Why would you care if you stayed here or not?
Why would you like the taste of my cooking?
Why would you want to get to know me?
Why would you tell me how scared you feel?
Why would you hope things will get better?
Why would you give me a chance?

Why not doubt my intentions?
Why not wait for me to hurt you?
Why not run and hide?
Why not think my house looks weird?
Why not expect to be thrown away?
Why not yell instead of cry?
Why not shake your fist at me, your foster
mom, and the world?

Thank you for giving me that chance.
Thank you for trying one more time.
Thank you for showing your strength.
Thank you for trusting me.
Thank you for laughing at my lame jokes.
Thank you for triumphing.
Thank you for making me
"happy to meet you."

Teamwork

"Never doubt that a small group of thoughtful, committed people can change the world. Indeed, it is the only thing that ever has." – Margaret Meade

Working With Caseworkers

By Veronica Brown

> ***I do try my best to make workers a part of our team.***

I often hear foster parents complain that their foster child's caseworker doesn't treat them like a part of the team. That's really not been my experience. However, I do try my best to make caseworkers a part of our team.

In my home, when a caseworker comes for a monthly visit, it's not a big deal or a big production. It's just a visit. Sometimes we even bake a little something to share. We sit back, relax and celebrate the child. I don't go down a list of all the things the child has done wrong in the last four weeks. If I've already dealt with the behaviors, why would I embarrass the child by rehashing it again? Most of the time, I've already called or e-mailed the caseworker anyway. And it usually goes like, "Hey, this happened... I've already dealt with it, but I just wanted to let you know."

There has been a child or two come to live with me from another foster home and they've really stressed out when their worker was scheduled to visit. It used to confuse me until I realized that they were used to being the only child in a room full of adults, listening to every awful thing they've managed to accomplish since the last visit. And one of those adults was writing it all down. I suppose this format gives the foster parent a chance to show off his or her halo, but that's not me. If I'm going to brag, it'll be about something awesome my kids have done, not all the grief I've had to put up with. Suffering doesn't make me great, or even that interesting. I guess it comes down to whether or not you want to spend your time complaining. If you look hard enough, you'll always find something to complain about. And so will your foster child.

Of course, I've had meetings where certain incidents or behaviors needed to be addressed. My philosophy has been for all the participants to know what's coming, almost like an agenda. I let the caseworker know what issues I need discussed and I let the child know what to expect. It usually goes like, "You know how your caseworker's coming over tomorrow after school? Well, I want to let you know that we're going to talk about that time when you . . ." No big deal, no drama, no "wait until your caseworker hears about this!" Very matter of fact; "we need to discuss this together." I'm not interested in making a social worker the bad guy.

I also try to give some of the glory to the worker. Usually, they have to be the bearer of bad news:

> "It looks like you're moving to another foster home."
>
> "Sorry, but the judge decided that you're staying in foster care for another six months."

"Unfortunately, we can't find your mom, so we don't know when you're going to be able to visit her again."

So when a caseworker approves funding for guitar lessons, baseball spikes, or basketball camp, I make sure the foster child knows where the money came from. Foster children need to know that their caseworker cares and is working hard for them. We're trying to build a support system for each child and the social workers are an important part of that.

Now, I haven't liked every caseworker I've encountered. But then again, I don't like every member of my family. And like it or not, a child's caseworker is an important part of the foster family. And just like I wouldn't trash talk a child's biological mother or father, I don't criticize a child's caseworker in front of the child. Besides, I'm sure there's been one or two caseworkers who hasn't liked me either!

Veronica Brown has been a foster parent in Canada since 1995. She primarily takes in boys aged 9 and older and usually has a handful at any given time. The drawing is how her 23-year old former foster son sees her which is far more important than what she looks like. Lucky for her...

What Inny Taught Us

By Allen Walker

Our story is one of love, passion, joy, heartache, and many tears. It's the greatest of stories and, at times, the most heart wrenching of stories.

In two short years we have experienced nearly every scenario in foster care. We have walked through reunification, adoption, children who you immediately bond with and children who stretch you in every possible way. Through our experience, we have learned that when we choose to unconditionally love a child, lives are transformed.

When we started foster care, we only took in newborns. Over the course of the first four months we had three different infants come to live with us. Our third baby was "Inny." This little girl has forever changed our lives. She taught us that love overcomes the most difficult of situations. Through her, we learned that when we choose to passionately, wholeheartedly, and unconditionally love someone, the struggles of yesterday can be washed away and hope can be resurrected. Inny has a special place in our heart, and her story has eternally affected our view of foster care.

Months before Inny was in our lives, we sat through foster parent training where I had a revelation that has stuck with me until this day. Our instructor said, "These children are not to fill a void in your life, but you are to fill a void in their lives." This phrase reconstructed the paradigm of my role as a foster parent.

There are many different reasons people pursue foster parenting. However, the foundational truth that we must hold onto is that we, as foster parents, are providing a need and filling a void in a child's life. The child is not to fill a void in our hearts, and if we have that expectation we are setting ourselves, and that child, up for disappointment and unnecessary heartache.

Inny helped teach us this lesson. We quickly fell in love with her, but each day we had to remind ourselves that we were the ones filling a void in her life. She was the one in desperate need of a stable, nurturing, and loving home, and we were the ones commissioned to give her that gift.

When we have the revelation that we are filling a void, unconditionally loving a difficult child becomes a little easier. When we step back and look at our children through different lenses, we no longer see the rebellious, indignant, and defiant child who has tested every boundary. Instead, we see a life that has had its innocence stolen, no longer trusts and is waiting to once again be disappointed. When we commit to love our children, trust is established, walls are torn down, and innocence is restored. Love is a powerful tool that we have been given as foster parents, and we must choose to use it so that lives are transformed.

Unfortunately, many people do not fully understand the reality of foster care. It is true that children are placed into the system for a reason. The state does not randomly go to a family and spontaneously take their children for no reason. Something happened that endangered the life of a child, and therefore, they are placed into foster care.

It is easy to pre-judge a biological parent. However, as easy as it is to pre-judge, it should be just as easy to believe that change can occur. Often times, the parents are children themselves who have never had support to help them learn to make right decisions.

We like to meet the biological families. This is typically discouraged. For us, though, we have learned that it helps us understand the family dynamic, and also eases the parents' concerns about where their child has been placed. When they realize that we are for them and not against them, they let down their guard and allow us to be an influence in their lives. We have seen this happen time and time again. However, Inny's Mom, "Grace" was different. Initially, she was not interested in us being a part of her life.

At first, it seemed as if Inny would be with us forever because her mom had not begun to do the necessary tasks required for reunification. However, at the last minute Grace showed up to the final court hearing and was given a second chance. Upon hearing this news, disappointment crept in. We allowed ourselves to go to a place that we were trained not to go. We began to dream about a future with Inny that was never intended to take place. Instead of growing disillusioned with the system, we chose to love Grace with the same intensity and passion that we had for Inny.

I will never forget sitting in the Miami courthouse in July 2009 waiting on a hearing on behalf of Inny. Up until that moment, our relationship with Inny's family had been strained and tense. Walking into the courthouse, I was convinced that the judge would remove Inny from our home so she could live with her grandmother. My heart was heavy, and my stomach in knots. After waiting for nearly an hour, I had the opportunity to talk to Inny's grandmother and Grace. I couldn't hide my emotions, and with tears running down my cheeks, I told them how special Inny was and how much we loved her. There was breakthrough at that moment. In their eyes, I was no longer an enemy, but rather someone who deeply loved Inny and only wanted what was best for her. The judge surprised us and allowed Inny to stay, and I remember leaving the courthouse knowing that something had changed, love was prevailing!

There was not an instant transformation, but within weeks a true friendship developed with Grace. We even celebrated Inny's first birthday together. I realized that a true transformation had occurred when Grace called in a moment of crisis. She needed someone to talk to, someone she trusted, and someone who loved her. We spent hours on the phone, and, in the end, love was displayed, honor and blessing were released and trust was deepened.

This was the breakthrough that people feel is impossible. In the eyes of many, it is not intended for the biological parents and foster parents to form a friendship. We are trained to stay far away and remain anonymous. However, imagine what would happen if more biological families felt a true, unconditional love coming from the foster family. Many times the birth families have no one to turn to. They have no one who believes in them, and have been told their entire lives that they are failures. What would happen if they had a foster family who blessed them, encouraged them and stood beside them during their journey? What if, for the first time in their lives, they had someone who believed in them and had faith that they could change? The inspiration and confidence that would arise could radically change an entire family.

In foster care, our goal is to see families reunified. However, I view my mission as much greater than that. I desire to see restoration occur. A parent can easily complete a check list, but if they change the way they live life, put destructive patterns behind them and provide a loving, stable home life for their children, then they are moving in a direction of success which decreases the chances of their children returning to the system.

The catalyst that will spur this transformation on is love. When foster parents choose to love not just the child, but the entire family, they are initiating restoration. It would be naïve to think that every situation ends with a happy family reunified. Unfortunately, birth parents may have their rights terminated. However, when they know that their children will be with a family that has honored and respected them, it is easier for them to let go and allow their children to officially become a part of a new family.

On June 8, 2010 our journey with Inny came to a close. We rejoiced in the courtroom as the judge declared reunification and wept as we drove away from her new home. It was the most joyous and terrible day of our lives. We were thrilled to see victory, but at the same moment our hearts ached knowing that Inny would no longer be with us.

We are thankful for the 18 months that Inny was in our family. She taught us about love, trust, and restoration. We learned a valuable lesson that we apply to every situation we now face. We choose not to judge the parents, but instead to love them. We choose to believe that they can be transformed and one day experience reunification. We know that Inny and Grace's story is not common, but our desire is to see it become the norm rather than the exception.

Allen Walker is currently a pastor at The Harbour Church in Fort Lauderdale, Fla. He and his wife have a daughter and are foster parents whose passion is to provide a place for children in need to receive love, safety, and stability. They believe that through unconditional love the lives of these children can be transformed in powerful ways. In 2010, they had 16 different children come through their home. The Walkers are advocates for fostering and adopting and share their story through speaking engagements and on their website at www.allenandeva.com.

Forever Family: My Daughter's Foster Mother is Still Part of Our Lives.

By Wanda Chambers

In 1998 I was pregnant with my daughter when I was arrested for possession of crack cocaine. I was given a conditional release to go to a drug treatment program but for a long time I could not get it right. First I ran away from that program. Then, when I was let out on bail to give birth to my daughter, I purchased some crack while I was bringing her home from the hospital and started using again. When she was 6 months old, someone reported me and the child welfare system put her in foster care. Honestly, I felt relieved because I knew I wasn't doing right with Ebony. Once she went into care, I didn't have to worry about whether she was safe.

When I look back today, I think, "Oh my God, I can't believe that was me." It's horrible how much I lied and connived. I was just so heavily into my addiction. I was in foster care as a child and, when I was 12, got involved in drugs with my mother. It was all I knew.

Praying for Strength

Soon after my daughter was removed, I got locked up. I got out in October and was back in jail in January. By then, I wanted to stop using but did not know how. I prayed, "God, I'm too stupid to get clean on my own." I was sent upstate to Bedford Hills Correctional Facility and by the time I got there I was more alert because I had been clean for months. I said to myself, "I'm going to start communicating with the agency." I could relate to my daughter's struggle and, once I was clean, I was committed to getting her out of foster care.

My daughter had been in care a year and a half at that point. I asked for reports and pictures of my daughter, but I never got visits. All I knew was that she was with a Spanish family and I was concerned that she wouldn't speak English. She was 3 years old when I saw her again.

Fighting Termination

While I was locked up, the agency filed to terminate my parental rights, and when I came home it was in progress. I told the caseworker, "I don't know what you're talking about. This is not abandonment! I wrote you letters!" The worker said, "Wanda, if you see the process as stretching between A and Z, you're at M right now. You can still turn this around." I said, "No, you still have a chance to turn this around. What do you need me to do?" I didn't have a struggle with the agency after that. I was compliant and had workers that worked with me. I graduated from a drug treatment program, took parenting classes, found my own apartment, and found preventive services. My grandmother was my backbone through it all. She supported me when I didn't believe in myself.

Slowly Reconnecting

When I began visiting my daughter, she couldn't stand my living guts. Ebony was afraid of me and was really not nice. She wouldn't talk to me, she'd scream when I got near her.

She'd sit under the desk for the whole visit, or keep running out in the hall to see her foster mother. I would keep reading, "And the bear said..." and if she looked at me I'd say, "Hello, Ebony." Of course I went home and cried.

At first, the foster mother and I did not get along. I felt that the foster mother's presence during visits was making it harder for us to bond. My daughter kept going out in the hall to talk with her foster mother, and it made me crazy. I said, "I'm going to ask them to remove the foster mother from the agency during the time of my visit." She fought me tooth and nail, one mother fighting another mother. She would say my daughter acted out after visits and she blamed me.

Still, I went step by step – I kept working on my relationship with Ebony and went from supervised to community visits to weekends. Ebony and I got closer when I was able to take her out to the park and then, when we had weekend visits, I could do little things like wipe her face and do her hair and put on her shoes. When I could sleep with her next to me I felt really connected with her. I'm emotional, and when her little hand would touch my leg, it would send chills through my body. As my daughter's foster mother realized that my daughter was really on her way home, she began to be a friend to me.

'We Can All Live Together'

The day my daughter came home for good, I felt like I should give Ebony back to the foster family because they loved her so much and she loved them. We'd had overnights, but it was nothing to prepare any of us for what felt like the final goodbye. That day, the whole foster family brought her to my door. They pulled up in a minivan with about 15 Spanish people in it, brothers and sisters, all crying – crying on the floor, crying in the street, taking all of her belongings out of the car, screaming, "My princess, my baby." I was like, "Oh my God, they're killing me." Part of me actually felt like I was doing something wrong by getting my daughter home. Another part felt overwhelmed.

I was actually planning to end their relationship with my daughter. I wanted her home with me, period. But later on, when I was bathing my daughter, she said to me, "This is what we can do. We can put your house and their house together and we can all live together." My heart went out to Ebony. I'm a woman of compassion, and I told myself, "There is no way I'm going to end this relationship. I can't do that to them or to her."

A Loving Connection

In the months after my daughter came home, her foster family continued to show love to us both. I called her foster mother once and said, "Why isn't this child eating?" We realized that Ebony was used to Spanish food and I cook black people food. So her foster mom would bring pans and pans of food. She taught me to cook pastelitos and peas and rice.

Today my daughter is 10 and she is an amazing little girl. I'm working as a parent advocate at the Brooklyn Family Defense Project, which represents parents in court and supports parents by assigning a lawyer, social worker, and parent advocate to each case. I tell the parents my story. I pull out my dispositions and my certificates and say, "You can sit on this side of the desk if you do what you need to do."

My daughter's former foster mother is still part of our lives. She often babysits since

I'm working and going to school, and Ebony stays with her in the summers.

We don't always agree – she thinks I'm too strict and that I don't feed my daughter enough, telling me, "She's too skinny! She needs to eat." I think she lets my daughter stay up too late eating anything. I'm big on boundaries because I didn't get any when I was a child. Even so, I truly appreciate her love for my child. I'll curse her out in a minute, but I love her, and I know she loves us both.

The Good Fight

By William Cuchens

When I became a foster parent, I had no idea how the role would affect me. Of course, I understood how radically my lifestyle would change, but I was not prepared for how radically I would change.

As a young adult, I never felt comfortable with confrontation. When I first got promoted to a supervisor position, I had to deal with employee performance issues like dress code, time, and attendance. When I had to coach someone's performance, I worried for days about the conversation; planning how I should phrase my words and preparing for their retaliation. Maybe I worried I'd lose the argument or that the employee wouldn't like me anymore, but I had a job to do and, through practice and some feeble trial-and-error, I improved and learned not to let their reaction bother me.

Nearly a decade has passed since I received my first taste of responsibility as a young adult. Since then, my wife, Laurie, and I have fostered five children, all younger than the age of 3, and adopted two – one from foster care and one from a private agency. Currently, we are a kinship placement for our oldest son's biological brother, a 2-year-old we called J.

J came to us with multiple medical issues; the most serious concern was his need for oral surgery. A week after he came home, Laurie booked an appointment with a reputable pediatric dentist who accepted Medicaid (a battle itself). The dentist found eight cavities and recommended the only oral surgeon in town who accepted Medicaid. Unfortunately, this surgeon worked on children once a month and was booked until the following month.

During the month we waited for his surgery, J had three head colds. Laurie took him to the doctor three times and each time the doctor sent her away with a prescription for over-the-counter medication. J's third cold came the weekend before his surgery and Laurie and I worried that if he were placed on an antibiotic, his surgery would be postponed. Our fears came true when Laurie took him in first thing Monday morning. The doctor diagnosed J with strep throat and said that his surgery would have to be postponed. Laurie called me at work and broke down crying. Had she been in good health herself, she might not have fallen apart, but she was on her way to her doctor who would diagnose her with strep throat as well.

I took a half sick day, rushed home, and booked an appointment for my three-year-old daughter, Vivianna, to see her pediatrician since she'd had a runny nose for a couple days. While I was gone, Laurie called the oral surgeon to cancel Thursday's surgery. The office informed her that the surgeon was booked the following month and we'd have to wait two months. When Laurie called me with the news, I lost my temper.

I called J's pediatrician's office and told the receptionist that if J had been put on antibiotics the two earlier times we'd brought him in, then he wouldn't have gotten strep, given it to his mother, I wouldn't have had to take a sick day, and J's surgery wouldn't have to be postponed. The receptionist transferred me to the doctor's assistant who asked me to repeat the entire story. I repeated everything at a higher volume and added, "This is your office's fault and you need to make it right." It was a pathetic bluff; this wasn't a restaurant that had messed up our meal and could comp the ticket. Nevertheless, it surprised me when she said I could bring him back in for a penicillin shot. "You want me to bring him back today?" I asked. The assistant said, "As long as he doesn't have a reaction to the shot he can still have the surgery."

I was more angry than relieved. "Why didn't you give him the shot earlier in the day when he was in?" I asked. She offered no explanation. She only said, "I'll have to check with the doctor to make sure we can fit you in today." By now, it was after three o'clock in the afternoon and I started to worry about rush hour traffic and what we were going to do about dinner. At 3:30 pm, the assistant called and said I could bring him in. I drove J myself and we were in and out in 30 minutes. He had no reaction to the penicillin and, three days later, had the surgery and came out fine.

I don't like that I got as frustrated as I did with the pediatrician's office. Had I not yelled at the assistant, she would not have offered the penicillin shot and J's surgery would be postponed two months. I have to remind myself that although the doctor's office takes Medicaid, it is still a business and the staff will not lose any sleep if my son cries and points at his teeth when he chews food. Laurie and I alone are emotionally invested in the well-being of this child. Like my role as a supervisor, I consider my role of a father as doing what I have to do because it's my job, regardless of how uncomfortable I am. I don't consider myself a fighter; rather I'm an advocate willing to do whatever it takes to ensure my children are taken care of.

William Cuchens and his wife, Laurie became foster parents in 2006 and fostered four children. Isaac, the second, was adopted just after his second birthday. Currently, they are foster parenting Isaac's biological brother. This article originally appeared in ***Fostering Families Today****. He writes about being a multiracial father at goggycoffee.blogspot.com.*

Teaching Sidney

By Denise Kendrick

On a typical Sunday morning, I peeked through the doorway of my foster daughter's class at our church. One of the teachers sat next to Sidney* helping her work a puzzle.

While I was delighted to find her so focused on a task, I realized the other seven children in class were listening to a Bible story. They fidgeted quietly, but seemed intrigued with the colorful pictures of Jonah and the whale. I soaked up a moment of discreet observation before the lead teacher noticed me standing outside the door. She abruptly told the circle of children to remain seated and came to the door.

"Sidney needs to move back to the toddler class. Her behavior is distracting to the other children," said Sidney's teacher, Jan, as she stepped into the hallway and closed the door behind her. I felt my face begin to flush. She continued, "Don't get me wrong, I love teaching Sidney, but I have to take the other children into consideration." Out of the corner of my eye I saw the other teacher leave Sidney to supervise the rest of the class. Sidney glanced around before gently tossing the final piece of the puzzle over her shoulder. I wanted to smile at her clever antic to avoid finishing the puzzle, but suddenly remembered we were being kicked out of Sunday School.

"I appreciate your concern, Jan, but this is the threes' and fours' class. Sidney turned four last month... this is her class." My voice trailed off a bit and I realized I was fighting back tears. "I know that Sidney can be a challenge, she is still learning to follow directions and participate in class. I think with more time, and positive reinforcement, she can do well. She needs to be with other children her age –" Jan cut me off, "The other children are cutting, gluing, drawing... Sidney needs to stay in a class on her level until she is ready to listen and participate." The flush on my face began to creep up to my ears.

Why didn't Jan want to help my child?

Why was she so insensitive?

Why isn't she being a team player for this child?

Eight short months before this tense conversation Sidney was placed in our home for foster care. She was found wandering around an apartment complex hours after dark in a man's undershirt and a diaper. A neighbor spotted her and began looking for her parents. No one in the complex recognized her or knew who she belonged to. The police were called, and finally found Sidney's mother and boyfriend passed out in their apartment, stoned on methamphetamine.

When the caseworker delivered her to our home for placement Sidney ran to me and yelled "Mommy!" Then she ran to my husband, and much to his surprise, yelled "Mommy!" Sidney was three-and-a-half years old, but functioned on the level of an 18-month-old. She only knew two words – "Mommy" and "TV." She had severe dental decay and asthma. Sidney did not know colors or shapes. She was delighted to play with the new toys and playmates she was surrounded by in our home, but would zone out and begin rocking in a trance-like state if the television was on.

Throughout the months in our home, Sidney learned dozens of words and began speaking in small sentences. Her underdeveloped body began to grow and strengthen. Tubes in her ears and breathing treatments for her asthma gave her newfound energy and health. She went to an early childhood learning program and took ballet lessons at the YMCA. She was diagnosed with Fetal Alcohol Syndrome, but amazed us with her wit and resilience.

Jan does want to help... but I've never shown her how.

Jan and I stood in awkward silence as I searched for a calm and loving response. Our church has always been a refuge for our family, a place of caring and acceptance. Of all the places I thought I might need to advocate for my child, to fight for her rights... I never dreamed it would be at my church. Why didn't Jan want to help my child? Why was she so insensitive? Why isn't she being a team player for this child?

It took only a moment of soul-searching for me to find answers to my questions:

Jan does want to help...but I've never shown her how.

Jan isn't insensitive...she is ignorant of Sidney's unique background and needs, and I've done nothing to educate her.

Jan isn't being a team player...because I haven't asked her to join Sidney's team.

I realized my pointing finger was pointing the wrong direction. In my haste to provide Sidney with every opportunity, and push for her inclusion... I had neglected to give Jan the tools and information she needed to help Sidney succeed.

I took a deep breath and asked Jan if we could speak in a more private setting. She feigned concern about leaving the class, but followed me to an empty classroom. We gingerly sat in child sized chairs. I reached out and took her hand. "Jan," I began, "You are a wonderful teacher. I know you want what is best for every child in your class. I know you want what is best for Sidney. This sweet child has faced so much hurt and neglect... " I continued to share my heart with Jan. I invited her to be part of our team, be part of the solution, and be an agent for healing during Sidney's time with us. Before I could finish, tears were rolling down Jan's face.

From that day forward, Jan was Sidney's biggest fan. She greeted her warmly at the door each Sunday morning. She stopped by the house to visit her, and made bows for her hair. Jan recruited volunteers to work one-on-one with Sidney and help her participate in class. And her efforts began to show.

One rainy Sunday morning in Spring I peeked in to Sidney's class. She listened intently to a Bible story in circle time, sitting in the lap of her volunteer. When Jan asked if someone wanted to pretend to put baby Moses in the basket Sidney's hand shot up. She gently placed the baby doll in a wicker basket, then began to rock it in her arms and sing. Her little voice carried to the door, and I immediately recognized the tune. "Jesus want me... I know. Jesus want me... I know." Sidney sang her version of "Jesus Loves Me" to the baby doll in the basket.

The next morning we got the call that Sidney would go home to her mother. After just longer than a year in our home she had begun transitioning back into her mother's life.

One hour visits with her mother had increased to half day, then overnight. Her mother had spent a long year staying clean, finding a new apartment in a safer community, and maintaining a wonderful job with benefits. She seemed ready to parent Sidney.

I called Jan to let her know that Sidney would be leaving Thursday afternoon, and her voice wavered as she thanked me for the call. The week rushed by in a whirlwind of packing, withdrawing from school, and last minute details. By Thursday at lunch Sidney was too nervous to eat and, instead, lingered in the entry of the house where the suitcases of her clothing, boxes of belongings, and hot pink bike sat expectantly.

I jumped when the doorbell rang, and went to answer. I was delighted to find Jan standing on our front porch, not the caseworker as I expected. Sidney yelled "Miss Nan!" and gave her a big hug. Jan stayed just long enough to give Sidney a colorful Bible. After Jan left I decided to read to Sidney from her new Bible. She climbed into my lap and we shared a few sweet moments together before it was time to go. Written inside the cover of the Bible was this note from Miss Jan:

"Dear Sidney,
You are a bright and wonderful child.
You have taught me so much this year in
Sunday School. I will never forget you!
Love, Miss Jan"

So many people invested in Sidney while she was in our home. From deliveries of hand-me-down clothes to home cooked meals, the generosity of our friends and family overwhelmed us. Sidney's school bus driver walked her to the front porch each afternoon, and often brought her tiny surprises. At her ballet themed birthday party a teenage ballerina came in a shimmering tutu and put on a show just for Sidney. This outpouring of love, and sense of community is something not every child is blessed to experience, especially children from Sidney's background.

While I know that Sidney benefited from the efforts of "our village"... it is the mutual growth on the part of the giver that makes these relationships so special. I taught Sidney how to button a sweater and she taught me what perseverance looks like. I taught her to fold her hands and pray, but she taught me that faith is something we choose. I taught her to point to each word as I read, she taught me sometimes it's okay to just enjoy the pictures.

Denise Kendrick is a long-time foster parent married to her high school sweetheart, Bruce. They lead a ministry called Embrace, www.EmbraceTexas.org, which encourages foster care, adoption, and global orphan care. Bruce and Denise have three biological children and just finalized the adoption of their oldest son. This article originally appeared in ***Fostering Families Today****.*

**Names hove been changed to protect privacy.*

Thanks to You

By Veronica Brown

More than one person has said to me, "Your foster son is doing so well, and it's all thanks to you." I know they are trying to be kind, and I appreciate the sentiment. But I usually respond something like, "Thanks, but if I take credit for the ones that do well, then I'll have to take the blame for the ones that end up in jail." The way I see it: if I did, then I'd have to.

Otherwise, what a great gig! I can sit back and own all the glory or toss the blame, responsibility, and disappointments in someone else's lap.

I'm also uncomfortable with the whole gratitude thing. Who's giving thanks? Is it supposed to be the foster kids? Should they feel indebted to me? I don't think so. If I honestly believe (as I do) that every child deserves a safe, caring childhood, why should they have to "thank me" for trying my best to provide that?

Of course, I think gratitude is an important core value and I try to teach my kids to show appreciation. I do not want them to develop a sense of entitlement, nor do I wish them to go through life feeling guilty. But, I require my kids to thank me for the things I do, not for who I am. They're expected to say thanks for the movie, thanks for letting me stay up later, thanks for making my lunch, thanks for letting my friend sleepover, etc. I remember thanking my mom for these things. I don't remember thanking her for loving me.

I am not keeping score. There is no debt. They owe me nothing. I wish for their success and happiness, but they owe it to themselves, not me.

And then, out of the blue, one of my boys brings a letter home from school.

Dear Ver,

Thank you for taking me into your Home and treating me So Special. it means a lot to me

you make very good meals. and you give me my allowance So I can buy Special thing.

and Even thouh your Singing make me happy it hurts my Ears.

You are very genarous especilly for a Yankees fan go Red Sox go!

you made my life so much better

I'll take this kind of thanks any day. Even if it's written by a Red Sox fan!

Veronica Brown has been a foster parent in Canada since 1995.

Foster parents and Court Appointed Special Advocates sometimes experience an uneasy and distrustful relationship but it does not need to be this way.

CASAs Can Make a Difference

By Randee Kaitcer

The woman's voice on the phone was polite yet emphatic. "I do not want yet another person visiting in my home. Thank you for the offer." She hung up.

"Yikes," I thought. "Now what?" The court appointed me as an advocate for children and part of that responsibility included seeing the children in their living environment. I did not anticipate this response from the foster mother, the person charged with day-to-day care and nurture of the children. I redialed the number.

"Mrs. Finnegan? I am so sorry to bother you again. Unfortunately, I do need to visit the children some time this month. Would it be more convenient for you if I piggy-backed my visit with the Child Protective Services worker's visit next week? Then we could sort of kill two birds with one stone," I laughed nervously. Mrs. Finnegan suddenly sounded tired. "Yes. That will be fine. See you Tuesday at 4 p.m., after the children get off the bus." Whew.

Foster parents and Court Appointed Special Advocates sometimes experience an uneasy and distrustful relationship but it does not need to be this way. After five years of CASA volunteer experience and more than two years of casework supervisory experience, I have seen the ups and downs, joys and challenges of working with both these amazing groups of generous-hearted and compassionate people.

When I interviewed for my current CASA position, one interviewer asked me if I would miss being an advocate. I thought for a moment and responded, "I will miss being an advocate – the contact with the children, the investigatory work, the in-depth research into new drugs, therapies, etc.; but as an advocate, I can touch only a certain number of children at a time. As a supervisor, I will be able to touch many more children by helping other advocates with their own cases." I was serious about my commitment to helping children then and I still am.

Listen to these words: "I want to make a difference. I never give up. I do what's in the best interest of the children. I have little control. The paperwork can be overwhelming at times. I want to give back. I get little respect. I learn a great deal about people and life. I feel unappreciated, the work is the most rewarding thing I have ever done. I get more than I give." A frustrated and dedicated foster parent? Yes. A frustrated and dedicated CASA volunteer? Also yes. We work toward the same dream and goal – creating positive change in the lives of the children placed in our homes and our lives by an overburdened system. We simply approach the challenge from slightly different directions.

All children need stability, security, and felt-safety, acceptance, discipline, respect, encouragement, and a place to call home. In a foster home, children experience, often for the first time, someone who cares enough to give them a consistent time to get up, eat, go to school, do homework, do chores, brush their teeth, and go to bed. It provides someone to teach them right from wrong, how to behave at church and at the store.

What happens when it is time for a court hearing, however? Many foster parents tell me they feel constrained and as if they have no voice – they are a forgotten member of the team. The foster parent knows the children better than anyone; yet despite the wealth of information at their fingertips, their opinion is not usually heard by the court. With a CASA volunteer, the foster parent's opinion is not only sought but heard. While any independent recommendation must be based on first-hand observations and be guided by what is in the best interest of the child, the foster parent is a critical source of a CASA's information gathering. We will disagree sometimes, but we do so with respect, courtesy, and professionalism.

Attorneys often find CASAs helpful as well. Lee Ryan Owens, a family law attorney in Arlington, Texas, said, "When a foster parent receives a new child into their home, a CASA who has been with the child through the three previous placements, schools and therapists can offer continuity and insights. They know the child's food likes and dislikes, their need for a night light and that they call their biological dad 'Big D.' By working with the CASA, a foster parent may gain a child's trust more readily, saving valuable time."

A CASA volunteer can help facilitate arranging sibling visits between separated brothers and sisters. The CASA can break through the impasse in obtaining specific services, such as grief counseling for a young girl whose mother committed suicide or post-traumatic therapy for a boy who witnessed horrors after a natural disaster struck his hometown. The CASA can be the "squeaky wheel" a foster parent needs, without fear of reprisal.

As foster parent Caren shared, "Our CASA works as a team [member] ....oftentimes personality conflicts become an issue [with] social workers. It might not even be from the current child in placement, but from something in the past. Each [child] is different and must be given individual attention."

Building relationships is the key to being a successful CASA volunteer. Listening, following through and making the promised phone call are all vital links in the chain of creating mutual respect and trust. The children and families we work with know they can count on us. As one custodial grandmother, Nancy, put it: "... I could tell [our CASA volunteer] was very observant... She made the children feel special and important, which assured me she was spending her Sunday afternoons with us for the right reasons. When it was time for court... I felt alone and scared of what the future held for my grandchildren... The CASA volunteer sat with me and provided support." A CASA can help ensure the court hears the foster parent's insights.

Foster families succeed in big and little ways, often without realizing it. An agency case manager shared the following success story: There are two sisters who are survivors of multiple traumas and are diagnosed with Complex Post-Traumatic Stress Disorder and depression. Their one and only foster family, by their love and patience, has cared for these

young ladies in their home for almost four years. The girls would be in a residential treatment center by now if it wasn't for this dedicated family.

We recently updated the girls' care plans and assessments. One sister's functioning level score increased by 30 points. The other sister's problem severity score decreased by 17 points. The foster mother struggled with the possibility the girls might never move past the stage they are at now. The foster family had been unable to notice the girls' improvement because the sisters have many ways they externalize their traumas.

Thanks to the persistent efforts of this committed family, these sisters are not only growing up together, they are also given the gift of healing together.

Collaborate with your CASA volunteer – allow him or her to help you help the children. While CASAs cannot always repair the children with whom they work, they can help minimize the damage and set the children on a course that will help them heal. It requires passion, energy, imagination, and love. It is unglamorous work but it is glorious. I know you can say the same.

Randee Kaitcer is a casework supervisor and former volunteer for CASA of Tarrant County in Fort Worth, Texas. She has a degree in economics from Franklin and Marshall College in Lancaster, Penn. In addition, she has served as a banker, lactation consultant, and public school reading teacher. At CASA of Tarrant County, Kaitcer has led efforts to expand continuing education for volunteer advocates of abused and neglected children throughout her community. This article was originally published in ***Fostering Families Today****.*

Birth Family Connections

"In all of us there is a hunger, marrow deep, to know our heritage- to know who we are and where we have come from. Without this enriching knowledge, there is a hollow yearning. No matter what our attainments in life, there is still a vacuum, an emptiness, and the most disquieting loneliness." – Alex Haley

Letter to My Mother

By J. A. Freeman

I should have written and given this to you a long time ago. Now there's no physical address for me to send this to you, but I'm hopeful that if I keep it in my heart, right next to where I hold your memory tight, you'll get it.

I don't know when I would have given it to you. Maybe the last time we were together, but who ever knows the last time they are going to see somebody in this life. I remember there was an undramatic rainfall that day which assured me that nothing out of the ordinary would happen. Your struggled breathing, the sound of it percussive against the walls of your empty apartment, penetrated me, not touching me but penetrating my body at the same time. Your beauty was grossly distorted but it never abandoned you. Long ago I learned to be strong for you, never shedding a tear. But your sadness was overwhelming, so much that I deserted my duty.

From an early age, I knew that I would be immune from the hardships that you faced, as if my childhood immunizations also guaranteed me a life free from suffering. I could always tell that my life was something both impressive and irrelevant to you because you never quite knew all that I did, but my success was your badge of honor and you reveled in it. You always drew strength from your children; we were your nourishment. In turn, I was dependent upon your praise. Somehow stealing from it what I needed, hoarding it, unwilling to let it go.

In life, we live and laugh and love for years and years and then just like that, in an instant, it's all gone and then we're invisible. The moment that you could no longer draw air in and out of your lungs or take me in through your weary eyes, I acquired an expression that set my features in a resigned way.

Afterwards I wandered alone, it felt as if I, too, had left this world, with people left to wonder where I was. I closed my eyes tight and thought of your face and thought of all our memories together, which eclipsed everything else. I also thought of all the things that I planned to do, including this.

I attempted to write a letter to you, and though the paper wasn't blank, there was no substance on it either, as if I had repeatedly tested the ink of my pen and had nothing to say. But it was really my sense of guilt that stopped me. I carried nothing with me from you or that part of my life when I was a child. Apart from the hometown area code that still lingered in front of my cell number, there was nothing to remind me of those years of my life. I allowed home to become an unfamiliar place, with unfamiliar people. It had become a piece of my past that strangely had nothing to do with my current life. That long involvement, becoming the man I am today, was rendered meaningless in the official chronicle of my past. I never wanted you to know this and I never wanted to admit this to myself.

I knew that you worried about me that without an involved mother, there would be no way I could survive in this world. But I wasn't only your son, I was a child of many mothers. Mothers who have children the same age as me but pulled double duty and helped me get into college as well, famous political mothers who helped adjust my tie before the bright flash of cameras, mothers in small towns who always keep a warm bed for me and my very own Christmas stocking hanging over the fireplace.

There are mothers who seamlessly incorporate me into Thanksgiving dinner and call me when they think of me, mothers who I've worked for that sing happy birthday on my voicemail and get me out of trouble, and mothers that I will always love for loving me but it never made me love you less.

And now, I remember you and carry with me invaluable lessons that you taught. You're gone, but I don't want you to worry about who will encourage me because all my mothers love me just as much as I know you did.

J. A. Freeman, foster care alumnus, age 28, from New York, was in care for nine years.

Before foster care, family meant my sister, my mother, my maternal grandparents, and occasionally an aunt or uncle. I considered them my family because I was biologically related and I spent a lot of time with them, including the holidays.

I left the system last year at age twenty. I was afraid that I would have to leave the life I worked so hard to create, afraid I'd lose the strong relationship that I had with my foster mother. I was afraid that I would have no place to live, no financial assistance, no health insurance, and most importantly, no emotional support or guidance. But my foster mother opened her home and her heart to me, and welcomed me into her family. I have met my biological father and relatives on his side; I have a friendly relationship with all of them, but I do not consider them family. Today, my chosen family is my sister, my foster mother, and my boyfriend of three years – these are the people who have stuck by me through the most difficult times of my life, and have supported me unconditionally. These are the three people that I can truly be myself around.

Family are the people who comfort, love, and support you, and I now know what it feels like to have a real family, and to feel that love. No matter how much support you have from others, you are your own best source of strength. It is so important to build relationships with people who inspire you to be a better person, but you have to be an inspiration to yourself as well.

– Jennifer Smith, foster care alumna, age 21, from New York, was in care for five years.

These thoughts are reprinted with permission from ***Flux, Life After Foster Care.*** www.fostercarealumni.org/resources/FLUX.htm

Children in Foster Care and Their Parents: Lessons Learned

By Eileen Mayers Pasztor, DSW

I have had the privilege of experiencing foster care over the past 40 years from the unique perspective of a child welfare social worker and a foster and adoptive parent. There also was a two-year period when my adopted son needed psychiatric hospitalization and residential treatment, so I learned the feeling of turning the care of my child over to others. Together, my foster daughter and adopted son experienced four foster families, five residential treatment facilities, abuse in care, a disrupted family reunification, a disrupted adoption, and reunification with birth siblings after 40 years of separation.

As a trainer, consultant, and curriculum developer (Nova, MAPP, PRIDE) serving nationally and overseas, I have worked with over 10,000 foster and adoptive parents, child welfare professionals, and advocates. There's an expression, "statistics are people with the tears washed off." I have learned first-hand about the dynamics of attachment, separation, loss, identity, and self-esteem. ***The following vignettes are examples of experiences that have left an indelible mark in my heart. Combined with research, policy, and best practices, here are some lessons learned for thinking about children in foster care and their parents. I am grateful to Carrie Kitze and Kim Phagan Hansel for the opportunity to share this perspective as you, in turn, think about the children you are working with and caring for.....and their parents.***

"Don't let them take me, Mommy."

I began my child welfare career as a county child welfare worker, directly out of college. My qualifications were a bachelor's degree in history and a driver's license. I "shadowed" a more experienced caseworker, who had gone to the emergency room to take custody of three siblings suffering from abuse (mother's boyfriend) and neglect (mother who, when drinking, could not protect and nurture her children.) After futile attempts to help the mother comfort her children, my colleague said, "We just have to leave with the kids. Take the little girl." As we tried to walk out of the hospital room with the children, the eight - year old collapsed on the floor sobbing, "Don't let them take me, Mommy." I was stunned. Why would these children want to stay with a parent who was harming them? My colleague explained, "They don't know where they are going. Some children prefer the security of misery to the misery of insecurity." ***Lesson learned: Parents are not consistently abusive or neglecting......there are good times, too. We have to help children remember the positives, without discounting or excusing the pain."***

"Take away my problems, not my children"

One of the birth mothers I worked with had come to the city from a rural neighboring state. Dual-diagnosed with schizophrenia and drinking to self-medicate, she was not able to care for her four children: two adolescents, and two others – four and six years old. Going to court for permanent custody of the little ones, she cried to the judge, "Take away my problems, not my children!" ***Lesson learned: Of course we couldn't take away her problems, and she never saw her children again.***

"I don't care who my biological dad is, I like the one I have now."
My husband and I adopted a ten-year-old boy in an open adoption. He would have regular contact with a maternal grandfather and 13 year-old sister living with Grandpa. Grandma and his birth mother were deceased. The birth father maintained contact with the birth sister. At about age 14, during a visit with his birth sister, she told him that the man he thought was his birth father wasn't actually that person. When he came home from seeing his sister, he recounted the story about "Sammy" not really being his Dad. I asked him what he thought about that. He paused for a moment and then said, "I'm so glad. Sammy is a jerk. I'm glad he's not my biological father. I'd rather not know who it is, than think it was him. Besides I like the Dad I have now." ***Lesson learned: Our son is 37 years old, he never brought it up again; follow the children's lead regarding how they want to identify with their parents.***

"Our three sets of parents"
Our foster daughter, well into her 20s and back living with us, along with her seven year - old son, hung up from a conversation with her birth mother. She was quite upset. "Bobbie" (her birth mother and she referred to her by her first name) heard me refer to you as my mother, and she feels bad." So I told my daughter that all of us have three sets of parents. There are those who birth us, those who raise us, and those who have legal custody of us. Most of us grow up with a Mom and Dad who fill all three roles. But for children in foster care, those roles are divided among the birth parents, the foster parents, and the agency/court system. So I told my daughter, "You call Bobbie back and tell her about the three kinds of parents. Tell her that she gave birth to you, I just gave you sandwiches and sent you to school, and scolded you. And the agency had the legal custody. You tell her that you got your beautiful eyes and pretty hair from her, along with your intelligence. Anyone could have done what I did: feed and discipline you. But her job was the most important, she gave you life. So we rehearsed this call. Afterward, she told me, "You know, I'm not sure she understood this – she's got so many problems. But I understand, and this made me feel better." Incidentally, our foster daughter calls my husband and me by our first names. But when she talks about us to others, she says, "My mom and dad." ***Lesson learned: Children should be able to choose what they want to call us. Most importantly: children should never have to choose between, or among, any of their parents. Just as parents with more than one child love all their children all at the same time, children who have more than one set of parents can love all of them – all at the same time.***

"I guess my hope for reunification is over now."
When our foster daughter was in her late thirties, she called to tell me her birth mother had passed away. I replied, "I'm so sorry, honey. How are you doing?" She paused and then said, "Well, I guess the chances for reunification are really over now." Children and parents who are separated but never reunified go through life with an unresolved grieving process. Children wonder, "Who am I? Why did I get separated from my family?" It is critical that we help children with loss and the resulting grieving process. This can take years. What can be more awful than, "My parents couldn't take care of me?" I've worked with my children to help them understand that parenting is a learned skill. For example, as we grow up, we learn to do more complicated things: tie our shoes, ride a bike, drive a

car. As we get older, we also learn how to make babies. And most people learn how to take care of the babies they make. But in some families, like theirs, the parents learned how to make babies, but not to take care of the ones they made. Social workers and foster parents try to help parents learn to take care of the babies they make. ***Lesson learned: Sometimes it doesn't work out: illness and, often, alcohol and drug abuse, prevent parents from learning to keep their children safe. Certainly, the children and the parents have a right to feel mad and bad and sad about what happened to their families. So we become time travelers: we use the present, to deal with the past, in order to go forward.***

"Give back the diploma"
Our son had his first psychiatric hospitalization on his 12th birthday. The social worker doing the intake learned, in the process of getting the social history, that he was adopted. She said, "Your son is catatonic. He may never come out of a back ward. You might want to think about giving him back to the agency." My husband and I were shocked. I noticed a diploma on the wall. It indicated that she was a Licensed Clinical Social Worker. I said, "You have a master's degree in social work. You should give that back." My husband and I hired a social worker in private practice to help us stay together as a family, deal with the awful reality of his illness, and help us find the best residential treatment center. Twenty-five years and many psychiatric hospitalizations later, we're still together. ***Lesson learned: Insist on working with professionals who are committed to keeping families together – however families are defined: birth, kinship, foster, adoptive.***

"Self-esteem and social justice"
These experiences and many more, have helped provide the framework for how I think about separation, attachment, loss, and identity, and how they relate to foster care. If there is one theme that runs through all these vignettes in this section, that would be self-esteem. Our challenge is to help children feel good about who they are, that the reasons they needed foster care were not their fault, or really anyone's fault. Sometimes, sad things happen in families because of social and economic conditions. It is hard to get adulthood right, if we don't get childhood right. So we protect and nurture children and, at the same time, try to enhance their self-esteem. If you look at the article the "Jigsaw Puzzle Child," (see page 29) you'll see that the parents are a lot like their children, just the chronological ages are higher. Most of them care for and love their children, and never intended harm.

Eileen Mayers Pasztor, DSW (Doctor of Social Work) is experienced as a public agency caseworker and supervisor; as a curriculum developer and trainer; and as a foster and adoptive parent for children with special needs who, now as adults, continue to require her support. She teaches child welfare and social policy advocacy courses at the School of Social Work at California State University, Long Beach (CSULB), and edits the journal ***Reflections – Narratives of Professional Helping****. She was the national program director for family foster care, kinship care, and adoption at Child Welfare League of America (CWLA). She is recognized internationally for her leadership to create programs to develop, train, select, and support foster and adoptive parents (Nova, MAPP, PRIDE), and she continues to consult and train nationally.*

Let's Have the Conversation....

With hundreds of thousands of children and families involved in foster care nationally, this is a billion dollar industry. Social workers have a National Association of Social Workers (NASW) Code of Ethics that we are mandated to follow. It has six main principles: being competent, having dignity, having integrity, believing in the importance of human relationships, providing service, and advocating for social justice. From this context, it is essential to consider:

1. Prevention: We need serious conversations in our communities about what can be done to help young people avoid having babies they cannot take care of. As my foster daughter once said, after having become a mother at age 17, "My life and that of my son would have been better, if I had a high school diploma and a driver's license before the baby."

2. Fatherhood: Child welfare continues to be overly female focused. Much of the emphasis is on the birth and foster mothers. Most of the workers are female. However, there are projects around the country that emphasize engaging fathers to have a role in the lives of their children. This can happen by building self-esteem, reducing social and emotional isolation, teaching them how to get along with the mothers of their babies, and getting jobs to pay child support.

3. Drugs, poverty, and institutional racism: Most children come into the foster care system because their parents abuse alcohol or other drugs. If we could get rid of the drugs, the foster care population would decrease dramatically. Poverty is not a reason for children and parents to be separated, nor should children of color be disproportionately represented. Education and jobs help keep parents and children together.

4. Skilled workforce and leadership: Child welfare is one of the few, if only, life-saving professions which lacks uniform standards for mandatory skills. Children with special needs require social workers and foster parents with special skills. There are proven models to recruit, select, train and retain competent foster parents who are committed to child protection. There are effective strategies to find and keep a competent workforce. But public and private child welfare agencies cannot manufacture foster parents or skilled social workers. We, as taxpayers, need to give them the necessary resources to develop and support therapeutic foster parents and skilled caseworkers, with agency and elected leaders who have a passion for compassion. I join many social workers and foster parents who know that our lives have been enriched by the experiences of working with, caring for, and caring about vulnerable children and their parents. All of us would, no doubt, give up all the lessons learned if these vulnerable children and parents could have been spared the pain of separation, loss, and trauma and, especially, the precipitating factors.

Co-Parenting/Working with Birth Parents

By Pamela Allen

"Hello, my name is Pam and I am not here to keep your children, I am here to help you get them back!" These are the words I always use when I meet the birth parent for the first time. I also always tell the children that my goal is to help get them back to their mommy or daddy. What better way to defuse what could start out as an adversarial relationship. I have NEVER met a birth mom or dad who didn't love their child, or a child who didn't want to go back to his or her birth mom or dad. The reality is, that is where they ultimately NEED to be if it is safe. I read somewhere that ninety percent of the children who are adopted or age out of the foster care system go back to their birth families. If this is the case, why would we want to deprive them of the opportunity to grow up with that family if possible?

When resource families (foster) and birth families work together from the start, children are able to go home more quickly and resource families, if a relationship is built with the birth parent, can stay in touch as a forever family and support for that child and his or her parents once the child goes home. When we look at "best interest" of children, we know that moving out of the foster care system in a timely manner is absolutely best. When the two families co-parent this can happen! What better way, than working together, can resource families model good parenting, appropriate boundaries and teach needed skills. Sometimes, children come into care because the parents do not have a support system outside of the system. After all, not all children come into care because of something their parents did. Sometimes parents just do not know where to seek outside help for their children... their family.

NFAPA (Nebraska Foster and Adoptive Parent Association) in collaboration with the Nebraska Federation of Families are working together with a pilot project to help resource parents and birth parents come together early on (within 72 hours if possible) when a child has been placed into foster care. The goal of this collaboration is to:

- Meet with families as early as possible.
- Build positive relationship between birth and foster parent.
- Statistics show increase in positive outcomes when positive relationship.
- Build informal supports.
- We will use practice based evidence (what works within our system in Nebraska).
- Identify foster families that believe in the philosophy.
- No protocol for birth families.
- Timely and successful reunification.
- Long-term collaboration.
- Begin to change the negative stigma, the perception of "foster families are bad" or "birth families are bad"

Shared parenting is building and maintaining relationship and communication between birth and resource families involved in a child's life with the goal of supporting family reunification or another permanency plan. One of the core philosophies of foster care families concentrates on the importance of family relationships in the treatment of children in care. While the foster family works with the foster child to develop positive changes, the biological family needs skills to support these changes and work on the family issues that initiated foster care. The relationship between foster parents and biological families can have a significant impact on the overall course of placement and/or treatment. When the relationship is respectful, nonjudgmental, and supportive, all parents are able to do a better job in meeting the children's needs. Birth parents experience less anger, feelings of shame, or worry about the care their children are receiving. With support the birth parents have more energy to focus on their own treatment issues.

When parents and foster parents work together, kids go home more quickly and stay home. Kids in foster care also get better care when the parent and foster parent exchange information about the child and work together to make visits positive. Kids also feel less worried about their families. Many kids are worried about loyalty – if they like the foster parent, does that mean they can't like their parent anymore? They feel better if they see the foster parent and parent getting along.

Reunification is also easier for the child if the relationship with the foster parent doesn't end, even if contact with the foster parent is just a birthday or Christmas card, a phone call, or occasional stopping by. The foster parent can become an ongoing support to the parent after reunification, someone who is an expert about their child. When things are tough and the kid is acting goofy, the parent can call and say, "What do I do?" The foster parent is able to say, "This worked for me." That can help prevent the child from re-entering foster care.

So, if we are truly working in the "best interest" of the child, why wouldn't we want to work with their parents?

Pamela Allen is executive director of Nebraska Foster & Adoptive Parent Association. She is a foster parent trainer. She and her husband, Randy, have eight children, two of whom were adopted. They have been fostering for 13 years. Allen was activities director/youth minister in a residential treatment facility before fostering.

We had one little boy who we'd hoped to work with his mom. She entered rehab as soon as he was born and we took that as a good sign that she would do her services. After looking at the services she needed to do I was discouraged for her. So we devised a plan to encourage her from afar, since we didn't have any personal contact with her. Each week we sent photos of her son and sent them to the visits. I often sent a camera to the visits as well so she could have the worker take photos of them together. I'd print them for her and send them the next time. I sent her the baby's first feeding and I'd send her letters letting her know how he was doing each week. Although she did not end up finishing her services, the worker said that out of her three kids that had been taken, she did more of her plan for this child than any other. It was a great feeling to know we did all we could to encourage her and help that bond between her and her son. I hope that even though she didn't get her son back that she was able to keep those photos and letters as a memento of her son.

Tracee Wagnon, foster, adoptive, and biological mom from a post on the list serve foster_parenting@yahoogroups.com

Eat, Play, Love

Visits helped me become a good mother.

By Anonymous

When my daughter, Lydia, was a year and a half, she was removed from home because my husband and I were using drugs. At our first visit, Hector and I were very anxious. I was scared that Little Mama would forget me, or would feel that I did not want her anymore.

Waiting in the hallway for our baby, we saw a Spanish man holding a little girl. The girl looked like my baby but she had bangs. Could that be her? My husband, Hector, said, "It is her" and he grabbed her from the guy's arms, saying, "Mama." She grabbed him back and put her little head on his shoulders.

When I saw my daughter's haircut, I was so upset. She did not look like my daughter. I confronted the caseworker and she told me that the foster parents could not see her eyes. I told her, "They should have put her hair up!"

"I'm sorry," the caseworker said. "It will grow back."

Sad and Confused

During the visit, Little Mama would not let go of us and was quiet. Her eyes gave a blank stare, moving ever so slowly. We tried to play toys with her but she just wanted comfort. She wrapped her body around me and rested her head on my shoulder. Her father and I rubbed her back and told her that we loved her very much and would fight to get her home.

At the end of the visit, it was hard to say goodbye. Little Mama was crying so much. Her face was full of agony. She screamed, "Mommy! Daddy!" I can still remember her arms stretching out to us.

When I looked into her eyes, I felt despair and guilt. I cried, hugged, and kissed Little Mama and told her we would see her again.

A Mom, But Not a Good One

Before my daughter was removed, I had a bad addiction for almost 20 years. At times, I barely slept or ate. I wandered the streets looking for my next hit. I had six children before Lydia and didn't raise any of them. Two of my sons ended up in foster care and were adopted by their foster mom, Tamera, who I asked to take Lydia when she went into foster care.

When I got pregnant with Lydia, I was determined to raise her. I stayed clean for six months. But I relapsed, even though I loved my daughter with all my heart.

While I was using, I tried to take care of Lydia. I put her to sleep by laying her on my stomach and rubbing her back until she fell asleep. I held her and comforted her when she cried. Little Mama liked to be tickled on her tummy and she liked rolling a ball back and forth. When she was old enough, I would take her to the park and push her on the swing and help her climb the jungle gym.

The best thing I remember during that time was Lydia's first birthday. I planned and saved money. I made tuna salad, baked macaroni and cheese, pernil, chicken and green salad. We had a big cake with Baby Minnie. I had capias made for each guest. We taped the trees with streamers and I even had her father hang a piñata stuffed with candy. All of

Working in the System, After Living in the System

By Adam Robe, MSW

I have never heard anyone say "Hey, let's really mess with this kid and move 'em again". Most of the time, everyone is really trying to give it their all and do the right thing. The truth as I see it, though, is that not much thought is really put into empowering anyone, including parents.

I was attending the first family support team meeting for a case just transferred to our organization. The meeting started out as they typically do. Everyone telling everyone else who is doing what and what progress is being made. About half way through the meeting, the children's mother jumps up and starts screaming at everyone in the room. She started cussing and telling everyone off. Several of the long time team members looked at me to take control of the situation, but I just let her go on. Her children were not present in the room and I thought, "If this is what this mother needs to do right now, well then, let's let her do it."

Several of the team members got up and said that they weren't going to sit in a meeting like this and left. After a few minutes, the mother sat back down and we finished the meeting. After the meeting, I took the mother to my office and told her that I was glad to see that she had some anger and frustration in her and that any time she needed to vent or yell at someone, to call me. I told her, however, that if she wanted to ever get her children back in her custody, that she could not rant and rave like that in front of anyone else. She looked at me in the strangest way, and got up and gave me a hug saying that no one in the system has ever talked to her that way before.

Never did she again explode in front of the other members of the team and over time, she didn't need to call me and vent either, because she had gained strength in herself and was able to pull her life together. Her children did end up going home with her, even after she was told that they never would. What people don't get is that the system doesn't empower you…it creates a sense of hopelessness and helplessness in those it is trying to help. Well meaning people who are high on themselves and their own opinions create barriers that seem impossible to overcome.

Adam Robe is a former foster child, social worker, trainer of foster parents and author of the Robbie the Rabbit books among other things.
www.robbietherabbit.com

These thoughts are reprinted with permission from ***Flux, Life After Foster Care.***
www.fostercarealumni.org/resources/FLUX.htm

my friends came and Tamera and her husband came with my two sons. That was the best thing – spending the day with my two sons and my baby.

Lydia was laughing and playing. I don't think she understood what was going on, but she was curious about her toys and ate a lot of cake. She even took her first steps that day.

Sometimes I was a good mom to Lydia but not always. Other times I would sell her milk and food stamps for money, and I would leave her in her crib while I got high. I hated when my high came down and I had to face that I'd messed up as a mother. That was the worst. I would lay on the floor with my daughter watching TV and I would cry. My guilt was tremendous. I always prayed to God to forgive me.

Getting Ready

After Lydia went into foster care, we had visits at an agency in the Bronx for two years. The visit room had a small red couch and some little chairs. There was a toy room but the lady in charge was rarely there. So basically, it looked like an office: no toys and very gloomy green paint on the walls.

A few days before each visit, I would pack a bag of toys, coloring books, and reading books. I tried to be ready for any activity. Hector and I would go shopping to buy Little Mama a new outfit and things for her hair.

Little Mama would come wearing clothes that were too small, and her hair was never done properly. So when Little Mama first came into visits, I would hug her and then take her to the bathroom to change her clothes and do her hair.

Eating and Playing

It made me feel better that I was still able to take care of my daughter. Even when I was using crack, I would get Lydia clothes from the church and wash them by hand so she would look like a clean little girl. With her hair done, she looked like my little angel again. I also loved to be in the bathroom with my daughter, away from everybody else. It was my time to comfort Lydia and let her know that I loved her.

Then Little Mama would usually eat a Happy Meal that Hector would bring for her, and for the rest of the visit, she and her father and I would play. Her favorite thing to do was color. She also liked us to bring kitchen things, like plates, spoons, and forks. We would pretend we were cooking. Every visit, I brought a camera and took pictures to look at during my week.

When it was time to say goodbye, I tried not to cry because I did not want Lydia to see me hysterical. I would tell her, "I love you and I'll see you next week." Hector would ask, "What do you want us to bring to the next visit?" As she got older, she could tell us if she wanted any candy or a toy. Then we would say goodbye with a hug and a kiss.

Smothering Her With Love

When the judge gave my family unsupervised visits, it was such a weight off to leave the agency. I was able to really hold my daughter and smother her with all of my love. She would call out, "Mommy!" and give me hugs and kisses. The more time I had with Lydia, the more connection I felt to her.

We would pick her up at 10 a.m. and bring her back by 4 p.m. We always made sure we were there early to pick her up and on time to drop her off. We would take her out to lunch, to the pool, the park and the playground, and to see all of our friends.

I loved taking her to the swimming pool. I bought her a little sky blue one-piece bathing suit. I would take her in the baby pool and watch her try to swim in the water. Now that I was sober, I was able to laugh and play in the water with her without any shame. My daughter's father would meet us at the pool and we would go for lunch. These were moments that I did not want to let go of.

A Good Mother

Being out with Lydia when I was sober was so much better. My thoughts were clear and I was able to take time to enjoy her laughter and her ideas.

I had never been sure that I could be a good mom. I was not raised by my mother; I was raised by the system. Not having a mom or dad for guidance when I became a mother was hard. During moments when I felt I needed advice, I felt empty. Feeling empty and alone had fed my addiction.

In parenting classes I learned that I could become a real parent to my daughter and have family activities with her and my husband. I learned about unconditional love and how to show Little Mama my love.

During visits, I was able to do motherly things with Lydia, like saying, "I love you" and playing with her. I learned that I could be a good mother. I also found out that I am a responsible person. I was proud that I was able to plan outings with Lydia and make sure that I had packed what she needed, like milk, juice, diapers, and a change of clothes.

The Little Things

The best parts of our visits were the little things: being able to hear her say, "Mommy" and feeling her hand in mine. Away from the agency, I felt safe with her, like no one could take Lydia from me.

Simple things felt good to me, like eating at a Chinese restaurant together, or asking Lydia about her brothers and Tamera and how things were in her foster home. The best was taking Lydia to church with me. I was able to put her in a nice dress and shoes and finally introduce her to people there. That was something I had wanted for a long time.

This article was originally published in RISE magazine and the author is a mother who is working toward reunification. Used with permission. Rise Magazine is comprised of stories by and for parents affected by the child welfare system. With each article comes study guides and tools for thoughtful reflection. Find more at www.risemagazine.org.

Strategies for Success in Working With Birth Parents

By Betty Daigle Hastings

The birth parents' ongoing involvement is a key element in successful foster care. The foster parents can do a number of things to increase parental involvement and to help build relationships.

The role of the foster parents calls for focusing on the family. Foster parents should reach out to the birth family, but sometimes the focus shifts to providing the child with a loving home. Many times there has been limited or no contact with the birth families and the foster families. Often, foster parents might wish that the birth families would just go away, but they don't always do so.

The push is on now to work harder than ever to reunite families. By focusing on the family as a whole the reunification becomes clearer. Foster parents, through training, are able to recognize how birth parents feel about the removal of their child, anger, frustrations, and resentment toward foster parents that someone else is replacing them in the care and custody of their child.

But it is important to remember that foster parents are a part of a team working together to reunite the family if at all possible. Once they are able to work through some of these difficult feelings, it helps birth parents to appreciate the care provided for their children.

Foster parents can become mentors, role models, help to prepare a child for a return home, and offer support to the birth parent in that eventual return home. There may even be times that after the child returns home that the foster parents may receive calls from the birth parents questioning how they handled certain circumstances that came up while the child was in care.

When a little girl returned home, after being in foster care for some time, the foster mom was surprised when the birth mom called to ask, "What did you do when my daughter had her bad behavior?" She said, "I know that you handled it, and I can't seem to get her to mind me." This may be a rare situation, but it happened.

- **Get involved in visitation**. This is an important area to participate in some way during the visit, even if it's no more than just bringing the child to the visit and meeting the parent.
- **Encourage the foster child to talk about positive things that are going on in the foster home.** For example, a 7-year-old came into care not knowing how to take care of chores, so during his visits after being in the foster home was able to share that he could make his bed, take out garbage and dry dishes. He's not always eager to offer, but he was happy to share the good news of what was going on in the foster home.
- **Do not judge the parent, particularly in front of the child.** Never let children hear anything negative about their parents, even if they make a comment, not to even agree with them. That will be one of the first things to ruin a relationship with children and ruin any possible chance of working with them and their parents.
- **Show love and concern for the foster child.** Foster parents should let the birth par-

ents see that they are interested in the child. Take pictures or any awards, copies of report cards, or things that are on a positive note for the child to show progress while in the home. Always stressing the reunification, foster parents should know the permanency plans for the child and stress the reunion of the family if this is what's in store for him or her.

- **Show respect to the birth parents.** Foster parents may not agree with what they did, or even some things that they're still doing, but show respect in the dealings with them, particularly during the regular scheduled visits. It can be a sticky situation, and it makes foster parents feel as though they're the enemy, but they have to look beyond this right now and realize what the birth parents are going through and try to show respect and consideration for them. Foster parents want to say, "this is your fault, don't treat me like this," but they can't. They have to rise above those feelings.
- **Open the lines of communications.** Let there be phone calls to the children, if approved by the caseworker. It usually gives the foster parent an opportunity to speak

One of my boys came home from an access visit, when he was 11 years old, pretty upset. His aunt (dad's sister) was talking about his (absent) mom and telling him that she was a drug addict and abandoned him as an infant and hasn't tried to see him since. My boy was caught in the middle. He was afraid of getting his aunt in trouble because she wasn't supposed to be gossiping about his mom. And, even though he has no memories of his mom, he still has a connection to her.

Luckily, he came to me . . . First I talked about his aunt. On one hand, being privy to family gossip made him feel grown up. But he was also mad that his aunt would talk so negatively about his mom. It was tricky, but I tried to reframe the conversation: I suggested that his aunt was not trying to hurt him. Perhaps she was trying to comfort him, trying to make him feel better for not having contact with his mom – that he was better off without her.

Next I tackled his mom. I was honest with him about his mother's issues with drugs. I told him that drug addiction can take over your life. When she 'abandoned him' by dropping him off at his grandmother's house, she was probably trying to keep him safe, even if safe meant not being near her and her problems. I have never met his mom, but I told him that the hardest thing for a parent is being separated from their child. But she did that for him, because she loves him and wants him safe.

Being non-judgemental is THE most important part of working with birth families. It's not only what you say to them, but also what you say about them.

– Veronica Brown is a foster parent to many.

to the birth parent. A friendly "hello" or "how have you been" can mean so much, even in the relationship with the foster child. Maybe Mom or Dad has had a birthday, an anniversary, or maybe a sad death in the family, so drop them a little note or card. There may not always be an appreciation note or even a comment that says "thanks," but foster parents will feel good that they've done their part. The foster child will appreciate this the most. The sending of cards can certainly apply to parents who are not present, or for one reason or another they cannot visit. They can be remembered also at a special occasion time. Remembering again, that the connection is there and the child will certainly notice.

- **Keep the caseworker informed.** Caseworkers play an important part in working with the birth parents. The worker can encourage or discourage, can listen to the concerns of the birth parent, and help to build a good relationship between the birth parents and foster parents. They can share information with foster parents. Foster parents should always keep the worker informed of all the contact with birth parents and the outcome.
- **Best Interest of the Child.** Working with birth parents and forming a good relationship is not an easy task, and foster parents may not be able to reach the majority of the parents of the children they foster. It's important that foster parents keep in mind that foster children must keep in touch with their parents, and always do what is in the child's best interest.

Every child's case should be handled individually. There is no perfect pattern to follow. Foster parents must just do the best they can and remember that a lot of responsibility rests on their shoulders, but in the end keeping the connections with birth parents is almost always in the best interest of the children.

Betty Daigle Hastings is a foster parent in Tennessee. She was a foster child in her teenage years. Betty worked for the University of Tennessee as a foster parent trainer and continues to train in Tennessee and across the nation. She and her husband have fostered more than 300 children and adopted two boys during this time.

While in care, my relationships were determined by the system. My relationships were based on a fee of service, business hours, contracts, a time frame, and background checks. Even biological family had to be scheduled and supervised. Relationships were not on my terms. Years after leaving care I struggle with how to create healthy relationships that last beyond a contract, business hours, or even a specific age like eighteen. Now in my thirties, I'm still learning how to stick around when relationships get tough, uncomfortable, feel too good, or even just feel like it's time to 'expire'.
– Angie Cross, alumna, age 33, from Texas, spent seven years in Canadian care

These thoughts are reprinted with permission from
Flux, Life After Foster Care. www.fostercarealumni.org/resources/FLUX.htm

Embracing the Importance of Birth Parents in the Lives of Adopted and Foster Children

By Ellen Singer, LCSW-C

Renowned adoption experts, Ken Watson and Miriam Reitz in their book, ***Adoption and the Family System*** defines adoption as "a means of providing some children with security and meeting their developmental needs by legally transferring ongoing parental responsibilities from their birth parents to their adoptive parents; recognizing that in so doing, we have created a new kinship network that forever links those two families together through the child, who is shared by both."

Joyce Pavao, author of ***The Family of Adoption***, states that in adoption, while birth parents no longer have the parenting role, they will always be the child's mother and father. How do families translate this understanding of adoption, with its unique joys and challenges, into the reality of their lives? Sometimes with great difficulty.

Such was the case with adoptive parents, Mr. and Mrs. Smith, and birth grandmother, Mrs. Jones, who had an open adoption arrangement around 3-year-old Steven. Over time, conflict between the Smiths and Mrs. Jones had developed around expectations for contact. The Smiths felt that Mrs. Jones desired a closer relationship and more contact than what they felt comfortable with. Mr. and Mrs. Smith initiated counseling with Mrs. Jones to sort things out. Both parties put forth a great deal of effort in separate and joint sessions to: 1) better understand each other, 2) repair the lost mutual respect and trust, and 3) strengthen their ability to negotiate. Visits were set to resume, but one sticking point remained. The Smiths refused Mrs. Jones' request that Steven call her "Grandma Betty." The Smiths insisted that Steven needed to be clear about who is "family" – that he had his two sets of "grandparents," and he needed to forever know that he was a "Smith," not a "Jones." Mr. and Mrs. Smith believed that Mrs. Jones's request meant that she did not accept what "adoption" means. Not wanting to undo all the progress that had been made in restoring her chance to resume visits, Mrs. Jones masked her hurt. Steven would call her "Auntie Betty" – since close female family friends were given the privilege of being called "Aunties."

Adoptive and Foster Parent's Attitudes Toward Birth Family

Mr. and Mrs. Smith are not unlike many foster and adoptive parents who struggle with difficult emotions around what birth family means to their children, let alone decisions around what role birth family should have in their children's and family's lives. This is because there are many complex forces that come into play in the journey of adoptive parenthood. While many adoptive parents have chosen adoption as first choice toward parenthood, or have adopted as a means to expand their families, many other adoptive parents have traveled the long and excruciatingly painful road of primary or secondary infertility. This road is filled with deep disappointment, loss, and grief. Adoption is therefore their second and often their third choice (the second being ART with donor assistance, etc.) toward parenthood. By the time they pursue adoption, these would-be parents are often battle weary. Their dream is to recover some sense of "normalcy" – to become parents, finally, or complete their families and be like every other parent they know.

During the process of adopting, especially domestically, birth parents can become another "potential source of more pain and disappointment." Jennifer Garner, a prospective adoptive mother in the 2007 movie, "Juno" captures the concern for the birth mother, but also the mistrust and fear that is inevitable. "Will she or won't she go through with the placement? Are my hopes going to be fulfilled or dashed?" It is not that parents do not have empathy for the birth parents, but the birth parents' loss is the adoptive parents' gain, making for a complex relationship indeed.

For prospective parents hoping to adopt through public adoption – from foster care, the question is: "Will this child be returned to her birth family? Will the birth parents agree to the placement if there is an open adoption agreement? Will the courts successfully get the TPR – termination of parental rights? How long will this take?" In these situations, parents must cope with the risk of losing a child who is already part of their family – a child they have become attached to. In addition, unless their foster child was placed at birth, the child has likely suffered neglect or abuse – and trauma. As a result, birth parents may be viewed in a negative light. Foster/pre-adopt parents may also be troubled by the impact of loyalty conflicts on their children. They want their children to be "free" to attach and connect with their new family, and leave their troubled pasts behind.

Often, adoptive parents do not get enough education, preparation, and ongoing support to understand the changes that have occurred in adoption practice. Many adopters still believe that traditional closed adoption is the norm and how it is "supposed to be." Most people do not know that, historically, adoption in cultures both here and abroad was informal and open. Adoption practice, or "closed adoption," began in the 1930s to protect against the shame and stigma of birth outside of marriage. It was not based on any research or knowledge of the impact of closed or open adoption on adopted children. In domestic adoption today, most adoptions have some degree of "openness," according to Evan B. Donaldson Adoption Institute, ***Safeguarding the Rights and Well-Being of Birth Parents in the Adoption Process*** by Susan Smith.

It is therefore not surprising that there is often a knee-jerk reaction by some adoptive and foster parents to deny the significance of birth parents. They don't want to compete for "realness – for authenticity." Adoptive and foster parents learn that they must "claim" their children – and develop a sense of "entitlement" – meaning they must ensure their right to parent their child and to fully embrace their parenting role, and create for their child a secure sense of belonging to the family. This is a process that takes time, as with the process of attachment. Again, not surprisingly, many parents do not know how to incorporate the significance of birth parents as they work to master these parenting tasks. Even the most secure parents can fear losing their relationship – their children's love – to birth parents. And finally, many parents just want to protect their children from painful feelings that might arise around birth parents – sadness, loss, hurt, confusion, being different and others. Parents who adopted at birth may wonder how a child can care about and grieve the loss of someone he or she never knew. Others wonder how a child can still care about or love a birth parent who mistreated him or her or allowed him or her to be mistreated by others.

Through the Eyes of Children

We know from years of research and practice, that adopted children think a lot about their birth parents. In C.A.S.E.'s federally funded research project, LIFELINES, services were provided to families with children moving to permanent adoptive homes. Parents were amazed by the results of a survey that was conducted with the children. The children reported that they think about their birth parents far more frequently than their parents would have imagined. In our individual and family counseling and groups, children and teens share their many questions: "Does my birth mother ever think about me? Why did she give me up? Where are my birth parents? Can I meet them? What do they look like? Do I look like them? Am I like them? Do I have any brothers or sisters?" The list goes on and on. We see grief behind their behavior – the anger, sadness and confusion. In counseling with adults, they share the pain they still feel at never being able to talk with their parents about their birth parents; how they have to hide their desire to search, or their experiences of reunion. Sometimes they struggle with loyalty conflicts, but often their loyalty conflict is based on reality – on sensing how threatened their adoptive parents feel at the mere mention of birth parents.

Pauline Boss, author of ***Ambiguous Loss***, explains the impact of loss of someone significant who is physically absent but psychologically present. She describes the anxiety and confusion that can be experienced when there is loss with no closure. In adoption, unless the birth parent is deceased, there is loss, but the possibility of undoing the loss remains. It is no surprise then that a study conducted by Harold Grotevant and Ruth McRoy called "Openness in Adoption: Exploring Family Connections" showed that children who had no contact with birth family spent more time thinking and fantasizing about them than children who had contact with birth family

How Parents Can Help Their Children

Helping adoptive parents cope with their fears, mistrust, and anxiety is critical for the well-being of adopted children and their families. It is imperative that parents reconsider their own needs – whether it's a need for simplicity, or to fulfill their dreams of what family life would or should be, or to protect their children from pain, so they can incorporate into family life what their children need. Adopted children and teens need their parents to be their guides in helping them identify, understand and cope with their feelings about birth parents. Continuously adopted adults tell us that what they needed as they were growing up was guidance and support, not protection.

Connections to birth family are critical for teens to form cohesive identities. Debbie Riley, C.A.S.E. CEO, and author of ***Beneath the Mask: Understanding Adopted Teens*** states, "It is especially hard for teens to figure out who they are without knowledge of their birth parents. For some teens, the need to search is really the need for information. For others, that need can only be satisfied through reunion with birth parents." Indeed, at C.A.S.E., we are receiving more calls from frantic parents whose teens have connected with birth parents through Facebook.

To assist their children, parents must learn how to communicate with their children around birth parents. There are many excellent resources available to assist parents. Parents are encouraged to read, attend workshops, and talk with other parents and professionals around sharing the adoption story, especially when talking about birth parents involves what they perceive to be "difficult information," such as mental illness, drug/alcohol abuse, incarceration, rape, and other issues.

Decisions regarding "open adoption" and maintaining connections with birth family is not a one-size fits-all phenomenon. The old "wait till you're 18" to connect with birth parents is a thing of the past. There is no right time or right way for these connections to occur. We also know that these decisions and these relationships can be scary and complicated, and that parents may need professional support to navigate these unique relationships. Especially in foster care adoption, post-adoption services need to include this assistance for everyone involved.

Obviously, many families will not have the opportunity for contact with birth family. (However, it is important to note that many families in international adoption are today finding ways to connect with birth family.) For children adopted through foster care, maintaining connections with previous foster parents may be equally important. Taking into account a variety of factors, every individual adoptive family will determine what is right for them. Sometimes the connection may only be through letters. Sometimes there will be face-to-face visits. A visit might take place only in a public place or only in a therapist's office. As family members get to know one another, hopefully trust will develop. And of course, decisions around contact may change over time.

In her keynote address: "Honoring Children's Connections," at C.A.S.E.'s 2005 annual Kids Adoption Network Carnival/Conference for parents and children, adoption expert and author of ***The Open Adoption Experience***, Sharon Roszia wisely advised the audience of adoptive parents that when they think about adoption and birth family, they should always remember to ask the right question: It is not "Who does this child belong to?" but, "Who belongs to this child?"

Ellen Singer, LCSW-C, is an adoption therapist and has more than 25 years of experience working with individuals, couples and families. She specializes in working with prospective parents, adoptive parents, adult adoptees, and expectant/birth parents. For more information, contact C.A.S.E. at www.adoptionsupport.org. This article originally appeared in Fostering Families Today.

Unnecessary Losses

By Joyce Maguire Pavao, EdD, LCSW, LMFT

Those of us involved in the worlds of fostering and adoption have become increasingly aware of how a child's relationship to his or her birth family continues to evolve after "surrender" "removal" and/or "termination of parental rights," and on into life. That awareness has challenged practices used for decades by adoption and child welfare agencies to help children transition from birth families into foster or adoptive families.

The "termination visit" has been one of those practices; steeped in notions that younger, and even older, children would establish better ties to their new families if connection to their first family was clearly ended. Professionals developed this notion out of their concern that children would be confused if there was any ambivalence conveyed about where their needs were to be met while in care and after adoption. Also, especially regarding children with a history of abuse or neglect, there has been concern that any ongoing relationship or correspondence would make emotional healing more difficult. Such contact was often viewed as being emotionally burdensome and potentially re-traumatizing. Sometimes that may be true, but we find that more often some thread of connection actually helps to heal and settle a child in his or her foster or adoptive family. We also find that a contained and careful plan for visitation leads to fewer cases of children running away (or running toward) their birth family in adolescence.

Termination visits have typically been seen as excruciatingly painful, but necessary in order to allow the children, birth mother, birth father and siblings to "go on with their lives" by having an unambiguous "terminal" farewell. With the change of thinking about attachment, and with more open adoption agreements being crafted, these visits are not as frequently done, but they still remain a vestige of the past and many professionals and parents still feel that emotional cut off from the past is good, rather than a step toward attachment disorder, as many of us see it to be.

The dilemma we face is that in many situations, the "termination visit" may exacerbate the confusion and trauma it has been designed to alleviate. Increasingly, members of the child welfare world, the adoption triad, and mental health professionals are raising the following concerns about the impact of cutting children off from the experience of birth family that may help them to heal and attach:

1. The word termination is powerful in that it is unmistakably absolute and final. It is over. But this word is not reflective of the child's inner reality or that of the birth family.

The Pre- and Post-Adoption Consulting Team Model at Center For Family Connections states that there is no such thing as true "termination" in the relationship between children and their birth families. Even if the birth parents die, it is never "over." An emotional and psychological bond is there, even if the child has never seen the birth family since birth. By creating a ritual that acts "as if" the relationship has ended, the child's internal world is at odds with his or her external one.

Many of the children and teens we see clinically are emotionally preoccupied with these dissonances. They may not have words to describe the depth of their confusion, or longing, or the rage that they feel. Compounding that internal upset, they may not have a neutral enough place to express thoughts and feelings that might be loaded for some of the other caregivers in their lives. Often, these children come up with answers to their questions that are bound in fantasy because there are no real life mirrors, or receptors, to help make sense of their experience.

2. Being terminally cut off from their birth family, children are not able to have that internalized love as part of their growing sense of self. It is much harder for the child to feel self-love when asking: "Why did my parents give me up?" or "Where are my siblings?" if there is no ongoing experience of birth family's positive feelings.

3. Even when birth parents continue to suffer from emotional or psychological difficulties and substance abuse, connection of some kind, sometimes supervised and sometimes clinically planned, can be healing and can build attachment with the new caregiver or the new parents.

As children mature, they can use their actual experience of their birth parents, even when disappointing, to make sense of why or how their birth parents could not take care of them. It would help to dispel the myths that often plague adopted children – such as:

- I am a bad child, or
- my adoptive family/Department Social Services stole me, or
- my birth parents just didn't like me.

Such fantasies may severely impede or complicate the child's ability to work through the actual losses and grief. He or she does not have the benefit of dipping into the real relationship, whether in person, or through correspondence, so that the actual love and awareness about what his or her birth parents couldn't provide is made real. However, the exposure to what is real will help children live authentically in their own lives. Establishing an overall formulation that holds all of the pieces of their shattered stories is essential to their forming of an integrated identity.

Certainly, there are circumstances where in-person contact or correspondence is not in a child's best interest. When a child has been maliciously or severely abused, for example, it could be seriously traumatizing to expose a child in any way to the perpetrator. When the birth family cannot see the reality of what led to removal and if the birth family cannot see that a child is in a permanent placement in the case of adoption or guardianship, then the messages will not foster permanence and will not be in the child's best interest.

Working with the birth family to help them to work in the best interest of the child is essential and yet the services for birth parents around and after a termination of parental rights are few. Each situation needs to be carefully and individually assessed. Any ongoing "openness" needs to fit the people who are in those relationships. The clinically supervised visits offered at Center for Family Connections are a structured and therapeutic way to have safe visits if they are warranted.

The prospect of the "non-terminational" approach may seem unsettling, and potentially destabilizing, to some child welfare workers, foster and adoptive parents who wish to protect their children and to establish boundaries around their families that are secure and clear. We need to develop and make available the most clinically supportive environments for foster and adoptive children and their many families, that reflect the changing face of child welfare and of adoption; environments that allow children and parents to explore their connections and losses out in the open, but with safeguards and boundaries where necessary and healing. We do not use the opportunity to teach children about "family" while in their foster home by providing family therapy to the fostering families during a child's stay in care. Without these supportive measures and without helping the foster families to heal from any of their own trauma, we are not giving the child all of the supports we possibly can.

Termination is a terrible word. We can terminate parental rights but we cannot terminate the feelings and emotions that go with them, nor should we for the sake of the child and for his or her attachment.

Joyce Maguire Pavao, EdD, LCSW, LMFT, is the founder and CEO of Center For Family Connections, Inc., Adoption Resource Center, Pre/Post Adoption Consulting Team, and Family Connections Training Institute, all of which are in Cambridge, Mass. Pavao is a clinical member and approved supervisor of the American Association of Marriage and Family Therapy and is a clinical member of the American Orthopsychiatric Association. She is currently serves on many adoption related boards. This article originally appeared in ***Fostering Families Today****.*

I wish...

By Mike Hollinger

I wish I knew my mom, I wish I knew my dad,
I wish I had the life that I never really had.

I wish I didn't worry all the time,
and that I knew that everything would be fine.

I wish I didn't go through foster care,
I wish when I needed someone they were there.

I wish I was never separated from my brother
and I didn't go through life without a mother.

I wish my dad would stop doing drugs,
I wish I knew how to show him love.

I wish I knew life like a regular kid,
not growing up wondering where I would live.

I wish I knew what the next 10 years hold,
and what life will be like when I'm old.

I wish I was closer to God,
going through this life alone can be hard.

I realize that not everything's set in stone...
But damn I wish I had a family of my own.

Foster care can be a scary experience, and for Mike, it was a 13 year reality. In March of 1998, at age 9, he became a ward of the state and entered foster care with his older brother. Nine years, nine foster homes, a shelter, and countless questions starting with "why me God" later he beat out many of the negative statistics and graduated high school. Later that year, he was selected as the 2008 fosterclub Allstar for Connecticut. It was a life changing opportunity, and he returned the next year as a "coach" for the new year of Allstars, which was one of the best summers of his life. Experiencing the positive impact of giving back has inspired him to think of starting his own non profit. He is currently working on his degree and plans to graduate soon.

Loss, Grief, & Anger

"Someone may have stolen your dream when it was young and fresh and you were innocent. Anger is natural. Grief is appropriate. Healing is mandatory. Restoration is possible." – Jane Rubietta

"Smart Enough" Parenting

By Susan Badeau

Every foster or adoptive child comes into a "new" family with a certain amount of baggage: rejection, loss, grief, trauma, identity issues, etc. As the child "settles" into the family, some of these issues will be best worked through within the family throughout the years, while others will require additional, outside help. How can you know when such help is needed?

When I went to an all-women's college in the 1970s, we were not encouraged to pursue "traditionally female" careers such as teaching, but rather to stretch ourselves toward the more "traditionally male" fields of law, medicine, engineering, or business. So, as our senior year approached, nearly all of my friends were busy scheduling their MCAT or LSAT exams, and, knowing that I didn't really want to go to graduate school, I too decided to take these tests.

I scored really well on both. So well, that my adviser was shocked when I decided not to apply to either law school or medical school like so many of my friends were doing. "Why not?" he asked, "Surely you can see that you are smart enough."

At the time, those words gave me a boost of confidence and added to my self-esteem. However, over the years, the words almost seemed to become a taunting refrain echoing in my mind every time I faced a challenging and troubling situation as a mom. "How could it be?" I would often ask myself, "that I am smart enough to be a doctor or a lawyer, but not smart enough to be a mom?"

Smart Enough or Not?

Not smart enough to know what to do when my bright son with the high IQ scores was failing in school. Not smart enough to figure out how to stop my talented son with the promising future ahead from descending into the pits of drug addiction. Not smart enough to prevent two of my young daughters from becoming pregnant within 3 months of each other. Not smart enough to help my handsome African American son avoid the stinging pain of racism and rejection when he got turned down for a prom date because of the color of his skin. Not smart enough to see the warning signs before a teen daughter's suicide attempt, or a teen son's runaway episodes. Yes, I have faced these and many more challenges in my years as a foster and adoptive parent. And there were many, many times when I just did not feel smart enough to conquer the challenges confronting me. At times sheepish or even ashamed when I had to reach out to others for help, resources and supports raising my own children.

And then one day, I had my proverbial "aha" moment. I was sitting in the driveway, in the car, about to drop off my young adult daughter and her 2-year-old-child. He had been giving her more than the usual run for her money that day and they were both exhausted. She turned to me with tears in her eyes and asked, "Do you think I will ever be smart enough to be a good parent?"

"Of course you are smart enough," I quickly reassured her, but added, "even smart people need help from time to time." I then thought of my professor all those years ago in college and I asked my daughter, "Do you think that I am smart enough to be a doctor –

or maybe a lawyer?"

"Oh yes, mom, you definitely could be a great doctor or lawyer."

"So, then, if you needed surgery today, you would trust me to wield the scalpel?"

She panicked for a moment, not knowing what to say. Finally, she quietly said, "Well, no, not really."

"Why not?" I asked, "I thought you just told me I was smart enough to be a doctor."

"True," she said, "But you have never been trained as a doctor. You never went to medical school or learned all that stuff."

Bingo. Being smart enough doesn't mean you have all the knowledge, training, equipment, or tools needed to handle every situation in life. If I could easily acknowledge that I, while smart enough to be a doctor, could not actually practice medicine without further education, experience, coaching, and support, why couldn't I also acknowledge that as a parent, especially of children with a range of special needs and early life exposure to trauma, I would also need further education, experience, coaching, and support to do a good job?

There is no shame in seeking help.

Once we overcome that mental hurdle and are willing to seek help, the challenges become knowing when to seek help, and how to find the right kind of help for the situation.

When many of my children were elementary school age, one of them broke his arm at school. The school nurse and I knew immediately that this was not simply a sore arm, but that he needed medical attention beyond the nurse's office and I promptly drove him to the hospital where his injury was diagnosed and a cast was set. But this did not mean that every time a child fell down on the playground, they needed to be rushed to the hospital. Nor that every sore spot could be fixed with a cast. Understanding this when it comes to the physical bumps, bruises, and ailments our children experience is pretty easy, but the challenge is harder when the injuries are less visible and more in the psychological and emotional realm.

When will a good pep talk, or going out for ice cream be enough to soothe an injured spirit, and when is professional help required? And even when we know that professional help is needed, how do we find the right kind? Certainly I wouldn't have taken my son with the broken arm to the eye doctor's office we passed en route to the hospital on the theory that expediency was essential so I had to get to the first, closest doctor I could find. Or the related theory that any doctor would do the trick. Yet in the world of mental health and trauma-related care, this is often what happens – we are referred to the closest therapist, or the one that takes our insurance and assured that "any therapy" will do. And yet, it does not work out so well when we take that approach.

Being a "Prepared Enough" Parent

So after many years stumbling along as a "smart enough" but not always "prepared enough" parent, I have concluded that parents who take the following four steps are not only "smart enough" but also equipped to handle even the most daunting parenting challenges:

1. **Learn, and keep learning, about normal child development.** So many times, sim-

ply knowing what behaviors or developmental milestones are to be expected of a two-year-old, nine-year-old or 15-year-old will help us assess our own child's behavior and development more appropriately. While it is not reasonable to expect a two-year-old to sit still for an entire two hour movie or church service, it is reasonable to expect a two-year-old to walk and begin to form thoughts into sentences. So the parent of a child that can't sit still doesn't need professional support, but the parent of the child that is not yet walking or talking probably does. We can apply this same principle to school age children and adolescents.

2. **Learn about the impact of trauma on children's development – and develop a tool-kit of trauma-informed parenting strategies**. Most children who come to us through foster care or adoption have experienced early life traumatic experiences. In recent years there has been an explosion of new science-based information about the impact of this exposure to trauma on the developing brain, and on the child's emotional regulation, behaviors, and social development. We also now know that typical parenting strategies that work well with non-traumatized children (such as time-out) not only do not work well with these children, but can often serve to trigger trauma reminders, increasing the child's vulnerability and undermining their opportunity to heal. Yet, we also know that children can heal from trauma and that parents and caregivers are the most important conduits for that healing. Not all trauma-exposed children need professional therapeutic interventions, just like not every playground tumble requires a trip to the ER. Sometimes they just need a different style of parenting at home. I have listed a few excellent resources at the end of this article for parents who want to learn more about trauma. Advocate with your agency to provide trauma-informed training for all foster, kin, and adoptive parents.

3. **Learn to recognize the warning signs of when a child needs more than parental support.** At the end of this article, I have provided a list of possible "red flags" that may indicate a need for outside resources. All children are likely to display some of these indicators at various times. The need for intervention is more likely if the child displays several at once, or some over longer periods of time. If you see these signs don't hesitate to seek help, just as I did not hesitate to seek medical help for my child's broken arm. Join a support group of other parents raising children with similar challenges. Peer support is one of the most effective and valuable ways to help parents know when some of the challenges they face are within the range of "normal development" or when extra help and support are needed.

4. **Know how to ask the right questions to get appropriate services and interventions for your child.** Never be shy at Individual Education Plan meetings, doctor appointments, or with your medical/mental health insurance provider. Ask probing questions about how and why the particular intervention they are proposing is appropriate for your child. Never settle for an eye doctor when your child has a broken arm. But when

Resources for Parents and Caregivers to Learn about Trauma:

www.nctsn.org/resources/audiences/parents-caregivers
www.projectabc-la.org/parents/
www.multiplyingconnections.org

your child needs an eye doctor, make sure you get the best one in town!

Red Flags Checklist

Things that Happened to the Child:

- Severe illness or forced separation from primary caregivers in the first three years of life.
- Neglect of physical needs, especially during the first two years of life, physical abuse at any time, but especially during the first two years.
- Sexual encounters of any kind during childhood.
- Child witnessed traumatic events, domestic violence, alcoholic or drug-addicted parents, a parental death, a sibling death, a destructive fire, etc
- Child is forced to participate in a group that practices frightening rituals, animal sacrifices, etc.
- Child is left alone for long periods or child is locked up.

Behaviors a Child may Exhibit:

- Indiscriminately (physically) affectionate.
- Refusal or fear of appropriate affection with parents, excessive clinging on, need for physical affection or attention.
- Pre-occupation with bodily functions, especially vomit, bleeding, urination, and defecation or sexual functions.
- Destructive to self, others, animals, material things. Lack of impulse controls, short attention span, hyperactivity beyond normal developmental stage.
- Difficulty and/or obsession with food, overeating, binging, refusal to eat, abnormal eating patterns, etc.
- Pre-occupation with images of death, violence, and gory, graphic details.
- Inability to discriminate between lies and realities and/or telling of crazy, obvious or outrageous lies.
- Extreme difficulty with forming peer friendships.
- Frequent bursts of seemingly unexplained anger, or outbursts of anger, fear or anxiety that is triggered by specific smells, foods, colors, people, sounds, situations or activities.
- Difficulty regulating emotions, inability or difficulty expressing a range of emotions.

Susan Badeau is currently director of Cross Systems Integration at Casey Family Programs and is a senior fellow within the US Department of Justice. Previously, Susan served as executive director of the Philadelphia Children's Commission and as deputy director of the Pew Commission on Children in Foster Care. She has been a child welfare policy consultant for agencies, universities, and court systems. Susan has worked for 33 years in child welfare and human services. She has developed curricula, writes extensively on topics related to children, and speaks frequently at conferences. She serves on several national boards and advisory committees related to the well-being of children and families, particularly those with special needs and challenges. Susan and her husband are the lifetime parents of 22 children, two by birth, and 20 adopted. They have served as foster parents for 50 children and hosted refugee youth from Sudan, Kosovo, and Guatemala. They have won numerous awards for their work on behalf of adoption and children in foster care. More information about Susan and her family can be found at www.badeaufamily.com.

Quiet or Defiant

Understanding the Foster Child's Behavioral Challenges

By Terry de Forrest, MFT, PhD

Foster parents open their homes and their hearts to children, hoping to give them everything they need to grow up to be appreciative, cooperative, grateful, and productive citizens. Unfortunately, that's not always how it works out. Foster parents are often confronted with angry, defiant children who refuse to cooperate and understand that they are acting in their best interests. Why? What goes awry?

Foster Child Perspective

To answer that question, foster parents must consider how a foster child sees the situation. Despite the fact that the child came to the foster parents because his or her biological caregivers were unable to provide proper support and safety, the child may not appreciate any help. Children often feel a strong sense of loyalty to their parents, in spite of the way they have been treated by them. They may want to stay with their parents. But they don't get a say in the matter. Strangers come in, take them away from their homes, and bring them to foster parents – complete strangers. The child is frightened, off balance, unsure and anxious about what is happening, not to mention angry. He or she may feel betrayed by all the strangers now in charge of his or her life, and the child may feel distrustful of everyone.

I have found that when young children intervene to protect their mother during domestic violence by standing between the mother and the abuser, or by calling 911, they take charge and become parentified. That is, they believe they have decision-making authority and are not subject to others' requests. An addendum to this process is that these young children develop contempt for adult women. The natural order is that mothers protect their children, and since these children have to protect their mother, they become confused. They think, "If you can't even protect yourself, how will you protect me?" From this, they assume all women are weak, and they lose respect for them. Even little girls feel this.

Quiet or Defiant?

When children are placed in a foster home, they initially react in one of two ways: quiet or defiant. Some children stay quiet and cooperative until they learn the rules and limits of the new home, which is called "the honeymoon stage." Then, after they are comfortable, they start to challenge the foster parents to see if their "new" parents are stable and truly in charge. Other children will be defiant right from the start, challenging authority and testing stability. So, what is behind all this? Why do children resist and cause conflict when they should be happy that they are in the safety of your home?

What Fear Looks Like

One reason is that they are fearful and angry, so they lash out. Another reason is that children will deliberately sabotage the success of the placement if they think doing so will force the foster parents and social workers to give up and return them to their parents.

Some children, out of a sense of loyalty to their biological parents, refuse any attempts for bonding, and actively avoid any feelings of attachment. The more they like their foster parents, the more they will resist.

Of course, there are a few children who are pleased or relieved to be placed in a stable home, and they may not have significant behavioral problems. And there is another group of children who have been "in the system" for many years and have had multiple placements. They have learned to use the system to get moved to a home that is more to their liking. But for those children who present behavioral challenges in a home, the situation can become a test of wills. Foster parents can feel just as frustrated and angry as the foster child – and both sides can feel lost about how to handle the situation.

I remember when I was 12 years old and I was crying in bed in one of the foster homes I lived in. I was terrified that night because I felt like there was no one who cared about me. Foster kids are forced to grow up and mature faster in a lot of different ways. But to be so young and to face the fact that you're all on your own is just devastating. I'm 20 years old and have friends who are only now going through what I went through when I had just become a teenager. Just to hold on, that's the advice I give other kids living in foster care. I'd tell them not to let this experience cast a shadow on the rest of their life. There are great things out there and you will find them eventually, but for now, just hold on.

– Ben, 20, foster alumnus

Consistency and Control

When faced with a challenging foster child, the first thing to remember is to maintain control. If foster parents get angry, then the child is in control of the situation. Don't get pulled into arguments, and don't try to explain why the child has to follow the rules. The child already understands why there are rules; he or she is simply using this argument as a diversionary tactic. Instead, work to develop trust by displaying consistency

The hardest thing about being in foster care is that you are scared about everything, especially if you don't know how they feel about you. Like if they want you to move or if they want you to stay like me. In the beginning, I had melt downs when something went wrong or when something didn't feel fair. Now I have been here in foster care for over four years, and sometimes I am still scared.

– Ivan, 12, current foster youth

and emotional stability. Consistency and stability are far more important than leniency. If foster parents are consistent, then the child knows they mean what they say, they are in control, and he or she can trust them. This also works to reduce arguments.

Set the tone of the home as soon as the child arrives; he or she knows that foster parents can't possibly "love" him or her from the first meeting, but a child can sense caring right from the start. Remember, the child is anxious and overwhelmed with all the changes, activities and strange adults now in charge of his or her life.

Give the child at least 24 hours to settle down and adjust to a new home. Initially, let him or her relax; then give out a few basic house rules. Don't confuse the child with a long list of expectations at first. There will be time for that later. Start simply.

Also realize that many children who come into a home will have behavioral and/or academic difficulties at school. While it may be tempting to try to "fix" everything, it's better to keep most school problems at school. Foster parents and the child have enough to deal with adjusting to the new home environment. Don't add to that stress. Imagine how it would feel having trouble at school, then coming home and having trouble there, too. Everyone needs a peaceful place. No one can live with being punished every day.

Be Realistic about Responsibility

There are two other points to mention. First, let the child know that he or she is expected to be responsible for his or her own behavior. If foster parents remind him or her to do what is expected, such as get up on time in the morning, finish chores or homework, then he or she never has to take ownership of the behavior. Second, remember that when a child is asked to do something, and he or she doesn't do it right, it doesn't necessarily mean he or she is being oppositional. Maybe the child doesn't know how to clean his or her room. Show him or her how it should be done.

Above all else, remember that learning anything new takes time. It's the foster parent's job to show the child the way to successful behavior. Consistency and patience are keys to improvement. Focus on small, but positive, changes you see in a foster child's behavior. And remember the old saying: Patience is a virtue.

Terry de Forrest, MFT, PhD, specializes in the treatment of childhood trauma, teen issues, and foster/group home consultation and support. He has been creating successful child behavioral plans for more than 15 years with logical, effective approaches to resolving children's behavioral issues and has conducted many seminars on the West Coast. He has written a short book: ***Improve Your Child's Behavior: Simple Strategies that Really Work.*** *This article originally appeared in* ***Fostering Families Today.***

Strategies to Deal with Anger and Power Struggles

By Christopher J. Alexander, PhD

Try lowering your voice instead of raising it. Imagine the impact on the child of hearing the parent gently say, "If the trash is not taken out in the next five minutes, I will put the video games in storage for a week." If a parent yells this, it sounds threatening. If, on the other hand, it is said in a matter-of-fact tone, the child receives the message, "Do as you will. I'm not going to battle with you. I trust you know the consequence for not complying."

Recognize when you are most vulnerable. If you are likely to be rushed, tired, or on edge on certain days or at certain times, this increases the chance you will get angry and reactive at those moments. What can you do to add a buffer during these times? How can you reduce the stress? Will it help to wake up earlier, avoid cooking on certain nights, or tell your partner you need more help? Will you need to set limits in advance with your child, such as saying, "No TV" or "No friends at the house" during those times?

Don't forget to breathe. When I'm angry, I hate hearing that one. But it really does work. Taking one second to breathe deeply or counting to five shifts the brain from "fight or flight," to "focus" (thinking of more rational responses). Remind yourself to breathe, focus attention, and to carefully think through what your reaction to stress/conflict will be.

Anticipate your child's triggers. Oftentimes, it is possible to predict when your child will get angry. This might be on Monday morning when shifting away from

Help Your Child Ward Off a Mad Attack

Things for Parents to Say:

- "Stop and think. Make a good choice."
- "Remember to breathe when your tummy gets tight. Breathe. Let's breathe together."
- "Use your words, not your fists. People are not for hurting."
- "You can do it. I know you can get your mads under control."
- "I understand, right now you are feeling mad. Still, you can't hurt people, things, or yourself."
- "You are the kind of kid who can take care of his own bad feelings."
- "Go to a safe place and draw out your mads."
- "You have a choice: Talk out your feelings or go to time out and get your mads under control."
- "Well, I'm feeling mad right now myself. I'm going to go cool off, then we'll talk."
- "I know how you feel. Sometimes I get mad myself. Then I tell myself, that it is OK to be mad if you are nice about it."
- "Thanks for sharing your angry feelings. Good choice in using your words!"
- "We are learning to be a 'Speak your feelings' kind of family. No more 'Mad Family' for us."
- "I believe in you. Sometimes it's tough, isn't it?"
- "You are one terrific kid!"

~ Excerpted from ***The Mad Family Gets Their Mads Out*** by Lynne Namka, EdD. Used with Permission
www.angriesout.com

weekend mode, on anniversaries or holidays due to the memories they raise, at bedtime, at mealtime, or when a child has to do homework. When you can anticipate these events, you are in a better position to think of how to defuse conflict before it arises. This might include giving the child advanced notice, such as, "I know tomorrow is your brother's birthday and it seems like that is always a rough day for you. What can we do in advance, to help make it a better day for all of us?"

Follow through afterward. Whether the conflict, power struggle, or rage episode with your child was major or minor, and whether it was expected (He always fights with me at bedtime) or unexpected, it is important to talk with your child about what happened. But do it after the tension has settled. For example, while bathing your child, tucking him or her in, or folding clothes together you can say, "You were really mad at me earlier when I said you couldn't have ice cream." Permit your child to share his or her thoughts or feelings, but try to educate him or her about the impact words or actions have on others: "When you throw things like you did, it scares the dog and that's why he doesn't want to sleep in your bed." "It hurt my feelings when you called me that name. Clearly, you wanted me to feel bad and you succeeded." "That ice cream was your father's and he had been waiting all night to have it. It's important that we share in this family. Tomorrow, we'll go out and buy treats that we can all have." "I'm sorry I called you a brat. I don't think badly of you. Your behavior makes me crazy at times, but I still think you're the best kid in the world."

Christopher J. Alexander, PhD, is a child psychologist, specializing in the treatment of foster and adopted children and the author of ***Welcome Home: A Guide for Adoptive, Foster, and Treatment Foster Parents.*** *This is excerpted from* ***Adoption Parenting: Creating a Toolbox, Building Connections****, ©2006 EMK Press.*

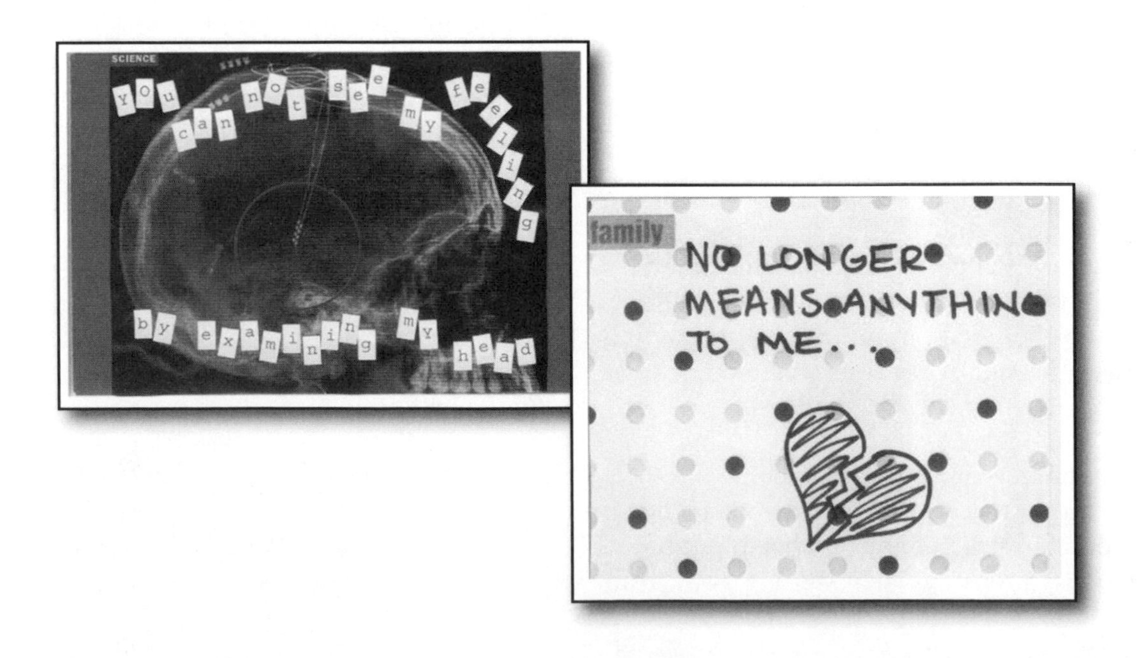

Being with Your Child in Public Places

Change Your Perspective on Tantrums and Change Your Child's Behavior

By Patty Wipfler, founder of Parents Leadership Institute (PLI)

We live in a society that has a demanding and judgmental attitude toward parents and young children. Often, the attitude toward children in public is that they should be seen and not heard, that the parent should be "in control" of the child's behavior, and that children who are having feelings in public are a nuisance. In short, children are not really welcome. Their freshness, curiosity, and frank expressions of feelings are not seen as a gift.

In addition, the child-rearing tradition that has been handed down to most of us sets us against our children when their behavior isn't convenient for adults. In the eyes of others, we are expected to criticize, grow cold, use harsh words and gestures, punish, isolate, shame, threaten, or physically attack a child who is "misbehaving." No parent really wants to act like an adversary to the child they love. We treat our beloved children in these ways when we can't think of anything else to do, or when we fear the disapproval of others.

There are certain situations in which young children often become emotionally charged. These situations include:

- Being with several people – with the whole family at dinner, a family gathering, a meeting, a birthday party, the grocery store, church, or temple.
- Moving from one activity to another – leaving home for daycare, leaving daycare for home, stopping play for dinner, going to bed.
- Being with a parent who is under stress – you can supply your own examples!
- At the end of any especially close or fun-filled time – after a trip to the park, after a good friend leaves, after wrestling and chasing and laughing with Mom or Dad.

When children become emotionally charged, they can't think.

They simply can't function normally. They become rigid and unreasonable in what they want, and are unsatisfied with your attempts to give them what they want. They can't listen, and the slightest thing brings them to tears or tantrums. Their minds are full of upset, and they can't get out of that state without help from you.

The help your child needs at this time is to have you set kind, sensible limits, and then for you to listen while he or she bursts out with the intense feelings he or she has. This spilling of feelings, together with your kind attention and patience, is the most effective way to speed your child's return to his or her sensible, loving self. A good, vigorous tantrum, or a hearty, deeply felt cry will clear your child's mind of the emotion that was driving him or her "off track" and will enable him or her to relax again and make the best of the situation.

How are we parents supposed to listen to a screaming, flailing child in the middle of the supermarket? Several adjustments of our expectations are necessary before we can allow ourselves to be on our children's side as they do what they need to do in a public place.

Every good child falls apart, often in public places. This is, for some reason, the way children are built!

Our society has trained people to disapprove of children doing what is healthy and natural. People disapprove of horseplay, noise, exuberance, too much laughter, tantrums, crying, and children asking for the attention they need.

As parents, it's our job to treat our child well. When other adults criticize him or her, it makes sense to do what we can to be on our child's side.

Being parents means that we will have to advocate for our children in many settings. We need to advocate when we are with doctors and nurses, teachers, relatives, and strangers.

Acknowledge that children legitimately need far more attention than it is comfortable to give. Adults who gave less attention to their own children, or who got little attention themselves as children, will be upset when they see you giving undivided attention to your child. We can expect these upsets, but we don't have to be ruled by them.

What do I do when my child falls apart in the supermarket aisle, or at the grandparents' house?

Spend one-on-one time with your child before you take him or her to a public place. Ensure that you both are connected with each other before heading into a challenging situation. Then, stay connected. Use eye contact, touch, voice, and short touches of your attention to stay with your child. This contact is deeply reassuring, and can sometimes defuse situations that your child often finds difficult.

When you see an upset beginning, immediately make real contact. See if you can find a way to play, so that your child can laugh. Laughter relieves children's tensions, and allows them to feel more and more connected. If, when you make contact, your child begins to cry or tantrum, do what you can to allow him or her to continue. The child's upset will heal if the feelings are allowed to drain.

Slow down the action, and listen. If getting into the car seat has triggered tears, then stay there, seat belt not yet done, and let the tears flow. Listen until he or she is done. Because of this cry, your whole day, and his or hers, will improve.

If necessary, move to a more socially acceptable place. Go to the back bedroom, or move your grocery cart out the exit to the sidewalk. Do this as calmly as you can. Your child isn't doing anything wrong. It's sort of like a car alarm going off accidentally – loud, but not harmful to anyone. These things happen!

Plan what you will say to people who express their opinions or concern. It's hard to come up with a comment that says, "We're okay – don't worry!" in the middle of wild things happening, so think ahead. You can adopt some phrase like, "We seem to be having technical difficulties," or, "My daughter really knows how to rip!" or, "It's that kind of a day!" or, "After he's finished, it's my turn!" or simply, "We're okay. I don't think this will last all day." A comment like this reassures others, and gives the message that you are in charge.

As one parent I know put it, "I've finally figured out that it's my job to set a limit when he's going 'nuts,' and it's his job to get the bad feelings out. As I listen to him, people might not be able to tell that I'm doing my job and he's doing his, but at least I know that's what's going on."

Patty Wipfler is the founder of Parents Leadership Institute (PLI) and Parenting by Connection. Parenting by Connection is the PLI approach to fostering close, responsive relationships between parents and children. For more information visit: www.handinhandparenting.org. This article originally appeared in ***Adoption Parenting: Creating a Toolbox, Building Connections*** *(EMK Press 2006)*

> It's important to look at the situation that a foster child comes from and try to not be like that. Just be patient because some of these kids who come to you are angry. No one wants to be taken from their parents or go through what many of these kids go through. Some kids aren't used to people caring for them or being nice to them. Have patience with them and don't give up on them.
>
> – *Angelina Chase, current foster youth*

Ten Ways to Help Children Feel Less Anxious

By Martha B. Straus, PhD, and Melanie Ernould, MA

Children in foster care tend to be among the most anxious kids around. It's understandable, of course, but that doesn't make them any easier to live with and teach. In our research and clinical experience, almost every foster child we've met qualifies for at least one kind of anxiety disorder; most of them fit the descriptions for several, at least in some part. These kids have specific fears, phobias, and obsessions – and a more general "free-floating" anxiety, too. They fear separations, as well as being too close, being controlled, as well as being out of control. They're afraid both of change and boredom. Some need nearly constant reassurance; others chew their cuticles until they bleed. Most adults can't even imagine how these children get through the day trying to manage such a relentless level of anxiety.

These children can become better self-soothers and problem-solvers. But in order to help them we first have to understand a bit about their wiring – everyone has their own way of being comforted that's based on temperament, experience, and ability to self-regulate. One child may need to run around the outside of the house three times to calm down, while another would prefer a bubble bath. Some kids are so intense they can't self-soothe at all once they're upset, while others regroup quite quickly with a hug and a little encouragement. Some of the children we know are aggressive and get angry in the face of stress; others are so sensitive they seem to crumple under the pressure of their lives. As you get to know your foster children, and they get to know themselves, you will be able to notice their patterns of anxiety and discover the strategies that work best for them.

Keeping in mind the fact that you and your children are going to have to figure out what specifically works best given their unique style of living in the world, we offer these ten tried-and-true general anxiety-management techniques for you to expand upon:

It isn't the child who is anxious and is a problem – it's the anxiety that's "visiting" the child that has a problem.

1. Take the Worries Seriously. Empathize with what children are experiencing. It is hard for them, and that's important to acknowledge. Sometimes kids calm quickly when they "feel felt;" they can sense that you do understand. It makes them feel less crazy and out of control to hear that you know they are suffering. When you take their worries seriously, you're also getting onto the same team as them, and putting anxiety on the other team that you'll oppose together. By the same token, it is usually pretty futile to admonish someone to "stop worrying" or to offer empty reassurances that, "there's nothing to worry about." It is not possible for most kids to turn off their anxiety like a switch, and this kind of approach is likely to make them feel worse anyway. Tell them, "I know you are feeling very worried and your stomach is in a knot." Or, "I'm sorry you're having such a hard time. I can try to help you feel better – may I?"

Together you might draw a "worry machine" based on how your child thinks his or her worry works. Then draw a "fear extinguisher" that includes a list of the strategies your child wants to use to calm down. Put it on the fridge to serve as a reminder.

2. Keep it Predictable. All anxious children are sensitive to change and foster kids have particularly good reasons to yearn for a predictable and routine life. They need warnings of transitions and even of small variations in schedule, though not too far in advance which can make them worry more. They benefit also from practice for the big changes — rehearsing the steps they will take. For example, when children make the switch from elementary school to junior high or middle school, they'll manage better if they already know their way around the new building. Kids who have a hand in their routines also seem to feel more in control. Have them draw their own calendars, make decisions about the order of events when they can, and review what they know. Use the most predictable schedule you can devise, and try to maintain it every day. Come up with some simple language that explains what happens next, and use that predictably, too. For example, say, "After dinner, it will be bath, story, then bedtime." Plan with children instead of for them — this can also reduce their anxiety.

3. Help Them Manage Their Bodies. Everything you've heard about exercise, a healthy diet, deep breathing and body awareness for reducing anxiety is probably true. It's a fact that kids who are in control of their bodies feel less anxious. Notably, children with physical trauma tend to be more anxious and cut off from their body signals. They will particularly benefit from strategies that get them to live more fully in their physical selves.

Exercise: All able-bodied children should be physically active. You and your child will have to figure out what kind of exercise is fun for them. They should also be aware that exercise is a great strategy for managing anxiety. Research shows that regular exercise releases endorphins, which are brain chemicals that help with relaxation. Exercise also improves sleep, which is frequently a casualty of anxiety. Eventually, exercise lowers the heart rate and blood pressure, builds muscles and stamina, and nurtures self-esteem. It has short-and long-term health benefits for both managing and decreasing anxiety. As an added benefit, exercise also exposes children to how it feels to have an increased heart rate during a typical circumstance. If you have a child who doesn't want to run around, dance, or get sweaty in a sporty way, you might also look at yoga or martial arts as alternative forms of exercise. For children who can handle team participation, group sports activities also help children develop confidence and social skills, reducing anxiety that way, too.

Diet: Foster parents frequently have their hands full dealing with food struggles and idiosyncrasies in their children. Food is often the symbolic and real family battleground where anxiety runs amok. To the extent possible, though, do avoid caffeine, which is shown to consistently increase anxiety and is found in soda, chocolate, tea, coffee, and some painkillers such as Excedrin and Anacin. Try to engage children in the discussion of why you are limiting treats and be prepared to offer enticing replacements.

Feeling awareness: Help children recognize and label their feelings, and know where they are located in the body. Use your language to aid them in pairing sensations with words, until they develop their own. Be prepared to guess and wonder, over and over again. "I wonder if you are feeling so worried that your tummy hurts?" "It seems like you are so mad that your head is hurting." The more they know how they are feeling, where it is located, and why they feel that way, the better your chances for helping them find self-soothing strategies. Your stance should be curious, not judgmental or dismissive.

Children can also learn to do "body scans," thinking about their feelings from head to toes, and trying to think about the messages their bodies are trying to give them. Do they feel like running away, freezing, fighting, or talking

Suggested Reading

Childhood Anxiety Disorders: A Guide to Research and Treatment by Deborah C. Beidel and Samuel M. Turner

Freeing Your Child from Anxiety: Powerful, Practical Solutions to Overcome Your Child's Fears, Worries, and Phobias by Tamar E. Chansky

What to Do When You're Scared and Worried: A Guide for Kids by James J. Crist

What to Do When You Worry Too Much: A Kid's Guide to Overcoming Anxiety by Dawn Huebner and Bonnie Matthews

Keys to Parenting Your Anxious Child by Katharina Manassis

Helping Your Anxious Child: A Step by Step Guide for Parents by Sue Spence, Vanessa Cubham, Ann Wignall and Ronald M. Rapee

The Anxiety Cure for Kids: A Guide for Parents by Elizabeth DuPont Spencer, Robert L. DuPont and Caroline M. DuPont

endlessly? Where is the trigger located and what does it seem to say?

It is also useful for children to know how much of a feeling they have. We ask, "On a one to 10 scale, with 10 being so anxious you could throw up, and one being totally cool and calm, how worried are you right now? What can we do to get the number one point lower?" Awareness of the intensity of a feeling, especially for kids who tend to be black and white thinkers opens the window to many useful techniques. Once children see they can reduce their anxiety even a little, they will start to feel much more in control of themselves.

Breathing: Deep breathing is essential for relaxation; shallow breathing makes anxiety much worse. When we're upset, it takes most of us about 10 minutes to get reasonably relaxed when we consciously start breathing more slowly and deeply. Children need to learn how to breathe deeply when they're anxious, following these general guidelines: First practice this when everyone is calm. Tell them to put their hand on their belly where a belt would sit, and push out while inhaling. They should try to only breathe nine times in a minute with long, deep breaths. They can do this by counting to four while breathing in. Then, they should exhale slowly. Make sure your child has relaxed shoulders while doing this exercise. Younger children can pretend they are blowing up a balloon and watching it float up into the sky. Be sure to notice and praise your children when they are breathing well so they can become conscious of what it feels like physically to be less anxious.

4. Practice Mindful Awareness. Parents and children can work together to stay in the present. Anxiety diminishes when we remain focused in the here and now, and in our bodies. Practice several times focusing internally and externally: alternating attention inward by saying "notice your breathing" and outward by commenting "now notice the chair you are sitting on," inward by saying "listen to your heart beating" and outward by saying "hear my voice speaking to you." Some children become so anxious they seem to forget where they are. Keep children attuned to the present by orienting them: "You are safe here in the living room, I am here with you." Give them permission to replace anxious thoughts with relaxing images that you've discussed before. "Remember the happy, safe place we talked about? Well let's go there in our minds. Imagine you're all wrapped in a cozy towel after a swim in the ocean, and the sun is warm, and I remembered to bring that beach chair with the cup holder you like so you can sit in it, and we're about to have a yummy picnic." When children learn they can remain present and have some control over what they think about, they become less anxious.

5. Don't Listen When Worries Come. Although this is a difficult technique for many children to master, it can be helpful for kids who tend to be obsessive worriers. First, children have to recognize when they are worrying. Then they can name it. It is helpful to give the worry its own name, for example some children we know have called it Mr. Anxiety, Worry Worm, Hornet, the Nudge, and Peanut Butter. The point here is that it isn't the child who is anxious and is a problem – it's anxiety that's "visiting" the child who has a problem. This strategy externalizes anxiety and lets kids see themselves as functionally independent of it. They can even cope with it by making choices to relax and have fun instead of letting worry take over. They can draw pictures of "Hornet," or make a puppet of him. Help your child think about ways to challenge and defeat worry: "Oh, Hornet is not going to let you enjoy going bowling even though you've been looking forward to it. What can you say to him so he'll go away for a while?"

6. Worry Well but Only Once. Some children and adults get on worrying jags, with one worry leading to the next. Anxiety can be a runaway train. It is helpful, therefore, to allot time for worry saying, "We'll talk all about it, and then be done." Some children even benefit from a designated worry time set aside each day for them to share everything on their minds. We can note and appreciate that the child has a big worry, but then after about 10 minutes we need to get them to agree that, "The worry department is closed for the day." When the worry returns, offer reassurance and reiterate that this is already a done deal. Try to get the child to focus on what's next: "We already talked about that and it's settled for the time being. Now I need you to count out five forks and five knives and put them on the table."

7. Tell Stories. Stories help children feel less isolated and defended, and they add logic and pattern to events. Tell them stories about people you know, other children, yourself as a child and now, and about themselves when they were younger. "I know a boy who... " "I sometimes feel... " "Last year when you ... " "When Sammy was at the baseball game he... " Talk with them about the characters they learn of in books and movies, about how these fictional people cope with worries and triumphs, too. One of the sources of anxiety in foster children is their difficulty developing coherent narratives – they struggle to tell stories of their lives that seem logical and linear. The lack of coherence provides fertile ground for worry. These kids need the chance to develop this cause-and-effect thinking to help them feel more in control. Thus, story telling is a critical component of anxiety management for them. The more they see the narrative logic of events, the less fearful they'll be about what is going to happen next.

8. Have a Little Fun. Most foster children have had less happiness in their lives than they should have so they benefit all the more from increased opportunities for joy and pleasure on a daily basis. Be silly by crawling on the floor, making faces and telling jokes. Help put laughter on the daily menu for your children. Make fun of yourself. Sadly, you may have to teach them to have fun. Are there television characters that hit a funny bone? What makes you laugh so hard that milk comes out of your nose? Anxiety and laughter are incompatible; children who are giggling are usually not too anxious. And the more time children spend having fun, the less they'll have for fretting.

9. Don't Overprotect. Some parents see the worlds of their children get smaller because the stress of transitions and novelty causes too many melt downs and conflict. Well-intended, these parents have gotten into the habit of protecting their children and themselves from the feared situations. It is important to gradually attack anxiety head on and not let it win over family life, either. Exposure to a fear is necessary for your child to begin to overcome it. Additionally, children need to learn that often the anticipation is worse than the actual experience. The exposure doesn't have to be drastic – it's more like slowly entering cold water a little bit at a time.

Begin by role-playing with your child through a feared situation, backing it up to the most comfortable starting point. For example, if a child is afraid of dogs, he or she might be able to role-play with a stuffed animal, or a picture of a dog to begin. You will need to figure out a ladder of steps, gradually ending with exposure to the feared object such as touching a safe dog. When a step becomes easy, move to the next.

Take your time, and never proceed until the child is completely successful and confident along the way. You may have to break a step into even smaller steps to make it successful. Don't push too hard, and make sure you're engaging in other, less stressful activities, too. At the same time that you're helping your child to face his or her fears, you'll want to build his or her confidence and competence elsewhere. Sometimes a little boost of self-esteem can make a worry get smaller all by itself.

10. Reward Brave Behavior. Many of the children we live and work with are heroes and survivors of frightening and tough lives. It is therefore important that we recognize their efforts, however small, to stay in control of themselves and their worries. Notice and praise brave behavior, being specific: "You got right in the car when I asked even though you were a little worried about seeing the doctor. Great job!" Keep your praise immediate and succinct. Over-praising and vague praising tend to backfire and make kids feel worse about themselves because they can't connect the words with their actual behaviors. If you use rewards such as money, points, activities and stars to get children to stay bravely on track, make sure you're clear and consistent about the behavior, and why you're reinforcing it.

These 10 strategies will help your kids become less anxious over time. Keep in mind that even after many successes, anxiety is likely to rear its ugly head again, especially in times of increased stress. We need to let our children know that when they feel overwhelmed by fear and doubt, it's time to revisit the strategies that worked in the past. Remind them with a hug. There's no need to worry about the worry, and there are many effective ways to manage and defeat it.

Martha Straus, PhD, is a professor in the Department of Clinical Psychology at Antioch University New England Graduate School in Keene, N.H., and adjunct instructor in psychiatry at Dartmouth Medical School. She maintains a small private practice in Brattleboro, Vt., and consults to schools, social service agencies and courts. Straus is the author of numerous articles and four books, including ***No-Talk Therapy for Children and Adolescents****, and more recently,* ***Adolescent Girls in Crisis: Intervention and Hope.*** *Straus trains and conducts workshops internationally on attachment, child development and treatment, and complex trauma.*

Melanie Ernould, MA, is a doctoral student in the Department of Clinical Psychology at Antioch University New England Graduate School. Ernould worked as a practicum student for a year at the clinic for the Study of Children at Risk at Brown University and is currently working at Advocates Community Mental Health Center in Marlborough, Mass.

Anger Everywhere!

By Sally Flintoff

I am intimately acquainted with anger.

There was my son's anger. I have never known anyone to hold more anger than my son, who joined our family at 4 years of age. When I say anger, I don't mean the kind of anger that the average person displays when they've reached the end of their tether, when they just can't take any more. I mean a deep, underlying, seething anger that is ALWAYS there ready to explode out in an instant with no warning and no provocation. He was angry from the moment he woke early in the morning to the moment he finally fell asleep late, late at night. And even during his sleep he was angry, tossing and turning in the bed like a whirling dervish. "Good morning sweetheart" spoken in a gentle, loving tone would be greeted with "I hate you" as he spat in my face, lashed out and hit me, or yanked a handful of hair out. "Would you like eggs [his favorite] for breakfast today?" would elicit profanity directed at me with such hatred and intensity that even a sailor would blush. Woe betide me if I put on his left sock before his right, or his right sock before his left, cut his toast or didn't cut it, spoke too loudly or too softly. In fact, it would be fair to say that generally the fact that I was breathing, was enough to send him into an uncontrollable rage.

Then there was my anger. Wow! Where did that come from? I would hold it together for so long, remaining calm in the face of constant, dire provocation and then wham, up out of nowhere it would come, exploding like a Mt. St. Helen's eruption. My normal, pleasant, friendly self would be replaced by a screaming banshee spewing forth hate, threats, and sarcasm. Who was this person who had taken over my body? Sometimes she frightened me, at other times she disgusted me. I tried to rationalize to myself that anyone would react in anger when faced with what I was living with day in and day out with no let-up, ever. And while this was absolutely true, it didn't lessen the shame I felt or the depth of the hatred I felt toward my own anger. I worked hard at holding it down, keeping it at bay, making it invisible. With therapy, perseverance, and determination my angry outbursts lessened. Over time that other mean, spiteful person only came to visit once in a while. I began to recognize when she was around, which was huge progress, but I continued to hate her presence and I fervently wished she would disappear forever.

It took a long time and a lot of hard work before I realized that I needed to befriend, embrace and welcome my anger rather than fear and hate it. Through this process the following highlights what I have come to understand about anger. First, I believe that how we deal with anger in our families is a really important piece in the overall picture.

Many of us have children who hold so much anger. For some of us, that anger spills over into pure, uncontrollable, terrifying, and dangerous rages that result in destruction of property, self-harm or harm to others, the intervention of police, removal from the family etc. Many of us also find ourselves filled with anger (and rage) provoked by our children and often directed at them for being so darn difficult to parent. We find ourselves doing or saying things in anger that can come out of nowhere and take us over, causing us to be someone who shocks us profoundly. Sometimes we snap at the small things, sometimes we spend hours (days/weeks/months) carrying around resentment and anger at the position we find ourselves in with our kids. Angry and resentful that no one else understands us, our situation or how devastatingly hard it is to parent a child with trauma – not the school, not the so-called professionals, not our extended family, not our friends.

Here's the thing though, anger is a perfectly normal emotion. Every single person on this planet experiences it. It's part of being human. It's healthy. The problem is that the majority of us have absolutely no idea how to express it in a healthy way.

The majority of people have been raised in homes where the expression of anger was not welcomed – in fact quite the opposite, it was repressed. To express feelings of anger was not acceptable. We were told off for expressing our anger, "Don't speak to me like that. How dare you behave like that. Don't you ever act like that again. Go to your room and don't come out until you are ready to apologize for xxx. It's not acceptable to speak/behave that way. You'll be in big trouble if you ever xxx again. You can't go through life doing xxx just because you don't like it. Suck it up."

Many of us are terrified of anger and have a deep sense of shame around it.

We were sent to our rooms, given consequences, had privileges removed or we were put in time-out for expressing anger. Essentially, love, relationship, and connection were withheld from us because we had feelings of anger. Many of us were even physically punished for expressing anger.

Some of us had parents who would withdraw, shut down, and stop communicating when they got angry. Some of us had violent, unpredictable parents who would blow up and shout or hit when they got angry. Neither of these expressions are healthy. We were told it was unacceptable to behave like this, yet that is what our parents modeled for us.

Our deepest blueprints have been programmed to find the expression of anger abhorrent, shameful, and totally unacceptable. Now we are presented with children who are so angry that it's difficult to comprehend. Little wonder then that we have no idea what to do with that anger.

Many of us are terrified of anger and have a deep sense of shame around it, due to the ways we have seen it expressed and the way we were treated when we felt anger as children. So we are horrified by our own anger – terrified to let it out because of what might happen if we do. Terrified to let our children let their anger out. So we exert enormous amounts of energy (subconsciously) holding our anger down, not letting it rise. When our kids start to express anger, we shut them down as quickly as we can.

Like all emotions, it is healthy to express anger in the moment as we feel it. When we do this, the anger is expressed, released and it's gone – forever. There's no major blow-up, no need to over-react to a situation. We feel the anger (feel it physically in our racing heart, our swirling stomach), we recognize it as anger, we express it in ways that are not harmful or dangerous to anyone else and then it passes.

When we bury it and push it down it gets stored (in our stomach, in our cells, in our subconscious memory). If we are never given the opportunity to express and release our anger, over time a huge amount of buried anger builds up. One day it will come out. When you bring a traumatized child into your home, it will trigger all that buried anger and it will come out. It's impossible for it not too.

The vast majority of us have stored anger – that is why we over-react to small situations, that is why we explode out of nowhere, that is why we say or do terribly mean and hateful things, that is where this 'other' person we don't know comes from. That is why we take our kids' behavior personally. That is why we can't stay present in the moment with our kids.

Before we can reach a place of being able to release our anger in the moment in a healthy, non-destructive way we have to have a really deep understanding of anger. It helps greatly also if we have released much of the old buried anger. Some of us need the help of a professional to do this. It depends on their individual and their past history. The anger can be stored beyond the reach of our conscious memory. Trying to reach it through the logical brain and thinking about it or remembering it doesn't work. Somatic therapies can be helpful with this.

Underneath the anger there is always fear or pain. Anger is a mask, a protective response. It is our responsibility to get underneath our own anger and find the fear and pain buried there so that we can stop holding onto it, stop burying it, or hiding from it. Instead, we must bring it to the surface, feel it, and then release it. Then we are free to do the same thing for our kids. To help them get underneath their anger to find the fear and pain behind it. To help them find ways to express it and release it, so they too can be free to express anger in the moment in a healthy, non-destructive way and not bring their entire store of anger to every single interaction they have.

When we can reach a place where we are not scared of anger, but recognized it as a normal part of who we are, accept it as part of ourselves then we are well on the road to total acceptance of ourselves. Then anger becomes no big deal. It's just another emotion, another part of ourselves. It holds no power over us. In the meantime, we can strive to honor our anger, and our children's anger. I know it sounds crazy at first, but really it is exactly what we must do. When we can truly honor our (and our children's) anger, accept it then we can begin the work of finding out what lies behind it – finding that pain and fear. So long as we continue to deny the anger and push it down, the pain and fear remain buried and the anger will continue. It will not just disappear just because someone tells us it's unacceptable to be angry.

A wise man I once worked with around my anger told me to say "I have anger" rather than "I am angry." Anger does not define who we are, it is merely an emotion we feel. By stating that we have anger we begin to be able to separate the anger from ourselves. Often we are deeply ashamed of our anger and identified with it. We feel there is something wrong us because we get angry, because we are angry. Once we can start to see that it just another emotion, that we are not bad because we have anger it becomes much easier to be able to feel the anger and to release it in healthy ways without the need to blame others for our anger.

Sally Flintoff is the mother of two adopted children. She has spent the past five years widely researching trauma, its impact on the developing brain, and the behaviors that can be displayed as a result. She founded Consciously Parenting Australia in 2008 (www.consciously-parenting.com) and is dedicated to educating and helping struggling families achieve the harmony and joy that is the birthright of every human being.

About Anger and Rage

By John Ross

Rage and anger are two things I do not care to deal with. They simply must go, either that, or the child goes. And since I would rather the child stay, 100 percent of my time is spent on dealing with rage and anger until it's either gone, or under control "in my home." It usually takes me about three to four months to get it under control "in my home." In my home means, as long as that child is around me, he/she will not rage or become so angry he/she is out of control. I must control me, and everything that goes on in my home. It is where I live, and if I cannot control what is going on, then whatever is causing me not to have control, must leave. If it's a child, and I chose to take that child in, then I have chosen to deal with that child's problems, so getting them under control is not an option, it is a must, and I have succeeded with every child that came to me, who rages out of control. They failed every placement they were in, until they came to my home, and there they remain until they are either returned home, adopted, or aged out of the system. Or, they become a danger to the other kids in my home, then that goes without saying, they need to be in a safer environment with more support staff around them.

I take these kids to places in public until they have a raging fit in public. From that time on, we are grounded, going nowhere except doctors, dentist, or school. Outside of that, we will go nowhere until that child can allow me to handle the rage or anger. I give consequences, and they will get a consequence without fail. You do A, I will do B, without fail. I am consistent, patient, nurturing, tough, long suffering, and I separate the behavior from the child. I don't like the behavior, but I love the child. A disorder is not the fault of the child, so I am not working against the child, I am working against the disorder, they are two different things. When they rage I am calm and quiet, one of us "has" to be. I can raise my voice, or lower my voice, it has to be timed right. When I raise my voice, I expect to accomplish something. If I see that raising my voice is not going to accomplish anything, then I will not do so, it is a waste of time.

For three solid months I am working on nothing else, except getting the rages and anger 100 percent under control "in my home." A child will come to my home kicking, screaming, throwing things, and raging for up to an hour. I have not failed yet, to get that under control within three to four months. That child may go to school and rage, but he/she will not rage with me around. Once I can understand it and control it, then I help the school. I have gotten rid of rages without the use of medication, but once kids are in school, that's a different story. A teacher has far too many other kids to deal with, so medication is sometimes needed for school to assist the child with rages and anger.

My first order of business when dealing with this is, I need to answer the question, "why." Why are they raging? I ask myself that question until I can't answer "why" anymore, and that's where I start working. Knowing why will assist me greatly in helping this child. From that, I look for triggers. What is triggering it. I make a mental note of every trigger. Then I start on body language from the child. What does he or she look like calm, and what does he or she look like during a rage. Then, what does he or she look like just before a rage. Then, what are the changes from calm to start of a rage, to full rage. Once I have this, I am well on my way to preventing rages "in my home." Once I know the triggers, and the signs, I then intercept the child "before" he or she get to the beginning of a rage. To do this, I have to constantly monitor the child during every waking moment in my home. So from the time the child gets up, I monitor him or her, I keep the child close to me, near me, in line of sight, always, 100 percent of the time. If there are other kids in the home and they are part of the triggers, if I need a bathroom break, each child has to go to their room and busy themselves until I come out. This too is part of helping them, teaching them to remain in their rooms until I come and get them. All of this takes an enormous amount of time, but it pays greatly in the end, and has done so for me through many kids. I have never gotten an easy kid, ever, long term. I pray each time I get one, just so I can see how it is to have one, but that day has yet to come.

Once I know how to keep the child from raging, I then start teaching how to self manage the time "before" the rage/anger. Sometimes this works, sometimes it does not. The times where it does not is usually with a child who is IED, (Intermittent Explosive Disorder). This is when the child doesn't know when he or she will rage, so it is sometimes, a shock even to him or her and he or she usually feel guilty after a rage. But that's another topic.

Once a child has gone through a month of no rages, it starts to build self-esteem back up. He or she feels good not having to rage, he or she has put some distance between the previous rage. We then do a test run in public. We go somewhere close to home. If the child asks for something and I say no, that is the first test. If the child responds with rage, we start over again by being grounded. Usually, at the end of three months, I can say no and the child becomes upset, but since I know this, I will usually already have taken the steps to avoid the triggers. So when I say the first "no," I have a backup plan already. "No, you cannot have that, however, I was thinking of getting you this instead." I want the child to hear "no," I want the child to accept "no" but I also want to quickly give a reward to avoid a tantrum/rage/anger, whatever. When it works, the child will feel more confident, one, for not having a rage, and, still getting something, just not what was originally wanted. Depending on the kid, there are a lot of things I will do once back in public, but I already know it will work because I will have tried it many times at home already.

It is draining, time consuming, and all encompassing, but the child wins when I win and that is the ultimate goal for me. There is a lot of detail I did not go into, it would take far too long, but this has worked for me with every child who was sent to me who has bounced from foster home to foster home. The bouncing stops here. When they get to me, it is now time for that child to "win," and I won't rest until they do, they deserve to win and they deserve to have someone who will be relentless in working with them.

John Ross has fostered more than 100 children in the 25 years he has been a foster parent. The children he has worked with have ranged in age of three months to 18 years old. He specializes in placements of children who have bounced from foster home to foster home. He loves working with these kids because they bring their worst and he helps them to become stable and get ready to hit the ground running if and when they leave his home. He has learned a great deal from the kids that have come through his home. They have taught him more than he could have ever learned at any university, for they are the best teachers around. No credentials, but wow, they can sure teach!

Trying to Shift a Child's Negative Behavior Pattern

By Cheryl A. Lieberman, PhD, and Rhea K. Bufferd, LICSW

After 10-year-old Matthew was officially adopted by Darcy and Judah, it was time to set up a meeting with his birth parents (court-mandated open adoption). There had been visits with his biological brother in another foster home, and it was decided that the families would meet at a Department of Social Services office. The session was difficult for everyone. The finality of the moment was overwhelming for Matthew, who realized that he would never go back to live with his birth mother; and this visit where he said goodbye with no hope of returning was devastating. For people who do not understand why a child would want to go back to a house where abuse and neglect were rampant, the situation might be compared to the witness protection program. The government promises you safety. All you have to do is give up everything that has been part of your life so far. It must be difficult to accept that offer.

Matthew's upset continued and finally resulted in his being suspended from school and after-school programs. He expressed no remorse, and often said that he didn't care about anything. His adoptive parents were stumped, and when it was suggested they do a ceremony they decided that they had nothing to lose.

Making Room For Good Messages

Preparation: Take several 3 X 5 index cards and put a bad message on each one. The messages should he based on knowledge of what had been said to the child in his or her past and what the child has said aloud about himself or herself.

- You are a rotten kid.
- You'll be the death of me yet.
- You'll never make it.
- You are unlovable.
- You are stupid.
- You are dumb.
- You are bad.
- You drive me crazy.
- You are a monster.
- You are clumsy.
- I hate you.
- Why can't you be good like (name)?
- It is your fault that you can't live here.

Then get another group of index cards. Cut each card into an interesting shape and put a colorful sticker on it. The messages used for Matthew were:

- You are good.
- You have a nice smile.
- You are unique.
- You try to do your best.
- You are super.

- You are huggable.
- You are lovable.
- You are smart.
- You are a terrific kid.
- You are kind.
- You have courage.
- You are special.
- You are brave.
- You are willing to try new things.
- You will be the best you can be.
- You are wonderful.
- You are helpful.
- You are clever.

The good messages should focus on basic characteristics, not on things the child did or did not do, such as, "You are good in math" or "You don't mess up your room." For Matthew's ceremony, two colorful folders were attached in such a way that the inside had three sections – enough to hold the good messages. The outside was decorated with colorful stickers and "Matthews Good Messages" was printed on the front cover. Also at hand were Scotch tape and a glue stick (so Matthew would have a choice later) and a small, reclosable plastic bag.

The Ceremony

Mama: Everyone at some time will hear good messages and bad messages from people.

Papa: Sometimes people say good things, such as, "You are a nice person." Sometimes people say bad things, such as, "You are a rotten person."

Matthew: People might be kidding around and say things like "Boy was that dumb," and you may feel like they said you were really dumb. That kind of kidding hurts. Sometimes people are angry or tired and they can say things like, "I could kill you" or "You are a monster." Children can take those messages and have them grow inside of them so that soon they believe that they are bad, rotten, or no good.

Papa: What kids have to learn is that just because people say bad messages, that does not make them true. Because kids are small and growing, they may not have room for good messages unless we get rid of the bad messages from time to time.

Mama: Today's ceremony will do just that – get rid of bad messages so that there can be room for more good ones. Matthew, are you ready to do that now?

Matthew: (Says his answer. If Yes, go on; if No, stop for the time being and do this ceremony later.)

If They Continue:

Mama: We have written on cards bad messages that adults and other kids sometimes give kids. If you have ever had that bad message given to you, let us know and we will put that into a pile.

Papa: If you can remember a time you heard it or a person who said it and want to share that, we will listen. If you have gotten messages that we have not written on cards, let us know and we will add them to the pile. After we do this, Mama will explain what happens to the bad messages.

(Matthew reads each message and puts some of them in a pile. When he is done, he decides to put all of them into a pile, just in case someone said one of these and he doesn't remember. Then Papa asks him to read each card out loud and then to tear each into tiny pieces and put all the pieces into the reclosable plastic bag. Papa closes the bag, has Matthew stomp on it, and then throws it into the trash. Since Matthew was having trouble with fire setting, they decided not to burn these messages. Matthew walks back, saying how much room he has for good messages.)

Mama: Now that we have started to remove the bad messages and there is room for good messages, we need to fill that space. We have written on cards good messages that we think apply to you. If you agree, we will make a way to push them into the space you now have for them. After each message is chosen and absorbed, we will put them in a special folder so that you can look at them often and share them with others.

(Mama shows Matthew the cards and he reads each of them, stopping to enjoy the stickers, too. He says he likes the stickers and doesn't want to eat them to get them inside. Mama assures him that he does not have to. They decide that Matthew will pick up each card in turn and Mama and Papa will read it. Matthew will put it next to his body at his head, upper chest, or abdomen. Mama and Papa will read it together and pretend to push it into his body at one of the three places he chooses. Then Matthew puts each card aside. Halfway through, Matthew throws his arms wide open and with a big smile says, "I am being so filled up with good messages." Papa shows Matthew the folder and helps Matthew put his cards inside the folder – this is not rushed, but done at Matthew's pace.)

Matthew: (Says how he feels now and what he thinks of the ceremony. Then he reads.) It is important for me to hold these good messages inside me. If I ever feel as though bad messages are trying to push them out, I will let you know that I need another ceremony to help me. I promise to try to believe the good messages people give me and to learn to manage the bad.

Papa: We promise to help you hold onto good messages. If I ever give you bad messages that hurt you inside, please tell me so that I can change the messages right away.

Mama: If I ever give you bad messages that hurt you inside, please tell me so that I can change those messages right away.

Papa: We will end the ceremony by reading the good messages in your folder because we believe they are all true.

(Mama and Papa read each message in turn.)

Group hug.

Afterward

At one point in the ceremony, Matthew threw his arms open and exclaimed, "I am really getting filled up with good messages!" His demeanor and behavior changed significantly after this ceremony. He stopped being oppositional and quieted down a lot. The ceremony had helped him cross a bridge from despair back to calm. It seemed to be one of the most behavior-changing events in this child's life.

Cheryl A. Lieberman, PhD, is a single adoptive parent. Her sons, Eric and Christopher, both from the same birth family, came to live with her when they were seven-years-old and six-years-old respectively. They have an open adoption arrangement. Cheryl earned a master's degree in social services and city planning and a doctorate in organizational planning from the University of Pennsylvania. She is founder and president of Cornerstone Consulting Group, Cambridge, Mass., which provides strategic performance enhancement and change management services to numerous profit and nonprofit organizations.

Rhea K. Bufferd, LICSW, has been an adoption social worker since 1974, when she joined the Massachusetts Department of Social Services. She went on to work with Cambridge Family and Children's Services and is currently an adoption therapist. Rhea earned her master's in social work at Boston University School of Social Work and did postgraduate work in family therapy at The Institute at Newton, Mass.

Healing Loss in the Traumatized Child

By Ellen Singer, LCSW-C

Thomas moved on and off between his birth mother and paternal aunt for the first seven years of his life. He was removed from that unstable situation after his aunt threw him down a flight of stairs, breaking his leg.

Now ten, Thomas has been in his pre-adoptive home for one year. As finalization nears, Thomas seems to be changing from a child who is eager to please, to one who is contradictory and noncompliant. He ignores many of his parents' directives and becomes anxious when reprimanded in any way. In addition, his school work is suffering, a turn of events that is particularly upsetting to his parents. His parents are wondering... Who is this child?

Many of the stories of children who enter the foster care system involve abuse – physical, sexual, or emotional – neglect or abandonment. Care-giving adults may be drug or alcohol addicted or mentally ill, unable to care for themselves, let alone children. In some instances, children have witnessed violence, even murder against loved ones. A large proportion of children lose connections with birth family members; others remain in contact with family members with whom they have ambivalent, conflicted and difficult relationships. For some children, placement occurs because a caregiver has died. Unfortunately, multiple caregivers and moves both prior to and subsequent to placement in foster care compound the experience of trauma and loss.

Amazingly, adults often expect children to move into adoptive placements smoothly, settling into their new lives with relief and minimal disruption. It is hoped that children can understand how the old and the new are separate worlds, and despite the considerable efforts of many people, those two worlds are permanently apart. These expectations, combined with the fact that adoptive parents may have had little knowledge of how prior trauma can cause depression, anxiety, or acting out behavior, may be a recipe for disaster.

Fortunately, much has been learned about the long-term impact of trauma on both children and adults. However, not all foster and adoptive parents are informed, and some mental health practitioners are unaware of the powerful, unique complexities of loss for children in foster care and adoption. It is critical that social workers learn how unresolved grief about previous losses can manifest itself in new home environments, and that information must be shared. Fears and worries grounded in former experiences must be recognized and addressed to diminish difficult or puzzling behaviors that challenge new families where safety and nurturing are present.

Last year, Thomas was referred to The Center for Adoption Support and Education, Inc., or C.A.S.E., in Silver Spring, Md., with his foster soon-to-be adoptive parents. Their therapist, Madeleine Krebs was not surprised by the route that Thomas had taken to reflect his anxiety and insecurity. She began by asking Thomas, "How did you get to this family?" She created a trusting relationship and a safe place where he could share his understanding of what had happened in his life and process his feelings related to his experiences and the losses he incurred.

Over time, through the use of activities designed to help him express his sadness and confusion, Thomas shared his anger. He made balls out of clay and threw them at the couch in Krebs' office, expressing fury at his aunt who had hurt him. Sometimes he would get angry at Krebs, who used the opportunity to help Thomas see that it was all right for him to get angry – healing his sense of trust in adults. He talked about his concern about the fate of a cat that had lived with him at his birth mother's home, eventually letting Krebs know that he was worried about his birth mother and wondered where she was.

Krebs also worked with Thomas' parents, coaching them to provide Thomas with what he needed, as well as how to respond appropriately to his difficult behavior. Krebs notes, "I needed to help his parents understand how his traumatic past resulted in a lack of trust which translated into anxiety, insecurity, and a hyper-vigilant stance in the world."

Thomas was testing his parents, and needed reassurance that he would be accepted and loved despite his misbehavior. In addition, Krebs helped Thomas' parents understand how his emotional challenges may have been interfering with his ability to learn and that throughout time, this might improve as well. In the meantime, she emphasized the importance of providing Thomas with support. The C.A.S.E. model of therapeutic support incorporates understanding of the impact of trauma, grief and loss in foster care and adoption as it relates to attachment. The concept of ambiguous loss, as described by Pauline Boss in ***Ambiguous Loss: Learning to Live with Unresolved Grief***, and the good grief model developed by Maria Trozzi in ***Talking with Children about Loss***, are important theories for treating children who continue to have contact with birth parents, as well as those who do not.

Ambiguous loss refers to loss which is uncertain and often unrecognized by others because it does not follow traditional patterns leading to closure. Unlike the finality of death, for example, ambiguous loss blocks the coping and grieving process because the loss situation may change. Children may believe they will reunite with birth families. Without more absolutes, the "family relationship freezes in place," Boss states in her book, complicating children's ability to move on and form new attachments, despite their need to do so.

The "good grief" model outlines the stages of grief for children and teens, and emphasizes that "grief shared is grief diminished," as stated in Boss' book. Trozzi believes that grief cannot be rushed, and that children need to be in trusting relationships to work through the pain of their losses.

The first of the four stages identified by Trozzi is understanding. At C.A.S.E., therapists help children to verbalize their perception of the situation that caused the loss. Sometimes information can be added or corrected, or different perspectives can be provided to help children comprehend why events occurred. Sometimes loss is not of a person, but of innocence, trust, or safety.

Lifebooks are helpful tools for concretizing the past for children. At C.A.S.E., therapists also help children identify "lifelines" that provided support to them at critical points in their young lives. Lifelines are clues for effective coping skills that can be useful again. They may be people, or activities such as playing sports, reading, phoning a friend, or they may simply be thoughts that were comforting or encouraging at a difficult time.

The second phase is grieving. Krebs notes that children can be helped to understand that painful feelings are normal, they can be expressed in healthy ways, and that they do not go on forever. "We need to help them keep faith and hope for the future."

The third phase, commemorating, helps children believe that there is value to their loss and that others will acknowledge the loss. Krebs emphasizes the importance of helping children keep and treasure photos of people and places. In addition, foster parents can maintain respect for children's losses through language. An example, "I was thinking about your birth father today, and I wonder if he had a good throwing arm when he was young – just like you!" Or, "I know your sister's birthday is this month. Would you like to make a card that we can send to her?"

Finally, the fourth phase is, going on, or moving forward with life by accepting and integrating the loss psychologically and emotionally within. However, children are likely to move back and forth through these phases; it is not unusual for them to return to intense grief when it has appeared previously that their sadness had waned.

The nature of loss for children in foster care is deep and often effects their self-worth. Many lose not only their birth families but possibly friends, teachers, and pets. Often they have moved from school to school and are unable to keep mementos or schoolwork that made them proud. They may lose things along the way, such as clothing, books, and photos. Grieving these losses is no quick or easy task.

The importance of grief work cannot be overstated. When children are not given the opportunity and assistance to effectively communicate their grief, as well as the feelings related to other traumatic experiences, the result can be a serious erosion of self-trust as well as trust in others. The result can be feelings of incompetence, and a belief that the world is unfair, unsafe, and unmanageable. These powerful emotions, if not recognized and alleviated, can have a serious negative impact on a child's ability to attach to a new caregiver.

Shana, 15, was removed from her biological family at age 10 after her mother failed to retrieve her and her 8-year-old brother from a babysitter's home. After living in several foster homes, she was placed for adoption at age 11. She entered therapy four years after adoption because she felt unattached to her adoptive parents and was asking to be removed from their home. Shana's parents had reached the point where they wondered, "She is so insistent about this, is there nothing we can do but let her go?"

Treating traumatized teens can be especially challenging because, according to Debbie Riley, Executive Director of C.A.S.E., teens frequently deny that they need the help of a therapist and that problems exist. Instead, teens may present self-injurious behaviors, depression, anxiety, anger-management issues, substance abuse, and relationship problems that stem from previous trauma. She notes that frequently, the situation is complicated because little information is available about the trauma the teen may have experienced in his or her early life. To heal, the essential components for recovery include the emotional support of the family as well as the therapeutic relationship. The adopted teen may have lived in environments where adults harmed and betrayed him or her, but helping build safe connections with others so that he or she may successfully attach to adoptive parents is crucial.

Riley describes the process of helping Shana share her story and express her emotions to be complicated. Although Shana tried to push her away, Riley remained steadfast and worked to slowly build the trusting relationship which helped her describe the sexual abuse she suffered at the hands of her stepfather. Riley sat with Shana as she poured out her pain, rage and fear that she was unlovable. The experience of sharing her memories led to Shana's ability to recognize and grieve the loss of the friend and other people she missed from her previous life.

Riley's work with Shana's parents centered on helping them understand Shana's traumatic past and the impact of the past on her ability to trust and attach to adults. Her parents had been unaware of the extent of Shana's experiences. Her rejection of her parents was an attempt to protect herself from future harm. Shana's parents were warm, loving people who did not want to lose her but had been hurt themselves by her behavior. They agreed to "hang in there with her" as long as she agreed to continue with them and her therapy.

"How kids work through the mourning process and grow from it is up to us," Trozzi notes. Children who are separated from birth parents and those who have been involved with the foster care system have experienced disruptions and losses that affect their ability to adapt to a family environment. It is up to adults – parents, social workers, nurses, doctors, and teachers – to anticipate, accommodate, and support these children as they grieve. Many children cannot maneuver through the complexities of their significant losses and their life stories without support that is enhanced by deep appreciation for the unique nature and challenge of those losses.

Ellen Singer, LCSW-C, is a therapist/educator for The Center for Adoption Support and Education (C.A.S.E.) in Burtonsville/Silver Spring, Md. She provides clinical services for prospective parents considering adoption/third party reproduction, foster and adoptive parents, adult adopted persons and their families, and expectant/birth parents and their families. Ellen facilitates adoptive parent support groups and provides training to parents, community groups, educators and other professionals. She is the editor of C.A.S.E.'s monthly e-newsletter and contributes articles to parent/professional publications. Ellen has served on the Board of Directors for RESOLVE of the Mid-Atlantic, and the Professional Advisory Council for RESOLVE. Ellen and her husband are parents to two children, by adoption and by birth.

Foster Parent to Foster Parent Resources

Beyond Consequences, Logic, and Control by Heather Forbes and B. Bryan Post covers in detail the effects of trauma on the body-mind and how trauma alters children's behavioral responses.

Parenting the Hurt Child by Gregory Keck talks about how the world is full of hurt children, and bringing one into your home can quickly derail the easy family life you once knew. Get effective suggestions, wisdom, and advice to parent the hurt child in your life.

Telling the Truth to your Adopted or Foster Child: Making Sense of the Past
by Betsy Keefer & Jayne Schooler
Answers the question of why adopted children need the facts about their history. This book presents why the truth – with all of its details – can help heal the hurt child. Adoptive and foster families will find this book helpful as they struggle with how to share the good, the bad, and the ugly with their children.

Fostering a Child's Recovery: Family Placement for Traumatized Children
by Mike Thomas and Terry Philpot
The overwhelming majority of children and young people in care today are fostered, but for some this only increases their problems through untreated trauma, ill-judged placements, poorly supported foster carers and multiple moves. This book outlines the principles of family placement on the basis of planning and evidence, and explores the qualities, skills and insights that create positive placement outcomes.

Making Children Feel Safe

Children need parents to set limits so they will feel safe.

In ***Parenting with Love and Logic***, Foster Cline, MD. and Jim Fay describe what firm limits feel like to a child:

Imagine yourself plopped down on a chair in a strange, totally dark environment.

You can't see your hand in front of your face. Your only security is the chair.

You don't know if you're on a cliff, in a cave, in a room, or wherever. Eventually you muster enough nerve to move away from the chair and check your immediate surroundings.

You find four solid walls. What a relief! Now you feel a little more secure and safe enough to begin exploring the rest of the room, knowing that you won't fall off the edge.

But what if you tested the walls and they crumbled? You would move quickly back to your chair for security. And there you would stay. Your entire environment is mysterious and threatening.

Some parents build walls in the form of firm limits for their children; others leave their kids to feel insecure and afraid by providing few limits, or limits that crumble easily.

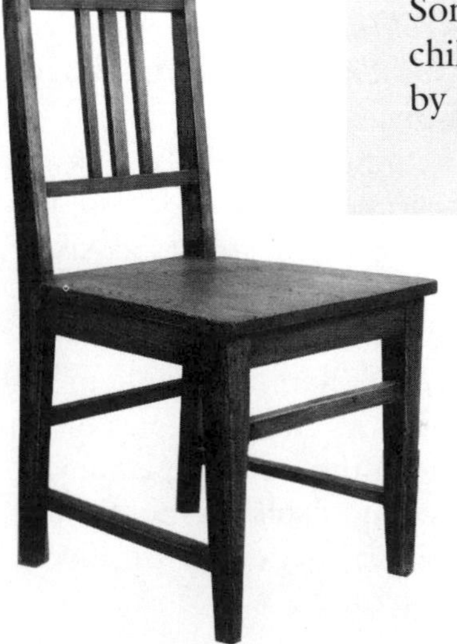

Attachment & Trust

If a child lives with criticism, he learns to condemn.
If a child lives with hostility, she learns to fight.
If a child lives with ridicule, he learns to be shy.
If a child lives with shame, she learns to feel guilty.
If a child lives with tolerance, he learns to be patient.
If a child lives with encouragement, she learns confidence.
If a child lives with praise, he learns to appreciate.
If a child lives with fairness, she learns justice.
If a child lives with security, he learns to have faith.
If a child lives with approval, she learns to like herself.
If a child lives with acceptance and friendship, he learns to find love in the world.– Dorothy Law Nolte

Now and Forever: Foster Parents Build the Bonds of Attachment

By Charlotte Simpson

More than 400,000 children currently live in foster care in the United States. Many are moved from one foster home to another with an average stay of two years. An estimated 51,323 children were placed in permanent loving families from foster care in 2005, many adopted by their foster parents. It is a slow and cumbersome system designed to help families stay together if at all possible.

More and more, legally and morally, the needs of the children are taking precedence over those of parents who have shown either through neglect or abuse that they are not able to adequately assume that role. Through the dedication of social workers, adoption advocacy groups, and foster parents, more children are finding stable homes sooner.

Every foster child experiences trauma. Most have been the victims of neglect and abuse; many experience the repeated loss of a primary caregiver, diminished connection with and sometimes permanent loss of birth parents, siblings, and extended family. With this history, any child would have difficulty learning to trust and attach within an adoptive or foster family. Temperaments, personalities, individual histories, and the extent of trauma vary from one child to the next, even among siblings.

The presence of loving caregivers at the right time can make a world of difference. But, for most children, extended time in foster care results in cognitive and developmental delays, anxiety and other emotional issues, and often sensory and motor development are impacted. First and foremost, their ability to attach to a primary caregiver, to love and trust, can be seriously damaged.

Sensitive caregiving during early childhood builds a healthy foundation for future development. When this foundation is damaged, children may have difficulty in forming loving, intimate relationships. According to the Association for Treatment and Training in the Attachment of Children, or ATTACh, "the inability to securely attach to the primary caretakers is called Reactive Attachment Disorder, or RAD." This manifests in many, sometimes contradictory, ways. We have drawn from the experiences of foster parent members of ASAP for examples.

M writes: A lot of my foster children who are age two to eight tend to be my "little stalkers." I often chuckle when they run into the back of me or can answer in one second where everyone in the house is and what they are doing. Because they have lost one mother, they now refuse to lose sight of me, the current substitute. To teach these children skills to be independent is often difficult and at times frustrating, especially when they stand outside your bathroom door. These children are often from abusive homes and their lives get even harder when you invite a new friend over and they cannot figure out whom to watch, the stranger whom they are worried sick about, or that new mom they do not want to lose.

The opposite could happen as well as I remember on a warm winter afternoon during a cookout at my house. I had two adorable little girls ages five and six. We had friends over for a cookout and my friend Lynn came with her new boyfriend Mitch. My two foster girls had always been shy and afraid of men due to their previous home life. My friend did introductions while I put out food. On my next trip through with more food I noticed both of my foster daughters sitting on this man's lap rubbing his chest hair – talk about inappropriate.

In an emergency, we once took in two girls, three and 18 months old, removed from their home during a drug bust. I thought these two girls were deaf because they would just sit and not respond. It became evident after a while that they were not deaf, but needed to learn that people were talking to them and they were calling their names. That same 3-year-old was afraid of grass. However, with baby steps, today they are living in an adoptive family and doing well.

B writes that she finally felt the five-year-old in her care was secure enough to take out shopping. She was cuddling and seemed to be forming a bond with her new foster mom. So they went to the mall where the child preceded to delight and engage every adult in sight, attaching herself to strangers walking past, eating up the "she's so adorable" from the shop clerks and passing out hugs and goodbye waves as though leaving life-long friends. That fragile thread between them was only a part of the net of ingratiation she was spinning to manipulate her world – she could not yet trust her foster parents to keep her safe.

Foster parents play a key role in helping children learn to trust. At the front line they begin the difficult and seemingly thankless task of helping a child who is removed from his or her home and may have nothing familiar to hold onto – no voices, clothing, toys, siblings – begin the process of recovering from the shame, fear, and sadness and the belief that no one can keep them safe.

If the child stays in a home long-term or ultimately joins the family through adoption, the parent's job is the continuing support and development of that trust, the nurturing of self-esteem and the re-building of the child's ability to connect and love through ongoing development and the normative crises of adoption. They lay the foundation that was missing in the birth family for the child's social, emotional, and developmental growth and ultimately success in life.

Professionals with the right background, training, and experience can help children and families attach. The accurate diagnosis and appropriate treatment of reactive attachment disorder can help children heal and families become strong.

Often this involves new ways of parenting, new ways of seeing and understanding a child, and a better appreciation for his or her true intelligence and abilities. With commitment, patience, and consistency there is much hope.

Charlotte Simpson is an adoptive parent and executive director of Adoption and Foster Care School Awareness Project, or ASAP. She is also the resource-liaison for her local special education parent advisory council and has her own website for parents of children with differing abilities at www.aboutmebooks.biz. She resides in Massachusetts with her husband and daughter. For more information on ASAP, the visit www.asapmass.org. This article originally appeared in ***Fostering Families Today****.*

Attachment 101

By Arthur Becker-Weidman, PhD

The attachment system and attachment behaviors are activated when the person experiences some threat, fear or discomfort.

A basic understanding of how normal and healthy attachments develop is important to help wounded children try to develop healthier patterns of attachment. So, what is attachment?

Attachment is a process involving a caregiver and a child. It does not reside in the child, but is reflective of the relationship between a caregiver and a child. In simplest terms, the attachment system is a "proximity-seeking" system. It operates like a thermostat; if everything is comfortable, you don't know if your heating and cooling system is operating, since it only comes on when the temperature is outside some pre-set range. Attachment behavior is proximity seeking behavior and is activated when a person feels some threat. In those instances, a person seeks the security and comfort of a preferred other person. For children, this preferred other person will usually be a parent. For you, this preferred other person may be your partner, the person you turn to when things get difficult.

The attachment system and attachment behaviors are activated when the person experiences some threat, fear or discomfort. What normally occurs during infancy is typical parent response to the child's distress, providing comfort and soothing the child. In the toddler years, the parent provides a safe base from which the child can begin to explore the world and learn. Without a sense of safety and security, learning can be difficult.

Why is Attachment so Important?

As the child grows and develops, attachment security provides the basis for learning, developing healthy relationships, positive self-esteem, effectively managing stress, learning cause-effect thinking, and many other important things. When a child is raised by a "good enough" parent who is committed to the child, sensitive to the child's emotional and physical states, largely responsive to the child's needs, and able to be insightful and reflective regarding his or her own mental states and how those affect the child, then that child is likely to develop a secure and healthy pattern of attachment. Once that pattern is formed, future relationships will be based on that secure pattern of attachment. If the parent is less than "good enough," lacking sensitivity, commitment and responsiveness, being harsh and punitive, or caught up in personal difficulties, then the child is likely to develop an insecure or disorganized pattern of attachment. In these instances, the child will show a variety of difficulties.

Another important and biologically based system is the fight-flight-freeze-appeasement system that is activated when a person experiences some threat. When faced with some threat, we may fight, flee, freeze or engage in appeasement behavior. So, what happens if the source of threat, which activates both the attachment and threat-response systems, is the source of comfort and security; the parent? In those instances, the child's psychological and mental processes will become disorganized. The child who experiences early, chronic maltreatment within a care-giving relationship, also known as Complex Trauma or Developmental Trauma Disorder, will develop a variety of difficulties and dysfunctions that the child will not grow out of, requiring specialized and therapeutic parenting.

What Happens When it Doesn't Work?

Children who have Complex Trauma and disorders of attachment will show low self-esteem. Their early experiences have "taught" them that they are unlovable, unwanted, defective, and bad. They will have problems with cause-effect thinking. Children learn, experientially, about cause-effect thinking because in early childhood their parents responded to their needs in a relatively consistent manner. The child "learned," "if I cry this way I get fed, if I cry that way I get picked up." The child learns cause-effect. In addition, the development of motivation and persistence comes from these early experiences. Why bother "trying" if your early life experiences have "taught" you that nothing you do matters? The stress of living in a chronically maltreating and threatening home causes real changes to the brain. Chronic high levels of stress hormones make it hard to learn and cause problems moving information from short-term to long-term memory. School and learning problems result. This high level of stress then becomes the normal "set point" for the child, who is now always on high alert. A child in a chronic state of high alert will have a difficult time managing stress and will easily become overwhelmed and dysregulated.

The child in your home has likely experienced chronic early maltreatment within a care-giving relationship and the resulting damage to this child's pattern of attachment, capacity to form trusting and healthy relationship with adults, capacity to form positive peer relationships, capacity to learn, ability to regulate behavior and emotions, and physical functioning will all be impaired. It is as if the lenses through which the child views the world and relationships have been distorted so that the child's experience and your experience of the same event may be vastly different. "Normal parenting," what you may have used with your birth children with great success will probably not be helpful with this child. That is not your fault. The child now in your home has a different history that causes the child to experience the world and act differently.

Think of it this way: A child is like a house. When you raise a child from birth you build the house from the foundation up. When a child is placed in your home, the foundation and some of the other structures may already be set. If the foundation is shaky, then no matter how beautiful the structure built on top of it, the building will likely be unstable and fragile, and may likely crack and crumble because of its poor foundation.

Attachment Facilitating Parenting

So what is a parent to do? We know that the four most important factors in placement stability are:

- The foster parent's own pattern of attachment, based on early relationships with the

people who raised him or her.
- The foster parent's commitment to this child.
- The foster parent's ability to be insightful and reflect on the child's experience as different from his or her own.
- The foster parent's ability to be sensitive and responsive to the child.

What these children need is a home that is stable, secure, free of physical and emotional threats, shame, or harsh and punitive methods.

A few principles for you to use are the following:
- It's about connections not compliance.
- Behavior has meaning.
- Fear is often the basis for much of what is problematic.
- Avoid saying "no."
- Keep the child close.

"It's about connections, not compliance" does NOT mean that compliance is not important. Being respectful, considerate and obedient are certainly traits that any parent would want in a child. But, how do you get that? Instilling fear, being punitive and harsh do not engender true compliance. When a child internalizes you, your values, beliefs, and approach, then you achieve true compliance; and this is achieved by creating a deep and meaningful relationship or connection with the child. Think of the story of Pinocchio. He only behaved if Jiminy Cricket was on his shoulder; when Jiminy was gone, Pinocchio got into trouble. Pinocchio only became a real flesh and blood boy when he and his foster father Gepetto developed a connection and an emotionally meaningful relationship; when Pinocchio went to rescue Gepetto from the whale. Gepetto was always there for Pinocchio. Gepetto was accepting, loving, and provided unconditional love and acceptance of the person.

All behavior is adaptive and has meaning. As a therapeutic parent you want to dig down below the surface to figure out for the child what is driving the behavior. Responding to the surface behavior of symptom will not be helpful; what helps is figuring out the cause of the problem behavior, and addressing that. Most often, what will be at the root of problem behavior will be fear and the child's difficult early experiences. Does the child take things that do not belong to the child? Well, that may be a good example of the child just not experiencing adults as helpful and of chronic early neglect. The child may be "help-blind" and not see the help that is right in front of the child. So, when the child needs something, the child takes what the child needs. It does not even occur to the child to ask for lunch money. So, why doesn't the child learn when you tell the child to "just ask me?" Even though the child may "know" to ask rather than "take," sometimes under stress, the child may not think clearly. Chronic stress can result in the child becoming easily dysregulated and unable to access information in memory; a real cognitive impairment.

Keeping the child close and interacting with the child is an important aspect of therapeutic parenting. By keeping the child close, you will be able to perceive what the child is feeling and experiencing, then put that into words for the child. Because the child cannot do it, you must do it for the child. Remove obstacles to the relationship as a means to avoid saying, "NO." Most often WHAT the child is asking for is acceptable, it is the timing that is off; so you can say yes to most things.

Child: Can I watch a movie? (Said at 8:30 p.m. on a school night.)
Parent: Sure, this Friday we'll rent a DVD and have popcorn.

Child: Can I go to Mary's house? (Asked on a school night before home work is done.)
Parent: You bet, after you clean your room and finish your homework.

Child: Can I drive the car? (age 14).
Parent: As soon as you get your license!

So, as a foster parent, you are the most important adult in this child's life at this moment. You can be a huge positive influence on this child, IF you understand the child and use the right parenting approaches. The child in your home has been the victim of awful things; you cannot make that go away, but you can go a long way toward fixing the foundation and helping the child build a better future.

Arthur Becker-Weidman, PhD, has been treating the families of adoptive and foster children for more than three decades. He has achieved Diplomate Status in child psychology and forensic psychology from the American Board of Psychological Specialties, is a registered clinician with the Association for the Treatment and Training in the Attachment of Children, and is a certified therapist, consultant, and trainer in Dyadic Developmental Psychotherapy®©. He is the director of the Center For Family Development and consults with governments, social services departments, residential treatment centers, mental health clinics, and professionals throughout the world. Becker-Weidman has published widely and he is the co-editor of the books, ***Creating Capacity for Attachment, and Attachment Parenting****. Art's newest book is* ***Dyadic Developmental Psychotherapy: Essential Practices & Methods****. Weidman has also published a number of DVDs useful for parents and trainers. More information can be found on his website at www.Center4FamilyDevelop.com. Material for this article is from several of his books, (in particular,* ***Attachment Parenting*** *edited by Arthur Becker-Weidman and Deborah Shell, Jason Aronson, Lanham, MD, 2010).*

People lie to you about your birth family: That some foster parents and case workers will tell you is your "parents died or didn't want you" instead of telling the truth that they made poor choices and are mentally ill and chose drugs, alcohol, and men over taking proper care of their children. You need to also hear some good things about your parents like they were good artists, musicians or were pretty.

– Mariah Berry,17, has beenin and out of foster care since age 3 and was in more than 30 homes. She was finally adopted at age 14.

The Attachment Spectrum

Attachment is a Long-term Process

Edited by Doris Landry, MS, LLP

Attachment Theory indicates that children do not break former attachments but rather, add more attachment figures, suggesting that parents of adopted and foster children need to understand how their child has been emotionally affected by a history that may have included multiple caregivers, loss, malnutrition, illness, abuse, and neglect. Helping our children move from the insecurity of less-than-adequate treatment to seek closeness as a means to a healthy and secure attachment is of primary importance. A child's secure attachment to his or her parents and foster parents will benefit every aspect of his or her life, and contribute immeasurably to the parent's joy in parenting. The following are styles of attachment:

Secure

Secure babies freely explore and even engage strangers while with their mothers. They will be visibly upset when separated from mom and greet her with pleasure and excitement when reunited. They mold to the shape of their mother's body when consoled, hang on to their mother when scared, and enjoy playful facial games and eye contact. Secure children develop trust and self-regulation, as well as learn self-reliance. The development of meaningful relationships and an ability to cope with stress and frustration allows for the attainment of their full intellectual potential.

Anxious/Ambivalent

Traits of an Insecure/Avoidant child:

- Anxious of exploration and of strangers in the presence of mother.
- Inconsolable and in distress when mother departs.
- Reunions with mother are resentful, yet needs closeness. ("hold me close/let go of me!")
- Resistant when mother initiates attention.

Older children may:

- Make parent work hard to find ways to satisfy child's needs; controlling.
- Exhibit extreme anxiety which may be exhibited by constant movement or chatter.
- Ask for hug, and then cry out "it hurts."
- Ask for help, then make the parent feel inadequate.

Insecure/Avoidant

Traits of an Insecure/Avoidant child:

- Avoids and ignores the mother.
- Does limited exploration even with mother present.
- Strangers not treated much differently than mother.
- Expresses little emotional range, less able to pretend play.
- Passively resists efforts to be soothed.

Older children may:

- Find ways to care for self, not needing others.
- Show little interest in parents; exhibits no fear of strangers.
- Exhibit stilted play; won't ask for help.

Insecure/Disorganized

Traits of an Insecure/Disorganized child:

- Lacks a coherent style or pattern of interacting due to erratic care.
- Perceives that caregivers are frightened (and are frightening).
- Acts alarmed, freezing in place under stress.
- Acts rejected or abandoned.
- Often behaves in ways indicative of abuse.

Older children may:

- Exhibit hurtful behaviors to animals or other people.
- Exhibit behaviors of former abuse with little or no remorse.

Reactive Attachment Disorder (RAD)

Children age five or younger can be diagnosed with Reactive Attachment Disorder if one of the following is present:

1) their behavior is reactive to care that had a persistent disregard for their basic emotional and physical needs, or

2) they had repeated changes of primary caregivers (i.e., no one to attach to prior to adoption). After the age of five, Reactive Attachment Disorder can manifest in children as Oppositional Defiant Disorder, progressing to more severe problems such as Conduct Disorder. These children may have little conscience or fear of consequence, will hurt, lie, and steal without remorse, and will not respond normally to nurturing or discipline. A baby or young child with Reactive Attachment Disorder is an extremely traumatized child, and requires intensive treatment and specialized parenting, as does an older child exhibiting opposition to authority, defiance, or general disturbed conduct behaviors.

The deprived infant/child, the one not held, fed, cuddled and "claimed," needs to be given the opportunity to experience missed sensations.
This is most often accomplished through occupational therapy but the missing component is usually the parent... treatment needs to be experienced within the context of a meaningful relationship.

Further, it is suggested that the treatment be through the parent.
This means the occupational therapist must work with the parent to teach them to do the interventions.

– Doris Landry, MS

Doris Landry, MS, LLP, is a psychologist with a master's degree in clinical psychology who maintains a full-time practice in Michigan. She privately treats children and their parents who are experiencing adoption or attachment issues. Her website is www.adoptionparenting.net. This article originally appeared in ***Adoption Parenting: Creating a Toolbox, Building Connections.***

Online Resources

Adoption Parenting
www.adoptionparenting.net

Adoption & Foster Care School Awareness Project (ASAP)
www.asapmass.org

A Forever Family
www.a4everfamily.org

ATTACh
www.attach.org

Attachment and Trauma Network
www.radzebra.org

Attachment Disorder Site
www.attachmentdisorder.net

Attachment Disorder Support Group
http://adsg.syix.com

Attachment Institute of New England
www.attachmentnewengland.com

Center for Adoption Support and Education (C.A.S.E.) www.adoption-support.org

Child Trauma Institute
www.childtrauma.com

Love & Logic
www.loveandlogic.com

Nancy Thomas Parenting www.nancythomasparenting.com

National Federation of Families for Children's Mental Health
www.ffcmh.org

Older Child Adoption Support
www.olderchildadoptionsupport.com

RADKID.ORG
www.RadKid.org

Fostering Regressive Behavior

By Corinne Watt

My daughter was placed with me at age five as a foster child. I had been pursuing adopting a child for three years, so I'd had plenty of time to read all the books and go to all the conferences, learning the current theories on dealing with these hurt and traumatized children from the system.

A lot of my education and support came from AdoptionUK, a British charity that promotes "The Wall." The Wall is a graphic illustration of how unmet physical and emotional needs early in life effect children's later development, requiring different parenting techniques and support for adoptive parents (see page 161). Foster and adoptive parents care for children whose emotional foundation will have missing or damaged "bricks." Allowing a child to go through early experiences again may help to repair his or her wall, and build attachment to a new family. My daughter had spent almost three years in a temporary foster placement, and was eager to have a permanent home and family. She had been well prepared by her social worker that I was her "new mummy."

And so I decided to take a regressive approach. I allowed her to revisit what it was like to be a young infant, but in a more consistent and safe environment. It also allowed me to experience what effectively I had also missed out on by being placed with a school-aged child.

Just as done for a newborn, I was the sole caregiver for my daughter in the first few weeks. For the six weeks until school began I was never more than a room away from her. She was small and underweight for her age, so I was able to carry her a lot. Most of this was at her request, as she was shy and overwhelmed by the changes around her, causing her to cling to me. I later discovered that her birth family had refused to carry her once she learned to walk, and had dragged her around with reins on.

I kept her world small and manageable for as long as possible. She had moved from a small village to a large town after just three weeks of visits with me. So we only visited the same local shops for some time, the same park, and we watched one television channel for preschool children, where familiar programs were often repeated.

She loved imaginative play, so it wasn't a great leap for me to offer her a bottle of warm milk and suggest she be the baby. This became something that she would request, particularly at times when she was upset. We would go through the whole process of checking how much she had eaten, and burping her, which she greatly enjoyed. It was obvious that she had not been fed in a way that encouraged attunement, as initially I would get no eye contact from her. It took many months for this to eventually happen and for both of us to be comfortable. It was 18 months before she was comfortable with me stroking her face or hair, and we had many other sensory issues to overcome.

She was a slow eater and would often get bored and want to leave the table even when still hungry. So feeding became a game that would keep her occupied and ensured she ate enough. Like a small toddler, she loved each mouthful to fly in like an airplane, or chug in like a train. Again her early feeding may have been forced as she found puréed food intolerable and would actually balk at eating it. She also did not seem to recognize when she was thirsty, so every drink required persuasion or was turned into a race between us, which of course she had to win.

When she was six she started losing her baby teeth. When she was seven, at one point she had five missing front teeth, which made biting difficult. This was another opportunity, and I bought soothing gel for babies' gums and little teething biscuits for when her new teeth started to work their way through.

Bath time was traumatic, or rather after bath time, which was probably linked to past memories. In the tub we had bubbles and a lot of toys and we would play together happily as I knelt beside her. As soon as I pulled the plug the problems started. She could not bear to be touched to be dried, so a soft hooded towel was necessary. I still can't imagine what the neighbors must have thought of the screaming, splashing, and accusations as I tried to get her safely out. Over time I discovered she liked the smell of a brand of antiseptic cream and baby talc. Eventually she would let me put it onto her scrapes and bruises, and rub talc on her back and feet.

For bedtime, she was delighted when I found lovely, soft, one-piece pajamas that had feet and zipped up just like an infant's jammies. She had never taken a pacifier before, but gathered a whole collection of them. I had made a soft quilt in the months waiting for a child to be placed, and this became her special cover. Falling asleep was a whole other issue…

Getting dressed was frustrating. Buttons couldn't be done or undone. She couldn't figure out which way round tops should go on. She wasn't always organized enough to take the old underwear off before putting on the clean pair. So there was more opportunity for mummy to help, showing her dressing can be done calmly, gently and with a few nursery rhymes thrown into the mix.

It is amazing how children of any age can engage in "peek-a-boo" or "round and

Building Relationships With Young Children:
Toddler Adoption: The Weaver's Craft
by Mary Hopkins-Best

First Steps in Parenting the Child Who Hurts
by Caroline Archer

Attaching in Adoption, Practical Tools for Today's Parents by Deborah D. Gray

Parenting the Hurt Child: Helping Adoptive Families Heal and Grow
by Gregory Peck and Regina M. Kupecky

round the garden" games. When most of my touch was not tolerated, we could still play "one potato, two potato." And she never considered herself too old to play with toys for a younger child. When just learning to read, board books with one word per page were ideal again. I found that in her awkward and argumentative moments I could engage with her in baby talk, making up words or talking in rhymes. We don't have hugs or cuddles, we have cuggles!

In the first couple of years we had some major behavioral issues to deal with, where triggers would set off intense rage and aggression directed toward me. This could be after contact with previous carers, or emotional events such as school starting after holidays, birthdays or even watching a movie that brought up feelings of loss or rejection. In these episodes I would have to try to protect both myself and my daughter from physical harm. I found the safest way was to wrap her in a blanket and hold her until it passed. At the time, these were distressing for me, but with hindsight I can see that they always led to a catharsis, where screaming, biting and kicking or punching would dissolve into tears, apologies and a desire to be held, rocked and soothed.

Developmental delays, Reactive Attachment Disorder, and Attention Deficit Hyperactivity Disorder have all been mentioned as explanations for her behaviors. Fetal Alcohol Spectrum Disorder could most likely be added to the list. But a label wouldn't help us in any way to have made this journey.

We have now been together for more than three years, and the "baby game" is played less often. My daughter is calmer, more confident and becoming more independent. She last asked for a bottle the night before she started her fourth year at school. But she said she was "no longer a baby," and sat in my lap to drink it like a toddler. My little girl is growing up and her Wall is getting stronger.

Corinne M. Watt, lives in the United Kingdom. She is a mental health nurse and single adoptive parent. She does voluntary work for her local church as a child protection coordinator and for AdoptionUK facilitating a local support group and family events for foster and adoptive families.

The Wall: Why adopted children need a different kind of parenting

With the majority of children adopted from the care system coming from an abusive or neglectful background, it is unsurprising that many adoptive parents struggle to overcome the consequences of this difficult start to life.

The Wall is a graphic illustration of how unmet physical and emotional needs early in life affect children's later development, requiring different parenting techniques and support for adoptive parents.

To view this helpful information, visit www.adoptionuk.org/information/103254/thewall/

The wall of a typical child:

5-9yrs	Roles	Choices	Tasks	Support	Love
	Learning	Opportunities	Friendships	Independence	Self-Reliance
2-5yrs	Interaction	Friends	Love	Trust	Boundaries
	Play	Language	Encouragement	Security	Social Skills
6mths-2yrs	Speech	Family	Security	Belonging	Love
	Boundaries	Friends	Understanding	Supervision	Safety
0-6mths	Stimulation	Eye Contact	Security	Belonging	Attunement
	Love	Cuddles	Milk	Warmth	Comfort

The wall of a child from a neglectful background:

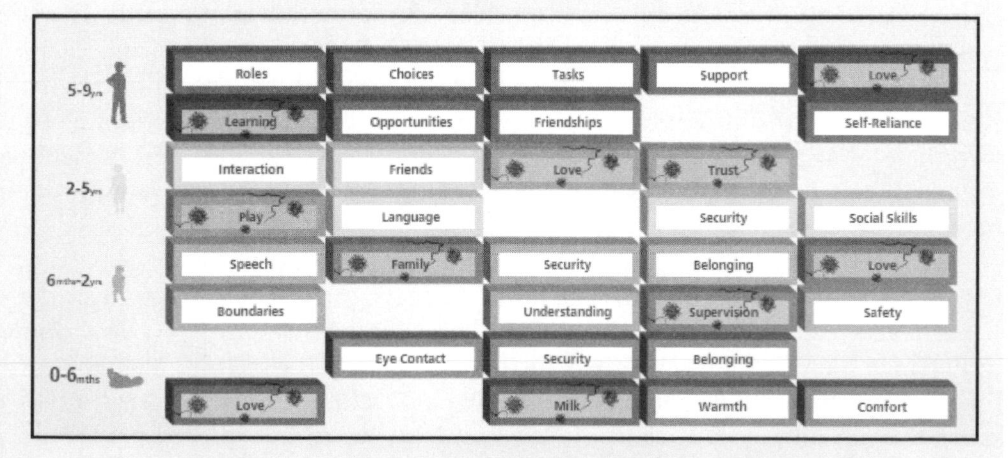

Breaking Through

By Erik A. Cooper

When he first arrived in my foster home, Rusty seemed painfully shy, quiet and withdrawn. Rumors of Rusty's fury were shared among his brothers, Richard, Ryan and Bryce. The second eldest of his family, Rusty had the temperament of a silverback gorilla. Rusty's older and younger siblings were both submissive and tamed around him, avoiding any spark of his temper while staying clear of his path. Slightly taller than most 11-year-old boys his age, Rusty was still just a boy to me. He was my foster child, someone I needed to understand, reach, and help break through.

Only two days after Thanksgiving, the four boys were surrendered by their mother to foster care. According to child welfare officials, Wal-Mart needed the land of their rented green house to build another Supercenter. I learned the boys were victims of neglect, sharing a tiny abode with the man their mother was currently dating. Rusty and his brothers reportedly shared the same bed and would later tell me they shared a toothbrush too. But when their mother's relationships ended, they moved on, changing schools once more, leaving neighborhood friendships behind, losing whatever clothes or toys they could not carry.

I knew these boys before we ever met. On my way to and from the county child welfare office, I'd drive past that tiny green home, seeing the boys cling to their mother's side while waiting for the school bus, swinging from a rope-strung tire beneath the protective branch of an old oak tree, or racing one another across the lawn on lazy summer afternoons. From my vantage point, in a car driving by, everything seemed fine. Like most people we never meet, I could never have known the boys' survival depended upon their mother's next short-term job, gratuities of a stand-in father, or handouts from the state. But inside that house, within the boundaries of this family's life, remained four hungry boys, a shared bed and a single frayed toothbrush.

Like many children we receive in our foster homes, these boys came with little information from the state. My only way of getting to know the boys was to hear from the boys themselves, their stories of Mom's abusive boyfriend who once threw Richard across the room and into a wall, how the boys helped hide an uncle on the run from police in an upstairs attic, and how Rusty's ears came off after a horrific traffic crash. Doctors sewed his ears back on, they said, and proved their tale with Rusty's scars.

Despite all of their challenges, these four were good kids who suffered greatly. Reaching them would require open ears, a soft heart and strong discipline. Together, they were helpful at home and eager to learn anything I could teach them. Reaching kids like Richard, Ryan, and Bryce was easy, but breaking through to Rusty would require much more.

The once sullen, withdrawn, and apprehensive young man finally opened up during our first confrontation in my kitchen. A homework assignment sent Rusty over the edge. While his brothers eagerly worked to complete their assignments and I prepared dinner, Rusty sat in defiance, pencil down, eyebrows furrowed. I pleaded with him, bargaining extra playtime before dinner and a later bedtime. He flatly refused. "It's too hard. I don't understand the questions. I just can't do it!" I sat with Rusty and offered help.

All of the obvious signs showed Rusty was capable of doing the work. But with my eyes fixed on the page and not on his, I missed the obvious – the growing impatience, his reddening face, his shortening temper. Frustrated, he snapped the pencil in half and threw it at me marking my shirt. He stormed out of the kitchen and upstairs to the playroom, yelling, "That's it! No more! I'm finished with my (expletive) homework!"

I gave him his space and returned to making dinner, until bodies began to bounce from the floor joists. I rushed upstairs to find Rusty pummeling his older brother, fists flying every direction, hitting me in the face, chest and arms as I approached. Without any training on how to calm an enraged child, I took Rusty by the wrists and collapsed with him to the floor. "Get off of me!" he screamed, flailing around like a suffocating fish out of water. "Get off! Get off you (expletive) (expletive)!"

"Are you going to calm down?" I asked, Rusty's face now enflamed, his once blue eyes now fiery red. He sucked what snot he had in him and flung it in my face. "I'll just wipe it off. You can't hurt me Rusty. You need to calm down."

"Get off! Get off of me!" he yelled, his brothers watching our exchange as Richard wiped blood from a cut Rusty's long fingernails made above his eye. How long could I do this? How am I supposed to stop an enraged boy? What do the police do with kids like this? Minutes grew longer, his panting slowed, and I finally released him from my grip.

This was not the Rusty I first met, the boy who seemed quiet, shy, and withdrawn. This boy was a ticking time bomb, angry to be separated from his mother, angry to be told to do homework, angry to be in foster care.

Weeks after this confrontation, Rusty's fingernails kept short to the quick, his teacher requested a conference. She received Rusty's Individual Education Plan, something his caseworker never shared, and said Rusty was in the wrong class. Through our meeting, I learned Rusty suffered learning disabilities and an IQ of 73. With this information earlier, Rusty would never have been placed in the wrong class, assigned homework he could never complete, or restrained to the floor by a foster dad trying to help.

Like many of our foster children, Rusty entered, left, and re-entered my foster care again. While I could not control his comings and goings under the state's direction, I knew I could reach this boy in small ways during each of our opportunities together. As his foster parent, I owed Rusty my patience, tolerance, and understanding.

During each of Rusty's return visits, I gained a greater understanding of his behaviors through our one-on-one time together. I realized Rusty exploded when he interacted with his brothers, classmates, and neighborhood kids. He suffered the tauntings all kids his age suffer, but for Rusty, he battled an emotional tug-of-war to do right versus wrong, and responded with violence much sooner than the situation demanded. At times, I believed I would never connect with Rusty, to help him help himself, to control his behaviors and, hopefully, keep him out of jail as an adult.

My breakthrough with Rusty didn't occur until our trip to a theme park with his brothers. We rode nearly every ride, from water flumes to haunted houses, bumper cars to arcade games. But when we approached the Dahlonega Mine Train, a roller coaster racing through vertical climbs and darkened tunnels, Rusty panicked.

"I don't wanna go," he said.

His brothers taunted him, the moment of excitement overwhelming the memories of their earlier taunts sending Rusty over the edge.

"C'mon Rusty! Don't be a ba-by!" they called.

I looked at Rusty, deep into his eyes, and saw the beginnings of a transformation from the boy having a great day to an emerging demon fighting to come out. Suddenly, I understood. The flood of our earlier battles, his fist-flying tirades, Rusty's relentless blasts of emotional baggage all made sense.

I knelt down within jab-striking range, took Rusty by the chin, looked deeply into his eyes and beyond the demon, reaching the boy who wanted to maintain his self-control and said, "Rusty. It's okay. I love you."

Those simple words shook this boy out of his rising fury and returned him to a safe place, a place with no challenge to ride a scary ride, no judgments that he's a wimp if he doesn't go, and no failures if he doesn't try. He was safe and he was loved. We skipped the mine train, leaving it behind for another day when Rusty wanted to ride.

Reaching through to our foster children requires a great deal of patience, tolerance, and understanding. As foster parents, we may not reach our kids the day they arrive, or even months after. But try and try again, and we will break through.

*Erik A. Cooper has served as a foster parent for 42 foster children. Cooper has written several articles for **Fostering Families Today** and **Adoption Today**, and is currently writing a memoir and screenplay. This article originally appeared in **Fostering Family Today** magazine.*

The most challenging aspect of transitioning from an abusive home life to foster care has been developing my trust for my foster parents. Regardless of their verbalized dedication and compassionate action, trust was undoubtedly a difficult obstacle for me to overcome. The trauma had shaped my foundation of trust more than I had ever realized. In general, I always had struggled to keep my brick wall standing. I wanted to protect my heart, that was all. Too many times, I allowed the adults around me to take advantage of my tolerance of abuse. So I didn't know how to handle such a transition, despite so many transitions. Parental support was a foreign experience for me, and trust followed in due time. Ironically, my foster parents (the people I had the most trouble trusting) became the people who have impacted my life the most since being in foster care.

– Kristine Burbano, foster youth

Creating PLACE

Parenting to Create a Sense of Safety
By Daniel Hughes, PhD

A child can best be understood by focusing not so much on the behavior that you can observe, but rather on the nature of the child's intentions which underlie the behavior. The child's intentions include the thoughts, feelings, perceptions, and motives that are associated with the resultant behavior. Often these features of the child's inner life are associated with previous events that were traumatic and/or shameful, so the meaning of the behavior is often closely tied to the meaning of those past events in the child's mind.

To ignore the child's inner life, we will have only the most superficial understanding of him or her. To encourage the development and expression of the child's inner life we need to first make him or her feel safe. If a child knows he or she will be judged negatively for his or her intentions, they will remain hidden. To provide the experience of safety, a parent might well consider PLACE. Representing the five parent attitude qualities of Playfulness, Love, Acceptance, Curiosity, and Empathy, PLACE creates a sense of safety that facilitates self-discovery and communication. PLACE also describes the nature of a home which serves both as a secure base for exploring the world, and a safe haven where one can return when the world becomes too stressful.

Playfulness. Playfulness characterizes the frequent parent-infant reciprocal interactions when the infant is in the quiet-alert state of consciousness. Both parent and infant are clearly enjoying being with each other while being engaged in the delightful experience of getting to know each other. Both are feeling safe and relaxed. Neither feels judged nor criticized. These experiences of playfulness – combined with comfort when a child is distressed – serve as the infant's original experience of parental love.

During frequent moments of playfulness, both parent and child become aware of how much they like each other. Playful moments reassure both that their conflicts and separations are temporary and will never harm the strength of their attachment. Playfulness also provides opportunities to convey affection when more direct expressions may be resisted. The child is likely to respond with less anger and defensiveness when the parent is able to convey a touch of playfulness in discipline techniques. While such a response would not be appropriate at the time of major misbehavior, when applied to minor behaviors playfulness keeps the behavior in perspective. The behavior is a threat to neither the relationship nor the worth of the child.

Love. When it is the central motive for the parents' interactions with their child, love enables the child to have confidence that what underlies the parents' behaviors involves the intention to do what is in the best interests of the child. Love, when it is expressed most fully, conveys both enjoyment and commitment. The child needs to know that basically his or her parent "likes" him or her, enjoys being his or her parent, and looks forward to having fun together. While at times enjoyment may not be obvious, for the child to feel loved, he or she needs to be confident that commitment is always present even when moments of reciprocal enjoyment are not. During these moments there remains an assumption that this basic "liking" will return.

Fundamental to the sense of being loved is the child's conviction that his or her parents will do what is in the child's best interest. The parent will do whatever it takes to keep the

Bubbles of Happiness

My goal is to create "bubbles of happiness" each day. As many as I can! I check in with my children often, and ask them regularly, "What's the best thing about today/this month/this week?" Then I ask them what they remember most in the same time frame.

What they will take with them into their adults lives are the small joys, celebrations, and successes – moments of fun and laughter. Creating these bubbles each day, both in thought, mind, and experience, and shaping the meaning my children are making from their lives is something that I have a lot of fun with. This brings things down to an achievable goal that is more often successful than not. Success encourages me to keep working; the more positive interactions I have with my children, the stronger our relationship becomes.

We each shape how our children make their own meaning and weave their own tapestry. How we frame things, how we teach values, how we weave our perception of their personal tapestry might be something that we haven't truly been conscious of before. How do we do that? What skills do we have? What resources do we have? How might we improve what we're doing now? Not in the "I have to be perfect" thinking, but in the spirit of continued self assessment and forward growth.

– Deborah Anderson, birth mom, biological mom, and adoptive mom

child safe and to ensure that his or her basic needs will be met and his or her rights will be respected. "Hard times" will pass without abuse, neglect, or abandonment because the child's welfare is at the core of the parents' daily motives, decisions, and behaviors with regard to their child. Children who have lost their first parents for whatever reason need ongoing signs that their relationship with their adoptive parents is permanent – that they will never be "given away" regardless of the crises or conflicts that lie ahead.

Acceptance. Unconditional acceptance is at the core of the child's sense of safety, value, and relaxed sharing with his or her parent. Within acceptance the child becomes convinced that his or her core sense of self is worthwhile and valued by his or her parents. The child's behavior may be criticized and limited, but not his or her "self." The child becomes confident that conflict and discipline involves behavior, not the relationship with his or her parents or his or her self-worth. While the behavior of the child may be evaluated and limited, the thoughts, feelings, perceptions, and motives of the child never are. The child's inner life simply "is;" it is not "right" or "wrong." Am I suggesting that if a child says to his or her parents that he or she does not like his or her brother and wishes that he or she lived somewhere else, such expressions are "Okay"? Yes – and the fact that your child disclosed hisor her inner life to you may well reflect his or her trust that you will not dislike him or her because he or she has such thoughts and wishes.

If the child is criticized for his or her inner life, the child will most likely begin to conceal it as well as feel ashamed of that aspect. When the child is safe to communicate his or her inner life, his or her parents will be able to understand the struggle with his or her brother, the reasons for the struggles, and possible ways to reduce them. When the child is not safe, the parent will be left with simply disciplining inappropriate behavior toward his or her brother, without addressing the underlying causes. When the child knows that his or her parents understand his or her dislike and wishes to have his or her brother "go away," often his or her experience of the brother begins to change on its own, the behavior problems reduce on their own, and there is no need for the parent to "fix" the problem. When the inner life is not expressed and accepted, the parent is often constantly managing conflicts between their children.

Accepting the child's intentions does not imply accepting the behavior. The parent may be firm in limiting behavior while at the same time accepting the motives for the behavior. In fact, this combination of making a clear difference between unconditional acceptance of intentions and presenting expectations regarding behaviors is probably the most effective way for your child to experience less shame toward self and more guilt toward others when engaging in inappropriate behavior.

Inner-directed guilt, in the absence of pervasive shame, is probably the most effective circumstance for facilitating socially appropriate behaviors.

Curiosity. Curiosity without judgment is crucial if the child is to become aware of his or her inner life and then communicate it to his or her parents. Curiosity does not mean adopting an annoyed, lecturing, tone and demanding, "Why did you do that?" Curiosity involves a quiet, accepting tone that conveys a simple desire to understand your child: "What do you think was going on? What do you think that was about?" The child most often knows that his or her behavior was not appropriate. The child often does not know why he or she did it or the child is reluctant to tell his or her parent why. With curiosity the parents are conveying their intention to simply understand "why" and to assist the child in such understanding. The parents' intentions are to assist the child, not lecture him or her nor convince him or her that his or her inner life is "bad" or "wrong."

With curiosity, the parents convey a confidence that by understanding the underlying intentions behind the behavior, they will discover qualities in the child that are not shameful. As the understanding deepens, the parent and child will discover that the behavior does not reflect something "bad" within the child, but rather a thought, feeling, perception, or motive that was stressful, frightening, and/or confusing and seemingly could only be expressed in behavior. As the understanding deepens, the child becomes aware that he or she can communicate inner distress to his or her parents. There is no need for the inappropriate behavior. The behavior does not reflect his or her being "bad." The child is much less likely to engage in that behavior again, since there is no need for it. The child is also more able to step back from the behavior, be less defensive about it, and experience guilt about it.

For curiosity to be experienced as helpful it cannot be communicated with any annoyance about the behavior. Nor is it presented as a lecture that provides an excuse to "process" a behavior in what amounts to rational blaming. Curiosity is a "not-knowing" stance involving a genuine desire to understand and nothing more. When it leads to the child developing a deeper understanding of himself or herself and a deeper sense that his or her parents understand and accept him or her, it will, when combined with empathy, naturally lead to a reduction in the inappropriate behavior much more effectively than will focusing on behavioral consequences.

Empathy. Empathy enables the child to feel his or her parents' compassion for him or her, just as curiosity enables the child to know that his or her parents understand him or her. With empathy the parent is journeying with the child into the distress that he or she is experiencing and then feeling it with him or her. Parents are demonstrating that they know how difficult an experience is for their child. They are communicating that their child will not have to deal with the distress alone. They will stay with the child emotionally, comfort and support him or her, and not abandon him or her in times of need. The parents are also communicating their strength and commitment. The pain that the child is experiencing is not too much for them. The parents are also communicating their confidence that by sharing the child's distress, it will not be too much for him or her. Together they will get through it.

Empathy enables a child to develop his or her affective resources so that he or she can resolve and integrate many difficult emotional experiences. He or she will be able to manage such experiences without being overwhelmed by anxiety, rage, shame, or despair. Curiosity enables a child to develop reflective resources that will enable him or her to understand himself or herself more deeply including intentions underlying his or her actions. With both empathy and curiosity parents lend themselves to the child for the purpose of developing the affective/reflective skills necessary for him or her to be able to act in ways that are in the best interests of both self and other. Researchers are increasingly clear that it is deficiencies in these affective and reflective skills that are often at the core of behavioral problems.

In essence, PLACE focuses on the whole child, not simply his or her behavior. PLACE facilitates attachment security and the closely related affective and reflective skills that are so necessary for maintaining a successful and satisfying life. The child discovers that he or she is doing the best possible, he or she is not "bad" or "lazy" or "selfish." Through PLACE and the associated attachment security, the child is discovering that he or she can now do better. The child can learn to rely on his or her parents and they will facilitate the development of his or her inner life and behavioral choices in a manner that he or she could never do alone. Then as he or she experiences PLACE first hand, time and again, these same qualities will become part of his or her stance toward others – now toward parents and friends, and later also toward a partner and children. The child will clearly know that both intentions and behavior matter. The child will also know that both "self" and "other" matter.

When we angrily lecture and scold a child about behavior and make assumptions about his or her equally unacceptable thoughts, feelings, perceptions, and motives, the child is not feeling safe. The child is likely to become shameful, isolated, and defensive, all of which will reduce the likelihood that he or she will change the behaviors. If instead, parents relate with PLACE, he or she will be likely to feel safe even when the child's behavior is being limited. The child too will strive to understand his or her inner life and associated behaviors. Feeling safe that the "self" is not being attacked and that his or her attachments with his or her parents are still secure, the child is likely to become motivated to change the behavior.

Daniel Hughes, PhD, is a clinician specializing in the treatment of children and youth with severe emotional and behavioral problems. His website is www.danielhughes.org.
This article originally appeared in ***Adoption Parenting: Creating a Toolbox, Building Connections.***

Bonding is a Vital Issue: Appellate Courts Agree

By James A. Kenny, PhD, and Mark Bontrager, MSW, JD

Bonding has too often been loosely defined. Mental health professionals, in their reports, have been vague and fuzzy, offering opinion rather than data, generalizations rather than facts. As a result, courts and case managers may not have given bonding the critical consideration it deserves.

Bonding Defined

Bonding must be practically defined in ways the court can accept and understand. The dictionary defines a bond as "a unique relationship between two people enduring for long periods, even a lifetime." The authors amplify this definition:

> ***"Bonding is a significant reciprocal attachment which both parties want and expect to continue, and which is interrupted or terminated at considerable peril to the parties involved."***

Bonding can be specifically defined in four concrete and evidentiary ways, any one of which is sufficient to indicate its presence:

1. Time in place.
2. The behavior of the child.
3. Reciprocal attachment.
4. Family identification.

1. Time in Place

Humans bond by sharing important events in daily life, such as eating, sleeping, and playing with each other. Time spent together is one factual way to measure bonding. In a parent-child setting, bonding is likely after three months. Research indicates that this is the length of time that normal human beings take to adjust to new and/or difficult situations. This three-month period is reflected in folk wisdom (the grieving time following a death), the probationary period when starting a new job, and in the description of many psychiatric disorders (the time allowed to "adjust" before an illness is diagnosed.) (DSM-IV-TR) In other words people usually take up to three months to adapt to a new situation.

Bonding is probable after six months. Normal children will adjust and attach well within this period. Indiana regulations for selecting an adoptive home recognize this fact. The Indiana Child Welfare Manual (805.12) recommends that preference for adoption be given to foster parents who have had the child in their home for six months or more.

Bonding is almost certain after one year, unless one is dealing with an unbonded (psychopathic) child. These children may be incapable of bonding with anyone. Even in the case of an unbonded child, the court may recognize the willingness of the prospective home to make a permanent adoptive commitment to the child. One year is a long time in the life of a child. For this reason, the Adoption and Safe Families Act (ASFA Summary) has attempted to set a limit on the time a child can be kept in temporary care. "A petition to terminate parental rights shall be filed for parents whose child has been in foster care for 15 of the last 22 months...." ASFA recognizes that it is harmful and even abusive to move a child who has been with a family for one year or more.

2. The Behavior of the Child

Bonding can be assessed by observing and documenting the behavior of the child. Interest and attentiveness, dependency, pleasure and joy, calmness, assertiveness, appropriate protest and anger, eye contact, copying mannerisms, staying close, etc. With children older than three: self-limit-setting and empathy (Belsky et al, 1988). Checklists such as the Randolph Attachment Disorder Questionnaire, Keck's list of Attachment Symptoms, and the Indiana Bonding and Attachment Checklist can be used to record behavioral evidence of bonding.

3. Reciprocal Attachment

Bonding flows both ways. A third way to measure bonding is to evaluate the promise expressed by the actual or potential parent. How well do they know the child? How strong is the promise they are willing to make? The potential adoptive parents can be asked to explain the depth of their commitment. The court should consider the quality of the commitment to permanence. "I want you for my forever child. I will always be there for you. As long as I live. Even after you are 18. You will never be 'emancipated' from my concern. When life hits you hard and you need a place to go. When you need money. When you go through a divorce. Or a death. My home is now your home. And when I die, you will have an inheritance."

4. Family Identification

Many state child welfare departments have definitions of bonding that consider how the relationship is viewed by the rest of the community. The Indiana Child Welfare Manual (805.12) lists three criteria for demonstrating a bond: "(a) The child identifies as a member of the family, and the family considers the child to be a family member. (b) The child is perceived to be a member of the family and is treated as such by the community, e.g. school, friends, neighbors, or extended family members. (c) The child has developed reliance upon and trust in the family, while in their care."

Bonding Outweighs Kinship

What determines a relationship? A relative is someone to whom you are related. There are many ways to relate or be related. Biological parents pass on their genes. Parents-in-place (de facto parents) pass on their culture and habits. Both are enduring.

Children form significant attachments to adults who meet their physical and emotional needs, regardless of any biological connection. This bonding outweighs biological kinship, not because the biological parents may not have certain "rights," but because these rights are superceded by the serious harm that can result from moving a bonded child. As ASFA says repeatedly, the child's rights are paramount.

The marriage bond is one example of a non-blood tie that is both significant and enduring. The relationship of husband and wife is an emotional bond amplified by a legal commitment. As such, it takes precedence over the spouses' biological relationship to their parents. Jesus commented on the precedence of the marital bond over that with the birth family: "...A man must leave father and mother and cling to his wife...." (Matthew, 19:5)

Interrupted Bonding

Bonded relationships are critical in child development. When a bonded relationship is threatened or severed, trauma results. Bowlby (1979) speaks eloquently of the resultant danger of losing the capacity for intimacy: "Many of the most intense of all human emotions arise during the formation, the maintenance, the disruption, and the renewal of affectional bonds...in terms of subjective experience, the formation of a bond is described as falling in love, maintaining a bond as loving someone, and losing a partner as grieving over someone. Similarly, threat of loss arouses anxiety and actual loss causes sorrow; whilst both situations are likely to arouse anger. Finally, the unchallenged maintenance of a bond is experienced as a source of security, and the renewal of a bond as a source of joy."

What is the cost of severing bonded relationships? Interrupted bonding takes a heavy toll on human health and well-being. It is as serious as divorce, brain surgery, or death. The younger the child and the deeper the bond, the more devastating will be the impact. The price tag is high, either immediately or later in adult life.

Interrupted bonding commonly contributes to or causes some of the following psychiatric disorders in children: Reactive Attachment Disorder, Oppositional Defiant Disorder, Attention Deficit Disorder, Adjustment Disorders, Developmental Delay, and Learning Disorders. (DSM-IV-TR) Interrupted bonding may also lead to later and more serious adult disorders. Separation and loss are critical life events for a child, but the traumatic reaction may be suppressed and delayed, only to emerge in adult pathology as homelessness, poverty, mental illness, and criminal activity. A case of pay me now or pay me later.

More than fifty percent of homeless persons in New York and Massachusetts were once foster children. Children emancipated without a permanent home are not only more likely to be homeless, but also poor. They have no financial support from a family and no inheri tance to anticipate. Schizophrenia, Depression, Anxiety Disorders, and other serious mental disorders have been significantly correlated with the loss of a significant attachment earlier in life. Multiply-placed and moved children are "psychopaths in the making." The unbonded child may become a "cold-blooded" adult who lacks compassion and empathy. Crimes without conscience are a common result.

Appellate Courts Continue to Choose Bonding

Fortunately, courts are recognizing the importance of bonding and attachment when considering placement decisions. The courts have used terms like "continuity of care" and "risks of transition" when describing the importance of attachment and keeping children in bonded relationships. Here are ten recent appellate court decisions from across the country:

Missouri

The Missouri Appellate Court upheld a ruling in favor of foster parents adopting their foster child over the objections of the child's grandparents and their Indian tribe. The child had multiple medical needs that required special medical equipment and training on its use. The foster parents became adept at providing for the child's medical needs and a strong bond developed. Although there is a statutory preference for the child to be placed with a member of his family and tribe, the court reasoned that his foster parents' ability to provide care for his special needs and the significant emotional bond between them overrode the statutory preference. (In re C.G.L. v. McDonald County Juvenile Office, 63 S.W. 3d 693) (2002)

Kansas

The Kansas Appellate Court ruled that a lower court erred, in part, when it discounted an emotional bond between a foster child and her foster parents, which is one factor in the best interests of child. The child was placed with a foster family by the custodial agency and the agency failed to pursue adoptive placement with interested relatives. The foster family and the child's relatives both filed to adopt. The lower court had ruled that the agency initially failed in its reasonable efforts to explore adoptive placement with the relatives and, therefore, the court ruled in favor of placement with relatives. The Appellate Court affirmed the lower court ruling that the agency failed in its reasonable efforts; however, the court reversed placement with the relatives until consideration could be given to the emotional bond between the child and her foster parents in determining her best interests. (In the Interest of D.C., 32 Kan. App. 2d 962) (2004)

In a separate case, the Kansas Appellate Court ruled a lower court erred when it granted an adoption by grandparents based solely on biological preference when the foster family had more of a relationship with the child. The child had resided with his foster family for more than two years when the competing petitions were filed. The court reasoned that the bond between the foster family and the child is a critical factor when determining the child's best interest. (In re Interest of J.A.,42 P. 3d 215) (2002)

Washington

The Washington Appellate Court affirmed a lower court that denied biological parents' preference to have a couple other than the family the children had been placed with to adopt. The court reasoned that the best interest of the child was to remain in the placement where he was thriving, not to undergo the risk of a transition. The record showed that the custodial family was prepared to adopt the child. They were experienced parents of three children. The child was observed to be happy and healthy in their care and was accepted by all members of their family. At the time of the trial court's decision, the child had lived with the family for 14 of his 19 months. The trial court did not abuse its discretion by concluding that the custodial unit was the family to whom the child bonded and that he should have remained in their care. Relevant discussion as to how a court should consider placement decisions was included in the opinion.

"Evidence relevant to an adoptive placement decision may include, but is not limited to, the psychological and emotional bonds between the dependent child and its biological parents, its siblings, and its foster family; the potential harm the child may suffer if severed from contact with these persons as a result of a placement decision; the nature of the child's attachment to the person or persons constituting the proposed placement; and the effect of an abrupt and substantial change in the child's environment. An important objective is to maintain continuity in the child's relationship with a parental figure, and to avoid numerous changes in custody if this is possible without harm to the child. Where possible, the initial placement shall be viewed as the only placement for the child." (p. 13) (In re Dependency of J.S., 111 Wn. App. 796) (2002)

California
The California Appellate Court upheld a ruling in favor of continuing placement with foster parents over placement with the children's tribe. In spite of the preference for Indian children to be placed with their tribe according to the Indian Child Welfare Act, the court ruled in favor of continued placement with the children's foster parents due to their significant attachment. The court reasoned that this extraordinary emotional bond falls under the "good cause" exception to the Act. (Fresno County Dept. of Children & Family Services v. Sup..., 122 Cal. App. 4th 626) (2004)

Pennsylvania
The Pennsylvania Supreme Court ruled in favor of foster parents adopting their foster child over placement with the biological grandparents. The child was "failure to thrive" when she entered foster care and made dramatic gains while with the foster parents. The court reasoned that the risks in moving the child from the foster home where she was secure and attached were too great. (In the Interest of C.J.R., 782 A. 2d 568)(2001)

Maine
Maine's Supreme Court upheld a lower court ruling that gave adoptive placement to the foster parents over the child's grandparents. The child had lived with the foster parents for two years while the grandparents had visited infrequently. The child had many developmental delays and the foster parents had a track record of meeting her needs. The court reasoned that significant bonding occurred between the child and her foster parents, and it was in her best interest to remain with them. (In re Annie A., 2001 ME 105; similarly In re Kayla M., 2001 ME 166) (2001)

Alaska
The Alaska Supreme Court ruled for a grant of adoption of a foster child by his foster parents, while denying the biological grandparents' petition. The child had continuously resided with his foster parents from the age of seven months to three years. Although the child had a relationship with his grandparents, the court reasoned it's in the child's best interests to be adopted by his foster parents due to the significant bond with them and recognizing the child's need for "continuity of care." (In re Adoption of Bernard A., 77 P. 3d 4) (2003)

Tennessee
The Tennessee Appellate Court ruled in favor of foster parents' adoption petition over that of the child's relatives – even though it permanently separated siblings. Siblings were initially placed together in the foster home, when the youngest, a four month old, was then placed in the custody of relatives while the older one remained in the foster home. This arrangement had continued for nearly two years when the competing adoption petitions were filed. The court granted the foster parents' adoption petition of the older child there-

by dismissing the relatives' petition. The relatives were able to adopt the younger child. The court reasoned that the continuity of care preference outweighed the preference for placing siblings together due to the age of the children and their respective attachment to their caregivers. (In re S.B., Tenn. App. LEXIS 308) (2000)

Indiana

The Indiana Court of Appeals recognized the importance of parenting and bonding when it comes to adoption. The Appellate Court held that biology is not more important than a child's relationship with a man who has been a father in the terms that matter most. The court upheld the adoption of a girl to a man who had cared for her as his daughter for five years while dismissing the biological aunt and uncle's adoption petition. (Gerweck v. Schoenradt, 793 N.E. 2d 1054) (2003)

Summary

More courts at all levels are recognizing the importance of bonding when making placement decisions. This consideration, however, remains far from universal. Many courts still fail to consider the documented bond between the foster parent and foster child and choose adoptive placement with a long lost relative, relying solely on the primacy of biological rights. Thanks to the Adoption and Safe Families Act (ASFA), the rights of the child are (or should be) considered paramount.

Hopefully, with increased understanding of child development and bonding, and a growing number of these appellate court decisions, judges will give bonding appropriate consideration in placement decisions.

Mark Bontrager, MSW, JD, was born and raised in Indiana. He obtained a master's degree in social work and a law degree from Indiana University. He has practiced in the field of mental health and social work for more than 15 years. His law practice focused primarily in the areas of adoption, child welfare, and special education law. He has authored numerous articles on such topics as attachment and bonding, and legal issues surrounding children in foster care. Mark has been the executive director of Aldea Children and Family Services since 2007.

James Kenny, PhD, is a retired clinical psychologist with doctorates in both psychology and anthropology. He and his wife are the parents of 12 biological and adopted children, and the foster parents of many more. They have co-authored several books on family and childcare. They are the founders of ACT, an organization devoted to helping foster children find permanent homes (adoptioninchildtime.org). Dr. Kenny is co-author of the recently published ***Bonding and the Case for Permanence.*** *This article originally appeared in* ***Fostering Families Today.***

Belsky, J. et al (1988) ***Clinical Implications of Attachment.*** *Hillsdale, NJ: Erlbaum.*

Bowlby, J. (1979) ***The Making and Breaking of Affectional Bonds.*** *London: Tavistock.*

Trauma & Abuse

"Children are like wet cement. Whatever falls on them makes an impression." – Dr. Haim Ginott

ADHD or Trauma?

By Robin D. Hayes, PhD

Children who have experienced trauma act a lot like children with ADHD when they are at school.

Do you foster a child diagnosed with Attention Deficit Hyperactivity Disorder who has made little or no progress with therapy and medication? Does a child you know have trouble paying attention in school and have a history of trauma stemming from abuse or neglect? Both examples could be the result of trauma – not ADHD. ADHD is diagnosed at higher rates among fostered and adopted children, but until recently, it was not known why. As researchers learned more about the psychological trauma that results from abuse and neglect, misdiagnosis of trauma was revealed with similarity of symptoms as the cause.

How Misdiagnosis Happens

Children who have experienced trauma act a lot like children with ADHD when they are at school. As Deborah D. Gray writes in "Attaching in Adoption," "Traumatized children are hard to teach. They are hyper-vigilant and hyper-aroused. Often, they are misdiagnosed with attention deficit disorder."

Hyper-vigilance, a common characteristic of traumatized children, means being on constant alert, monitoring the body language of the teacher and fellow classmates, listening for sudden sounds, and paying attention to everything except schoolwork. The child appears to have problems paying attention when in reality, they are paying a lot of attention – but to the wrong things. The teacher does not realize what the child is doing and judges it at face value; it looks like the child is not paying attention.

"These children [traumatized children] are hyper-vigilant because they are looking for dangers or threats," says Frank Putnam, MD, professor of pediatrics and psychiatry at Cincinnati Children's Hospital. In an article by Maia Szalavitz, Putnam states, "They become exquisitely attuned to sights, sounds and especially facial expressions or tones of voice that might be linked with impending trouble."

The teacher sees a child who does not appear to pay attention in class and starts sending notes home; perhaps the teacher even mentions attention issues at a parent teacher conference. The ball is set in motion for a diagnosis, but will it be accurate?

Consequences of Misdiagnosis

Bruce Perry, MD, PhD, of the Child Trauma Academy of Houston, Texas, is leading the charge, investigating the frequent misdiagnosis of trauma as ADHD. Perry is the co-author, with journalist Maia Szalavitz, of the acclaimed book, "Boy Who Was Raised as a Dog," and a frequent speaker on the topic of misdiagnosis of trauma as ADHD. The main consequence for misdiagnosed trauma is that treatment for ADHD will not help a child suffering the effects of trauma. "Medication and talking therapy will not work. The part of the brain that is impacted by trauma is not… easily influenced or changed by talking," Perry said in an interview with TES newspaper.

Putnam agrees with Perry's findings. "Many children who are diagnosed with ADHD… may actually be suffering from trauma. There is probably a significant group of kids with traumatic hypervigilance or dissociation that interferes with attention and increases arousal and activity levels," Putnam states in an article by Maia Szalavitz. "What's worse, children suffering trauma symptoms actually have higher than normal levels of neurotransmitters like adrenaline and noradrenaline (norepinephrine)," according to Putnam. "These same transmitters are raised even further by stimulants like Ritalin that are commonly prescribed for ADHD." So not only will ADHD treatments not work for kids with trauma, they may actually hurt.

Yet many practicing children's therapists remain unaware of the potential for misdiagnosis. Perry explains in the TES interview that the field of trauma is new and still evolving, thus new information is being discovered all the time. In a rapidly evolving field, it is difficult for therapists to keep up with the influx of new information.

What to do if Misdiagnosis is Suspected.

If a child you foster has a diagnosis of ADHD but does not seem to improve after one year of treatment or if that child has a diagnosis of ADHD and a history of trauma, educate yourself about the confu-

Resources About ADHD and Trauma:

Articles:

'Trauma often misdiagnosed as ADHD' by Emma Seith (January 9, 2009) in TES www.tes.co.uk/article.aspx?storycode=6006919.

'Diagnosis: ADHD – or Is It Trauma?' by Maia Szalavitz for MSN Health and Fitness online at www.health.msn.com/health-topics/adhd/articlepage.aspx?cp-documentid=100191637.

'Child maltreatment, other trauma exposure, and post-traumatic stress symptomatology among children with oppositional defiant and attention deficit hyperactivity disorders.' by J. Ford, R. Racusin, C. Ellis, W. Daviss, J. Reisers, A. Fleischer, (2000, August). Child Maltreatment, 5(3), pp 205-217.

'Stress, trauma, and PTSD in ADHD-diagnosed children. A biopsychosocial perspective' by E.A. Bennett from the California School of Professional Psychology – Berkeley/Alameda, US. Dissertation Abstracts International: Section B: The Sciences and Engineering, vol 60(9-B), Mar 2000. pp 4875.

Books:

Attaching in Adoption
by Deborah D. Gray

ADHD: The Great Misdiagnosis
by Julian Stuart Haber

Boy Who Was Raised as a Dog
by Bruce Perry and Maia Szalavitz

sion between ADHD and trauma and then consider having a conversation with the child's therapist. Keep in mind that both ADHD and trauma are clinical diagnoses that must satisfy stringent criteria.

Talking with a Therapist about ADHD and Trauma. Should you feel compelled to discuss this issue with your foster child's therapist, remember that psychological trauma is a new and rapidly evolving field and that it can be difficult for busy working therapists to stay current on all new developments. Schedule time to sit down and speak privately with the therapist without children in the room. Bring reference materials with you, such as information printed from Perry's website (www.childtrauma.org). Remain calm and present your concerns without blame. You may or may not be correct in your suspicions, but by remaining calm and presenting this concern dispassionately, your concerns will be heard.

Misdiagnosis of trauma as ADHD occurs when symptoms are misinterpreted or when histories of trauma are ignored or unknown. Unfortunately, children who struggle due to trauma do not benefit from treatments designed for ADHD. Foster parents who are aware of the similarities in symptoms of trauma and ADHD will be better able to advocate for the needs of the children in their care. New information about trauma will benefit many children who were previously misdiagnosed.

Robin D. Hayes, PhD, is the parent of three children by adoption, she writes about adoption, education, and life in a multiracial family. She is the founder of www.adoptingtheolderchild.com. This article originally appeared in ***Fostering Families Today.***

Connecting with the Hurting Foster Child

By Betty Daigle Hastings

How often do foster parents put themselves into the life of that hurting, traumatized, devastated child to feel as they feel and to consider what they can do to help reach the child? Are we truly passionate about their pain, their hurt feelings, and the terrific tragedy that they are going through as they are removed from their home and placed in strange, unfamiliar settings?

Children come into care with problems, scared, hurting, and so many times, just simply angry and upset. Sometimes foster parents unintentionally push the wrong buttons that result in confused and upset children. This in turn makes foster parents wonder if they can handle parenting or if they should continue even trying. Sometimes foster parents simply think foster children will just be so thankful for being in a new, safer home. But if foster parents look at foster care through the eyes of a child, perhaps they will find a connection that hadn't been thought of before.

When a child is placed in a new home, foster parents know to provide love, food, shelter, clothes, safety, and work for a brighter future, but do they need to consider more?

For a foster child, coming into a strange, new home can be scary, horrible, terrifying, and frightening. Children who come with their baggage of problems, hurts, and low self-esteem may not understand why they've been removed from their parents and everything they know. Can you imagine being suddenly taken from your familiar surroundings, snatched up from family, school, and friends and moved to a strange and unusual place to live with a family that you don't even know?

It's no wonder that children come into care with low self-esteem. Children need to feel useful, valuable, important, and as if they belong to a family. If they don't find that sense of belonging, sometimes they turn to gangs, drugs, or other destructive measures. There are some things foster parents can do to make this transition go more smoothly.

1. Foster parents need to have all of the information available about the child. The more information shared, the more prepared parents will be to address the issues that arise and deal with hurt and problems as they are revealed.

2. Foster parents need to make sure their expectations of the child are not too high. Expectations that are too high will make a child feel like he or she is a constant failure. This may result in physical illness or withdrawal from relationships or depression. Foster parents should give praise daily, and when possible give the child an opportunity to make his or her own choices with guidance in the right direction and consequences of wrong decisions. It is important to encourage plans for permanency.

3. Foster parents need to always treat the child with respect, acceptance, and willingness to show unconditional love. Foster parents should not only share their home with a child, but also their lives – taking time to walk with them or go for an ice cream. Having private time can make the child feel important and like a significant part of the family. Foster parents who can show that they will be available in bad times, as well as good times, can create a tremendous step toward connection with a child.

4. Never give the foster child a feeling that foster parents never make mistakes. Promoting the idea of the "perfect couple" can make a child uncomfortable. Recognize and admit mistakes. Soon a child will readily recognize leadership abilities, strengths, mistakes, and shortcomings. Children are like tape recorders, they listen, record and keep the information inside, often to be played back at a later date. Always be real and honest with a child.

5. Give each child the opportunity to start with a clean slate as he or she enters a new home. Do not live in the past with what previous foster children in the home have done.

6. New foster parents have to learn that the way they were raised in their own birth homes may not be the way they should parent foster children. Foster children should be handled differently. Foster parents need to be careful not to judge the child by his or her behavior, reactions to food served, and hygiene, remembering that he or she may come from a completely different environment, home setting and certainly different discipline techniques.

Children coming into care have experienced traumatic removals from their homes, and they may not understand their situation. They may feel that the judge is the enemy even though he may be acting in the best interest of the child at the moment. If the child happened to be present to see the anguish, pain, and distress that goes on in the courtroom, this may only add to the child coming into a new home scared, upset, angry, and depressed. Often children do not understand what has happened or why, resulting in a troubled child.

Foster children may try to hide their feelings and one of the best connections with children is communication to help them discover that they are worthy of respect and understanding. Foster parents should always be willing to listen regardless of busy schedules.

Ultimately, realize what foster children have gone through, what they have experienced, and the hurt that they feel. We desperately need to let these children know they have someone on their side who will try to look at the situation from their perspective, focusing on their needs. Throughout that, foster parents need to show unconditional love through the problems and interruptions while a child is in their home. Foster parents have a lot of influence.

It's difficult to bring children from different environments, attitudes, cultures, and lifestyles together. But foster parents can make a difference, connect with the feelings and touch the heart of the foster child for a brighter future. We just have to connect!

Betty Daigle Hastings is a foster parent in Tennessee. She was a foster child in her teenage years. Betty worked for the University of Tennessee as a foster parent trainer and across the nation. She served as state president of the Foster Parent Association in Tennessee for six years. Presently, she serves as chair of the National Foster Parent Association States Affiliates Council and was elected as vice president of Tennessee Foster Adoptive Care Association and to the Tennessee Supreme Court Improvement Committee. She served on committees, meeting the needs of children in the welfare system. She and her husband have fostered more than 300 children and adopted two boys during this time.

Ten Keys to Healing Trauma in the Adopted and Foster Child:
By B. Bryan Post, LCSW

1. Trauma creates fear and stress sensitivity in children. Even for a child adopted from birth, their internal systems may already be more sensitive and fearful than that of a child remaining with his biological parents. You must also consider the first nine months in which the child developed. These early experiences as well could have major implications.

2. Recognize and be more aware of fear being demonstrated by your child. Be more sensitive and tuned in to the small signals given such as clinging, whining, not discriminating amongst strangers, etc. All are signs of insecurity which can be met by bringing the child in closer, holding, carrying, and communicating to the child that he is feeling scared, but you will keep him safe.

3. Recognize the impact of trauma in your own life. One of the single greatest understandings parents can have is a self-understanding. Research tells us that far more communication occurs non-verbally than verbally. Understanding the impact of past trauma in your own life will help you become more sensitive to when your reactions are coming from a place other than your existing parent/child experience. Re-experiencing past trauma is common when parents are placed in an ongoing stressful environment.

4. Reduce external sensory stimulation when possible. Decrease television, overwhelming environments, number of children playing together at one time, and large family gatherings. When necessary that these events take place, keep the child close, explain to him that he may become stressed and he can come to you when needed.

5. Do time-in instead of time-out. Rather than sending the stressed out and scared child to the corner to think about his behavior, bring him into to you and help him to feel safe and secure. Internally this will then permit him the ability to think about his actions. Though time-in is not a time for lecturing, it will allot your child an opportunity to calm his stress and then think more clearly. Another effective key is to let the child decide how much time-in he needs.

6. Do not hit traumatized children. Doing so will only identify you as a threat. The biblical verse spare the rod, spoil the child speaks to the raising of sheep. A rod is used to guide the sheep and the staff to pull him back into line when he strays. Hitting children, just like sheep, will cause them to become frightened of you and in many instances to runaway or hit back.

7. There is never enough affection in the world. A very simple technique for time is the affection prescription 10-20-10. Give a child 10 minutes of quality time and attention first thing in the morning, 20 minutes in the afternoon, and 10 in the evening. Following this prescription of time has proven to have a great impact on the most negative behavior.

8. Encourage an Individualized Education Plan in the classroom developed in or with an understanding of the child's stress and fear. This may assist in addressing such vital areas as homework, playground, peer interaction, lunchtime, and physical education. All common areas of reduced structure and increased stress.

Trauma, Anxiety, and PTSD Resources

Books:
New Families, Old Scripts by Caroline Archer and Christine Gordon

Trauma, Attachment and Family Permanence by Caroline Archer and Alan Burnell

Parenting the Hurt Child: Helping Adoptive Families Heal and Grow by Gregory Keck and Regina M. Kupecky

Websites of Interest:
ChildTrauma Academy (Bruce D. Perry, MD, PhD)
www.childtrauma.org

National Center for Post Traumatic Stress Disorder
www.ptsd.va.gov

The Child Trauma Institute
www.childtrauma.com

9. Educate yourself regarding the impact of stress and trauma on families. Try not to scapegoat your child for his difficulties, but rather take responsibility for creating the environment necessary for healing his hurtful experiences. There are many resources available. A few of note are: www.postinstitute.com; www.beyondconsequences.com; www.ChildTraumaAcademy.org; and www.traumaresources.org

10. Seek support. Parenting a child with trauma history can take its toll on the best of parents. Seek out a support system for occasional respite care, discussing of issues, and the sharing of a meal. Such small steps can go a long ways during particularly stressful times.

B. Bryan Post is a Licensed Clinical Social Worker in the states of Virginia and Oklahoma and is registered to practice within various other states. He specializes in working with adults, children and families who struggle with issues related to early life trauma and the impact of trauma on the development of the mind body system. He lives with his wife Kristi and their three daughters in Virginia Beach, Va.

To Download a Free copy of this new book ***From Fear to Love: Parenting Difficult Adopted Children*** *visit:* **www.postinstitute.com/feartolovehelp/**

Child Trauma Academy has free online courses to help understand how children cope with traumatic events **www.childtraumaacademy.com**

Courses they offer:

- The Amazing Human Brain and Human Development
- Surviving Childhood: An Introduction to the Impact of Trauma
- The Cost of Caring: Secondary Traumatic Stress and the Impact of Working with High-Risk Children and Families
- Bonding and Attachment in Maltreated Children

What Does PTSD Look Like in Children?

Researchers and clinicians are beginning to recognize that PTSD may not present itself in children the same way it does in adults.

Criteria for PTSD now include age-specific features for some symptoms.

Very young children may present with few PTSD symptoms. This may be because eight of the PTSD symptoms require a verbal description of one's feelings and experiences. Instead, young children may report more generalized fears such as stranger or separation anxiety, avoidance of situations that may or may not be related to the trauma, sleep disturbances, and a preoccupation with words or symbols that may or may not be related to the trauma. These children may also display post-traumatic play in which they repeat themes of the trauma. In addition, children may lose an acquired developmental skill (such as toilet training) as a result of experiencing a traumatic event.

Elementary school-aged children may not experience visual flashbacks or amnesia for aspects of the trauma. However, they do experience "time skew" and "omen formation," which are not typically seen in adults. Time skew refers to a child mis-sequencing trauma related events when recalling the memory. Omen formation is a belief that there were warning signs that predicted the trauma. As a result, children often believe that if they are alert enough, they will recognize warning signs and avoid future traumas. School-aged children also reportedly exhibit post-traumatic play or re-enactment of the trauma in play, drawings, or verbalization. Post-traumatic play is different from re-enactment in that post-traumatic play is a literal representation of the trauma, involves compulsively repeating some aspect of the trauma, and does not tend to relieve anxiety.

Other Signs of Trauma in Children

Besides PTSD, children and adolescents who have experienced traumatic events often exhibit other types of problems... fear, anxiety, depression, anger and hostility, aggression, sexually inappropriate behavior, self-destructive behavior, feelings of isolation and stigma, poor self-esteem, difficulty in trusting others, and substance abuse. Children who have experienced traumas also often have relationship problems with peers and family members, problems with acting out, and problems with school performance. Along with associated symptoms, there are a number of psychiatric disorders that are commonly found in children and adolescents who have been traumatized. One commonly co-occurring disorder is major depression. Other disorders include substance abuse; other anxiety disorders such as separation anxiety, panic disorder, and generalized anxiety disorder; and externalizing disorders such as attention-deficit/hyperactivity disorder, oppositional defiant disorder, and conduct disorder.

From PTSD in Children and Adolescents, A National Center for PTSD Fact Sheet by Jessica Hamblen, PhD. This article originally appeared in ***Adoption Parenting: Creating a Toolbox, Building Connections.***

Practice Camping

By Veronica Brown

Once my younger boys are in bed, my favorite way to relax is watching a baseball game on TV with a novel to read between innings. It was on one of these evenings that my 17-year-old sat down next to me, which is a sure sign that he wants to talk. I muted the game and marked my place in the book.

"What's up, Sam?"

"Ian hasn't unpacked yet," Sam said.

"It's only been a couple of weeks and in his nine years, he's moved a lot and lived with a lot of different people. It'll take awhile," I responded.

"I know, but when I asked Ian when he was going to unpack his stuff, he said that he wasn't going to unpack because he'll end up annoying you and you'll end up kicking him out," Sam offered.

"What did you say?" I asked.

"I said, 'Dude, Veronica's been fostering longer than you've been alive.' I told him that you've put up with a lot of crap and that he's not going anywhere," Sam added.

"Wow... thanks," I responded. "You know, that means so much more coming from you than it would from me. I'm just another adult making a lot of promises. Ian has no reason to believe me. But you've been there, you know what it's like. That'll be a big help to Ian."

Well, Ian eventually did unpack his belongings. He took care decorating his bedroom and really made it his own. Ian found a place in our family as well. Unfortunately, once he decided to stay, he didn't want to go... anywhere. The home became his haven. Ian had to be coaxed and encouraged to leave the house, even to go somewhere fun. His anxiety levels spiked when we went out and it really stopped him from enjoying new experiences.

One of these new experiences was a two-day train trip to Toronto during March Break. In the days leading up to the big day, Ian was really excited. And the train was an awesome adventure until we could see the city as we approached the station, then Ian started kicking, throwing things, and yelling "I want to go home! You can't make me stay! I never wanted to come in the first place!" It was shocking, unexpected and sad to witness.

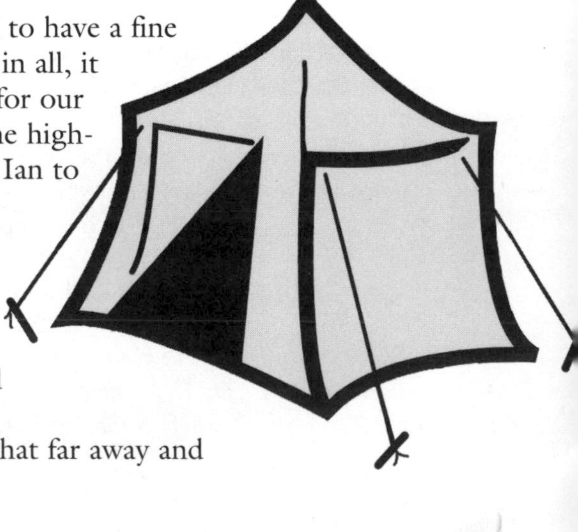

Ian eventually calmed down and we managed to have a fine time in Toronto. There were a few issues but all in all, it was fine. Seeing Ian's struggle, my concern was for our annual week-long camping trip in August. It's the highlight of our summer break and we really wanted Ian to come with us.

A few weeks later, Sam again sat next to me on the couch. He was excited to tell me about the Harry Potter Exhibition that he had found on the Internet. I asked him where the exhibition was being held and when he said Chicago, it was in a tone that suggested Mars.

When I let Sam know that Chicago was not that far away and

that we could easily drive there, perhaps do some camping, he was stunned.

And so a plan was developed. We ordered tickets to the exhibition and booked a campsite. We checked out the museum on the Internet and mapped our route to Chicago. Tents and sleeping bags were dragged out of the attic and packed in the minivan. As it was explained to Ian: the family was going on a two-night rehearsal for our big trip in August. No stress, no expectations, and no chance of messing it up – it would be practice camping.

And as the saying goes, practice makes perfect! Ian handled himself and managed his anxiety. I know it couldn't have been easy for him, and I was proud of him and the other boys who helped him out in many little ways. Ian enjoyed his trip, and gained enough confidence to join the rest of the family for our big August camping trip. It was a full week of new experiences well-documented in dozens and dozens of photos. The best one was enlarged, framed and hung in a place of honor in the family room.

I believe that when you open your door to a child, it should swing into a home and out to the world.

Veronica Brown has been a foster parent in Canada since 1995. She primarily takes in boys aged 9 and older and usually has a handful at any given time.

Stress Free Kids: www.stressfreekids.com

Stress Free Kids® is a website that has products designed to help children, teens, and adults decrease stress, anxiety, and anger. These books and CDs will introduce you and your children to the proven techniques of deep breathing, progressive muscular relaxation, visualizations, and affirmations/positive statements. This unique storytelling format has been embraced by psychologists, doctors, child life care specialists, yoga instructors, teachers, counselors, parents, and most importantly… children. Two of their books are below.

Bubble Riding by Lori Lite
A Relaxation Story, designed to help children increase creativity while lowering stress and anxiety levels

Sea Otter Cove by Lori Lite
A Relaxation Story, introducing deep breathing to decrease anxiety, stress and anger while promoting peaceful sleep

A Journey With Jason

By M. Kim Combes, LBSW, MEd

"Will You Abandon Me?"

These words haunted me well into the holiday season following the initial meeting of my future foster son, a young man with no perceived security or stability in his 16-year-old life. In an ideal world, this question would never have passed his lips.

It was in July 1995 that I was first made aware of Jason. Because of my experience as a human service worker and a foster parent, his juvenile court officer believed that my personality might best match with the problems this teen may manifest in my home, should I choose to foster this challenging client. At the time, he was living in a residential facility, needing to work its program before he could graduate, be discharged, and placed in my foster home. His juvenile court officer would keep me posted on his progress.

Jason wanted to meet me after hearing there was a foster parent potentially willing to parent him. A staffing was held in November. The juvenile court officer drove Jason's mother, who he had not seen in more than a year, and me to the facility. While making conversation during the more than three-hour one-way drive, I realized that I had met Jason's extended family several years prior while employed with the Iowa Department of Human Services. His mother and I concluded it was a small world.

Upon seeing his mother, Jason hugged her and wanted her close to him as the assembly of social workers and treatment staff gathered to discuss his progress. He watched me intently, seemingly trying to get a grasp on who I was. Was I someone to be trusted?

When the reporting was done regarding Jason's behaviors he was given an opportunity to "interview" me. His longing look, coupled with his first words, tugged at my heartstrings. His inquiry underscored his first and foremost priority. Rather than delve for information regarding rules, home life, brothers and other related issues, his predominate concern popped out with no apparent effort – "Will you abandon me?" His affect disguised the vulnerability underlying the words. What if I said, "YES," or couldn't convince him I wouldn't? He wanted to trust, but history was not on his side. Why should he believe I would be different than others to whom he had given his susceptible heart?

I can't remember my response to this pointed and poignant request for a "forever" relationship. The intensity of it took me aback. I had been in the human service arena for more than fifteen years. I thought I had seen and heard it all. However, in this context, I could not rid myself of the echoing memory of those four powerful words. It was as if I held his life in the balance.

Jason spent some time with me and the foster siblings in my home during the Thanksgiving and New Year's holidays during his pre-placement visits. He was anxious to graduate so he could become a member of my household and family. This was not to happen until February, however. It was then that his still-echoing words were going to be put to the test.

He initially hated the court-ordered day treatment program in which he was placed. This program provided him some structure so he could more easily transition into having the freedom most teens his age have. Because he had been in a locked facility for so long, he would need some bridge to ensure a smoother transition into the real world again. The frustration of having to spend twelve hours a day in another therapeutic environment, coupled with the influence of a negative foster brother, sparked the explosive combination of ingredients that was a recipe for trouble.

Within five weeks of placement in my home, he bolted from his court-ordered structure. He was found within two weeks and subsequently spent a month in a short-term group facility. Tearfully, he asked me over the phone if he was able to return to my home. "Most assuredly so," I told him. Six months and many power struggles later, he was once more placed in a short-term facility for "regroup time" due to some poor decision-making on his part. A visit and several phone calls again gave him the confidence that I was still there and still family. He was placed back with me for round three.

Fall turned into winter. Jason began to trust that I was committed to his well-being – and to him. Progress was being made. Jason's increasing maturity was reflected in his making better life choices and decisions. His desire to be reunited with his mom grew stronger as they spent time together getting re-acquainted. They had been separated for various reasons for much of his short life.

Winter gave way to spring – a season of rebirth. It would seem appropriate, then, that this season of positive growth and change would see Jason back with his mom full-time. It was an emotional moment when his worker remarked at a monthly team meeting that she saw no reason for him to stay in foster care. He and his mom were speechless as tears streamed down their cheeks. They had not anticipated this reunification until summer at the earliest. Jason was to see his hopes realized.

Prior to leaving my home, Jason gave me his goodbye letter. The following is an excerpt from this touching farewell:

> *"I do not know how to thank you so much. I came in here thinking that this was going to be another foster home that will abandon me and not help me much with anything. You have worked with my mom and I so much and helping us to get back together soon because you always told me that you would bring up to [the caseworker] to have me move in with her at the beginning of the summer and it happened sooner than we both thought. I think you did a very good thing by becoming a foster parent for many kids. God must have said to you at an early age to help out all these kids because they need a home to go to and a loving foster parent like yourself."*

As with many things in life, desire alone does not always make dreams come true. It eventually became apparent that familial love was not enough to make this long-awaited living situation work. Jason once more entered my home. He hadn't lost the trust of our relationship after eight months of living elsewhere. We were thus able to continue to build on the pre-existing foundation we had both struggled hard to cement during the last two years.

The holidays once more came and went. Jason would be 18 in six months and was biting at the bit to be independent. Being on his own was priority for him. However, he wanted it to happen now. Thus, in tribute to Martin Luther King, Jr.'s birthday, he ran "free at last" – for one night. He was found and placed in detention during the holiday weekend. Yes, in answer to his question, he could come back. But, he was told by his workers and me that should he decide to abscond again (and be caught) he would spend the remainder of his minor years in lock-up to keep him safe until he reached the age of majority.

This did not deter Jason's obsession with freedom. His final break occurred on March 4, almost four months before his 18th birthday. It wasn't until mid-May that he found either the courage or desire to call me. However, he was initially deceptive regarding his whereabouts for fear of losing the freedom he had enjoyed the last two months, and wanted to keep until the end of June, when Juvenile Court would no longer have jurisdiction.

It was during this conversation that his assumption was validated – he was still my "son" and running away again had not broken that bond. I did give him a parental chewing, but past that he felt secure in his relationship with me. He reassured me that he didn't run because of me, but because he wanted independence and a chance to be with extended family while he was still "a kid."

By mid-July, Jason was almost a month into adulthood. He came back from his uncle's ranch in South Dakota and spent a night and a day with me. Today, he calls me "Kim," but refers to me as his dad when speaking with others. What an honor that is!

It has not been an easy road for either of us. Nothing of value really is. The father-son relationship was borne with tears and great frustration on both sides. But this young man now knows the answer to his long-ago asked question.

M. Kim Combes, LBSW, MEd, is a private practice counselor and national presenter, as well as a former foster dad to 40-plus teenage boys since 1994. Currently, he and his wife, Diana, live in Colo, Iowa with their five adopted children who range from 10 to 17. Combes can be reached at kcombes@netins.net.

Sexual Abuse: How to Get (and Give) Help!

By Amy Lang, MA

Sadly, children in foster care are four times as likely to be sexually abused than children not in the system.[1] Some children are abused by their foster parent, another familiar adult who has access to them, or by other children in the family. The good news is that children who receive treatment can and do recover and go on to lead healthy and happy lives.

The following are some simple steps you can take to help a child in your care. Remember, a child's safety is an adult's responsibility and if you know a child is being abused, it is your responsibility to get help and report the offender.

If a child discloses sexual abuse to you:

1. Remain calm and go to a private place to talk. If you get upset about the situation or offender, the child may believe you are upset with him or her.
2. Believe them. Only 2 percent of disclosure of sexual abuse is false. Kids don't lie about this.[2]
3. Treat the child like a crime scene and don't cross examine the child. Ask simple questions – Where? When? Who? Has someone touched you in a way that hurts you or feels uncomfortable? The interview specialist will investigate fully. This isn't your responsibility. Less questioning is better.
4. Tell the child you will need to tell other people and the number one priority is to make sure the child is safe.
5. Don't congratulate or chastise the child for confiding in you.
6. Quickly report what you've been told and call Child Protective Services (in home molestation) or the police (out-of-home). If they aren't responding fast enough, complain.
7. Write down what the child said and describe his or her attitude and behavior.
8. Get support for everyone – the child, yourself and anyone else in the family who may need it.

If you suspect a child has been sexually abused, but they haven't disclosed it, it's better for them to be interviewed by a professional, rather than by you. This is called a "forensic interview" and it is not traumatic for the child. The people who do these interviews are amazing, kind, gentle and know just what to say and do to draw a child out.

Some sexual behaviors that would be considered "concerning" and worthy of at least a phone consultation are:

- Adult-like sexual activity – anything that seems like adult sex in any way. This can be "humping" another child or adult repeatedly, oral contact, attempted penetration, explicit language, too much knowledge for their age, and other similar sexual displays.

- Your gut or intuition tells you – in a loud voice – that there is something off, unusual or wrong about the child's behavior.
- The sexual behavior is with a child who is not a regular playmate, is much younger or older, is more powerful (smarter, bigger, etc.), or involves aggression, violence, threats, or bribery.
- The behavior happens a lot – over and over again and the child doesn't respond to correction.
- The behavior is directed at an adult.

Other behaviors that can be considered warning signs that abuse may have occurred:[3]

- Nightmares, trouble sleeping, fear of the dark, or other sleeping problems.
- Extreme fear of "monsters."
- Spacing out at odd times.
- Loss of appetite, or trouble eating or swallowing.
- Sudden mood swings: rage, fear, anger, or withdrawal.
- Fear of certain people or places such as a child may not want to be left alone with a babysitter, friend, relative, or some other child or adult; or a child who is usually talkative and cheery may become quiet and distant when around a certain person.
- Stomach illness all of the time with no identifiable reason.
- An older child behaving like a younger child, such as bed-wetting or thumb sucking.
- Sexual activities with toys or other children, such as simulating sex with dolls or asking other children or siblings to behave sexually.
- New words for private body parts.
- Refusing to talk about a "secret" he or she has with an adult or older child.
- Talking about a new older friend.
- Suddenly having money.
- Cutting or burning herself or himself as an adolescent.

Physical warning signs a child may have been sexually abused:

- Unexplained bruises, redness, or bleeding of the child's genitals, anus, or mouth.
- Pain at the genitals, anus, or mouth.
- Genital sores or milky fluids in the genital area.

Sexual abuse is something no one wants to deal with, but for many children and adults it is an enormous problem. Being a supportive, open, and approachable parent is the best thing you can do for any child. And if you were sexually abused yourself, imagine what your life would be like if just one adult in your life stepped in to protect you and offer help and support.

A sexual health educator for more than 20 years, Amy Lang teaches parents and other people how to talk to kids of any age about the birds and the bees. She is the author of the Mom's Choice Award® winning ***Birds + Bees + YOUR Kids – A Guide to Sharing Your Beliefs About Sexuality, Love, and Relationships*** *and* ***The Ask ANYTHING Journal****. She created the lively and engaging video* ***Birds + Bees + Kids: The Basics*** *so parents can learn how to talk to their kids about sex and values without leaving the couch! Learn more at BirdsAndBeesAndKids.com.*

For more help contact any of the following resources.
You can usually call anonymously.

Stop it NOW! –
1-888-PREVENT or
www.StopItNow.org

PEACE of Mind –
www.POMWA.org

Darkness to Light –
1-866-FOR-LIGHT or
www.D2L.org

Birds + Bees + Kids –
www.BirdsAndBeesAndKids.com

[1]www.cfrc.illinois.edu/pubs/Pdf.files/childmalretro.pdf
[2]www.sldran.org/pdf/Falsereportsbychildren.pdf
[3]www.stopitnow.org/warnings

I struggled for many years with flashbacks and nightmares. I also found myself dealing with feelings of grief. I would mentally re-experience the horror of my trauma every night. I was hurt so deeply it caused me a great deal of stress. I was agitated and felt I caused it to happen. I was shameful and thought something was wrong with me. I was extremely sensitive and experienced panic sensations several times a day. I felt helpless and began to withdraw from people. I was carrying around such intense fear that I struggled to cope with my life experiences. I needed to make sense of what happened to me and once I could understand my trauma, I was less fearful and finally able to start managing it.

– Armond DeGasperis is a former foster child. He wrote ***The End is the Beginning*** *at the age of 13 detailing his experiences with abuse.*

You Are Safe Here

By Cheryl A. Lieberman, PhD, and Rhea K. Bufferd, LICSW

Ceremonies are powerful ways to communicate with children. This ceremony lays out concrete information that is relevant for a child who has been abused.

Situation:
Making safety clear for a first-time foster child.

Spring, 11 years old, had been living with her biological father since her mother died two years previously. The father drank heavily and had been abusing his daughter sexually. Spring became known to the Department of Social Services through a report from her favorite teacher, who wanted to help her. Spring did not want to live with her father, but she also did not trust anyone else. Connie, the social worker, said that sexual boundaries in the home of the foster parents, Donald and Rosalie, should be clear from the beginning.

Special Note: Some people might find the language and approach in this ceremony shocking. At a conference sponsored by Project Impact (now known as Special Adoption Family Services) in Boston, a social worker from Texas shared her approach to introducing foster children who had been sexually abused to a new family where they would be safe. Her approach cut down on false accusations by angry or confused foster children against foster parents. Her main idea has been incorporated into this ceremony.

"You Are Safe Here"

Connie: The purpose of this ceremony is to set up some clear ground rules for this home.

Rosalie: We know that your father was being sexual with you in ways that a father is not supposed to be with his daughter.

Donald: We want you to know that no matter what you do or say, we will not be sexual with you.

Rosalie: I have sex with Donald and no one else.

Donald: I have sex with Rosalie and no one else.

Rosalie: It is not your fault that your father had sex with you.

Donald: While you may be mad at your father for what he did sexually to you, you may still love him for other reasons.

Rosalie: We are here to help you in any way we can and in any way you will let us.

Donald: We are not here to say bad things about your father.

Rosalie: We know how to hold and hug children without being sexual. We will help you learn this, too. And we know how to set limits even if you are sexual with us.

Spring: What if I get worried about my father or about what might happen to me?

Connie: I will stop by and you can ask me any questions. You can talk to Rosalie and Donald. They can call me if you have any questions or concerns that they cannot address.

Spring: I don't want other kids to know why I left or why I'm here.

Rosalie: Kids will not know anything you do not tell them. You might think about saying that your father is having some problems right now and cannot take care of you, so you are staying here.

Spring: What if I do not like it here?

Donald: There will be times when we expect you to do things that you don't want to do, like make your bed, and you will want to leave. We will have good moments and bad moments and we will work out together. If we need help, we will ask Connie to help us.

Spring: What if I wake up in the middle of the night with bad dreams?

Rosalie: We are there to help you.

Spring: What if I need to talk about things?

Donald: We will be here to listen.

We want you to remember that you are safe here.

No one here will try to have sex with you.

Rosalie: This ceremony is over. We want you to know that the talk can continue outside the ceremony. We would like to end this ceremony by shaking hands with everyone as a way of saying we will keep our promises.

Afterward

Rosalie and Donald together showed Spring around the house. They showed her their bedroom and said that if their door was closed, she should knock and wait to be invited in. They would extend the same courtesy to her as long as they knew she was all right. She said that she wanted to spend some time alone in her room, and Rosalie agreed. She told her that she would call her when it was time to go grocery shopping so they could buy some things Spring liked, too. When Donald asked Spring to come downstairs, she did so at the first request. She looked guarded for the first week but then started to relax and talk.

Cheryl A. Lieberman, PhD, and Rhea K. Bufferd, LICSW, are the authors of ***Creating Ceremonies: Innovative Ways to Meet Adoption Challenges.*** *Reprinted with permission.*

Don't Make Kids Wait

By James A. Kenny, PhD

Waiting is painful, even torturous for adults. Ignorant of the outcome, one is likely to imagine every possibility, and especially the worst.

Imagine you are awaiting the results of your breast exam or prostate test. You call daily but they still don't have the results. What are you thinking, feeling?

Pretend you are working as a temp, hoping to get a full-time job so you can have access to benefits and support your family. The months slip by. You are doing a good job but are afraid even to inquire whether they plan to hire you. Nothing is happening. You are worried but try not to let it show.

Imagine that you are camping deep in the woods and the ranger comes to tell you there is an emergency phone call for you. He does not know what it is about, only that you need to come at once. The ranger station is 45 minutes away. What is going through your mind as you are driving to take the call?

Waiting is much worse for a child living in a home with no permanent commitment. Adults have other life experiences, memories of times when patience was rewarded with good results. Adults learn to hang in there on the big issues and not to "sweat the small stuff."

The foster child's whole life and future are on the line. He will not understand all the bureaucratic reasons we may provide to explain the delay. He is much more likely to interpret a lack of results as a lack of love. "If you loved me, you would promise to be there forever for me."

Children view the world differently. In some primitive cultures, when meeting a person for the first time, the pair will circle around. One will get behind the other in order to see what their "partner" sees, to see the world from the other person's point of view before saying hello. We need to do the same thing with our children in waiting, to try to see the world the way they do.

Several years ago I received a phone call from a lady in a nearby Indiana city who said she wanted to volunteer for ACT, our organization to help foster children find permanence. I asked her why. She explained that they had had their foster son since he was six. He was now ten. Each time they tried to adopt, the caseworker or the court were not prepared. Four times they tried and four times the judge dismissed the case after a lapse of time, suggesting that they refile. She went on: "Two months ago I came home from court and my son again asked me: 'Mommy, am I going to be adopted yet?' I had to answer no, tried to explain, promised him we would keep trying. He went upstairs and hanged himself."

I was speechless, could not talk for a full minute. More than anything else it brought home to me how easy it is for adults to miss the fear and pain that live behind a foster child's mask.

Being parked in a foster home for an indefinite period is not safe. Waiting can cause serious psychological damage. From my clinical work with foster children, I have identified five emotional stages that these vulnerable children pass through.

1. **Hope.** At first the child has hope. "Maybe this family will be the one. If only..." But in time, hope hurts.

2. **Fear.** As hope fades, fear sets in. "What if it will always be like this? What if no one really wants me? What if I never have a home? What if..."

3. **Anger.** After fear comes anger. The child gets mad and often expresses his feelings by acting out. Temper tantrums. Foot-dragging. Stealing. Destroying property. Failing "deliberately" in school to frustrate the foster parents.

4. **Depression.** The anger may fade into darkness. The child becomes quiet and sad.

5. **Indifference.** In time, the depression may be replaced by a coldness, a lack of caring. "So what! What's the use? Who cares? I don't."

Delay is destructive. The delay is not simply about some isolated anticipated event. The delay for the foster child, and the way the child perceives the delay, concerns his or her whole life. So what can we do to minimize delays?

Here are four obvious ways that can be implemented immediately. Three of them involve the two systems designed to protect our children in care. The fourth is something foster parents can do.

1. **Start Immediately.** Within 24 hours of removal, the caseworker should provide the birth parents with a case plan for them to remedy the abuse or neglect. This is not brain surgery. What the caseworker needs to do is directly address the problems that led to the removal. If the housing is substandard, find new housing. If the parents have little parenting skills or the child was left alone, attend parent training classes. If a boyfriend abused the child, get rid of the boyfriend. If one or both parents were on drugs, they may need to pass a few random drug screens. And so on. The plan can later be approved or improved in court, but the clock will already be ticking, either on the way to reunification or toward termination.

2. **Locate Any Relatives Within Two Weeks.** One major cause of delay is the eleventh-hour relative, sometimes referred to as kin-come-lately. Just when a termination of parental rights is about to happen, a relative from far away emerges – an uncle, grandmother, or half-sibling. This throws a monkey wrench into the mix. The proceedings come to a halt while this new matter is being considered. An immediate and thorough search for potential relative placements will avoid this delay.

3. **Follow the Deadlines.** The court generally reviews the status of children in care every three months. If the birth parents do not appear to be making a reasonable

effort for reunification by six months, the permanency plan can be changed to adoption. Federal law (ASFA) requires that a termination of parental rights be filed after 12-15 months. These deadlines are vitally important and need to be honored. One year is a long time in the life of a child. When you're in third grade, it's a long time until lunch.

4. **Keep Daily Records**. Foster parents can shorten the time in care by keeping a written track of daily events. Maintain a daily journal. Record visitations or failed visitations and what happened. Keep track of school achievements and medical appointments. Make careful notes about any misbehaviors or incidents that may later evoke other interpretations.

If, as most of us would agree, delay is destructive, and further, there are obvious steps to take that would minimize delays, why aren't we doing something? Many reasons can be given, from bureaucracy to court continuances for trivial reasons, from casework overloads to a concern about giving the birth parents every opportunity to make an effort. Two reasons, however, stand out.

First, many of us remain ignorant about the seriously destructive psychological impact on the child of waiting in limbo. More so than for adults, waiting tears at a child's fabric of life. Hopefully, this article has provided some insight into the foster child's view.

Second, many caseworkers have argued with me that they need time to get the case plan right. Then the judge needs to approve the plan before the birth parents can get started. This is wrong. The best thing for caring birth parents is to give them an immediate opportunity to correct what went wrong.

If a child protection worker took my child, I would beg on the spot for a preliminary plan and I would begin at once to do what was required to get him or her back. There is no reason for the child welfare system to delay in providing the birth parents with a beginning remedy. The one thing you can be certain of if you wait too long to get it right is that you are already wrong.

James A. Kenny, PhD, has doctorates in psychology and anthropology and is the author of 10 books on child care and family life. He and his wife have raised birth, adopted, and foster children. He is on the ***Fostering Families Today*** *advisory board. This article originally appeared in* ***Fostering Families Today.*** *He is shown here with his granddaughters.*

Family Impact

"When we seek to discover the best in others, we somehow bring out the best in ourselves." – William Arthur Ward

An Island of Calm

By Denise Kendrick

In many ways Russ* was a typical seven-year-old. He loved to wear baseball hats and swim. He could count to 10 in Spanish and cheated when we played Candy Land. It was no surprise then that the first time he had ever heard the words "foster care" was when he and his baby brother, Joshua, arrived at our home.

Russ walked in at 11:30 pm carrying his little duffle bag and his brother's diaper bag. He was only weeks from his eighth birthday, but confidently shook our hands when introduced by his bleary-eyed caseworker.

The caseworker looked confused as to where to set the chubby baby buckled in an ancient infant carrier, and seemed relieved when I offered to take him. My husband ushered Russ into our bedroom to show him the pack-n-play I had set up for Joshua, then took him upstairs to show him where he would stay. The CPS worker unloaded the crumpled Happy Meal boxes in his hands onto our counter and pulled out a manilla folder. He wearily explained that he would not be the ongoing worker. He had simply been asked to "make the delivery." From upstairs I heard a shout "Bunk beds?!!? No [expletive] way!!" The caseworker seemed not to notice the outburst of profanity and continued shuffling through the placement papers. I, on the other hand, made a "note to self:" explain "nice words" and "not nice words." The caseworker showed me where to sign while summarizing how these children came into care. As the days went on, Russ would often share random details of life with his parents, which helped us fill in the gaps of their story.

The boys' parents, Joshua Sr. and Melanie had been evicted from their apartment. Melanie had dropped out of high school while pregnant with Russ. Joshua Sr. had only made it to 8th grade and had served time on and off for drug and assault charges. Joshua Sr. had been making repairs and acting as a superintendent for their building to cover the rent, but the landlord had recently fired him.

Russ often recounted stories of how difficult life was for his young family – how his pregnant mother fell half-way through the rotting floor of the apartment unit; how her leg was scratched and bleeding when his father lifted her out. He proudly told about helping watch his baby brother to make sure he didn't get into his dad's tools, or eat the construction waste and bugs that littered the apartment floor.

When the family was finally evicted Joshua Sr. carried the baby, Melanie carried a single suitcase and Russ carried the diaper bag as they began walking down the highway. They hitched several rides and ended up at a bus station. Russ told us about the night they slept on the tile floor where "no one would turn out the lights so we could sleep." Russ said his mother complained that it was hot and his dad complained that his back hurt. Russ explained that he was tired from the walking too, but it was his job to watch the baby so his parents could rest.

The family ended up staying with a friend for a few nights. When they had worn out their welcome there they moved on to a homeless shelter. Russ mentioned he liked the staff and the food there. CPS came to investigate when his mother and father left him and Joshua in the care of another woman living at the shelter. They said they were going to look for jobs and an apartment. After two days with no word from their parents, the woman told the shelter she could no longer care for the children... and so here they were, in our home now. With that the caseworker abruptly stood up, gathered his copies of signed paperwork and showed himself to the door just as my husband and Russ returned from the upstairs bedroom in time to say goodbye to the worker. The caseworker told Russ to "be good." Russ replied, "you be good too," and with that the caseworker left.

I asked Russ if he would mind taking a bath. He quickly sniffed under his arms and said "no, thank you." I elbowed my husband who quickly stifled his laughter and explained we had a wonderful selection of bubble bath Russ might like to check out. Russ winked at me, grabbed my husband's hand and said, "let's go!"

Baby Joshua had fallen asleep eating cheerios in his high chair, so I wiped him off with a warm wash cloth, changed his diaper and laid him in the pack-n-play. He never opened his eyes, just moaned softly and pulled at his ear with chubby fingers.

In a new pair of Superman pajamas, a cleaner, more hyper Russ zoomed into the kitchen to show me his cape. When he smiled widely I noticed for the first time that one of his front adult teeth was broken and half missing. Under the glare of the kitchen fluorescents I could see several scars on his nose and chin, and one on his forehead that cut through the tight, black curls on his head like a little river. I caught myself wondering if these were the proud badges of an active young boy, or scars from neglect and abuse.

While he dug through his Happy Meal box searching for the last few cold fries he talked nonstop. He offered a story about helping his uncle change a tire on the truck followed by a story about nightmares he has after watching "grown-up scary movies." He shared about a painting he had made in school, and then about the night his parents fought so loudly and violently that he had carried his baby brother out to the car and slept there for the night.

But as sudden as it all started, it was now time for them to go.

In the six months that Russ and Joshua lived with us they both celebrated a birthday. Russ blew out eight candles on a Spiderman cake and learned to ride a bike without training wheels. I have pictures of Joshua covered in icing from head to toe at his first birthday, and video of him taking his first steps on round little feet. Russ completed an entire level in our church children's program and earned six patches for his vest. Joshua's lone tooth was joined by five more, he began feeding himself solids and saying "uh-oh," "no," and "puppy." Russ stopped spending every moment trying to meet Joshua's every need and began to learn how to enjoy being a little boy. Instead of sitting on the floor, making silly faces to keep Joshua entertained, he played soccer at the park with friends and drew pages and pages of his favorite superheroes. Joshua finally cried when I left him in the church nursery, and during that same week Russ sang with the children's choir in a Christmas program and took his first piano lesson.

But as sudden as it all started, it was now time for them to go. After three days of moody apprehension on all sides, and the early opening of Christmas presents, the boys were packed and ready to go. I loaded four duffle bags and a box of toys into the trunk and front seat of a burgundy Ford. Joshua sipped juice from a cup and picked at the buckle on his car seat. Russ hugged us both, hopped into the back seat and buckled up. I saw him flipping nonchalantly through a magazine he'd found on the floorboard. After my husband and the transportation worker managed to cram Russ's bike and scooter into the trunk and tie it closed we knocked on Russ's window and waved. He struggled to find the right button for the window, but was finally able to roll the window halfway down.

I don't know what I was expecting him to say in our final moments together, but he held up the magazine and showed us the ad for Six Flags amusement park printed across the page. "I remember when we went there! Remember I would go on the big rides you're too scared to go on?!? I want to go back some time." A sober look flashed across his face and he told us goodbye and rolled the window back up before we could respond.

When I walked back into the house a flood of relief and sadness washed over me. I had dozens of kids come and an equal number go, but as always I found myself full of mixed emotions. We spent the next few weeks gathering up the remnants of Joshua and Russ' stay with our family – a remote control to a robot, a tiny sock behind the couch, a soccer ball in the bushes, pictures that just arrived from the JC Penney portrait studio. We gathered them in a box and delivered them to the boys' caseworker with promises they would be sent to their new home.

I have often wondered what Russ was thinking when that last big smile faded from his face. In many ways, Russ was not a typical eight-year-old. He had seen pornography and domestic violence. He had feared for the safety of his parents and been the primary caregiver for his baby brother. The people he trusted most had failed to protect him and eventually abandoned him. And even as he had learned to trust again, he had been forced to move on to yet more unknown.

I hope and pray that while they were "ours" the boys got a little dose of normal in their transient lives – a tranquil season of routine and typical. I hope that as he grows, Russ will continue to choose "nice words" over "not nice words." That he will pray. That as a young man he will remember the way he should treat his family and wife. I pray that as a father he will choose to love his children the way he was loved... if only for a short while. If we gave him nothing else, I pray that we gave Russ a choice. A choice between what he experienced early in life, and the kind of life he shared with us.

Two weeks later our phone rang, and shortly after a grungy toddler wearing a man's under shirt was handed to me with a trash bag of her belongings. Another child from a stormy past welcomed into our "island of calm." And so, we continue to open our lives, our home, and our hearts to these hurting children without reservation or regret, trusting that our offer of love, care and protection will yield a lifetime of hope and healing.

* The names of foster children in this story have been changed to protect their privacy.

Denise Kendrick is a long-time foster parent married to her high school sweetheart, Bruce. They lead a ministry called Embrace which encourages foster care, adoption, and global orphan care. Bruce and Denise have three biological children and just finalized the adoption of their oldest son. You can find more information at www.EmbraceTexas.org. This article originally appeared in ***Fostering Families Today.***

Family Holidays

By Adam Robe, MSW

I remember Christmas Day as a child in care; my sister and I (both in the same placement) would race to the tree to see if Santa brought us everything we wanted. After we demolished the living room, I'd look around and see everyone laughing and having a good time. But inside, I felt that I didn't belong and all I wanted was to be at home with my family. I'd head to my room, wondering what my mom and brother were doing. Were they thinking of me? I knew I missed Christmas at home with them. Sadly, no one in my foster home knew (or publicly acknowledged) that I was struggling with these feelings. My foster parents never talked to me about my biological family, nor did they ask how I used to celebrate the holiday with my family. I believe those conversations were never held because the professionals in my life feared what could come of them. Would I start misbehaving? Would it make me sad? Starting this conversation with me could have opened the door to a more meaningful relationship. It may have helped me open up about how I was feeling inside. As professionals in the foster care system, we have a responsibility to the children in our care to recognize – and acknowledge – each child's history. We should help children embrace their identity by recognizing their past as an important part of who these children are.

So, where do you start? Here are a few examples you can use this holiday season:

- Don't assume that a child celebrates Christmas.
- Find out what traditions the child had in his or her home and incorporate one or two into your celebration (with their permission). Even if you have a number of foster children in your home, this is possible with little work.
- Start a new tradition and explain how they are a part of it.
- Share stories of previous Christmases.
- Document the night with pictures and create a scrapbook for the child to take with him or her.
- If it is okay with the treatment team and court, allow the child to call his or her parent(s) and sibling(s).
- Treat each child the same in your home, regardless of whether the child is a biological or foster child.

In my house, we pick a night to hang ornaments on the tree, listen to Christmas music and decorate the living room with knick-knacks. At the end of the night, when everything is ready, my children climb to the top of the ladder and gently put the Christmas Angel on the tree. These are memories that we'll all share forever. Remember, no matter what the reason was for the removal of a child from his or her biological family, the child has good memories, too. Let the child share them with you.

Adam Robe is a former foster child, social worker, trainer of foster parents and author of the Robbie the Rabbit books among other things. His website is www.robbietherabbit.com.

Prince Charming:

Growing Up with Foster Siblings Teaches a Young Woman a Powerful Lesson
By Alexeah G. Smith

The hot July sun burned high above the light blue sky as white puffy clouds slowly danced by. Dozens of suntanned children scrambled around me, blurting out shrieks of joy as they plunged into the transparent waters of the Phillipsburg Municipal Swimming Pool.

Holden meandered on the cracked cement, moving closer to the white picnic tables full of young teenagers. I watched his every move. I felt as if I rested on a six-foot stand, dressed in a cherry-red bathing suit monitoring the numerous tiny bodies splashing around me, the way I focused on my 10-year-old foster brother. Vanilla ice cream accompanied by melting chocolate, saliva, and peanuts streamed off of his chin onto his plump, chocolate-colored tummy.

Little eyes curiously stared in our direction as we found a seat in the crowded mess of junior high students at the white table covered with residue from weeks-old treats. I recognized their questions by their facial expressions: "What happened to him?" "Why does he slobber like that?" My bright-blue eyes stared back; I interrupted their thoughts and made the teens quickly turn away. Angry thoughts started to fill my mind as I noticed the many eyes once again glued on us.

My family started doing foster care at the end of my sophomore year. I guess that's when I noticed my small-town neighbors paying excess attention to my always-changing family. We accepted children from all different backgrounds, anywhere from African American teenage mothers to beautiful Spanish toddlers. Many strangers, not knowing our situation, would stare and give unappreciative looks.

The looks weren't the hard part in foster care, or even close. The youth and infants coming and going impacted my life; I parted from many people who I wanted to keep in my family forever. After 14 foster siblings leaving though, Holden wandered into the life of my family.

As with every other child or teen we accepted in our home, we knew little about Holden in the beginning. Reports and caseworkers quickly informed us. They started with Holden's horrible past. Because of the severe abuse since his birth, specialists diagnosed Holden as mildly mentally retarded. He also had oppositional defiant disorder, making it hard for anyone to handle him. Holden's problems only grew. A few weeks before his placement in our household, his grandmother, the only one of Holden's family members strong enough to take care of him, died.

Not knowing what to expect of my family, Holden tested us with misbehavior and occasional defiance. My mom and dad quickly let Holden know this behavior would not happen in our home. My parents also told Aubreah, Trevor, and me that our laughter would not be acceptable, since it only encouraged him; but we had never seen such an entertaining and ornery little boy. Misbehavior came naturally to the 10-year-old, but deep down he had a mind jam-packed with imagination. Whether Holden rocked out on a guitar like Elvis, making up songs that always started out with, "Everybody clap your hands;" or had incredible strength like the Hulk, his mind carried him anywhere. My personal favorite of Holden's characters defined himself as Prince Charming, which magically made me

Cinderella.

As I sat at the white table filled with junior high kids and Holden that bright July day, tears began to fill my eyes. I quickly hid my face in hopes Holden would not notice his Cinderella crying. As the cold tears continued to slide down my cheeks, I finally realized at the age of sixteen the unfairness of life. I pondered why life turned out the way it did. Why could Holden not ride his new red scooter down the driveway without falling, yet my siblings and I all play sports effortlessly? Why could kindergartners know they had a messy face, yet Holden had to be told, "You're drooling?" These questions piled up on my brain. Fury boiled inside of me. I wanted to rage at the entire world right then, but suddenly I turned the anger toward myself – not that I made Holden mildly mentally retarded, but because I never saw life the way he did.

Holden educated me about himself while he lived in my house, but he taught me even more about myself.

As I pulled myself together and tried to camouflage the tear streaks on my face the best I could, I looked at Holden. Ice cream and hot fudge now covered his chin, face and the hands that once held the sugar-cone villain, which created this dark milky mess. I rushed Holden over to the chrome water fountain by the swimming pool entrance, so I could wash him off before he hopped in the pool and left the job of removing the sticky dessert to the chlorine. After he washed the warm water all over himself and the cement, letting the ice cream make a new temporary home on the ground, Holden looked up at me with his mouth of many missing baby teeth and smiled. In that moment, I knew exactly why Holden had come to my family.

Holden educated me about himself while he lived in my house, but he taught me even more about myself. Not only did he teach me to reach out more and help those with greater needs, he also taught me about true strength. Holden received every curve ball in life, but instead of giving up, he would ride his scooter even after scraping his knee and flash a true smile even after someone else teased him because he drooled. The same smile appeared after he cannon-balled back into the cool waters of the swimming pool creating a mediocre splash, even if he needed my helping hand. Other people may say the sun brightened that July afternoon, but I believe Holden's smile did, just as Cinderella's did when she first saw Prince Charming.

Alexeah G. Smith graduated from Phillipsburg High School. She is second to the youngest of five biological children in her family. Smith's hobbies include dancing, acting in school plays, being with friends and family, basketball, and track. Smith is actively involved with her church, through youth group, working in children's church and the nursery. She also volunteers as a Big Sister for Big Brothers, Big Sisters. Her future plans include attending college and pursuing her education to become an elementary special education teacher. This story originally appeared in ***Fostering Families Today****.*

The Unexpected Teacher

By Tom Osterbuhr

It is amazing that life's greatest teachers often come when you least expect them. In fact, they are often the least likely candidate. My greatest teacher almost didn't enter our life because of my selfishness. Thank God my family persuaded me to rethink my decision and not give into my first answer. Let me explain in greater detail.

It was July 11, 2003; my wife, Chris and I were celebrating our 22nd wedding anniversary. We had finished dinner and were walking around Eagle Scout Lake in Grand Island, Neb., when my wife hit me with a life-changing proposition. She said, "don't answer me now, pray about this tonight and let's talk tomorrow. There is this little boy that really needs a loving home and I think ours is the one. He is non-verbal, in diapers, but a sweet little guy and he deserves a stable home like ours." Now I didn't wait and I didn't just say no, I said, "NO WAY! It's not fair to our five children and I'm just too old." She responded with, "OK we'll talk more tomorrow.

The next day was Sunday and it started like most Sundays with mass and then I went for a run. I had a lot on my mind so I went a little longer than normal; a 10-mile run would allow me time to think. I was running around the lake when I felt a strong conviction say, "Tom how dare you back out on this boy, you have five healthy children, a wonderful wife, loving parents and in-laws of your own and though you don't have all you want, you have all you need in life." Now, this should have been enough for me to say, "OK Chris, he's moving in." But no, I had an angle.

I went home and told my wife that if all five of our children voted yes we would take this new boy in.

I went home and told my wife that if all five of our children voted yes we would take this new boy in. I just knew that my 16-year-old would vote with me. She was already intolerant of her 12-year-old brother and 10-year-old sister. So the meeting and the vote took place and to my surprise the vote was unanimous, 5 to 0 that he should move in.

That would be enough for most people to say, "OK." Me, being selfish, however took the low road and pulled my daughter aside and said, "Have you gone crazy, this kid will make your life hell, he will get in your stuff and trash your room. What are you thinking?

She looked at me and said, "Dad, we have a pretty nice family and a real nice home, it's the right thing to do." I immediately realized that I was being selfish and my family, then my daughter, had humbled me; it brought me to tears. I called everyone together and said we would bring him in, which we did Sept. 7, 2003.

I was angry the first 30 days Brandon lived with us. I wasn't ready to give up my lazy life I had envisioned as I grew older. What I couldn't see was how much this non-verbal four-year-old boy, still in diapers would bring to our family and especially to me. He was diagnosed mentally retarded, Autistic with Cerebral Palsy, as well as having Reactive Attachment Disorder. In the end, we discovered he does have RAD and a seizure disorder, but none of the other diagnoses were accurate. Since his arrival, this young boy has done nothing but change our lives. We went through being bit, hit and pinched in the early days. Brandon found little or no comfort with us because we were just another home – his fifth in just a little more than four years. To say those early days were easy would be a flat out lie, but I will say they laid the foundation for future teachings for me and my family.

As time went along, we would have small victories and large losses. It was one step forward, then five backward. But Brandon has charisma, a smile and laugh that can win over the toughest critics. On Oct. 7, 2004, just one year and one month after joining our family as a foster son, we adopted Brandon. He officially took on our last name. It's hard to believe he has now been a part of our family for more than eight years. But it would be even harder to imagine our family without him!

This is where the teachings of Brandon come in. I have always been worried about money, status, moving up and what others think. I have always prayed for patience. I was in the third year of a sales position and making more money than I had my entire life when my wife said one of us would need to stay home with Brandon. It ended up being me, again, a bitter pill at first. However, after two years of being Mr. Mom, I wouldn't trade it for any position on earth. I can now add excellent wagon puller and train rider to my resume, (we rode a miniature train at Stolley Park every day, Tuesday through Sunday all summer. No one rides it better than us). I am learning patience, but most important have found my purpose in life.

As for my children, the impact has been equally amazing. They have learned life is about helping others. It has changed how they view life and what is important. My oldest, 25-year-old Kate, went to the local community college, so she could be close by to help with Brandon for two years. She graduated with a consumer family science degree from the University of Nebraska in December 2008. She just took a job in New Orleans with Boys Town and will work with teenage youth. Twenty-three-year-old Denise is at the University of Nebraska studying sociology, and wants to help others. She just finished up a 10-month stint with Ameri-Corps in August and graduated the same month. Meghan, 19, now works in Lincoln. She had a position as a home health care worker, however her client is in a nursing home now. She used to think she had a hard life, then she met Brandon and realized hers wasn't as bad as she thought. My 18-year-old son Jason graduated from Grand Island Central Catholic and is looking at possibly teaching elementary education. My youngest daughter, 16-year-old Alyson, will be a senior at Grand Island Senior High and has done research papers on abuse and neglect.

Brandon has made them all aware of disabilities and rising above those obstacles. They see value in a person, all people. My son Jason wrote a paper about how he and his sisters thought they had a hard life, but since Brandon came to live with us they didn't complain anymore, because they realized he had it tough, not them.

*Tom Osterbuhr is the father of six children. He and his wife have five biological teenagers and one adopted, non-verbal, special needs son whom Tom helps to home school. His son's disability is a seizure disorder brought on by neglect prior to being in foster care. Osterbuhr worked at Girls and Boys Town and Boys Town affiliated sites for 15 years. He currently works as a trainer for youth care organizations. He volunteers as an announcer for his son's school athletic teams and speaks locally for foster/adopt, civic, community, and church groups. This article originally appeared in **Fostering Families Today.***

"Why Do You Ask?"

Questions from Total Strangers and Strategies to Handle Them
By Cheryl Leppert

"Where are your kids from?" It happens at least once a week. Total strangers approach me in the grocery store, at the park, in the library. Most days I'm happy to answer, but sometimes I admit I just want to shout, "It's none of your business!" Locally – for example in our church – everyone knows who we are: We're the family with the two girls from India. They may not always remember our names, but our faces are indelibly etched into their consciousness. That's not necessarily a bad thing. The response has been overwhelmingly positive. One family from our church even chose to adopt after seeing the joy our children have brought to our family. But that feeling of being on display never goes away. So how do we handle invasion of our privacy?

I have learned some strategies to help me evaluate which questions are OK, and which invade the privacy of our family and ask for information private to my children. I also am teaching my children how to evaluate situations – essentially, teaching my children how to speak for themselves. This is really important. One day soon, if it's not happening already, your daughter or son will start moving around in this world without you. It may begin at preschool, dance class, scouts, or elementary school. But when that day arrives, your kids are going to need to be prepared with some idea of how to handle the questions when you are not there to help answer them. Here are my tools for teaching my kids how to evaluate situations:

- Model good responses.
- Ask their opinions. "How could we have handled that differently?" "Were you comfortable with me answering that question?" "Is it okay for me to share that information?" See **W.I.S.E. Up in School** chapter page 271.
- Role play with them. Ask what situations they've encountered and work together to come up with responses that might work.
- Let them know it's okay to ask for help. If a child at school is too persistent in his/her questions, who can your child turn to for help in deflecting the problem?
- Let them know it's okay to not give an answer, and demonstrate this when out in public. It's parents' jobs to defend their children, it establishes boundaries and it teaches how to establish them.

Five great strategies for formulating a response:

Strategy 1: Give a brief, but honest answer, when appropriate. More often than not, this will end the conversation quickly. "Where is she from?" "She was born in India."

Strategy 2: Answer their question with a question. "Why do you ask?" This puts the ball back in their court. If they're being inquisitive, they'll probably feel uncomfortable saying so and will let it drop. If they have a good reason for asking, you can decide where to go from there.

Strategy 3: Show them how invasive the question is. "Do your children get their looks from their father?" A quip is in order sometimes: "I don't know. I never met him." And a snappy response to "Are they really sisters?" is to reply with, "Yes, they are now. Thanks for asking! And do all your children have the same father?" The point here is not to cast doubt upon the questioner's virtue, but to help her see a comparably personal question.

Strategy 4: Defer to your children. Depending on their age, you can make a point of asking them if it's okay for you to answer the question, or, if they're a bit older, you can invite them to do the answering. It's good for the children to see that you respect their ownership of the information, and it can be a good chance for them to practice how they want to answer when strangers ask.

Strategy 5: Invoke the cloak of privacy. Privacy is different from secrecy. Secrecy connotes that there may be something to be ashamed of. Privacy is the barrier that allows you to keep personal information to yourself. Would a total stranger walk up to a woman with a newborn and ask how many stitches she received after childbirth? No. Some things are personal and private and it's okay to say, in as tactful a way as fits the occasion, that it's none of their business.

One thing I have discovered is that my primary obligation is to my children, not to the person who has asked the questions. Using that premise to set boundaries and to model responses for my children has been the key to handling intrusive questions for my family.

Cheryl Leppert is a freelance writer and adoptive parent of two children. This article originally appeared in ***Adoption Parenting: Creating a Toolbox, Building Connections.***

Using your Body to Communicate

Turn. Allow your body language to indicate the question is out of order with a look or by physically turning. Your children will come to learn from you that boundaries are important for matters that are personal and private.

Silence. Sometimes the sound of silence is most expressive. When someone asks a question which in your view is outrageous and simply violates family privacy, it isn't necessary to answer.

Look. You can also add a slow gaze slipping over the person questioning you as you disengage. That tells the person your view more directly than words.

What I've learned about myself while being a foster parent:

I'm an emotional eater.

I trust too many people with my heart.

I am strong and can advocate for myself, my child, and my family.

I try to please people and by so doing, I lose myself in the process.

That I love the tough cases, the kids who really need someone to stand by them.

I sometimes need a reality check into the whys of my decision to continue foster parenting. Is it for my own selfish desire to be a hero or for the attention? Those reasons will not sustain a long-term placement of a troubled child. If I can look at myself and my motives and feel good about both, I know I'm in a good place to continue on and to work to help children in need.

Carrie Craft first saw the need for foster care in 1996 while working at the Wichita Children's Home. Craft has been the Guide for Adoption and Foster Care on About.com since 2004. She also trains foster/adoptive parents in Kansas on various issues that affect their families and the children they parent. She can be reached at adoption@about.com or visit her on the Web at www.adoption.about.com.

Choosing Teens

By Denise Kendrick

My husband and I had fostered younger children for several years before we discovered the need for families to adopt older children. While looking for information about training on the Child Protective Services website, I stumbled upon a link to the profiles of children waiting for adoption in our state. I scrolled more than 90 pages crowded with the photos of sibling groups, teens and children with special needs all waiting for adoptive families.

The profile descriptions accompanying each photo gave vague insight into lives shattered by abuse and neglect:

"Johnny, 14, loves to ride his bike and play outdoors. He struggles to build relationships with his peers. Johnny is making progress in counseling, and will flourish in a consistent, loving home. Johnny would do best as an only child, in a home with experienced parents."

"Marissa, 12, and her sister Margo, 9, are girly girls who love to play dress-up and have their nails painted. Both girls have been diagnosed with Fetal Alcohol Syndrome and receive special services in school. These girls are looking forward to being part of a family, and would do best with a single mother. These sisters have a sibling who will be adopted separately, and would like to have contact with him."

Sparkling eyes and smiles concealed hurt and healing souls. We had never considered adopting, but the faces I saw that day planted a seed in my heart that would not sprout into action for several more years.

Scrolling through the pages of waiting children became a habit for me. I celebrated when a child's photo would disappear, assuming he or she had been adopted, but was startled the first time I saw a picture reappear a few months later. Did an adoptive placement fail? Had this child endured more broken promises? One day a teenage boy's photo caught my eye. Daniel was 14, had a mop of red hair and freckles, and a brief profile praising a child who was helpful, kind and played trumpet in the band.

The last sentence revealed he was in treatment for leukemia. I knew that these children were living and growing while "on hold" and waiting for adoption, but the realization that a child could face the fight of his life in foster care was a shock to me. I didn't feel "sorry" for Daniel, but pouring over his photo I thought "this child needs a mother."

I introduced my husband to Daniel's profile the next day, and he felt a connection to him as well. We began praying for his healing and safety, and two weeks later we contacted Child Protective Services about adopting him. I wondered how many people would consider adopting a child who was not only older, but suffering from a severe medical condition.

When we shared our interest in adopting a teen with our family and friends, their reactions varied but were overwhelmingly concerned. They were worried that this child would bring too much "baggage" into our home. That the peaceful life we had built with our biological children would be wrecked by a destructive or violent teen. These thoughts had crossed my mind as well, but a small and persistent voice deep inside reminded me "this child needs a mother." Two months later we were notified that Daniel had been adopted by an out-of-state relative. It was bittersweet news that felt like disappointment and relief at the same time.

I began to wonder how many families shared our same heart for these teens, and why so few stepped up to adopt them. Did they worry, like our friends and family, that an older child might put their biological children at risk? Were they worried a child who had endured so much could not assimilate into a family? The next week, after much prayer, we set our concerns aside and contacted our foster agency.

"We would like to adopt a boy between 10 and 15 year old." Our caseworker piped in that we were a wonderful family, and she wished more people would consider older children. We spent the next 30 minutes discussing our motivations to adopt and defining more clearly the parameters the agency would use to match us with a child.

We talked about the special needs an older child would face, and how to prepare our home and family for adoption. Our agency knew our family well, and we trusted that they would match us with the right child. We knew their goal was for this to be a safe and successful placement for everyone involved.

The call came two days later. We had been matched with a 15-year-old boy named Brandan. Our worker shared that Brandan had spent many years in foster care after being abandoned by his birth mother. He had been in a failed adoptive placement, and was currently living in a group home. He loved sports and music, to which my husband elbowed me in the ribs because these are two things he is also passionate about. He was tall with dark hair and brown eyes. We took a deep breath and told them we would like to meet him. After the call, we realized even with the information the agency had shared, this child was a stranger to us. But it didn't matter, he was already becoming our son in our hearts.

I would like to tell you that after a few weekend visits and Brandan's moving in with our family, that we all lived happily ever after. We quickly found out that Brandan was not just 15 – he was weeks away from his 16th birthday. He was a charming and playful young man who was helpful around the house. He had rugged good looks and began to shed his extra pounds with a more active lifestyle and home-cooked meals.

He quickly settled into the routines of our home. But Brandan also struggled with a variety of learning and attachment issues and psychiatric diagnosis. He did not know how to nurture friendships with his peers or interact appropriately with adults. Brandan could not control his temper and went into rages that, although not directed at people, were hard on the furniture.

Happily ever after is not something that comes easily for children like Brandan. There are no easy fixes, no guarantees. But choosing a teen has brought so much to our lives. We are teaching a young man that he is lovable and worth loving. He is a wonderful big brother to his younger sisters and brothers. He calls us Mom and Dad, and occasionally wakes up early on a Sunday morning to make the family French toast. When I think back to the first days after he moved into our home I marvel at how much he felt like "company" and how much he fits in now. He still has much to overcome, but now he has a family supporting him along the way. He has his own cheering section at JV football games (complete with little sisters in cheerleading uniforms with pompoms).

Brandan is finding joy in the little things these days, like a dad who knows how he likes his burger cooked, and a mom who packs his lunch. The clock is ticking toward Brandan's eventual independence, a time that for teens who are never adopted brings great hardship and for many, grim outcomes. But Brandan is a teen who was chosen. A teen who carries the last name of his family and the confidence this safety-net awards him.

Denise Kendrick is a long-time foster parent married to her high school sweetheart, Bruce. They lead a ministry called Embrace, www.EmbraceTexas.org, which encourages foster care, adoption and global orphan care. Bruce and Denise have three biological children and just finalized the adoption of their oldest son. This article originally appeared in ***Fostering Families Today****.*

Can't Live With Them, Forced to Live Without Them

By Kasey Carty Jordan

Michael and Jennifer, whose names have been changed to protect their privacy, two siblings separated in foster care, rode horses and climbed rock walls together this past summer after not seeing each other for four years. The normal highs and lows of a sibling relationship were condensed into their one week together, as they argued over not wanting to sit next to each other or to swim in the same section of the swimming pool. Yet Michael's sincere "I love you, but I'm just not used to being around you," brought to light the sad situation of the foster children in America who live apart from their siblings.

Of the nearly 600,000 children in foster care in the United States, approximately 75 percent are separated from at least one sibling. When removed from their homes and placed in a new home, family and life, these children lose not only their family identity but also their relationship with brothers or sisters who are likely to be the only ones who truly understand what they have been through.

Although this problem may seem to pale in comparison to other issues that these children face, the isolation that foster children experience after losing a sibling relationship has far-reaching effects on their ability to connect with others. Studies have shown that up to 25 percent of the homeless population in the United States are former foster children. Of those children who leave the foster system without being adopted, up to 45 percent will be homeless within a year, many will live without health insurance, and a large number will be incarcerated. The lack of connection and responsibility that these children feel toward others creates the sense that their actions do not matter. In their eyes, if nobody cares about what they do or how they live their life, their failure will be a disappointment to no one.

This silent minority lives in a situation that is, for the most part, unknown to the average American. Yet what happens when one person decides to take the broken pieces of her childhood and transform the lives of thousands of siblings in this situation? Camp To Belong.

Until the age of eight, Lynn Price didn't know she had a sister. At that time, her adoptive family took her into a room where she met the mother who was responsible for her placement in foster care, and another little girl they called her "older sister." Price refused to believe that this was her sister, because, after all, this other girl did not look anything like her.

Nearly a decade later, when Price and her older sister went to college, these two women finally began to form memories together as sisters. Because of this experience, Price decided 13 years ago to start a camp to provide the opportunity for children just like herself to create the memories that were absent from her own childhood. Camp To Belong now operates in the states of Nevada, Maine, Massachusetts, Georgia and the Northwest region made up of Washington, Oregon, Alaska, and Idaho. Camp To Belong has extended beyond the borders of the United States with an affiliate in Canada, and has initiated planning committees in Australia and the United Kingdom

Camp To Belong provides foster and adoptive children, age 8 to 18, the opportunity to come together with their separated siblings for a week of "normal" summer camp activities that include horseback riding, rock climbing, swimming, hiking, and arts and crafts. These activities are designed to build each camper's sense of self-esteem, belonging, accomplishments and pride to address the issues that accompany the isolation and loss associated with being separated from siblings. Children build long-lasting bonds with their siblings and others who are familiar with the same type of separation.

Those attending the camp have been separated from siblings for a variety of reasons and Camp To Belong provides a positive environment where children can face some of these causes. One cause of separation is "parentification." Responding to the neglect by their parents, older siblings often step into a parental role to provide for younger siblings physically and emotionally. They often do this at the expense of enjoying their own childhood. When taken into foster care, they are given the "chance" to be children again by being separated from their siblings.

During their week together at Camp To Belong – Georgia in July 2008, Raven, whose name has been changed to protect her privacy, a 15-year-old separated from her younger siblings for this reason, sat between her 11-year-old and 8-year-old brothers at each meal, talking with them about the foods they currently liked and encouraging them to eat their vegetables. She admitted that this was one of the first times that she felt she could be herself, and that no one reprimanded her for taking care of her brothers. "I don't want to be their mother, I want to be a role model for them," she says.

Volunteer counselor Julie Stevenson saw this freedom to be themselves in many of the campers during her experience at Camp To Belong – Georgia. She says, "The camp provides an opportunity for the kids to get away from everyday life, focus on the relationship with their siblings and just have fun."

Jonathan, Rachel and Mary, whose names have been changed to protect their privacy, three siblings from a sibling group of ten, also attended Camp To Belong-Georgia. Rachel was afraid of water and announced that she would not go canoeing with her siblings. At Jonathan's prompting, she timidly stepped into the canoe, trusting that her older brother would take care of her. Although she saw other children tipping canoes around her, she chose to trust this brother. While seemingly small, this step built Rachel's trust in another person and increased Jonathan's realization that his actions mattered to someone.

By taking these steps, teenagers are better equipped emotionally to have a successful future. To further help these children to attain educational success, campers participate in the Life Seminar Program. This program is designed to educate older campers about the options available to them after high school graduation and to support them as they approach emancipation from the foster care system.

Campers aged 14 years and older complete career interest surveys; learn about grants, scholarships and financial aid; discuss school and job applications; and receive informational notebooks for future reference. Guest speakers, college advisers and recruiters present options regarding college, vocational or technical school, community service organizations, and the military. One week is not long enough to address every opportunity that these children have available to them, but the relationships formed at the camp provide mentorships that last long after the camp is over.

As the bus pulled away from the camp, Michael and Jennifer – well-known throughout the week for their constant arguing – sat together in silence and told each other "I love you" before walking through the parking lot toward the two cars that would take them in different directions. Their week together had brought four years of separation to a close, and they were going back to their separate lives. Yet there was an understanding and a depth to their relationship that had been absent just a week earlier.

Five days of camp do not seem like they can change the world, but for these children they do. One foster or adoptive parent, one caseworker, one set of siblings at a time, we can all make the tiny steps necessary for these children to be the brothers and sisters to each other they were meant to be. Those interested in starting new affiliates, volunteering at existing camps, or involving your separated foster or adoptive children and their siblings at a summer camp, contact Camp To Belong at www.camptobelong.org.

Kasey Carty Jordan serves on the board of directors of Camp To Belong-Georgia as the chair of camper recruitment and fundraising. Before joining the founding board in 2007, she served, and continues to serve, as a Court Appointed Special Advocate for children in Cherokee County, Ga. In May 2009, she completed a master of arts in professional writing degree at Kennesaw State University. During her time at KSU, she served as a teaching assistant, using a service learning approach to teach civic involvement to her students. She also served as an intern for the KSU College of the Arts, contributing weekly feature stories, and serves as the primary grant writer for CTB-GA. Find out more about Camp to Belong at www.camptobelong.org. This article originally appeared in ***Fostering Families Today.***

Ensuring Family Fit for Foster Families

By Betty Daigle Hastings

When the final approval has been given to newly approved foster parents there is that feeling of excitement, enthusiasm, and the desire to demonstrate that they are now ready to begin immediately fostering a child needing placement. There are many areas that need to be addressed prior to the placement of a child in a home. Is this the right child for our foster home, is an important question to ask before acceptance of a child. Hopefully, time will be given to consider this important decision.

Accepting a Child Into Your Family

During the licensing process, foster parents must determine the age of the child they want to consider. Due to the desperate need to place children, foster parents are often called to consider children who do not fit within that age limit or type of placement families feel comfortable handling. With all the love, training, and what they may feel they have to offer, it's important to understand that every child may not be best suited for placement within a particular family setting. Careful consideration should be given to each request.

The foster parent must be able to understand that every child will likely suffer a devastating loss associated with his or her removal from the biological parents and being placed in state custody. Every child who comes into care has a different situation. The circumstances surrounding the process of treatment and success to a permanency plan will vary from child to child. Therefore, it is important that the potential foster parents be informed and have the knowledge of the child's prior history. They need to be allowed to review any and all information to assist in determining if the child would be a proper placement for their home. The child's health history is an important fact as there are the foster parents who are not able to deal with the special needs of a particular child. Lack of this information will definitely jeopardize the successful permanency work that the foster parent must offer to a child.

Consideration should be given to the ability to preserve the continuity of the child's racial, ethnic, and cultural identity in a positive manner. A key component to effectively foster children of other cultures is for the foster parents to become aware of their own culture and the difference and similarities between their culture and that of the child's. There may be cultural bias within the foster parents' extended families, the community, the school system, or other areas. The child will need the support of the foster parents to be able to navigate through this emotional time. Understanding these facts is important and where there should be great consideration if the placement would be in the best interest of the child in the home.

Foster care is temporary and foster parents must determine if they can work effectively with the birth parents if reunification is the goal of the child. Children placed in legal custody, when given the right to visit with their birth parents, need the support and shared parenting responsibilities of the foster parents. Foster care is a partnership which involves the agency, birth parents, child and foster parents. To effectively meet the best interest of the child, all components of this partnership must work together. No matter how troubled or difficult the birth family may be, they are the roots of the child's origin and identity.

Inability to work with a foster child's birth family, when the goal is to return home, would certainly prove to be detrimental to the placement the child.

In considering the placement, it is important to recognize the other members of your immediate family, the effect that it has upon your spouse, birth children, extended family, and others in order to work effectively with the foster child. Certainly, there are often those unexpected circumstances that will arise after placement, and perhaps movement from the home may be inevitable. Understanding that each movement of a child sets the child back possibly six months, nothing good can come from multiple moves. Therefore, this makes it even more important to take all areas under consideration prior to placement to keep disruptions from happening.

Refusing a Child

When the decision has been reached by foster parents to refuse a placement, it is important to clearly express to the agency the reasons why. One of the most important pieces of good relationships is communication.

Communication opens doors for foster parents and workers. It is the responsibility of all involved to share information and certainly understand the reason for refusing to receive a placement is a part of the good relationship between the agency and the foster home.

If foster parents refuse a placement they should not fear they may never be called for a placement again, unless refusals occur numerous times over a period without good reason.

Siblings should not always be kept together

That the state believes that siblings should be kept together in adoption, even if they were thriving as individuals with their foster families who wanted to adopt them. In my case, our family was very violent with each other. My siblings are very violent with brain damage. I was violent, but learned how to control my anger. When you put violent kids who learned a pattern of abusing each other back together in a new family, it's a recipe for diaster. Both of my siblings have RAD. They have both been returned to foster care by the second set of adoptive parents. I believe if they were left with the people that loved them when they were toddlers, they would have been okay today. My brother tried to kill me when he was 12 and our adoptive parents dissolved his adoption. My sister tried to kill her second adoptive mom when she was 11 and she was removed from that family.

– Mariah Berry, age 17, was in and out of foster care since age 3. She was finally adopted at age 14. She was in more than 30 foster homes in Florida, is hearing impaired and has overcome much.

A placement should never be accepted with the feeling, "if I don't take this child, I may never be called again." Foster parents must keep in mind the best interest of the child which is what fostering is all about. There will certainly be another call eventually because there are so many children in need of care. It's just as important that when a home is needed, it also be the right placement for the child and family.

Changing Roles

The role of foster parents has made a tremendous change within the past few years. Foster parents in some states today are able to receive information and assurances of participation prior to placement due to the adoption of the Foster Parent Bill of Rights. Even though the Bill of Rights may differ somewhat in wording in the individual states, the intent is to give foster parents an understanding of their rights, but also it has opened the door to give foster parents an understanding of the responsibilities associated with those rights mandated. In some states as adopted by the Bill of Rights, foster parents have the right to refuse placement without the threat of retaliation. This move has made it easier for foster parents to be able to truly give that request for placement deeper and more consideration of how it will affect their lives and the life of the child needing placement within their home.

Foster parents should always keep in mind that if the child is placed in their home, they hold a part of that child's future within their hands. If placement is not in the child's best interest and placement is denied, they should never feel bad. There will be another child needing a home. The excitement, enthusiasm and desire to foster will return when a good fit is found.

Betty Daigle Hastings is a foster parent in Tennessee. She was a foster child in her teenage years. Hastings worked for the University of Tennessee as a foster parent trainer and continues to train in Tennessee and across the nation. She serves as state president of the Foster Parent Association in Tennessee for six years. Presently, she serves as chair of the National Foster Parent Association States Affiliated Council and was elected as vice president of the Tennessee Foster Adoptive Care Association and to the Tennessee Supreme Court Improvement Committee. She serves on committees, meeting the needs of the children in the welfare system. She and her husband have fostered more than 300 children and adopted two boys during this time. This article originally appeared in ***Fostering Families Today.***

Where are the Laws to Protect Foster Families?

By Jay Paul Deratany, JD

A True Story

I was in my office one afternoon when the phone rang. It was a potential client and she relayed and all too common heart-breaking ordeal:

"Mrs. Smith" and her husband had long wanted to bring a foster child into their home. The Smith's registered with a private placement agency which advertised that it could place foster children into the homes of welcoming families. The private placement agency had a contract with the Department of Children and Family Services to facilitate the placement of children. The Smiths had three other children ages 4, 5, and 7 and wanted to make sure that accepting an older foster child into their home would "cause no harm" to their biological children.

The Smiths met with the private placement agency caseworker, "Sandy," who advised them that she had a "perfect child for them" named "Billy." When the Smiths asked if the child had a history of sexual or physical abuse, the caseworker denied that the child had any such history. The caseworker also represented that the child had been in "two or three" prior homes.

Serious Problems Arise

After a couple of months, Mrs. Smith begins to notice that Billy appears to be more verbally abusive and that her own children are withdrawn and easily upset. When she asks her children if anything is wrong, they deny that anything is bothering them. She takes her three biological kids to their grandfather's farm, hoping that a week in the country will be good for them. At the end of the week, when it comes time for the Smith children to come home, they scream and cry to their grandfather that they "do not want to go back home." Mr. and Mrs. Smith take their biological children to a child therapist where it is disclosed that the foster child repeatedly raped and sexually abused the Smith's younger biological children and threatened to kill them if they told.

Failure to Disclose

After Billy is removed from the home, the Smiths, through their attorneys, discover that Billy did not have "two or three" prior placements as they were told, but rather there were 14 prior homes, where he had been rejected because of physical and sexual abuse to other children. The Smiths also discover that the foster care agency had medical records in its possession that indicated Billy had a history of physically and sexually aggressive behavior toward other children. The Smiths also learn that the foster care agency worker "Sandy" was told by other caseworkers that Billy was schizophrenic and sexually abusive to other children. In short, Sandy and her agency intentionally placed a sexual perpetrator into a home with three younger children, without telling the parents. Sandy admits that she is compensated by the agency with bonuses for quickly placing "hard to place" children.

Frightening Pattern

Unfortunately the above has become a much too common theme in the placement of children by agencies contracting with various State Departments of Children and family Services. Part of the problem is that the state is abrogating or repealing its right by entering into contracts with private agencies and then failing to provide the proper oversight. The result is that many foster parents are not only left in the dark, but are deceived with regard to a foster child's mental health background, as well as to the child's history of abuse or perpetration. The consequences of the foster placement agency's failure to disclose full information concerning the child being placed is devastating for both the child and the recipient family. In the Smith's case, had Billy's condition not been ignored, he would have received psychological treatment and most likely would not have been placed in a home with younger children.

Many States Do Not Adequately Protect Foster Families

Most states have no law which specifically mandates that the foster parents must be given all medical, psychiatric, and psychological information pertaining to a child who is about to be placed in the foster parent's care. This lack of specific and coherent laws that protect both the foster family and the child being placed is a problem throughout the country. This has resulted in some placement agencies simply disregarding the foster parents rights statutes and providing information of their own choosing to the foster family, or simply misinforming the families to make a placement.

Redrafting the Statues to Protect All

We need a national standard for the placement of children in foster homes. Specifically, in order to protect both the child and the foster family, there needs to be a uniform code which is adopted in each state. At minimum, there must be no exception to a full and complete disclosure of a child's mental health, medical history, biological, familial medical and mental health history to the potential foster home. Foster care agencies must not be allowed to continue "hear no evil, speak no evil" way of doing business. The statute should also set forth specific civil and criminal penalties for failure to disclose information to a foster family. Those agencies which choose to misrepresent a child's history to a family purely to make a profit should be held liable in a court of law for their violations. Failing to implement a national standard which requires full disclosure of the child's physical and mental condition to a foster family, will only increase the likelihood of severely emotionally, mentally impaired or sexually abusive foster children being placed into a family and causing physical harm to himself and/or to others in the house.

*Jay Paul Deratany, JD, is a partner in the Law Offices of Deratany & Carend in Chicago, Ill. He has successfully prosecuted cases ranging from medical malpractice to nursing home abuse. He also does extensive charitable and pro bono work, including involvement with the Perspectives Charter School for need children and Community Support Services for individuals with developmental disabilities. He has a juris doctorate degree from DePaul University College of Law in Chicago, Ill. His website is www.lawinjury.com. This article originally appeared in **Fostering Families Today.***

Torn Hearts: When Foster Children Leave

By Gail Valence

My oldest son was three when my first two foster children, twin 1-year-old girls, were returned to their biological mother. They had lived with us for eight months, a substantial part of my son's life. Their return home was sudden, as swift as a judge's signature on a court order. I was notified at 11 am on the day they were to return home. I was told that social workers would come by 12:30 pm to pick up the girls. I remember wondering how I could possibly give them enough hugs and kisses to last a lifetime.

My husband was at work and the social workers did not even want to wait for his return home. I called him and asked him to come home immediately. My husband arrived just as the social workers were carrying our foster daughters out the door. I'll never forget the looks in the girls' eyes as they cried and held their arms out to us as virtual strangers took them to a car. My husband only had time for quick hugs and kisses. As we tearfully said our goodbyes, our son, bewildered, cried in response to his foster sisters' cries. The pain for me is as fresh and raw today as it was 19 years ago.

This makes me wonder what effect it had on our son and what effect, if any, it had on his future relationships, with his unborn siblings. Although my son had been toilet trained for five months before the girls left, he reverted to wetting the bed at night and had to wear diapers for an additional six months. He walked around for weeks looking and calling for his foster sisters. He asked repeatedly if he were going to be taken away, too. He often awoke from nightmares, crying out in fear.

Even though we had always told him that the girls were our foster children and that they may not always live with us, this concept was too difficult and abstract for him to grasp. Psychologist Albert Goldstein writes that "Unlike adults, children have no psychological conception of blood-tie relationships until late in their development." If this is true, how could he understand that the children living in our house were not his sisters, no matter what we say?

When our second son was born seven months later, our oldest son looked at him with little interest. The first thing he asked was, "How long are we going to keep this baby?" Even with our assurances I am not sure he was convinced.

According to Nancy Millichap Davies, "The experience of being taken away to a foster home is traumatic for any child. Children show signs of emotional stress during the early weeks and months of placement. These may include nightmares, trouble in sleeping, bed-wetting and eating problems. Most such physical symptoms disappear after the first few weeks of placement, but the emotional problems continue."

It is the last sentence that frightens me most. How long do the emotional problems continue? I've often read of the detrimental effect that repeated separation on the biological children in the foster home. The physical symptoms and emotional stress appear to be identical. Is the outcome also similar?

In my search for answers, one foster parent told me, "When a foster child returns home, my sons become very antagonistic toward each other for awhile. They don't say so in so many words, but I wonder if they think the other is to blame for a child going home." I wonder if she could be right. Children often blame themselves when parents divorce so it seems reasonable that they could blame their parents, or their siblings, when a foster child is taken away.

Another foster parent shared that her biological children seem to maintain an emotional distance from the foster children in her home. She thinks they do this as a form of self-protection, because it is painful for them when foster children leave their house.

According to psychologist Joseph Goldstein, continuity of relationship is essential for a child's healthy development. Yet, we are taking the "continuity of relationships" away from biological children in foster homes whenever a foster child leaves. How does this affect the relationship between the siblings? Is their sense of trust or security compromised as a result? Did taking foster children into our home when my own children were young compromise the trust and security of their long-term relationships as siblings? Is it better to take in foster children when your own children are older?

The human spirit is remarkably strong. Just as some families appear easily to handle the issues of separation and loss as children enter and leave their home, so do some children, resilient by nature, cope better than others. This natural resiliency extends to all children, whether they are foster children or the biological children of the parents opening their home to foster children. However, we must work to understand the impact of separation and loss on the biological children in our own family and be prepared to deal with the after effect.

It would be so easy, God
To make the simple decisions
That convenience, the desire
To be like,
And momentary peace
Dictate.
And just as I withdraw the hand
Which offers pain, adversity,
And exhaustion, You remind me
That no one ever grows,
Never blooms when things are easy.

– Gordon MacDonald

Gail Valence is a teacher in Rochester, NY. Her master's thesis on foster children was groundbreaking research questioning the effects that foster children have on families. Many foster care agencies are using her research. This article originally appeared in ***Fostering Families Today.***

Discipline

Children need love, especially when they do not deserve it.
– Harold Hulbert

Don't Use an Elephant Gun To Shoot a Mouse

By Walt Piszchala

I was experiencing my first baptism under fire with an angry and oppositional 15-year-old boy who was telling me, in plain English that would make any sailor or truck driver proud, what I could do with my rules.

I remember sitting in the office of my first supervisor as a young and inexperienced child care worker, in Warehouse Point, Conn., at the State Receiving Home. This is a facility run by the Connecticut Department of Children and Families, the year was 1975. Silas W. Davis, a man I would come to view as both a mentor and a father figure was speaking to me about his personal philosophy of disciplining children for inappropriate behavior. The words he spoke to me seemed strange and it was a while before it registered with me. He said, "I want you to remember this, 'Don't use an elephant gun to shoot a mouse... "

Fast forward several months later, I was experiencing my first baptism under fire with an angry and oppositional 15-year-old boy who was telling me, in plain English that would make any sailor or truck driver proud, what I could do with my rules. Enraged by this blatant lack of respect, both for myself and the rules of the cottage, I proceeded to operate on pure emotion and adrenaline and totally ignored what Davis had told me in his office. You see it is one thing to remain calm reviewing a programmatic rule and even possibly role playing a situation in training under controlled circumstances, but it is quite another experiencing it in real life. It didn't just affect the young man in question and me; it was in front of 17 other children and several of my co-workers.

Being young and inexperienced, I did what every parent since the dawn of time has done when their child goes into a meltdown, and does something either at home, school, or church to embarrass both themselves as well as their family, I brought out my own personal elephant gun. Needless to say I turned a routine verbal intervention into an exasperating incident which damaged not only my relationship with this child, but everyone who was witness to it. I always want to remember my personal elephant gun story so I can help every person I train to never have to experience what I did.

I would like to share with the readers, one specific area of my own Verbal De-escalation Curriculum that I teach to foster and adoptive parents in local and national conferences. I offer a five-step approach to setting limits that can be adapted to any age, population or functioning group.

Step One: Use Language That Calms

Tell your child in language that I refer to as "affect neutral" what it is that you are asking, not telling, them to either start, or stop doing. An example of each would be:

A. Your child gets into a heated argument with a sibling and becomes increasingly aggressive with both body language and verbal threats. In this situation you are setting limits to have them "stop" engaging in an inappropriate behavior. It's not the argument that is our issue; it is the aggressive body language as well as the threats. If you start trying to intervene and stop your child from typical age appropriate behaviors, or sibling rivalries, you will never get anything accomplished. In addition to my "elephant gun" metaphor I always stress that in order to act in the best interest of the out-of-control individual we need to clearly be in control of our own feelings and emotions first. Have you had a bad day at work? Are there existing marital or financial problems in your relationship? These personal issues can exacerbate the situation and cause you to bring out your own personal elephant gun to try to settle a situation.

B. The second example of asking them to, in this case, "start" doing something is at 7 p.m., dinner is finished, the table is cleared, and chores complete, it is now homework time. Tommy has seated himself in front of the TV and is about to play his favorite video game while everyone else has gone to their rooms and cracked open their books. In this situation, an example of bringing out your own elephant gun would be to go over to the TV, take the remote, and "click." We all know it is not going to end there. A line in the sand has been drawn and someone is going to lose. And, the unfortunate reality is it is going to be you!

Step Two: Tell them why...

You must clearly and concisely inform the child why you are asking, not telling, him or her to do something. The reason "why" should always go back to the common theme of "because the rules of the house" say that from 7 to 9 p.m. it is homework time and nothing else. Do not let the situation become personal, keep the focus on them, not you.

Step Three: Review the consequences.

(This can be a deadly minefield for a parent to navigate through)

The classic elephant gun, "negative consequence," is an empty threat. For instance, "if you don't go to your room right now you are going to lose TV for one month!" Now you know full well there has never been a parent in the history of the world who could stick to their guns for an entire month of no TV. Isn't the primary point of consequences – both positive and negative – to teach children a lesson? What lesson are you imparting to your child if you bring out the negative consequences first? They begin thinking back on all of the times that the adults in their lives have yelled, screamed, and used negative reinforcements to try to change their behavior. Always try to remember, "in order to change a child's behavior you have to first fundamentally change the way they view their world." What are we doing if all we engage in are threatening, negative consequences using our own elephant guns?

So what else can we rely on instead of negative consequences? How about starting your intervention with a positive consequence for complying with your request, not demand, first? Sometimes the positive consequence will be a tangible reward, however other times the positive consequence may simply be not earning a negative consequence. Try it sometime; it may surprise you with its effect on your child.

Now, once you've gone over the positive consequences for complying you must then let them know what the negative consequences will be for failure to cooperate.

Step Four: Give them some time.

You have to give them a brief cooling off period, no more than a few minutes. Trying to coach an answer out of children after all of this is too overwhelming. They need a few minutes to process everything, to make the best possible choice for them as well as lose the least amount of face with their siblings.

Step Five: Be prepared to enforce.

You need to be ready to do what you said would happen, both positively as well as negatively. The two biggest mistakes you can make at this stage is to not follow through with the positive consequence you said would happen, and being a parent that says, "This is it! No more chances! You better not do that again!" If this is your personal elephant gun, then I say give them your car keys, your Visa or MasterCard with directions to the nearest shopping mall, because at this point they own you. You have lost your credibility with the child as well as the rest of his or her siblings.

You all have a profound impact on your children's lives. You are welcoming children into your homes, who in many cases have been damaged beyond our own imaginations and we are charged with the task of nurturing them into healthy and productive citizens of our society.

*Walt Piszchala worked for The Connecticut Department of Children and Families for 33 years, specializing in working with children in a variety of capacities, primarily in residential care. For 27 of those years Piszchala worked as a trainer in the field of Crisis Intervention and Health and Safety, teaching both verbal and physical intervention techniques and CPR, AED, First Aid, Blood Borne Pathogens. Piszchala retired from the Connecticut Juvenile Training School as a full-time training coordinator. His main focus had been in the development and implementation of a comprehensive behavior management and crisis intervention program. From 1997 to 2006 Piszchala was an adjunct staff trainer at the Department of Children and Families training academy. Since 2007, Piszchala has become a member of the training faculty for the Connecticut Association of Foster and Adoptive Parents. He offers courses in verbal de-escalation and works with oppositional and defiant children. For more information, visit www.piszchala-associates.com. This article originally appeared in **Fostering Families Today**.*

The Value of Consistency

By Jo Ann Wentzel

If I could give only one word of advice to parents, it would be consistency. A consistent parent gives the child the gift of always knowing what to expect. Neither the rules nor the consequences change from day to day.

I had foster kids who called this "nagging," but they knew what they could or could not do and what would happen if they made the wrong choice. They would come in the door and before discovering we already knew what they had been up to, they were discussing the consequences. They knew them in advance. I knew I had hit home with a message when the kids started to finish the sentence. No kid, upon learning that he or she was in trouble, could claim ignorance because I had heard them repeat the rule.

They claim the average attention span for teens being talked to is about 30 seconds, so that is the time you have to get messages across. If that is the case, a complete message needs to be broken down into small, short bits, and repeated often.

Teens dislike sermons so these short bursts are best, but more important than length is content. Being consistent means telling the exact same thing in the exact same way until it sticks in their memories like an advertising jingle for a product on TV. You begin to remember the exact words; the phrase goes together without even thinking about it. Have you noticed the new trend in advertisements? The first few weeks you get the complete ad with every gruesome detail. Later on, they shorten it to just the punch line, but the entire ad is already playing in your mind. Commercials have something to teach parents!

Consistency means nothing to kids if you don't follow through in practice. This means a parent should be sure of what policies they want to implement. Consistency implies no change without a good reason.

I have been a foster parent in organizations where every day there were policy changes. As foster parents, we were confused. Now, consider a foster child who has never had stability. Suddenly, the pattern is repeating itself and he or she does not know what the rules are anymore. Most foster kids came from families that were inconsistent. For the first few years of parenting, these parents were often so lenient, set few rules, and never expected kids to pay consequences for their action.

Suddenly, they decide it is time to be firm and go so far the other direction as to almost be abusive. They certainly are not realistic. It takes months before they admit this approach is not working and midstream; they change direction again. Their kids are confused, and by this time probably dizzy.

Another scenario involves the parents who say "if you do this, you will be punished in this way." When the kids do (let's say lying), the punishment for that is grounding for a month. Unfortunately, the kids are driving them crazy so they let them out in two weeks. These kids have learned not to believe what you say. They figure they should not worry about rules or consequences since you will weaken or they can get around you. It is always better to keep grounding to a minimum that you can live with, but be consistent.

This does not always work. I had one young man who was grounded for two weeks every time he got drunk. He had the pleasure of my company every two weeks. He would pay his consequence without complaining, then immediately do it again. It eventually took, but we did not back down. This young man has since attached himself to our family and for all intents and purposes, he is our son. We all lived through it. In some rare instances I also allowed kids to work their way out of grounding for the sake of both our sanity. But the work was in addition to regular chores, time-consuming, and difficult.

Consistency is important in scheduling for the same reasons as in rules. These kids never knew if they would eat or when, what time they would finally go to bed, or if they would actually see the parent that day. We tried to keep to a reasonable schedule in our foster home. It is difficult, but not impossible. Crisis and a tremendous workload make it a challenge, but keep to a schedule if you want calm kids. The unpredictable former lives they have led are a leading factor for problems they have. They might complain to you, but they tend to thrive on set times for everything.

Kids learn to associate certain things with other events, such as homework being done directly before or after supper. Other examples include the bus coming for school exactly one hour after their morning shower, and lights out or quiet time at specific times, followed by sleep.

Consistency should also carry over to love. No matter what kids do, they still need attention and love. That should never be withheld from them as a treatment to help the situation, punishment when they mess up, they need it most of all. See how consistency helps you deal with your kids. And foster parents, thank you for being there.

Jo Ann Wentzel is the mother of three: two children born to her and one foster kid who never left their family, grandmother to five, foster mom to more than 75 kids, and mother, friend, guardian angel, or their worst nightmare, depending on which of the other hundreds of kids whose lives she has touched. This article originally appeared in ***Fostering Families Today.***

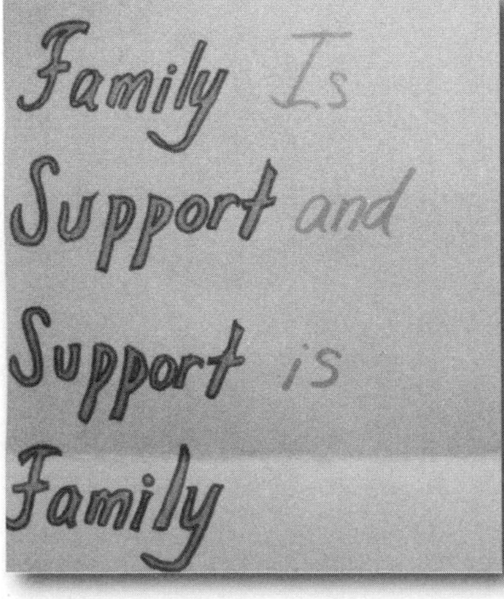

Appropriate Boundaries in Parenting

By Sue Laney

What do parents most want from children?

Is it obedience – for children to do what parents think is best whether for the benefit of the child or for the parent? Could it be love – that parents want their children to love them unconditionally as parents try to love their children unconditionally? What about becoming good citizens who are responsible, pleasant to be around, non-offensive to others, and working toward success and independence? And, does love equal respect? So, how do parents get what they most want from their children? The answer is setting appropriate boundaries. These boundaries look and feel different depending on the chosen parenting style. There are typically three styles of parenting with some parents jumping from one style to the other depending on what point or convenience they believe is important to make at the time.

Lines in the Sand

The first boundary style is called "lines in the sand" and the following story will illustrate this parenting style.

> *Four-year-old Jody and her mother are eating lunch at a local restaurant. Jody wants some gum out of the gum ball machine and asks her mom for some money. When mom says, "Not now, sweetie," Jody continues to ask and mom continues to deny the request. Mom decides to call a friend on her cell phone and while mom is distracted Jody goes into her mom's wallet, gets a handful of change, puts the coins in the machine and comes back to the table with some gum in her mouth. After a bit, Mom finally notices Jody chewing gum and tells her friend the whole story as Jody listens. Mom expresses to her friend she just doesn't understand why Jody doesn't obey her. Jody is never personally scolded for her poor choice or instructed how to make a better choice.*

Although many parents want to have fun with their children, when a parent draws a line in the sand as the boundary for the child to follow, the relentless waves of the tide come in and wash the line away each time it is drawn. Therefore, what did Jody learn? If this parenting style is used often, Jody will relentlessly test her mom and other authority figures just to see where the boundaries actually are. Often, foster parents are unsure of where to place boundaries on foster children and may be overly lenient to compensate for the hurt foster children have experienced. "Lines in the sand" parenting tells foster children that 1) they are not good enough to have set or standard boundaries and will need to set their own, 2) the parent is incapable of setting appropriate boundaries, or 3) they are special and don't need to follow the same boundaries as other family members. This parenting style leads birth and foster children toward rebellion breeding chaos, fighting, disrespect, and a low sense of self-worth.

The Brick Wall

The second style of parenting is described as a "brick wall." Picture it... a tall, thick, red brick wall. Does it signify protection, strength, a sense of durability; or could it be described as more cold, looming, harsh, and impenetrable?

> *Susan has been parenting for a number of years and now has three teens in her house. "I have to make sure I can maintain order and discipline so we are very strict with the children. We have a very strict curfew and have learned that if we let one child get away with something, everyone else will try to do the same thing. Rules are important and must be obeyed or there is punishment. If there is no punishment for misbehavior, how will these children learn to behave?"*

Children need the protection and strength from parents but never do they need parents to be unwelcome, forbidding, rigid, or unforgiving. Children also need the opportunity to learn to make good choices. A safe and comfortable home environment is where children can experience many opportunities to practice making choices. Being allowed to make choices encourages confidence. If children find the answer to their requests always being "no," or a place where guilt and unforgiveness is the rule of the day, then those children will seek acceptance elsewhere and usually in unfavorable settings. This parenting style also leads children to rebellion breeding chaos, fighting, disrespect, and a low sense of self-worth.

Often children run from rigidity because their inherent sense of free will or freedom of choice is being squelched. Foster children have often been reared in homes which have neglected their needs either through moving or non-existent boundaries, such as "lines in the sand;" or strict boundaries described as "brick wall" parenting.

The Deep Rooted Tree

The two extremes in parenting have been explained leaving the third parenting style of the "deep-rooted tree." Picture a tall, sturdy tree whose branches spread out over the yard giving shelter, shade, beauty, freedom, creativity, recreation, and a feeling of being tested over time.

> *Megan is excited to finally get out to the store. Her children, ages five and three keep her jumping most days and she is looking forward to seeing a new comforter that is currently on sale. As she puts her little one in the cart, her oldest starts to scream that he wants to be in the seat, not his sister. No amount of conversation seems to be able to dissuade his desire and a full melt-down ensues. Megan glances at her watch and realizes that it is getting close to supper time and they have been pretty busy all day. She lets her son know that she understands he is tired and hungry and that they can try to do this store another day when everyone is in a better mood.*

One of the benefits of this parenting style is the manner in which life's storms are weathered – with grace, flexibility, and wisdom. There's no room for arrogance, impatience, or pity. A quiet strength is rooted in good soil, rich with healthy nutrients expressing the importance of taking care of oneself and others. There are no inappropriate expectations nor judgement but a joy when family members choose to spend time together under the tree. Delightful flowers and foliage often bring forth delicious fruit allowing others to share from the bounty and the beauty this style offers. When the storms come, deeply planted roots hold the tree upright with a strong trunk. The branches know just how far to bend without breaking from the wind. And so it is with this parenting style.

Creating Strength and Flexibility

As children need strength and wisdom from their parents, they also need flexibility. "Deep-rooted" parenting has a strong foundation supporting children to learn from their personal experiences through proper guidance in making effective choices. These teaching moments become life lessons which mold children's character and prepare them to respond appropriately in future situations.

As foster parents, strength with flexibility offered to all children shows parents care about children as individuals, that parents believe in children and trust their ability to make good choices for their level of development. Children experience freedom and peace when acting within appropriate boundaries. In return, through time, parents will receive the love and respect that they demonstrate to others.

Although flexibility is the key element in appropriate boundaries, determining how far a parent is willing to go and being consistent in not going beyond the boundary limit is crucial. A rubber band has several uses but is most commonly used for holding things close or together. It can only be stretched so far before it pops. When the band does pop, it is no longer as useful; it stings anything near it; and if the ends are tied together again to resume its initial purpose, there is less room to perform its purpose inside the band. Therefore flexibility has its limits.

Appropriate parenting boundaries are defined as: the structure from which to operate, which is geared for protection and effective living, offering freedom to act within the limits, while encompassing positive, and negative consequences for reinforcement of the structure. Without boundaries we have chaos, conflict, and confusion.

When setting boundaries ask the question, "Is this boundary used for protection and teaching or is it for my comfort?" Keeping the child's best interest at heart will help to ensure boundaries remain appropriate. Use boundaries suitable for the appropriate age and stage of the child's development and use reasonable punishment to fit the crime. Pay attention to the behavior you want to see by using many more rewards than punishments. The best rewards are praise, hugs, or a pat on the back, which don't cost any money. And if you want children to obey, they have to trust in you – not just trust you, but in you – trusting that you always have their best interests at heart.

*Sue Laney is the author of "**Nurturing God's Way Parenting Program for Christian Families®**," "**Basic Home Visitation Skills™ Training Curriculum and Survival Kit for Parents™**" and "**Nurturing Your Home® Training Curriculum**." She is the president and CEO of the Family Nurturing Center of Georgia and a national trainer/consultant for Nurturing Parenting Programs®. Currently she is the project director of Nurturing Georgia's Families® Project. This article originally appeared in **Fostering Families Today.***

Cycle of Want

Assuming emotional needs continue to be met, an older child learns to calm and self-regulate through a parent's yes or no response to their "want." The circle must be completed for positive learning to take place.

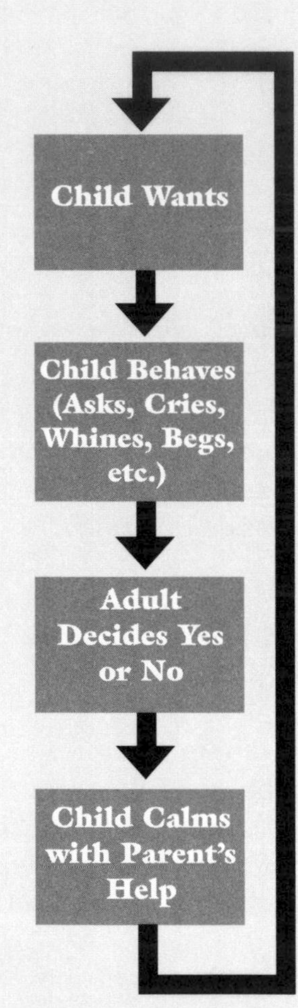

Parents say yes or no based on what is best for their child. Calming is what completes the cycle, not saying "yes" for peace and quiet. You teach self-control and belief in parents.
Doris Landry, MS

The Extra Layer and Discipline Strategies

By Deborah Moore
Based on the work of Doris Landry, MS with permission.

Successfully disciplining an adopted or foster child takes the extra layer of adoption/loss into consideration. On top of whatever method of discipline you choose, therapist Doris Landry, MS, suggests adding these three basic tools to dramatically increase its effectiveness.

Understand. It is important for parents to help children understand the meaning of their actions. For instance, children who were hit, slapped, kicked or restrained in their previous life experiences may replicate those behaviors under duress, without understanding why. When a child misbehaves, and you can recognize where the behavior comes from, it can be helpful to explain the relationship between his or her actions and his or her past.

Express empathy. With empathy, parents you can help children see that while their behavior is bad, they are not bad. When children are taken into your parents' arms and engage in meaningful dialog about the "why" of what happened, parents are not condoning the misbehavior, but rather helping children understand the origin and the meaning of the behavior.

Re-attune. The child's understanding and the parent's empathy together lead to a re-attunement between parent and child, allowing for the child to express sorrow for hurting the other person. The child is then able to learn, change, and openly accept guidance and correction.

The past experiences of these children necessitates considering different models for discipline. Some of the best advice I ever received about disciplining my children, was to have a "toolbox" of techniques. Landry, in her "Discipline with an Adoption Twist" workshop, outlines seven different discipline "tools." These are all basic, well-known methods, but with an explanatory adoption/loss "twist" for our children's extra layers.

The Toolbox...1-2-3 Magic.

This book, written by Thomas W. Phelan, PhD, asserts that parents often treat children as little adults, and often spend way too much time trying to persuade our children that we are right. Parents talk too much and with too much emotion, which actually provokes the child. This can lead to yelling and even eventually to hitting. The 1-2-3 Magic philosophy:

1) A parent gives one explanation only.

2) A parent's authority is not negotiable.

After giving the one explanation, the parent then begins to count. If the misbehavior doesn't stop as a result of the explanation, the parent warns, "That's one." If the misbehavior continues, the parent says, "That's two." If the child is still misbehaving the parent says, "That's three" and gives the child a time-out. The parent is not to argue with the child, or lecture the child. After the time out, the child re joins the family.

The Adoption Twist: Parents should not send the child off to another room as suggested in 1-2-3. Rather, by keeping them close and modeling calm, controlled behavior parents help the child regulate by not allowing him or her to escalate. This method takes the emotion out of the discipline, which will help the child re-attune with the parent.

How to Talk So Kids Will Listen & Listen So Kids Will Talk.

This popular book written by Adele Faber and Elaine Mazlish gives parents four techniques for successful listening (a key piece of communication and attunement):

Listen with full attention. When you only half listen, children just give up even trying to talk with their parents. But when you give them your full attention, they feel special and want to talk with you even more.

Show a caring attitude. Children don't always want you to fix their problems. They may just need to know that you care about them and what they're feeling. You can often communicate your caring with just a word, such as "Oh" or "I see," or "Mmmm..." The child will know he or she was heard.

Deal with feelings, both the parents' and child's. How often do we as parents try to deny what our children are feeling? Our child will try to express emotion, and we quickly jump in telling him not to feel that way. Instead we need to help them deal with their feelings by naming those feelings. Statements such as "you are sad," "what a shock that was for you," or "you really cared about your friend" will help your child feel that you understand him or her.

You don't need to fix it. Don't try to solve the problem. Parents often try to explain things with adult reasoning. Telling a 2-year-old that you don't have any Toastie Crunchies in the house doesn't mean anything to him or her. All the child knows is that he or she wants them now! Instead, give into the child's wishes and fantasy. How much easier it is for a child to go along with you when you fantasize right along with him or her about how wonderful a box of Toastie Crunchies would be. When mom wants it as much as the child does, how can he or she argue?

Faber and Mazlish also offer help in gaining cooperation from our children. Parents can talk to their kids in such a way that the kids will naturally listen.

Describe the problem. Simply stating the problem as you see it is much better than blaming, yelling, or coercing. The point is made without blame and without emotion. It does not put the child on the defensive. Instead of "You haven't taken the dog out all day. You don't deserve to have a pet," try "I see Rover pacing up and down near the door."

Use one word. Instead of yelling at your child again for walking out without his or her lunch, simply say "lunch." Again, you don't express blame or accusation toward your child.

Talk about your feelings. Instead of yelling at your child for pulling on your sleeve, tell him or her calmly, "I don't like having my sleeve pulled." It is more difficult for a child to argue with how his or her behavior makes you feel.

The Adoption Twist: The goal of the Faber/Mazlish method is to help children change unacceptable behavior without making them feel threatened, attacked, or rejected, and also to help parents learn to listen so children feel genuinely heard. This is particularly important for the adopted child, who may have a heightened sensitivity to not being heard or understood. The parents need to be mindful of not falling into the adoptive parent discipline trap, and should avoid:

- Giving in to the child's demands out of fear that the child won't love them.
- Being overly dismissive of the feelings that an adoptive child is trying to express (not really listening).

Behavior Modification.

This relies on rewarding positive behavior in order to increase the frequency of such behavior. Any behavior will increase if followed by something pleasant. The reward can be either material, verbal, or time spent together. Parents need to be careful when using this approach, and consider whether not reaching a reward will wrongly affect their child's self-esteem, and if the system is reinforcing the correct behavior.

One way to use the behavior modification technique is with the use of a reward chart. Once the problem behavior has been identified and agreed upon by the parents, it then needs to be discussed and agreed upon by the child. Allowing your children to help select the rewards and help in designing the chart is usually greeted with great enthusiasm. It's important to set a start date, and commit to a consistent time of filling out the chart. For some kids, behavior modification doesn't work. If, after implementing this technique, you see that it is not working for your child, then you need to question why. Perhaps it is because your child has significant control issues, or doesn't truly trust his or her parents to know what's best for him or her, both of which are not uncommon in adopted children. Parents may need to seek professional help.

The Adoption Twist: An important thing to remember about this discipline technique is that the rewards should be only positive, such as more time spent together, or choosing dessert for that night, or playing a favorite game together. Behavior Modification is really just a helpful indicator to measure if your child can be amenable to change…or if the problems run deeper. If a simple additional story at bedtime is motivation for a reward you are well on your way to a healthy relationship. If nothing motivates the child, then there is cause for concern; children normally are motivated by positive incentives.

Time-Out.

Time-out is a common discipline technique that often needs modification in order to be appropriate for a child who:

- has been recently adopted
- has not fully attached to his or her parents
- struggles with anxiety related to separation from his or her parents

Time-out involves separation of the child and parent by sending the child to a designated room away from the family. But a child who has attachment issues, or who is just learning to trust a new family, should never be forced away from the parents. Using time-out, but with the adoption "twist," the parent still disciplines the child, but places him or her in a location close by.

Another adaptation of time-out takes place with the child sitting in the parent's lap to calm down and "think." A tantruming child can be kept safe in a parent's arms and lap while mom or dad is sitting on the floor. An out-of-control child may scream to get away, but desperately needs the calm, safe physical security of his or her parent.

The Adoption Twist: Time-out minimizes the shame response that adopted children are so easily prone to. This type of time-out is a positive example of disciplining a bad behavior, while always helping the child feel emotionally and physically secure.

Time-In.

Time-in is a variation of the time-out technique mentioned above. According to Landry, the goal of time-in is for a chronically misbehaving child to experience a successful day. When a child repeatedly misbehaves and does not respond to other disciplinary methods, a time-in may be appropriate. The parent explains to the child that he or she is going to help him or her have a good day by keeping the child nearby, and helping him or her make good decisions throughout their time together. The child is kept physically close to the parent, usually within arms length, for as long as the parent thinks necessary. As the parents go about their day with their child beside them, they are able to talk together about the child's misbehavior and the feelings that caused it. The parents are also able to correct any subsequent misbehavior or bad attitude, because they can address the issues immediately, as they surface. The key to the success of this technique is for the parent to be loving and empathetic toward the child, as the parent helps the child make good choices.

The Adoption Twist: The physical closeness of the parent and the time spent together gives the parent and child an opportunity to process the child's feelings and surfacing behaviors. The parent must present a time-in as a help to the child, not as a punishment. The idea is to promote a "we are going to do this together" team feeling. Time-in is a wonderful opportunity to practice and strengthen attunement between parent and child.

Love and Logic.

Love and Logic parenting, created by Foster Cline and Jim Fay, is an approach to raising children that puts parents in control and teaches responsibility to children. This is accomplished by parents setting firm limits in a loving way, and making sure the child knows in advance exactly what is expected of him or her. The child then experiences natural consequences for his or her actions, both good and bad, and is held accountable for his or her actions and for solving his or her own problems. The parent expresses empathy toward the child for making a bad choice, but does not bail the child out of the problem or try to solve it for him or her. The Love and Logic approach is normally a positive technique, yet for the post-institutionalized child, or the child who has been neglected, abused, or shuffled from family to family, the "natural consequence" may not be known to him or her. Time is needed for the parent to teach and train the child, and to establish a basis of trust. If trust has not been established, then natural consequences can be shaming rather than instructive.

The Adoption Twist: Coaching the child may be a necessary adjunct to implementing Love and Logic, as some of life's lessons may have been missed, especially if the child was adopted from an orphanage or from foster care. Coaching focuses on teaching the child appropriate behavior. Instead of just telling a child to stop a behavior, the parent teaches the child societal expectations, and what appropriate behavior looks like. This builds an alliance between the child and his or her parent.

60-Second Scolding.

A 60-second scolding is another highly effective discipline technique. When the child misbehaves, the parent comes close to the child and makes eye contact, even gently holding his or her face if necessary. The parent tells the child, firmly but without shouting, how the child's actions affected the parent. The parent then softens his or her voice, hugs the child and tells the child how much he or she is loved and assures him or her it is the parent's job to take care of the child, and together they will work through the problem.

The Adoption Twist: The 60-second scolding is intense and honest, provides immediate intervention and ends on a nurturing note, affirming the parent's love and commitment toward the child. Most parents scold, walk away, and proceed with life as though nothing has happened. The adopted child is profoundly affected by disciplinary action, so the re-attunement "twist" is vital. This technique is powerful in its simplicity and works well for the adopted child, as it fosters a quick re-attunement between parent and child.

Deborah Moore is an adoptive mom of two daughters. This article is excerpted from the article titled, "Discipline with an Adoption Twist," which originally appeared in the book ***Adoption Parenting: Creating a Toolbox, Building Connections*** *(EMK Press 2006) and is based on the work of Doris Landry, MS, LLP.*

Dealing With Control

Living with a child-sized control freak can be frustrating. Battling a child's tenacious will over endless inconsequential interactions is wearying work. Giving the child many choices over his or her daily life doesn't seem to end the ongoing problem, either. How can a parent help a child deal with a need for control that has invaded home, school, and the child's friendships?

Remove Yourself. It's not about the parent finding a way to eradicate the problem, it's about the child. A child's continued need for control is indicative of his or her feeling intrinsically out-of-control, and has nothing to do with what you might have attempted to do to help your child change.

Ask Your Child. Create a dialog with your child to really find out what is fueling the undesirable control-behavior. How does the child feel inside when he or she has the need to take control? What is going on within the child that needs to be addressed? A child who is helped to recognize the fear or anger his or her need for control is masking, can take steps toward awareness and consciously work at letting go of the need for control. A securely attached child cares about what his or her parents think and feel, and wants to please them. Parents who understand the true issue of control can deal with the issue at its core, and not waste time and effort on the resulting symptoms. Needing control is a tough behavior to break, but a child who knows that his or her present negative behavior is based on feelings and experiences in the past, will be able to work on a new pattern with the guidance of his or her family.

– Doris Landry, MS, LLP

Becoming Your Foster Child's Emotional Tutor

By Allison Maxon, MS, MFT

Children in foster care have all experienced varying degrees of abuse, neglect, and multiple placements. They typically have increased social, emotional, and behavioral problems, most often due to their inability to modulate internal affective or feeling states. These children have experienced overwhelming amounts of internal emotional distress at an age when they were ill-equipped to manage their emotional states. The end result is that children in foster care have increased behavioral problems, and these behavioral problems create distress for the families with whom they are living.

We know that punishing these children is ineffective, as punishment does not actively add or teach anything. In fact, when parents use negative reinforcement, it most typically reinforces negative behaviors. What these children most need to learn is how to regulate or manage their internal emotional states. They need to develop the skill of returning to a state of calm after a stressful experience. But how does a child with social and emotional deficits learn these critical life skills? Hired for the job – foster parents who are willing and able to become their foster child's emotional tutor.

Emotional Intelligence

Becoming your foster child's emotional tutor is no easy task. It requires that parents have increased emotional intelligence. This does not mean that parents have to be perfect and never show any negative emotion, such as anger and frustration. In fact, it is quite the opposite. Your child needs you to express all of your emotions – not just the warm fuzzy ones, so he or she can see how it's done. The difference here is that parents with increased emotional intelligence are not just "emotionally reacting" to external stressors, they are able to model healthy ways to manage their own internal distress.

A parent with increased emotional intelligence might say, "Mom is frustrated right now, I'm going to take a few minutes to calm down before we talk about how we're going to solve this problem." With increased emotional intelligence, we begin to see and understand that most of our emotional reactions are the result of our own internal perceptions and interpretations. So instead of saying, "you make me so mad," we would be correct in saying, "I make myself so mad when I perceive or think about..." The golden rule when emotionally tutoring your child is to be mindful that we, as parents, are modeling our own emotional intelligence all the time. Children in our care are always learning from our example. It is much like teaching your child a dance. Our own dance is the dance we teach. Is that dance reactive and impulsive, attentive and loving, or busy and detached?

The Emotional Dance

When a parent is emotionally tutoring a high-needs child, it is critical that the parent leads the emotional dance. So when the high-needs child is in a state of distress, anger or hyperarousal, it is imperative that the parent responds to the needs of the child by providing the external regulation that is necessary to return the child to a state of calmness. Because the child's early attachment needs were not met, they cannot "internally" regulate their affective states. So using interventions like room time or time-outs are often ineffective because this would assume that the child could auto-regulate or self-soothe.

In emotional tutoring, the parents are always thinking about what they are actively teaching, or adding to the child's skill repertoire. What does the child's behavior indicate that he or she needs? It is important to note that the question is always, what does the child need to learn? Is this behavioral issue related to a skill deficit? What is the underlying need? What the child is saying verbally he or she wants and what he or she needs are not the same thing. The child is most often stuck in a defensive pattern of reacting, and does not have increased insight into what he or she needs.

The goal here would be to increase the child's ability to return to a state of calm after a dysregulating event, so the parent would use a time-in, where the parent provides the external structure the child needs to return to a state of calm. The parent would remove the child from the stimulating environment and proceed to down-regulate the child. With a small child this would involve rocking, singing, deep pressure rubs down the spine; with an older child it might involve taking a walk together, exercising, listening to music or expressive arts.

Once the child is in a state of calm, a re-do is always the consequence, as the child learns most quickly through experience. A re-do is where the desired behavior is practiced. Once the child is successful, the parent bathes the child in affective pleasure – "good job, look how smart you are!" or "Wow, look what you can do, I'm so proud of you!" When children's early attachment needs are not met, their ability to relax, attend and think through solutions – is greatly diminished.

Foster children desperately need their foster parents to actively tutor them emotionally, but this requires that parents think non-traditionally about how they are responding to misbehavior. When a parent can remain calm in the eye of the storm, and model for their child in care how to manage internal distress, the child learns the dance of increased emotional intelligence, which is how to think before one reacts.

Emotions Are Contagious

Emotions are contagious; it's easy to "catch" an emotion. This is perhaps the most difficult challenge for foster parents today. Children in foster care live with chronic, overwhelming emotional distress, which means foster parents live in an environment where their emotional states and skills are being constantly taxed. It is most typical to respond to an angry child with anger, a defiant child with defiance and a distressed child with distress.

Emotional tutoring requires that the foster parent does the hard work of not following the child into a negative emotional state, but becomes the leader of the emotional dance between parent and child and actually pulls the child out of distress, frustration, and anger. This is most easily done when parents model their own healthy emotional coping skills, like using humor to help alleviate stress, "Can anyone tell mommy a joke right now, because I sure need to laugh?"

Emotional tutors are aware that they are setting the emotional tone within the family and develop a bag of tricks to alleviate the stress that the child in care brings into the home. This bag of tricks can include things like: joke night at the dinner table, all-day pajama day, costume night where all members have to dress up and stay in character, role-reversal night at the dinner table where the kids fix dinner and the parents get to whine, or playing feelings charades. Foster parents who are able to be creative and playful, will find that they are teaching the kids in their care how to cope effectively with life's stressors.

The Healing Power of Play

One of the biggest problems for many children in care is that they have not experienced enough pleasure. The first five years of life are supposed to be filled with loads of pleasure, fun and play. In fact, play is the language of children. They learn best through play. But what if the child does not know how to play? This may sound like a small problem, but in reality, it is enormous for the child in care.

Giving and receiving pleasure is one of the most important things the child learns in the early parent and child attachment relationship. Human connections are supposed to be pleasurable, but what if the child has not learned this, and subsequently does not know how to give and receive pleasure? And what if the child is stuck in chronic states of distress, and does not know how to pull him or herself out of these states? Again, what the child most needs is emotional tutoring.

One of the best ways to tutor the child is to engage him or her daily in play. Each time you play with the child in care, you replace distress with pleasure, frustration with laughter, and isolation with connectedness. In addition, you will provide the child with the experiences that he or she needs to strengthen emotional and social development. The child will learn good impulse control when he or she is playing a board game where he or she is required to take turns. The child will learn how to think in a more organized way when playing structured games that have a beginning, middle, and end. They will learn how to express their feelings with words when they play "feelings charades." They will learn how to be sensitive to other people's needs and cues as they play social games.

Cooperative games are best because the players together are playing against the game rather than competing against each other. They will learn how to attend and focus when they are engaged in games like Concentration, Clue, and other similar games. But most of all, they will slowly learn how to replace chronic distress with pleasure, fun, and play. They will develop coping skills that will last a lifetime. In fact, social and emotional skills have been found to be more critical to life's success than one's intellectual ability.

Yes, it is true that children in care have been negatively impacted by abuse, neglect or multiple placements. Children in foster care come to families with social and emotional skill deficits. These deficits create parenting challenges for foster parents. The good news is that children change, grow, and heal within the context of a healing relationship. So now we have another skill to add to the foster parents' resume. You are hired for the job – emotional tutor.

Allison Davis Maxon, MS, MFT, is currently a licensed therapist at the Kinship Center in Santa Ana, Calif. Allison is the program supervisor and group educator for the Bridge Builders Program, which provides therapeutic services and group education to parents who are adopting special needs children. She specializes in family attachment therapy. This article originally appeared in ***Fostering Families Today****.*

Foster Parents can best help the children they care for by actually caring for them and not treating them like a business. The children would be better behaved and more open to rules if they were treated like they were loved...

– Ashley Radford, former foster youth who was in the system for 11 years.

Dear Dr. Kenny: Family Talk and Discipline

By Drs. James and Mary Kenny

Family Talk is a regular column in ***Fostering Families Today*** magazine. Drs. Kenny and Kenny offer a pragmatic perspective on discipline from their own experience with parenting 12 children and fostering many.

Kids Need Discipline, Not Punishment

Dear Dr. Kenny: *Is spanking kids child abuse? What's wrong with a good swift swat to a well-padded bottom? Let the child learn that misbehavior will result in punishment. If more parents took their responsibility seriously, we would have far less delinquency today.*

– New Hampshire

If punishment was effective, advertisers would use it.

Dear New Hampshire: I agree with your last statement, that parents need to take child rearing seriously. Punishment, however, is a poor way to motivate and discipline children.

Is spanking child abuse? Technically, in most states that depends on whether the spanking leaves marks that can be seen a day later. Whether or not spanking qualifies as child abuse, it is wrong-minded. Many states forbid foster parents to use physical punishment. Verbal abuse can be even worse. Whether the tongue-lashing involves obvious demeaning and put-downs or whether the abuse is more subtle, inducing guilt in the child, verbal abuse strikes at the soul. Punishment itself is questionable. Punishment is not good discipline because it does not work well to obtain the desired result. Discipline includes many more effective techniques for stopping misbehavior and obtaining compliance.

Discipline is the total character-molding of the child through love, example, praise and attention for good behavior, and ignoring punishment for bad behavior. Punishment may provide a short-term deterrent so long as the parent is bigger, stronger, and in control. Usually, punishment is the last resort of a frustrated and unskilled parent. If punishment was effective, advertisers would use it. Have you seen or heard an ad that threatened bad consequences such as loss of popularity or financial insecurity unless you use the product? No, because such an approach would not induce us to buy what they were selling. Ads stay positive.

Too often children are subjected to a barrage of what's wrong with them. The child, confronted with constant yelling, scolding, moralizing and spanking will learn that either he or she is a bad character or that parents are to be avoided. Or more simply, the child will turn off and tune out. Punishment, with its focus on misbehavior, fails to inform a child what he or she should do. Identifying the misbehavior, targeting its opposite and rewarding being on time with small privileges is more likely to be effective. The rewarding indicates clearly what is required and gives attention to the appropriate behavior.

The most serious indictment of punishment is that it encourages the behavior that parents are trying to eliminate. By focusing on the undesirable behavior, parents are providing valued time and attention for the wrong thing. The time and attention that accompany punishment is called "secondary gain." Too often the secondary gain outweighs the primary painfulness.

What parent has not exclaimed, "The more I get after him, the worse he gets. He's just doing it to get attention." Of course he is, so try a better way.

If punishment worked well, parents would not have to use it so often. So why do parents punish? Probably because they believe that punishment hurts and children will behave to avoid the hurt. The key question parents should ask however, is does punishment work?

Curing Bad Language

Dear Dr. Kenny: *My 12-year-old grandson uses foul language, words that I could never even write in my letter to you. He has been punished at school, but he thinks it's cool. His mother has tried everything. How can we get him to clean up his mouth?*

– Pennsylvania

Dear Pennsylvania: One of the biggest mistakes that all of us make is to give too much attention to bad behavior. We explain, correct, threaten, and punish our children when they use foul language. We fail to understand that in providing attention to bad behavior, we are rewarding it. I am sure that's the last thing your daughter wants to do.

Every one of us has complained, "The more I get after that child, the worse he gets." Then in exasperation we add, "He's just doing it to get attention." Of course that's exactly what he is doing. So why do we keep getting suckered in?

We keep on being ineffective for two reasons.

- First, we confuse our parenting goal with our strategy. The goal is fine. The strategy is counterproductive. But it sounds so right to our adult ears.
- Second, it's the only way we know, talking the misbehavior to death. If that doesn't work, we talk louder. If it still isn't working, we punish. And if that worked, you wouldn't be writing us. Your grandson is getting too much attention for his bad language.

The trick is to identify the opposite behavior and reward that with your time and attention or with some small token. If the opposite occurs, then the foul talk does not happen. What is the opposite of foul language? The answer is "not using foul language." So simple and obvious. Yet it is hard to reward a nonoccurrence. Here is a plan for doing just that. I call it the "happy mouth" plan.

> *Johnnie will clean up his mouth. Each third of one day – before school, after school and after supper – that he does not use any of foul language – make a list of the inappropriate words – or raise his voice, he will earn one happy-mouth point.*

Parents score his success, or lack thereof, immediately with a 1 or 0 on the wall calendar. The points are worth a small token reward.

My most popular rewards are slips of paper concealed in a love jar. The child may select a slip for every five points. The slips allow for endless possibilities: breakfast in bed, a slice of pizza, dad will stand on his head and sing the school song.

Other possible rewards might be awarded for each point and include: Five minutes of closely supervised drawing time, five cents, a handful of trail mix, staying up late for 10 extra minutes. Including the child in the planning is a good strategy. By asking the child what rewards he values, you are enlisting his cooperation. The rewards should be immediate and small. They are not a bribe. They are simply a way of reversing the attention factor and responding with a token thank you when the desired behavior occurs.

We need to catch our children right in the act of being good and let them know we notice. Good luck.

Teaching Respect to Your Children

Dear Dr. Kenny: *Adults are rude to one another, and children are even more so. Politicians, talk show hosts, everyone seems to enjoy being hurtful and confrontational. Music lyrics are mean. Why have we become so uncivil? Are we failing as parents to teach our children respect? What can I do as a parent?* ***–New Jersey***

Dear New Jersey: You are right. We are going through an uncivil time in our country. I suspect that it is related to our desire for dominance. As we compete with one another for more and more goods, we adults find that meanness works. Putting down the other person is effective in battling for a prize. Smaller families may amplify this tendency. With fewer or no siblings, children grow up without the normal give-and-take between brothers and sisters. They have less opportunity to learn social skills.

Teaching children respect is high on every parent's list of requirements. Parents can deal with this epidemic of rudeness in several ways. Parents teach mainly by example. Parents should keep careful watch on their own language and gentility. Here are some things to look for:

- Use "I" messages. (I don't like hitting.) Speak your own mind and wishes without putting your partner or your child down. Assertiveness is certainly possible without offending or hurting.
- Avoid judging or blaming. The best way to achieve this is to avoid using "you" when making a request by confronting someone.
  "I want the table set now" is better than, "You get busy and set the table."
  "It's bedtime and I want lights out" is better than, "You get to bed right now before I have to come in there."
- Avoid put-downs. No name-calling and no sarcasm. No one should be called "stupid" or any of the many crude and obscene slang terms.

One way to help raise your own parental consciousness might be to list the words and phrases to be avoided. Offer to put a quarter in a "fun jar" every time your children catch you using one of these terms.

Teaching respect can be turned into a game. Identify nice ways of saying things. Award "nice" points and keep score. Some obvious social graces include:

- Saying "thank you," "I'm sorry," and "please."
- Asking to be excused from the table.
- Making requests in the proper manner, without demanding.
- Going for specified time periods without any name-calling or other put-downs.

Finally, parents might use the restate technique. When a child is rude or disrespectful, don't respond with anger. Instead, ask your child to restate his or her request or comment in an acceptable and civil way. For example, if your son calls his brother "stupid" help him restate what he means. Perhaps he might say: "That's not the way I would do it," or "I am mad at you."

If your daughter demands you do something right now, help her restate the request in an assertive but less hurtful way. She might say "please" or "I would like it if I could."

Parental example, making manners a game and requiring children to restate their disrespectful remarks in an acceptable and more effective style are good ways to combat rudeness.

*James Kenny, PhD, has doctorates in psychology and anthropology and is the author of ten books on child care and family life. He and his wife have raised birth, adopted, and foster children. He is on the **Fostering Families Today** advisory board.*

*Mary Kenny is the mother of 12 birth and adopted children, grandmother of 28, and foster mother of many more. She is also a volunteer reading tutor, CPA, and author of five books on family and child care. These articles originally appeared in **Fostering Families Today**.*

Picking Your Battles

By Jo Ann Wentzel

Foster kids rarely have just one area where problems exist. Most kids, in fact, have several bad behaviors to correct, issues they must overcome, and goals they must reach. The foster parents see their job as mender, fixer, or repair person. We are never content to just let these issues resolve themselves, and rightly so. We arm ourselves with ideas, solutions, and prayer to battle the various problems.

One thing wrong with this strategy is the fact that we attack on all fronts, instead of focusing on just one enemy at a time. Foster parents must pick their battles carefully. There are two basic reasons that this is best. Number one is the fact that kids cannot usually successfully work on a whole array of problems at one time. The second reason is for the sake of the foster parent. You will burn out too quickly if you don't reserve your strength.

But you say, these kids have soooo many problems. They need so much help. You count off the problems on your fingers, but before you get to your toes, slow down. Try to remember it took many years for these problems to develop. You cannot fix this kid by Friday. You will need to pick your battles.

This assessment to decide which war you wage may take a bit of time. It is also hard to do when you still don't know the child well. Until you truly connect with a kid, you must rely on first impressions and what you have actually witnessed.

It is necessary to prioritize this child's needs when deciding which behaviors to conquer, and help him meet challenges necessary for a functional life. We developed a system. First, list all the major problems. Put things in perspective, this is usually not going to include things like he does not make his bed, or he forgets to brush his teeth. If these are this kid's most pressing problem, pat yourself on the back, give him a big hug, and be content that you are so lucky. I'm thinking more in the terms of items like he is violent toward others, he uses pot, he steals, or he cannot stay in school. You know – the kinds of issues foster parents deal with every day.

Next, start to prioritize them. I tend to divide them into the following categories.

1. Behaviors, activities, or problems that are dangerous to other's well being.
2. Behaviors, activities, or problems that are dangerous to the foster child's physical well-being.
3. Behaviors, activities, or problems that are dangerous to other's mental/emotional well being.
4. Behaviors, activities, or problems that are dangerous to the foster child's mental/emotional well-being.
5. Behaviors, activities, or problems that are against the law.
6. Behaviors, activities, or problems that interfere with the foster child's education.
7. Behaviors, activities, or problems that interfere with the running of the household.
8. All other negative behaviors, activities, or problems that you need work on.

Start at the top and work your way down. Work on one problem to its solution before tackling another one. The only time you should break this rule is when you are getting nowhere after months and months of work then focus on another problem for awhile, going back to the first after the new one is solved.

You may see this list differently than others do and change the arrangement of priorities. Even foster parents have pet peeves, pet projects, or their own things that drive them crazy. I remember one foster mom who took really tough kids. The only ones she would refuse were those with blue hair. Drove her crazy. We can laugh about such a silly thing, but if the child is where you can see him, day after day and a little thing sets you off, you will be unable to parent that kid effectively. I believe foster parents should always have the option to decide if a child will fit into their home and lifestyle. There are so many kids out there; we should be able to accommodate most parents. I also believe their requests should be reasonable, blue hair is probably not a real valid excuse, but I can understand it just the same.

I feel any behavior that can lead to death or injury for anyone must be number one on your list. That battle has a high chance of casualties if you do not attack there. One battle at a time, unless the problem will prove to be a small, little skirmish. Kids can work effectively on correcting one behavior. They will be more successful if they believe this is the one thing that will please you (and shut you up). When you approach with a long list in hand, they don't fight, they don't surrender, and they just play dead. They don't hear you or even care what you are saying. It is impossible to redirect them. It is impossible to implement a plan or develop a procedure. They have turned you off, and they will not be part of your little war since they are sure they cannot win. Make it easier on them by giving them one front to battle at a time. Then, everyone wins.

To all foster parents who have taken up arms to battle for our kids, I commend you.

Jo Ann Wentzel is mother of three, two children born to her and one foster kid who never left their family, grandmother to five, foster mom to more than 75 kids, and mother, friend, guardian angel, or worst nightmare, depending on which of the other hundreds of kids you ask.

How to Use The Behavior Management Strategy of The Re-do

By Carol Lozier, LCSW

Karyn Purvis, PhD, and David Cross, PhD, wrote **"The Connected Child: Bring hope and healing to your Adopted Family."** This book has great behavioral management tools including, the re-do. Purvis and Cross state, "The beauty of a re-do is that it catches an inappropriate action in progress and says, "Whoa! Let's go back and do this again differently." Immediate practice is an aid to developing mastery, just like any skill – whether it's riding a bicycle, learning to read, or playing a game. By actively replacing misbehavior with correct behavior in your child's memory banks, you can help the child encode competency."

To further explain, parents use a re-do when their child is in the middle of, or immediately following, an inappropriate behavior. In a re-do, ask your child to stop the inappropriate behavior and try again, but this time choosing an appropriate behavior. We want children to re-do behavior because it provides the opportunity to learn healthier behavior and it allows their brains to experience the correct behavioral choice.

You may wonder, "Why is it important to let my child's brain experience the correct behavior?" The answer is, the child has to experience the correct behavior for his or her brain to translate it into habit. Parents also need to verbally explain the better choice but the most effective way for a child to learn new behavior is to repeatedly do the appropriate behavior.

Let's look at the example of six-year-old Jesse and her mom, Mary. In a therapy session, Mary learns about the re-do and quickly puts it into practice. In public, Jesse runs ahead of mom even though the family rule is: We hold hands and walk together. The next time Jesse runs ahead mom catches up to her and asks her to re-do this behavior. Mary says, "Jesse, our family rule is to hold hands and walk together. Let's go back to the beginning and try it again." Together, they go back to the beginning and re-do the walk in an appropriate way. At the end of the re-do, Mary verbally praises Jesse's cooperation and appropriate behavior, "Thank you so much for following our family rule about walking."

Re-do's are an invaluable behavioral strategy to use with foster and adopted children. And it is a powerful tool for children from preschool age through the teen years. Look for the next chance to help your child's brain turn behavior into habit!

Carol Lozier, LCSW is a psychotherapist in private practice; she specializes in helping foster and adopted children and families. She graduated from Florida State University in 1989 with a master's degree in social work. Visit her blog at www.fosteradoptchildtherapist.com.

Experience

By Veronica Brown

Not so long ago, my nine-year-old was about an hour into an episode in his bedroom.

My older foster son came into my room. "Geez, is he still at it?"

"Yup."

"How much longer?"

"Well, after he broke his glasses, he came up to his room and when he slammed his door, the trim came off. So now he's mad and panicking. I think Jason thinks he's going to get kicked out."

"Did you tell him he's not getting kicked out?"

"A bunch of times. But he's not hearing me. In his experience, this sort of stuff gets him moved. I keep going in to try to talk to him, but it's not helping. I'll just let him get it out of his system."

"Isn't that driving you crazy?"

"Kinda."

"He's been doing this a lot lately. Is it going to get better?"

"Of course it's going to get better. I've been here before."

If you focus, absolutely, on putting one foot in front of the other, oftentimes you look up and can't believe how far you've come.

I had been there before. But I hadn't always been that calm or confident.

Early in my foster parenting career, I had a boy who was prone to rages. I remember all the different ways I dealt with him. I tried calmly talking him out of his temper and I tried shouting back. I tried ignoring him and I tried standing there watching. And sometimes I would sit on the floor outside his bedroom door, head in my hands wondering "what do I do now?"

I remember the overwhelming feeling of failure. I remember the fear, the despair, the hopelessness. I remember thinking that I hadn't been able to reach this child at all. It seemed that he had a meltdown every day. And I couldn't picture that changing. I grew up in a loving, supportive home and had many successes in my life. I've experienced hardship, but I've always had my family to help me stay positive. And still, I had difficulty picturing success with this boy. I had a hard time seeing the situation getting any better.

But it did. Support from social workers, a very special therapist and several schools all combined to make that placement successful. I don't even remember the tipping point. I don't remember when things started getting better. They just did.

If you focus, absolutely, on putting one foot in front of the other, oftentimes you look up and can't believe how far you've come.

I've had more than a few foster kids since that boy. And now I have all that experience to draw from. Not only the skills I developed, but also the mistakes I made. Strategies learned in training classes and from individual sessions with professionals. I've discovered my strengths and my weaknesses and how to use both. Most important of all: I've seen healing. I've been a participant and a witness and I have known success.

Jason had never experienced that kind of success. Small accomplishments, sure, but not the kind of achievement that brings personal confidence or a sense of optimism. He never had the chance to work through problems with the help of someone else. He never witnessed things getting better; hard work paying off; someone standing by him through thick and thin, sick and sin.

Jason's experience included being picked up early from school and told he was moving to a new foster home right now. He knew what the world looked like when turned upside-down. He knew failure. He knew the beginning of the end. And while he was throwing his clothes and toys around his room, he knew it was the end. In his mind, if he was going to get kicked out – he was going to go out in a blaze of glory. You can't fire me – I quit!!

Well, I didn't fire him and I didn't let him quit.

And eventually the identified objects stopped flying. The mad got tired and the panic wore down. All that was left were the tears. The awful, gasping sounds of grieving. Mourning the past, regretting the present, and unable to imagine a future. And that was my cue. I knocked and was granted permission to enter. "Do you want some help putting your stuff back?" A nod was all he could manage.

And as we cleaned I asked him, "Have I ever told you about my first year with Shawn?"

Veronica Brown has been a foster parent in Canada since 1995. She primarily takes in boys aged nine and up and usually has a handful at any given time.

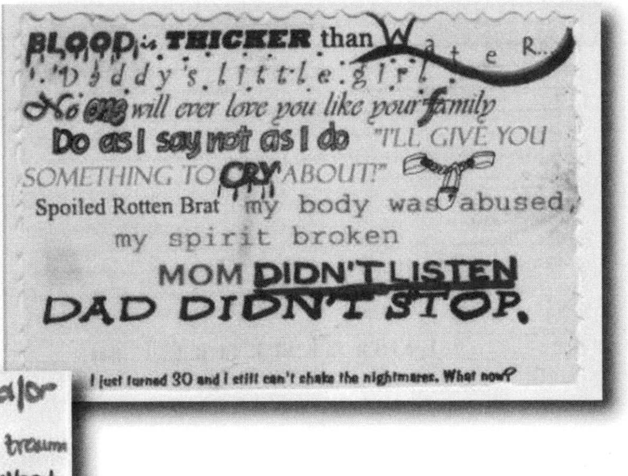

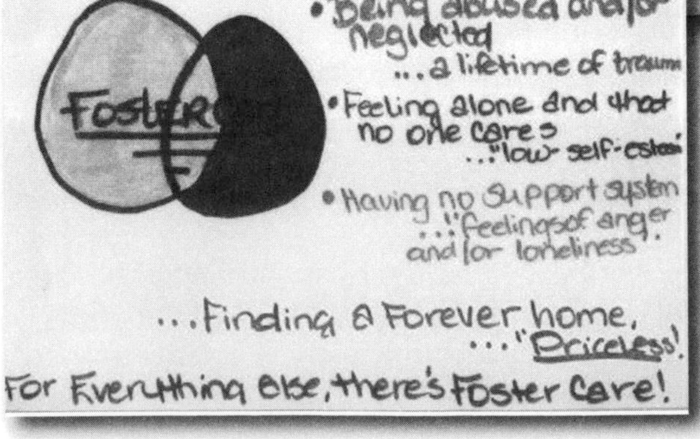

BLOOD is THICKER than WateR..
Daddy's little girl
No one will ever love you like your family
Do as I say not as I do
"I'LL GIVE YOU SOMETHING TO CRY ABOUT!"
Spoiled Rotten Brat
my body was abused,
my spirit broken
MOM DIDN'T LISTEN
DAD DIDN'T STOP.
I just turned 30 and I still can't shake the nightmares. What now?

FOSTER
• Being abused and/or neglected
...a lifetime of trauma
• Feeling alone and that no one cares
..."low self-esteem
• Having no support system
..."feelings of anger and/or loneliness"
...Finding a Forever home,
..."Priceless!
For Everything else, there's Foster Care!

School Tools

"If the only tool you have is a hammer, you tend to see every problem as a nail." – Abraham Maslow

Supporting Foster and Adopted Children in the Classroom

By Christine Mitchell

School Issues for Foster and Adopted Children

The school years play a critical role in shaping children and their futures. For many foster and adopted students, emotional, behavioral, and learning difficulties can significantly affect their school experience. Children's issues stem from prenatal substance exposure, abuse, neglect, institutional care, loss of birth family, and multiple foster care moves.

Schools can help students by being sensitive to the effects of trauma as well as issues such as foster care, adoption, and diversity. Teachers can also broaden family-based assignments to accommodate non-traditional families, and help children cope with intrusive questions. Many parents choose to educate their schools about respectful foster care and adoption language. Most importantly, caregivers can help teachers to understand the child's unique learning, social, emotional, and behavioral challenges.

Before School Starts

When enrolling a child at a new school, foster and adoptive parents need to have all of the required paperwork for enrollment. This generally includes immunization records and/or a record of the child's last physical exam, prior school information, the child's social security number, emergency contacts, and doctor's contact information. Foster parents will want to be sure the school understands exactly who is to receive information regarding the child (foster parents, birth parents, social worker) and who is to participate in school conferences and Individual Education Plan meetings (if applicable).

If a child has been recently placed, it is important to ensure that he or she knows the foster parent's full name, address, and phone number. The child also needs to know the drop-off and pick-up routine, and the route to and from school or the bus stop.

It can be helpful to practice with a child how he or she might respond to difficult or intrusive questions from classmates. Caregivers should also help children understand which information is appropriate to discuss with peers and which details are private. The more personal details that classmates know, the more likely the child is to be teased or bullied.

Talking with the Teacher

It is wise to schedule a conference with the child's teacher shortly before or after the start of school, to discuss the child's unique needs. Parents and guardians should disclose only information that will help the school to meet the child's needs. Many details about the birth family's situation or the child's history are not relevant to the child's current issues, and thus should not be shared. Teachers can be reminded that information about the child's history should be kept confidential.

Emotional and Behavioral Issues

A foster or adopted child may grieve the loss of birth family and other prior caregivers. The child may have experienced neglect, abuse, separation from siblings, and multiple foster care moves. These factors can significantly influence school behavior and performance.

Students dealing with trauma and complex emotional issues often have less energy to pay attention in class and focus on lessons. They may have behavior issues such as low impulse control, defiance, wetting/soiling, stealing, lying, and destructiveness. When teachers understand that grief and loss are playing a role in a child's troubles they are in a better position to support the child.

Both at home and at school adults need to establish clear rules, behavioral expectations, and consistent consequences. Additionally, if parents notice certain warning signs before their child erupts, or discover a particular disciplinary, calming or re-directing technique that works well, they can pass the information along to the teacher.

Children in foster care, and those adopted at older ages, may also lag behind in social skills. If a child is having trouble making or keeping friends at school, he or she may need help developing social skills. Perhaps the child could benefit from some coaching about sharing, taking turns, and not hurting other children's feelings.

It is important to note that sometimes children who have been abused are confused about memories, and which caregiver (current or past parent) actually perpetrated the abuse. If a child has shown any tendency for confusing memories or caregiver names, it might be wise to inform the teacher of this before a serious misunderstanding occurs.

Grief Triggers

Parents and teachers will want to look out for changes in a child's mood such as increased anger, sadness, or anxiety that may be tied to grief from past trauma and losses. Grief often resurfaces as children reach new developmental stages, and it can be triggered by various events.

Changes in routine, such as vacations, field trips, or substitute teachers can be difficult for a student with a history of instability. The child may also be more sensitive or likely to act up near his or her birthday or Mother's Day. Even holidays like Thanksgiving and Christmas can stir up feelings for kids who remember spending those holidays with their birth family. Parents should notify teachers of any new losses the child is experiencing (loss of a pet, changing therapists, etc.), which may remind him or her of the separation from birth family, triggering grief reactions and behavioral changes.

In many classrooms, students watch non-educational movies from time to time. Parents may want to ask teachers about plans to share movies or books that feature orphans, foster care, or adoption. Many children's movies involve themes of parental loss – which can trigger grief or anxiety in some children. The caregiver may wish to discuss the film with the child beforehand, or offer to supply an alternative movie for the class.

If parents and teachers recognize that emotional issues can be triggered by changes in routine, holidays, and other reminders of past losses, they can offer extra patience and support during these times.

Transitions

Children who have experienced multiple moves and caregivers may have intense anxiety during transitions such as moving to a new school, and the beginning or end of the school year. As the end of the school year looms, children worry about losing what is familiar – both their friends and teacher. Children also worry about what their new teacher will be like and fear that the new teacher will be mean or scary. They may demonstrate increased anxiety and behavior problems, and have difficulty focusing on academics.

As with other issues, parents can talk to the child about feelings and acknowledge that school transitions are tough for many children. These kids may also be reassured to some degree by being given information about their new teacher, and any friends who will be in their class the following year. Ideally, the student should visit the new classroom and teacher before summer vacation. Keep in mind that children may be particularly apprehensive about the start of school if they have experienced difficulties in the classroom in the past.

Special Education: Learning and Developmental Disabilities

Foster and adopted children may be more likely to have speech and language delays, learning disabilities, developmental delays, and emotional or mental health issues. Therefore, it is important that parents and caregivers educate themselves on services that may be available to children as well as applicable laws and protections such as IDEA, ADA, IEPs, 504 Plans. The Individuals with Disabilities Education Act (IDEA) is the federal legislation behind most of the rights guaranteed to children with learning disabilities. It includes terms such as FAPE (free, appropriate, public education), IEP (Individualized Educational Program), and (LRE) Least Restrictive Environment.

Wrightslaw.com is an outstanding source of information on special education rights, and a great place to start is with the book **Wrightslaw: From Emotions to Advocacy**, 2nd Edition, by Peter W. D. Wright, Esq. and Pamela Darr Wright.

Parents and Schools Working Together

Because children spend a great deal of time at school, their school experience plays a significant role in their future and their self-worth. By making educators aware of the challenges faced by foster and adopted children, parents and guardians can help schools become a source of support for these students rather than an additional hurdle. Schools can offer flexibility in challenging family-based assignments, encourage positive foster and adoption language, and be sensitive to grief triggers for traumatized children. Foster and adoptive parents can educate teachers about their child's unique issues and strategies that are effective with him or her. Open communication between caregivers and teachers will enable them work as a team to meet the educational and emotional needs of foster and adopted children.

Christine Mitchell is the author of ***Welcome Home, Forever Child: A Celebration of Children Adopted as Toddlers, Preschoolers, and Beyond****;* ***Family Day: Celebrating Ethan's Adoption Anniversary****; and* ***A Foster-Adoption Story: Angela and Michael's Journey****, co-authored with Regina M. Kupecky, MSW. You can find out more about Christine at www.christine-mitchell.com.*

Making Sense of the Letters
By Christine Mitchell

Because adopted children may be more likely to have speech and language delays, learning disabilities, developmental delays, and emotional or mental health issues, it is important that parents educate themselves on services that may be available to their child as well as applicable laws such as IDEA, IEPs, 504s, and the ADA. The Individuals with Disabilities Education Act (IDEA) is the federal legislation behind most of the rights guaranteed to children with learning issues. It includes terms such as FAPE (free, appropriate, public education), IEP (Individualized Educational Program) and (LRE) Least Restrictive Environment.

IDEA: The Individuals with Disabilities Education Act is the federal legislation behind most of the rights guaranteed to children with learning issues. It includes terms such as FAPE (free, appropriate, public education), IEP (Individualized Educational Program) and (LRE) Least Restrictive Environment.

IEP: The Individualized Education Program is a document which spells out the components of a child's special education. It lists educational goals for the student and details the services and accommodations the child will receive to help him achieve those goals.

ADA: The Americans with Disabilities Act (ADA). Title II of the ADA prohibits discrimination on the basis of disability.

504 Plan: Section 504 of the Rehabilitation Act of 1973 is designed to protect individuals with "handicaps" from denial of benefits or discrimination from any program receiving federal funds – which includes public schools. Students may qualify for accommodations under a 504 Plan if they have a health, mental, or emotional disability which does not qualify for an IEP.

NCLB: The No Child Left Behind Law of 2001 provides for testing accommodations for learning disabled students in regard to NCLB assessments:

- "Presentation (example: repeat directions, read aloud, use larger bubbles, etc.)
- Response (example: mark answers in book, use reference aids, point, use computer, etc.)
- Setting (example: study carrel, special lighting, separate room, etc.)
- Timing/Scheduling (example: extended time, frequent breaks, etc.)

:

Overcoming Difficult Comprehension Challenges

By Lee Tobin McClain, PhD

"This is boring," mutters your teenaged foster son, slamming shut his science book. "That quiz wasn't fair," whines your 10-year-old foster daughter. "I read the chapter but I still flunked!"

These are typical kid complaints, but be alert. Sometimes remarks like these reveal that your child is having trouble reading. "But he reads just fine," you may say, having seen your child spend hours perusing the TV guide. Her teacher may concur. If your child did well with reading in the early years, the school most likely concluded that no special help is needed. But as kids get older, their reading material becomes more challenging, and new strategies are needed to comprehend the harder stuff. That's when kids with smaller vocabularies and fewer background experiences – most foster kids – start to struggle. In addition to sharing your concerns with your child's teacher, there are ways you can help at home. Here are several:

Share Your Reading Process. When you're reading assembly instructions, talk yourself through them within hearing of your kids (omitting swear words!): "That doesn't make sense. Let me read it again" or "Now wait – this is just like that table we put together last month." By re-reading and using background knowledge, you're demonstrating important skills.

Keep Highlighters Handy. A major part of comprehension is figuring out what's most important and what can be safely skimmed. If you ever cut articles out of the paper or a magazine to show family members (a wonderful way to share reading enthusiasm), highlight two or three important sentences. Keep highlighters near the magazine piles in your home, and your kids may start to follow suit. For school textbooks, keep a jar of sharp pencils handy: kids can be coached in drawing a light line beside the most important text and erasing it later.

Pre-read With Your Kids. Pre-reading is what many of us do naturally, browsing through a book or article, skimming chapter titles and subheadings to get a sense of what it's all about. Kids who've been in the system may have missed out on this training, but you can casually replicate it at home. "Let's see what you're doing in science," you can offer. Then pick up the book and run a finger down the table of contents. When you reach an interesting-sounding chapter, flip to it and page through, reading aloud some subheadings and captions. Talk about what your child already knows about the topics. "Did you ever see a lemur at the zoo?" or "remember when we watched that hurricane on TV?" Since foster kids often lack experiences other kids have had, you may have to dig a little, or plan a quick trip to the natural history museum right before the class hits the archaeology chapter. That's a comprehension strategy too.

Ask Questions. This one requires some delicacy, especially with sullen teenagers; it helps if you have a real interest in what they're studying. Many people learn better by discussing a topic with others, so once your child has done a bit of reading on a topic, see if you can engage him or her in conversation about it. "What's going on in Africa these days, anyway?" or "I've always wondered why heat rises" might get the ball rolling. If your child knows a little bit more than you about something, his or her self-esteem mounts, and he or she might even get eager to learn more.

Read Aloud and Get Him or Her to Read Aloud to You. Reading out loud fosters fluency, an important aspect of reading comprehension. Set the example yourself by reading tidbits from your newspaper or magazine to whoever's around. Ask a kid to read you the assembly instructions while you're putting something together or the recipe while you are cooking. Have them re-read it a couple of times. Encourage doing homework at the kitchen table, and ask your kids to read the interesting parts to you while you're fixing dinner.

Make Reading a Priority. Comprehension strategies like these may seem obvious, but in the busy rush of family life, conversation about books and active engagement with reading can often get sidelined. Bring reading back to center stage and you'll give your children a boost in many areas of schoolwork and adult living.

Stages of Reading

Learning to read isn't a one-time event. Instead, kids go through predictable stages in the journey to becoming an excellent reader. The trick is that, if one stage isn't mastered well – likely for children from troubled or chaotic homes – a reader can get stuck there, which affects his or her ability to understand and learn for years to come. Check out these brief descriptions of the stages to see where your foster child fits, and how you might nudge him or her on to the next stage. Descriptions of these stages were developed by pioneering Harvard researcher Jeanne Chall, who also attached ages and grade levels to the stages. Many children from disadvantaged backgrounds will lag behind the stated age and grade levels.

Pre-reading: Birth-6 During this stage, children are learning about the world and sounds in language. Both are important to later reading skills. Children need to experience many people, places, things and activities so when they start to read, they can link words on a page to something they know in real life. They also need to hear many words and sounds, so that when they run across the word "veranda" in text, they've sat on one – and talked about it – at Grandma's house. To support this developmental stage, talk to your children a lot and read them a lot of stories, running your finger along the text as you read to emphasize the link between those squiggles on the page and the words you're saying.

Decoding Stage: Grades 1-2, Ages 6-7 This is the stage where kids "learn to read." Laboriously at first, they begin to connect letters to sounds and decode words. Kids at this stage need practice to remember vowel and consonant sounds. They may need to point at each word or use a straightedge to keep their focus on a line of text; reading researchers say they are "glued" to the text. Since they are working so hard to decode, they often lose the bigger thread of the story; illustrated texts or an adult's gentle summary of what's happened so far can help with comprehension. Show your kids how to sound out harder words and give them plenty of chances to practice. Also take the time to read to them; at this stage, their ability to read lags behind their ability to understand and enjoy, and listening to more complicated stories reminds them that becoming a better reader is worth all the time and hard work they're putting in.

Fluency Stage: Grades 2-3, Ages 7-8 During this stage, kids start to recognize whole words automatically without sounding out each letter. Such automatic decoding allows a child to read fluidly without focusing on the act of reading itself. His or her mind now has space for higher-level concepts and more complicated stories. At this stage, young readers need to practice. Reading easy books for pleasure builds fluency and speed, so don't worry if your child wants to read every book in a silly series, or to read books that seem overly simple to you. Your job is to keep plenty of reading material at just the right level close at hand, a challenge when the "right level" is changing every month or two. This is the time to trade books with friends or make weekly visits to the library for stacks of Magic Tree House books or A-to-Z Mysteries.

Reading: Grades 4-8, Ages 8-14 Now that the child is a fluent reader, things get more complicated. In the middle grades of school, children are no longer learning to read; now they read to learn. All the previous stages come into play: children must have ample background experiences so they can understand new information; they must be able to decode unfamiliar and complex words; and they must read fluently enough to focus on the meaning of a complicated text. It's at this stage that many foster kids run into trouble. Yes, they can read; but due to impoverished backgrounds, they may not have the life experience to put what they read into context. They may be poor decoders or less than fluent. And now, they're being tested on their ability to make sense of a textbook in social studies or health. How can you help?

Before your child starts reading a chapter in his or her science book, talk about what he or she already knows about the subject. Remind him or her of the television show on elephants or the way oil and water don't mix when baking a cake. Have him or her skim the subheadings in the chapter, and talk about learning expectations in the chapter. Look at the pictures. After the reading is complete, have him or her tell you some of the things learned.

Stages of Reading for Teens

The following are the higher stages of reading useful for high school and older students – and how you can help your foster kids, who may have missed out on some stages, improve their skills.

Reading To Learn After your child has learned to read, he or she begins to read for information; vast percentages of what we end up knowing comes through the written word. Materials children read in middle school build vocabulary and add to background knowledge. Now they're reading about topics that don't come up in ordinary conversation – the characteristics of the solar system or the *War of the Roses* – so they must be able to use skills from all the other stages: discovering main ideas, decoding new words, and applying background knowledge. They may need help with strategies like pre-reading, skimming and note-taking from texts. Frequent conversations about what they've read can promote comprehension and help them make links to prior knowledge.

Multiple Viewpoints: High School Reading As readers become comfortable with gaining information through reading, they are able to understand multiple viewpoints – reading several books and articles about Michael Jackson, for example, and realizing that some of the information and attitudes conflict. Such conflicts force them to analyze and critique what they read, rather than accept it all at face value. This "critical comprehension" stage is where students learn to deal with layers of facts and to correct their own previous ideas if new material proves them wrong.

Constructive Reading: Age 18 & Older
In the most advanced stage of reading development, learners construct knowledge by taking information from various sources and skillfully interpreting and combining it. They create their own truth from the truth of others. They use texts for their own purposes, knowing what to read closely and what to skim. They form their own educated view based on various sources. Obviously, our culture benefits from having many readers at this stage who can make informed judgments about political candidates, serve on juries, decide on school curriculum, and evaluate and solve social problems.

What Can Go Wrong
Effective reading at each stage depends on adequate knowledge of the previous stages, and herein lies the problem for many kids in the system. If they've missed out on decoding-stage skills, reading for information is laborious: instead of having the mental energy to learn new concepts and complex ideas, they're stuck trying to remember what sound goes with which letter. Reading becomes a frustrating experience, so they don't want to practice, which means they don't improve. Likewise, if teenagers haven't learned the vocabulary and background information of "read-to-learn" texts, it's harder for them to understand and analyze the multiple viewpoints encountered while researching for a high school paper.

What You Can Do
If you notice your child is struggling with reading, schedule a meeting with his or her teacher right away. Sometimes, they'll suggest ways you can help at home: more practice reviewing the reading story each week, or a computer game that improves decoding skills. Teachers can start the ball rolling on intervention services or place the child in a more appropriate reading group. Though we often think of reading specialists as an elementary-school phenomenon, in fact, most middle and high schools offer reading support as well.

Almost always, one part of the solution is to encourage pleasure reading. Find texts your child can read easily, preferably matching his or her interests, and encourage frequent stints of reading. How? Baskets of books in the bathroom and at the kitchen table; a good reading lamp and a couple of magazines on the night stand; audiobooks in the car. All build vocabulary and fluency, and with these skills solidified, older kids have the mental space to wrestle with difficult concepts.

It can be a challenge to focus on a child's reading skills when the future is uncertain. Maybe he or she will go back to his or her birth family in a few months, or be moved to a different placement. And reading skills sometimes seem like the least of a troubled teen's problems. But reading can help teens do better in school, escape from home problems, and build self-esteem. Even a small boost may be enough to push kids to the next stage. Reading well will serve the kids we care about for their whole lives. It's worth all the effort we can put into it

Lee Tobin McClain, PhD, teaches writing and literature at Seton Hill University. She's the author of three novels featuring teens in foster care, ***My Loco Life****,* ***My Abnormal Life*** *and* ***My Alternate Life****. For more information, visit www.leemcclain.com. This article originally appeared in* ***Fostering Families Today*** *magazine.*

I entered foster care in fourth grade. That year I switched schools five times before I finally entered foster care. My foster mother ended that chaos. She and my grandparents pushed me to get good grades. My grandmother would always tell me that "leaders were readers." They taught me that if I wanted to succeed in life I needed to succeed in school. My foster mother went to all the school meetings and had relationships with the teachers. They had high expectations of me and they knew I was capable of meeting them. Because of their support, I did well in school and I love to learn. I graduated from high school as the salutatorian of my class and have gone on to college and graduate school.

– Daniel Knapp, 27, New York alumnus

Encouraging Education

By Misty Stenslie, MSW

Through my years of bouncing from one placement to another, one set of losses and questions to the next, the only constant in my life was that I was good at school and could find a place to fit wherever I went as "the smart girl." Being good at school saved my life a time or two – pulled me from the brink of suicide as a 12-year-old who desperately needed something to grasp, brought me positive attention as a 14-year-old caught up in dangerous situations at my home, on the streets and in the juvenile justice system. Though I never successfully found a forever family during my journey through the system, I did find a love of learning and people who took interest in me, occasionally told me they were proud of me, through my academic achievement.

> *My foster parents were great. I was on the honor roll all the time I was with them. They put education first regardless of the situation.*
>
> *– De Annrea Carter, 26*
> *Colorado alumna*

For those of us who grow up in foster care, loss is a constant companion – loss of family, familiar people and places, and identity. Even in the best of foster care situations, living in placement comes with a predictable set of questions: Where do I belong? Who really loves me? What's wrong with me that all of this has happened? Will I ever get over this? How?

Supporting young people to build their internal and external sources of strength should be our first goal as foster parents. Too often, case plans and court orders are focused on identifying what's wrong with children and how to fix it. As the people who spend the most time with children, who know them the best and who have the most daily influence on them, foster parents are in the unique position to provide a different focus.

> *My mom was clear that she expected me to do the best I could, and she was always ready to provide support when needed. I think it helps when foster parents have high educational expectations of their children – reasonable and appropriate for the child, of course.*
>
> *– Samatra Doyle,*
> *30-year-old*
> *Washington alumna*

We can work on helping young people figure out what's right with them and how to use that to claim an identity for which to be proud. As the losses pile up, so does that sense of anything being right. One of the few things that can't be lost is what we've learned – both formally and informally. Creating a culture of learning in the home is among the most important opportunities foster families have to ensure our children have something to hold onto now and forever.

Some ideas for how to support young people by creating a culture of learning in your home:

- Actively pursue your own learning and share what you've learned. Perhaps you can start a dinnertime ritual of each family member talking about one new thing they learned that day.

- Broaden your idea of what "education" means – make time for listening to public radio, reading news magazines, participating in civic and community activities, visiting museums and trying new food. Curiosity and a willingness to try new things are among the most useful habits you can teach your children.
- Hold high expectations – people live up or down to our expectations of them. Your expectations for every child should be based on his or her strengths – so make sure you're looking for those and telling your child what you see.

Misty Stenslie, MSW, is the former deputy director at Foster Care Alumni of America. She has worked in the child welfare field since 1988. She spent many years in care as a child. As an adult, she became a licensed foster parent and has a lifelong love for the three teens she parented. All three of Stenslie's children are now adults and her inspiration. This article originally appeared in ***Fostering Families Today*** *magazine.*

I didn't have anyone show an interest in my grades and homework until I was placed with a relative and then it was a HUGE adjustment.

– Jordan Brooks
Arizona alumnus

For me, school was my safe place... a place where I felt like I could control my environment when everything else was being controlled for me. If I applied myself with hard work – I got an A. Getting A's was further rewarded because it also brought positive teacher and peer attention. At home, when I was being abused, it never made sense when it was going to happen so I started thinking there was something about me and it affected my self-esteem. Getting A's improved my self-efficacy and facilitated my self-esteem. I know for me, there is no one that is going to "beat me up" as bad as I when I make a mistake.

— Sharon Stone, 42, Illinois alumna

Motivating Challenging Foster Kids

Turning Difficult Kids into Productive Citizens
By Shemille Brown, LCSW-C

Youth who display symptoms of learned helplessness, depression, anxiety, aggression, explosive and other challenging behaviors can be difficult for foster parents to engage and motivate. As a result, these children have a high risk of multiple placements including group homes, residential treatment centers, and foster care. In my ten years of experience working with youth in residential, institutional, and educational settings, I learned that once you understand the "why" behind the youth's behavior it is much easier to identify the appropriate intervention and easier to use the youth's own internal motivation to engage him or her. At BSquared Trainings and Consulting Services, we share with foster parents the meaning behind some of these most challenging behaviors exhibited by today's youth.

The brain is involved in everything we do. So we start there, by looking at how the brain and chemicals in the body impact learning and behavior. In addition, we take what is known about child development, learning, behavior, and relationships and present the information in a clear, concise, interactive method to foster optimal learning.

A key part of the brain is called the amygdala. The primary function of the amygdala is to alert the brain of potential danger. It is often referred to as the "fear center" of the brain. When this area of the brain senses danger, real or perceived, it sends a chemical known as cortisol through the body. Cortisol is known as the "stress hormone." In small, controlled doses cortisol is helpful; it allows the body to react to dangerous situations in an efficient manner. For example, it will "shut down" non-essential parts of the brain to allow increased focus on the situation at hand. It also increases the heart rate and blood pressure, thus increasing oxygen to be directed to vital body parts like the legs in order to run from danger and decreases sensitivity to pain which allows the youth to focus on fleeing from danger and not becoming immobilized by the distraction of pain or injury.

When the body is exposed to cortisol in large or prolonged doses the result is harmful. When this occurs, youth can have impaired memory and increased difficulty with focusing, maintaining attention, and learning. Additionally, individuals with significant prolonged exposure to cortisol have serious health issues including high blood pressure and excessive weight gain.

Generally speaking, this means that as a foster parent you want to reduce the amount of stress and anxiety youth in your care experience. You can do this by using a calm and soothing voice when communicating, having a warm and inviting home environment, and establishing clear and concise rules. Expectations should be clear, consistent and have reasonable consequences. In general terms, the less the amygdala is activated to release cortisol in the body, the more receptive the youth will be to engaging with you and learning new information.

Try It, You'll Like It

The next thing we encourage foster parents to do is to look at one specific behavior and try to understand the meaning behind it. In its simplest explanation, "behavior either gets you more of something or less of something."

Let's take the behavior of hitting others when upset. The meaning behind a behavior like this may be that the youth is not feeling heard or validated – he or she wants more of an opportunity to be heard.

Once you have developed a plausible explanation you are then in a position to think about how to intervene. The question you want to ask yourself using our example is, "How do I give the youth more opportunities to feel heard without resorting to hitting?" By focusing on this question you can eliminate the need for the unwanted behavior – hitting. However, this is frequently where foster parents resort to feeling as though they have to punish the youths for their behavior and "make" them learn they can't hit people. The problem with this thinking is that you are working against the youths and what is motivating their behavior; and you are just addressing the behavior, not the meaning behind the behavior.

Keys to Remember

1. Is the youth not being heard because he or she is having difficulty expressing him or herself? If this is the case, then your interventions are going to be focused on increasing the child's ability to express him or herself in a socially acceptable way. This may be related to a disability with language expression. The youth may need testing to rule this out.

2. We, as caregivers, are not listening. The youths may give subtle signs they are in need of your attention to express themselves. It may be a comment like, "I'm bored." If our response is along the lines of "What do you mean you're bored? You can clean your room, read a book or do your homework, etc.," we are shutting down the lines of communication and are not allowing space for youths to fully express themselves which could lead to aggressive behaviors like hitting others.

The intervention would need to focus on creating time to allow for appropriate self-expression. A working solution may be for you to say something like, "I'm busy right now. I can give you five minutes now or 30 minutes when I'm done in an hour."

These interventions are proactive. That means you are putting things in place to minimize the need to become aggressive. You are providing them with the opportunity to be heard and decreasing the likelihood that they will hit to be heard.

Why It Works

As with any behavior, especially dangerous ones, you will need to establish consequences to assist in communicating that behavior is not acceptable, and create an opportunity to teach alternative methods. Keep in mind that consequences are rarely accepted with welcoming arms (think about your response the last time you got a traffic ticket). That is OK, because your role as a foster parent is to be clear, consistent and make sure your consequence is connected to the behavior. Below is an example for how you might handle the next situation.

The first thing to address is any safety concerns. This may include separating the individuals involved, tending to any medical injuries or seeking additional assistance. After the immediate safety concerns have been addressed, you may ask the youth to take some "cooling down" time in a safe place such as a special area away from distractions. Ask him or her to come up with two or three alternative behaviors that could have been used; instead of leaving the youth there and telling him or her to think about what he or she did, as he or she will only spend the time replaying the event and finding ways to justify the behavior. Once he or she has the ideas he or she can come out of "timeout" and talk about the solutions. Once he or she has shared ideas ask, "Which one would you like to practice?" Role play with the youth and allow him or her to practice this new skill or strategy. Remember, if the youth doesn't have the opportunity to practice the desired skill, he or she will not learn. If the youth is not willing to practice a new skill he or she should be asked to return to a safe place until he or she comes up with an alternative.

So how and why might this work? Having the youth focus on alternative behaviors reinforces the cooling-down period by shifting attention from what went wrong, which was emotionally charged to what can go right, forcing him or her to let go of some of the highly charged emotional energy, and leading him or her to use some of the higher functioning reasoning and processing skills. Depending on the youth and the situation, the amount of time he or she needs will vary. Be patient and keep in mind that this approach allows an objective way for both the youth and foster parent to know when the youth is ready to constructively process the event. Having the youth practice the behavior provides an opportunity for learning. It allows the youth to see the skill in context and begin to lay the skill down in long-term memory pathways.

Remember, change doesn't happen overnight. Just as it will take you time to become comfortable using this approach, it will take the youth time to adjust as well.

*Shemille Brown, LCSW-C, earned a masters in social work from Smith School for Social Work in Northampton, Mass. She has more than 10 years of experience providing therapy and working with children and adolescents in a range of settings including residential treatment centers, therapeutic foster homes, classrooms, outdoor educational programs, and athletic facilities Brown is the founder of Bsquared Training and Consulting Services where she provides trainings, workshops and consultations to parents, foster parents, mental health. Learn more at www.bsquaredtrainings.com. This article originally appeared in **Fostering Families Today** magazine.*

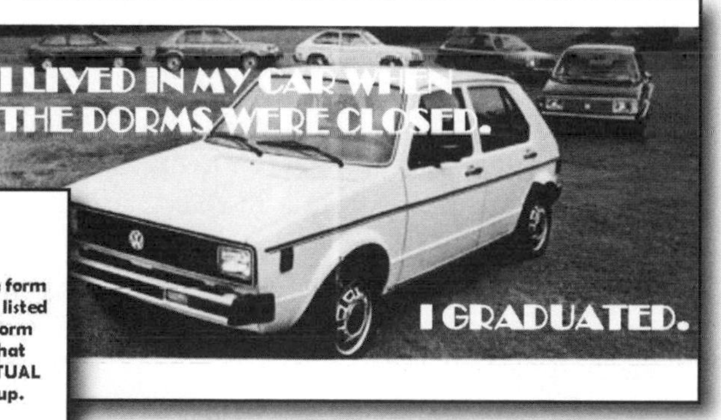

I LIVED IN MY CAR WHEN
THE DORMS WERE CLOSED.
I GRADUATED.

During freshman orientation, the form asked for 'permanent address'. I listed my new college PO Box and the form was returned to me with a note that the business office needed an ACTUAL permanent address. I made one up.

I didn't have one of those.

Special Education 101

The Basics for Fostering a Child with Special Education Needs

By June Bond, MSW, and Mary Eaddy

Advocating for your foster child in the school system may be one of the most daunting tasks that a foster parent undertakes. This is especially true for a first time foster parent who may have a wealth of child rearing experience, but no experience in the world of accessing special education services. This article is designed to help parents understand the basic programs offered in special education and how their programs may benefit children in their care.

What is Special Education?

Special education is instruction that is specially designed to meet the unique needs of children who have disabilities. This is done at no cost to the parents in the public school system. It should be noted that private or parochial school systems may not have a wide array of special education programs or may charge for added services. Special education can include special instruction in the classroom, at home, in hospitals or health-related institutions. It is estimated that more than 5 million children receive special education services each year in the United States. So, take heart, you and your child are not alone.

Many of the programs that are included in special education are related to the Individuals with Disabilities Education Act. This federal act is often referred to as IDEA. There are 13 general categories of disabilities listed in IDEA. These categories include autism, deafness, deaf-blindness, hearing impairment, mental retardation, multiple disabilities, orthopedic disabilities, emotional disturbance, speech and/or language impairments, traumatic brain injury, visual impairments, and "other health impairments," which can be defined as affecting a child's life functions, of which learning is one of life's functions.

The first initial steps to receiving special education services are: 1) to ascertain that your foster child has one or more of the disabilities that fall into one of the 13 designated categories AND 2) that this impairment affects the child's school performance. Many of the foster children who come into your home may already have been evaluated and deemed eligible for special education services. However, a young child or a child who is in foster care for the first time may not have been evaluated for special education services. Likewise, it is not unusual for a child who is in America illegally to not have been in the school system long enough to have a full and thorough evaluation. Consequently, it is critical that families understand the evaluation system that leads to special education services. A good understanding of the evaluation system and rules relating to the evaluation of a child can open doors to access the services to the fullest extent and benefit for the child.

Having the Child Evaluated

The first stepping stone to receiving special education is to ask the school to evaluate the child. The guidance counselor or director of special education can assist in the request and paperwork. Request in writing that the school evaluate your child as soon as possible. Remember to date and save everything that relates to your requests. A slow evaluation will lead to a slow implementation of extra help. In most cases, the school will evaluate your child at no cost to you. You should be aware, however, that the school does not have to evaluate your child if they do not think your child has a disability or needs special education. In times of budget crises, this can be a real issue. If the school refuses to evaluate your child, the school must outline its reasons in written form. A parent has two rapid fire responses to a denial for evaluation:

1. Request the school system's special education policies, as well as parent rights to disagree with decisions made by the school system. The stated policies should have added steps to take and

2. Get in touch with your state's Parent Training and Information Center, which is an excellent resource and advocacy for parents to learn more about special education, their rights and responsibilities, and the law. To locate your state's Parent Training and Information Center, go to www.parentcenternetwork.org.

Required Reading for Parents with Special Needs Children in School

Wrightslaw: From Emotions to Advocacy The Special Education Survival Guide
by Peter W. D. Wright and Pamela Darr Wright

How To Compromise With Your School District Without Compromising Your Child: A Field Guide For Getting Effective Services For Children With Special Needs
by Gary Mayerson

What happens during an evaluation for special education services? The full evaluation team should look at a host of factors to ascertain how the child is affected by the disability. This evaluation should include assessing the child's health, vision, hearing, social and emotional well-being in addition to general intelligence, performance in school, and communication and physical skills. The evaluation must be complete enough to identify all of your child's needs for special education and related services. Thoroughly evaluating the child can provide a great deal of information that can help decide if your child has a disability and how an individualized education plan can be specifically designed for your child's needs.

You are one of the most significant people on the evaluation team. In addition to you, there should be at least one regular education teacher, a special education teacher, service providers, a school administrator who is familiar with all programs at the school for both regular and special education, a professional who can interpret the evaluation results and talk about what instruction may be necessary, as well as individuals who have knowledge about your child, such as the foster care worker. Do not forget about other qualified professionals who are familiar with your child's situation. These professionals may include a school psychologist, an occupational therapist, a speech and language pathologist, a physical therapist, or a medical specialist.

What makes up a good evaluation? Individual and group tests scores, observations of your child's teaching team – your observations and concerns can provide a starting point. Medical records, psychological reports, birth parent information, counseling observations can also provide a more global picture of the child's disabilities. The evaluation team, with your permission, should collect information about your child from many different people and in many different ways. Tests are an important part of an evaluation, but they are only a part.

Once the evaluation is completed, many foster parents are uncertain as to what should happen next. The evaluation team will determine if your foster child meets the definition of a child with a disability as determined from the IDEA and from the policies your state or district uses. If so, your child will be eligible for special education and related services. In most states, the caseworkers and the foster parents have the right to receive a copy of the evaluation report. If the group decides that your foster child is not eligible for special education services, the school system must tell you this in writing and explain why your child has been found "not eligible." Make certain that you know what policies the school district has for rebuttal to a contested decision for receiving special education.

Developing an Individualized Education Program

If your child is found eligible for special services, the next step is to develop an Individualized Education Program to address the child's basic disabilities. Once eligibility is established, a meeting must be held within 30 days to develop the IEP, which is a written program statement of the educational program designed to meet a child's individual needs. Every child who receives special education services must have an IEP. The IEP will: (1) set learning goals for your child; and (2) state the services that the school district will provide for the child. Please bear in mind, that it is important that children with disabilities participate in the general curriculum as much as possible. In addition, participation in the mainstream extracurricular activities and other nonacademic activities is also important. Your child's IEP needs to be written with this in mind.

A child's IEP will contain:

1. Present levels of achievement and educational performance. This statement describes how your child is currently doing in school. This includes how your child's disability affects his or her involvement and progress in the general curriculum.

2. The IEP must state annual goals for your child. Annual goals reflect what the team thinks he or she can reasonably accomplish in a year.

3. The IEP must also list the special education and related services to be provided to your child. Related services can include, but are not limited to transportation, speech-language pathology, audiology services, psychological services, physical therapy, occupational therapy, early identification and assessment, counseling services, orientation and mobility services, medical services for diagnostic or evaluation purposes, school health services, social work services in schools and parent counseling and training.

4. The IEP must also define how much of the school day the child will be educated separately from nondisabled children or not participate in extracurricular or other nonacademic activities such as lunch or other activities.

5. The IEP should also address testing modifications or changes in how the tests are administered.

6. In addition, the IEP must state (a) when services and modifications will begin; (b) how often they will be provided; (c) where they will be provided; and (d) how long they will last.
7. Finally, no later than when your child is 16, the IEP must include measurable post-secondary goals related to training, education, employment, or independent living skills.

A meeting must be scheduled with you to review your child's progress and develop your child's next IEP at least one time per year. The team will discuss your child's progress toward the goals in the current IEP and what new goals should be added. There can be changes if need dictates in the special education and related services. This annual IEP meeting allows you and the school to review your child's educational program and change it as necessary. Remember, you don't have to wait for this annual review. You may ask to have your child's IEP reviewed or revised at any time. Under the IDEA, your child must be re-evaluated at least every three years. The purpose of the re-evaluation is to find out if your child continues to be a "child with a disability."

Remember that you do have a role in this process. The law is clear that parents or their surrogates such as caseworkers and foster parents have the right to participate in developing the child's IEP. Your input is invaluable. You know the child well, and the school needs to know your insights and concerns. It's important that you attend these meetings and share your ideas about the child's needs and strengths.

Mary Eaddy is executive director of PRO-Parents of South Carolina; the South Carolina PTI. She has been affiliated with PRO-Parents since its inception in 1990 when it became the parent training and information center for South Carolina. She serves on multiple task forces and committees with the South Carolina Department of Education, South Carolina Department of Mental Health, South Carolina Department of Social Services, South Carolina Developmental Disabilities Council as well as other state and local agencies. Eaddy's most relevant knowledge and passion for her work comes from parenting two children with learning disabilities and attention deficit disorder and being grandmother to a grandchild with developmental delays.

June Bond, MSW, earned a bachelor of arts in psychology and a master of education in early childhood education from Converse College. She is the executive director of Adoption Advocacy of South Carolina. She has published numerous articles that relate to adoption, education, and family issues and speaks nation-wide on adoption-related issues. She was South Carolina Adoption Advocate of the Year in 1995. She is also the 2006 Congressional Angel in Adoption recipient. She is the mother of six children. She resides in Spartanburg with Bill, her husband of 30 years.

This article originally appeared in ***Fostering Families Today*** *magazine.*

Troublesome Family-based School Assignments

By Christine Mitchell

Several common school assignments can make foster and adoptive children feel sad, left out, and uncomfortable. Children may lack the information for some projects like the "Family Tree," "Family History," and "Bring-a-Baby Picture." Basing lessons on a traditional family model not only excludes these students, but may also trigger strong grief reactions.

Teachers are generally not aware of the impact of these projects on foster and adoptive children, unless the subject is brought to their attention. Fortunately, these assignments can be easily modified to work for children in all different types of family configurations, by broadening the scope of the assignment and offering students wider choices.

Caregivers are advised to ask the teacher about any upcoming family-based projects at the start of the school year, or when a child starts a new school. The outline below lists some common assignments and the corresponding challenges they present, as well as solutions to make them more inclusive.

"Bring a Baby/Family Picture" Assignments or "Bring Photos at Each Age from Birth"

Problem: An adopted or foster child may not have baby or family photos.

a) This assignment emphasizes an issue that is already painful for children.
b) It puts the child in the difficult position of explaining to other kids why he or she doesn't have baby or family pictures.

Solution: Present the assignment as a choice. Bring a pictures of:

a) The child as a baby or any younger age or
b) Of the child on various holidays or doing various activities.
c) Important people in the child's life.

Family Tree Assignments

Problem: The standard format does not allow for foster, adoptive, birth, or step parents and siblings.

Solution: Rather than avoiding the family tree assignment, parents and educators can use it as a tool to teach children about the many varieties of family structures. Offer a choice of the following formats like:

a) The Rooted Family Tree, where the roots represent the birth family, the child is the trunk, and the foster, adoptive, and/or step family members fill in the branches.
b) The Caring (or Loving) Tree, where the child can fill the branches or leaves with all sorts of important people in his or her life.
c) The Family Wheel Diagram, where the child is in the middle and the outer rings of the circle represent the birth, foster, adoptive and step family relationships.
d) The Family Houses Diagram, which uses houses instead of trees to show connections between birth, foster, adoptive, and step family members.

Autobiographies and Family History Assignments

Problem: Many foster and adopted children lack information about their early years, or the information is painful and private.

Solution: Offer students a choice to write about:

a) My life
b) When I was younger
c) My summer vacation
d) A special event or person in my life

Create a Timeline of the Student's Life

Problem: Some children have little or no information about their milestones. Other children may wonder if they need to include private information like foster care moves.
Solution: Do not require that the timeline begin from the child's birth, just that it cover a period of time. Alternatively, allow children to create a timeline for a historical or fictional character.

Superstar, VIP, Student-of-the-Week Projects

Problem: Having students share information about themselves is intended to be a fun activity that helps students get acquainted. But it can be uncomfortable for children who have limited access to pictures and information about their early years. Some children may also have painful memories of their early childhood.
Solution: Instructors can provide students with a list of many alternatives for the information to be shared, including more innocuous choices such as interests, hobbies, sports, or pets.

Tell About Your Name

Problem: Some children will not know why their birth parents chose their name, and may even have gone through a name change.
Solution: Call the assignment "What's in a Name?" and let students choose between writing about their own name or interviewing a friend or relative about their name.

Write About Your Birth

Problem: This assignment can be fun for children being raised by their biological parents, who can interview their parents about and learn interesting details of their birth. This project is difficult or impossible for many foster and adopted children to complete.
Solution: Ideally, eliminate this assignment altogether, as the questions tend to be intrusive even for families formed by birth.

Assignments revolving around family and personal history can prove troublesome for many types of students. Increasing numbers of families differ from the "traditional" configuration in one or more ways: single-parent and step families, same-sex parents, transracial families, foster and adoptive families, and kinship caregivers. By modifying assignments, teachers will be exposing all of their students to positive messages about adoption, diversity, and respect for all types of people and families.

Christine Mitchell is also the author of ***Welcome Home, Forever Child: A Celebration of Children Adopted as Toddlers, Preschoolers, and Beyond; Family Day: Celebrating Ethan's Adoption Anniversary; A Foster-Adoption Story: Angela and Michael's Journey****, co-authored with Regina M. Kupecky, MSW. You can find out more about Christine at www.christine-mitchell.com. This article originally appeared in* ***Fostering Families Today.***

Bullying

A Real Problem/Some Real Solutions

By Sherryll Kraizer, PhD

Bullying is an integral part of our culture. It happens every day in classrooms, in bathrooms and hallways, on playgrounds and in the neighborhoods of all communities. It is insidious and it is hurtful. Children who are bullied, physically, emotionally or socially, are deprived of their right to go to school and to live in communities where they feel safe.

Being bullied is linked to depression and low self-esteem. Many adopted and foster children suffer with these also – linked to loss, feelings of "not being good enough" to remain with birth family, and also feelings of being different to their (often white) adoptive or foster parents. Some adopted or foster children are vulnerable with regard to social skills. The baggage that being adopted or of living in foster care brings these children means that they are open to becoming bullied or bullies. Some children present as easy prey to classroom bullies, while others bully as a means of bolstering faltering esteem.

What can foster parents do to help things in the classroom change? Most adults easily remember a specific bullying incident from their past. If they were the victim, they remember the panic, the sick feeling, wondering why no one was helping. If they were the bully, they remember the feeling of power and perhaps the shame for what they did to others. Some were bystanders. They remember the anxiety of not wanting to be the next target and often guilt for failure to intervene, even though they didn't know how.

Is Bullying Really That Harmful?

Bullying is the deliberate and repeated infliction of harm on another person. It takes many forms. It may involve one child bullying another, a group of children against a single child or groups against other groups. Bullying includes many behaviors. Common forms of physical, verbal, emotional, and social bullying are shown below:

Physical	Verbal	Emotional	Social Bullying
Hitting	Name-calling	Exclusion	Peer pressure
Pushing	Teasing	Rumors	Exclusion
Kicking	Belittling	Acting superior	Making fun of
Shoving	Making fun	Being mean	Taunting / Baiting
Pinching	Bad language	Not caring	Set up to get in trouble
Violence	Verbal abuse	No conscience	Threats
Abusive	Mimicking	Thoughtlessness	Ganging up on someone
Destructive	Shouting	Gossip	Name-calling
Spitting	Taunting	Threatening	Pranks
Tripping	Cursing	Belittling	Internet harassment

Whether the bullying is direct or indirect, perpetrated by an individual or a group, the key component of bullying is that the physical or psychological intimidation occurs repeatedly over time and is designed to hurt. Young people who are bullied are more likely to be depressed, to feel isolated, anxious, to have low self-esteem and to think about suicide.

Bullying, as most children know, starts early and it is devastating. And as we have seen, it impacts all the harder on adopted and foster children with their intrinsic vulnerability as regards self-esteem, and damages these children all the more.

What Is the Role of Adults?

All forms of bullying are opportunities to teach children how to get along, how to be considerate of all people, and how to be part of a community or group. But, children do not learn to solve conflicts and get along with others naturally. They have to learn specific skills that will prevent and thwart problems with bullying. As soon as children are old enough to interact with others, they can learn not to be bullies and not to be targets. This includes giving them the words to express their feelings, skills to monitor and change their behavior, and conflict resolution strategies.

When preschoolers begin to call people names or use unkind words, we should intervene immediately and consistently. In kindergarten, children learn the power of exclusion. We begin to hear things like, "She's not my friend and she can't come to my party." Respond with, "You don't have to be friends with her today, but it's not all right to make her feel bad by telling her she can't come to your party."

In the early elementary grades, cliques and little groups develop which can be quite exclusionary and cruel. Children need to hear clearly from adults, "It's not all right to treat other people this way. How do you think she feels being told she can't play with you?" Kids don't have to play with everyone or even like everyone, but they can't be cruel by excluding others. Children who are not bullies or victims have a powerful role to play in shaping the behavior of other children. We need to teach these children to speak up on behalf of other children being bullied. "Don't treat her that way, it's not nice."

What Is Role-Play?

Role-play is the tool that turns theories about prevention into reality. It is the game parents and teachers can use to coach children to better life skills. It is the way to find out what children think about the social problems they encounter and how they actually handle them. It is the primary skill-builder for prevention of bullying. It's also a lot of fun!

Role-play is really just practice for life. It's a way of preparing for what we can anticipate. Everyone does it. If you are going to your child's school to discuss a significant problem with a teacher, you probably rehearse what you are going to say, or mentally practice how to approach the issue, thinking through how to respond if the teacher says this, or that. It is perhaps the most powerful way to prepare to be effective.

Learning to speak up is also a skill learned by doing. When a child is able to say, "Don't do that to me, I don't like it," in a tone of voice that is clear and assertive, while standing up tall and looking directly at the person, you will know that role-playing has worked.

How Do I Get Started?

Initiating role-play is as simple as asking a "What if…" question or responding to a child's "What if…" question. For example, you might begin with, "I heard that there was a problem in the lunchroom with one of the boys taking other kids' desserts. What would you do if that happened to you?" When the child begins to tell you, suggest, "Show me what

Role Play

Some Good Ways To Respond To A Bully

It is helpful to have a range of statements, behaviors, or actions in mind as children are role-playing. The following chart will help you get started.

Statements	Behaviors
"That wasn't nice."	Walk away
"Don't do that."	Join another group
"I'm going to tell if you do that again."	Laugh and leave
"That really hurts my feelings."	Ignore them
"That's not a very nice thing to say."	Act like you don't care
"Give that back or I'll tell the teacher."	Avoid the bully
Make a joke –"Whatever," "No kidding"	Get away and tell
"Leave me alone"	Ask a friend to help

Children should also develop action plans to get help. This might include:
- Go and tell a teacher.
- Tell a parent or another adult.
- If they are really afraid, run to someone who can help.

Practice, Practice, Practice

Role-play takes these concepts and makes them skills. Be sure to have fun putting an end to bullying with role-plays. Children love to role-play and will rapidly use it as a way to address other concerns they have. This is invaluable for parents and teachers. The "What if..." questions or scenarios kids suggest reflect their fears, concerns, anxieties and curiosities. Children hear stories about things that have happened to other children, or they witness something in school or on the playground. They naturally think about what they would do. They want to role-play so they know how to handle a similar situation. By eliciting children's ideas through role-play, we discover how they think, how they solve problems, their concept of how the world and their social groups work, and what they know and don't know about solving interpersonal conflicts. Always look for the skills children are bringing to these problem-solving, "What if…" scenarios and acknowledge them. These are the building blocks for all future skills.

Role-play scenarios are easy to create and modify according to the situation or the skills and needs of an individual child or group. Always keep the experience positive, empowering, and fun! Remember that interpersonal skills are learned a little bit at a time, so each step a child takes in the direction of being a clear, powerful, and assertive communicator is important.

you would do, I'll be the kid trying to take your dessert." Play it out. See what resources the child already has.

If the child isn't particularly effective, suggest you switch roles. The child is now the bully. You should model standing up straight, looking the bully in the eye and clearly saying. "Do not touch my lunch." Then change roles and let the child try it again. If he or she gets part way there, provide coaching. Whenever you role-play, remember, it is a process. You are learning what the child's skills are and helping to develop new ones. Avoid judging or making an issue over any part of the role-play or the value will be lost. Role-play is never a confrontation. It is an opportunity to share ideas, initiate discussion, and learn new strategies.

The three key elements of role-play are:

1. **Speaking** – this includes deciding what you want to say and then saying it in an assertive manner, paying attention to tone of voice, volume, pitch, clarity, etc.
2. **Body language** – this includes posture, facial expressions, the distance between the people involved, use of hands, etc.
3. **Eye contact** – communication that is delivered face-to-face, eye-to-eye is more powerful.

Consistently combining all three of these elements takes time and practice. Children most often learn the skills one at a time and then integrate them. Practice and successive approximations is the key. Role-play teaches children how to communicate effectively and consistently so they can utilize the skills automatically.

Family Ethos

Perhaps your child isn't being bullied or isn't a bully, but children are aware of it occurring. Ask any children from kindergarten through high school who is bullying whom. A teacher or parent may not know, but the children always know and they don't want to be next. They are also highly conflicted because they don't want to be marked as a "tattle tale." Okay – let them become **advocates**. Children like to speak up for others!

Advocates are those children who are neither bullies nor targets and they have the most powerful role to play in shaping the behavior of other children. They tend to have better social and conflict management skills. They are more willing to assert themselves without being aggressive or confronting. They suggest compromises and alternate solutions. They tend to be more aware of people's feelings and are the children who can be most helpful in resolving disputes and assisting other children to get help. Often adopted and foster children who have proactive parents will have already been discussing the key elements of bullying (difference, weakness) with their parents, because adoptive and foster parents are aware. Maybe they will have discussed the effects of difference and feelings of inability, loss and vulnerability.

Schools need a policy and an educational plan regarding bullying that targets the entire student body. It should include:

- A clear statement regarding bullying: that it is unacceptable.
- A plan for student and parent education about the policy.
- Adequate and active supervision, especially at times when students are moving about

freely during recess, class breaks, lunchtime, and after school is dismissed.

- A policy of immediate and early intervention (always too early rather than too late).
- Training that makes every child an advocate for every other child.

We should scrutinize our schools for diversity and empathy for difference. And, we need to become advocates against bullying. If each of us is willing to speak up and to learn the skills to intervene effectively against bullying, this can no longer be a culture of meanness and violence.

Sherryll Kraizer, PhD, is the founder and director of the Coalition for Children. This article originally appeared in ***Adoption Parenting: Creating a Toolbox, Building Connections*** *(EMK Press 2006)*

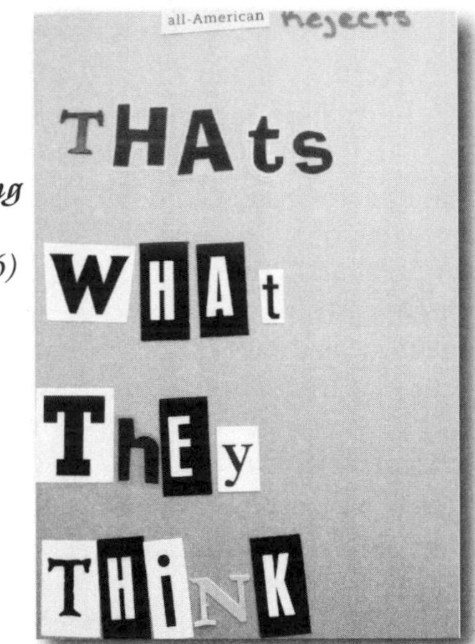

Some Additional Resources:

Bullying At School: What We Know and What We Can Do, D. Olweus

Take A Stand Prevention of Bullying and Interpersonal Violence Program **www.safechild.org/bullies.htm**

The Safe Child Program, **www.safechild.org/program.htm**

Women's Educational Media, uses film to train parents, staff, faculty, administrators and students in schools. **http://groundspark.org/our-films-and-campaigns/lets-get-real**

www.tolerance.org

What If a Child Wants To Disclose Bullying?

Children use "What if..." scenarios as a way to tell their parents and teachers things that have happened. It seems less like tattling to them and makes incidents easier to talk about. For example, "Mom, what would you say if some of my friends were making the little kids miss the bus and blaming it on someone else?" To follow up, you would want to explain that telling about a problem is not tattling and that you would like to help without making the situation worse. You might role-play your child talking to someone at the school, with or without you. Or decide together that this is a situation you should handle with the school directly. Always remember to thank your child for speaking up and for being an advocate for another child.

W.I.S.E. Up! For Foster Care: A Tool to Empower Children

By Ellen Singer, LCSW-C, and Debbie Riley, MS

This story on the right is just one example of the kind of situations children in foster families may face when they are out in the world, away from the protection of their foster families. Questions like the ones Callie asked are loaded with meaning and emotion for foster children. They can go right to the heart of their self-concept, challenging who they are and where they belong.

"Why are you in foster care?"
"How come your family couldn't keep you?"
"I heard that kids who live in foster care were bad and got in trouble."
"Did your parents do drugs?"
"Where is your real family? Don't you want to see them?"
"Why are you a different color from your family?"
"If you and your sister live with different families, then you're not really sisters."

These questions and comments are just samples of the ones hundreds of children and teens have shared with us at The Center for Adoption Support and Education (C.A.S.E.). These kids have told us that answering others' questions about their foster families and being in foster care is among their major concerns. Sometimes they are asked about their own stories. At other times, they are asked to offer expert commentary about some media event connected to foster care. Throughout the years, children and teens have shared with us how difficult and uncomfortable this can make them feel. They report feeling caught off guard as they frequently don't know what to say. They often later regret what they did say and are left with a mixture of emotions: confusion, anger, embarrassment, shame, sadness, or frustration.

As foster parents, you might also feel this range of emotions when questioned. And, while you may feel comfortable talking about foster care and about your decision to become foster parents, you too, can be caught off guard by an acquaintance's or stranger's comments or questions. Later, you may wonder if you handled the situation appropriately. Your positive and negative experiences help to make you more aware of how important it is to help prepare the chil-

Anthony picked up his poster board and headed for the front of the class. It was his turn to be Grade 5 Star of the Week. He had drawn some artwork and added a photo that his new foster mom took of him with her digital camera.

At the end of his talk, the teacher said, "That was terrific, Anthony! Does anyone have questions?"

Callie piped up. "That's just one picture! Why don't you have more? We all saw you at the hay ride last week! How about showing us some from before you came to this school?"

"I don't have any pictures from that time," Anthony said.

The teacher shifted uncomfortably in her chair. She couldn't do anything to help Anthony. Even if she could say something – what would it be?

dren to respond to questions and comments about foster care.

Empowering Foster Children

No matter what situation brings on a question or comment, children in foster families are more confident when they feel in control of their responses. This is precisely why The Center for Adoption Support and Education created W.I.S.E. Up! for Foster Families – to give children and teens the tools they need to take control.

W.I.S.E. kids can:

- Make quick choices about how they want to handle each situation as it comes up;
- Decide how much information they want to share (if any) about foster care, their foster family or their personal story;
- Use their considerable knowledge to understand why others might say or ask the things they do;
- Feel certain that, no matter what they may experience, they're not alone – many other kids have been through the same thing!

Why is W.I.S.E. Up! Needed?

Friends, neighbors, relatives, teachers and strangers ask questions about foster families for a variety of reasons. For starters, people whose lives have not been touched by foster care have little understanding about it. (Can you remember what you knew about foster families before you became a foster parent?) More often than not, others' knowledge about the topic is shaped by limited personal experience and by societal myths. For some, the topic is interesting because they have heard heart-warming stories about foster care. For others, the topic is interesting because the media sometimes focuses on, and sensationalizes, negative stories. While some good can result from such stories, focusing only on the negative tends to spread misunderstanding about foster families and the foster care system, in general.

Children who have never been exposed to foster care exhibit a natural curiosity about how and why foster families are formed. Not surprisingly, children have difficulty understanding all of the complexities involved. Unfortunately, it is difficult for them to obtain factual answers to their questions. They may wonder if being placed in foster care is something that could ever happen to them. For all children, the idea that one can "lose" their parents or can be "taken away" from their parents is a frightening thought. Consequently, other children might ask a lot of questions and even tease a child who lives with a foster family to try and reassure themselves "it can never happen to me."

Whatever the reason, children in foster families benefit from knowing that they are WISER than their peers and others about foster care. It helps them to understand that others do not have the knowledge they do about the topic. The W.I.S.E. Up! program empowers children to help educate others – to W.I.S.E Up! the world about foster families.

W.I.S.E. Up! also helps children to understand that nearly all children in foster care are asked questions about it. On those days when being in foster care makes them feel different from their classmates, W.I.S.E. kids can remember that hundreds of thousands of kids are working to meet the same challenges!

How Does W.I.S.E. Up! Work?

W.I.S.E. Up! is simple. The letters in WISE stand for the four options children have for responding to questions or comments about adoption:

W	Walk away or ignore what is said or heard.
I	It's private and I don't have to answer it and I can say that appropriately, even to adults.
S	Share something about my personal story.
E	Educate others about foster families.

W.I.S.E. children are taught to memorize their options, assess each situation and choose the letter – one of the four choices – that feels most comfortable to them, based on 1) their mood, 2) the person who is asking the question (e.g. best friend or just a classmate), 3) their feelings about the question being asked, and 4) the context in which the question is being asked (e.g. alone with the questioner or in front of other children). It's important for children to know that choosing ANY of the options is perfectly acceptable; however, practice helps children exercise their personal choices to suit situations more effectively.

For example, when a child does not want to answer a difficult question posed by a classmate, he or she has every right to choose the letter I (It's private). While politeness is preferred, as in, "I don't want to talk about my personal story right now," the reality is that children will talk like children and it is perfectly acceptable for them to say, "It's none of your business." Other children like to get that message across by quickly changing the subject. They might respond, "What did you think of the math test?"

Years of experience with children has shown us that the third choice – share something – requires considerable review time. We encourage you to help your children practice the "S" responses, paying particular attention to helping them to decide when, with whom, and how much they want to share about their personal history. Children should also be advised that just because they share something personal to one question, they are in no way obligated to continue "sharing" – to follow-up questions. For example, in response to the question, "Why don't you look like your parents?" a child who feels comfortable choosing the S might say: "These are my foster parents; I look like my birth parents." But that child may not wish to offer an explanation to a follow-up question, "Why aren't you living with your 'real' parents?" In that situation, the child needs to know that responding with any of the other three choices W, I, or E is perfectly appropriate.

When children want others to know about foster care without sharing their personal story, they can choose the E – Educate others. E involves providing general information about foster care. For example, to the child who asks, "Why do you live with foster parents?"... the foster child might respond, "Children live with foster families because their birth parents did not or could not take proper care of them." Or, "Did you know that 12 million people have grown up in foster families? Eddie Murphy, Ice T and John Lennon all were in foster care."

The W.I.S.E. Up! Powerbook For Children in Foster Care

The original W.I.S.E. Up! Powerbook written by Marilyn Schoettle, an educator and former director of publications and education at C.A.S.E., was created so parents could teach this empowering tool to their adopted children. Recognizing the need to provide this powerful tool for foster children, C.A.S.E. was pleased to revise the book to create the W.I.S.E. Up! Powerbook For Children in Foster Care. If you are interested in learning more about this book, visit the C.A.S.E. website at www.adoptionsupport.org.

Ellen Singer, LCSW-C is a therapist/educator for The Center for Adoption Support and Education (C.A.S.E.) in Burtonsville/Silver Spring, Md. She provides clinical services for prospective parents considering adoption/third party reproduction, foster and adoptive parents, adult adopted persons and their families, and expectant/birth parents and their families. Ellen facilitates adoptive parent support groups and provides training to parents, community groups, educators, and other professionals. She is the editor of C.A.S.E.'s monthly e-newsletter and contributes articles to parent/professional publications. Ellen has served on the board of directors for RESOLVE of the Mid-Atlantic, and the Professional Advisory Council for RESOLVE.

Debbie B. Riley is the CEO of The Center for Adoption Support and Education, Inc. (C.A.S.E.), an independent adoptive family support center, and co-author of the book, ***Beneath the Mask: Understanding Adopted Teens.*** *She is also an adoptive mother. Debbie holds a master's degree in marriage and family therapy from the University of Maryland. Since 1993, she has focused exclusively on the field of adoption. She has created a continuum of pre and post-adoption innovative and effective clinical and training programs to address the complex needs of families from all adoption backgrounds, including public and private, international and domestic. Ms. Riley presents locally, nationally and internationally on numerous topics related to adoption and adolescent mental health.*

Parenting Teens

And yet, parenting teens is so often about having the good judgment to withhold one's better judgment. – Robert Brault

Parenting Teens

By M. Kim Combes, LBSW, MEd

Many of us remember Redd Foxx in the 1970s sitcom *Sanford and Son.* He and his son co-owned a junk yard and interacted with various comedic individuals on a weekly basis. Fred Sanford had a trademark gesture for which he was well noted when excited. He would look to the heavens exclaiming, "It's the big one, Elizabeth" to his deceased wife as he held his hand over his chest feigning near death by heart attack. Bystanders rolled their eyes as they witnessed this hyperbolic response to whatever it was Fred was reacting to in this overly melodramatic way.

A while back I attended a workshop called *Teenage Brains: Engines Without Drivers.* Gloria and Lee Daniels presented research showing that as children hit puberty and negotiate adolescence, their brains "morph" much as brains do in the first five years of life. The turbulence of hormone surges, changing bodies, roller coaster relationships and the angst that is associated with young adulthood makes parenting these aliens in our home challenging at best. Since parenting is sometimes a "crapshoot" we must have a full toolbox of ideas as to how to successfully negotiate teen life with our young charges. What works one day with our children may not work the next. So where do we start?

I believe children and teens respond to what they get the most response from. For example, sadly, my own children sometimes see the more frustrated side of my parenting rather than the delight I have in them when they are making good choices. If we continue to show more intense emotion for the negative choices our teens make, then show little or no emotion for good choices, we likely will get the behaviors that manifest our more emotional side. Thus, we need to learn to "parent with pizzazz," doing the Fred Sanford imitation when good choices are made.

We can stop making a federal case about chores not being done on time, grades being less than what we expect or attitudes being defiant. Rather, we can learn to exaggerate our responses to positive behaviors such as bringing home a good test score, starting a chore without being reminded, being nice to their brother or other similar behaviors. Imagine our teens' response if we would grab our chest and celebrate loudly the fact that they were up on time without being awakened, cleaned up a mess without prompting and showed initiative by starting homework before their designated time period for doing so. Yes, they may initially think we've finally "lost it," but done without sarcasm, with a playful smile and a hug or high five afterward, these responses may motivate them to do more behaviors that have us responding as the fools they sometimes think we are. Moreover, it will give them something to razz us about in the presence of their kids someday, saying things like, "Hey Junior, you should have seen how funny Grandpa looked back when I was a kid when he'd grab his heart like he was having a heart attack."

Teens are really no different than adults when it comes to wanting respect and dignity from significant others. As difficult as it might seem sometimes, we need to remember that we wouldn't treat our boss, friends, co-workers, or members of the community the way we sometimes react to our children when they fail to meet our expectations. We need to come up with ways to discipline – lead, guide, teach, correct – our teens in ways that they feel respected, gently yet firmly.

Drs. Gary Chapman and Ross Campbell co-authored ***The Five Love Languages of Children*** while Chapman alone wrote ***The Five Love Languages of Teens.*** The premise of these books is that our children need all five love languages incorporated into their lives, but are hardwired for a primary love language – one that "fills their love tank." The authors believe it's not a question of "do we love our children, but do our children feel loved?"

The five love languages include physical touch, words of affirmation, quality time, gifts, and acts of service. Many people give the same love language they desire to receive. For example, a parent who enjoys physical touch and close proximity to significant others will show their love by touching and being close. Teens, however, may try to avoid touch with parents; the parent subsequently feels rejected and the teen's own love language is overlooked. The teen may greatly desire quality time with a parent while the parent is blissfully ignorant of this yearning while the teen may manifest anything but that longing. Consequently the teen does not feel loved even while touchy-feely parents are trying diligently to convey their affection by hugging, high fives, hair mussing, and other actions.

Many young people respond well to words of affirmation such as praise for good choices, high marks at school, random acts of kindness and the like. Some youth enjoy gifts such as little tokens given them for the aforementioned choices – it doesn't have to be monetary, but can be rewards such as a later curfew, friends over night, a 10-minute backrub, or doing a chore for them. Teens would greatly love parents to volunteer to do their dishes for them, or better yet, wash while the teen dries, thus spending some quality time with him or her simultaneously.

I have learned in the 15 years of being a foster/adoptive parent that, contrary to parental popular belief, teens want adult interaction. There is an old adage that states "people don't care how much you know until they know how much you care." My teens have taught me, and research bears this out, that our young people need us to be actively involved in their lives, thus showing them that we care by spending time with them. Having quality time with parents is of paramount importance to teens floundering in society today. They look for direction from adults who don't just "talk the talk, but walk the walk." Remembering "Cats in the Cradle," the 1970s song by Harry Chapin, gives us insight as to how important it is to honor our children by giving of our time and selves.

There is a plethora of information via books and websites geared toward parenting our next generation. I can but only scratch the surface, even from my own personal experiences, when it comes to discussing parenting techniques for molding our young adults into successful societal members. However, I have seen for myself the success that can be gained by incorporating the five love languages into everyday discipline while also utilizing the Fred Sanford approach to motivating our teens to rethink the wayward direction they may be heading.

We are indeed making a positive difference in the lives of our teens, so hang in there. We're all in this together.

*M. Kim Combes, LBSW, MEd, is a private practice counselor and national presenter, as well as a former foster dad to 40-plus teenage boys since 1994. Currently, he and wife, Diane, live in Colo, Iowa with their five adopted children who range in age from 10 to 17. This article orignally appeared in **Fostering Families Today**.*

Adolescence: Surviving and Thriving

By Brenda McCreight, PhD

The Evolving Challenge

The teen years – we've only considered this time of life, carved out between childhood and adulthood, since the late 1890s. Prior to that, boys and girls matured later with menstruation rarely beginning before age 16. By that age, youths were considered to be young adults and they were expected to undertake the responsibilities of work and marriage. As the demands of the workforce changed with industrialization and the availability of food increased, puberty onset began earlier and entry into the workforce was delayed, thus creating a time in life that was not defined by economic need or biological function. So there we were, for the first time in recorded history, with a socially defined life stage that held no particular value beyond the emotional place the youth had in the family.

It may seem like we should have figured out what to do with this life stage by now, but 120 years is a pretty short length of time for people to develop a new set of social constructs and role definitions. And, to make it more complicated, this life stage isn't generalized throughout all societies; it's mainly evolved in North America and has been shaped by, and reflected back into, the values of Western society and culture. So, we stand almost alone in this historical journey, inventing and re-inventing adolescence with each generation.

Today, this stage of life has become negatively associated with rejection of parental values, drugs and alcohol, a separate set of music and cultural idols, and its own use and interpretation of language. Indeed, with the rapid expansion and dissemination of technology, the younger generation often knows how to use current communication devices before parents. That the young have access to more ways of communicating and defining how these are used is unprecedented in history.

With adolescence continuing to evolve, parenting has also had to change with each generation. Few parent the same way they were parented, and it's doubtful anyone does it the way their grandparents did. The demands and expectations placed on children have also changed and increased. Today's children and youth are expected to learn more in school, achieve highly, participate in a myriad of after school activities, and avoid peer pressure that might lead them astray. With the dangers of easily available drugs and alcohol, and the fear of other negative influences ("What do I do with a 16-year-old who has become the queen of Goths at school?" and "How will I know if my son is beginning to experience annihilation type delusions brought on by overexposure to violent video games?") adolescence has become a time that creates fear and uncertainty in many parents and in society.

The Adolescent Brain

Those who foster teens, or adopt older children and teens, often find that these fears are compounded by the fact that these teens' brains were negatively impacted and indeed, altered in structure and function, by the prenatal exposure to drugs, tobacco, and alcohol, and by their early experiences of neglect, abuse, and multiple caregivers. So, not only are there the general problems of raising youth in a culture that doesn't know what to do with

Practical Methods in Caring for Teens

By Mary T. Keane

- Listen more and speak less. Let them talk and be non-judgemental – no matter what they tell you. Bite your tongue.
- Be patient. Kids always say when asked, "what parents need to be is patient." Patience should infuse everything.
- Maintain a sense of humor and try to employ it in the middle of your anger.
- Try to say "yes" as much as possible, or try not to say "no" often.
- Tread softly with your words. You never know what connections they make in their heads or what history your words trigger.
- Be as real as you can. They can spot a phony in a second even when they don't tell you to your face.
- Stick to your word – almost always, no matter what.
- Always let them become who they are and not who you want them to be.
- Always be willing to apologize for being a fool because you will be.
- Never take anything they do personally because you were probably the last thing on their mind when they were doing it.
- Take a time out immediately when you feel yourself losing control and do something to keep from talking and sticking your foot in your mouth or worse.
- Work with the kids where they are and take the time to find out where that is. Don't assume anything, especially based on age.
- Focus on the "important" stuff and let go of the rest.
- Focus on the positives and away from the negatives. Their whole lives have emphasized the negatives.
- Put aside your ego. It will get stomped on anyway.
- Let the kids teach you. They are patient and tolerant teachers.
- Be "fair" and just.

Mary T. Keane is an adoptive and pre-adoptive mother. Her nine children, all from the foster care system, range in age from 18 to 36 years old. She works for You Gotta Believe! the Older Child Adoption Agency and Homelessness Prevention Program. www.yougottabelieve.org. This was originally published in ***Fostering Families Today.***

this life stage, but there is the added factor of raising youth who may not have the capacity to respond and react in a healthy manner to the demands of today's world.

Some people question why there is a need to understand the adolescent brain. Isn't it enough, they ask, to simply deal with the behaviors? The answer is, no, it isn't enough. There isn't a technique or approach that is right for every single foster or adopted teen, or for every parent and every family. Different people use and respond to different things. In order to understand the foster or adopted teen, a basic understanding of what makes them tick is important so we can devise, in the moment it's needed, the best way to handle difficult situations and even reduce some of the potential problems.

There isn't a technique or approach that is right for every single foster or adopted teen, or for every parent and every family.

The adolescent brain undergoes a massive change beginning at about age 13 and finally finishes its work by age 25. During this time, the brain connections grow and interconnect in a way that selectively changes over time to meet the needs of the environment and to respond to the incoming stimuli – that is, the family, peer scene, school, overall culture, and others. For foster or adopted teens, this also may include the additional emotional tasks of dealing with birth family, foster/identity issues, or abandonment and lack of attachment, as well as the almost overwhelming tasks of an altered brain undergoing basic change. At this stage, it begins with the grey matter volume increasing in the pre-teen stage, followed by sustained loss and thinning starting around puberty, which happens at the same time as advancing cognitive abilities. This process results in greater organization of the brain as it prunes useless or underused connections, and enhances the tissues that transmit brain messages.

At the same time, areas associated with fairly basic functions, including the motor and sensory areas, mature rather early in the process. Areas involved in planning, decision making and the cognitive or reasoning area of the brain (which are important for controlling impulses and emotions), seem to develop much later, more toward the end of the process. The part that leads to so much risky behavior, is rooted in the brain's reward center which becomes more active during adolescence, so the adolescent brain still is strengthening connections between its reasoning- and emotion-related regions.

Parents Do Make the Difference

In a nutshell, the brain grows massively, and the parts that are underused are basically pruned off, while the parts that are regularly used and stimulated are allowed to grow and shape the personality of the youth. What does that mean for foster and adopted teens? Well, to begin with, many of them are still stuck in behaviors that are rooted in trauma. The early traumas will have dug deeply into the youth's brain and are regularly stimulated by a life of uncertainty. For example, the worry, "Will I be moved from this foster home before the end of the school year?" is going to further entrench and activate the abandonment issues. So is, "Will my foster mom think I'm just like my birth mom if she finds out

I smoked pot last weekend?" and "If I don't sleep with my new boyfriend will he leave me just like everyone else in my life has?" and "Is my foster dad going to yell at me again when he sees the make-up I'm wearing?" and "Will my foster parents dump me when they find out I've been stealing again?"

The sexual or physical abuse traumas are triggered constantly by the sexual pressure placed on teens by society and peers. If the parents don't address the underlying trauma openly, then the teen's attempts to meet expectations while repressing the memories will also dig the trauma deeper into the maturing brain so that these memories become the foundation of the brain structure and the subsequent behaviors. The teen begins to experience what has been called "emotional self-mutilation," which is demonstrated by rages, running away, drug and alcohol abuse, and other forms of self-harm.

It often seems like foster and adopted kids don't give any thought to how or what parents are feeling. In reality though, they consider their behaviors constantly. Parents or caregivers have to realize that how they choose to interact with these teens will influence what genes and neurons are activated in the teens' brains. Reactions to their behaviors will, to a large part, determine whether their brains are flushed with the destructive stress hormones which shut down reasoning and communication, as well as destroy any potential for resolution; or, whether parents' behaviors toward the teen will decrease the stress hormones and bring in the self-soothing and calming hormones and chemicals which allow for attachment, communication, and resolution – and most importantly, healthy relationships and positive behaviors. Maybe the situation can't be resolved as in, "You aren't going to the party tonight even if every other teen in town is allowed" may have to stand, but the conflict and the emotional energy can be toned down and the relationship left intact so that there can be resolution tomorrow, or even a year from now, and the relationship remains strong.

Key Parental Behaviors

Regardless of what parenting methods and behavioral approaches are used in a family, they will only succeed if they are created from an emotional attitude on the part of the parent that allows for nurturing, calm, and provides a general feeling of wanting the best for the child or youth. That may seem impossible at times, and once again, the burden is on the parent to set the tone even in the face of a youth who is hurling the "f" word around or a 10-year-old who is raging and throwing chairs against the window. However, if the parent follows some basic steps in emotional climate control, most of the more severe outbursts can be avoided.

To begin, as soon as there is any escalation on the part of the child or youth, the parent needs to do a quick mental survey to determine his or her own level of anger or bad mood. It's always going to be up to the parent to get to the right emotional space quickly. Taking some deep breaths, focusing on the child, clearing the area, and sitting down are first steps to sidetracking a raging youth. Follow that with a lowered voice tone, and a calm appearance. Most importantly, the adult has to remember that this is about building and maintaining relationship and changing to emotional state – it's not about drug abuse or school failures or sexual acting out or any other topic that led to this particular conflict. Foster and adopted children and teens are simply larger versions of an angry 6-month-old,

FAMILY TALK: How to Handle Teen Lying

By Drs. James and Mary Kenney

Q: Dear Mary: My husband and I are feeling betrayed and hopeless because our 16-year-old daughter lies to us. She seems sincere, but on several occasions we found out later that everything she said was untrue. I fear we cannot be close as a family if we cannot trust each other. Is this likely to pass? Is there anything we can do?

– Pennsylvania

A: Dear Pennsylvania: You describe well parents' feelings of dismay. Most often children lie to keep from getting in trouble. Another reason may be to get their way. As a teenager might put it: "If I told the truth, you wouldn't let me do what I want." These reasons do not excuse lying, but help to recognize why it may occur. Lying frustrates parents like no other misbehavior because lying is totally within the child's control. The usual suggestions about rewarding good behavior and disciplining misbehavior firmly and promptly do not work with lying. Often parents do not even know when the misbehavior is occurring. The parents' only recourse is to take away the payoff for lying. If lying works for the child it is likely to continue.

To take away the payoff for deception a parent must verify everything from other sources. Is Lisa staying overnight with her girlfriend? Call the girlfriend's parent. Has Larry skipped school and lied when you questioned him? Contact the school counselor and set up a program to check on and discipline attendance. Call the counselor personally whenever your child is going to be absent. Does Tim come home after curfew with the excuse:"We had a flat tire?" Establish that curfew is curfew. If he is late because of a misfortune, sympathize but impose the penalty anyway. You will have taken away the reason to make up an excuse. Next, when some activity cannot be verified from another source ignore it. You ask: "Where were you?" And he or she responds: "We went to a movie." In most cases the parent cannot verify this. Of course, you could grill the child: "What time did the movie start? Tell me the plot?" Such questioning focuses time and attention on lying.

Ideally, you want to ignore lying. Ignoring is an effective way to stop behavior. Suppose each morning on your way to work you meet your neighbor. Each morning you say, "Good morning." Your neighbor, however, never returns your greeting. Rather quickly, you will probably stop your greeting. Ignoring can have the same effect on lying. Will lying stop eventually? Some adolescents who lie grow into adults who are open and honest with their parents. While no one can predict the future, human behavior suggests that lying will stop most quickly when it proves useless and is ignored. Some parents try to "nail" a lying child by setting him or her up. They get evidence from outside sources, let the child lie, then confront him or her with the facts. While such a practice may give the parent a grim satisfaction, it destroys the child's self-respect. It is the cruelest of put-downs and leaves the child no way out. For these reasons it is not a good way to handle lying.

Verify your child's activities from outside sources. Disregard what cannot be verified. With no reason to lie, lies will likely stop.

Drs. James A. and Mary Kenney host a regular column in ***Fostering Families Today.***

with the same inability to self-regulate. No matter how angry teens are, no matter how foul-mouthed, or aggressively dressed they are, they are victims of a rotten childhood that left them unable to self-regulate and in need of the external regulation a parent provides as a six-month-old. If they could do better, they would.

It's always important to remember in times of escalating conflict, that if a youth's emotional state is changed, the change in behaviors will follow. Once foster parents have regulated their breathing, lowered their voice tone, and removed the audience, their mirror neurons will start to help. What are mirror neurons? These are neural circuits located in the frontal lobes that fire off in response to the people we are with. While watching a football game, a fan's pulse can get as high as that of his or her favorite player on the field. If foster parents get into an argument with their teen, the emotional arousal of the teen will be "mirrored" in the foster parents' own neurons, escalating the foster parents' own behavior. However, foster parents have minds that can exert control, so it becomes the parental responsibility to use the mirror neurons to regulate those of the teens.

This takes considerable self-awareness on the part of the parent. It's not easy to withstand the anger and chaos that is launched from the angry and unreasoning teen. Still, it can be done. And, if the parent practices this state of mindful interaction and self-regulation on a daily basis, it sets a tone in the relationship that often prevents further angry escalation and confrontations. The teen needs to find the same stability in the foster or adoptive parent that he or she should have found in the birth parent. As the foster or adoptive parent becomes better at creating this positive relationship-based connection with the teen, the brain of the adolescent can begin to change and resolve into the more mature version that is supposed to be developing.

Brenda McCreight, PhD, RSW, is an adoptive parent, therapist, and the author of ***Recognizing and Managing Fetal Alcohol Syndrome/Effects: A Guidebook; Parenting Your Adopted Older Child*** *and the childrens' book* ***Eden's Secret Journal: The Story of An Older Child Adoption****. Brenda is the mother of 14 children, 12 of whom are adopted and are considered to have special needs. Since 1982 Brenda has worked as a therapist with children and families facing issues such as sexual abuse and family violence as well as adoption and foster related concerns. Brenda is a writer and a sought after speaker in the area of behavior disorders. Her website is www.theadoptioncounselor.com.*

Passing The Test

By Tanya Reid

I have always imagined getting married, having children, and adopting. My plan was to adopt a young child, maybe five years old or younger, but adopting a teenager wasn't part of what I imagined. I got married and my husband and I had three children. My husband always knew I wanted to adopt a child, so we took the next step. We went through the training and completed our homestudy. After our homestudy, my husband and I were approached about adopting a 15-year-old boy.

We were given his history. George was born drug exposed, abused, and neglected by various family members. His father died when George was 11. George lived with his grandmother most of his life until she died when George was 13. He was then placed in foster care. We were told that he had no behavioral problems and that he excelled in school. I thought to myself, "how could a teenager with his history have no behavioral problems?"

After we agreed to meet George, we met him and his caseworker for lunch. When I met him, I wanted to immediately take George home and protect him from anyone who would hurt him. He was so shy, awkward, and quiet. He made no eye contact and his caseworker did most of the talking for him.

Next, my husband and I talked to the kids about him. They were excited and we all agreed that we wanted to have a visit. Our first visit was at a bowling alley and then we spent several hours at our home. He seemed to fit right in. George wasn't as shy, awkward, or quiet. The kids seemed to really enjoy his company. Several more visits occurred and eventually sleepovers and several weeks later George moved in with us.

My husband and I understood that there would most likely be a "honeymoon" period where things would be great with George, but that there would also come a time when George would test our commitment to him. George began testing our commitment one month after he moved in with us.

First test: Every night when he thought we were all sleeping, I would hear George sneak downstairs to the kitchen where he would consume enormous amounts of food. That behavior was easy to understand after talking to George about it. He said in his previous foster home he was given three small meals a day and then a padlock was put on the refrigerator. I let him know that he didn't have to sneak food because he would never be denied access to food in our home. George continued to sneak food and I continued to meet him in the kitchen in the middle of the night to remind him that it was okay to stop eating late at night. After many late night meetings in the kitchen with me, George eventually trusted that he would not be denied food and our middle-of-the-night meetings in the kitchen stopped. We passed the first test.

Second test: We had no time to study for the second test because it happened almost immediately after the first one. We discovered that George was stealing money from us. It wasn't a lot of money, but the fact that he was stealing wasn't okay. I lectured him about stealing and told him that if he needed money for something he had to ask for it, then I grounded him. We passed the second test.

Third test: My daughter came in the house crying and said George hit her on the head. I called him in and George admitted to hitting her, saying she wouldn't stop singing, "George of the Jungle." I explained to him that it was not okay to hit the kids and sent him to his room. My daughter went back outside after I explained to her that it's not okay to tease anyone and she should have listened to George when he asked her to stop.

I went upstairs to talk to George who was lying face down on his bed. I asked him why he got so upset and felt the need to hit her. He wouldn't speak. After lecturing him, I told him to think about what he did and when he was ready to talk to me he could come downstairs. I went downstairs and George began to throw things around his room. I went upstairs to try and calm him down. He broke a lot of stuff and also broke some of the kids' stuff. I hardly knew what to say, so I told him that he needed to find a way to talk about how he was feeling and not destroy things. I told him that we all cared about him and wanted him to remain in our family, but in this family we talked things out and didn't hit or break things and then I grounded him.

In between the commitment tests I questioned, wondered, and worried about George being able to bond with us; to truly feel that he was part or our family and accept that we wanted him to be a part of our family forever. During my uncertainty about his placement with us, George gave us another test of commitment.

Fourth test: There are times when I send George to the store to pick up things like milk and bread. To make things easy, I gave him my PIN for my bank card because the store wouldn't let him use it as a credit card, or so I thought. With my debit card and PIN in hand, George would happily go to the store for me every time I asked him. Little did I know that he was happily withdrawing money from the ATM on his way to the store. After five ATM withdrawals I realized what he was doing and confronted him. He admitted it and when I grounded him, he flipped out. He smashed a glass jelly jar on the kitchen floor, then went upstairs and threw his television and cable box down the stairs and completely trashed his room and the upstairs' bathroom. I didn't know what to do. My husband was away on business and I was failing this test. While he destroyed everything upstairs, my kids were outside and thankfully not witnessing this craziness.

Eventually things calmed down and the next morning I told George that he needed to work off the money he took from me so I told him to rake up all the leaves in the back yard. He went quietly and began raking and I watched him through the window while he raked with rage. After a while he came in the house and went to his room. I called him downstairs a few times before he said, "I'm sorry, but I am not coming down." I asked him what he meant and he said, "I don't want to live here anymore." I calmly told him it was his choice and that he could call his caseworker. A few minutes later, without a word said, George was back outside raking the leaves.

I called his caseworker who came right over after he heard what was going on. I spoke to the caseworker outside and then George came to talk to him. I watched through the window as his caseworker lectured him and George held his head down and cried. I felt bad for George. After a while George told me his caseworker wanted to talk to me. I told his caseworker that I would be right out after I talked to George first. I brought George into my room and told him that taking money from us was unacceptable and that I wanted to help him find a better way to get his needs met. I told him that he was a great kid with a lot of potential. I told him he was smart and could have a bright future. When I told him that he was worth it and deserved to be happy with a family who loved him he started to cry. I told him that we all cared for and loved him and wanted to adopt him.

I called his therapist who was meeting with him that evening and told her everything. After I picked him up from therapy he was quiet. I simply asked if he was okay and he said yes. When we got home he went right into the back yard, in the dark and rain, and began raking more leaves. After a while I went out check on him and he was asleep on the deck stairs with the rake in his hand. I sent the poor kid to bed.

A couple of weeks later after all that, I approached George about a paper I had to write about my experience being a foster parent and wanted his input. I knew he liked to write and thought this would be a good way for him to express his true feelings. I asked him to write down his feelings about being in foster care and his feelings about being adopted. He readily agreed and wrote:

> *"My experience living in foster care has not been a good one. The problem is that whenever I was in a foster home the thing they don't do is that they don't get to know me. It can be really troublesome when you are living in a place for a long period of time and the people don't know a thing about me. Now, living in an adoptive home has the same beginning feeling. Like when I started living here for the first three weeks and they had yet to get to know me. Right now my biggest problem is that they think they know me and what I've been through. If they did know, they would know that I did not have a father to teach me the things that a normal child should have known. And that as I was growing up I had to learn these things on my own, which was not easy. I'm still trying to learn. School is easier for me, which would explain why I feel more comfortable in school than at home. If they just took the time to get to know me and for me to get to know them, everything would be a lot better. As for becoming adopted by their family, I don't know how I really feel because as far as I see it, it's the same as living in a foster home."*

I wanted to defend myself to George and explain to him that I have been trying for eight months to get him to talk to me, really talk to me about his history and feelings. I wanted to remind him that we actually have had talks about his birth family and how he feels. I wanted him to know, rather validate my own efforts, that I am a good adoptive parent and completely understand how he must feel. But the truth is, I am not perfect and my efforts to get to know him have not satisfied him. Looking back, I did most of the talking when trying to get to know George, I thought I understood him and his feelings and I told him that I know how he must feel and let him know what I thought his feelings were. He always just listened to me, sometimes his eyes would fill with tears and thinking I hit an emotional nerve, I would continue to try getting him to talk. But I really never gave him a chance to talk because all I wanted was to make him feel good and feel better about himself. I thought that by lecturing him, a light bulb would go off in his head and he would realize that we are a good fit for him. But I was wrong.

So, that night George and I talked for a long time about his history. I let him talk and I just listened. He set the record straight about what we were told about his history before he was placed with us and the truth – his truth. Until the night we talked, I honestly thought I was doing everything right. But I realized that night that George had wanted us to know the real him, not the sanitized version we were told by his social worker who hoped to find an adoptive home for George. That night I felt like I was starting over with George after eight months of "knowing" him.

There were more tests given to us by George throughout the year and I am sure there will be more to come. George has a traumatic history and he is also a typical teenager. So, with a lot of patience, love, understanding, and forgiveness (as parents of any teenager needs to have) we have made George a permanent part of our family

Tanya Reid enjoys reading, writing, and spending time with her family. She is a social worker living in New Jersey who recently adopted her son.

I remember being unable to exercise my VOICE! While growing up in foster care, I just did what people told me to do and worried about survival, rather than using my VOICE about what was wrong with the system. Once I reached my early twenties, I became connected with new mentors! One particular person sticks out as a positive influence and that's my last foster home. Throughout the nine foster homes and three group homes, the Wades took the time to provide foster parenting but they were guardian angels to me. Despite the harsh and tormented reality of my childhood, I have been able to up rise from those hurts and turn my future into becoming a strong advocate for those currently in care. To my foster care brothers and sisters, know that your past can allow you to become the most passionate person in the world. Know that you're loved and you have a foster alumni family! We must stick together and bring about change within the foster care system. Foster parents must be MENTORS……not just a foster parent. Fostering is a true art!

Nicole Lawrence, 29-year-old foster alumni

The Broken Child

By Anne Birdsong Giberson

With the help of my other sons, we righted the table.

Rolling fruit was gathered and washed.

Jagged ceramic lay in pieces on the floor.

The dish, a gift, looked broken beyond repair.

I gathered the fragments together and began placing them in a sack to be discarded.

The dish wasn't the only broken thing here.

My son, full of teen angst and layers of past traumas, had flipped this table over in a moment of rage – not a rage over the losses in his life or the hurts he's endured, but over the latest insurmountable injustice. He didn't get the seat he wanted when it came time to watch a movie, and this insignificant precipitator had escalated and swollen until its enormity could not be contained.

Sweeping up the broken bits too small to be gathered by hand, I wondered, "Could I fix my child?"

Such arrogance to pose that question.

Logical Me knew well enough that you can't undo the hurt caused by years of neglect and drug use, as well as physical, mental and emotional abuse simply by gifting a child a room of his own, nice clothes, a pool, and a family vacation down the shore.

But Melodramatic Me fantasized that by showering him with our unconditional love and support (and a good dose of professional therapy), maybe, just maybe, he could turn whole again. I thought if the light of our love could seek out and illuminate the darkest recesses of his hurt, it would be enough to negate all that had happened in his past.

Could love, support and stuff fix what's broken?

Listening to the muted rumble of him trashing his room upstairs, it looked as if the answer was no.

Still, I had to believe that all this drama is part of the healing process he must go through to recalibrate. He was functioning just fine in his old life until I came along and opened up his wounds. He barely gave a thought to his scars, or his lack of a family. A pack of rowdy boys roaming the streets and doing the things unsupervised boys do served fine as a family. And scars were just that, scars. They had long ago healed and were nothing more than part of his physical terrain. He gave them no more thought than he would one of his freckles.

A person could walk along impaled by a staff. Perhaps once in a while, if he weren't careful, it might become a problem, it might hurt if he got it caught on something. But if it spared organs and arteries, a person could function, certainly. Remove that staff, and now you've got exposed, raw, painful flesh. That wound will ache. It will heal, but it will take time and it will hurt like the dickens for a good, long while. And without proper care, the gash could become worse before it gets better, becoming inflamed and infected.

Of course this is Melodramatic Me at my finest here, but I'm trusting that's what we're dealing with. A case of old wounds opened up and aggravated. Every instance of loss of control becomes like a cattle prod in the bared gash. On a good day, he can bite the bullet as he controls himself and the pain subsides. On a bad day he becomes a wounded, cornered, wild animal acting out in self-preservation.

I cut my finger on a piece of the shattered ceramic. I watched the blood trickle down my hand and drop to the floor, mingling with the dust of the broken dish and my tears, which had been raining down steadily. I stood and moved to the sink, and washed the blood from my negligible nick. It probably wouldn't even need a Band Aid.

In a moment, my son appeared, standing at my side.
Through his own tears, and barely able to look at me, he murmured his apologies, then walked outside. I completed my task, then went outside to talk to him, big lectures beginning to form in my mind. But as I closed the kitchen door and walked into the night, I turned and found my son leaning against the deck railing, looking out over the pond and illuminated by the light of the moon. He was crying – sobbing.

The lecture could wait. I stood beside him and reached up to put my arm around his shoulders. And we stood together like that for some time, quietly crying together.

Anne Birdsong Giberson is the mother of six children. Three of her kids joined her family by birth, and three were born to other mothers and joined the family later in life, at the ages of 5, 10, and 13. Anne lives on a small hobby farm in rural Pennsylvania with her husband of 20 plus years where she and the kids watch over their horses, goats, dogs, and other assorted critters. Most of all she loves to watch her children as they learn and grow, making their own mistakes along the way, but figuring things out better than she could. Between mucking out the barn and resolving disputes between children, she occasionally updates her blog at www.bringingboryahome.blogspot.com.

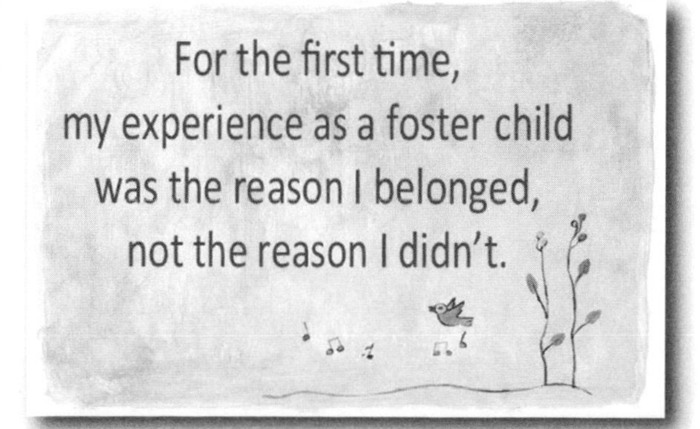

For the first time,
my experience as a foster child
was the reason I belonged,
not the reason I didn't.

T. and We

By Amy Heibel

My partner and I decided to become foster/adoptive parents in our late 30s. We had always intended to foster/adopt, and chose not to have biological children. I suppose we were moved by the plight of children in long-term foster care seeking adoption; as they cycle through the system, they so often remain without a stable permanent connection to an adult, and the statistical fate of those who "age out" of the system is grim.

What we did not expect was to fall so perfectly in love. We met a teenage boy who lives with us now and blows our minds on a daily basis. Adopting him turned out to be the best thing we've ever done, and by far the most difficult. In the course of getting to know him, we did seventeen consecutive weekend overnights, endured a singular moment of crisis when he got mixed up in some serious trouble, followed him through a brief and frustrating stay in a group home, made ourselves a thorn in the side of county child services until he was "placed" with us, and became his parents.

It reminds me of science. I once interviewed a research chemist. He described disease as a keyhole, and likened his work to investigating tens of thousands of chemical "keys," seeking the one that would fit the disease target exactly. He said it always seemed incredibly unlikely and at the same time inevitable that he'd find a match, and that science depends on the confidence that eventually one will emerge.

By whatever odd miracle of chemistry and personality, T. and we fit like that; it seems both impossible and inevitable. He'd been searching for adoptive parents for two years when we met him. We met him at the first "matching" event we ever attended. I looked around the room and thought, well, I feel like I could probably parent any one of these

I think the best way foster parents can best help the kids they care for is to stay open minded, patient, don't take much personally, and be prepared for a little (or a lot) of chaos. I know I've bitterly pushed away my foster parents when I really just wanted to be closer to them. It's taken me a while to come around and realize everything they do for me and show gratitude. And even years after placement old issues still come up, so be open minded to whatever is going on and be patient with us.

We just want to know that you're not going to leave us too.

– Foster Youth, entered the system at the age of 14

kids. Then I saw T. and something inside went, "fascinating!" He smelled good to me. His eyes showed a busy brain, and his facial expression showed tremendous, probably excessive, self-discipline. The slight tremor in his hands gave away his fear and the importance he attached to being adopted, but his dignified reserve suggested that he would be the one deciding on the circumstances. I couldn't stop thinking about him.

The first three months after he moved in were hard. He wasn't used to feeling attached to authoritative adults. He understood rules, but he hadn't experienced the coercive emotional pressure of love. It was confusing to him. It made him feel trapped to find that he cared what we thought. We worked through it. We continue to work through it. We aim for a mix of flexibility and consistency, but really it's mostly sheer innate compatibility that works most of the time. One night, driving in the car, he said from the back seat, "I think God sent you a message that it was me." Perhaps that's it. That's certainly how it felt, and I'm not a religious person.

A good friend of mine said recently, "It's his ego that saved him" and that struck me as being very true. At some point, when he might have broken, he decided, "This is shit. I'm going to find something better." And he did. He doesn't feel grateful to us he feels satisfied. He was right.

I do love the frank honesty of parenting a kid like that. It's as if we met in the middle of a vast, busy, often indifferent world and looked at each other and said, "Okay, what have you got?" We had to put our emotional cards on the table. My partner and I might have expected to be overwhelmed by his needs. He might have expected to be cruelly disappointed or rejected – that's what adults had taught him to expect. Instead, it turned out that we had the potential to create a soulful, life-altering connection to each other. We know each other in a deep way, as if we have known each other for much longer than we actually have.

I do think people are spooked sometimes by the "knowing" child. Our cultural cliches of family suggest sometimes that parents are all powerful, and the process of parenting is one of transmitting values and knowledge from parent to child. Kids like T. are not like that. It's a much more democratic process of negotiation. He knows a whole lot of things I will never have the misfortune to understand. I know things he could care less about. We have to sort out tremendously complicated issues together, like why he should follow our rules, and how to balance love and loyalty to more than one kind of family.

I love being that kind of parent. It makes me a better person. Nobody told us this was a good idea, and a lot of people told us it was impossible. But it totally works for the three of us. It makes me think that the world is a much more nuanced, multi-dimensional, profound place than I would otherwise have realized.

Amy Heibel and her partner decided to become foster/adoptive parents in their late 30s. They had the great good fortune of being "picked" by an amazing teenage boy who blows their minds on a daily basis. Adopting him turned out to be the best thing they've ever done, and by far the hardest. Amy is a wrier and editor living in Ca. In her free time, she enjoys surfing and Chinese food. Follow her musings at lafosterblog.blogspot.com.

My Journey

By Adriana Borris

Being a teenager is one of the hardest things in life. Being a teenager in foster care is 10 times more difficult. When I got to my foster parents' home, I was broken. I felt hurt, abandoned, and I had no trust. To protect myself, I had covered my body in tattoos and gotten a violent reputation. I had been placed in a high risk group home before being placed back into foster care. And when my foster mother came along, I had my reservations as far as going into her home. She was a single mother of a baby girl, a Jewish white lady who knew absolutely nothing about a life like the one I was living.

I had a lot of insecurities from the moment I moved in. I craved the attention and the love of a parent, so I started trying to do good. I was trying to stay out of trouble and go to school. She was giving me the positive attention that I needed and I loved being around her baby girl. But a couple of months after being there, I got the most horrible news that sent me spiraling down. My roommate from the group home, who was five months pregnant, was beaten to death and her body was discarded at an old military base. They found out who she was because of a tattoo I had given her while I was at the group home. Soon after that, I began hanging out with gang members again. At school I would get in fights and was constantly in trouble.

> *With their love, patience, persistence and comprehension they helped me change my whole style of living.*

Then I received news that another one of my friends was stabbed to death. At that point, my foster mother's partner took me aside and talked to me. She told me that they lived in fear that I would be the one to go next. She told me that they did not want anything bad to happen to me. They couldn't understand the violence happening around us and that if it didn't stop that we were going to move to another city about an hour away.

They did not take long on sticking to their word and in less than a month we moved to Santa Cruz. There, I started going to a new school but began hanging out with my old gang member friends. However, my foster parents made it clear that at "our home" we have rules and I was to follow them. I also had to do chores. Even after all of the changes they made for us, I was afraid that something bad was going to happen and I would end up having to go some place else to live. I was mostly scared because I had become extremely close with their little girls – they were like my little sisters.

Not long after we moved to Santa Cruz another friend of mine was murdered. I started fighting again, and one evening as I was visiting friends I decided to start using drugs and drinking alcohol. That night I ended up with alcohol poisoning and overdosing. The next morning when I woke up in the hospital room I was informed that I was going back to Juvenile Hall and losing my placement. My foster parents were in the room with me. They tried to talk to my probation officer and asked her to give me another chance, but she told them that it was not up to her. I had to go back to court and talk to the judge before anyone determined what to do with me.

For the next couple of weeks I stayed in Juvenile Hall. What affected me the most was that their little girl, the one I was closest to, was so upset with me. Watching her tears broke my heart. They were my sisters and I never wanted to hurt them. My foster parents did not give up on me. They went to Juvenile Hall to visit me and that's when they talked to me. They told me that they had gone to my school and managed to keep me enrolled and my teacher was willing to work with me, but I needed to put more effort on doing things if I wanted to continue living with them. I also needed to get my tattoos removed and find a job. I had to do my part if I wanted them to talk to the judge so I could live with them.

When the time came to go to court they talked to the judge and became completely responsible for me. They told the judge our plans and the judge allowed me to go home with them. At home they made sure I went to school and gave me job leads. One morning as we stopped to get a bagel, one of my home girls walked in with her mom. Her mother had just gotten out of prison and she was working at a fast food restaurant. Her mother told me that she was having a party to celebrate being out of prison.

I turned around after they were gone, looked at my foster mother and I told her, "I don't want to be like that when I grow up, I never want my children to have to see me that way." My foster mom responded, "you don't have to be that way, there is so much more to life, and you are so much better than that." That's when I made a promise to myself that I was going to do my best to just be better than I had been. They were my family and for the first time I could see that I had someone who really cared about me.

I got a job and started going to school. They were teaching me responsibility. They took me to open a bank account with the money I was earning and encouraged me to look into a trade school. Then one day they told me that we were going on vacation to Victoria, Canada.

With their love, patience, persistence, and comprehension they helped me change my whole style of living. They treated me like a human being, like their child. They wanted me to succeed. Because of their efforts I went to school to get my certificate of office skills. They talked to the judge so I could stay at their home through the foster care system until I turned 19 years old so I could finish my education. Because of them I learned a different lifestyle. They showed me to communicate whenever I am upset instead of punching people.

After that last episode I never went back to Juvenile Hall. They became my parents and I became the big sister to their children. I was never legally adopted, but now they are grandparents to my children. I am really thankful to them for all of their efforts and love that they have given me.

Adriana Borris entered foster care due to an abusive parent. She got caught up in the foster system living in a variety of placements including foster homes, juvenile hall, and group homes. She struggled with major anger issues and lack of respect for authority and even became involved with gangs. She is certain that her last foster parents found her to be a very challenging child but with their support and unconditional love, they helped her to let down her guard and learn to trust and love again. She hopes that sharing her story will help others understand and give older foster children a chance.

Ten Things Parents Should Know About Raising Teens

By Aileen Rosario and Anni Keane

Every teen is different from the next one and their issues and attitudes vary from simple to extremely complicated. For parents who need some help working and building a relationship with their teen here are some tips. Hopefully these tips will help you and your teen navigate through the adolescent years with the tools to survive them.

1. Times will get hard. There will most likely be conflict and disagreements. Parents will not always agree with their teen's choices and behaviors. Parents must learn that they cannot control their teen but they can help him or her see what is best. Never let the behaviors or decisions affect how you love and show love to your child.

2. It is OK to be a detective. You have to know what your teens are doing, friends they have, and what sort of things they are into, in case they are doing things that are dangerous to their health or well-being. Through a good, solid, open relationship, parents can get to know their teens better. Teens do like to hide even good things. Parents should ask a lot of questions and always pay attention to what their children are doing and where they are going. Don't search through their personal items unless they are acting suspicious or you happen upon something while cleaning their room.

3. Listen to your teen. Some teens are not good at expressing their thoughts or feelings when going through a rough patch and they expect you to be mind readers and body language experts. You can pick up clues to their feelings by listening to their tone of voice and demeanor when they speak to you. Also, when you watch them closely enough you can pick up on their body cues, such as finger tapping, blinking a lot and fidgeting when they are fibbing.

4. Do not be straight laced and rigid all the time. There are times when seriousness is necessary and the demeanor of a prison guard is warranted. But you also need to have fun with your teen by being a friend. Take them to the movies, a play, shopping, or take a class together. If you show your teen that you can be someone he or she can talk to about anything, he or she is likely to come to you when there are problems. He or she will feel comfortable enough to confide in you.

5. Allow your teen to make mistakes. Do not make a big deal when he or she makes mistakes. Help your teen realize where he or she went wrong and help him or her figure out how not to do it again. Do not be judgmental or accusatory when aiding him or her through mistakes. Every mistake can be corrected. Nothing is worth losing the relationship you have with your teen.

6. Do not impose unrealistic expectations on your teen. Every human is different and teens are no exception. He or she will no doubt have different goals and aspirations than what you have for him or her. He or she will also achieve these things at a rate that is comfortable, so parents have to come to terms with this and help him or her achieve his or her own goals. This may be hard to accept, but we cannot all be doctors, lawyers, teachers, or Nobel prize winners.

7. Be careful how you advise your teen. Don't be too pushy, preachy or demanding when giving advice. If you do, he or she will lock up like a clam and completely ignore your input. Remember parents, you can only help him or her see what is best, but you can't make him or her do it.

8. Always tell your teen that you love him or her and only want what is best. Like the *You Gotta Believe!* teen prayer says "May you love me the most when I deserve it the least because that is when I need it the most." If you are not reminding your teen that you love him or her despite poor behavior he or she will forget it. If teens do not feel the security of unconditional love and commitment then they might feel like they have nothing to lose and their behavior might get worse.

9. Be honest. Parents have the tendency to have this saying "do as I say and not as I do." The problem with this is that teens do as you do, so lead by a positive example. If you get caught in your lie, your teen will distrust you and your words will hold little to no weight. In others words, a great amount of respect will be lost.

"May you love me the most when I deserve it the least because that is when I need it the most."

*Teen prayer from **You Gotta Believe***

10. Do not give up on your teen. If you do, you will never know what a great adult he or she will become as a result of your parenting.

Aileen Rosario and Anni Keane are sisters who were adopted in February 2007 at 23 and 24 years of age. They had been placed with their mother, Mary Keane, at the age of 17. Both now work for You Gotta Believe! and attend Lehman College. This article originally appeared in ***Fostering Families Today.***

Words of Encouragement for Children and Teens

By Homer Kiracofe

You Do A Good Job Of... Children should be encouraged when they do not expect it, when they are not asking for it.

You Have Improved In... Growth and development is something we should expect from all children. They may not be where we would like them to be, but if there is progress, there is less chance for discouragement. Children will usually continue to try if they can see some improvement.

We Like (Enjoy) You, But We Don't Like What You Do... It is important to distinguish between the child and his behavior, between the act and the actor.

You Can Help Me (Us, Others, Etc.)... A child's self-esteem is built through usefulness. The more useful he feels to himself, the better he feels about himself.

Let's Try It Together... Children who think they have to do things perfectly often are afraid to attempt something new for fear of making a mistake or failing.

So You Make A Mistake: Now What Can You Learn From The Mistake?... Mistakes are for learning. There is a great deal a child will learn if he is taught not to feel embarrassed about making a mistake or missing the mark in some way.

You Would Like Us To Think You Can't, But We Think You Can... This can be used when the child conveys that something is too difficult for him and he hesitates to even so much as try. If he tries and fails, he has at least had the courage to try.

Keep Trying. Don't Give Up... When a child is trying but not meeting much success, a comment like this might be helpful.

I'm Sure You Can Straighten This Out (Solve This Problem, etc.) But If You Need Any Help, You Know Where To Find Me... Expresses confidence in child's ability.

I Can Understand How You Feel (Not Sympathy, But Empathy), But I Am Sure You Will Be Able To Handle It... Pity seldom helps, but understanding his situation and believing in the child's ability to adjust to it is of much greater help to him.

Remember, no words are magic in themselves. The intent and spirit of speech precede it.

Homer Kiracofe is a therapist and pastor.

Nurturing Identity

An old Cherokee told his grandson, "My son, there is a battle between two wolves inside us all. One is Evil. It is anger, jealousy, greed, resentment, inferiority, lies, and ego. The other is Good. It is joy, peace, love, hope, humility, kindness, empathy, and truth." The boy thought about it, and asked, "Grandfather, which wolf wins?" The old man quietly replied, "The one you feed."

I'm Not Invisible! I'm Valuable!

By Cile Cogburn, MSW, and Joseph Galata, PhD

A lifebook is like a security blanket, a teddy bear, a concrete tool, that details a physical, psychological, emotional, and social record of a child's individual and community identity.

A child deserves to know that his or her self-identity is of value to both self and others, especially if he or she isn't living with his or her family of origin. In the foster care system, a lifebook is both a wonderful process and a tool of a child's existence.

A lifebook provides an opportunity to honor a child's life through the use of visual reminders. The process of creating an individual lifebook promotes positive self-esteem, forms and solidifies identity formation, strengthens self-acceptance; assists in resolving separation issues; facilitates a child's attachment to foster/adoptive families; identifies positives about the family of origin; helps recognize and differentiate between past, present and future; increases normalization of foster care and adoption language and keeps "issues" from becoming taboo conversation; distinguishes reality from magical thinking; reduces psychological tensions and divided emotional loyalty between birth parents and foster/adoptive parents; allows recognition and resolution about strong emotions pertaining to past events; and provides constancy regardless of the number of placements that a child may be forced to experience.

One of the most successful lifebook projects is that of "Saving A Life: The Lifebook for Every Child Project" in Reno, Nev. Started in 2003, this collaborative project is sponsored by the Washoe County Department of Social Services, the Sierra Association of Foster Families and Treasured Memories. Facilitated Monday through Friday at the Sierra Association of Foster Families, the scrapbooking supplies are donated by customers of local scrapbook stores and also purchased with generous grant funding from an educational foundation that supports the academic needs of children in foster care.

What is a Lifebook?

A lifebook is a collection of words, photos, graphics, artwork, and memorabilia that creates a chronological record of the child's life. It is about the child, for the child, by the child, and hopefully will reflect a simple, truthful story written through the child's eyes. It is a visual record that captures and preserves, with pride, an entire life. A lifebook is a combination of a scrapbook, photo album, and memory box put on 8½ by 11 pages that focus specifically on the child and his or her life.

Many people initially say, "But I'm not a crafty person." One need not be a Martha Stewart, Picasso, or Ansel Adams, to create an artistic lifebook. With pictures from magazines, any type of paper, photos, glue sticks, stickers, and other tools inexpensively purchased in a dollar store, a foster/adoptive parent can work with the child by starting with what he or she likes to eat, favorite activities, dreams and hopes, family members, television shows, and other identifying aspects of individual, family, school and community "likes and dislikes." One photo can create a page of memories.

If a child doesn't know where he or she came from and who he or she is, it's hard for the child to grasp a current self-identity and acceptance of the foster/adoptive home and family. A lifebook allows a child to think and feel, "I'm not invisible, because I'm valuable." A lifebook is like a security blanket, a teddy bear, a concrete tool that details a physical, psychological, emotional, and social record of a child's individual and community identity.

Joseph Galata, the executive director for the Sierra Association of Foster Families, and major promoter of lifebooks, tells prospective foster/adoptive parents in PRIDE trainings, "Truthfulness is an important element of healthy psychological functioning. It is imperative that a child in foster/adoptive families understands the truth about him or herself. A lifebook records a truthful story, usually beginning with the child's birth. By including a birth certificate, photos and drawings of birth parents, bio-grandparents, siblings, family pets, school chums, the animated pages of a lifebook establishes a foundation for the truth about a child's life."

He goes on to say, "Adults may say, 'But I know nothing or very little about the child's history.' What the foster/adoptive parent knows or doesn't know about the child's earliest years is of no importance, because the child knows both cognitive and emotional truth. A child remembers, even remembers 'secret things,' and the task of the adult is to help that

My Second Foster Home

On ______ I moved into this home.
(Date)
Address:
The name of the Foster Parent(s): ______
The color of the house/apartment building was: ______
I attended the ______ school.
Some of the foods I liked in this home were: ______
______ and ______
I ______ this home because: ______
(liked/disliked)

On ______ I left this family.
(Date)
The reason I moved is because:

Baby Pictures

If you have a baby photo— keep it safe. Get a color copy.

If you don't—here are a few ideas:

Do you know which hospital you were born in?

Take a picture of you in front of the hospital.

Maybe go inside and visit the baby nursery. Get a picture there. If you're feeling brave, take a picture of you in the baby section so you remember where you started your life.

Draw your baby self (in the box below). Can't draw? Cut out some baby images from a magazine.

Hate the whole baby thing? Place a photo of you now in the box instead.

My Feelings

...en I think about some of the things that have happened to me I feel:

___angry ___happy ___sad ___other (feeling)
___confused ___mad ___scared ___other (feeling)
___frustrated ___no feeling ___upset ___other (feeling)

...eelings are very normal for anyone, especially a kid, ...gone through BIG changes.

...get upset from thinking about some of the big ...that have happened to me, I know that there are ...ngs that I can do to make myself feel better. ...these things are:

These are sample pages from two lifebook resources for foster children created by Beth O'Malley, MEd: ***My Foster Care Journey*** and ***For When I'm Famous, a Teen Foster Adoption Lifebook***. Visit her website for more information www.adoptionlifebooks.com.

child put those 'memories' into poems, drawings, photographic captions, and statements reflecting the truth as the child has witnessed it, sees it, feels it."

There is documented research about the benefits a lifebook can offer a child in foster/adoptive families. Working on a project with enormous and intense benefits is a front-load process for a child to feel in control of his or her life, especially when a foster child is constantly hearing orders and mandates from social workers, judges, court masters, attorney's, "this is what you have to do," "these are the people you have to live with," "this is the school you have to attend now," "these are the things you can have or keep," "this is when you have to visit your bio-parents," "this is the law you have to obey," and other similar comments. The process of creating a lifebook is not only fun but a front-loaded creative journey in discovering "who am I?" "where do I come from?" "what are my roots?" and "how did I get here?"

A lifebook is... a creative journey in discovering "who am I?" "where do I come from?" ... "how did I get here?"

Kathy Hovore, a lifebook specialist at the Sierra Association of Foster Families and a foster mom, has been scrapbooking for more than two years. "I have such a love for family history. When I discovered lifebooks, I was hooked right away. I've seen my foster children learn to acknowledge and appreciate their past, even the most difficult moments in their past. Because of painful circumstances, children in foster care don't have a love or appreciation for their past. Rather, they often substitute what therapists call 'magical thinking' for reality. But with lifebooks, reality is not something to deny or be ashamed of any longer. Working on a lifebook becomes a magical process."

And finally, when a foster parent receives a child to care for and that particular boy or girl brings to the new home and family a lifebook, the foster parent has an easier and faster opportunity to learn about the kid. A lifebook provides a starting point that helps the foster parent refrain from playing ad hoc investigator.

*Cile Cogburn, MSW, is an adoption social worker with Washoe County Department of Social Services in Reno, Nev. She specializes in adoptions of special needs children who are in the foster care system. Cile was previously in private business and was a volunteer Court Appointed Special Advocate. She started the **Lifebook for Every Child** project in 2003 as a collaborative project that was designed to help all children in foster care, not just children entering the world of adoption.*

*Joseph Galata, PhD, is the executive director for the Sierra Association of Foster Families in Reno, Nev. He is a retired faculty member, a former international educator for hospice, an Arts-in-Education Specialist, and a cultural awareness specialist focusing on how races, ethnic groups, and religious/spiritual groups use arts, rituals, and ceremonies in healing from grief. His newest DVD is **From Institution to Family**, an educational program on medically fragile, delayed-disabled, and terminally ill children needing foster care and adoption. His newest book is **Linda: Our Eyes and Her Soul**.*

Fostering Firsts

By Veronica Brown

I usually foster boys aged nine and older. Taking in boys this age means I miss a lot of firsts: first step, first word, first day of school and so many others. But I am lucky enough to witness some other firsts:

1st time he packed for a vacation – and not just to move again.

1st time his photograph was framed and hung on a wall – by anyone.

1st time he made Christmas cookies from scratch and ate most of the dough.

1st time I picked him up from the principal's office – and it wasn't the end of the world

1st time he realized I was serious when I told him he had to do housework while suspended.

1st time he didn't flinch when I put my arm around his shoulders.

1st time he was sent to his room and didn't slam the door.

1st time he laughed at an inside, family joke.

1st time I looked him in the eye and said, "I trust you."

1st time he went to a birthday party – with a really cool gift that he wrapped himself.

1st time he went to the same school for three years in a row.

1st time he realized that there were other foster kids who knew what he was feeling.

1st pair of Nikes – which he slept with for a week.

1st time he believed me when I told him "you belong" for the thousandth time.

1st time he earned a later bedtime than his foster brother, and danced around the house.

1st time he thought he "talked" me into going to Dairy Freez for ice cream.

1st time he told me about that awful secret that he kept hidden inside.

1st time he had a friend sleep over.

1st time he looked like an ordinary kid – with no cares in the world other than learning that new trick on his skateboard.

Veronica Brown has been a foster parent in Canada since 1995.

Lifebooks: Every Foster Child Needs One

By Beth O'Malley, MEd

Foster children so often have that sense of missing pieces. I should know. I spent my first five months in foster care before being adopted.

Information is gold to any child separated from biological family. Every tiny piece is precious, whether it's a photo or quote from a child's first foster parent. Lifebooks help put all the pieces together in a way that helps a child make sense and ultimately feel good about his or her history.

"...My second foster family reported that I used to make these funny lip smacking sounds as a baby...and that the entire family would watch and laugh. This is one of my favorite pieces of information, discovered in my foster care notes..." (Beth O'Malley)

This story never appeared in any lifebook. Instead, my foster parents took the time to share it with my social worker. She found the time to write it in her case notes. The adoption agency then managed to hold onto my case record for 35 years. And the post-adoption social worker thought I might find the anecdote amusing. Talk about teamwork. I'm grateful that every person followed through, giving me this "baby picture" in words that I carry in my heart today.

I'm convinced that my entire life would have been different if I had been given a lifebook. The absence of information about my birth family meant I had nothing with which to connect with my history. A blank screen. A feeling of floating, or that numb sensation that so many foster children later describe.

"...Lifebooks remain important to my children... They show that their biological connections are still important... They will never be forgotten..." (Michelle Braxton, single foster/adoptive mother of seven)

Imagine what would be important to you ten or twenty years later in life. Including school papers, awards, copies of report cards, the birth certificate, locks of baby hair, baby teeth, and mementos increases a lifebook's value. These volumes will fill in gaps, with words, art work, and photos, if available. Your words can create pictures if none are available. Speaking of pictures, can you imagine going through life without ever knowing what your mother or father looked like? Foster parents often have the unique opportunity to get photos of birth parents. Foster mother Sandy Parker shared the following story:

"...I took three-year-old David for a visit with his birth mother while she was incarcerated. They didn't allow cameras inside the facility. Shortly thereafter she was released, overdosed, and died. So I learned a lesson. At the next visit with a different child I took pictures...His birth mother also died abruptly, but Sam will know what she looked like!"

One foster parent recently lamented that with five foster children, one being medically involved, coupled with caring for an aging parent and her 150-pound dog, she didn't always have the time to complete her children's lifebooks. It is a tall order.

A team approach to lifebooks may be the wave of the future. If foster parents can capture a few pages of the child's life, perhaps grabbing a picture of the birth family (regardless of the goal), then the lifebook has begun. Social workers, CASA volunteers, and/or therapists can add in additional information. Don't forget the birth certificate, which children in foster situations love at any age. Here are a few suggestions from Dr. Vera Fahlberg, national adoption expert:

- Start with the child's birth.
- Always discuss the birth mother and birth father (even if you know nothing, say you don't know).
- Talk about the reason for separation from the biological family.

Lifebooks help reduce magical thinking and fantasy. This frees up a foster child to pay better attention in school or be more available to focus on developing painting skills or playing soccer.

Lifebooks help answer questions, increase self-esteem, and teach children the truth. They are the ultimate teaching tool. Lifebook facts become "memory pegs," says Mimi Robins, originator of lifebooks in Massachusetts. If children are given the basics, the essentials, then hours of therapy later in life can be saved.

Children need to feel proud of their strengths and those of their birth parents. A lifebook page on birth parents really helps in those tough adolescent years when identity issues begin to peak. Foster care periods are often the only time when birth parents are usually available to answer questions and discuss talents and hobbies.

The ultimate magic to creating a treasured lifebook is to start it, work on it with a child, and give it to him or her, or to the social worker, when the child moves on. Even if it only has five pages, it is tangible proof to that child that they is precious enough to deserve this treasure.

Beth O'Malley is a speaker and the author of ***Lifebooks: Creating a Treasure for the Adopted Child, My Foster Care Journey,*** *and* ***For When I'm Famous: A Teen Foster/Adoption Lifebook****. To learn more about the books, call 800-469-9666. To receive free lifebook tips, visit www.adoptionlifebooks.com.*

An Adoption / Foster Care Collage: Putting the Pieces Together

A way to manage, memorialize, and make visual poetry of the past

By Mary Anne Cohen

Of all modes of art, adoption most resembles the collage: a collection of mixed materials, already pre-existing, brought together to make something new, interesting, and sometimes beautiful. The whole becomes greater than the parts. This is true at the beginning, especially in open adoption, but it is there in a less tangible way in closed or international adoptions as well and for the child in foster care; the inhabitants of the 'Ghost Kingdom,' as author Betty Jean Lifton calls it, cluster around the everyday reality of birth parents, adoptive parents, foster parents, and adoptees.

Collage Works Well. One big advantage of using the collage in art therapy is that it truly is something anyone can do, and those who are intimidated by the thought of having to draw or paint may be more comfortable with scissors, glue, and a pile of old magazines or found objects. Anyone can put stuff together, and often a surprising amount of emotion comes out in the process, the selection and combination of images, and in the finished product. Any adoptee or birth/adoptive family-member can privately make her or his own collage, or it can be done as a group activity at a meeting, at a conference or at a workshop It can be big or small, simple or elaborate, flat or three dimensional. It can be done as fine art (even Picasso did some collages), or as a strictly therapeutic tool with little thought to its artistic merit. It should be fun to do, although sometimes the emotions evoked by art done this way are strong and painful. There should be time to talk about those emotions, and about the finished product and the process, as well as time to do the actual work. The group leader should be available after the workshop for anyone who is distressed and needs further care because of the depths of emotions evoked. Sometimes we need help coming back to the world from that other place where dreams and art are made.

Advance Preparation Pays Off. I find that it works well to prepare in advance to do the collage, although it can be done on the spur of the moment with just a diverse pile of magazines to cut up, clean construction paper on which to assemble the images, scissors, and glue sticks. If you plan a collage meeting, instruct your group members to look through their adoption memorabilia, documents, and photographs:

- birth certificates
- surrender papers
- decree of adoption
- search notebook
- baby pictures, family photos, reunion pictures

Adopted children may also possess a certificate of abandonment, medical records, finding ad, police report, original passport and a certificate of citizenship. Foster children might have photos of caseworkers, CASAs, judges, foster family photos, and photos of places they have lived.

Make copies of anything that might be interesting or meaningful to use. Some may want to make color copies which can get expensive. I like the look of black and white copies of photos, and prefer them for collage work. Depending on how elaborate you wish to get, people can also use small objects, cloth, ribbon, buttons, and junk jewelry. Craft stores are a good source of all kinds of little things (even tiny dolls) that can be used in many ways in collages. Junk drawers at home often have great and weird things, too. If you are

Everyone's Collage will be Unique:

Some people will have just a few images, and a lot of blank space, where others will have filled every inch, and have items overlapping. Some will have mostly text, a mix of text and images, or all pictures and no text. Some will tell a story, while others will be more abstract and just create a mood.

making a three dimensional work, a glue gun is a good idea to have. They are cheap and can also be found in craft stores. If you are working in a group, bring several, along with enough glue sticks.

Once you have gathered your materials, you can gather your group. You may want to play a tape of some calm and unobtrusive music in the background. Start with getting everyone to relax and quietly think about their adoption or foster care experience, while looking through the material they have brought with them and the magazines and other objects that are available to share. You can reassure the group that nobody will be graded or judged, and that what is important is to express inner feelings, and to have a good time working with a variety of images. Once things get rolling people should feel free to talk and compare, and ask for what they want if they are not finding it, as in "did anyone see a picture of a cat?" or "I need a red rose."

Conversation is as Important as the Art. When everyone is done, leave enough time for participants to show their work, talk about the images, and talk about what feelings came up in the process. There is something reassuring about the concreteness of the finished work, and the use of images that already exist gives a bit of emotional distance not present when one must draw or paint one's own images from scratch.

There is no limit to how photos, documents, words, pictures, and objects can be manipulated and combined in an adoption collage. It is a project that can be done again and again, always with new results. It can be a way to chart the progress and the shifting configurations of family and connectedness for the adoptee. It can be a way to manage, memorialize, and make visual poetry of the past. It can be a way to envision the future, to create fantasy, and to come terms with reality.

No Special Skills Required. Unlike written poetry, or most visual arts, it requires no special skill to create something that is eloquent, inventive, and often a source of continued insight into the mind and heart. It is often chaotic and messy, like real life, but there is still an element of choice and control over the situation that is helpful to adoptees, who had so little actual control over adoption, in most cases. It is a means, once removed, to explore the landscape of dreams and the subconscious, and to connect to archetypal and personal imagery that has deep meaning for the individual. What is unique about the collage is that those images can be collected and frozen in place, to be looked at again and again for deeper meaning.

Mary Anne Cohen is a birth mother who has been active in adoption reform since the mid 70s. She is the former editor of Origins Newsletter, an essayist and poet with a degree in art, and has presented at many adoption reform conferences. Mary Anne is married and has three adult sons whom she raised; she has also reunited with her surrendered son. This article originally appeared in ***Adoption Parenting: Creating a Toolbox, Building Connections*** *(EMK Press 2006.)*

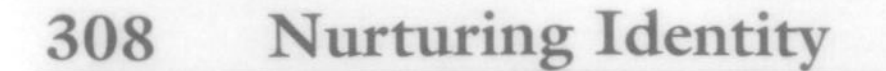

Past: What words or images can be used to describe the past?

Present: What words or images can be used to describe what is happening right now?

Future: What words or images can be used to describe what the future can hold?

The Collage

By Julie Craft

My daughter Lauren was 1,500 miles from home in a therapeutic boarding school when she was ready to examine her feelings. Her therapist assigned her a project, a series of collages; and she chose the topic of adoption. They were rough. Nothing was cut with scissors or perfectly aligned. Pictures were limited and carefully chosen. She scoured through magazines tearing out photos, phrases, headlines, and pictures that spoke to her. What she found was spooky.

These were much more than words she would have chosen, more than words she had chosen in the past to explain her feelings about adoption. She created three collages that represented her PAST, PRESENT and FUTURE. In the PAST collage, "sophomore slump" represented the year in school when she crashed, her first suicide attempt. "Jones" was her birth mother's name and ironically slang for drugs. "Lost in Space" and "Children need help to develop" were phrases that cleverly described her feelings. Her PRESENT collage included words and phrases of advice and inspiration. "It's your life – fill it up," "Take comfort," and "The chemistry's just beginning" – these spoke of the transition she was feeling as she absorbed new information about her birth family. Her page on the FUTURE was totally upbeat – "A dream come true," "Being me," and "The greatest experience of my life" showed her optimism and excitement. And imagine finding this phrase, "The day seemed magical. They opened up their hearts to each other. They confided intimacies, confident of each other's acceptance." These are the words that spoke to her, for her. The collages were a way of finding the words she couldn't find.

Try making your own collages. Use magazines and newspapers looking for words, images, and pictures that represent the Past, Present, and Future. Use scissors, glue and construction paper, it doesnly have to be complicated. These work best if time is taken to think and reflect and then find the perfect word or image that describes that part of the child's story. You don't even have to be a child in foster care. What would your collage look like?

Julie Craft is the co-founder and president of The Adoption Support Center, Inc. in Indianapolis, Ind. Craft is the biological parent of Lindsey and adoptive parent of Lauren. Both daughters involved themselves in work at the agency. Lindsey became an international homestudy specialist (then later a pediatric registered nurse), while Lauren openly shared her struggles and triumphs as an adoptee and became peer support for birth mothers. This article originally appeared in ***Pieces of Me: Who Do I Want to Be?*** *(EMK Press 2009.)*

Connecting through Ceremony: *Rituals Add to Family Glue*

By Carrie Kitze

On days when children might think more about all the parts of their families and where they fit, (birthdays, anniversary days, holidays, life milestones, Mother's and Father's Days) we can try to talk a bit more on how they came to be with us – and we can make a special ceremony. Children are ritualistic; being claimed as well as claiming by rite matters to them. A ceremony doesn't need to be complicated to be effective. Ceremonies are living pictures – short action narratives that help children grasp complex meaning. Here are some easy ideas which help make new rituals and ceremonies for families like yours:

Write a Letter. Letter writing is powerful as children get older and can articulate their thoughts and wishes better. It can be an update on what they are doing, If you have an address, you can send the letter or you can burn the letter and send the wishes up in smoke, or save it in a file for later. If you have birth parent contact, this is a nice time to send this letter and let them know what the child is doing/thinking. These snapshots of feeling make great additions to a co-created lifebook.

Create an Honoring Ceremony. Kids love ceremonies – especially the ones that they get to participate in and that make them be at center stage. My littlest one loves to blow out candles. So for us, a ceremony with candles is a great choice. Here's what we have done. Each of us has one candle for our parents (all of them) and one for ourselves. We also have one main candle, which is the family candle. Help your little ones to light their parent candles and the candles representing themselves from the family candle. Talk about how each person (moms and dads, too) joined the family. Mom and dad through marriage, biological children through birth on their birthdays, adopted children on their adoption days, foster children on the day they came to your house. Have them blow out the candles with thoughts or wishes. This can be repeated as many times as you need until all the thoughts and wishes are out on the table. This is one to follow the lead of your children. There are no right or wrong answers.

Share Thoughts With the Moon. Another powerful symbol of connection is the moon. Regardless of where we call home in the world, we all look at the same moon and this can be a wonderful way to allow your child to create a personal and private tool for connection. We sometimes sit on our back porch and gaze at the moon and send wishes to people we aren't with at the moment. Do it for grandparents, cousins, or aunts and uncles who don't live close and also for birth relatives, past foster parents and other important people in your child's life.

It's important to be able to voice and accept the feelings that come from memories. Ceremonies and rituals will help your family do that.

Carrie Kitze is an adoptive mom who has used many matches and candles to honor all the people in the lives of her children. She has written two children's books, ***We See The Moon*** *and* ***I Don't Have Your Eyes*** *both written for adopted and/or fostered children. She is the owner of EMK Press, the publisher of this book and other resources for foster and adoptive families. Visit her website at www.emkpress.com.*

Self-Esteem Building in Families

By Cheryl A. Lieberman, PhD, and Rhea K. Bufferd, LICSW

Children become used to receiving stars and other stickers in school. Teachers continue to give them out because children respond well. From time to time, you might present simple and colorful awards to your child for being kind, having a nice smile, comforting a sad person, cleaning his room especially well, learning to ride her bike without training wheels, and so on.

You can take time to provide verbal recognition for doing well: "Thank you for being so patient," "You certainly are clever," "You have a good eye for color," or "What you said is very interesting." Also take time to make positive statements to your child, especially when your remarks are unexpected and not tied to any achievement: "I am lucky to know you," "I like you," It's good to see you." "I love you," "Thanks for being you," "I am glad you are here," "I enjoy being with you." Look into your child's eyes when you say these things.

The members of one family, for example, used a Sunday lunch time when the family was usually together after church, to describe one thing they appreciated about each person in the family each week.

They kept the rules for speaking simple:

- Say only positive things.
- Be serious, and don't make jokes.
- Try to be specific.
- Only say things that are true from each person's perspective.

The listening rules were also simple:

- Listen carefully to what each person says.
- Don't joke or put yourself down.
- Enjoy what you hear.

They even found a way to involve young children. Someone might say, "I like the way you try to feed yourself," or if spoken language was still a problem, they would use a special smile or touch or voice tone for the person – still remembering to use eye contact.

If you have more than one child, rotate the honor of being child of the day. The child of the day gets to choose the book that is read at night and has his or her picture put in a frame labeled "Child of the Day." That way, every child in a family with more than one child gets his or her chance to feel special and singled out.

Rhea K. Bufferd, LICSW, has been an adoption social worker since 1974. She is an adoption consultant to the Adoption Resources Program at Jewish Family and Children's Services.

Cheryl A. Lieberman, PhD, is an adoptive parent. She holds a masters in Social Services and City Planning and a PhD in Organizational Planning. She is Founder and President of Cornerstone Consulting Group, Cambridge, Mass. Cheryl and Rhea are the authors of ***Creating Ceremonies: Innovative Ways to Meet Adoption Challenges.*** *This ceremony is from that book, reprinted with permission.*

The Picture Book Fix for Emotional Challenges

By Lee Tobin McClain, PhD

Want a fun, non-preachy way to help foster kids deal with emotional issues and improve their reading and artistic literacy as well? Grab good picture books and read them together. Parents, teachers and others who work with youth often bemoan their focus on television. The upside of this focus: today's kids are highly visual. Picture books play to that strength, attracting kids' attention and interest in the way that pure text doesn't.

Learning from Stories

Picture books provide easy-to-read stories that can help children understand and deal with difficult emotions. Research by Dr. Debby Zambo of Arizona State University shows multiple ways picture books teach emotional regulation strategies:

- Picture books are familiar and accessible.
- Favorite characters help children feel less alone in their emotions.
- Stories gain kids' attention and engage their emotions.
- Most picture books portray techniques children can use to manage emotions and solve problems.
- Children are more willing to listen to new ideas in the context of a character's life.

As Zambo points out, youngsters learn from stories in every culture and throughout history, and typically find such learning enjoyable and rewarding. Stories are a powerful and effective way to teach without lecturing. And of course, the more you read with your children, the more they'll value reading, which leads to academic gains, which leads to higher self-esteem, which helps with all kinds of emotional problems.

The Value of Visuals

What's the best thing about picture books? The pictures, of course! The art in picture books can help children learn to read body language and facial expressions, important skills for social success. Studies have shown that kids with disabilities, in particular, often fall behind in this type of visual literacy. Additionally, research indicates that those who lack skills in reading faces and body postures tend to interpret others' behaviors as negative, even when no negative intention is present. Improving kids' skills in these areas can reduce conflicts with schoolmates and teachers – and make your kids' world a friendlier place. Another benefit: some of the best original art being done these days is between the covers of picture books. Exposing kids to art can develop their appreciation of painting, drawing, collage and color, giving them a permanent source of enjoyment and pleasure.

But My Kids are Too Old

If you're fostering teens, you may think picture books can't apply to them. But you'd be surprised. It's common practice in some high schools to read Judith Viorst's "Alexander" and the "Terrible, Horrible, No Good, Very Bad Day" as a way to lighten up adolescent moodiness. Some books targeted for teens are now cast as picture books or comics. Reading specialists have found picture books effective in teaching concepts, skills and moral reasoning skills to low-performing young adults or to learners who struggle with English. The great benefit of picture books for teens is that you can teach without lecturing, and thus avoid the adolescent "off" switch that's flipped at the merest hint of adult sermonizing. A side benefit is the accessibility of most picture books, which enables weak readers to gain confidence and make progress in reading skills. If you assume teens want nothing to do with the world of young children, think again. Today's teens buy up Dora the Explorer and Strawberry Shortcake paraphernalia by the cartload, seeming to relish the nostalgic return to a simpler time of their lives.

How Do I Get Started?

Picture books demand a different style of reading than most adults are used to, especially if they're being used to teach emotional regulation strategies. Make sure to pause every few pages to discuss what you're reading. Talk about an illustration before moving ahead with the text, asking questions like "How do you think Wemberly feels now?" and "Have you ever been laughed at like Leo?" Study facial expressions together to help your child analyze what they mean. Focus particularly on strategies characters use to work through their emotions and problems, and ask if there are ways your child could employ such strategies. Don't overdo the discussion. Many children prefer to get on with the story, and they'll internalize characters' ways of dealing with problems by hearing the story a few times.

Most kids in foster care struggle with emotional challenges, and fortunately, most receive ongoing therapy to help them cope. Picture books aren't a substitute for professional help, but they are a useful adjunct that can be used at the family level in small, daily doses. Best of all, picture books can facilitate a pleasant bonding experience, helping to fill children's reservoir of need in a way that's fun for both parent and child.

*Lee Tobin McClain, PhD, is the author of **My Loco Life**, **My Abnormal Life**, and **My Alternate Life**, a series of novels featuring teens in foster care. She teaches writing and literature at Seton Hill University. This article originally appeared in **Fostering Families Today**.*

Picture Books to Try:

Anger:

When Sophie Gets Angry — Really, Really Angry
By Molly Bang

Where the Wild Things Are
By Maurice Sendak

Sometimes I'm Bombaloo
By Rachel Vail

Fear and Anxiety:

Wemberly Worried
By Kevin Henkes

There's an Alligator under My Bed
By Mercer Mayer

Brave Irene
By William Steig

Sadness:

Tough Boris
By Mem Fox

The Blue Day Book for Kids: A Lesson in Cheering Yourself Up
By Bradley Trevor Greive

A Gift for Tia Rosa
By Karen T. Taha

Guilt and Shame:

Leo the Late Bloomer
By Robert Kraus

Thank You, Mr. Falker
By Patricia Polacco

No, David!
By David Shannon

Being Different, Facing Discrimination:

I Don't Have Your Eyes
By Carrie Kitze

The Story of Ruby Bridges
By Robert Coles

Daisy and the Doll
By Michael Medearis and Angela Shelf Medearis

The Story of Ferdinand
By Munro Leaf

The Right to Grieve

If it's unmentionable, it's unmanageable – Maria Trozzi

By Sheena Macrae

Children in foster care suffer loss of birth family, friends, and surroundings that are known to them. It can be harder for them to resolve or "find closure" for that grief because they have no absolutes to pack away. Will they be reunited with their families again? Will they see their friends or school again? How would they feel if they were reunited?

Foster parents need tools to understand a child who might feel grief and loss. They need to help children move to form fresh attachments, and help to place their grief and loss in perspective. Sometimes children need guidance in order to understand the story of their grief, and may need to be given "different endings" and different ways of viewing what happened to them.

Foster parents need to understand children's grief. To do that, we need to listen to what they tell us. Foster parents then can help them re-process it by offering different ways of looking at the loss, basically offering a new perspective. Lifebooks can be helpful in making the past available to the child – the book is literally in the child's hands. So also are "lifelines." Therapists at CASE believe that grieving children need to be taught coping skills, which help work through patches in their life when grief is strong. "Lifelines" can be people, sports, thoughts or simply permission to call a friend and talk...

Grief is normal after loss. Parents need children to know that painful feelings are appropriate for hurts, and that with time and understanding, the feelings will diminish to a manageable size.

Children need to have the right for respect of their history. Foster parents can help children find pride in what has been lost. Foster parents can respect birth parents, and ensure children have access to whatever personal property is brought to the foster parents' home. Foster parents can celebrate the connection between children, their birth family, and the foster family.

Children need to find a way to integrate their loss and move forward. If we work with our children to honor their loss, it can be incorporated, and children can function as a whole again. Grief and loss are still part of children, but no longer the dominant part.

Sheena Macrae is a senior editor at EMK Press, an adoptive mother, and she serves on a local authority Adoption Panel in the UK. This article originally appeared in ***Adoption Parenting: Creating a Toolbox, Building Connections*** *EMK Press 2006.*

Recommended reading: ***Talking with Children about Loss***, by Maria Trozzi. ***Healing Loss in the Traumatized Child***, by Marilyn Schoettle, MA, and Ellen Singer, LCSW-C, free download from The Center for Adoption and Support Education, Inc. (C.A.S.E.) www.adoptionsupport.org.

The Sad Rabbit

A therapeutic story presenting the idea that children can express their grief through one or more actions or activities that represent their loss.

By Susan Ward

"Shaggy, the brown and white bunny sat… and sat… and sat. He didn't do anything. He didn't eat. He didn't play. He didn't think. He didn't cry. He just sat. Shaggy's grandmother had died last week.

Friends came by Shaggy's house. They asked him to come out and play. He said "no." They asked if he wanted to go for a walk. He said "no."

After several weeks of feeling a big hole inside him, he decided he needed to talk to someone. Someone who would help him feel better.

One person told him to be active, to play, to get outside, to stay busy. So, he spent a week running, and hopping, and playing, and running, and hopping, and playing. He still felt the same… like he had a big hole inside him.

Another person told him to not think about it, not to be sad. So he spent weeks pushing the memories and thoughts of his grandma out of his mind. Every time he started to think of something nice or funny his grandma had done or said, he squashed that thought away. But, it didn't help. He still felt like he had a big hole inside him.

Another person told him to wait and the sad, bad feelings would go away. He thought to himself. I've been waiting. My grandma died weeks ago, and I still feel like I have a big hole inside me.

One morning he woke up and said, "I know who will help! I need to talk to Mrs. Owl." He hopped out of bed, hopped out the door, hopped down the path, hopped along the river, hopped through the woods, and came to Mrs. Owl's house. She was SO glad to see him!

Just as he had guessed, Mrs. Owl knew exactly what Shaggy needed. First, she told him that that big hole inside him was normal. That everyone who has someone die, or move away, or who has a person go away from their life feels that big hole. Some people can't eat. Some people cry a lot. Some people feel lonely. Some people can't sit still. Some people are grumpy. She explained that everybody's sad is different. And, that's okay. "There are three things you need to do," she told him, "to feel better inside."

She sent him off to visit Mr. Turtle. Mr. Turtle was pleased to see him. Mr. Turtle sat down with Shaggy and explained that one thing he needed to do was to tell his grandma that he was mad that she had died. "How can I do that?!" Shaggy yelled. She's gone! She's dead!" Mr. Turtle said, "Yes, that's true. But still, you need to say that you're mad."

All of a sudden, Shaggy's eyes got big, his chest puffed out, and he yelled, "WHY DID YOU DIE, GRANDMA?! WHY DID YOU LEAVE ME?! I'M SO MAD AT YOU! I MISS YOU!!" As soon as the words were out of his mouth, he began to cry. Softly at first, then loudly, he cried big tears, and more tears, and even more tears. Mr. Turtle just sat quietly and patted his head. After a long time, Shaggy looked up and said, "I think I… Maybe I feel… Why do I feel… a little bit better?" Mr. Turtle said, "Sharing your inside feelings help you feel better. And, crying helps you feel better, too."

Then, Mr. Turtle sent Shaggy off to visit Miss Robin.

Miss Robin was pleased to see Shaggy. Miss Robin sat down with Shaggy and explained that one thing he needed to do was to tell his grandma what he missed about her. "How can I do that? She's gone.

She's dead." Miss Robin said, "Yes, that's true. But still, you need to share all the things that you miss about her.

Shaggy curled into a little ball. His eyes almost closed. He whispered, "Grandma, I miss your cookies. You made the best cookies in the world. And, Grandma, I miss your voice. Your funny voice when you read silly stories to me. And, Grandma, I miss being in your garden with you. You had such pretty flowers and you used to tell me all the flower names…" After he stopped talking, he got very quiet. Then he began to cry. Softly at first then loudly, he cried big tears, and more tears, and even more tears. Miss Robin just sat quietly and patted his head. After a long time, Shaggy looked up and said, "I think I… Maybe I feel… Why do I feel… a little bit better?" Miss Robin said, "Sharing your inside feelings help you feel better. Remembering why the one you love was special helps. And, crying helps you feel better, too."

Then, Miss Robin sent Shaggy to visit Mr. Bear. Mr. Bear was pleased to see Shaggy. Mr. Bear sat down with Shaggy and explained that one thing he needed to do was to build or draw or make or plant something that would help him remember his grandma for a long time. "But what can I do," said Shaggy, "I'm just a little rabbit?" Mr. Bear said, "Well, let's think about it… What could you do so that every time you look at it, you will think of your grandma, and smile?"

Shaggy thought and thought. "I could draw a picture or I could make something with clay or I could write a poem… I know! I'll plant some flowers! The kind Grandma liked! I can plant them, and water them, and look at them, and smell them…and it will make me smile because I will think of my grandma!" He got a big smile on his face, then the smile faded, then he looked sad, then he cried. Mr. Bear just sat quietly and patted his head. After a long time, Shaggy looked up and said, "I think I… Maybe I feel… Why do I feel… a little bit better?" Mr. Bear said, "Sharing your inside feelings helps you feel better. Thinking of ways to remember people who aren't in our lives any more helps. And, crying helps you feel better."

Slowly Shaggy got up. He stretched. He said, "I feel soooo tired… and maybe I feel a little tiny bit better.

As Shaggy walked home, he thought about the three things he had done. He had told his grandma he was mad at her for dying. And he had cried. He had shared what he had missed about her. And he had cried. He had thought of a way to remember his grandma in a nice, long-time way. And he had cried.

He did feel a little tiny bit better.

When he got home and told his mom and dad about his idea for making a garden to help remember his grandma, they agreed that it was a wonderful idea! During the next few weeks, Shaggy picked out seeds and planted them. He watered them. He pulled out weeds. And, soon, he had a beautiful garden. It wasn't exactly like his grandma's garden, but every time he looked at it, or pulled out weeds, or cut pretty flowers to put into a vase, he thought of his grandma, and he smiled. The nice memories of his grandma were with him every day. He still missed his grandma, but he felt a tiny bit better inside.

Susan Ward is the founder of Heritage Communications, a writer/lecturer, an adoptive mother, and runs Older Child Adoption, a site with many resources for adoptive parents. Her website is www.olderchildadoptionsupport.com. This article originally appeared in ***Adoption Parenting: Creating a Toolbox, Building Connections*** *(EMK Press 2006).*

Allegations

"The only source of knowledge is experience."
– Albert Einstein

Preventing Allegations in Provider Homes

By Jodee Kulp

Foster care providers are vulnerable to charges from both the children they care for and the birth parents that have been denied custody. Allegations can be made because of good faith mistakes, come from angry or hurt parents or children, or be maltreatment of a child or vulnerable adult. Statistically 65-70% of all allegations are false. If this happens to you remain calm and cooperate. Child protection is mandated to keep the child/children safe. That means children may be removed from your home. They are also mandated to investigate the allegation to make sure the child/children are not being abused and this process can takes weeks and sometimes months. The time between the first call and the final results can feel like eternity. If you have an allegation take care of yourself and your family. If you have not yet had an allegation prepare, prevent, and protect.

Here are some steps care providers can take to protect themselves from allegations and the resulting bureaucratic nightmare:

Steps a provider family can take to prevent maltreatment:

Understand and follow all licensing regulations. When a provider is accused of neglect or abuse and has not been in compliance with regulations, the likelihood of a negative licensing action is increased.

Get as much information about the child as possible. Before you accept a placement, it is important to get as much information as you can and write it down or get it in writing. Keep a separate notebook for each child, a colored 25¢ pocket folder with a stitched notebook inserted in the pocket will do. A stitched notebook is good because pages cannot be torn out without upsetting the sequence of events. Don't use a computer because changes are too easy. Invest the time to handwrite. Use an ink pen. Include information on the following:

- Behavioral, emotional, physical, and school issues.
- Medical attention needed (current doctors/previous specialists).
- How many prior foster homes and placements has the child had?
- Ask to speak to previous foster family before the child comes to your home.
- What respite is available? How are they related to the child?

Say no to a placement that will put you at risk. If you are concerned that this placement will put your family at risk or if you are unsure if you are capable of handling this child or set of siblings, you will need to say no to the placement. No one has skills to care for every type of child. Say no to an inappropriate placement. Children need as much continuity of care as possible, and saying yes to a potentially unhealthy placement could damage your family and harm the child.

Relationships are important. Maintain a positive relationship with the licensing caseworker and the child's caseworker.

Get it in writing. Make sure any predetermined variance from regulation is approved **in writing** beforehand.

Call the licensing worker and the child's caseworker when positive things happen with the child. Don't make all your calls to the agency sound like problems or complaints. Let them enjoy some of your successes and good days.

Safety guidelines cannot be compromised:

Pay careful attention to safety issues, especially for younger children. Conduct daily safety checks and make sure all hazardous materials are put away.

- Never leave curling irons out.
- Always fasten seat belts.
- Always lock medicine cabinets.
- Never leave child unattended in vehicles.
- Routinely checks to assure the well-being of ALL members of the household.

Closely supervise children at all times.

- It is unwise to allow children to play unattended at any time.
- Do not have too many places where children can hide.
- Leave nap room doors open and periodically check on children during these times.
- Check above child's bed for cords, books, lamps, etc. that could fall onto a child.
- Make sure all safety latches are in place and working.
- Do not leave child alone with pets.

Develop consistent family policies. Develop family policies and follow them concerning discipline, children's developing sexuality, toileting, napping routines, and how substitutes will be hired. File a copy of these with the licensing agency.

Be careful how you play. Do not tease, roughhouse, wrestle, tickle or use sarcasm as children can easily misinterpret all these.

Do not use discipline prohibited by licensing. Never use, or threaten to use, corporal punishment as a means of discipline. This form of discipline cannot be delegated to non-parent guardians, and is prohibited by licensing regulations.

Use appropriate behavior and communication skills. A foster parent is a model of appropriate behavior and a teacher of problem-solving and communication skills to the children they care for. If methods of discipline vary between birth children and foster children, discuss the variances with the social worker.

Screen those you use to help. Carefully screen all helpers/substitutes including relatives and friends; make sure they understand licensing regulations, house rules, and any specific restrictions about individual children because of court orders, and other reasons.

Foster Parent Bill of Rights

Foster parents play a vital role in each state's efforts to care for children and it is essential that each state strengthens the partnership between the governmental agencies and foster parents who are providing those services. In general, Foster Parent Bills of Rights affirm the dignity of foster parents, require that they be given notice regarding child placement decisions, allow them to participate in planning visitation with a child's biological family, and give them priority consideration if adoption becomes an option. It is also provides guidelines on the working relationships between the agencies and foster parents.

According to the National Foster Parent Association (NFPA), 16 states have a Foster Parent Bill of Rights or its equivalent. These states are: Alabama, Arkansas, California, Georgia, Illinois, Kentucky, Louisiana, Maryland, Missouri, Mississippi, New Mexico, Oklahoma, Oregon, Pennsylvania, Tennessee, and Washington. The text of each state's legislation is available on NFPA's website. The NFPA has drafted a model bill that states may look to for guidance when creating a Foster Parent Bill of Rights.

In general, Foster Parent Bills of Rights' outline the privileges and obligations of foster parents, clarify the relationship between foster parents and the state division of child and family services, and provide for the well-being of children. Common provisions give foster parents the right to:

1. Be treated with dignity and respect.
2. Receive adequate training and ongoing support.
3. Obtain all biographical and medical information on a child prior to or at the time of placement.
4. Refuse placement of a child in the foster home or request the removal of the child from the foster home without reprisal.
5. Obtain timely financial reimbursement.
6. Help plan visitation with a child's parents and siblings.
7. Receive notice of department plans or court proceedings affecting a child's placement.
8. Have priority consideration when a foster child becomes available for adoption.
9. Be provided a fair and timely investigation of foster home complaints and an ability to appeal decisions of the placement board.

More information and detailed bills are on the NFPA website and can be found at: www.nfpainc.org/faq.asp?page=69.

View yourself as part of the co-parenting team:

Be a part of the child's team. Keep parents informed of positive progress their child is making and any interesting things they might like to know about their child's activities. View yourself as a part of a co-parenting team that is attempting to reunify a family, not as a competitor for their children's loyalty.

Get help with troubling behaviors. Seek outside resources and assistance immediately if behaviors or issues arise beyond your ability or desire to deal with. Avoid blaming others if possible, and actively seek a solution to resolve the problem to the benefit of all concerned.

Document, Document, Document! Don't trust your memory.

Document both progress and problems. Document progress and problems, medical needs, behavioral patterns, or changes and efforts to teach acceptable behavior.

Use a calendar. Document on a calendar – date child enters your home, changes in the child's behavior; the child's behavior following visits and any patterns of behavior that seem to follow specific events or times of the year (i.e. anniversaries of certain past events).

Use a Journal or notebook. Document in your journal/notebook (spiral bound or perfect bound) – of situations, reactions, and behaviors.

- Document visitation, medical appointments, school meetings or issues.
- Changes in behavior in children including severity and length of these changes, especially after visitation or any changes at school.
- Inappropriate words, unusual statements or actions during or after birth parent visits. Include any action taken to deal with inappropriate behavior.
- Document and report any sexual acting out to the social worker and child's therapist.
- Any unusual behaviors after visits with social workers, police or medical personnel.
- Document and identify conflicts that arise with parents, children, teachers, social workers, etc., because of value differences. Be respectful of individual rights to their own point of view. Negotiate and work toward a compromise.
- Always document any serious conflicts with parents, children, social workers, licensors, teachers, etc., and keep these records in a file. Request copies of these to be kept with the licensing agency.
- Provide a visitor page for signatures in the notebook. Many times a biological parent will claim a foster parent won't let them visit their child. A dated list with signature will do two things: protect you from false allegations of non-compliance and provide support for reunification of family by proving the child and parent have been working on the relationship.

Report suspected abuse. Always report suspected child abuse to local child protection authorities or the social worker assigned to the case, especially after parental visits.

Invest in a camera. If you have a child that visits mom and dad on weekends take before and after pictures. Make sure the camera has data function. This is also handy for positive

Allegation Resources

For more information on training about preventing and surviving allegations of abuse, e-mail North American Council on Adoptable Children's Diane Martin Hushman at hushman@nacac.org.

National Foster Parent Association
www.nfpainc.org

National Child Abuse Defense & Resource Center –
PO Box 638 • Holland, OH 43528
419-865-0513

National Foster Parent Coalition for Allegation Reform – www.nfpcar.org

Foster Parent Legal Solutions –
www.foster-parents-legal-solutions.com
PO Box 175 • Yarnell, AZ 85362
928-427-0088

You Gotta Believe has an article posted at www.yougottabelieve.org/articles/allegations.htm

Adopting and Advocating for the Special Needs Child by L. Anne Babbs & Rita Laws, PhD.

relations for the child to have pictures of parents coming to get them and visiting if things are progressing positively. If the child returns with scratches, bruises or other injuries document the cause.

Be the best parent you can be.

No one can be a perfect parent every day and under every circumstance. There is no way to completely avoid allegations. Understanding your own personal needs and the needs of family members is crucial in being able to develop a supportive and strong foster family.

Avoid being stretched. Know and respect limits. Don't overload your home. Establish appropriate boundaries. If the child is not a good family fit, ask for help before any negative situation can develop. Take breaks from the children and the situation. Make sure to get away alone with your support team or significant other.

Be a team member. Work for the best interest of the child in your care. Build a support system. Foster parenting cannot be done in isolation.

Know your rights.

Document allegation details in your notebook. Include every phone conversation, personal interview, and correspondence related to the allegation.

- During interviews behave appropriately: be on time, make your point and then stop talking. Be factual, honest, and objective. Avoid emotional language. Bring a support person with you to provide a perspective on how the meeting went.
- Find out what will happen during the investigation and what your rights are. Get a copy of your state's laws.

- Request written copies of the written charge against your family.
- Request a written copy that formally states the allegation was unfounded.
- Find out how you can appeal if you disagree with the findings, ask for a waiver or proceed with a grievance procedure.
- Hire legal counsel, especially recommended for sexual abuse allegations.

Life will continue.
As hard as living through an allegation is, you will one day wake up and be on the other side of it, regardless of the outcome. Take care of yourself through this process. Give yourself 15 minutes of joy each day, look for the miracles in the tiny things – watch a sunset, look at the details in a rose, talk to a friend, do a kindness for someone else. Thankfully tough times don't last forever and when it is over you are wiser, stronger, and better able to walk alongside another parent.

Jodee Kulp is the author of ***Families At Risk, A Guide to Understanding and Protecting Children and Care Providers Involved in Out-Of-Home or Adoptive Care.***

This was originally published in ***Fostering Families Today.***

"We're Being Investigated for Child Abuse"

By Michael Weisberg

Our trainers warned us that foster parents face a risk of having to defend against false accusations, but I never worried about being investigated by Child Protective Services until it happened to us. My secretary found me in a side hallway near my office and told me that my partner was on the phone with an "emergency." Returning to my desk, I sat down just in case the news might be more than I could handle standing upright. Then he told me, "we're being investigated for child abuse."

I burst out laughing. The idea was preposterous. I knew that neither of us had done anything wrong, but then my partner explained to me how the Child Protective Services worker had called him at work and bullied him into agreeing to leave his office and go to the nursery school to defend us. My partner wanted me to go with him.

Fortunately, we both had jobs that we could leave in an emergency. My partner works for a software company, and I was working for a law firm as an attorney. I told my secretary that I had to leave, and off I went.

My partner and I met in the nursery school parking lot. Once inside the building, we found that the investigator who bullied my partner was a petite woman in her early twenties who had learned to do her job by establishing a commanding presence that outsized her skinny body. Upon learning who we were, she strode up to us and demanded, "all right, where do you want to go? The doctor's office or the emergency room?" Having spent a significant portion of my legal career defending clients in government investigations, I answered more as a matter of reflex than of thought. "Just a minute," I shot back. "I want to know what the allegation is and what your process is."

"Oh," she answered, surprised at my questions, "do you want to know that?"

The investigator led us into the office where she and the boys' caseworker apparently had spent several hours before we arrived. On the screen of her digital camera, she showed us the photographs she had taken of our foster son's buttocks and asked us whether we understood why she was concerned about possible abuse. The pictures showed purplish markings that neither of us had noticed when we changed our foster son's diapers. Apparently, our foster sons' mother and the case supervisors discovered the markings during a supervised visit. I pointed out that the pictures could just as easily show a heat rash, and noted how our two-year-old foster son would struggle as I tried to buckle him into his carseat, which might make him sweaty on a hot July day. Maybe because I was calm and took a problem-solving approach, the investigator backed down and listened. Adopting a more conciliatory tone, she told me "we're not doctors," and explained that the reason she and the caseworker needed to have our foster son seen by a physician was to obtain a professional medical opinion regarding his symptoms.

I phoned our pediatrician's office number by heart, and obtained the last appointment of the day. Then I calmly turned to the investigator and told her, "every complaint gets investigated, so let's go." Only at this point did my partner and I get to see our younger foster son and his older, 3-year-old brother. We also got to talk briefly with the nursery school director, who told us that the investigator had already interviewed our older foster son, although he had little of value to say. Before we left the building, my partner and I peeked inside our younger foster son's diaper. What we saw was strange. Our foster son had black-and-blue speckles from one side of his bottom to the other, with small clear patches between the marks. Could these speckles be the result of abuse?

When we finally got to the doctor, one look was all the pediatrician needed before announcing a diagnosis that the rest of us had never heard of. Our foster son had a petechial rash. To prove that the rash wasn't caused by abuse, the doctor pressed down on the purpled area, which then turned white. Also, our foster son didn't cry. If our foster son had actual bruises, the markings would have stayed purple as the doctor pressed on them, and our foster son would have cried out from the pain. The cause of the rash wasn't clear. It could have been caused by our foster son playing on a home-made water slide at a party the weekend before, or by a virus, or for no identifiable reason at all. (Later that week, our foster son was diagnosed with Coxsackie virus.)

Even after the pediatrician cleared our names, we still had to comply with the rest of the investigative process. The investigator and caseworker came back to our house. We showed them where the boys slept, and we opened our refrigerator to prove that we had food. Satisfied that we were providing a safe home, the investigator warned us that we would receive an unpleasant form letter in the mail advising us that we were targets of an abuse investigation. Six weeks later, another county worker came to our house for a follow-up visit. Two weeks after that, we received another letter advising us that the allegation against us was unfounded and that the investigation was closed.

I subsequently learned that the photographs of our foster son's buttocks had circulated around the county office. Everyone who saw the pictures expressed the opinion that the pictures reflected abuse. Having seen the pictures, as well as the real-life markings, I understood why the possibility of abuse had to be investigated. What I didn't anticipate was how quickly the investigation would focus on my partner and me to the exclusion of every other person who provided care to this child. By the time we met the investigator, she had already decided that our foster son had been abused and that the foster parents were the abusers.

In our case, we were fortunate that the investigator was open to changing her mind as new information challenged her hypothesis. The process of changing her mind included having both foster parents accompany her and our foster son to our doctor's office. I know other foster parents who weren't as lucky as we were. In their case, the county's caseworker took their foster child to the emergency room without the foster parents. When the caseworker told the doctor how the child's injury supposedly had occurred, the caseworker's story was different from what the foster parents had told her. Because the caseworker changed the story – intentionally or not – the doctor concluded that the injury did not match the explanation he was given, which was true because the explanation he was given was inaccurate. The doctor also could not exclude abuse as a possible alternative explanation for the child's injury. This combination of findings was enough to result in an "indicated" report of abuse being issued against the foster parents. The foster parents eventually succeeded in overturning the indicated report, but the foster parents and their foster child never saw each other again. This outcome never would have occurred if the foster parents had been permitted to talk to the doctor directly.

When I think of these stories, I'm reminded of how vulnerable foster parents are. Most of the time, we're too busy taking care of the children to think about the possibility that an investigator might show up at our foster kids' school or day care center and conduct interviews and physical examinations without our knowledge, or that well-meaning or overly defensive county workers might decide that keeping the children "safe" requires them to remove the children from our homes abruptly, perhaps with no notice at all, and with no closure either for the children or for us. Further, we tend to receive little information about what our rights might be in such circumstances.

To ensure that our foster children's needs are met, and keep our own and the caseworkers' minds at ease, my partner and I try to follow some simple routines. If a school nurse calls to tell us that one of our foster kids has been hurt, we ask the nurse to send a note home that we can produce if anyone questions us. If our foster child has a visible injury, we advise the caseworkers before the children visit their mother so that the workers know how it happened. And if anyone advises us to take our foster child to a doctor, we take him. It's true that we've been to some doctor visits that turned out to be pointless, but we've never had to explain why we decided not to obtain medical care. If anything, we've established that abuse and neglect don't happen at our house.

Michael Weisberg lives in upstate New York with his partner of 15 years and their two foster sons, who should finally be adopted by the time this book is published. They are all looking forward to reaffirming and making permanent the family relationship they have formed during the past six years.

Allegations Happen: How to Prevent and Survive Them

By Diane Martin-Hushman

Whether false or confirmed, allegations arise for different reasons. We hope that children who are abused by their caregivers will notify a teacher, social worker, or someone else in authority. But sometimes children whose backgrounds include abuse are highly sensitized to triggers that they associate with abuse. You may just be leading a child to a time out after he kicks his sister; but the instant you grab his arm, your foster son may flash back to times when he was dragged to a room and whipped with his birth father's belt. As children age through the foster care system and grow in street wisdom and anger, many also learn that allegations are a ticket out of a placement, a means of getting attention, and a way to keep parents who are starting to get too close a safe distance away.

The general public is concerned about child abuse and neglect, but not very knowledgeable about how parents must try to deal with some difficult behaviors presented by abused children. The media is quick to shine the spotlight on a few foster and adoptive parents who abuse children in their care, and say little about those who are diligently working to improve children's live. Once they happen, allegations are hard to live down.

Consequences of Allegations

When I was a social worker, a 13-year-old girl in my caseload alleged that her 71-year-old foster grandfather had sexually abused her. The grandfather had a heart condition and I thought the reports would kill him. After looking into the charges, investigators discovered that the girl was distorting the situations and re-enacting a previous abuse situation with birth grandfather.

Though not substantiated, the charge became part of the family's case file, and the stress family members experienced lingered on. Many parents describe allegations and subsequent as a process of loss and grief. Parents may lose their sense of identity, their self-esteem and their trust in the worker or agency. Children may be removed – another painful loss for both the children and parents. Even after child protection closes the case, a parent may feel that the family's good name is forever tarnished and the episode will never be resolved.

Allegations that uncover licensing violations or substantiated abuse claims can cause additional stress. Depending on the severity of the infraction, foster parents may be placed on probation, be issued a correction order, or have their license temporarily suspended or permanently revoked. Serious allegations may result in a criminal charge that could land a parent in jail, and forever ruin chances of fostering or adopting another child.

Allegation Prevention Strategies

Foster and adoptive families who have several children, including children of different races, and who have been fostering for a long time, are at greater risk of being reported for alleged abuse. All families who care for children with special needs face some risk, and every parent can take steps to keep situations from turning into allegations. Below are ideas for parents to consider.

Know your limits. If you are not comfortable handling children with certain challenging backgrounds and behaviors, don't set yourself up by bringing such children into your home.

Learn all you can about each child before he or she is placed with you. You have a right to know about previous abuse and allegations. Ask: "Has this child been abused? In what way? Who were the perpetrators? Have there been any abuse allegations? "Had the foster family whose 13-year-old girl charged the grandfather with abuse known about her abuse history, they would never have left the foster grandfather alone with her.

Make sure that men and boys in your house are never alone with a girl who has been sexually abused. Proactive precautions are important in this situation, especially at the beginning of the placement. Talk with your partner and others in the household about this safety plan, and stay proactive.

Give each sexually abused child his or her own bedroom. I know this is difficult, but why put another child in your home at risk? If a child's boundaries have been invaded, he or she needs to relearn proper boundaries.

Be crystal clear about rules for dress, privacy and touching. Caregivers must agree on house rules, boundaries, and consequences. Each child comes from a different culture of parenting , sexuality, sleep habits, dress, touch, and other rules. Each child will need to learn the rules and understand what is appropriate. As a foster mom, I talked about sexuality as one of the house rules. "In this house," I would say, "my husband gets sexual needs met with me and only me." Sound crude? Yes, but I said it in a matter-of-fact tone and set a clear boundary that teenage girls we worked with needed to hear.

Never use physical discipline. Corporal punishment is not allowed in foster care, but I know some people think that once the kids are adopted, physical discipline is OK. Don't do it. Children with a history of physical, sexual or emotional abuse often misinterpret physical discipline and an allegation is likely. Physical discipline can also undermine attachment.

Avoid teasing, horseplay, wrestling, and suggestive language. These are acts of intimacy, and intimacy is what abused children resist. In addition, the child may get a different message than you intend during the close physical contact involved.

Document sexual acting out in writing. Send reports to the child's social worker and therapist. Then, if another incident comes to light, the worker and therapist can see that there might be a pattern to the child's acting out that perhaps relates to past experiences.

Document behavior patterns. When a child enters your home, use a calendar to record changes in the child's behavior; inappropriate words or actions during birth parent visits; the child's behavior following visits; the cause of scratches, bruises or other injuries; and any patterns of behavior that seem to follow specific events or times of the year, like anniversaries of certain past events.

Participate in a support group. As foster and adoptive parents of children with special needs, we need to share the struggles and joys that are part of our lives with those who can empathize and support us. We need people who can laugh and cry with us and understand foster and adoptive parents' journey.

Reserve personal time to reduce stress. Know what pushes your buttons, and establish a calming plan. Post 20 calming tips on your refrigerator and model stress-reduction techniques for your children. Then, make plans for a weekly – yes, weekly – time away from the children. Take care of yourself; you are the child's greatest gift.

Allegation Survival Strategies

Sometimes, despite a family's efforts to prevent them, allegations will happen. Maybe things are going a little too well with Jimmy – a 12-year-old with a history of sexual abuse – and he starts to get scared. The week after a lively game of Twister with his foster dad, Jimmy tells his worker that the foster dad was touching and pressing his body against Jimmy's. Jimmy claims it was sexual abuse, and soon child protection opens a case file to investigate Jimmy's allegation. The foster family is looking at weeks or months of investigation, and Jimmy moves to an emergency shelter. What can the parents do to take care of themselves?

- Try to stay positive. Assume that the charge will be proven false, and try not to presume guilt. Statistics I've seen say that about 65 to 70 percent of all allegations are false. Child protection has to investigate to make certain that the child is not being abused. The best thing you can do is cooperate.

- Document everything. Start a notebook to record details of every conversation, personal interview and correspondence related to the allegation. Write in pen, and be prepared to use the notebook to back up your story in court if needed. Request copies of the written charge against your family, as well as the letter that formally states that the allegations were unfounded.

- Educate yourself. Insist on getting a copy of your state's foster care rules and laws pertaining to allegations and abuse, and learn about county or agency policies and procedures too. Find out what will happen during the investigation, what your rights are, and how you can appeal an investigator's determination.

- Behave appropriately. During interviews, make your point and then stop talking. Speak with confidence, and be factual, honest, respectful, and business like. Avoid emotional language when telling your side of the story. It may be extremely hard, but you must try to be objective.

- Meet with people who are gathering information. If an investigator asks to meet with you, don't keep him or her waiting. If you need to, bring along a friend or someone from your support group who can give you perspective on how the meeting went.

- Communicate with your partner. Allegations, especially those of sexual abuse, can drive a wedge between partners. The husband thinks, "How can they think I would do something like that?" The wife wonders, "Could it possibly be true?" If not openly discussed, these questions can pull couples apart just when they need each other's support the most.

- Know your rights. Don't be afraid to appeal, request a waiver, and learn how the grievance procedure works. If need be, hire legal counsel. I would especially recommend hiring a good attorney for sexual abuse allegations.

How Support Groups Can Help

In addition to counseling new foster and adoptive families about taking conscious steps to prevent allegations, support groups can be helpful when a family is going through or has just concluded an allegation investigation. Sometimes, the best help is just being there to listen and talk. To support family members who are going through an investigations:

- Offer a sympathetic ear. This is a time when families need the support. Make them feel welcome by respectfully listening.
- Stay neutral. It is not the group's job to fix the problem. There are many sides to the story, and the group should be objective. Agency bashing helps no one.
- Share information. Encourage members to talk about their experiences with allegations, share local allegation policy and procedural information with the entire group.
- Suggest resources. Direct the family to legal services and suggest how they can obtain agency policies concerning allegations.
- Assign a mentor. Parents going through an allegation may have an easier time talking to one person who has experienced an allegation rather than the whole group. A call from someone who can say, "I've walked the walk," can mean so much during this time.

After the investigation is over, ask for help to regain your equilibrium, rebuild and move on. Take good care of yourself. Think hard and give yourself some time off before bringing a child back into your home, or accepting another placement. Take care of the children still in the home. Difficult times can be therapeutic and healing, showing children that we can have tough times, but as families are strong and resilient. If you can't prevent an allegation, at least do what you can to survive, learn, and thrive.

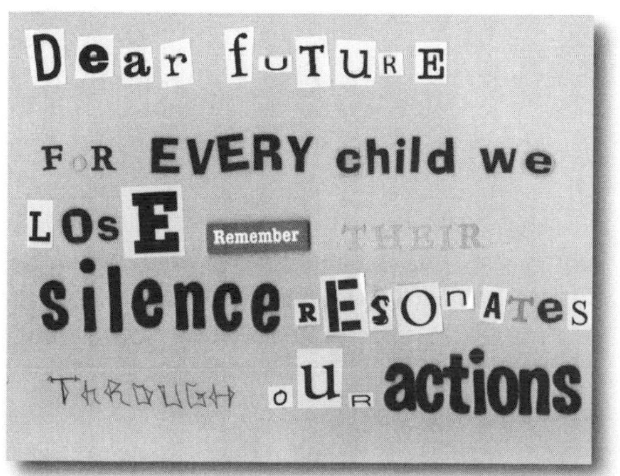

This article reprinted with the author's permission from the Spring 2002 ***Adoptalk****, published by the North American Council on Adoptable Children for more information visit www.nacac.org.*

Criminalizing Foster Parents

By Lori Groves, MMFT, and James Kenny, PhD

The United States foster care system has a higher turnover rate than most fast food industries. Of the estimated 150,000 licensed foster homes, from 30 to 50% drop out each year. With about 408,000 children in foster care, we have a critical shortage of homes. Why are foster parents leaving? Of all the reasons, the biggest by far is that they are treated poorly.

Being a foster parent can be the toughest job you will ever love. Foster children often come with serious issues. They may lie and steal. They have behavior problems and learning difficulties. They may suffer from a variety of physical and mental illnesses. Foster parents quickly learn that a nurturing love is often misunderstood and is not always enough. Yet, they generally rise to the challenges, knowing that they have the chance to make a difference in the life of a child.

Foster parents must be vetted initially by a thorough homestudy, which usually includes a background social history, psychological testing, a police check, medical records review, and collateral information from references. Then they must complete hours of parent training and they must keep up their skills with annual continuing education. They are professional parents.

So, here you are as a new foster parent. You have welcomed your first foster child and you are excited. Your caseworker is supportive. You are dealing with the multiple issues that neglected and abused children bring with them. Your own children have adjusted and welcomed a new member to the family. As time passes, you and your foster child are bonding.

Then, often as a surprise, an allegation is made. No one warned you that this was likely. Someone has called in to say that you spanked your child. The child may have told his teacher that you touched him "improperly" during a bath. The birth mother may have charged that you left the child alone or locked him in his room. The caseworker may even charge you with neglect for failing to keep a doctor's appointment or for not taking the child for visitation, even though he was sick. The allegations may not be what we normally consider abuse or neglect, but simply reflect a violation of welfare policy. Any and all allegations, however, must be taken seriously.

What is the Charge?

The Division of Family and Children's Services (DFCS) reminds you that they have additional rules and policies. As a professional parent, you are held to a higher standard of care. Here are some examples: DFCS Manuals may forbid physical punishment. The Manual may require that babysitting and respite care are provided only by another licensed foster parent, or by someone older than 21. Since the child is a ward of the state, failure to follow any direction given by the caseworker may also be construed as abuse or neglect. Can you imagine getting charged with neglect for leaving an eight-year-old with a 19-year-old to babysit? It happens! A serious problem for foster parents is that these charges (failing to follow policy) are lumped with and labeled as child abuse, no matter how minor they may sound.

How Allegations Are Made

Allegations can be made by anyone. In order to encourage the reporting of abuse, the accuser is granted complete anonymity. Consequently, the foster parent can never examine or confront the accuser. To further the effort to assure the safety of the child, no strong proof is required. Hearsay is allowed. The standard is "credible evidence," believable but not necessarily true evidence. This is a sad joke because even the word of a four-year-old or the word of the biological mom who is a drug addict and wants a fast way out may appear credible to the caseworker. And that word alone can be sufficient to remove the child from the home.

Once the caseworker with Child Protective Services (CPS) has substantiated any charge(s), your child may not only be removed, but in many states, you are placed on a LIST, the same list with sex offenders and others.

The consequences of being listed are severe. Foster parents will lose their license. They cannot work with children. The authors know people who have lost their jobs as a case manager in a mental health clinic, a prison guard, a school bus driver, coach, scout leader, and other jobs because of this stigma. All they have done is allegedly fail to follow a policy that required exceptional parenting. Unproven allegations can and often do lead to a criminal-sized penalty for a mere policy violation.

The welfare department faces no reciprocal accountability. Although they are a party to the foster care contract, no charges are laid when they fail to follow their own Child Welfare Manual and Policies. Caseworkers are required to make home visits, to file permanency plans in a timely manner, to disclose to foster parents detailed background information about the child; to respond to certain requests made by the foster parents and other mandates. When DFCS fails to follow their half of the contract, nothing remotely comparable happens to them. Even worse, when a foster parent complains; they may be "blackballed" by the caseworkers and DFCS, which means they will not get any more child placements in their home.

Foster parents begin with a love of children. Most of them leave, not because they cannot face the challenges of handling troubled youngsters, but because they fail to receive support from the system. Here are a few of the extraneous issues they must deal with:

Foster care receives negative publicity. Children may be threatened: "If you don't behave, we will have to send you to a foster home." Then there is always the occasional neighbor or friend who does not want "those kinds of kids playing with our kids."

They get caught in a power struggle with the DFCS over what is considered best for the children in their care. They will lose this battle, because the children are officially wards of the state, and even long-term foster parents have no legal standing. Although foster parents do all the hard work, they have a minimal say in planning the child's future.

They must face allegations from anonymous accusers and may have charges substantiated against them with one-sided minimal evidence and no due process procedure to defend themselves. If they need an attorney, they must pay for one themselves

Finally, a substantiated charge of child abuse or neglect will place foster parents on an accessible LIST that may well cost them their job. In most cases, it is extremely difficult to get one's name removed from the LIST.

In corporate America, contracts impose civil obligation that both sides are meant to follow. Foster parents have entered into a contract with DFCS. However, in the business world, contract violations must be proven by a preponderance of the evidence. This is not so for foster parents. Foster parents who break this contract may be given felony-sized penalties without due process.

What Can Be Done?

In order to stop the drain of good foster parents, we propose three changes to the way that allegations of abuse and neglect are handled.

Raise the standard of proof. If hearsay is acceptable, have the CPS worker require at least three sources to back up the complaint. Make the foster parents aware of the charges in writing and get the foster parents' written response before substantiation. "Credible evidence" is too weak and an unfair standard. Raise the level of proof required to a "the preponderance of evidence."

Separate criminal child abuse from a civil policy violation. The CPS worker would then have two options: 1) To substantiate a charge of "Improper Professional Parenting," a policy violation. 2) A criminal charge of child neglect or abuse. Improper parenting, a mere policy violation, might be handled with a reprimand, a requirement for corrective action, or even the loss of a foster parent license. But it would not lead to a foster parent's name being placed on the LIST.

Criminal child abuse should be subdivided into misdemeanors and felonies. With criminal charges, foster parents would have the right to defend themselves in a trial court where due process procedures are followed. Hearsay evidence is not permissible. You can face your accusers. The state must prove its case "beyond a reasonable doubt." Conviction of child abuse would merit being placed on the LIST.

We must cherish our foster parents for their unselfish willingness to tackle a task that few others take on. Unfortunately, they are leaving the system because of the way they are treated. All foster parents are vulnerable daily to allegations of child abuse. Failing to follow DFCS policy and/or to meet a high standard of parenting is a civil violation with a criminal-sized punishment. Being on the accessible LIST of child abusers is a heavy penalty with serious consequences.

When foster parents are accused of failing to meet acceptable standards of parenting, they deserve all the rights that our legal system guarantees. They deserve better treatment than the substantiation of unproven charges based upon hearsay. We must cherish our foster parents for their unselfish willingness to tackle a task that few others will take on.

Lori Groves, MMFT, has a master's degree in marriage and family therapy. She recently co-authored a book called ***Bonding and the Case for Permanence****. Lori and her husband have been foster parents to more than 50 children. They also have adopted and birth children.*

James Kenny, PhD, has doctorates in psychology and anthropology and is the author of 10 books on child care and family life. He and his wife have raised birth, adopted, and foster children. He is on the ***Fostering Families Today*** *advisory board. This was originally published in* ***Fostering Families Today****.*

False Allegations of Abuse in Foster Care

Position Statement from the National Foster Parent Association

The National Foster Parent Association's first concern is to ensure that no child suffers harm while in foster care. The Association does acknowledge that some foster parents are capable of maltreatment.

Foster and adoptive families are at risk and vulnerable to charges of false allegations because they are so visible in the community. They frequently have large families, children from culturally diverse backgrounds, or children with physical and/or emotional disabilities. There is a need to care for the children but also to address the issue of protection and retention of foster and adoptive homes.

Currently, an estimated 150,000 foster families are providing care for more than 408,000* children in placement across the nation. These children frequently exhibit a wide variety of behavior problems including making false allegations of abuse toward their foster/adoptive parents. Research has shown that children who have been abused, particularly children who were sexually abused, may make false abuse allegations against subsequent parents or caregivers. It is estimated that in 2009, there were approximately 50,000**allegations with less than 0.5% being substantiated.

NFPA believes foster parents, upon being licensed and/or approved, should always be provided with a manual that gives specific clear directions on how allegations and investigations of abuse in foster care are handled in their agency. NFPA believes foster parents, in order to function with maximum effectiveness as a part of the team, need helpful, relevant and current information, the best and most skilled agency support services, and a clear view of expectations to enable them to perform their role as competent parents.

*The AFCARS Report: (Adoption and Foster Care Analysis and Reporting System) Report, released in June 2011 by the U.S. Department of Health and Human Services.

**Administration for Children and Families statistics (www.acf.hhs.gov)

When Might Foster Parents Need an Attorney?

Two times when legal representation may be advisable are: when you have been accused of abuse or neglect and/or when the agency has scheduled a hearing to revoke your license.

The Child Protection Office (CPS) of the Department of Family and Children is required to investigate all allegations of abuse or neglect. That requirement protects foster parents against frivolous or mean-spirited charges levied by an angry child or birth parent. You want CPS to hear your side.

Many such complaints are found to be unsubstantiated. If, however, CPS substantiates a charge of abuse, you may want to go to court to have the charges investigated more thoroughly and to defend yourself. For this you need an attorney.

Another time you may need an attorney is at a license revocation hearing. Some foster parents have felt that threats to revoke their licenses were made in retaliation for disagreeing with the agency. Your foster parent license is a property right and not something that you can be deprived of by whim. An attorney who knows the laws and policies related to licensing and the appropriate penalties for violations, which may well be less severe than revocation, may save your foster parent license.

How Do I Find an Attorney?

There are two good ways to find an experienced foster parent attorney. Check with other foster parents who have been through the process you face, and ask if they were satisfied with their attorney. The best recommendation will come, not from a family friend or your family attorney but from someone who has been helped through the same process you face.

The second way is to call ACT's toll-free number (877-ACT-4KIDS) outside Indiana call 1-812-339-7403 and get the names of three attorneys in your area who have taken our ACT seminars.

The purpose of ACT is to promote early permanence for foster children. One of the main ways that ACT tries to achieve this purpose is by training attorneys in the area of foster parent adoption. ACT has offered seminars and provided literature for attorneys throughout Indiana on foster care adoptions.

James A. Kenny, PhD, has doctorates in psychology and anthropology and is the author of 10 books on child care and family life. He and his wife have raised birth, adopted, and foster children. He is on the ***Fostering Families Today*** *advisory board.*

Respite & Support

"Stressed souls need the reassuring rhythm of self-nurturing rituals."

– Sarah Ban Breathnach

Schedule free time in your day: Yes, I said free time! Free time to do fun, carefree activities like: write in your journal, swing on a swing set, rest or relax . . . you've earned it.

Self-Care for Adoptive and Fostering Parents

By Carol Lozier, LCSW

While the day-to-day caretaking of children is certainly draining, foster and adoptive parents may find daily life even more exhausting. Ongoing pressures can cause stress to your behavior, body, thoughts and feelings. Sometimes we are so accustomed to the symptoms of stress, we don't even consider them to be out of the ordinary. An article written by Mayo Clinic staff, "Stress symptoms: Effects on your body, feelings and behavior*," points out some common symptoms:

Body: Headache, back pain, heart palpitations, high blood pressure, sleep problems, and stomach aches.

Thoughts and Feelings: Anxiety, irritability, depression, anger, insecurity, and forgetfulness.

Behavior: Overeating or undereating, angry outbursts, crying spells, and relationship problems.

Therefore, it's imperative that parents practice self-care to keep their stress at a healthy level. While it's important to follow the strategies that include proper nutrition, exercise, meditation and yoga, I have found some other strategies that are helpful as well.

1. Practice saying, "No, thank you."
Pay attention to how many volunteer and extra curricular activities you and your kids are involved in. Of course, it's important to volunteer and participate, but too many activities deplete your energy. Practice saying, "No, thanks for asking," when you have reached your limit.

2. Laugh.
Laughter relaxes your whole body and keeps your outlook positive. As a family, watch funny movies or TV shows (we find "America's Funniest Home Videos" provides a good belly laugh) or buy a good joke book and take turns reading jokes.

3. Maintain a detached viewpoint.
Detaching with love is a strategy to practice when others instigate stress. Next time, try this: Imagine a protective glass wall around you, so that your love can go out to this person, but his or her negativity cannot come back to you.

4. Reduce the amount of time you spend with technology.
Electronics, gadgets, computers, games, and cellphones all require an inordinate amount of our attention. Reduce the amount of time you spend with technology outside of work.

5. Create a priorities list and stick to it.
Create a list of priorities for work, home, family, and spirituality. Which priorities are a daily must for your serenity? Postpone activities that create more stress than calm.

6. Find inspiration.
Feeling inspired improves your mood and energy level. Take time each day to quietly focus on your personal source of inspiration whether it's antique cars, nature, knitting, dogs, gardening, and so forth.

7. Faith.
Relieve your stress by relying on your higher power (however you define it) in times of trouble or uncertainty.

8. Make Your Dreams Come True.
Do something you've dreamed about but haven't done yet. Maybe you've talked about learning a foreign language or a new hobby; don't put it off any longer.

9. Schedule free time in your day.
Yes, I said free time! Free time to do fun, carefree activities like: write in your journal, swing on a swing set, rest, or relax... you've earned it.

Carol Lozier, LCSW, is a psychotherapist in private practice; she specializes in helping foster and adopted children and families. She graduated from Florida State University in 1989 with a masters degree in social work. Visit her blog at www.fosteradoptchildtherapist.com.

The Power of Connecting

Whether it's online or off, the most powerful thing we can do for ourselves is to connect to other parents with shared experiences. Being able to talk in person or online to a mom or dad who has shared or is sharing similar parenting experiences can really make a difference. Ask your caseworker for local on the ground support groups, or join one online. Yahoogroups (found at yahoo.com) have a wide variety of groups to meet many specific family needs. Our favorite? Foster_parenting.

Find it at groups.yahoo.com/group/foster_parenting/

It's a topic driven group that changes topics regularly. There's lots of thoughtful discussion. Don't forget to keep the privacy requirements of your state when sharing any information online.

Other groups?

FosterCare Central
www.fostercarecentral.org

NFPA Foster Parent Forums
www.fosterparentforum.org

Adoption.com
www.forums.adoption.com/foster-parent-support/

Put Your Own Oxygen Mask First

By Susan Badeau

Parenting can be stressful.

Caring for our children can be difficult, draining, and exhausting. So, as the flight attendants on planes always remind us – we need to put our own oxygen masks on first if we expect to be able to help anyone else. Taking good care of ourselves is one of the most important skills we can develop as parents or caregivers. Yet, it is easy to let that slip to the bottom of our priority list in the face of the immediate demands facing us every hour, every day. When we neglect our own "internal thermometer" we often will find ourselves over or under reacting to situations in ways which come back to haunt us later on. Scientists teach us that the mind (brain), emotions, and body are all involved when we experience or respond to trauma or stress.

Sometimes, stress causes us to feel "hot and bothered" – our personal thermometer is totally out of whack and when that happens, we may become distracted, or respond out of the "heat of the moment" rather than out of rational thinking. Good self-care strategies can help prevent these meltdowns.

I am convinced that all parents, regardless of how their family came together, experience certain amounts of stress, and that self-care is a necessary component of all good parenting. Yet, I am also aware that parenting in the foster, adoptive, or kinship family brings with it additional and unique stressors that need special attention. Think about a "typical" family life cycle in the modern-day United States. Starting with a single "unattached" adult who eventually joins with a partner and becomes a couple. Children are added and the couple goes through many adjustments during the early years of parenting. Eventually, everyone is in the rhythm of their work-home-school lives for a number of years until the child moves through the teen years and starts to feel that "itch" for independence. Soon, the parents are "launching" their young adult children out into the world – perhaps to college, the military, jobs, independent single life, or marriage. The parents and their children develop a new level of relationship now that they are all adults.

Many of us may have experienced this cycle in our own relationships with our parents and siblings, and with some of our children. But we know that the circumstances that brought us into the world of foster, adoptive, or kinship care represent a variation on this cycle which can cause some shifting of expectations and transitions in roles. We don't typically get our children at the moment of birth. We don't always get to parent them through all the developmental stages through to adulthood. We have not experienced, with them, the developmental stages that came before their entry into our home. Their lives, and ours with them, are a constant swirl of change, and every change brings the possibility of added stress.

Throughout the years, I have identified the following six ways that people typically react to significant changes and stressors in their lives. These are not mutually exclusive, many times people will do two or more of these things in the face of a single change – in fact most of us will mix up our own personal recipe blending several of these possible "change reactions.".

Do nothing: Sometimes changes seem so overwhelming or beyond our control, that

I Cannot Give Away That Which is Not Mine to Give

I cannot provide peace, tranquility, and calm to a wounded child,
if I am not at peace and calm.

I cannot provide safety to a child, if I do not feel safe inside.

I must remember my child's eyes, before they were far away eyes,
before they looked right through me, before they were vacant.

I must remember that my child has seen what no child should have ever seen;
that my child has heard what no child should have ever heard;
that my child has felt what no child has ever felt.

I must remember that the lens through which my child sees life, love,
family, and relationship is not the same lens through which
I see life, love, family, and relationship.

My child comes from a land of hurt, shame, abuse, and neglect.
My land is foreign to her.

My child comes from a home of anger. My home is foreign to her.

My child comes from a life of fear. My love is foreign to her.

We simply cannot expect our children to move into our worlds when we cannot
spare a few moments to join them in theirs.

We simply cannot expect our children to trust us, because we say so.
Many before us have said many things.

We simply cannot expect our children to obey us, because we are right.
They have been wronged too many times prior to our right.

If we are to become the conduit to healing such pain
in wounded children, we must first heal ourselves.
We simply cannot give away that which is not ours to begin with.

Peace,
Juli Alvarado
Foster Mom
www.coaching-forlife.com

we simply cannot or do not react. Or some people have a laid back personality and take a "go with the flow" approach to change.

Rebel or protest: Some of us just don't like change. Period. We dig in our heels, get mad, refuse to budge and say "No way, not me, I'm not going there." – We spend a lot of energy protesting the change at hand.

Seek calming or comforting: It's a ***very normal*** reaction during times of stress and change to need to be soothed, comforted. Why do we call certain foods "comfort foods?"

Ask for help: This is actually less common – it is often hard for people to ask for help until the situation becomes a crisis.

Try to fix the problem: Many of us have never met a problem we didn't want to solve. Problem solving skills are essential to successful parenting in any family, including foster, adoptive and kinship families.

Adjust, internally: This is a high level skill and one that many of us struggle with. It goes beyond the external work of fixing the problem to some internal work and often means changing the way we think.

These varied approaches to coping with change and stress became real for me as we welcomed four school-age siblings, each a year apart into our home. Prior to joining our family, these children had experienced abuse and neglect during the years in their birth family home and then four years in more than seven foster care placements. They had multiple exposures to trauma during these years. When they arrived in our family, they each presented a different coping mechanism.

Franny, the youngest, was the soother. She sucked her thumb, twirled her hair, rocked and found other ways to soothe herself.

Geoff, next in line, was the rebel. He protested every chance he had – acting out at home and at school, even throwing a school desk out the window on one occasion.

Sylvia, the oldest girl, was the nurturer and fixer. She wanted everything to be better and everyone to be happy. She mediated arguments, did extra chores, braided her sister's hair, got all A's.

Marcus, the oldest, adjusted. He didn't want to make waves. He settled in and fit into each new foster home and school and including our family like he was born there. He was a chameleon.

For their part, many of the adults around the children throughout the years were in the "do-nothing" category. Act like everything is normal and it will be so. But slowly, in our home, we decided to try the "ask for help" approach and as a result of this modeling, the children began to learn to ask for help too.

Learning to ask for help is an important part of what I will call the "Self-Care ToolKit." I tend to think of each tool in this toolkit as a "stress buster" – and the toolkit needs a variety of types of tools – including those designed to prevent stress and emotional burnout, as well as those required to help with the healing from difficult emotions that accompany caring for our children and teens.

Our family has taken many road-trips and camping trips through out the years. One thing I have learned is that when you take a trip, you better take along a really good toolkit. You know, when we set out to drive from the East Coast to the West, through hills and valleys, big cities and small towns, highways and dirt roads, we needed to learn that we would experience flat tires, we would get lost, the air conditioner would quit, and so on. We needed a good toolkit. So here are some of the tools that I have learned to put in my own personal "self-care" toolkit and maybe it will help you to think about what goes into yours.

Into my toolkit goes touch and affection, a whole box of different communication styles, a lot of anger management techniques and stress relievers, a set of advocacy weights to pump, a boatload of jokes, and laughter, a bottle to collect my tears, and friends to share the journey with – its my AAA plan – and all of these tools going into a "toolbox" provides the safety net I need to dare to set out, one more time, on a new leg of the journey.

When developing your own "self care toolkit," don't forget to think of multiple outlets that use your mind, body, and emotions. Sometimes it helps to be with other people in a social or supportive situation, other times a little time alone can be just what the doctor ordered. Know yourself and what situations require which kinds of supports. I have also noticed that sometimes the tools that work well for women are not the same as those that work for most men, or for people raised in different decades. Also, race, culture, ethnic and religious traditions may play a part in guiding what kinds of "stress busters" are most effective for each of us. So don't let anyone else dictate what should or shouldn't go in your personal toolkit. As long as your "tools" are not self-destructive or harmful to others, they can work for you even if they don't make it on your friends – or pastor's, or therapist's, or caseworker's lists of suggested tools.

A "self-care toolkit" should include some of the kinds of activities we can engage in as often as daily (walking the dog, reading, prayer, exercise), some that are less frequent but still regular like weekly or monthly (date night with our spouse or partner, book club, bowling night, getting nails done, etc), others that are reserved for special occasions (vacation, retreat, conference) and finally those few things we might have handy to employ "whenever" there is a need for a brief break (listening to favorite music, deep breathing, cup of tea, call a supportive friend, punch a punching bag). Don't forget to nurture your own adult relationships and find opportunities for laughter and play.

By creating and then using our own self-care toolkit, we will not only be better equipped to care for our children, but we will also be modeling for them one of the most important strategies they will need in life as they continue their journey of healing and wholeness.

Susan Badeau has worked for 33 years in child welfare and human services. She has developed curricula on many topics used to train child welfare professionals, adoptive and foster parents, judges, attorneys, and youth. She writes extensively on topics related to children and speaks frequently at conferences. She serves on several national boards and advisory committees related to the well-being of children and families, particularly those with special needs and challenges.Sue and her husband, Hector, are the lifetime parents of 22 children, two by birth and 20 adopted. More information about Susan and her family can be found on the family website, created by their daughter Chelsea, at www.badeaufamily.com.

Bring Me Hope: Foster Parenting Through Tough Times

By Terra Trevor

The blue dress reminded me of the kind of silk my great grandmother used to trim her blankets. Seventeen-year-old Eva stood at the edge of the dressing room drowsy with possibilities. I bury the thoughts about the sensible everyday clothes we were "suppose" to buy. The results of sensibility, I reminded myself, were the white Bermuda shorts purchased two summers ago, which were never worn.

"Can I buy this dress?" Crow black hair fell folded into the small of her back, and the Morning Glory blue material rippled like wind walking across grass. I nodded my head yes, and her face lit with a thousand-watt grin. Two seconds later her smile faded. "But what if something happens and I do something bad, will I still get to keep the dress?"

"Honey, there is nothing you could ever do that would cause me to take this dress away from you. It will be yours no matter what." Unlike my son and youngest daughter who needed to be held lightly, this child needed to test the strength of my grip. Perhaps there is no adequate description for some older foster children whose trust has been damaged time and time again. This kind of love needs to stay molten. In its lifetime it will often need to be thrown back into the fire, recast, reshaped.

When we arrive home she puts the dress on again, and leans hard into the mirror's reflection, pushing aside all that thick black hair. The mail arrives bringing me the latest issue of a newsletter featuring foster kids in need of a family. I glance at the photos of waiting children. Lisa's high-cheeked face stares at me. She is eight, and has experienced extreme neglect in her birth family. An athletic girl, Lisa enjoys sports, and she also likes to cook and bake, but she can be bossy, and stubborn. It says a two-parent family, where at least one parent is Native American is needed; that she'd do best in a family experienced in parenting children who have been abused and neglected.

I'm an instinctive mother with a lot of hard-won parenting experience, and my heart tells me they are looking for another mom like me, for I know what it is like to parent children whose needs are almost beyond my strength. I remember when I used to think that all a troubled child needed was to be brought into a loving family and be loved. Now I know better. Eva came to me at age eleven, after years in multiple foster placements. Although we eventually adopted her, the word forever when it came to family was a source of anguish for her. She was a smart girl, beautiful, with a loving heart, but also with unresolved emotional and behavioral problems stemming from abuse, deprivation, and rejection in early and middle childhood.

When she was first placed with us, my husband and I must have reflected the ability to provide an older child with guidance, our household a place to truly experience family. We liked children and enjoyed the challenge of parenting. Most importantly, we knew that children didn't say thank you. But we were verbally bright, well-read, without a shred of practical parenting experience to prepare us for what was coming. We had years of what felt like at the time as getting-no-where counseling. Never one to waste money, or admit defeat, I spent those sessions discovering my own thorns – we all have them.

There is much agreement that same race, same culture placements offer children the best opportunity for a connection to their own heritage. Yet, the child we received had been so abused and neglected, she didn't feel a connection to anything or anyone. In the world as I've come to know it, emotionally healthy families of all races and cultures have similar characteristics. The side effects of abuse are also pretty much the same in every culture.

Because of strong ties to my own Native American community, I firmly believe we need to outline specific steps to ensure cultural ties do exist within a foster family. But I also believe a person of any race and culture, who is willing to make a racial and cultural commitment, can be a good foster parent to kids from any racial ethnicity. Too often race and culture are in the forefront while less effort is spent preparing new foster parents about the child's past living experiences. In our daughter's case, her days were spent alone, watching endless hours of television. At eleven, she could barely read and write. Because she was the youngest in the majority of her previous placements, contact with members of her own peer group was something she had little experience with prior to being placed in our family.

Foster parenting an older child requires a strong support system throughout the parenting years. You must teach yourself to work at creating positive memories. Learn to think of parenting your child as a relationship waiting to be built rather than a wall needing to be torn down. It's important to be aware of common behavioral problems of older children, who have lived in multiple placements, and to find a therapist and begin family counseling – before you need it. I stress this because once the new child becomes an "identified patient" in the family; it takes much longer to get to the root causes of the emotions they experienced with birth and foster family members prior to becoming placed within your family. It is better to establish family counseling soon after an older child arrives, even if everything is going smoothly, so that everyone in the family has equal opportunity to learn and grow together, rather than waiting until a difficulty surfaces.

Give up any notion you might have of changing your child's personality into your ideal. Instead, meet them where they are. Find the good and praise it, and chances are on some days that child will rise to your standard. Most days you won't be as lucky, so be kind to yourself. Treat yourself as you would a beloved aunt or uncle, and the ripple effect of love you show yourself will have a trickling down effect on the children within your household.

For older kids who have experienced much loss, those losses and abandonment issues will surface at holidays, on anniversaries, and at other times when we least expect it. Milestone events bring out an old sadness (ones that we usually don't even know about) and it gets mixed up in our current family life, and masked sadness often surfaces as anger.

Still, there are those of us bound for the older foster child placement trail. We saddle up, and get ready to ride. Violet water bathes our thoughts of what could be. Lisa, the child in my mind's eye, learning to accept the consequences of her behaviors, tenderly loved, dancing in a beam of sunlight, with a billow of fringed jersey shall around her. This time I know the dream giver comes to me not with a child, but instead with this story.

Terra Trevor is a contributing author of 10 books. Her memoir, ***Pushing up the Sky****, is widely anthologized with excerpts included in* ***Children of the Dragonfly: Native American Voices on Child Custody and Education****, and in* ***Birthed from Scorched Hearts****. With her husband she raised three children who are now grown. In addition to writing, Terra has worked at a group home and youth crisis shelter with runaway, homeless, and foster youth in transition.*

A Knock at the Door: Recognizing Depression

By Karen J. Foli, Msn, PhD, RN

Loss. The word seems to echo through us when we say it aloud and resonant in our hearts when we experience it. Many people who work in the areas of adoption, foster parenting, and the placement of children outside their birth homes feel immersed in loss.

The child certainly has experienced extensive loss, although it varies in intensity and duration. Birth parents, whose children have been removed, lose the right to parent their child for a period of time, and many times have lost their ability to regulate their body's physical needs, their ability to control their emotions, and the direction of their lives.

And you, the foster parent, open the door to say "good-bye" as often as "hello" as each child passes through. With good-byes, a bit of relief, ambivalence, joy, anger, or loss may be felt, depending on the depth of your attachment. You have become the sponge, the confidante, the person who is supposed to be strong, perhaps stoic. You are the person who is sought out to help, when help is really needed. On one level you offer a primal assistance: to care for a child's basic needs, such as shelter, sustenance, and necessities for living, such as clothes. On a different level, you meet the needs of the soul: love, concern, advocacy, information, hope, faith, and much more. You are a chameleon of caring, changing what you have to offer the child in order to meet changing needs as the child grows more trusting of you and as each new face walks through your door.

A Cup of Coffee and a Piece of Pie

From the primal to the personal, you support, nurture, feed the children. This was made clear to me a long time ago when I was a student nurse and enrolled in my community health course. Each student was assigned a family in the community to follow, to assess their needs, and to compose a plan of care for that family. My family happened to be a foster family, with several birth children, one of whom was a little girl in the third grade with spina bifida (an incomplete closure of the spinal cord). The little girl with brown, magnified eyes that peered out from her thick lenses was paralyzed from the waist down, mildly mentally handicapped, and required urinary catheterization several times per day. After many years, I still remember her sweet innocence and patience with my awkwardness.

My entrée into the family was tentative, influenced by my fear more than by their unwillingness to let me in. But it was clear that the mother was the gatekeeper, the one who guided, instructed, and in general kept the family functioning. By the end of the semester, I had identified the father's hypertension, the unhygienic practices of the school staff who catheterized the girl midday (and which had led to numerous urinary tract infections), and had spent several hours with the mom, who continues to inspire me with her ability to carve out a balance in her life. Although busy with several foster children, one an infant, a daughter with severe disabilities, and a husband with a chronic health condition, she managed to understand how necessary it was to – for lack of better words – continue to heal from what life tended to throw at her.

Knowing resources were scarce, she accomplished this in an ingenious way: she walked to a small diner about half a mile from her home and ordered a cup of coffee and a piece of pie. My youth blinded me to what value she was getting for her money, that it wasn't mere crust with some fruit, and water mixed with ground java beans that she was receiving. Sitting at a chair and lingering at a table and murmuring a few words here and there to others allowed her to then stand, and push the stroller back home, fix dinner, and greet the children under her care. It was time without distractions, to sit, to be waited upon, and to enjoy tastes and sips. While the setting wasn't as exotic as Italy or Spain, it was enough.

She had fought depression in the past, she told me, and knew that she was vulnerable to it. Again, my youthful mind was unable to comprehend what she communicated to me. Today, I do. Today, I know that depression can appear suddenly or slowly, with an insidious, shadowy growth. It can make you feel that you are physically sick and so very, very sad.

Signs and Symptoms of Depression

The signs and symptoms of depression are important to know. According to the Diagnostic and Statistical Manual (Fourth Edition), the book that professionals use to diagnose individuals, the signs and symptoms of depression include[1]:

- A depressed mood; feeling sad or empty
- Loss of interest or pleasure
- Significant (unintended) weight loss or weight gain
- Difficulty sleeping or wanting to sleep all the time
- Feeling like you can't sit still/restless, or feel like you're slowed down/can't physically get going
- Fatigue or loss of energy
- Feelings of worthlessness or excessive guilt
- Diminished ability to think or concentrate or indecisiveness
- Recurrent thoughts of death or thinking about suicide/acting on these thoughts

*Five of the nine symptoms above should be present for the past two weeks and at least one of these five symptoms should include depressed mood or loss of interest or pleasure.

What To Do

First, it's important to ensure that physical problems aren't the real contributors to the symptoms above, so a visit to your primary care provider is the first step. For example, hypothyroidism may contribute symptoms that mimic or contribute to symptoms of depression.

Second, by helping yourself, you're helping those you care about the most. Years of research make one point clear: when a parent struggles with depression, the children are also negatively affected. As a foster parent, you need to make sure there is enough of "you" to meet the constant needs of others. When you struggle, others will be affected. The sooner you reach out for help, the better – for everyone's sake.

Third, reset your internal voice: it's not selfish to want a balance in your life. Knowing your limits isn't easy, especially when the need for foster parents is so great. While gentleness is often given by way of a tender touch, a soft word of encouragement, an acceptance of an apology from others, we often withhold it from ourselves. Humans make mistakes. At times, they lose their tempers, find trust in another difficult to extend, and become so tired. Sometimes forgiving yourself is the most important step to finding help.

Four, share what you're experiencing with a trusted individual, perhaps a significant other or a mental health professional. Expression of thoughts and feelings to an individual can assist in making sense of what you're experiencing, add perspective, and link you to resources that you might not have been aware of.

Five, help build a support system through sharing and education. Many parents – birth, foster, adoptive – have found virtual support networks and groups to be useful. Books such as this one are also of great benefit in learning about beneficial ways to cope and decreasing the sense of isolation that can come with depression.

Six, if you feel yourself losing control, seek help immediately. Don't hesitate to call for assistance if you feel you've entered a place where you know you need professional intervention. The safety of yourself and the children under your care is Number One Priority.

These six points are by no means inclusive. Often, the severity, duration, and depressive symptoms you experience will guide what will be the most helpful to you. Remember, you have learned to be a chameleon of caring for others. Extend some of that care to yourself – everyone will benefit if you do.

*Karen J. Foli, MSN, PhD, RN, is an assistant professor at the Purdue University School of Nursing in West Lafayette, Indiana. She is the co-author of **The Post-Adoption Blues: Overcoming the Unforeseen Challenges of Adoption** (Rodale, 2004) and is currently conducting research that examines depression in adoptive parents. Karen has been interviewed by journalists from **The New York Times, The Philadelphia Inquirer,** and **O! The Oprah Magazine** for articles discussing post-adoption "blues" and/or depression.*

Footnote:

[1] American Psychiatric Association (2000). *Diagnostic and Statistical Manual of Mental Disorders*, Fourth Edition, Text Revision. Washington, DC: American Psychiatric Association.

Respite Works for Everyone

By Stacey Leidner

What is respite? Respite is a temporary break, given to caretakers, that provides a period of rest and renewal. The respite guide, ***Taking a Break: Creating Foster, Adoptive and Kinship Respite in Your Community***, is intended to help parent support group leaders develop and provide respite programs to the families in their communities, or to partner with public agencies in their program development and implementation.

Respite care is a much needed service for all families, especially foster, adoptive, and kinship families. Scheduling time for respite allows primary caregivers an opportunity to plan activities and most importantly, it helps to keep families from becoming overwhelmed by their many ongoing responsibilities. It is imperative for all families to take time to refuel and re-energize.

Parents can utilize different respite providers as caretakers for their children. However, for children in foster care, finding respite caretakers can sometimes be challenging. All respite caretakers must have thorough background checks completed, which includes finger printing, to provide respite for foster children.

Some of the children in foster care have emotional, behavioral, or medical challenges. Respite caretakers for these children need extra training to work with the many challenges these children may have.

Respite is not only a great opportunity for primary caregivers, but it is just as important for the children in foster care. Often when the children are in respite, they are able to build healthy relationships with other children in foster care, pursue a special interest, or have fun doing an activ-

The respite manual outlines step-by-step guidelines for developing any type of respite care program and includes sample forms that groups can use in the day-to-day operation of their program.

Sample forms:

* Respite Billing
* Emergency Service Authorization
* Emergency Care Information
* Child Information
* Family Care & Provider List
* Primary Caregiver Information
* Group Care Information
* Parent Checklist
* Payment Agreement
* Event Evaluation
* Recreational Respite Evaluation
* Respite Provider Agreement
* Training Evaluation
* Respite Fact Sheet
* Committee Meetings

Download the guide here
www.adoptuskids.org/resourceCenter/publications/respiteManual.aspx

ity they enjoy. They get the opportunity to build onto their social skills and self-esteem. This allows them to learn to trust others and to trust that the caregiver is going to come back to pick them up. This is often important for children who are in foster care because many have often been abandoned by people earlier in life and they fear they will be left again. Ultimately, respite leads to healthier families and less placement disruptions.

The respite guide has three major sections. The first section is devoted to exploring the benefits of respite. These include: (1) allowing the caregiver to get some much needed free time, (2) a decrease in child abuse and neglect, and (3) a decrease in disrupted placements. One adoptive parent quotes, "Now, 10 years later and after adopting six more children, we know when we keep ourselves healthy we can help our children heal and bond to our family. If we let ourselves get so drained we have nothing to give our children, we are in fact letting them down. Our health and the health of our marriage have to be intact so we can be a good parent to our children."

If we let ourselves get so drained we have nothing to give our children, we are in fact letting them down. Our health and the health of our marriage have to be intact so we can be a good parent to our children.

Although the respite is beneficial to families and children it is not always available. First of all, one must also find a provider who can properly and safely care for the child. It is important for the family and the child to feel comfortable with the provider, so the experience does not feel like punishment for the child, and that it is a wholesome and positive experience for all.

The second section of the guide explores the various respite care options that might be developed for families. There are several model respite programs around the country. The models are designed to inform parent support group leaders about the programs that are available and helps them develop a program that is right for their families. What works in one area may not work in another area. There is also an emphasis placed on the parent groups conducting a needs assessment. This allows the parent group leaders to receive feedback from the families regarding the types of respite the families need.

The Continuum of Respite Care is based on the needs of the families. Respite can include in-home care which allows the child to stay in his or her own home and have a trusted adult come to the home. Group child care is another option and it allows the child to go to a daycare center with other children while the parent is at a parent group meeting.

Special interest and mentor relationship experiences are also a great option. These include the child being involved in an activity that they enjoy such as sports, music or Girl Scouts. Camps can also provide a planned form of respite care. Camps can be day-long, overnight, weekend, or week-long. It is up to the family and what the family needs are to determine what type of program would be best.

Therapeutic care is another option available to families. This is a much more restrictive type of respite care that is provided by trained professionals or experienced caregivers.

Again, it is all based on the needs of the child and the family.

The final section of the guide shows the applicant how to develop a plan. Using the parent assessment tool, parent group leaders would design their respite program. Additionally, applicants are provided the guidance to ensure they have addressed all the legal requirements for a respite program. Finally, this section emphasizes how important it is for the provider of respite care to form a good relationship with the public child welfare agencies in the jurisdiction of the program.

The group leaders must also determine the number of children to be served, the type of respite program desired, how often families can request the services, how many staff members are needed and where the program will be housed. With the plan outlined, the budget can and must be developed. Last but not least, once a provider receives a grant, they will need to locate and train respite care providers.

Evaluations are a must. They are important for the group leader to gather information from the group to find out if the program met their expectations and needs, and to determine if the program should continue.

The evaluation is also a good way for people to share their ideas and discuss any changes they would like to see in the program. The evaluation can be done by survey, interview or just general conversation.

Finally, the Respite Guide also provides forms that groups can use for their program. Medical history, billing information, authorization forms, and child information forms are a few examples of the forms that are included in the guide.

Additionally, there are also several organizations and websites listed that can provide additional resources to the respite groups.
www.adoptuskids.org/resourcecenter/atcpublications.aspx.

Stacey Leidner began her career in child welfare 10 years ago. After graduating from college, she worked at a group home for children with severe emotional disabilities for four years. There she gained significant experience with and knowledge of the children in foster care. She met a child she adored so much she brought him home to provide him with a family. Although he no longer lives with her, she is his family and he is her son. For the past seven years she has worked at AdoptUsKids. Her work with the families and the children is quite rewarding and it has been a learning experience. She has been a mentor for another child for the last four years and she is a foster mother to two little boys. This was originally published in ***Fostering Families Today****.*

Taking Advantage of Respite Foster Care

By Carrie Craft

One of the things we have enjoyed doing during our years of being foster parents is offering respite care. "Respite," as it's commonly called, gives us a chance to meet other kids on a short-term basis while giving foster parents a short break from fostering. Usually respite is only for a weekend, but we have had the children for as long as 10 days or more while a foster family went on vacation.

One such respite adventure didn't go as smoothly as either party would have liked. There weren't enough diapers or clothing provided, and the dates for pick-up were off by 24 hours. This resulted in much stress for both me, as the respite provider, and the family who needed the break. ***If we all would have followed a few pointers this respite could have been a true break for the foster family in need and smoother for us as the respite providers.***

Setting Up and *Finding* Respite

The first step, of course, is setting up the respite weekend. A good rule of thumb is to initiate this about two weeks prior to the days you are seeking off. If the desired dates fall during a holiday weekend, then start talking to your social worker well before two weeks. This gives your worker time to locate another foster family who can provide the respite. If you happen to locate your own respite provider, be sure to clear it with your worker first.

> ***Each foster care agency handles respite foster care differently. Ask your social worker who locates the respite provider. Can you utilize a family member? Does the family member need a quick background check first? If you can locate your own respite provider, here are a few ideas on great places to look:***
>
> - ***Church***
> - ***Your family***
> - ***Friends***
> - ***Other foster families you've met at trainings or support groups***

Whether you are the seeker of respite or the provider, be sure to clarify drop off and pick up dates for the children when setting up the respite. This is where we made our mistake. I had the daycare calling me wondering why I hadn't picked up the children, while I was calling the foster mom who thought she was still on vacation. She was enjoying a bubble bath.

Make sure when preparing for respite to record any important appointments such as visits with birth family or therapy. Clarify with the foster family if these are appointments that need to be kept during respite. If not, then the foster family should be sure to reschedule any missed appointments for after the respite. We chose to keep the children in their routine of going to daycare, but some respite providers may not be able to run appointments or maintain a visitation schedule. If this is the case, it may be in the child's best interest to find another respite home. Talk to your social worker about any missed appointments.

Preparing the Child for Respite

It is common knowledge that multiple moves during a child's stay in foster care can be traumatic. Respite doesn't have to be a negative for a foster child. There are a few things we can do as fostering families to help children prepare for a weekend with another foster family.

- Try to visit the respite family before the overnight stay.
- Get some basic information about the family and share it with the child. Does the family have pets? Do they have other children? Have any special plans been made for the weekend? Share these fun facts with the child before the respite date. This allows the child time to process and ask questions about the upcoming stay.
- Allow the child to take a special stuffed animal or toy, but keep the number of special friends down to one or two. This will help prevent missing items and the respite provider will have fewer items to keep track of, thus leading to fewer headaches.
- If dealing with a sensitive child or a longer respite break, consider packing a little photo album for the child. Include pictures of birth family, foster family, friends, and pets in the book.
- When packing for the child, be sure to include enough underwear, socks, night clothes, and toiletry items. If sending a younger child for respite, be sure to pack adequate diapers, wipes and formula for the stay.

Being a Great Respite Provider

I have been known to snub respite opportunities. Yes, I know, not a great way to avoid burnout. But in my defense, I have sent great kids off to respite on a Friday, only to have returned on a Sunday to pick up the remnants of former great kids. It became too big of a stressor to have to deal with behaviors afterward. Respite weekends are supposed to be relaxing, not taxing. Here are some ideas on how to be a great respite provider.

- Try to keep any schedule or routine as outlined by the foster family. For example, if the foster family has a set bedtime for a child, try to adhere to the bedtime. It may be difficult when a fun Saturday night has been planned, and that is perfectly understandable. But, when it comes to longer stays, following a routine becomes more critical. This is particularly true for toddlers and infants.
- Remember the sensitivities of some foster children due to past abuse or neglect. If the foster family shares that the child has certain fears, remember these fears. Some of my past foster children were treated with a screening of the movie "Scream." Needless to say that came back to haunt us, literally.
- Remember medication and to keep any needed medication logs. It wouldn't be foster care without paperwork.
- Confirm the dates of respite. For example, if you are to do respite from the fourth to the seventh, does that mean that the child stays the night of the seventh or is picked up on the seventh? Also remember to clarify pick up and drop off locations.
- Have fun and plan activities for the kids, but don't feel that you have to turn your

weekend into a trip to Disneyland. Trips to the park, rented movies with popcorn, or just free time with a new group of friends can be a hit. Simple is great!

- Throw in some added perks if the mood strikes you. I often do the children's laundry so that they return to their foster family with clean clothes. Who likes to return home to more laundry? I have received many compliments on my mini-laundry service.

Respite Information Packet

One of the perks of fostering is meeting new fostering families and learning new things. One of the best things I learned from a foster family was how to make a respite information packet. It was a simple gallon sized zip-lock baggy that contained all the needed and critical information on the foster child.

How to make a respite information packet:

- One large zip-lock baggy.
- Typed list of the child's basic information: full name, birth date, social security number, foster family's name and numbers, social worker's name and number, doctor's contact information, and any other emergency numbers.
- Any daily schedule, especially helpful for little ones. Include fears, noted behaviors, likes, dislikes, allergies, and appointments.
- Medical card and consent to treat.
- Medication instructions, medication log, and medication bottles.
- Latest physical.

Now, whenever I am ready for a break, my packet is already made. I just update it with any appointments or medication changes, throw in the medication bottles and we're ready to go. This packet is also great when heading out to a doctor appointment or other meetings where information needs to be shared.

Some days it seems like a short walk from sane to insane. Thus, we have respite. So, once you find great respite providers to work with, start a list of those you can call on as needed, especially those who stick with your schedule and work to keep your foster children on track.

If it's been a long week and the weekend just can't get here fast enough, take a break from the issues and drama of foster care and get back to basics. Get some rest! You have earned it. I know you have, you're a foster parent.

Carrie Craft first saw the need for foster care in 1996 while working at the Wichita Children's Home. She and her husband, Matt, began fostering for the state of Kansas in 1977 two months after the birth of their daughter, Jordon. Craft, Matt and Jordon adopted three teen/pre-teen brothers – Gary, Alan, and Christopher in 2002. Craft has been the guide for adoption and foster care on About.com since 2004. She also trains foster/adoptive parents in Kansas on various issues that affect their families and the children they parent. She can be reached at adoption@about.com or visit her on the web at adoption.about.com.

Shifting Gears Gracefully

By Cheryl Petersen

"Can you go get Tina, now?" The social worker asked me over the phone.
I mentally shook off my plans for the day and told the social worker,
"Yes, I will go pick her up right now."

As a licensed foster parent, I was often called to provide respite care. In this case, Tina and her foster parents were not getting along. I was told that exasperation had escalated terribly, to the point where they needed a break from one another, starting right now. Tina would stay with us until things cooled off.

Tina was a few months away from turning 18, when she would begin living on her own. The social workers were preparing her for the move. But in the meantime, her behavior at home insinuated, loudly and obnoxiously, that she should not be treated as a child, and not be told what to do. She could take care of herself. Needless to say, the foster parents were drained. Counseling, talking, reasoning, all went down the garbage shoot.

Privileges had already been taken away from Tina. Tina got madder. So, in retaliation, she threw her cell phone on the ground instead of handing it over to the parents reasonably. The atmosphere in the home was unbearable.

While driving over to the home, I thought, "This is a typical example of human logic with one person's "logic" being "illogical" to another person. This is because people interpret things differently – filtering new information through their own human experiences and knowledge."

Probably, Tina's foster parents knew Tina needed to learn better self-discipline because she would be on her own soon. But, Tina knew she had already survived being passed around from home to home

– without her consent or willingness

– and so now figured she was ready to prove she can live on her own, make her own decisions. Their logic and therefore their realities were conflicting. However, humanity has the ability to put aside the logic built on melodrama. We can connect with a spirit that communicates an inspired logic built on the reality of Love. From ***21st Century Science and Health***,"[Love] is true, and interprets reality to us."

When I arrived at the foster home, we introduced ourselves. I was told that Tina needed to be chauffeured to her part-time job at McDonalds during the next few weeks. And that was about it for talk. Resentment and sadness spoiled any further conversation. Tina got in the car with me, which was a good sign, unlike a runaway. I told her we lived on a farm. Then, she started talking, basically reaffirming the thinking that she can take care of herself and her foster parents had no right to think she couldn't.

Then, I impressed her. Not with words, but with an action. I took her to the shopping mall – a privilege she had taken away. She thought I was cool.

Tina was impressed enough not to get fiercely angry with me. Because I didn't take her to the mall to shop or hang with her friends, but to support her logic that she can take care of herself, which she knew required getting another job. Her surprise fed her willingness. She filled out half a dozen applications and spoke with managers, discovering it isn't all that easy to get another job.

Just before she reached a point of frustrated disappointment, I said, "Let's go home."

We drove up to our house on the farm. I said little, just listened. Until Tina asked me about TV. I told her, "Oh, we don't have TV reception on the farm." Her face went white with shock. No TV!

But without a TV to add to her brain already full, Tina had the opportunity to quiet down. Tina began telling me her dreams as we put her stuff in her room. As we started making cookies from scratch, I reminded her we weren't allowed to bad talk her family. Tina was a good gal — smart, lovely, and strong. Her part-time job at McDonalds was going well, and she had just finished high school; except she would not get her diploma if she didn't return a school book. Tina did not have a driver's license. And, maybe she was a little afraid about living on her own. But, so I didn't really hear her admit that, she changed the subject quickly and mentioned she was interested in law.

The next day, we returned the school book before I took her to McDonald's for work. I picked her up after work and took her to businesses where she could fill out more job applications. Her confidence was shifting from confidence in self-righteousness to poise in being a useful potential employee. When we got home, we asked my husband if we could borrow his farm pickup. He said, "Yes."

Tina and I spent hours driving around the farm, me teaching Tina how to shift gears and pay attention, her practicing the art of learning pleasantly. In the evening, she read the driver's license study book I had picked up while she was at work. Days later, she took and passed her test. Now, with a driver's permit, she chauffeured me around.

I had also made arrangements for her to spend a day with a lawyer. Tina was motivated now with the desire to do a good job, to learn, instead of proving other people were wrong about her. At the end of the career day, I went a bit early to pick her up. It was humbling to watch her behave as a mature young woman in a court room. When we got home she noticed the Father's Day card I had left on the table for her to send to her foster dad, who I know she wanted to forgive. She filled it out gracefully and we sent it off in the mail. A greater peace came over her.

Within a few more days the phone rang. "We know it's earlier than planned, but can we come pick you up? We want you to come home now," the foster parents said to Tina. She was ready. It was a beautiful moment.

Cheryl Petersen and her husband, Doug, were licensed foster parents in the state of Washington for 15 years. They have two grown daughters. Peterson is now a writer, and also works at a daycare. For more information, visit her web site at www.HealingScienceToday.com. This was originally published in ***Fostering Families Today****.*

Reunification, Adoption, & Beyond

"When you have come to the edge of all the light you have
And step into the darkness of the unknown
Believe that one of the two will happen to you
Either you'll find something solid to stand on
Or you'll be taught how to fly!" – Richard Bach

Foster Parents: A Barrier to Permanency?

By Bart and Claudia Fletcher

Most foster parents begin their journey with the desire to help children who have been hurt. Playing the unique role of "temporary provider" can become difficult when a child's parents' rights have been terminated and the child becomes legally free. Should the child be adopted? Is he or she better off staying in foster care with people he or she knows even if it is not legally "permanent?" Should an adoptive family be selected? Is adoption the only type of "permanency" there is? What is "permanency?" What do kids approaching the age of 18 require in their lives?

Pat O'Brien, founder of You Gotta Believe, an adoption agency in New York City, makes it clear in his trainings that kids need one adult who is permanently and unconditionally committed to them for life. Teens may not be ready for an adoption plan, but parents must be ready to make that commitment when the child, teen or even adult is ready. Many foster parents believe there is no difference between foster care and adoption, but there is – both for the parents and kids.

There is a difference for the parent who provides permanency through foster care or the parent who legally adopts a child or teenager. Parents who adopt accept legal responsibility for the child even as that child grows into adulthood. The children become their legal heirs. They assume all rights as if the child had been born to them. There is no other option, without great difficulty, to have this relationship legally dissolved prior to the child's 18th birthday.

A foster parent's role is distinctive. The custody of the foster child remains with the state, which is legally responsible for the child until the age of 18 or 21, varying by state. Foster parents receive compensation to provide care for the child until the age of legal adulthood, at which time they are legally free to cease providing care for the child. The whole concept of what has been called "permanent" foster care is really an anomaly; "foster" care is always for a specific, temporary time period, no matter how seemingly long its duration.

As far as the children are concerned, adoption claims a child in a way that is different from foster care. The claiming of adoption involves the parent saying, in more ways than one, "I want you to belong to me, carry my name if you wish, to be in my will, to have a relationship with me like my other children."

As an adoption professional, I have heard many horror stories about foster children who were told they were "a part of the family" and then discover, as time goes on, that they were not. For some it happened the day they were asked to move out because they had reached the age when the foster care compensation ceased. For another, it came years later when a wedding was taking place a great distance away, and the parents bought tickets for everyone in the family to attend but the former foster child.

There are many foster parents who will say, "My commitment to this child is no different than if I were to adopt them," to which I have to ask, "So why don't you adopt them?"

I am not suggesting every foster parent adopt every child in their care. There are a myriad of situations in which a child or teen does not want to be adopted. In that case, being open to adopting them when they are ready is an equal commitment to adopting now. There are other situations where no one else is willing to provide foster care or adopt the child, and in those cases being in foster care is certainly superior to a group home or residential treatment center, even if the permanent commitment does not exist.

There are several appropriate reasons not to adopt a difficult teenager who is in foster care. While no one wants to talk about the financial aspect, it is a fact that in many states, adoption ensures that a family's income will be reduced significantly.

Another serious concern is the number of services that will, upon finalization, become something fought for, instead of something automatically granted if the child is a ward of the state. Finally, potential child protection investigations become a possibility upon finalization. Adoptive parents, no longer "protected" by the social services system which selected them as foster parents, are often scrutinized or blamed for seeking the same services which had previously been built into the (former foster) child's case plan.

There are times when foster parents make valid decisions not to adopt. However, there are times when the adoptive home has parents who are willing to accept legal responsibility. It is in these situations where foster parents, unwilling to adopt, become barriers to adoption. During my seven years as a matching specialist, I have seen foster parents become barriers to adoption or sabotage many placements in several different ways:

1. Taking time to decide if they would like to adopt a child. In some cases, I have seen foster parents take 12 to 18 months following termination to decide if they wish to adopt. I understand the dilemma of that decision, as my husband and I have made it a number of times personally, but the decision must be made expeditiously. Extended time for decision making is a luxury the family may be able to afford, but it is not in the best interest of the child. In a case where the foster family decides to adopt, it has little impact on the child.

It is simply making legal what has already become an emotional reality. In cases of ploddingly slow deliberation when the foster family decides not to adopt, the child's social worker is now a year or more behind in the race to secure a permanent family. Every day the child grows older, it becomes increasingly more difficult to find an adoptive family for a child who has now lingered a year or more in what has become a temporary setting.

2. Exchanging current comfort for future impermanency by diligently convincing foster children that they would be better off living with their foster parents because they are "fine where they are." In this scenario the relative ease of the present compromises the opportunity for a lifetime parental commitment for the child. Since in many states, teens can choose whether or not they wish to be adopted at the age of 14, many foster parents encourage teens not to choose adoption. If the foster parents are committed to parenting these children for life, this issue is a moot point. All too often, well-intentioned foster parents eventually choose not to help the young adult navigate college, plan a wedding, or be grandparents to the grandchildren. This results in little disruption for the parents but significant setbacks for the former foster "child," now a young adult with no legal and little emotional recourse.

3. Communicating mixed messages to foster children headed to an adoptive placement. "If things don't work out with the family you're going to, you can always come back here," or even more blatantly, "If your behavior is really bad when you are there they will let you come back and live with me." I realize that this does not happen often, but it does happen. Creating an emotional environment in which a child wants to return to a foster home, or where he or she feels in some way a "need" to return to a foster home, is not in a child's best interest. Foster parents, unwilling or unable to provide permanency for a child, need to see beyond themselves to provide the closure the child will need to create a permanent bond with a forever family.

While I have experienced foster parents who have been barriers to permanency, I have, fortunately, witnessed many good examples of foster parents who are great assets when helping foster children transition into an adoptive home. They grieve appropriately, stay in touch, remain supportive, and free the children emotionally to bond with their adoptive family.

The permanency that adoption offers is in the best interest of a child, but it is perhaps even more significant as the child grows into young adulthood. Most children would do equally well in foster care as children, but they begin to need a parent when in their twenties and thirties.

If you are a foster parent who has made an unconditional commitment to your foster children for the remainder of your life, then formal adoption may be inconsequential. However, if you question your ability or willingness to be involved as the committed adult in that child's life on a permanent basis, your foster son or daughter deserves the benefit of your candid self-assessment.

If there is another family willing to provide a permanent commitment by building upon the care you have already provided the child, allow yourself the painful, freeing choice of letting him or her go. It may be the hardest thing you have ever done, but it may be the best thing you can do for this child, who will, sooner than you realize, become a young adult needing a permanent family connection in ways neither of you ever envisioned.

Bart and Claudia Fletcher are parents of 12 children, born between 1986 and 1998, 10 adopted domestically from the child welfare system and two adopted internationally from Guatemala. Bart is a United Methodist pastor, a board member for the Minnesota Association for Children's Mental Health, and a parent trainer for Mental Health Behavioral Aides. Claudia is an adoption worker for Permanent Family Resource Center and an adoption specialist for the Adopt America Network. They published their first book in 2009: ***Out of Many, One Family: How Two Adults Claimed Twelve Children through Adoption.*** *For more information, visit www.outofmanyonefamily.com. This was originally published in* ***Fostering Families Today.***

Post Reunification and Beyond

By Michael Weisberg

Seeing our foster children return to their mother was devastating. After four years in care, almost three years with us, our four and five-year-old foster sons no longer remembered living with their mother. They didn't want to go back. We didn't want to see them go, either. Their mother wasn't ready. Privately, one worker told us the boys wouldn't be safe.

The county's caseworker tried to put a positive spin on the lack of safety. She predicted that the boys' mother wouldn't be able to hold her family together for more than a few months, and then the boys would come back to us. "Hopefully," she told us, "they won't get hurt too badly." When I became a foster parent and envisioned helping a troubled family stay intact, I never imagined a reunification like this one.

Numb with grief and fear for the boys' safety, and clinging to the hope that the boys would soon come back, my partner and I went to our only meeting to discuss the reunification plan. The boys' mother treated us warmly that day, a dramatic turnaround from her hostility toward us throughout the preceding month. She was looking forward to achieving her goal of having her children with her, but she knew she was going to need help. As we sat around the big conference table with her, her partner, and too many caseworkers, our boys' mother asked us whether we would be willing to be part of her support network and continue to see the boys after their return.

Caseworkers had posed this question to us before, and it always felt unfair that they would ask us to hold this family together when the birth parent was supposed to stand on her own again and our job was supposed to be over. When the boys' mother asked us the same question, however, we welcomed her overture even as we questioned the wisdom of responding in kind.

To answer her, I explained that we had provided respite care to two other foster children who eventually returned to their mother, and we saw what happened when the foster mother helped the birth mother too much. The foster mother wound up keeping the kids all weekend every weekend. When the foster mother finally tried to back away, the birth mother got overwhelmed, and the family collapsed. We told our foster kids' mother that we definitely wanted to see the boys, but during our first few visits, we would want her to be present. We weren't going to provide her with respite until she showed that she could manage without our help. To our surprise, she told us that our concerns made sense.

The boys went back to their mother, and we didn't hear from them at first. After two weeks, we had a phone conversation. Then we all met at a park. The older boy's kindergarten was down the street, so I made sure we walked over to the building. He showed us his classroom window, and we looked inside. Our foster son needed to know that my partner and I knew where to find him.

More weeks went by, and the family was still intact. Before long, my partner suggested that the boys' mother let us take the boys every Sunday afternoon for swimming lessons that we would pay for. She agreed, and welcomed the break that we were giving her. After swimming lessons, we sometimes took the boys to visit some of their old friends or went out to dinner together. Periodically, we took the boys shopping, especially if they needed new sneakers. Buying things for the boys helped us make sure their needs were met. It also gave their mother a reason to stay in touch with us. As my partner's boss told us, "people always come back to money." Of course, we were still trusting the prediction that the boys would come back to live with us soon.

As months passed, we saw signs that the boys' family wasn't thriving, but the situation wasn't bad enough to trigger a removal. Eventually, a social worker from one of the voluntary agencies we worked with told us that we needed to start thinking about moving on with our lives. We couldn't live in a holding pattern waiting for the boys to come back to us. When I countered that the county's caseworker predicted that the boys would be back within a few months, the social worker answered that a few months had already passed. What's more, if the family moved across county lines again, the boys wouldn't come back to us even if they were taken back into care. At the least, the worker told me, we had to move on with our emotional lives. Another social worker took the issue a step further, saying, "you have to do something more sophisticated than that. You have to move on and still be available." A third social worker scoffed, "I don't think that's possible. Not just for you," he clarified. "For anybody."

The question of whether to stay involved with our foster sons or move on with our lives might have been more complicated if my partner and I had been committed to finding children to adopt, but adoption wasn't necessarily our goal. For me, I found it more meaningful to maintain an ongoing relationship with our now-former foster children than to sever that relationship in the hope of finding permanency with some other children. I considered what it would be like to "move on," but there was nothing I wanted to move on to. My attachment to the boys wasn't stopping me from doing anything else. When I told my partner that I preferred to stay involved with the boys and be a stable presence in their lives, my partner agreed.

Even so, sometimes it was hard to know whether the relationship would last. Although the boys' mother valued us as a support, she also found us threatening. So did some of the other adults in her innermost circle, and we never knew whether one person or another was encouraging her to push us away. Nobody answered the phone when we tried to call our older foster son to wish him a happy sixth birthday. When we finally saw him a month later, he told me that his mother saw our name on the caller ID and refused to answer. She also had no qualms about canceling the swimming lessons that she had told us we could pay for. Several times, we wondered whether the boys' mother had cut us off forever.

On the other hand, if she felt overwhelmed, the boys' mother would call us with no warning and ask us to take the boys for a few hours, overnight, or all weekend. Sometimes she would put our younger foster son on the phone, and we could hear her coach him to ask us to come get him because he missed us. Taking the boys under these conditions, we wondered whether we were just propping up a family that should be allowed to fall apart. Sometimes we claimed to be unavailable just to force the boys' mother to face the responsibilities of parenting.

Despite her struggles, the boys' mother surprised everyone and maintained custody of her children, but the situation wasn't good. We suspected that the caseworkers wanted us to stay involved with the boys in part so that we could keep tabs on whether they were still safe. As the county closed the family's case, we continued to pass information along to the county's legal department through our lawyer, who knew the county's attorneys well. In the most extreme circumstances, we called the child abuse hotline as several workers had instructed us.

We later found out we weren't the only people reporting serious safety issues regarding this family. Sixteen months after the boys left our home, they finally came back into care. Because the boys' relationship with us remained intact, the boys returned to our home pursuant to the county's policies. My partner and I went to work getting to know the boys' teachers and other providers and setting the boys up for all of the medical appointments they had missed. Because we knew the boys' histories, we were able to fill in gaps in the boys' stories for the providers who lacked information that they needed.

The boys have been living with us for ten months, and we still don't know what the future holds. All we can do is give the boys stability and a structured routine that encourages them to learn and grow. Even without an assurance of permanency, there's nothing else I'd rather do.

Michael Weisberg lives in upstate New York with his partner of 15 years and their two foster sons, who should finally be adopted by the time this book is published. They are all looking forward to reaffirming and making permanent the family relationship they have formed over the past six years.

A Second Chance for a Background

By William Cuchens

When our son, Isaac, came home as a sixteen-month-old foster child, my wife, Laurie, and I had to accept that whatever happened prior to him coming to us would remain a mystery. Unfortunately, all we ever learned were the names of his birth mother and his biological siblings.

At first, we wanted to know Isaac's history in order to better parent him and explain some of his behaviors. But we made do with the resources we had. We read books on toddler adoption, got involved with other foster and adoptive parents, and sought advice from doctors, play therapists, and behavioral specialists. After only a few months in our home, Isaac quickly bonded with us and caught up on his development.

Then our curiosity shifted and we wanted to provide him some background for his own sake. In our foster and adoptive parents' playgroups and support groups, parents shared stories about their children asking about their birth parents. Some kids grieved the loss of their former family while other children couldn't have cared less. Laurie and I knew that a relationship with Isaac's birth family was unrealistic. But we wished we had some pictures or maybe even a letter or a card – something that would make them real people rather than simply names on pages of official court documents.

Nevertheless, Laurie and I made our peace with the mystery of Isaac's birth family. We adopted him just after his second birthday and his baby sister, Vivianna, was born four months later. As we developed an open adoption with Vivi's birth mother, Laurie and I prepared ourselves for any potential questions or grief Isaac might have watching his sister look at pictures, read cards, and even play with birthday and Christmas presents from her birth family. We expected this to one day bother Isaac. But what we did not expect was the phone call we got from his former caseworker on a warm June morning, informing us that Isaac had a younger brother who had just entered foster care.

"We want to place him with you as a kinship placement," the caseworker said.

Laurie called me at work to tell me. "I told her I'd have to talk to you," she said.

It took me less than two seconds to say absolutely. "I told the caseworker you'd immediately say yes," she said. "But can you believe it? Isaac has a little brother!"

Laurie called the caseworker back and learned that J had been in foster care for more than a week and that he and his birth mother had already had one visitation meeting. Moreover, the caseworker had supervised the meeting and took pictures of J and the birth mother he shared with Isaac.

When I got home that night, I sat at the computer and watched the slideshow with Laurie sitting next to me. I saw little two-year-old J playing a toy piano in baggy blue clothes. His skin complexion and forehead matched Isaac. "That's him?" I said to Laurie. She nodded.

I clicked on the next picture and saw a woman feeding him out of a fast food bag. "That's her?" I said to Laurie. She nodded.

The next few weeks passed like molasses. J's caseworker required a homestudy on us before she could place him, which took two additional weeks to approve. Finally, six weeks after entering foster care, the caseworker brought Isaac's two-year-old brother to our home.

Friends donated a bunk bed for the boys to share, which they loved almost immediately. In fact, I had to forbid use of the ladder within five minutes of assembling it.

J adapted to our routine quickly. He ate nearly everything we put on his plate and slept soundly. He had a limited vocabulary, which developed quickly under the influence of an older brother and sister. Both Isaac and Vivi accepted him immediately, with Vivi telling everyone within earshot, "He baby brudder." She followed him around the house all day asking him, "You come play in my room?" At three years old, she's only nine months older than he and they make a great pair. She suggested her favorite games – princess dolls and makeup – and he complied unconditionally.

Meanwhile, Isaac accepted his role as the protective big brother. He worked diligently to teach J the word "gentle." From the other side of the house, we heard Isaac shout, "No, J. Gentle with the dogs" or "gentle with Vivi's hair." Then, as Vivi rushed to tattle on him, Isaac shouted, "No, Vivi. Don't tell Mom and Dad." We thought it's sweet that Isaac didn't want him to get in trouble.

People often asked us whether we're going to adopt J. When we said we hope so, their follow-up question was, "Aren't you afraid of the effect it might have on the kids if he leaves?"

It's a legitimate question, one their mother and I took seriously. Ultimately, even if we knew he wouldn't stay with us permanently, we still never could have turned him away. He is our family too. If he leaves, we'll be devastated and mourn losing him and what could have been. Then, once time has passed, we'll look back on the time we spent with J and the pictures we have of Isaac's birth mother and brother and find comfort that at least we have that.

On the other hand, if we do get to adopt him, then one day Laurie and I will have a great story to tell. We'll share with the boys that we were told their birth mother was thrilled when she found out they had been united.

J came home almost a month ago. So we have no idea what's going to happen to him in the long term. But we're grateful for the memories we got to build with J in our lives, moments like Isaac's first day of kindergarten with us, Isaac's sixth birthday. We had spent years praying for a letter or a photo from his birth family. We didn't expect we'd get another son.

William Cutchens and his wife, Laurie, became foster parents in 2006 and fostered four children. Isaac, the second, they adopted just after his second birthday. A few months later, Vivi, whom they adopted from a private domestic agency, was born. Currently, they are foster parenting his son's biological brother. Billy writes regular articles and stories about being a multiracial father on his blog, goggycoffee.blogspot.com. This article originally appeared in ***Fostering Families Today.***

Our Adoption Story

By Chris and Pete Moses

> ***Often times we are told how these children are so blessed to have us as their forever parents but it is us who are blessed to have them in our lives.***

My husband and I married late in life, so we wanted to start a family right away. We spent many years trying and many years of infertility and a journey that would prove much tougher than we thought. Therefore, after many years of being unsuccessful, we needed to change our plan. We decided that adoption might be our way to become a family.

We signed up and took the extensive MAPPS training sponsored by our local Department of Social Services and had made the decision to adopt and not foster a child. The ink wasn't even dry on our applications when they called to tell us that they had three small children who needed a home right away. Not ever having any children prior to this our decision to do so was a huge one. Could we really do this? I left the final decision up to my husband and he said yes.

So on a Friday night in August 2000 we picked up three children ages 2, 3, and 5. They came bolting out to our car and hopped in, two boys and a little girl. The youngest one had second degree burns (partial thickness burns) down the front of her chest. It had happened while on a birth visit and their birth parents had sent them back to the previous foster home in this condition.

So, this is how we began our foster care journey. For the next three years we struggled with being a family, we struggled with all the legal aspects of it and we also dealt with the birth parents. It was such a journey, but today we are so grateful for the Department of Social Services and the court systems for making the best decision possible for these children.

On a sunny day in April 2003 we adopted our three children. We also had been blessed with a fourth child even though doctors said we would never give birth to a child. Though we never dreamed we would have four kids, we did. We were so happy to finally have a family we could fully call our own.

Eighteen months later we took another child into our home, who was a week older than our youngest. She stayed with us for a month, went into a pre-adoptive home, and then was back with us after another 18 months due to unforeseen circumstances. We were able to help her birth father get his life together and so her plan again was to be reunified with her birth father. She went home to live with him and we thought and prayed that this would be a permanent situation; however this wasn't the end of our journey with this special young lady. We had kept in contact with her and her father and one day in the middle of the afternoon we received a call from a neighboring city's sheriff's department asking if we could come get her. Her father was in the middle of a drug bust in his residence. He went to jail for a couple of years and we diligently took care of "his" daughter. He knew as well as her birth mother, that they were unable to care for their child as well as she had been cared for in our home. So in the spring of 2009 her parents relinquished their rights and we adopted her in July 2009. Our family, though large, was finally complete.

Though I am ready for another little one, my husband is not and so we wait and if it is meant to be it will happen. We have been so blessed in our quest to have children. All five of our children are thriving and great kids. Often times we are told how these children are so blessed to have us as their forever parents but it is us who are blessed to have them in our lives. Adoption is not for everyone but EVERY child deserves their forever home.

Chris and Pete Moses are parents to five beautiful children, four adopted from foster care.

Jennifer

By Amy Bates

You, me, somehow turned into we.
Our lives, so different,
a familiar thread stringing us together.
Two women with little in common
living separate, yet permanently intertwined.

Yours a life of heartache, pain, struggle.
Into adulthood you went screaming
learning, doing, much too young.
Becoming a mom
before you were done being a child.

Butterflies, rainbows
and the tooth fairy dotted my skies
Although, not recognized, a life of ease was mine.
Motherhood came natural
with generations to pattern
Overabundance meant to share.

Our worlds crashed together
Yours an ending, mine a beginning.
He has your eyes, he remembers your smile,
visits, treats, fairytale endings
invade his daytime dreams.

Yet he has my last name, shares my life
Fills my day with skinned knees,
stomping feet, a beautiful smile
In confusion he yearns for what never was
He treasures, underestimates the life given.

One gave all, sacrificing, for a child to live
her dream
Another gives all, sacrificing,
for a child to live his dream
Through differences, combining in force
to love as mothers do, completely.

He is your son
He is my son
He is our son
Forever

What I Wish I'd Known about Adoption

By Rita Laws, PhD

In 1985 as the mother of five children younger than six, I wanted to meet older parents who had adopted children from the foster care system, as I had done. I wanted to ask, "Now that your kids are grown, what do you wish you had known when you started out?" This article is my attempt to answer that question more than 25 years later.

Everything was going great in 1985. We were building the large family we wanted. I had "retired" from teaching to stay home and spoil the kids in the best sense of the word. The two adopted "high risk" babies arrived right after the births of our second and third biological children. They were sick due to drug exposure and lack of prenatal care and nutrition. One of them was allergic to every known baby formula and rapidly losing weight. Being a La Leche League Leader (a lactation volunteer for other mothers in the community) was a big advantage. The sick babies took to breastfeeding quickly and were healthy in no time. Slowly but surely, they began to catch up on developmental milestones.

The days were busy but idyllic. We used cotton diapers so we spent a lot of time at the clothesline, but it wasn't all laundry. We played games, watched cartoons, and read books. We bought a used VCR and rented Disney movies from the town library for free. We had a lot of animals on our mini-farm. It was a happy, laid-back, hippie-like experience and it was among the happiest times of my life. I had no way of knowing that everything would soon change.

Five of the next seven adoptions would turn out to be ill-advised for our particular family. Our naiveté and lack of experience led us to say, "Sure, we'll try," instead of, "No, this child's needs are too great or are not a good match for our growing young family." Successful adoption starts with a sound two-way match. For the most part, we were matched to high-risk and older children whose behavioral and mental health needs were so extreme, they should never have been placed into a large family.

For a while, we had almost as many counseling sessions scheduled each week as we did sporting and band events. We were constantly adjusting medications and trying new ones to deal with depression, mood swings, rage and hyperactivity. The physical and learning disabilities like asthma, arthritis, speech delays and developmental disabilities were, comparatively speaking, easier. There are no instant cures, but there were ways to deal with these problems that were effective. The emotional and behavioral problems did not respond as well to treatment, however, at least not for long.

We struggled with issues of chronic deceit, defiance, theft, sibling abuse, mood disorders, rage, and violence. Some of the children eventually ended up with several different diagnoses that affect behavior, such as FAE, ADHD, OCD, ODD, Conduct Disorder, Bipolar, and RAD. Five of my 12 children would eventually spend some time in residential treatment for behavior that made them a threat to themselves or others.

A sudden divorce and a no-show father further complicated things. Nine kids were still at home at the time. Overnight, I had twice the work and half the income. Family counseling and a lot of late-night family chats got us through the grief but there were days when I worried that the physical and emotional exhaustion would kill me.

Summers were the toughest and summertime became my stress barometer. For years, each mid-year season was tougher than the year before but then one year, it was easier. As certain children grew up and moved out, I knew we'd turned the corner.

Today, I have just one son still at home. We truly enjoy spending time with each other and spoiling our dogs. I have seven beautiful grandchildren that I don't get to see nearly enough. I'm busily self-employed and my life is almost serene. I'm thinking about returning to teaching, my first love. I don't take a single day for granted. I haven't been this happy since, well, since 1985.

In short, I survived my choices. So what have I learned that should be passed along?

1. I wish I had known to insist on a full psychological evaluation on each potential addition to the family, no matter how young the child.

The opinions of social workers, teachers and foster parents are important, but a comprehensive "psych eval" uses a team approach with objective tests. It contains diagnoses and recommendations from medical doctors, mental health professionals, and educators so it compliments the opinions of the people who have personal relationships with the waiting child.

2. Foster and adoptive parents MUST be creative.

Sometimes, an adoption is final before the parents realize they are in over their heads. When this happens, they have to roll up their sleeves and get creative. It amazes me how many parents keep yelling and threatening even when, clearly, these techniques are not working for them. If a discipline technique doesn't work, you have got to keep trying something new and different until you find something that does. Seek professional help, read a shelf full of parenting books but stay one step ahead of the kid. Residential treatment is a last resort, of course, but if that's what you have to do to help the child and keep the rest of the family safe, then don't hesitate.

3. I wish someone had told me that, generally speaking, deeply troubled kids turn into deeply troubled teens who turn into deeply troubled adults.

There are exceptions, of course, but I believe they are few. I'm not saying that my hard work was for nothing. I believe that my son who has been in and out of jail for non-violent theft crimes might have murdered someone by now had he not known unconditional love. I know the outcomes are better because of adoption. But with some of my kids I had to continually lower my expectations and alter the definition of success. The traditional idea that a child is successful who gets a college degree and lives happily ever after became for some of mine, "If only he can finish high school and do so without a felony record." This is no exaggeration.

4. Troubled kids may never understand your values, even after they are grown, much less adopt them.

Take pets, for example. I've loved animals my whole life and I'm passionate about treating them right. We had a lot of animals when the kids were growing up, mostly rescues, and every dog and cat was spayed or neutered. The only puppies we ever had were the ones born to a stray a short time after we took it in. All of our animals had their shots, and fenced-in room to run, and were cherished. Being cruel to an animal was one of the worst things you could do in our home.

My adult troubled kids act as though they know nothing about how to treat them. Not one dime is spent at the vet. Dogs are tied up or allowed to roam the neighborhood, animals breed, and they suffer from preventable diseases and from parasites they should never have to put up with. When I asked one of my adult children once why his dog was tied to a tree, the response was laughter and this explanation, "Spoiling dogs is a mistake I will never make. I'm not you, Mom!" What I saw as an important value to impart, my child saw as foolishness.

5. I believe that "tough love" type boundaries keep us from becoming co-dependent with our addicted or mentally ill adult kids.

I have to practice "tough love" with some of my adult children, and it is tough. I have to tell them that I cannot and will not be their ATM machine or their anger doormat. If they want me in their lives at all, they have to:

- Be sober.
- Have no outstanding felony warrants hanging over their heads.
- Take care of their mental health needs. If they need medicine and/or counseling to maintain their mental health, they have to be on their medicine and/or seeing a counselor.

6. Cherish the friends who understand as their value will only grow over time.

One of my dearest friends and I had an argument we couldn't resolve. She sent me flowers to break the impasse. We agreed to disagree and made up. I'm so glad she had the wisdom to recognize the worth of our friendship when I did not.

7. Take the time to appreciate your efforts even if no one else does.

Foster and adoptive parents should never forget that they are a priceless resource and society needs them just as much as ever. It's true. The greatness of any nation is measured by how well it treats its most vulnerable, especially children and animals.

Rita Laws, PhD, of mixed American Indian and European ancestry, lives in Oklahoma and has been a freelance writer for 25 years. She is the author of several books about special needs adoption. Her doctoral dissertation in psychology studied the interests of adoptive parents in the nature-nurture debate. She is a mom to 10 sons and two daughters and eight grandchildren.

Helping Youth Succeed as Adults: The Challenge of Aging Out

By Charles Redell

Whether a child is able to return to safe and loving parents, moves in with another family member or is adopted, the goal for all youth in the child welfare system is permanency. Unfortunately for many 15- and 16-year-olds, the goal of permanent placement gets replaced with "independent living."

Many young people turning 18 might consider themselves adults. The reality, however, is that most youth this age are far from ready to live on their own. A 2003 study by the National Opinion Research Center found that most Americans do not consider a person to be an adult until he or she reaches 26 or finishes school, lands a full-time job and starts a family. Another study found that parents spend an average of $44,500 on their children after they turn 18. And the Midwest Evaluation of the Adult Functioning of Former Foster Youth: Outcomes at Age 21, released by the Chapin Hall Center for Children at the University of Chicago, estimated that parents provide $34,000 in "material assistance" to their children between the ages of 18 and 34.

Of course, a young adult who turns 18 while in foster care does not have this kind of support available. Often he or she has been in a group care facility or has moved from one family to another many times. In some cases, a young person is lucky enough to stay in one foster home for a long time, but many jurisdictions say 18-year-olds can no longer live with foster families or will no longer finance care. Suddenly, a young adult who has never lived on his or her own and has no idea what it takes to do so has nowhere to go. Often, the young adult feels like he or she has no options.

"I needed extra time to prepare," says Amanda Metivier, a former foster care youth from Alaska. "I didn't start working on independent living until I was 17½, so I had six months to become a fully independent adult. That's ridiculous." Metivier was able to extend her stay in care to age 21.

A Group at High Risk

The problem of aging out is not a small one. In 2005, the number of youth in foster care fell, but the number who aged out rose to more than 24,000, according to ***Time for Reform: Aging Out and On Their Own***, by The Pew Charitable Trusts-Kids Are Waiting Campaign and the Jim Casey Youth Opportunities Initiative (2007). The study also found that in fiscal year 2005, close to 32,000 youth had a goal of "emancipation" and more than 37,000 had a goal of "long-term foster care."

According to the Midwest Evaluation, "On many dimensions that would be of concern to the average parent of a young adult in the United States, these young people are faring poorly as a group." The Pew study backs this assertion up. It found that one in four young adults who age out will be incarcerated within the first two years of leaving the system and one in five will become homeless after turning 18. Only 58 percent have a high school diploma at 19, and fewer than 3% earn a college degree by 25.

All is not lost for these young adults though. The Midwest Evaluation found that, "As a group, they exhibit extraordinary optimism." Interviews with former foster youth and volunteer advocates bear this out. But aging out of the foster care system (which often happens at 18 but may be extended in some states to 19, 20 or even 21) is not an easy path to follow.

Creating Connections

Like all young adults, older foster youth must get and keep a job, find a place to live, pay their bills, go to school, manage a budget and perhaps keep their car running. However, they often do it all without a social circle acting as a safety net. While creating connections for foster youth is the role of social services, this task often slips through the cracks. CASA of Orange County Executive Director Gregory Bradbard thinks solving this safety-net problem could help solve some of the root issues youth face. He led his California-based program to develop the Family Connections project. "We hear from a lot of youth that they don't have any permanent relationships with someone who they know is going to be in their life today, tomorrow and 20 years down the line," he says.

Family Connections is modeled on a project of Catholic Community Services in Seattle. In addition to their advocacy role, CASA volunteers are trained to locate close family friends, neighbors and family members with the goal of creating a permanent connection for the youth they serve. The first step is to mine the youth's file to find information about "anyone who loves, could love or has loved the child," Bradbard says. They look for names and phone numbers in the margins of letters or other notes in a social services file. "We've found it to be much richer than a court file," Bradbard notes.

If they cannot find anything that way, volunteers will use the names, birth dates and social security numbers of parents to do an internet search for an aunt, uncle or someone else willing to connect with the child. Once a name and contact information are found, "This is where the training comes in," Bradbard says. "With a lot of people, a wall immediately goes up and the volunteer must have a very sensitive conversation."

Bradbard stresses that the key is communication and taking it slowly. For more information about methods to establish permanent connections for youth, see "*8 Skills for Building Family Connections*" in the Winter 2008 issue of **The Connection** (www.casaforchildren.org and click on News & Events to find The Connection and archives). Amanda Metivier, the former foster youth in Alaska, entered the system at 17 and emancipated when she turned 21. She agrees with the need for a permanent adult connection. "Being someone who is there to stay and letting youth know you're available to have a relationship and really be there for them is key," she says. According to National CASA Chief Program Officer Sally Erny, "The CASA volunteer can be an important support in helping youth find these connections."

Real Life Demands Real Solutions

As important as connections are, the practicalities of life also demand attention. According to the Pew report, youth emancipated from the system do not know how to create a budget or understand the need for one. Many cannot drive because their states do not allow foster youth to get a driver's license, and the maze of paperwork necessary to take advantage of education benefits can be daunting. Even setting realistic goals is often beyond the scope of their skills simply because they are 18.

To help youth learn how to set realistic goals, Orphan Foundation Executive Director

Eileen McCaffery says they need to be taught the concrete steps it takes to achieve a goal. "You'll have an 18-year-old who wants to be a rock star but doesn't play an instrument, or one who wants to be a lawyer but can't write a sentence," she says. "It's a major gap between goals and planning." Telling a young person things he or she does not want to hear is vital to teaching him or her how to reach established goals. "Nobody says, 'But wait a minute, you skip school every day.' No one calls them on that," McCaffery states. Finally, she believes that most adults realize nothing comes without work, but young people do not know this yet. "They may feel as if they have to jump through hoops, but everyone has to jump through hoops," she says. "We've got to start talking in very concrete ways that help them mature and understand the amount of work it takes."

Cathy Netter, a CASA volunteer in Ohio, agrees. She worked with a young person who received a stipend for going to school and completing chores.

"In the real world, you don't get paid for doing what you're supposed to do," she says. "That's a big jump for kids of that age." Metivier says she was ready to move out when she turned 18, but her foster mother convinced her otherwise by sitting her down at the

Ways for Youth to Afford College

ETV=Education for Foster Youth
(www.statevoucher.org) The Education Training Voucher (ETV) program awards grants to current and former foster youth to help pay for college or specialized education. ETV grants are funded by the federal government and administered by the states. In most states, eligible students may receive grants of up to $5,000 per academic year.

Foster Care and Education
(www.casey.org/Resources/Publications/FosterCareAndEducation.htm) For the almost 500,000 children and youth in foster care in the United States, a quality education is vitally important. It not only provides children with a roadmap for future success, it can also serve as a positive counterweight to abuse, neglect, separation and instability. Produced by the National Working Group on Foster Care and Education, this brochure identifies key resources and tools to increase understanding and provide ways to advocate for positive educational outcomes for children and youth in foster care.

The Orphan Foundation
(orphan.org) offers year in scholarships for foster youth to attend college. Recipients are also assigned a dedicated mentor who works with them.

Chafee Funds
Chafee funds are intended to provide youth with opportunities to learn needed independent living skills and increase the likelihood of successful transition from foster care. They are federal funds administered by individual states.

Other resources to check out: www.casey.org or www.abanet.org/child/education and www.voice-for-adoption.org.

kitchen table and writing a sample budget.

"Once I saw those numbers on how much it would cost to live on my own, I started to panic," she says. "I was afraid of being on my own." Metivier extended foster care twice. She is now 23 and on her way to becoming a social worker.

Getting Ahead

One of the biggest practical hurdles youth must overcome is paying for school. The Orphan Foundation helps older foster youth and the adults who work with them do this. McCaffery explains that the Orphan Foundation administers the Chafee Act federal education training voucher program in nine states. The vouchers are worth up to $5,000 per year and are available in all 50 states. The foundation also awards $1.5 million in scholarships each year, including $1 million from the Casey Family Scholars Program. McCaffery says the Orphan Foundation is a holistic program and offers family support.

Each recipient gets a trained and supported mentor as well as three care packages a year and cards recognizing their birthday and other notable events. "They hear from us when times are good and when they're bad," McCaffery says. She stresses that a lot of money and other resources are available to students. Youth just need help looking for resources and understanding the long-term benefit of writing an essay for a scholarship versus taking out a loan. "Arm them with real information, real consequences, and real opportunities," she says. "Really be proactive. These are the things that make a difference."

While CASA and GAL volunteers carry out their mission of advocating for young people to find safe, permanent homes, they can also play an important role when a permanent home is not found and youth age out on their own. Advocates and other concerned adults can help make sure that young people do not leave the foster care system without permanent connections. After all, how many of us who grew up in much better circumstances could succeed in the long haul without ongoing support and encouragement from people who care about us?

Charles Redell is a Seattle-based writer and editor with 10 years of experience. He has worked as a journalist for a variety of publications, covering many different topics. This article is reprinted from the Spring 2008 ***The Connection*** *magazine, produced by the National CASA Association. National CASA supports a network of more than 50,000 volunteers across 900 local program offices that serve 225,000 abused and neglected foster children.*

The following organizations, programs and tools are helpful in understanding the scope of concerns of older youth in care. They are also resources to support youth in creating permanent connections and preparing for independence.

California Youth Connection (www.calyouthconn.org)
This group's Speak Out Report is a compendium of foster youth voices on the challenges they face and ideas for addressing those challenges. Visit the "Resources" section of their site to find the report.

Casey Family Programs (www.casey.org)
With a variety of programs focused on the child-welfare system, Casey Family Programs is a treasure trove of facts and guides. The following are three of their resources helpful in life-skills preparation:

1. **Foster Care Independence Act FAQ** Casey's three-part list of frequently asked questions is an excellent summary of the Chafee Foster Care Independence Program. Search for "Chafee FAQ" from casey.org.
2. **It's My Life: A Framework for Youth Transitioning from Foster Care to Successful Adulthood** Casey offers a series of guides for older youth and advocates who work with them called It's My Life. Download a free PDF of this out-of-print resource from http://www.casey.org/Resources/Publications/pdf/ItsMyLife_PostsecondaryEducation.pdf.
3. **Ansell Casey Life Skills Assessment** To help young people learn more about the challenges of independent living and discover where they are in the process, encourage them to take the online Ansell Casey Life Skills Assessment. Go to caseylifeskills.org, click on "Assessments" in the menu and select the first option to determine the appropriate assessment for your needs.

Family Search & Engagement: A Comprehensive Practice Guide
This guide was developed by Catholic Community Services of Western Washington and EMQ Children & Family Services in Northern California. It is designed to help locate, engage, connect and support family resources for youth. It is available at www.emqff.org/press/docs/FSE_guide.pdf.

FosterClub (www.fosterclub.org)
FosterClub is a national network supporting young people in foster care. Their Permanency Pact is designed to encourage lifelong, kin-like connections between a young person and a supportive adult.

Represent: The Voice of Youth in Care is a national bimonthly magazine written by and for young people in the foster care system. They sponsor a website www.youthsuccessnyc.org filed with excellent resources on a variety of topics for youth and the people who work with them.

You Gotta Believe (www.yougottabelieve.org) is a homeless prevention program that seeks to find permanent adoptive homes for teens and preteens in foster care.

Seven Things Emancipated Youth Need to Know About Money Before Leaving Care

By Shay Olivarria

I emancipated out of foster care at age 17. I thought I knew everything there was to know about money because I had been living on my own for a while and working full time while finishing high school. Looking back, I didn't know anything about being responsible with money. I was living paycheck to paycheck with no savings, no money saved for retirement, and no idea what I would do if I lost my job. Over time I learned the tips that I'm going to share with you. I share them in hope that you'll start your adult years with a knowledge that many of us never learn.

1. Open a Checking Account at a Credit Union

Most people I come in contact with don't know what a credit union is, what it does, or why they are more beneficial to users than traditional banks. Let's begin at the beginning. Credit unions are financial institutions that are owned by the members (customers) of that specific credit union. Credit unions are not-for-profit organizations. That's right, the goal of credit unions is not to make money. This is a key difference between credit unions and traditional banks. Since all the money that is lent to members comes directly from other members' loan rates, fees are lower than traditional banks.

Wouldn't you loan a friend money at a better rate than you'd loan a stranger? Also, credit unions are smaller than traditional banks and tend to have better customer service. It's possible that because I didn't come from a stable home and I have a lot of trust issues, I like credit unions mostly for this reason. I like working with people I know and who I'm familiar with.

Takeaway *– Credit unions have the same financial products as traditional banks, but tend to offer lower interest rates for loans, have lower fees and have better customer service. Most credit unions are linked through the co-op system, so you can make withdrawals and deposits at other credit unions and not be charged out-of-network fees.*

2. Housing Should Never be More that 30% of your Gross Income.

According to OnTheMoveBayArea.org, "Up to 50 percent of former foster/probation youth become homeless within the first 18 months of emancipation." What that means is that it's imperative that those leaving foster care understand how to choose a place to live so they are able to afford it. Many of us have never had a room to ourselves and the thought of having our own space, be it an apartment or a house, is too exciting to pass up. We want the space that we never had regardless of how much it costs, but that's unrealistic. You need a place that's safe, clean, and affordable.

The amount of money that you earn from a job is your gross income. What you have left over after taxes are taken out of your check is your net income. The goal is to find a place that you can afford on 30 percent or less of your gross income so you don't overextend yourself. There's no greater feeling than walking into a home that you are paying for yourself and no worse feeling than having that place taken from you and not knowing where you'll go next.

***Takeaway** – Find a place that's safe, clean, and costs less than 30 percent of your gross income. Get a roommate if you have to.*

3. Buying a Reliable Used Car is Always a Smart Move.
I have never bought a new car and I don't think I ever will. Vehicles depreciate as soon as you drive them off the lot and cost too much new. The key is to find a car that's safe, reliable, and in your price range. Great places to start are Craigslist.org and AutoTrader.com. Take a look around and see what cars are available in your price range and which ones you like.

Once you think you know the make, model, and year of car that you'd like to purchase, visit Kelly Blue Book at Kbb.com or Edmunds at Edmunds.com to find out the value of the car. You don't want to find out you've overpaid once the deal is done. You can use the information you find on the car to negotiate with the car owner.

You have a car you like, it's in your price range, and you think you're ready to buy. The next step is to make sure that the car you want is reliable. The easiest way to do that is take the car to a AAA approved mechanic to take part in the Vehicle Inspection Program. It'll cost you about $89, but it's better to spend the $89 to find out a car is a lemon than hundreds of dollars to fix a broken down vehicle.

***Takeaway** – When you find the car you like, look up the value of the car on Kelly Blue Book to make sure you're paying a fair price, ask the car seller for the vehicle identification number (VIN) and get a used car report from a AAA approved mechanic to make sure the car has been taken care of and will serve you well. Don't ever take out a car loan longer than three years and it's easier to buy the car outright than make payments.*

4. Know the Loan Information.
People take out loans for a myriad of reasons. It's important that when you go to take a loan (personal, car, mortgage, etc.) that you know what the loan terms are that you are agreeing to before you sign anything. It's a cold truth, but no one cares about how you, "didn't understand" or "didn't know" what you were signing. Find out the principle, interest rate, and length of the loan with every loan, every time.

The principle is the amount of money for which you are taking out a loan. For example, if the car costs $4,000 then the principle amount is $4,000. It's important that you know the principle amount because some car dealers will entice you to make a bigger purchase than you can really afford by focusing on the monthly payment instead of the total amount. Thinking that you have to pay $150 a month may not sound bad, but once you realize that will pay $5,400 when you meant to only spend $4,000 may make a difference in your choice.

The interest rate is the amount of money you'll have to pay back in addition to the principle. Let's stay with the $4,000 example. If your interest rate is 5 percent, then you'll pay $119.88 per month for 36 months. If your interest rate is 9 percent, you'll pay

$127.20. If your interest rate is 12 percent, you'll pay $132.86. The numbers may not seem like a lot, but over the lifetime of the loan you'll pay an extra $467.28.

The "length of the loan" means how long you'll have to pay the loan back. Taking out a loan is a commitment that will have long-term consequences for the borrower. None of us know where we'll be in one year, let alone three years or five years. It's critical that you know how long you'll be expected to pay back any loans that you take out.

***Takeaway** – It's up to you to know, and understand, what you're signing. Make sure you know the principle amount, interest rate, and length of the loan term before you sign.*

5. Start an Emergency Fund.

In life, something will always come up. Whether it's your car needing new brakes or an illness that keeps you from work, everyone needs a little financial cushion. Having at least $500 in a money market account at a credit union or bank as an emergency fund is a smart move.

When you open a checking account the customer service representative will usually also suggest you open a savings account. The problem with the savings account is that it's too accessible. That means that you can easily deposit and withdraw money from the account, so a savings account doesn't really act as a savings vehicle for most Americans.

The better decision is to open a money market account at a credit union or bank. A money market account is like a savings account, but better. You can usually make up to six deposits or withdrawals a month. The fees are low and the interest rates that you are paid for keeping your money in the credit union or bank are higher than savings accounts. You can have checks and an ATM card if you'd like, but consider how much space you'll need from the money to make sure you don't spend it.

***Takeaway** – Start saving money in a money market account at a credit union or bank as soon as possible. Earmark it as your emergency fund. Leave the money in the account and only use it for actual emergencies. Once you use it, start building the emergency fund back up again as quickly as possible.*

6. Save for Retirement Now.

The reality is that most of us will live to an old age, so you'd better start thinking about how you'll pay for your expenses in retirement. Social Security may or may not provide enough money for you to live on. Pensions have gone the way of the dinosaur. If you want to make sure you'll be able to live comfortably in retirement, you'd better start saving. Now.

There are several options on mutual funds, no-load funds, and load funds. A no-load fund has shares which are sold without a commission or sales charge. Load funds typically charge a commission at the time of your purchase and at the time you sell it. Most no-load mutual funds require that you either have a significant amount of money to open an account or that you promise to add at least $50 a month to your account. Adding at least $50 a month is the easiest way to save for retirement. When the cost of shares of your mutual fund are high, you'll purchase fewer shares. When the cost of shares of your mutual fund are low, you'll purchase more shares. Over time, the costs of the shares will appreciate and you'll make money. Adding the same amount of money every month is called Dollar Cost Averaging. The earlier you start, the more money you'll make.

Takeaways *— The earlier you start saving, the better. Use Dollar Cost Averaging to your advantage. Put at least $50 away in a no-load mutual fund every month and you'll be a millionaire by age 65 with little-to-no effort.*

7. Love Will Get You in Trouble Financially if You're Not Careful.

Many young people start making money mistakes because of a person they think they love. When people start asking you to purchase them things or let them "use" or "borrow" money, cars, or credit cards that's a warning sign. People who care about you want to see you do well in life. They don't want to take from you, they want to add to your life. If you feel funny about a request from someone, go with your gut and don't honor it.

Takeaway *– People who really love you don't need you to buy them lavish gifts or spend a lot of money on them.*

Shay Olivarria is a motivational speaker, financial literacy coach, former foster care youth, and author of ***10 Things College Students Need to Know About Money and Money Matters: The Get It Done in 1 Minute Workbook****. As an ambassador for financial freedom, Olivarria travels throughout the country to educate people on responsible financial decisions. She has partnered with several community organizations including Independent Lens, Promise House of Dallas, Texas; Los Angeles Urban League; San Diego Urban League; and the Latino Student Business Association of the University of Southern California. For more information, visit www.BiggerThanYourBlock.com. This was originally published in* ***Fostering Families Today****.*

Knowing When to Stay Committed and When Your Job is Done.

By Carrie Craft

This is the tough question, the tough spot to be in as a foster parent. It's often hard to think that there is someone out there who may have more skills than you as a parent, or be a better match for a child, especially if you've put a lot of time, energy and love into a child. For us mothers, there is also a lot of guilt associated with calling it quits and saying, "I can't do any more." What does "done" look like? When is it time to say, we're done?

Several years ago, we took in a beautiful 18-month-old baby boy as a foster child. He was gorgeous with big brown eyes that would just melt your heart. Our daughter was two at the time. I thought I could handle the two children together. However, I wasn't prepared for his reaction to being in a strange home, a reaction that lasted for three weeks. This little guy screamed and wailed. I was a relatively new foster parent and this was my first toddler placement. The only time he quit screaming was when he was in my arms or touching me somehow. I quickly could see the impact it had on my daughter. There was no longer any room left for her in my arms, the new little guy needed me and I really wanted to be there for him.

One evening I went to pick my daughter up from my parents as she had spent the night. When I entered the room and called for her, she ran from me crying, "No, home. Home, bad. Baby there." She refused to come home with me that night. I returned to my home, without my daughter. I knew then that this placement needed to end. My husband asked where our daughter was and after I told him what had happened he too simply said, "When our daughter doesn't feel comfortable in our home due to a foster child, it's time for that child to move on." We were done.

I cried for days over this decision. I know how important attachments are for a child and I couldn't help but think we did more damage to this little boy; however, I also know that we were doing damage to our own daughter. His constant screaming had taken its toll on her and on us. I, too, was loosing my patience. We had to say goodbye to him and our agency was able to find another foster placement for him that same weekend.

There have been other instances when we and other foster parenting friends have had to ask for children to be placed into other foster homes as the needs of the child outweighed the strengths of the home. We can't give what we don't have or don't know to give. When a child's behavior or needs has a negative impact on:

Yourself. Do you find that you're feeling overwhelmed by the child? Are you losing your patience and feeling on edge? Have you lost contact with the reason why you wanted to be a foster parent in the first place? It may be time for someone else to work with the child.

Marriage. Does the subject of the child initiate an argument between you and your spouse? If we lose our own families while trying to help another family – what have we truly gained? I know many foster parents who have divorced while fostering. Many say that the stress of fostering added to the dismantling of their relationship.

My husband and I have been pitted against each other by foster children as well, this is not something to allow into your relationship. Stay strong with date-nights and open communication. Be open and honest with each other. My husband had a child removed from our home without my knowledge. He could see the damage the child was doing to our family – something I could not see. While I was upset to learn about what he had done, I understood his reasons, but we had to agree to never make such big decisions again without the other. It's important to remain open and honest about what we see happening in our homes and relationships. Remember many of these children have survived years of abuse and their survival and coping skills are often maladaptive and unhealthy – but effective. It's difficult to say that a 9-year-old can tear down a family – but a 9 year old can.

Allow each foster child time to transition into your home. The amount of time needed will be different for each child. Once a child has grieved losses he or she will be better able to move on and integrate into your home and family. As long as this transition time does not become unhealthy for your children, it may be best to hang in there with the foster child.

Other children in the home. Be aware of how your children are doing in the family around the new foster child. When a child's behavior is upsetting or damaging to your children, it may be time to let your agency know. Like with my daughter, she didn't know how to communicate with me that the constant screaming was adding to her stress and unhappiness, but when she finally was able to deliver that message, we both heard her – loud and clear.

Overall happiness of the home and family. Sometimes a fostering family just needs a break and not just a short respite weekend. Take a few months off or maybe a few years. The need for foster families will still be there if and when you are ready to re-license and return to the work.

When the child has difficult periods remember the positive time and the growth that the child has experienced prior to the current situation that is making you consider disruption. Are these little glimpses of hope that a child is making progress overshadowing the hard days?

Also know that sometimes the overall attitude or atmosphere of the case is not a good fit for a family. We have disrupted due to the constant miscommunication and overall negativity of a case and the caseworkers. It's important in my opinion to maintain the happy spirit within your home and family and to make adjustments where needed to guard your home and heart.

Carrie Craft and her husband began fostering in 1997. They adopted three teen/pre-teen brothers in 2002. Craft has been the Guide for Adoption and Foster Care on About.com since 2004. She also trains foster/adoptive parents in Kansas. Visit her at adoption.about.com.

Disruption: When it Becomes Necessary

By Veronica Brown

One evening, my 12-year-old foster son told me that our newest foster child (older and much bigger) had cornered him, bent back his wrist until he was on his knees, took out his penis and told him to 'suck it.' Although the older boy released him and told him he was 'just joking,' "Adam" was scared. I immediately called the caseworker and it was confirmed that the older boy had a history of this kind of behavior. I had him moved that night.

Disrupting a placement is seldom that black and white. It's easy to make the call when someone's safety is at risk. There are children that need a higher level of supervision or expertise than can be offered in a mere foster home. There was no shame or guilt in that situation - I had no second thoughts. But many factors contribute to the 'success' or 'breakdown' of a foster home placement, as I have learned over the years. . .

Shawn was my very first foster child. About age 11, his struggle at school was translating into trouble at home. He had come to my home from a treatment facility with an attached school. The transition to a community school, even with supports, was not working out. He had a very committed therapist and social worker, however I still found myself wondering, "What I have to offer this child may not be enough for his needs. BUT, maybe it would be enough for another child. When do I throw in the towel?"

Shawn had been through multiple foster homes before landing in the treatment facility before coming to me. I was very conscious of being positive about his placement. With the school worries, I didn't want him stressing about his safety and security with me. But my natural optimism, and the idealism only new foster parents have, were starting to wear down. It had been a year and a half of constant struggle and I was thinking of asking my worker for re-placement. I sat Shawn down and told him I wasn't sure if I could do it anymore. I wasn't threatening him, I was trying to be upfront and honest. He looked me in the eye and asked, "Can you give me a second chance?"

"Second chance?" I was shocked. "I've given you 10, 15, 20 chances!"

"You never told me that! You never told me that you gave me a second chance."

He was right. I hadn't. I thought I was protecting him, but I was actually shielding him from the truth. Shawn had no idea that I was also struggling. So we gave each other a second chance, and what we had to offer turned out to be enough.

Fifteen-year-old "Richard" had been with me for four months and had no challenging behaviors. He came to me from a foster home that had decided to close. He was in a regular school program and had just gotten a part-time job locally. Richard was trustworthy, honest and polite. But, he had a personality that clashed with mine. He was very similar to a teen that I had fostered years before, and that kid drove me nuts. By the time I asked for him to be removed, I could barely even look at him. The fact that I had let it get that bad was totally my fault and was due to pride and arrogance in my ability to connect with any child.

When I started recognizing my inability to connect with Richard in a way that he deserved, I called the case workers involved. We met to openly talk about our differences (I don't think Richard was any happier than I) and we gave ourselves a trial period. At the end of two weeks, we decided that Richard needed another foster home. Since we had started this process early, there was no rush to find just any home, but to look for the best situation. A foster home was found close to his job, and we were able to start with pre-placement visits, overnight stays, and then weekends. We were able to let Richard move forward, not just move away. And when Richard stopped in to visit after the disruption, I can honestly say I was pleased to see him.

"Ben," a 17-year-old young man with an intellectual disability was becoming more and more challenging. He had been with me for nearly three years and for the first half, a steady improvement was seen both in his behavior and emotional stability. But situations beyond my control, plus some medical issues, were making him more and more agitated. I knew that if he was to move, it would be to a group home and there would be the real chance that I'd lose contact with him.

How Can You Avoid a Disruption?

Ask for help. Social workers report that placements sometime disrupt because families wait too long before they seek help. Ask for help before you are past the breaking point.

Use respite. Respite care should not be reserved for emergencies. Respite allows foster parents to renew their energy, which can enhance the quality and the longevity of placements.

Learn. Research suggests that foster placements are more stable when foster parents have a clear and realistic understanding of the issues their children are struggling with, and when they have the knowledge and skills needed to successfully parent their children. In particular, foster parents should take steps to learn all they can about:

- Trauma and other mental health issues that affect children in foster care
- Their children's right to receive mental health and educational services
- How to advocate effectively for these services
- Appropriate discipline techniques, especially for children struggling with trauma, mental health issues, and oppositional/aggressive behavior

Maintain family connections for the child. Sustaining connections between children and their siblings, friends, and other family members can add to their sense of stability.

Build and maintain your own support system. Keep strong connections to your family, friends, faith community, other foster parents—all the resources you need to stay healthy and keep fostering.

I was barely hanging on with Ben, but a referral to a specialist had just come through and we were waiting to see if it would be enough to help. All through the process, I felt this clock ticking, knowing that one major episode would take the decision out of my hands. And it happened. It was the bridge that couldn't be uncrossed. The caseworker pulled the trigger and Ben was moved to a group home in a different community. And I wasn't allowed to see him because they wanted him to get used to the new situation, and then Ben was transferred to a new caseworker, one who didn't return my phone calls. Ben's old caseworker couldn't discuss him with me, citing confidentiality, and now I am reduced to scrounging around for gossip, hoping to hear that he is okay.

A social worker arrived with 10-year-old "David" who was being moved from another foster home. I was contacted ahead of time and had three days to prepare for this move. He was in the backseat of the worker's car and he looked FURIOUS. The worker let me know that the foster parent was nervous about telling David about the move because she didn't want his behaviors to escalate. He only found out he was being 're-placed' when he was picked up from school at lunchtime by his foster mother under the pretense of 'going shopping.' They passed the store and just went straight home, where all his belongings were packed and his worker was waiting for him. And then David was told that he was being moved to a new foster home.

We brought in David's bags, introductions were made, documents were handed over, and a seven-day visit was scheduled. Then the workers left. And I was looking at a boy who had just learned that in foster care, even if you go to school in the morning, you may not sleep in your OWN bed that night. I believe it took a full year before David finally felt secure in his place with our family. This was confirmed when I picked him up from school one day, out of the blue. He was called to the office and when he came in and saw me, the only expression on his face was confusion. No worry or anxiety. He just asked, "Hey, what are you doing here?" I had the happy privilege of surprising David and his foster brothers with tickets to an afternoon baseball game. With a whoop, David turned and ran to his classroom to get his backpack. As I stood there waiting for David, I hoped that this afternoon could somehow balance out that awful day when he was blindsided by the people responsible for his care.

Foster home placements may breakdown for many reasons. Whether initiated by the foster parents, foster child, social worker or agency, the challenge for everyone is minimizing the impact and trauma of disruption.

Veronica Brown has been a foster parent in Canada since 1995. She primarily takes in boys aged 9 and older and usually has a handful at any given time.

Tips for Disrupting a Placement

Know Your Skills

The best disruption is the one that never happens. Be realistic about the types of children and levels of behavior your family is best suited for. Keep taking training courses to explore your comfort zone.

Define the Placement

Give foster children the opportunity to protect themselves by explaining the context of the placement. If it's an emergency or short term transitional placement, be honest with the child. "Your caseworker is looking for the best foster family for you. So you'll stay here until we find that family."

Communicate with the Caseworker

Be open and honest about the placement. If appropriate, bring the child in on the conversation. Give the caseworker a chance to help and (hopefully) arrange additional services or supports. And sometimes just venting (and being heard) helps diffuse tense situations. If a disruption is inevitable, give the caseworker a chance to really search for the best alternative instead of making a quick, emergency decision.

Plan the Move

When moving a child, tell them ahead of time and make sure it's with a caseworker that is known to them. Give the child as many details about the new placement as possible and give the new foster family personalized information about the child's likes, dislikes and routines. Arrange pre-placement visits if at all possible.

What's Theirs Is Theirs

Make sure foster children are able to take all their belongings, especially mementos and pictures. Promise that you'll send along anything you might find after they leave and DO IT. Try to minimize their loss.

Moving with Dignity

NO GARBAGE BAGS. That is their life being packed up and carted away, so take care. Every child deserves to be treated with decency and respect, no matter what has happened. A foster parent may never see that child again, so make sure the last message is of positive good wishes for their future.

Lessons Learned

Disruption is personal and emotional. The child should be told by the foster parents and caseworker together. And if the child has a lesson to learn from the breakdown of the placement, the lesson should come from the caseworker. A foster parent should not stand in judgement.

Give Yourself a Break

Let yourself mourn. Remember the successes. Reflect on the challenges. Continue to learn. Remember: there is no such thing as a perfect foster parent.

My Daughter

By Amy Bates

I lost my daughter today.
Sadness threatens to overwhelm me.
Grief consumes my every thought.
Pain fills my entire body.

The words send a shock to my heart.
My legs fail me as I fall to the floor
Knowing it was to come,
Realizing it is God's will,
Nothing makes it easier to hear.

My heart crumbles under the weight
I know all the pieces will never be found.
A wound created that will never heal.
A constant reminder of what is gone.

Desire to become a forever family.
Hope of taking away too much pain.
Dreams of her eyes filling with child-like joy.
Plans of holidays, birthday, and special events
All cause to mourn, all will never be.

I long for the comfort others might have,
Joy with her in the arms of the Father,
Peace in knowing she is cared for,
Sure knowledge that we will be together again.

I lost my daughter today.
There are no flowers to brighten my soul.
No grave to visit and seek refuge at.
The rest of the world will never notice,
For the daughter I lost was never really mine.

Amy Bates is mom to 10 kids who miraculously came to her through adoption, birth, and foster care. She and her husband have been foster parents for 11 years to over 40 wonderful children. She works for a non-profit agency that emphasizes family preservation and child safety, both of which are incredibly important to her. She is continually amazed at the strength of the children who pass through her doors and is honored to get to know each and every one of them. This was originally published in ***Fostering Families Today****.*

Resources

Additional resources can be found at www.emkpress.com

1. Why Foster?

Another Mother: Co-parenting with the Foster Care System by Sarah Gerstenzang

Is Eight Enough – God Knows and He Ain't Telling by Kate Thompson

Foster Parent Association
Valuable information and support. The NFPA website will link you to many excellent resources, such as each state's requirements for training; it will also give you general answers to some typically asked questions about foster parenting.
www.nfpainc.org

Foster Parent Links
For Links to Foster Parent Associations in your city or state, visit these websites for the most up to date listing:
www.nfpainc.org/reploc/
www.fosterparents.com/states3

National Foster Care Coalition (NFCC)
605 North Carolina Avenue, SE, Unit #2
Washington, DC 20003
(202) 280-2039
The National Foster Care Coalition (NFCC) is a broadly based national, nonpartisan partnership of individuals, organizations, foundations, and associations dedicated to improving the lives of children currently in the foster care system and all of the others who have been, or will be, involved in the foster care system.
www.nationalfostercare.org

National Foster Parent Association (NFPA)
(253) 683-4246
(800) 557-5238
info@nfpaonline.org
The National Foster Parent Association (NFPA) is a nonprofit volunteer organization. The NFPA's purpose is to bring together foster parents, agency representatives, and people in the community to improve the foster care system. NFPA promotes coordination, cooperation, and communication among foster parents, foster parent associations, child care agencies, and other child advocates in an effort to encourage the recruitment and retention of foster parents.
www.NFPAonline.org
For a state-by-state listing of foster parent organizations, visit **www.nfpainc.org** and click on the affiliates tab.

Walk Me Home is a fund-raising and awareness event for foster care in America. Each year, walkers participate in Walk Me Home events across the country, raising funds to support the life changing programs and activities of foster care associations throughout the United States. For more information, please see **www.nfpaonline.com/wmh**

National Resource Center for Permanency and Family Connections (NRCPFC)
Hunter College School of Social Work
129 East 79th Street – Suite 801
New York, NY 10021
(212) 452-7043
gmallon@hunter.cuny.edu
The NRCPFC customizes an array of services for each request to support States, territories, and Tribes in sustainable, systemic change efforts producing greater safety, permanency, and well-being for children, youth, and families.

The NRCPFC also offers onsite technical

assistance and indepth information services in collaboration with family partners to assist in the implementation of new strategies, expand knowledge, increase competencies, and expand commitment to family-centered practice by child welfare professionals at all levels.
www.hunter.cuny.edu/socwork/nrcfcpp

2. Perspectives

FLUX: Life After Foster Care by Leigh Ecke and Misty Stenslie and was written to support young people during the emotional transition from foster care to adulthood. Available from **www.fostercarealumni.org**

Adoption Learning Partners
Online courses that assist families in understanding and address challenges of parenting and fostering.
www.adoptionlearningpartners.org

3. Transitions

Trail through Foster Care by Adam Robe

Moving to Another Foster Home Adam Robe

Meeting my CASA Adam Robe

Out of Many, One Family: How Two Adults Claimed Twelve Children through Adoption Claudia and Bert Fletcher

Inward Bound, LLC
psychotherapist for individuals, couples, and families. Primary clinical focus is on adoption and foster care issues, including the impact of early trauma and the spectrum of relationship difficulties that results from disrupted attachments.
www.InwardBoundCo.com

4. Teamwork

Tools to help children in the foster care/adoption system: **www.robbietherabbit.com**

National CASA
100 West Harrison Street
North Tower, Suite 500
Seattle, WA 98119
(800) 628-3233
www.casaforchildren.org

National Association of Social Workers
750 First Street, NE • Suite 700
Washington, DC 20002-4241
(202) 408-8600
www.naswdc.org

Healthy Foster Care America (HFCA)
c/o American Academy of Pediatrics
141 NW Point Blvd
Elk Grove Village, IL 60007
(800) 433-9016
fostercare@aap.org
The Healthy Foster Care America (HFCA) website utilizes the expertise of a large, multidisciplinary coalition to improve the health and well-being of children and teens in foster care. HFCA addresses a wide range of health issues and needs of children and youth in foster care, provides resources on health systems of care, and makes available a Resource Library that links to other resources related to the health and well-being of children and youth in foster care.
www.aap.org/fostercare/index.html

5. Birth Family Connections

The Family of Adoption
by Joyce Maguire Pavao

Adoption and the Family System
by Ken Watson & Mirriam Reitz

Beneath the Mask: Understanding Adopted Teens by Debbie Riley

Rise Magazine – A magazine by and for parents affected by child welfare system - **www.risemagazine.org**

C.A.S.E. - The Center for Adoption Support and Education
4000 Blackburn Lane
Suite 260
Burtonsville, MD 20866
(301) 476-8525
caseadopt@adoptionsupport.org
C.A.S.E. was created to provide post-adoption counseling and educational services to families, educators, child welfare staff, and mental health providers in Maryland, Northern Virginia, and Washington, D.C. In addition, C.A.S.E. is a national resource for families and professionals through its training, publications, and consultations. C.A.S.E. is a private, non-profit adoptive family support center. Its programs focus on helping children from a variety of foster care and adoptive backgrounds to receive understanding and support which will enable them to grow into successful, productive adults.
www.adoptionsupport.org

6. Loss, Grief, and Anger

Improve Your Child's Behavior: Simple Strategies that Really Work by Terry de Forrest

The Mad Family Gets Their Mads Out by Lynne Namka

Welcome Home: A Guide for Adoptive, Foster and Treatment Foster Parents by Christopher J Alexander

Childhood Anxiety Disorders: A guide to Research & Treatment by Deborah C. Beidal and Samuel M. Turner

What to Do When You Worry Too Much: A Kid's Guide to Overcoming Anxiety by Dawn Huebner

What to Do When You're Scared & Worried: A Guide for Kids by James J. Crist

Freeing Your child from Anxiety: Powerful, Practical Solutions to Overcome Your Child's Fears, Worries & Phobia by Tamar E. Chansky

Helping Your Anxious Child: a Step by Step Guide for Parents by Sue Spence, Vanessa Cubham, Ann Wignall & Ronald Rapee

Keys to Parenting Your Anxious Child by Katharine Manassis

The Anxiety Cure for Kids: A Guide for Parents by Elizabeth DuPont Spencer, Robert L. DuPont, Caroline M. DuPont

No-Talk Therapy for Children and Adolescents by Martha Straus

Ambiguous Loss: Learning to Live with Unresolved Grief by Pauline Boss

Talking with Children About Loss by Maria Trozzi

Beyond Consequences, Logic & Control by B Bryan Post and Heather Forbes

Parenting the Hurt Child: Helping Adoptive Families Heal and Grow by Gregory Keck and Regina M. Kupecky

Telling the Truth to Your Adopted or Foster Child: Making Sense of the Past by Betsy Keefer, Jayne Schooler

Fostering a Child's Recovery: Family Placement for Traumatized Children by Mike Thomas and Terry Philpot

Parenting With Love and Logic by Foster Cline, MD and Jim Fay

Resources for Parents and Caregivers to Learn about Trauma

www.nctsn.org/resources

www.projectabc-la.org/parents

www.multiplyconnections.org

www.angriesout.com

Talk, Trust & Feel Therapeutics provides innovative toys and books to help parents, teachers and therapists teach children to express uncomfortable feelings, take responsibility for their own behavior and learn positive social skills. Our commitment is to develop products to help children feel good about identifying and breaking into their acts of power and replacing them with acts of love. Our unique mission is to help children and adults learn how to deal with their anger and express it in safe, constructive ways. Our philosophy is that changing our world is possible when adults approach children's misbehavior with love and compassion and teach them better ways to act. We are a mom, pop company determined to make a difference on the planet.
www.angriesout.com/catalog/index.htm

Parenting by Connections
Hand in Hand Parenting works with parents of young children providing resources, training, and lots of support. For over 20 years, our Parenting by Connection approach has given parents practical tools to resolve universal family challenges. Unlike other parenting methods, which rely on systems of rewards and punishment, our philosophy is centered on children's strong, innate desire to love and be loved. Our fresh and effective framework is consistent with the latest research and results in long-term family success.
www.handinhandparenting.org

Consciously Parenting Australia – dedicated to educating and helping struggling families achieve the harmony and joy that is the birthright of every human being.
www.consciouslyparenting.com

7. Attachment and Trust

Creating Capacity for Attachment edited by Arthur Becker-Weidman, PhD and Deborah Shell, MA, LCMHC

Principles of Attachment Parenting by Arthur Becker-Weidman, PhD

Toddler Adoption: The Weaver's Craft by Mary Hopkins-Best

Parenting the Hurt Child: Helping Adoptive Families Heal and Grow by Gregory Keck and Regina M. Kupecky

First Steps in Parenting the Child Who Hurts by Caroline Archer

Attaching in Adoption, Practical Tools for Today's Parents by Deborah Gray

Adoption and Foster Care School Awareness Project or ASAP **www.asap-mass.org**

Center for Family Development
Specializing in the treatment of adopted and foster families with trauma and attachment disorder.
www.Center4FamilyDevelop.com

A Forever Family
www.a4everfamily.org

ATTACh – www.attach.org

Attachment & Trauma Network Inc.
Provides Support - Education - Advocacy
(240) 357-7369
info@attachtrauma.org
www.attachtrauma.org
Attachment Disorder Site www.attachmentdisorder.net

Attachment Disorder Support Group
adsg.syix.com

Attachment Institute of New England
Provides treatment, education, and support for children and families experiencing trauma and attachment issues.
www.attachmentnewengland.com

Child Trauma Institute
Training, consultation, information, and resources for those who work with trauma exposed children, adolescents, and adults. Information on trauma, loss, and treatment for adults and for parents. **www.childtrauma.com**

Love & Logic
Provides simple and practical techniques to help parents with kids of all ages
www.loveandlogic.com

Nancy Thomas Parenting **www.nancythomasparenting.com**

National Federation of Families for Children's Mental Health
www.ffcmh.org

RADKID.ORG – **www.RadKid.org**

Adoption in Children Time
Organization devoted to helping foster children find permanent homes
www.adoptioninchildrentime.org

8. Trauma and Abuse

Boy Who was Raised as a Dog by Maia Szalavitz and Bruce Perry

Attaching in Adoption, Tools for Today's Parents by Deborah Gray

ADHD: The Great Misdiagnosis by Julian Stuart Haber

From Fear to Love by B. Bryan Post

New Families, Old Scripts by Caroline Archer and Christine Gordon

Trauma, Attachment and Family Permanence by Caroline Archer and Alan Burnell

Parenting the Hurt Child: Helping Adoptive Families Heal and Grow by Gregory Keck and Regina M. Kupecky

Creating Ceremonies: Innovative Ways to Meet Adoption Challenges by Cheryl A. Lieberman, PhD and Rhea K. Bufferd, LISCW

The Body Remembers: The Psychophysiology of Trauma and Trauma Treatment by Babette Rothschild

Child Trauma Academy
(Bruce D. Perry, MD, PhD) **www.childtrauma.org**

National Center for Post Traumatic Stress Disorder
www.ptsd.va.gov

The Child Trauma Institute
www.childtrauma.com

Attachment & Trauma Resources ATTACh
1268 W. Main St.#2
Sun Prairie, WI 53590
(866) 453-8224
questions@attach.org
www.attach.org

Fight Crime, Invest in Kids
1212 New York Ave. NW, Suite 300
Washington, DC 20005
(202) 776-0027
info@fightcrime.org
Fight Crime: Invest in Kids is an anti-crime organization of over 5,000 police chiefs, sheriffs, prosecutors, and violence survivors. We take a hard look at the research about what prevents kids from becoming crimi-

nals and put that information in the hands of policymakers and the general public.
www.fightcrime.org

Attachment & Trauma Network Inc.
ATN Provides Support -
Education - Advocacy
(240) 357-7369
info@attachtrauma.org
www.attachtrauma.org

Foster Family-Based Treatment Association (FFTA)
294 Union Street
Hackensack, NJ 07601-4303
(201) 343-2246
(800) 414-3382
ffta@ffta.org
The Foster Family-Based Treatment Association is a membership organization committed to enhancing the lives of children and their families by strengthening family-based organizations. Treatment foster care is a model of care that provides children with a combination of traditional foster care and residential treatment centers, with the treatment occurring within the foster family home.
www.ffta.org

Child Trauma Academy
They have free online courses to help understand how children cope with traumatic events. Courses they offer:

- The Amazing Human Brain and Human Development
- Surviving Childhood: An Introduction to the Impact of Trauma
- The Cost of Caring: Secondary Traumatic Stress and the Impact of
- Working with High-Risk Children and Families
- Bonding and Attachment in Maltreated Children

www.childtraumaacademy.com

Stress Free Kids®
Has products designed to help children, teens, and adults decrease stress, anxiety, and anger. These books and CDs will introduce you and your children to the proven techniques of deep breathing, progressive muscular relaxation, visualizations, and affirmations/positive statements. This unique storytelling format has been embraced by psychologists, doctors, child life care specialists, yoga instructors, teachers, counselors, parents, and most importantly... children.
www.stressfreekids.com

Sexual Abuse Resources
Stop it NOW!
(888) PREVENT
or www.StopItNow.org

PEACE of Mind
www.POMWA.org

Darkness to Light
(866) FOR-LIGHT
www.D2L.org

Birds + Bees + Kids
www.BirdsAndBeesAndKids.com

Prevent Child Abuse America
500 North Michigan Ave. Suite 200
Chicago, IL 60611
(312) 663-3520
(800) 244-5373
mailbox@preventchildabuse.org
www.preventchildabuse.org

Specialized Alternatives for Families and Youth (SAFY)
SAFY of America
10100 Elida Road
Delphos, OH 45833
(800) 532-7239
Specialized Alternatives for Families and Youth (SAFY) cares for children who are victims of abuse and neglect.
Headquartered in Delphos, Ohio, SAFY has offices in eight States, focusing on treatment, intervention, adoption and the placement of children whose intensive needs cannot be managed through traditional foster care.
www.safy.org

Youth Law Center (YLC)
200 Pine Street
Suite 300
San Francisco , CA 94104
(415) 543-3379
info@ylc.org
The Youth Law Center works to protect children in the nation's foster care and juvenile justice systems from abuse and neglect, and to ensure that they receive the necessary support and services to become healthy and productive adults. The Center's efforts have focused on strengthening families and advocating for education, medical and mental health, legal sup port, and transition services needed to assure children's success in care and in the community.
www.ylc.org

9. Family Impact

Creating Ceremonies: Innovative Ways to Meet Adoption Challenges by Cheryl A. Lieberman, PhD and Rhea K. Bufferd, LISCW

Neighbor to Family
Brown & Brown Building
220 South Ridgewood Ave.
Daytona Beach, FL 32114
(386) 523-1440
www.neighbortofamily.org
Works to keep siblings in foster care together or connected to facilitate reunification and well being.

Boys Town
14100 Crawford Street
Boys Town, NE 68010
(402) 498-1300
(800) 448-3000
Boys Town provides a continuum of care for children and families.
www.boystown.org

Camp to Belong
P. O. Box 1146
Marana, AZ 85653
info@camptobelong.org
(520) 413-1395
Camp To Belong Summer Camp was created to offer siblings in foster care and other out of home care the opportunity to create lifetime memories while reunited at camp.
www.camptobelong.org

One Simple Wish
1977 North Olden Ave, #292
Trenton, NJ 08618
609.883.8484
info@onesimplewish.org
Granting simple wishes to children and families in need.
www.onesimplewish.org

10. Discipline

1-2-3 Magic: Effective Discipline for Children 2-12 by Thomas W. Phelan, PhD

How to Talk so Kids Will Listen and Listen so Kids will Talk by Adele Faber and Elaine Mazlish

Parenting With Love and Logic: Teaching Children Responsibility by Foster Cline, MD and Jim Fay

The Connected Child: Bring Hope and Healing to Your Adopted Family by Karyn Purvis, PhD, and David Cross, PhD

Building the Bonds of Attachment by Daniel Hughes, PhD

Parenting by Connections
Hand in Hand Parenting works with parents of young children providing resources, training, and lots of support. Our Parenting by Connection approach has given parents practical tools to resolve universal family challenges. Unlike other parenting methods, which rely on systems of rewards and punishment, our philosophy is centered on children's strong, innate desire to love and be loved.
www.handinhandparenting.org

Hearts for Families
P.O. Box 385
Snellville, GA 30078
(770) 972-3664
To strengthen families and those that serve families with nurturing parenting education.
www.heartsforfamilies.org

11. School Tools

For Parents with Special Needs Children in School Wrightslaw: From Emotions to Advocacy The Special Education Survival Guide by Peter W.D. Wright and Pamela Darr Wright

How to Compromise With Your School District Without Compromising Your Child: A Field Guide For Getting Effective Services For Children with Special Needs by Gary Mayerson

The Legal Center For Foster Care & Education
It serves as a national technical assistance resource and information clearinghouse on legal and policy matters affecting the education of children in the foster care system.
ccleducation@staff.abanet.org
www.abanet.org/child/education.

Christine Mitchell's website
Resources for families fostering and adopting out of fostercare.
www.christine-mitchell.com/adoption_and_school_assignments

Bsquared Training and Consulting
Providing training, workshops and consultations to parents, foster parents, mental health professionals.
www.bsquaredtrainings.com

12. Parenting Teens

The Five Love Languages of Children by Gary Chapman and Ross Campbell
The Five Love Languages of Teens by Gary Chapman
Recognizing and Managing Fetal Alcohol Syndrome/Effects: A Guidebook ; Parenting The Story of An Older Child Adoption by Brenda McCreight, PhD

You Gotta Believe!
Older Child Adoption Agency and Homelessness Prevention Program
www.yougottabelieve.org

Brenda McCreight, PhD, RSW
Therapist working children and families facing issues such as sexual abuse, family vio-

lence, adoption, and foster related concerns
www.theadoptioncounselor.com

Foster Care Alumni of America
901 North Washington Street
Suite 208
Arlington, VA 22314
(703) 299-6767
(888) ALU-MNI0
admin@fostercarealumni.org
The mission of Foster Care Alumni of America is to connect the alumni community and to transform policy and practice, ensuring opportunity for people in and from foster care.
www.fostercarealumni.org

FosterClub
753 First Avenue
Seaside, OR 97138
(503) 717-1552
(877) 216 7379
FosterClub provides encouragement, motivation, information, education, and benefits for foster youth. The website provides information relating to foster care including articles, questions and answers (q+a), message boards, contests, discussion of foster care topics, and biographies of famous people who grew up in care.
www.fosterclub.com

Jim Casey Youth Opportunities Initiative
222 South Central, Suite 305
St. Louis, MO 63105
(314) 863-7000
The Jim Casey Youth Opportunities Initiative is a national foundation whose mission is to help youth in foster care make successful transitions to adulthood. Formed by the Annie E. Casey Foundation and Casey Family Programs, the Initiative brings together the people and resources needed to help youth make the connections they need to education, employment, health care, housing, and supportive personal and community relationships.A s a grant-making foundation, the Initiative supports successful community-based efforts that create opportunities and build assets for youth leaving foster care through grants, technical assistance, and coalition building with multiple stakeholders. Grants are made to qualified nonprofit organizations or governmental agencies by invitation only.
www.jimcaseyyouth.org

John H. Chafee Foster Care Independence Program Administration for Children and Families
370 L'Enfant Promenade, SW
Washington, DC 20447
www.acf.hhs.gov/programs/cb/programs_fund/state_tribal/jh_chafee.htm

National Resource Center for Youth Development (NRCYD)
College of Continuing Education
4502 East 41st Street -- Building 4W
Building 4W
Tulsa, OK 74135
(918) 660-3700
dansell@ou.edu
The National Resource Center for Youth Development (NRCYD) helps States incorporate youth into all areas of programs and services, implement services that address legislative requirements, and prepare for Child and Family Services Review (CFSR) and Program Improvement Plan (PIP) development and implementation.
www.nrcys.ou.edu/yd

Orphan Foundation of America (OFA)
21351 Gentry Drive
Unit 130

Sterling, VA 20166
(571) 203-0270
help@orphan.org
The Orphan Foundation of America's mission is to provide opportunities for America's foster youth to continue their education, to increase awareness of the number and plight of older teens leaving the bureaucratic maze of foster care, to highlight the potential of America's foster youth and the importance of supporting their dreams, and to offer direct opportunities for citizens, business, and civic organizations to assist older foster youth.
www.orphan.org

13. Nurturing Identity

Families Change: A Book for Children Experiencing Termination of Parental Rights (Kids Are Important Series) by Julie Nelson

Maybe Days: A Book for Children in Foster Care by Jennifer Wilgocki, Marcia Kahn Wright and Alissa Imre Geis

Kids Need to Be Safe: A Book for Children in Foster Care (Kids Are Important series) by Julie Nelson

My Foster Family: A Story for Children Entering Foster Care by Jennifer Levine

The Dandelion Seed by Joseph P. Anthony and Cris Arbo

The Boy Who was Raised as a Dog: And Other Stories from a Child Psychiatrist's Notebook: What Traumatized Children Can Teach Us About Loss, Love and Healing by Bruce D. Perry, MD, PhD, and Maia Szalavitz

Lifebooks: Creating a Treasure for the Adopted Child by Beth O'Mallery

My Foster Care Journey by Beth O'Mallery

For When I'm Famous: A Teen Foster/Adoption Lifebook by Beth O'Mallery

Talking with Children About Loss by Maria Trozzi

Healing Loss in the Traumatized Child by Marilyn Schoettle, MA and Ellen Singer, LCSW-C

Lifebook Resources
Foster children's lifebook resources & lifebook tips
www.adoptionlifebooks.com

C.A.S.E. - The Center for Adoption Support and Education
4000 Blackburn Lane
Suite 260
Burtonsville, MD 20866
(301) 476-8525
(301) 476-8526
caseadopt@adoptionsupport.org
www.adoptionsupport.org
C.A.S.E. was created to provide post-adoption counseling and educational services to families, educators, child welfare staff, and mental health providers in Maryland, Northern Virginia, and Washington, D.C. In addition, C.A.S.E. is a national resource for families and professionals through its training, publications, and consultations. C.A.S.E. is a private, non-profit adoptive family support center. Its programs focus on helping children from a variety of foster care and adoptive backgrounds to receive understanding and support which will enable them to grow into successful, productive adults.
A site with many resources for adoptive parents - **Olderchildadoptionsupport.com**

14. Allegations

Adopting and Advocating for the Special Needs Child by L. Anne Babbs and Rita Laws, PhD.
For more information on training about

preventing and surviving allegations of abuse, e-mail North American Council on Adoptable Children's Diane Martin Hushman at hushman@nacac.org.

National Foster Parent Association
www.nfpainc.org

National Child Abuse Defense & Resource Center
PO Box 638
Holland, OH 43528
(419) 865-0513
www.falseallegation.org

National Foster Parent Coalition for Allegation Reform
www.nfpcar.org

Foster Parent Legal Solutions
PO Box 175
Yarnell, AZ 85362
(928) 427-0088
www.foster-parents-legal-solutions.com

You Gotta Believe has an article posted at **www.yougottabelieve.org/articles/allegations.htm**

Journal resource for foster parents
www.adoptioninchildtime.org/journal.php

North American Council on Adoptable Children
970 Raymond Ave.
Suite 106
St. Paul, MN 55114
(651) 644-3036
info@nacac.org
www.nacac.org

Legal Advocates for Permanent Parenting (LAPP)
1840 Gateway Drive
Suite 200
San Mateo, CA 94404
(650) 712-1442
info@lapponline.org
www.lapponline.org
The Legal Advocates for Permanent Parenting (LAPP) provides self-help legal information, training, referrals, and consulting on issues of interest to foster parents, kinship caregivers, and pre-adoptive families of children in foster care. In addition, LAPP works to improve communication between child welfare workers, CASAs, attorneys, and the courts and to educate the general public about the fostering and adoptive process, with the goal of encouraging permanence for children in the public child welfare system.

15. Respite & Support

E-Groups to connect with other foster parents:
groups.yahoo.com/group/foster_parenting

It's a topic driven group that changes topics regularly and is a great place to ask questions about your particular situation. Many of the contributors to this book are on this forum. There's lots of thoughtful discussion. Don't forget to keep the privacy requirements of your state when sharing any information online.

FosterCare Central
A forum for foster parents, social workers and foster alumni. **www.fostercarecentral.org**

NFPA Foster Parent Forums www.fosterparentforum.org

Adoption.com Foster Parent Forums
www.forums.adoption.com/foster-parent-support/

Boys Town
14100 Crawford Street
Boys Town, NE 68010
(402) 498-1300
(800) 448-3000
Boys Town provides a continuum of care for children and families.
www.boystown.org

Camp to Belong
P. O. Box 1146
Marana, AZ 85653
info@camptobelong.org
(520) 413-1395
Camp To Belong Summer Camp was created to offer siblings in foster care and other out of home care the opportunity to create lifetime memories while reunited at camp.
www.camptobelong.org

One Simple Wish
1977 North Olden Ave, #292
Trenton, NJ 08618
(609) 883-8484
info@onesimplewish.org
Granting simple wishes to children and families in need.
www.onesimplewish.org

Downloadable respite manual outlines step-by-step guidelines for developing any type of respite care program and includes sample forms that groups can use in the day-today operation of their program.
www.adoptuskids.org/resourceCenter/publications/respiteManual.aspx

16. Reunification, Adoption & Beyond

FLUX: Life After Foster Care by Leigh Ecke and Misty Stenslie and was written to support young people during the emotional transition from foster care to adulthood. Available from **www.fostercarealumni.org**

10 Things College Students Need to Know About Money by Shay Olivarria

Money Matters: The Get It Done in 1 Minute Workbook by Shay Olivarria

Taking a Break: Creating Foster, Adoptive and Kinship Respite in Your Community by AdoptUsKids

Voice for Adoption (VFA)
VFA develops and advocates for improved adoption policies. Recognized as a national leader in special needs adoption, VFA works closely with federal and state legislators, as well as other child welfare organizations, to make a difference in the lives of the 107,000 children in foster care who are waiting to be adopted and the families who adopt children from foster care.
www.voice-for-adoption.org

California Youth Connection
This group's Speak Out Report is a compendium of foster youth voices on the challenges they face and ideas for addressing those challenges. Visit the "Resources" section of their site to find the report.
www.calyouthconn.org

National Resource Center for Youth Development (NRCYD)
College of Continuing Education
4502 East 41st Street -- Building 4W
Building 4W
Tulsa, OK 74135
(918) 660-3700
dansell@ou.edu
The National Resource Center for Youth Development (NRCYD) helps States incorporate youth into all areas of programs and services, implement services that address legislative requirements, and prepare for Child and Family Services Review (CFSR)

and Program Improvement Plan (PIP) development and implementation.
www.nrcys.ou.edu/yd

Orphan Foundation of America (OFA)
21351 Gentry Drive
Unit 130
Sterling, VA 20166
(571) 203-0270
help@orphan.org
The Orphan Foundation of America's mission is to provide opportunities for America's foster youth to continue their education, to increase awareness of the number and plight of older teens leaving the bureaucratic maze of foster care, to highlight the potential of America's foster youth and the importance of supporting their dreams, and to offer direct opportunities for citizens, business, and civic organizations to assist older foster youth.
www.orphan.org

Shay Olivarria
She is a financial education speaker, weekly newspaper columnist, former foster youth and author of *All My Mistakes: Money lessons for emancipating youth, 10 Things College Students Need to Know About Money* and *Money Matters: The Get It Done in 1 Minute Workbook.*
www.helpshayspeak.com
www.biggerthanyourblock.wordpress.com

Children Available for Adoption

Adoption Exchange Association
8015 Corporate Dr. Suite C
Baltimore, MD 21236
(410) 933-5700
(888) 200-4005
www.adoptea.org

AdoptUsKids
Adoption Exchange Association
8015 Corporate Drive Suite C
Baltimore, MD 21236
(888) 200-4005
info@adoptuskids.org
www.adoptuskids.org

Association of Administrators of the Interstate Compact for the Placement of Children
American Public Human Services Association
1133 Nineteenth Street, NW, Suite 400
Suite 500
Washington, DC 20036
(202) 682-0100
ICPCinbox@aphsa.org
The Interstate Compact for the Placement of Children is a uniform State law establishing a contract among party States to ensure that children placed across state lines receive adequate protection and services. The primary function of the ICPC is to protect the interests of both the children and the States by requiring that certain procedures be followed in the interstate placement of children who are being adopted, placed with relatives, or going into residential care or foster family homes.
www.icpc.aphsa.org

Heart Gallery of America
Gracie Station
PO Box 516
New York, NY 10028
(212) 965-8699
www.heartgalleryofamerica.org

The Adoption Exchange
1423 East Evan Ave.
Aurora, CO 80014
(303) 755-4756
(800) 451-5246
www.adoptex.org

Child Advocacy Organizations

A.C.T. In Child Time
815 Gardenbrook Circle, Apt. D
Indianapolis, IN 46202
Attorney Peter Kenny, ACT Exec. Dir.
(317) 924-4963
Psychologist James Kenny, PhD
(317) 635-5220
www.adoptioninchildtime.org

American Foster Care Resources, Inc. (AFCR)
PO Box 271
King George, VA 22485
(540) 775-7410
afcr@afcr.com
AFCR is a publisher of resource materials for foster care providers, the children in care and their families, and the placing agency's staff and administration. AFCR's publications cover such topics as ADHD, discipline, sexual abuse, independent living, recruitment, and support groups.
www.afcr.com

Annie E. Casey Foundation (AECF)
701 St. Paul Street
Baltimore, MD 21202
(410) 547-6600
The Annie E. Casey Foundation works to build better futures for disadvantaged children and their families. The primary mission of the Foundation is to foster public policies, human service reforms, and community supports that meet the needs of today's vulnerable children and families.

Major Program(s)/Initiatives(s):
www.aecf.org/MajorInitiatives.aspx
Family to Family
KidsCount
Family Economic Success
Making Connections
www.aecf.org

Casey Family Programs
1300 Dexter Avenue North
Third Floor
Seattle, WA 98109-3542
(206) 282-7300
(800) 228-3559
info@casey.org
www.casey.org
Casey Family Programs provides an array of services for children and youth, with foster care as it core. Casey services include adoption, guardianship, kinship care, and family reunification. Casey is also committed to helping youth in foster care make a successful transition to adulthood.

Children's Rights
330 Seventh Avenue, 4th Floor
New York, NY 10001
info@childrensrights.org
212) 683-2210
(888) 283-2210
www.childrensrights.org

Center for Child and Family Programs (CCFP)
Institute for the Study of Children, Families, and Communities/CCFP
203 Boone Hall
Ypsilanti, MI 48197
(734) 487-0372
iscfc@emich.edu
The Center for Child and Family Programs (CCFP) has replaced the former National Foster Care Resource Center. The goals of the CCFP are to enhance the lives of vul-

nerable children and families and to shape local, State, and national policies by working with public and private agencies to conduct research, demonstrate new models of service, develop training curricula and provide T/TA, conduct program evaluations, and develop policy recommendations.
www.iscfc.emich.edu

Center for Family Finding and Youth Connectedness
Seneca Center Training Institute
2275 Arlington Drive
San Leandro, CA 94578
(877) 380-5300
familyfinding@senacacenter.org
The mission of the Center for Family Finding is to support systemic changes that block children in out-of-home care from maintaining or reestablishing contact and relationships with those that love them. The Family Finding model offers methods and strategies to locate and engage relatives of children living in out of home care. The goal of family finding is to provide each child with the life long connections that only a family can offer.
www.senecacenter.org/familyfinding

Center for Family Connections
350 Cambridge St.
Cambridge, MA 02141
(617) 547-0909
cffc@kinnect.org
Offers training, education, consultation, advocacy, and clinical treatment to families touched by adoption, foster care, kinship, and guardianship.
www.kinnect.org

General Resources

Child Welfare Information Gateway
Children's Bureau/ACYF
1250 Maryland Avenue, SW 8th Floor
Washington, DC 20024
(800) 394-3366
info@childwelfare.gov
www.childwelfare.gov
Child Welfare Information Gateway connects professionals and the general public to information and resources targeted to the safety, permanency, and well-being of children and families. A service of the Children's Bureau, Administration for Children and Families, U.S. Department of Health and Human Services, Child Welfare Information Gateway provides access to programs, research, laws and policies, training resources, statistics, and much more.

Child Welfare League of America (CWLA)
Headquarters
1726 M St. NW, Suite 500
Third Floor
Washington, DC 20036
(202) 688-4200
The Child Welfare League of America (CWLA) is the oldest national organization serving vulnerable children, youth, and their families. CWLA provides training, consultation, and technical assistance to child welfare professionals and agencies while also educating the public on emerging issues that affect abused, neglected, and at-risk children. Through its publications, conferences, and teleconferences, CWLA shares information on emerging trends, specific topics in child welfare practice (family foster care, kinship care, adoption, positive youth development), and Federal and State policies.
www.cwla.org

Children's Bureau (CB)
1250 Maryland Avenue, SW 8th floor
Washington, DC 20024
The Children's Bureau, the oldest Federal

agency for children and families, is located within the Department of Health and Human Services' Administration for Children and Families, Administration on Children, Youth and Families. The Bureau is responsible for assisting States in the delivery of child welfare services designed to protect children and to strengthen families. The Bureau provides grants to States, Tribes, and communities to operate a range of child welfare services including child protective services, family preservation and support, foster care, adoption, and independent living.
www.acf.hhs.gov/programs/cb/

Congressional Coalition on Adoption Institute (CCAI)
311 Massachusetts Avenue NE
Washington, DC 20002
(202) 544-8500
info@ccainstitute.org
www.ccainstitute.org
The Congressional Coalition on Adoption Institute is a nonprofit, nonpartisan organization dedicated to raising awareness about the foster children in this country and the orphans around the world in need of permanent, safe, and loving homes; and to eliminating the barriers that hinder these children from realizing their basic need of a family.
Major Program(s)/Initiatives(s):
- Angels in Adoption Program
- Foster Youth Internship Program
- Congressional Resource Program
- CCAI International Program
- National Adoption Day

Dave Thomas Foundation for Adoption
525 Metro Place North, Suite 220
Dublin, Ohio 43017
1-800-ASK-DTFA (1-800-275-3832)
info@davethomasfoundation.org
Finding forever families for children in care
www.davethomasfoundation.org

FosteringConnections.org (FC.org)
4301 Connecticut Avenue, NW
Suite 350
Washington, DC 20008
(202) 572-6000
info@fosteringconnections.org
The Fostering Connections Resource Center was established to provide data, online tools, and technical support to aid States and Tribes in the implementation of The Fostering Connections to Success and Increasing Adoptions Act (Fostering Connections), Public Law 110-351 (October 7, 2008). The Fostering Connections Resource Center is supported through contributions of the Annie E Casey Foundation, Casey Family Programs, Dave Thomas Foundation for Adoption, Duke Endowment, Eckerd Family Foundation, Jim Casey Youth Opportunities Initiative, Sierra Health Foundation, Stuart Foundation, and Walter S. Johnson Foundation.
www.fosteringconnections.org

Freddie Mac Foundation
8250 Jones Branch Drive
Mailstop A40
McLean, VA 22102
(703) 918-8888
freddiemac_foundation@freddiemac.com
The Freddie Mac Foundation provides funds for various nonprofit organizations that work on behalf of children, youth, and families. The Foundation focuses on children and prevention-oriented programs. Typically, grants are awarded to programs that build strong families, prevent child abuse and neglect, and recruit foster and adoptive parents. Among the Foundation's major programs are Healthy Families

America and Wednesday's Child USA, a campaign to promote adoptions.
www.freddiemacfoundation.org

National Indian Child Welfare Association
5100 S.W. Macadam Avenue, Suite 300
Portland, Oregon 97239
(503) 222-4044
www.nicwa.org

Pew Charitable Trusts
901 E Street, NW
Washington, DC 20004-2008
(215) 575-9050
(202) 552-2000
info@pewtrusts.org
The Pew Charitable Trusts' goal is to improve public policy, inform the public and stimulate civic life through partnering with a diverse range of donors, public and private organizations, and concerned citizens who share the commitment to fact-based solutions and goal-driven investments to improve society. One of the areas of work for the Pew involves Children and Youth. The Pew supports initiatives, grounded in research and evidence, that aim to help children and youth become active, contributing members of society. At the national level, Pew addresses issues that impact the lives of children, including foster care reform, home visiting, health and dental needs, and educational programs.
www.pewtrusts.org

Voice for Adoption
1220 L Street NW
Suite 100-344
Washington, DC 20005
(202) 210-8118
voiceforadoption@gmail.com
Voice for Adoption (VFA) develops and advocates for improved adoption policies.
voice-for-adoption.org

Social Learning.com
Has training resources to help foster, adoptive and kinship care providers, agencies and schools, backed by attentive customer service and a hassle-free return policy.
www.sociallearning.com

Kinship Resources

Kinship Center
124 River Road
Salinas, CA 93908
(831) 455-9965
(800) 4kinship
Kinship Center provides the full spectrum of family-centered support to strengthen the families and communities we serve.
www.kinshipcenter.org

Casey Family Programs
2001 Eighth Avenue, Suite 2700
Seattle, WA 98121
(206) 282-7300
At Casey Family Programs, we support and assist child welfare systems in their efforts to protect children and create strong families. Children do best in stable families and familiar environments. This gives them the best chance to grow into successful adults. With a variety of programs focused on the child-welfare system, Casey Family Programs is a treasure trove of facts and guides.
www.casey.org

EMQ Families First
251 Llewellyn Ave.
Campbell, CA 95008-1940
(408) 379-3790
They help children and families in need through innovative programs that make a real difference in people's lives.
emqff.org

FosterClub
753 First Avenue
Seaside, OR 97138
(503) 717-1552
A national network supporting young people in foster care
www.fosterclub.org

You Gotta Believe
1728 Mermaid Avenue,
Brooklyn, NY 11224
(718) 372-3003
Their mission is to find adoptive parents for young adults, teens and pre-teens before they age out of the foster care system and run the extremely high risk of becoming homeless.
www.yougottabelieve.org

Jordan Institute for Families,
UNC-CH School of Social Work
John McMahon, Editor
1459 Sand Hill Rd., No. 6 (NCDSS)
Candler, NC 28715
A publication dedicated to making foster care and adoption in North Carolina the best they can be. Online resources and magazine.
www.fosteringperspectives.org

Coaching for LIFE!
15400 West 64th Avenue, #E9-171
Arvada, CO 80007
(303) 431-0604
(866) 570-0604
Juli Alvarado at Coaching for Life! teaches organizations, families and individuals trauma informed and necessary skills for creating and maintaining peaceful systems where healing is ever-present.
www.coaching-forlife.com

Carol Lozier, LCSW
The primary aim of my blog is to educate parents and others on the unique needs of foster and adopted kids with specific strategies tailored to their needs. **www.fosteradoptchildtherapist.com**

Magazines, Books & Other Resources

Fostering Families Today
541 E. Garden Dr. Unit N
Windsor, CO 80550
(888) 924-6736
(970) 686-7413
editor@adoptinfo.net
www.fosteringfamiliestoday.com

Fostering Media Connections
P.O. Box 2343
San Francisco, CA 94126
info@fosteringmediaconnections.org
www.fosteringmediaconnections.org

Youth Communication NY Center, Inc.
224 W. 29th Street
New York, NY 10001
(212) 279-0708
info@youthcomm.org
The mission of Youth Communication is to help teenagers, including foster youth, develop their skills in reading, writing, thinking, and reflection, so they can acquire the information they need to make thoughtful choices about their lives.
www.youthcomm.org

Represent Magazine
224 W. 29th St
New York, NY 10001
(212) 279-0708
Written by and for teens in foster care, Represent provides them a voice to share

personal experiences, to plan for their future, and to help them negotiate the present.
www.representmag.org

Blogs

Blogs can come and go as interest in blogging changes. There are many blogs by current and former foster parents and former foster youth. Search for foster parent blogs or former foster youth blogs to find current ones.

Carrie Craft
Adoption/Foster Care Guide at About.com
www.adoption.about.com

Alan and Eva Walker
Advocates for fostering and adopting and sharing their story through speaking engagements and on their website.
www.allenandeva.com

Anne Birdsong Giberson
She blogs about family, adoption, farm stuff and animals. **www.bringingboryahome.blogspot.com**

Embrace Ministry
A ministry which encourages foster care, adoption, and global orphan care
www.embraceTexas.org

Veronica Brown
Blogs about her foster parenting experience by request from one of her former foster children.
www.redlightworms.com

William Cuchens
Blogging about being a multiracial father
www.goggycoffee.blogspot.com

Amy Heibel
A candid account of her experience with foster/adopting a teen in Los Angeles
www.lafosterblog.blogspot.com

Susan Badeau
Information and stories about her large family formed by fostering and adoption.
www.badeaufamily.com

Research Organizations

Chapin Hall Center for Children
1313 East 60th Street
Chicago, IL 60637
(773) 753-5900
webmaster@chapinhall.org
Chapin Hall is a research and development center focusing on policies, practices, and programs affecting children and the families and communities in which they live. The Center devotes special attention to children facing significant problems such as abuse or neglect, poverty, and mental or physical illnesses, and to the service systems designed to address these problems.
www.chapinhall.org

Child Welfare Research Center (CWRC)
University of California at Berkeley/School of Social Welfare
120 Haviland Hall
Berkeley, CA 94720-7400
The Child Welfare Research Center (CWRC) provides research on a variety of child welfare issues including adoption, case management, foster care, and welfare reform. For access to information on current and archived projects, please see
www.cssr.berkeley.edu/ucb_childwelfare

Children and Family Research Center (CFRC)
1203 W. Oregon
Urbana, IL 61801

(217) 333-5837
(800) 638-3877
cfrc@uiuc.edu
The Children and Family Research Center (CFRC) is dedicated to supporting and conducting research that contributes to keeping children safe, assuring permanent homes for children, and supporting child and family well-being. The CFRC is an independent research organization created at the School of Social Work by the University of Illinois at Urbana-Champaign (UIUC) and the Illinois Department of Children and Family Services (DCFS).
www.cfrc.illinois.edu

Fostering Results Children & Family Research Center
150 North Wacker Drive
Suite 2120
Chicago, IL 60606
(312) 641-2505
fosteringresults@uiuc.edu
General Scope: Fostering Results is a public education and outreach campaign that will work at the national level and in selected States to highlight the need to address the Federal financing mechanisms and to improve court oversight of child welfare cases. Fostering Results is supported by a grant from the Pew Charitable Trusts to the Children and Family Research Center, School of Social Work, University of Illinois at Urbana-Champaign.
www.fosteringresults.org

Institute for the Study of Children, Families, and Communities (ISCFC)
Eastern Michigan University
203 Boone Hall
Ypsilanti, MI 48197
(734) 487- 0372
iscfc@emich.edu
The Institute for the Study of Children, Families and Communities, at Eastern Michigan University, explores contemporary issues and enriches family and community life through the application of scholarly research and practical expertise, innovative projects and leadership in collaborative problem-solving efforts. The Institute operates through four Centers, including the Center for Child and Family Programs (CCFP). The CCFP has replaced the National Foster Care Resource Center at the Institute. While the CCFP maintains a strong commitment to child welfare and foster care, it has broadened its focus to reflect diverse community needs as well as children and youth in crisis.
www.iscfc.emich.edu

Institute for Human Services North American Resource Center for Child Welfare
Gwinn House
1706 East Broad St.
Columbus, OH 43203
(614) 251-6000
The North American Resource Center for Child Welfare (NARCCW) is an umbrella organization of agencies working to achieve best practice in child welfare by providing professionals with the resources necessary to help children and families.
www.ihs-trainet.com

Index

On the following pages you will find CEU quizzes for each chapter. These are "open book" quizzes. As you read the articles identified in each of the questions, you should be able to answer the questions. Once you have completed the questions for the chapter, photocopy or tear out the completed pages, **attach your essay on a separate sheet of paper** (it may be typed or handwritten), send to the address below with the correct processing fee. **Be sure to check with your placement agency to see if they will credit you for completing the CEU Quiz.** You will be mailed a Certificate of Credit for each completed quiz.

Downloadable copies of these forms are available at www.emkpress.com/FPCEUquizzes.htm

Mail them to:

EMK Press
16 Mt Bethel Road #219
Warren, NJ 07059

Pay by check with a processing fee of $5.00 for each quiz make the check payable to EMK Press.

Fax them or email them to:

732-469-7544 or scan and email them to ceuquiz@emkpress.com and use Paypal to pay the processing fee. Send paypal payment to ceuquiz@emkpress.com. Please be sure to include your name in the payment information.

Please include the following information when you send in each completed quiz (this is at the bottom of each quiz):

Name____

Address ____

City ______________________________**State** ______**Zip** ________

Private or State Agency Contact______________________________

Office Address/PO Box __________________________________

City ______________________________**State** ______**Zip** ________

Learning Objective: to increase foster and/or adoptive parents' ability to apply and respond to new information and conceptal frameworks to their work with children in their care. Please rate the following on a scale of 1-4 (1 is poor, 4 is excellent):

The information was informative: (1-2-3-4)

The information was useful/helpful in my role as a foster/adoptive parent: (1-2-3-4)

The information was thought-provoking, (1-2-3-4) especially the story on page(s)

____

I would be interested in reading more on the topic(s) of: ____________________

Foster Parenting Toolbox CEU Quiz: Why Foster?

1. **The article titled "The Day That Changed My Life" by Michele Burnette talks about her expectations when she first started fostering. Which of the following did she realize were inaccurate:**

a. Foster parenting is a way to save a child.

b. A child should feel comfortable right away because of her "gingerbread" house filled with toys and fresh cookies.

c. It is important as a foster parent to give a child the chance to be a child.

d. Foster care is about making a connection intended to last a lifetime.

2. **According to the article, "Selecting Foster Parents: What to Expect and Ask," by Eileen Mayers Pasztor, DSW, and Donna D. Petras, PhD, on page 4, which of the following questions typically are asked by potential foster parents?**

a. How many children am I required to foster?

b. In what ways is fostering similar or different from parenting birth children?

c. What kinds of references are needed?

d. How much does it cost to be a foster parent?

3. **Which of the following definitions of out-of-home care is TRUE based on the "Definitions" article on page 5?**

a. It is the overall term for child welfare services that are not provided for children.

b. A mandated child welfare services for children and parents who must live apart while maintaining legal and, almost always, affectional ties.

c. The overall term for child welfare services that are provided for children and parents who are not living together, including family foster care, kinship care, group homes or residential treatment facilities.

4. **In the article "Selecting Foster Parents: What to Expect and Ask," by Eileen Mayers Pasztor, DSW, and Donna D. Petras, PhD, on page 7, what items can you expect to be required to provide for a child placed in your home:**

a. A safe and nurturing environment.

b. Age appropriate structure and discipline.

c. Support for birth family visits.

d. Participation as part of a team.

e. All of the above.

5. **According to the article, "Foster Parent Stipends: Are They Doing it for the Money?" by Sarah Gerstanzang, MSW, on page 13, why does the "doing it for the money" stereotype exist?**

a. Negative perceptions are drawn because many of the people who step forward as foster parents are poor.

b. Negative perceptions exist because social workers believe most foster parents do it for the money.
c. Many foster parents depend on foster care stipends as their primary income.
d. The media is to blame for focusing on negative stories where foster parents abuse or neglect children in their care.

6. According to Crystal Frazier, foster youth, on page 15, what is the most challenging thing about being in foster care?

____

7. List one of the things author Emily Parks recommends to new foster parents trying to understand how fostering works according to the article, "Navigating the System," on page 16.

____

8. In the article "Why I Stay" by Amy Bates, a friend of hers has a personal motto. What is it?

____

What is her hope for every child she touches with kindness?

____

9. Essay: Why did you become a foster parent? What have you learned about yourself on your foster parenting journey? What advice would you give to other foster parents? Please use a separate piece of paper.

Please print clearly:

Name ______________________________

Address ______________________________

City ______________________________ **State** ______ **Zip** __________

Private or State Agency Contact ______________________________

Office Address/PO Box ______________________________

City ______________________________ **State** ______ **Zip** __________

Learning Objective: to increase foster and/or adoptive parents' ability to apply and respond to new information and conceptal frameworks to their work with children in their care. Please rate the following on a scale of 1-4 (1 is poor, 4 is excellent):

The information was informative: (1-2-3-4)

The information was useful/helpful in my role as a foster/adoptive parent: (1-2-3-4)

The information was thought-provoking, (1-2-3-4) especially the story on page(s)

____

I would be interested in reading more on the topic(s) of: ______________________________

Foster Parenting Toolbox CEU Quiz: Perspectives

1. In "We Need More Than the Obvious" by Tamarra Lestage on page 24, she talks about how she wanted to be treated and introduced. What introduction did she feel put her in an awkward position?

____

2. Which of following "tough starts" should foster parents understand about a child's behavior, according to the article, "Tough Starts Matter," by Adoption Learning Partners staff on page 26?

a. Ignoring children's past helps them move on.

b. Recognizing the importance of early diagnosis.

c. Learning the causes of domestic violence.

d. Neglect causes brain damage to children.

3. Which of the following are among the eight parts to children's development according to the article, "The Jigsaw Puzzle Child," by Eileen Mayers Pasztor, DSW, on page 29?

a. Life experience age.

b. Age of puberty

c. Academic age

d. Ethnic age

4. In the "Jigsaw Puzzle Child," Eileen Mayers Pasztor suggests that you create a jigsaw puzzle diagram and place it where?

____

5. List two of the eight people you can turn to with your shortcomings and frustrations as a parent, according to the article "Taking off the Mask" by Anne Birdsong Giberson, on page 33.

a. ____

b. ____

6. In the article "To the Honorable Judge Michael Usan " by Mackenzie Ramsay on page 36, what is the one critical ingredient for a foster youth's success?

____

7. **In "Be There" by Veronica Brown, what was the lesson she learned?**

___

8. **Tina Severance-Fonte writes in "Foster Care Reflections" on page 43 that while she was sad her foster child would leave them for reuinfication with her biological mother, her family did not suffer psychological and emotional pain with this placement because**

___

9. **How can foster parents best help the children they care for, according to the article by Mariah Berry on page 45**
   a. By letting children feel like they are just a job.
   b. By keeping in touch after they leave.
   c. By actually taking them to dental and doctors appointments like a real parent.
   d. By feeling sorry for the kids and letting them get away with stuff.

10. **Essay: What do you do to make the children in your care comfortable in your home? What have you learned in your years of foster parenting**

___

Please print clearly:

Name ___

Address ___

City ___ **State** ___ **Zip** ___

Private or State Agency Contact ___

Office Address/PO Box ___

City ___ **State** ___ **Zip** ___

Learning Objective: to increase foster and/or adoptive parents' ability to apply and respond to new information and conceptal frameworks to their work with children in their care. Please rate the following on a scale of 1-4 (1 is poor, 4 is excellent):

The information was informative: (1-2-3-4)

The information was useful/helpful in my role as a foster/adoptive parent: (1-2-3-4)

The information was thought-provoking, (1-2-3-4) especially the story on page(s)

___

I would be interested in reading more on the topic(s) of: ___

Foster Parenting Toolbox CEU Quiz: Transitions

1. **Which of the following are some of the common circumstances when children are moved through the foster care system, according to the article, "Life Links: Transitioning children in Foster Care with Less Trauma," by Jennifer Winkelman, MA, LPC, NCC, on page 48?**

a. Having new clothes packed in a suitcase upon arrival.
b. Bicycles and other belongings left behind.
c. Belongings transported in trash bags and items are sometimes lost in transit.
d. Arrival at the new home in desperate need of a bath or with untreated illness.

2. **Which of the following are some things to keep in mind to promote the long-term success of a child who has experienced foster care, according to the article, "My First Night" by Adam Robe, MSW, on page 53?**

a. A child's self-esteem and identity are affected.
b. Children in foster care are happy to be safe and protected.
c. Children will go through the stages of grief and loss.
d. Children will ask many questions about their new family and environment.

3. **According to the article, "Easing the Pain of Separation," by Noelle Hause, EdD, LPC, on page 55, what can foster parents do to help a young foster child adjust to a new situation?**

a. Children should share a room so they are not lonely.
b. Be an advocate for developmentally appropriate skills, expectations, and practices for the young child in your care.
c. Tell the truth appropriate to the child's gender.
d. Listen to concerns and questions posed by your child.

4. **In "Feeling Fostered" on page 57, Missy Kenny Corron learned a lot from looking at photos of her when she was in Kindergarten. What did she learn?**

____

5. **In "To Be Concerned? Or Not To Be Concerned? That is the Question!" by Nicolle Hause on page 61, if you have unanswered questions or are interested in learning more about your foster child's behavior, what are two of the suggestions she has for you?**

____

6. **List two of the nine social milestones for the end of 48 months, according to the article, "To Be Concerned on Not to Be Concerned," by Noelle Hause, EdD, LPC, on page 61.**

a. ____
b. ____

7. According to the article, "Preparing for Adoption," by Claudia Fletcher on page 69, what must foster parents do once children are legally free until an adoptive family has been identified?

a. Re-affirm your love for the child and explain that it is okay to love many people.
b. Keep hope alive.
c. Help them pack their bags.
d. Look through photos of potential families together.

9. Which of the following are among some of the unanticipated emotional challenges that come with raising a kin member, according to the article, "To Grandmother's House We Go," by Ron Huxley, LMFT, and Catie Hargrove, MS, on page 73?

a. Dealing with choices their child has made and how this affected their grandchild.
b. Holding onto child rearing practices that may conflict with current social standards and from the child welfare system.
c. Confusion about who has final say on the welfare of the child.
d. Feeling forced into a role of honesty to avoid legal conflict and having children placed in the "system."

10. Essay: What have you done to help foster children transition to and from your home?

____

Please print clearly:

Name ____

Address ____

City ______________________ **State** ______ **Zip** ________

Private or State Agency Contact ______________________________

Office Address/PO Box ______________________________

City ______________________ **State** ______ **Zip** ________

Learning Objective: to increase foster and/or adoptive parents' ability to apply and respond to new information and conceptal frameworks to their work with children in their care. Please rate the following on a scale of 1-4 (1 is poor, 4 is excellent):

The information was informative: (1-2-3-4)

The information was useful/helpful in my role as a foster/adoptive parent: (1-2-3-4)

The information was thought-provoking, (1-2-3-4) especially the story on page(s)

____

I would be interested in reading more on the topic(s) of: ______________________

Foster Parenting Toolbox CEU Quiz: Teamwork

1. Which of the following statements is TRUE based on the article, "Working with Caseworkers," By Veronica Brown on page 78?

a. In my home, when a worker comes for a monthly visit, it's a big deal and a big production.

b. My philosophy has been for all the participants to know what's coming, almost like an agenda.

c. I also try to give some of the glory to the child.

d. Foster children do not need to know that their worker cares and is working hard for them.

2. According to the article, "What Inny Taught Us," by Allen Walker on page 79, what did the family learn while foster parenting "Inny?"

a. The pain to your heart when foster parenting is not worth the trouble.

b. It does not hurt to let go of a foster child.

c. We choose not to judge the parents, but instead to love them.

d. The judicial system is unfairly slanted toward reunification.

3. In Wanda Chamber's article "Forever Family: My Daughter's Foster Mother is Still a Part of Our Lives", after reunification with her daughter, she wanted to end any contact with the foster family. Why did she change her mind?

___

4. What has William Cutchens in his article, "The Good Fight" learned about himself on his role as a father to foster children?

___

5. What did author Denise Kendrick learn about advocating for children in her home, according to the article, "Teaching Sidney" on page 86?

a. I put the emphasis on myself rather than Sidney.

b. I felt called to help foster children like Sidney.

c. I needed a break to be a better foster parent.

d. I had neglected to give Jan the tools and information she needed to help Sidney succeed.

6. In "Teaching Sidney" What three things does the author say that Sidney taught her?

a. ____

b. ____

c. ____

7. In Veronica Brown's article " Thanks to You" , She states that if she states that if she takes credit for all the children who do well, What else must she take credit for?

____

8. Which of the following statements is FALSE according to the article, "CASAs Can Make a Difference," by Randee Kaitcer on page 90?

a. Foster families fail in big and little ways often without realizing it.

b. Building relationships is key to being a successful CASA volunteer.

c. All children need stability security and felt safety, acceptance, discipline, respect, encouragement and a place to call home.

d. A CASA volunteer can help facilities arranging sibling visits between separated brothers and sisters.

9. Essay: How have you seen members of a foster child's team work together? What role should foster parents play in that team?

____

Please print clearly:

Name ____

Address ____

City ______________________________ **State** ________ **Zip** ________

Private or State Agency Contact ______________________________

Office Address/PO Box ______________________________

City ______________________________ **State** ________ **Zip** ________

Learning Objective: to increase foster and/or adoptive parents' ability to apply and respond to new information and conceptal frameworks to their work with children in their care. Please rate the following on a scale of 1-4 (1 is poor, 4 is excellent):

The information was informative: (1-2-3-4)

The information was useful/helpful in my role as a foster/adoptive parent: (1-2-3-4)

The information was thought-provoking, (1-2-3-4) especially the story on page(s)

____

I would be interested in reading more on the topic(s) of: ______________________

Foster Parenting Toolbox CEU Quiz: Birth Family Connections

1. **Eileen Mayers Pasztor, DSW, writes about lessons she learned as a foster parent in "Children in Foster Care and Their Parents: Lessons Learned." What lesson did she learn about what foster children should call their foster parents?**

___

2. **Which of the following statements if FALSE according to the article, "Let's Have the Conversation," by Eileen Mayers Pasztor, DSW, on page 99?**

a. Child welfare continues to be overly female focused.

b. Most children come into the foster care system because of their parents' mental illness.

c. Child welfare is one of the few, if only, life-saving professions which lacks uniform standards for mandatory skills.

d. We need serious conversations in our community about what can be done to help young people avoid having babies they cannot take care of.

3. **Which of the following are the goals of the collaboration between the NFAPA and the Nebraska Federation of Families to bring resource parents and birth parents together early on, according to the article, "Co-Parenting/Working with Birth Parents," By Pamela Allen on page 100?**

a. Build positive relationships between birth and foster parents.

b. Allow foster parents to better understand where children in foster care come from.

c. Change the perception that "foster families are good" and "birth families are bad."

d. Long-term collaboration.

4. In "Eat, Play, Love" written by a mother whose child was removed by the foster care system on page 102, name one thing that Lydia's mother learned in her parenting classes that she had not learned from her own childhood?

___

5. **Which of the following are among the "Strategies for Success in Working with Birth Parents," by Betty Daigle Hastings on page 106?**

a. Make it clear how you feel about drug abuse and violence.

b. Open the lines of communication.

c. Show respect to the birth parents.

d. Create a lifebook with the foster child.

6. **Angie Cross, a foster care alumna, on page 108, is still learning what?**

___

7. List the three things that people in the stories from the article," Embracing the Importance of Birth Parents in the Lives of Adopted and Foster Children," by Ellen Singer, LCSW-C, on page 109, did in order to better work together.

a. ____________________

b. ____________________

c. ____________________

8. Joyce Maguire Pavao, EdD, writes in "Unnecessary Losses" on page 113 about the word termination and creating a ritual "as if" the relationship has ended. What does she believe is the internal reality of the child?

a. Even if birth parents die, it's never over

b. Termination helps children understand they can never have a relationship with birth family again.

c. If a child has never seen the birth family, no connection will exist between them.

d. The internal realities for the child are at odds with the external realities.

9. Essay: How has your perception of birth families changed since becoming a foster parent?

____

Please print clearly:

Name ____________________

Address ____________________

City ____________________ **State** ______ **Zip** ______

Private or State Agency Contact ____________________

Office Address/PO Box ____________________

City ____________________ **State** ______ **Zip** ______

Learning Objective: to increase foster and/or adoptive parents' ability to apply and respond to new information and conceptal frameworks to their work with children in their care. Please rate the following on a scale of 1-4 (1 is poor, 4 is excellent):

The information was informative: (1-2-3-4)

The information was useful/helpful in my role as a foster/adoptive parent: (1-2-3-4)

The information was thought-provoking, (1-2-3-4) especially the story on page(s)

____

I would be interested in reading more on the topic(s) of: ____________________

Foster Parenting Toolbox CEU Quiz: Loss, Grief & Anger

1. Which of the following are among the steps to be a "smart enough" parent, according to the article, "Smart Enough Parenting" by Susan Badeau on page 118?

a. Learn to recognize the warning signs of when a child needs more than parental support.

b. Learn your child's triggers and responses to stress.

c. Create a positive learning environment for your child.

d. Know how to ask the right questions to get appropriate service and interventions for your child.

2. Which of the following are two points to remember about being realistic about responsibility, according to the article, "Quiet or Defiant," by Terry de Forrest, MFT, PhD, on page 122?

a. Children should have chores to earn an allowance.

b. When a child is asked to do something and he or she doesn't do it right, it doesn't necessarily mean he or she is being oppositional.

c. Let children know they are responsible for mowing the lawn.

d. Let the child know what he or she is expected to be responsible for his or her own behavior.

3. Terry de Forrest, MFT, PhD, suggest several methods to maintain when working with a challenging foster child's control in the article, "Quiet or Defiant," on page 122. What is one his suggestions?

____

4. What are three things a parent or caregiver could say suggested by Lynne Namka, EdD, in her article "Help Your Child Ward Off a Mad Attack" on page 125.

a. ____

b. ____

c. ____

5. Which of the following should you do if you start to see your child fall apart, according to the article, "Being with your Child in Public Places," by Patty Wipfler on page 127?

a. If necessary, move to a more socially acceptable place.

b. When you see an upset beginning, promise your child a treat if he or she behaves.

c. When you see an upset beginning, immediately make real contact.

d. Stay home to avoid conflict in public places.

6. List two of the "10 Ways to Help Children Feel Less Anxious," according to

the article by Martha B. Strauss, PhD And Melanie Erould, MA on page 129.

a. ______

b. ______

7. Which of the following bad messages about children could be included on index cards for the making room for good message activity, according to the article, "Trying to Shift a Child's Negative Behavior Pattern" by Cheryl A. Lieberman, PhD and Rhea K. Bufferd, LICSW, on page 140?

a. You are a good kid, I just need to get my act together.

b. You are a lovable child.

c. You drive me crazy.

d. It is your fault you can't live here.

8. In "Trying to Shift a Child's Negative Behavior Pattern" by Cheryl J. Lieberman, PhD, and Rhea K. Bufferd, LICSW, what are four of the recommended good messages they suggest for Matthew?

a. ______

b. ______

c. ______

d. ______

9. Essay: What are some ways you've worked with your foster children on their anger, loss or grief?

Please print clearly:

Name ______

Address ______

City ______ **State** ______ **Zip** ______

Private or State Agency Contact ______

Office Address/PO Box ______

City ______ **State** ______ **Zip** ______

Learning Objective: to increase foster and/or adoptive parents' ability to apply and respond to new information and conceptal frameworks to their work with children in their care. Please rate the following on a scale of 1-4 (1 is poor, 4 is excellent):

The information was informative: (1-2-3-4)

The information was useful/helpful in my role as a foster/adoptive parent: (1-2-3-4)

The information was thought-provoking, (1-2-3-4) especially the story on page(s)

______

Foster Parenting Toolbox CEU Quiz: Attachment & Trust

1. Which of the following statements is TRUE based on the article, "Now & Forever: Foster parents Build the roots of Attachment," by Charlotte Simpson on page 150?

a. The presence of living caregivers at the right time cannot make a difference.

b. Foster parents cannot play a key role in helping children learn to trust.

c. Tough parenting during childhood builds a healthy foundation for future development.

d. More than 500,000 children currently live in foster care in the U.S.

2. List two of the four most important factors in placement, according to the article, "Attachment 101" by Arthur Becker-Weidman, PhD, on page 150.

a. ______________________________

b. ______________________________

3. Marian Berry, a former foster youth, talks about how she had been lied to about her birthparents on page 155. What does she think is important for foster parents and caseworkers to share about birth parents?

____

4. Which of the following are traits of an insecure/disorganized child, according to the article, "The Attachment Spectrum," by Doris Landry, MS, LLP, on page 156?

a. Exhibit hurtful behaviors to animals or other people.

b. Smears feces on the walls.

c. Cries uncontrollably.

d. Acts alarmed, freezing in place under stress.

5. In "Fostering Regressive Behavior" on page 158, Corinne Watt shares a graphic illustration called "The Wall". What kinds of "bricks" are included in a child's wall?

a. ______________________________

b. ______________________________

c. ______________________________

d. ______________________________

6. In "Breaking Through" by Erik Cooper on page 162, what was the sentence

that Erik said to Rusty that shook him out of his rising fury?

____

7. **Which of the following represents the five parent-quality attitudes of PLACE, according to the article, "Creating PLACE," by Daniel Hughes, PhD, on page 165?**
   a. Playfulness, Love, Attitude, Curiosity and Empathy
   b. Playfulness, Love, Acceptance, Curiosity and Empathy
   c. Playfulness, Love, Acceptance, Creativity and Empathy
   d. Playfulness, Longevity, Acceptance, Creativity and Empathy

8. **According to the article, "Bonding is a Vital Issue: Appellate Courts Agree," by James A. Kenny, PhD and Mark Bontrager, MSW, JD, on page 169, which of the following are the concrete, evidentiary ways bonding can be defined?**
   a. The affection shown.
   b. Reciprocal attachment.
   c. The behavior of the child.
   d. Number of children in the family.

9. **Essay: What do you do to build attachment with your foster children?**

____

Please print clearly:

Name ____

Address ____

City ______________________ **State** ______ **Zip** __________

Private or State Agency Contact ______________________________

Office Address/PO Box ______________________________

City ______________________ **State** ______ **Zip** __________

Learning Objective: to increase foster and/or adoptive parents' ability to apply and respond to new information and conceptal frameworks to their work with children in their care. Please rate the following on a scale of 1-4 (1 is poor, 4 is excellent):

The information was informative: (1-2-3-4)

The information was useful/helpful in my role as a foster/adoptive parent: (1-2-3-4)

The information was thought-provoking, (1-2-3-4) especially the story on page(s)

____

Foster Parenting Toolbox CEU Quiz: Trauma & Abuse

1. According to the article, "ADHD or Trauma?" by Robin D. Hayes, PhD, on page 176, misdiagnosis of trauma as ADHD occurs when?

a. Children have been in foster care.

b. Symptoms are misinterpreted.

c. Histories of trauma are ignored or unknown.

d. Clinicians have not worked with foster children previously.

2. According to the article, "Connecting with the Hurting Foster Child" by Betty Daigle Hastings on page 179, what can foster parents do to make transitions go more smoothly?

a. Foster parents need to always treat the child with respect, acceptance and willingness to show unconditional love.

b. Create a welcome scrapbook for the child.

c. Give each child the opportunity to start with a clean slate as he or she enters a new home.

d. Foster parents should prove to foster children that they do not make mistakes.

3. List three of the "Ten Keys to Healing Trauma in the Adopted and Foster Child," by B. Bryan Post, LCSW, on page 181.

a. ______________________________

b. ______________________________

c. ______________________________

4. Jessica Hamblen, PhD, writes in "What Does PTSD look like in Children" that young children may present with few of the PTSD symptoms. Because

a. Eight of the symptoms require a verbal description of feelings and experience.

b. Children report more specific rather than generalized fears like stranger danger

c. Children repeat themes of the trauma in play

d. Children do not lose any acquired developmental skills due to the trauma.

5. On "A Journey with Jason" by M. Kim Combes on page 186, what was the one question Jason asked Kim as he "interviewed" him before deciding to move to be part of Kim's foster family?

____

6. According to the article, "Sexual Abuse: How to Get (and Give) Help by Amy

Lang, MA, on page 189, which of the following can be considered warning signs that abuse may have occurred?

a. An older child behaving like a younger child such as bed-wetting/thumb sucking.

b. Losing money.

c. Clinging to adults for attention.

d. New words for private parts.

7. **The ceremony, "You are Safe Here" on page 192 by Cheryl A. Lieberman, PhD, and Rhea K. Bufferd, LICSW, uses frank language that specifically sets boundaries for sexual conduct. According to Project Impact in Boston, what impact has using this sort of boundary setting had?**

____

8. **Which of the following are the five emotional stages that vulnerable children pass through, according to the article, "Don't Make Kids Wait," by James A. Kenny, PhD On page 194?**

a. Sadness, solitude, hope, indifference, anger

b. Hope, fear, anger, depression, indifference

c. Encouragement, anger, sadness, hope, fear

d. Calm, anger, depression, sadness, hope

9. **Essay: What do you do to help your foster children deal with their past trauma?**

____

Please print clearly:

Name ____

Address ____

City ______________________________ **State** ______ **Zip** ________

Private or State Agency Contact ______________________________

Office Address/PO Box ____________________________________

City ______________________________ **State** ______ **Zip** ________

Learning Objective: to increase foster and/or adoptive parents' ability to apply and respond to new information and conceptal frameworks to their work with children in their care. Please rate the following on a scale of 1-4 (1 is poor, 4 is excellent):

The information was informative: (1-2-3-4)

The information was useful/helpful in my role as a foster/adoptive parent: (1-2-3-4)

The information was thought-provoking, (1-2-3-4) especially the story on page(s)

____

Foster Parenting Toolbox CEU Quiz: Family Impact

1. In " Island of Calm" by Denise Kendrick, on page 198, she shares the experience her family had fostering Russ and Joshua, name two milestones that each of them celebrated/accomplished in their home?

a. ____________________

b. ____________________

c. ____________________

d. ____________________

2. How can you help children embrace their identity during the holidays according to the article, "Family Holidays," by Adam Robe, MSW, on page 201?

a. Bake cookies to give to their birth family.

b. Start a new tradition and explain how they are part of it.

c. Document the night with pictures and create a scrapbook for the child to take with him or her.

d. Sing Christmas carols together.

3. In "Prince Charming" by Alexeah Smith, on page 202, one child who entered their family named Holden, educated them about the issues he faced but also taught her an important lesson. What was it?

____

____

____

4. Which of the following tools for teaching kids how to evaluate situations does author Cheryl Leppert use in the article, "Why Do You Ask?" on page 206?

a. Show how to access emotions to create a response.

b. Create a book with a list of responses.

c. Model good responses.

d. Role play with them.

5. List two of the five strategies for formulating a response when strangers ask questions according to the article, "Why do You Ask?" by Cheryl Leppert on page 206.

a. ____________________

b. ____________________

6. **In "Choosing Teens" by Denise Kendrick, on page 208, after reading about a waiting child named Daniel, she learned he was fighting the battle of his life without a mother, What was Daniel fighting?**

a. ________________________________

7. **On Page 217, the article" Can't Live With Them, Forced to Live Without Them" by Kasey Carty Jordan, describes one reason for separating siblings as "parentification". According to Jordan, what is parentification?**

____

____

8. **According to the article, "Ensuring Family Fit for Foster Families" by Betty Daigle Hastings on page 214, when foster parents decide to refuse a placement, what is important for them to do?**

a. Clearly express to the agency why.
b. Not let the decision haunt them.
c. Create a secure home for the next child.
d. Pray the child is placed with a better family.

10. Essay: What impact has foster parenting had on you and your family?

____

Please print clearly:

Name ____

Address ____

City ______________________ **State** ______ **Zip** __________

Private or State Agency Contact ______________________

Office Address/PO Box ______________________

City ______________________ **State** ______ **Zip** __________

Learning Objective: to increase foster and/or adoptive parents' ability to apply and respond to new information and conceptal frameworks to their work with children in their care. Please rate the following on a scale of 1-4 (1 is poor, 4 is excellent):

The information was informative: (1-2-3-4)

The information was useful/helpful in my role as a foster/adoptive parent: (1-2-3-4)

The information was thought-provoking, (1-2-3-4) especially the story on page(s)

____

Foster Parenting Toolbox CEU Quiz: Discipline

1. Which of the following are among the five steps to setting limits, according to the article, "Don't Use an Elephant Gun to Shoot a Mouse," by Walt Piszchala on page 222?

a. Review the consequences.

b. Create a list of rules.

c. Be prepared to enforce.

d. Don't bend the rules of the house.

2. Jo Ann Wentzel writes about how to be a consistant parent in " The Value of Consistency" on page 225. That consistency means nothing to kids if what?

____

3. What do "lines in the sand" parenting tell foster children according to the article, "Appropriate Boundaries in Parenting," by Sue Laney on page 227?

a. The are good enough to set their own boundaries.

b. The parent is incapable of setting appropriate boundaries.

c. They need to follow the same boundaries as other family members.

d. The parent is capable of setting appropriate boundaries.

4. Which of the following are among the four techniques for successful listening, according to the article, "The Extra Layer and Discipline Strategies," by Deborah Moore on page 230?

a. Offer your opinion.

b. You don't need to fix it.

c. Take notes.

d. Describe the problem.

5. On page 230, Doris Landry, MS, illustrates the Cycle of Want. In her opinion, what completes the cycle?

____

6. Allison Maxon, MS, MFT, writes about how to become your Foster Child's Emotional tutor, on page 235. In the article, she talks about which emotions you should allow your child to see you express. Which ones does your child need to see you express? And why ?

a.____

b.______________________________

7. **In Drs James A. and Mary Kenny's "Family Talk and Discipline" article, on page 239, how do they feel about punishment?**

____

8. **Which of the following are categories you can use to prioritize which behaviors to work on with a child, according to the article, "Picking Your Battles," by Jo Ann Wentzel on page 242?**

a. Behaviors, activities, or problems that interfere with the foster child's education.
b. Behaviors, activities, or problems that others find fascinating.
c. Behaviors, activities, or problems that are against the law.
d. Behaviors, activities, or problems that are funny or entertaining.

9. **Essay: Which discipline strategies have you used with your foster children? Which have been the most beneficial? Which have not worked?**

____

Please print clearly:

Name ______________________________

Address ______________________________

City ______________________________ **State** ______ **Zip** __________

Private or State Agency Contact ______________________________

Office Address/PO Box ______________________________

City ______________________________ **State** ______ **Zip** __________

Learning Objective: to increase foster and/or adoptive parents' ability to apply and respond to new information and conceptal frameworks to their work with children in their care. Please rate the following on a scale of 1-4 (1 is poor, 4 is excellent):

The information was informative: (1-2-3-4)

The information was useful/helpful in my role as a foster/adoptive parent: (1-2-3-4)

The information was thought-provoking, (1-2-3-4) especially the story on page(s)

____

Foster Parenting Toolbox CEU Quiz: School Tools

1. **According to the article, "Supporting Fostering and Adopted Children in the Classroom," by Christine Mitchell, on page 248, what can caregivers do to help teachers understand a child's unique learning, social, emotional and behavioral challenges?**

a. Give teachers full disclosure of a child's past.

b. If a child has shown any tendency for confusing memories or caregiver names, it might be wise to inform the teacher before a serious misunderstanding occurs.

c. Create a book of information about the child in your care for teachers to reference.

d. It is wise to schedule a conference with the child's teacher before or after the start of school to discuss the child's unique needs.

2. **What is the definition of IDEA, according to the article, "Making Sense of the Letters," on page 251.**

____

3. **According to the article, "Overcoming Difficult Comprehension Challenges," by Lee Tobin McClain, PhD, on page 252, what ways can you help children with reading comprehension at home?**

a. Read aloud and get him or her to read aloud to you.

b. Keep books throughout the house.

c. Let children choose books that aren't too difficult.

d. Make reading a priority.

4. **Also in "Overcoming Difficult Comprehension Challenges", what are the three higher stages of reading that are useful for high school and older students?**

a. ____

b. ____

c. ____

5. **List one of the three ways you can support young people by creating a culture of learning in your home, according to the article, "Encouraging Education," by Misty Stenslie on page 257.**

____

6. **In "Motivating Challenging Foster Kids:", on page 259, Shemille Brown, LCSW-C, suggests three ways to reduce the amount of stress and anxiety in your home. What are they?**

a. ____

b. ____

c. ______________________________

7. What should a child's IEP contain, according to the article, "Special Education 101" by June Bond, MSW, and Mary Eaddy on page 262.

a. A list of additional local resources for children.

b. No later than 16, your child's IEP must include measurable post-secondary goals relating to training, education, employment or independent living skills.

c. The IEP should address testing modifications or changes in how tests are administered.

d. IEPs must include a year-by-year list of annual goals for your child.

8. In school, there will be assignments which surface that might be difficult and trigger reactions from children in your care. List three that are detailed in "Troublesome Family-based School Assignments" by Christine Mitchell on page 266.

a. ______________________________

b. ______________________________

c. ______________________________

d. ______________________________

9. Essay: What have been some of the positive and negative experiences you've had working with teachers/schools concerning your foster child's educations?

Please print clearly:

Name ______________________________

Address ______________________________

City ______________________________ **State** ______ **Zip** __________

Private or State Agency Contact ______________________________

Office Address/PO Box ______________________________

City ______________________________ **State** ______ **Zip** __________

Learning Objective: to increase foster and/or adoptive parents' ability to apply and respond to new information and conceptal frameworks to their work with children in their care. Please rate the following on a scale of 1-4 (1 is poor, 4 is excellent):

The information was informative: (1-2-3-4)

The information was useful/helpful in my role as a foster/adoptive parent: (1-2-3-4)

The information was thought-provoking, (1-2-3-4) especially the story on page(s)

____

Foster Parenting Toolbox CEU Quiz: Parenting Teens

1. Which of the following are included in the five love languages, according to the article, "Parenting Teens" by M. Kim Combes, LBSW, MEd, on page 278.

a. Positive encouragement.
b. Words of affirmation.
c. Acts of service.
d. Eating meals together.

2. Which of the following are among the several "Practical Methods in Caring for Teens" according to the article by Mary T. Keane on page 381.

a. Let the kids teach you.
b. Always take anything they do personally.
c. Try to say "no" as much as possible and try not to say "yes" often.
d. Maintain a sense of humor and try to employ it in the middle of your anger.

3. Which of the following statements is TRUE based on the article, "Adolescence: Surviving and Thriving" by Brenda McCreight, PhD, RSW, on page 380.

a. During this time, the brain connections decrease and disconnect in a way that selectively changes over time to meet the needs of the environment.
b. With adolescence continuing to evolve, parenting has not changed with each generation.
c. The adolescent brain undergoes a massive change beginning about age thirteen and finally finishes its work by age 25.
d. Today, this stage of life has become positively associated with rejection of parental values, drugs and alcohol, a separate set of music and cultural idols and its own use and interpretation of language.

4. Dr. James A. Kenny advice in "How to handle Teen Lying" is to:

a. Verify activities from outside sources.
b. Ignore it.
c. Disregard that which cannot be verified.
d. All the above.

5. In "Passing the Test" by Tanya Reid on page 286, George tested his new family often. What was the one thing George believe that his foster family didn't do?

____

6. In "The Broken Child" by Anne Birdsong Giberson, she wondered if she would be able to fix what was broken. Her son, full of trauma and teen angst had exploded. What did she feel was the cause of the explosion?

a. Old wounds that were opened up and aggrieved
b. Years of neglect and drug use
c. Not enough unconditional love
d. Not getting the seat he wanted to watch a movie

7. Adriana Borris shares the story of her struggles in "My Journey" on page 294. What things that her foster parents did for her helped her change her whole styles of living?

____

8. Which of the following are among the "Ten Things Parents Should Know About Raising Teens," by Aileen Rosario and Anni Keane on page 290.

a. Do not be straight-laced and rigid all the time.
b. Do not allow your teen to make mistakes.
c. Always tell your teen that you love him or her and only want what is best.
d. Time will always be easy.

9. List two of the ten "Words of Encouragement for Children and Teens" according to the article by Homer Kiracofe on page 292

a. ____
b. ____

10. Essay: What is the most important thing you have learned from foster parenting teens?

____

Please print clearly:

Name ____

Address ____

City ____________________ **State** ________ **Zip** ________

Private or State Agency Contact ____

Office Address/PO Box ____

City ____________________ **State** ________ **Zip** ________

Learning Objective: to increase foster and/or adoptive parents' ability to apply and respond to new information and conceptal frameworks to their work with children in their care. Please rate the following on a scale of 1-4 (1 is poor, 4 is excellent):

The information was informative: (1-2-3-4)

The information was useful/helpful in my role as a foster/adoptive parent: (1-2-3-4)

The information was thought-provoking, (1-2-3-4) especially the story on page(s)

____

Foster Parenting Toolbox CEU Quiz: Nurturing Identity

1. **According to the article, "I'm Not Invisible! I'm Valuable!" by Cile Cogburn, MSW, and Joseph Galata, PhD, what is a lifebook?**

a. A collection of words, photos, graphics, artwork and memorabilia to remember a child by once he or she leave your home.

b. The creation of a child's life work.

c. A collection of words, photos, graphics, artwork and memorabilia that creates a chronological record of a child's life.

d. A compilation of mementos from a parents' fostering journey.

2. **On page 303, Veronica Brown lists a number of firsts in her article called "Fostering Firsts". What are two of the most surprising firsts that you might want to look for in your fostering?**

a. ______________________________

b. ______________________________

3. **According to the article, "Lifebooks: Every Foster Child Needs One," by Beth O'Malley, MEd, on page 304, how do children benefit from having a lifebook?**

a. Lifebooks help reduce magical thinking and fantasy.

b. Lifebooks help answer questions.

c. Lifebooks help create a positive picture of a child's foster care experiences.

d. Lifebooks help give children a should to cry on.

4. **List one of the things that can be used to create a foster care collage according to the article, "An Adoption/Foster Care Collage: Putting the Pieces Together" by Mary Anne Cohen on page 306.**

____

5. **In the article, " The Collage" by Julie Craft on the page 309, what are the three types of collages her daughter created to help her understand her feelings?**

a. ______________

b. ______________

c. ______________

6. **"Self Esteem Building in Families" an article by Cheryl A. Lieberman, PhD, and Rhea Bufferd, LICSW, on page 311, has a number of suggestions to help build up self esteem. What are their three listening rules?**

a. ______________________________

b. ______________________________

c. ______________________________

7. How can picture books teach emotional regulation strategies, according to the article, "The Picture Book Fix for Emotional Challenges," by Lee Tobin McClain, PhD, on page 310?

a. Children will gain valuable educational benefits from reading or being read to.

b. Children are more willing to listen to new ideas in the context of a character's life.

c. Favorite characters help children feel less along in their emotions.

d. Books create a make believe place where children can avoid dealing with reality.

8. How can foster parents help their children grieve, according to the article, "The Right to Grieve," by Sheena Macrae on page 312?

a. Foster parents needs to create a safe place for children in their care.

b. Foster parents need to understand children's grief.

c. Children need to attend counseling.

d. Children need to have the right for respect of their history.

9. Essay: How have you helped to nurture the identities of children in your care?

____

Please print clearly:

Name ______________________________

Address ______________________________

City ______________________________ **State** ________ **Zip** __________

Private or State Agency Contact ______________________________

Office Address/PO Box ______________________________

City ______________________________ **State** ________ **Zip** __________

Learning Objective: to increase foster and/or adoptive parents' ability to apply and respond to new information and conceptal frameworks to their work with children in their care. Please rate the following on a scale of 1-4 (1 is poor, 4 is excellent):

The information was informative: (1-2-3-4)

The information was useful/helpful in my role as a foster/adoptive parent: (1-2-3-4)

The information was thought-provoking, (1-2-3-4) especially the story on page(s)

____

Foster Parenting Toolbox CEU Quiz: Allegations

1. List three of the several things you should document in a journal or note-book, according to the article, "Preventing Allegations in Provider Homes," By Jodee Kulp on page 318.

a. ______________________________

b. ______________________________

c. ______________________________

2. Which of the following should be included in a foster parent bill of rights, according to the article on page 320?

a. Help plan visitation with a child's parents and siblings.

b. Receive an adequate reimbursement rate.

c. Receive adequate training and ongoing support.

d. Be considered part of the child welfare team.

3. In the article, "We're Being Investigated for Child Abuse" on page 323, what is one of the simple routines that Michael Weisberg does that keeps his and the caseworkers' minds at ease as well as ensure their foster children's needs are met?

____

4. According to the article, "Allegations Happen: How to Prevent and Survive Them", by Diane Martin-Hushman on page 326, which of the following are strategies to prevent allegations?

a. Create a sign in and sign out sheet for everyone living in your home.

b. Give each child his or her own bedroom.

c. Document sexual acting out in writing.

d. Be crystal clear about rules for dress, privacy and touching.

5. Also in the article, "Allegations Happen: How to Prevent and Survive Them," by Diane Martin-Hushman on page 326, sometimes despite a family's efforts to prevent them, allegations may happen. What are some of the survival strategies that the parents can do to take care of themselves? List three of the suggested strategies.

a. ______________________________

b. ______________________________

c. ______________________________

6. Do you know where the nearest foster and adoptive parent support group meets? When? And how often?

a. Yes or No (circle one)

b. When?____

c. How often?______________________________________

7. Which of the following are among the three proposed changes to the way allegations of abuse and neglect are handled, according to the article, "Criminalizing Foster Parents," by Lori Groves, MMFT, and James A. Kenny, PhD, on page 330?

a. Separate criminal child abuse from a civil policy violation.

b. Change the people who are mandated reporters.

c. Require accused foster parents to be added to an offender registry.

d. Raise the standard of proof.

8. In "False Allegations of Abuse in Foster Care" on page 333, what percentage of the allegations made in 2009 was substantiated?____________________

9. How can foster parents locate an attorney according to the article, "When Foster Parents Need an Attorney," by James A. Kenny, PhD, on page 334?

a. Search the Internet

b. Check with other foster parents.

c. Contact the North American Council on Adoptable Children

d. Go to your local courthouse.

10. Essay: What things have you done to prevent allegations in your home? What advice would you give to a foster parent going through an allegation?

Please print clearly:

Name ____

Address ____

City ______________________________**State** ______**Zip** ________

Private or State Agency Contact ______________________________

Office Address/PO Box ___________________________________

City ______________________________**State** ______**Zip** ________

Learning Objective: to increase foster and/or adoptive parents' ability to apply and respond to new information and conceptal frameworks to their work with children in their care. Please rate the following on a scale of 1-4 (1 is poor, 4 is excellent):

The information was informative: (1-2-3-4)

The information was useful/helpful in my role as a foster/adoptive parent: (1-2-3-4)

The information was thought-provoking, (1-2-3-4) especially the story on page(s)

____

Foster Parenting Toolbox CEU Quiz: Respite & Support

1. Which of the following are strategies to practice self-care according to the article, "Self-Care for Adoptive and Foster Parents," by Carol Lozier, LCSW, on page 336?

a. Go out to dinner with your spouse.

b. Make your dreams come true.

c. Join a book club.

d. Reduce the amount of time you spend with technology.

2. List two of the ways people typically react to significant changes and stressors in their lives, according to the article, "Put on Your Own Oxygen Mask First," by Susan Badeau on page 338.

____

____

3. In "I Can't Give Away That Which is Not Mine to Give" on page 339, the author states that she can't provide peace, tranquility, and calm if

____

4. Terra Trevor shows some wise advice in "Bring Me Hope: Foster Parenting Through Tough Times" on page 342. She talks about how foster parenting requires a strong support system and that you need to think about parenting your child as a relationship waiting to be built instead of

____

____

5. Which of the following are signs and symptoms of depression according to the article, "A Knock at the Door: Recognizing Depression," by Karin J. Foli, PhD, RN, on page 344?

a. Diminished ability to think or concentrate or indecisiveness.

b. Little interest in your children.

c. Difficulty staying awake.

d. Difficulty sleeping or wanting to sleep all the time.

6. In "Respite Works for Everyone", Stacey Leidner defines respite as

____

____

____

7. In that same article, "Respite Works for Everyone" by Stacey Leidner, what kinds of options are available on the Continuum of Respite Care?

a. In home care

b. Neighbor babysitting

c. Group Child Care

d. Therapeutic Care

8. In "Taking Advantage of Respite Foster Care" on page 350, Carrie Craft lists some tips to help children prepare for a weekend with another foster family. List two of her suggestions.

____

____

9. Which of the following are ways to be a great respite provider, according to the article, "Taking Advantage of Respite Foster Care," by Carrie Craft on page 350?

a. Feed the kids only foods they like.

b. Confirm the dates of respite.

c. Try to keep any schedule or routine as outlined by the foster family.

d. Keep a log of the children's misbehaviors.

10. Essay: Have you used respite care? What was good and bad about the experience? What would have made the respite more effective?

Please print clearly:

Name ______________________________

Address ______________________________

City ______________________ **State** ______ **Zip** ________

Private or State Agency Contact ______________________________

Office Address/PO Box ______________________________

City ______________________ **State** ______ **Zip** ________

Learning Objective: to increase foster and/or adoptive parents' ability to apply and respond to new information and conceptal frameworks to their work with children in their care. Please rate the following on a scale of 1-4 (1 is poor, 4 is excellent):

The information was informative: (1-2-3-4)

The information was useful/helpful in my role as a foster/adoptive parent: (1-2-3-4)

The information was thought-provoking, (1-2-3-4) especially the story on page(s)

____

Foster Parenting Toolbox CEU Quiz: Reunification, Adoption & Beyond.

1. According to the article, "Foster Parents: A Barrier to Permanency?" on page 356, which of the following ways have foster parents become barrier to adoption or sabotaged placements?

a. Telling foster children they don't deserve a family.

b. Encouraging foster children to keep in contact.

c. Communicating mixed messages to foster children headed to an adoptive parent.

d. Providing additional emotional support to children even after they've moved to a new home.

2. In "Post Reunification and Beyond" on page 359, Michael Weisberg and his partner's reason for not "moving on" are

a. They preferred to stay involved with the children.

b. They wanted to be a stable presence in the boys' lives.

c. They want to remain the birth mother's respite choice.

d. They are not committed to finding children to adopt.

3. In "Second Chance for a Background" on page 362, William Cuchens and his wife consented to be a kinship placement because they

a. Wanted birth family connections for their adopted son.

b. Are grateful for the memories they are building.

c. Want to expand their family.

d. Wanted to provide some background for their son's sake.

4. List two of the seven thoughts author Rita Laws, PhD, passes onto the readers of the article, "What I'd Wish I'd Known About Adoption," on page 366.

a. ____________________

b. ____________________

5 Which of the following statement is TRUE according to the article, "Helping Youth Succeed as Adults: The Challenge of Aging Out, by Charles Redell on page 369?

a. One in four young adults who age out will be incarcerated within the first two years of leaving the system.

b. One in six young adults who age out will become homeless after turning 18.

c. Only 62 percent of young adults who age out will have a high school diploma.

d. Fewer than one percent of young adults who age out will earn a college degree.

6. **Which of the following are among the "Seven Things Emancipated Youth Need to Know About Money Before Leaving Care," by Shay Olivarria on page 374?**

a. Housing should never be more than 40 percent of your gross income.

b. Buying a reliable used car is always a smart move.

c. Put off saving for retirement.

d. Start an emergency fund.

7. **On Page 371, The Jordan Institute for Families lists steps to take to avoid disruption. List 2 of the steps that most hit home for you and your family.**

a. ______________________________

b. ______________________________

8. **According to Veronica Brown, author of "Disruption: When it is Becomes Necessary", placements break down for many reasons. The challenge is for everyone to minimize the impact and trauma of the disruption. List four of the tips that she offers to minimize the trauma of disruption?**

a. ______________________________

b. ______________________________

c. ______________________________

d. ______________________________

9. **Essay: What has been your involvement in the adoption or reunification process? What did you learn from that experience that you would like to pass along to others?**

Please print clearly:

Name ______________________________

Address ______________________________

City ____________________ **State** ______ **Zip** ________

Private or State Agency Contact ______________________________

Office Address/PO Box ______________________________

City ____________________ **State** ______ **Zip** ________

Learning Objective: to increase foster and/or adoptive parents' ability to apply and respond to new information and conceptal frameworks to their work with children in their care. Please rate the following on a scale of 1-4 (1 is poor, 4 is excellent):

The information was informative: (1-2-3-4)

The information was useful/helpful in my role as a foster/adoptive parent: (1-2-3-4)

The information was thought-provoking, (1-2-3-4) especially the story on page(s)

____

About the Publisher:

EMK Press:
Resources and books for families formed by adoption

16 Mt. Bethel Road, #219
Warren, NJ 07059
732-469-7544
732-469-7861 fax

Titles currently in print:

I Don't Have Your Eyes

We See the Moon

At Home in This World, A China Adoption Story

Adoption Parenting: Creating a Toolbox, Building Connections

The Foster Parenting Toolbox

Forever Fingerprints

Pieces of Me: Who Do I Want to Be?

We publish books for families formed by adoption and foster care.

www.emkpress.com

Please advise us if a link listed in this book is broken or not working.

To reach us via email:

info@emkpress.com